CHRISTIAN L

Christian Law: Contemporary Principles offers a detailed comparison of the laws of churches across ten distinct Christian traditions worldwide: Catholic, Orthodox, Anglican, Lutheran, Methodist, Reformed, Presbyterian, United, Congregational and Baptist. From this comparison, Professor Doe proposes that all denominations of the faith share common principles in spite of their doctrinal divisions; and that these principles reveal a concept of 'Christian Law' and contribute to a theological understanding of global Christian identity. Adopting a unique interdisciplinary approach, the book provides comprehensive coverage on the sources and purposes of church law, the faithful (lay and ordained), the institutions of church governance, discipline and dispute resolution, doctrine and worship, the rites of passage, ecumenism, property and finance, as well as church, State and society. This is an invaluable resource for lawyers and theologians who are engaged in ecumenical and interfaith dialogue, showing how dogmas may divide but laws link Christians across traditions.

NORMAN DOE is Professor of Law and Director of the Centre for Law and Religion at Cardiff University Law School.

CHRISTIAN LAW

CONTEMPORARY PRINCIPLES

NORMAN DOE
*The Centre for Law and Religion,
Cardiff University Law School*

CAMBRIDGE
UNIVERSITY PRESS

University Printing House, Cambridge CB2 8BS, United Kingdom

Cambridge University Press is part of the University of Cambridge.

It furthers the University's mission by disseminating knowledge in the pursuit of education, learning and research at the highest international levels of excellence.

www.cambridge.org
Information on this title: www.cambridge.org/9781316500651

© Norman Doe 2013

This publication is in copyright. Subject to statutory exception and to the provisions of relevant collective licensing agreements, no reproduction of any part may take place without the written permission of Cambridge University Press.

First published 2013
First paperback edition 2015

A catalogue record for this publication is available from the British Library

Library of Congress Cataloguing in Publication data
Doe, Norman.
Christian law contemporary principles / Norman Doe, Professor of Law and Director, The Centre for Law and Religion, The Law School, Cardiff University.
pages cm
Includes bibliographical references and index.
ISBN 978-1-107-00692-8 (hardback)
1. Canon law.   2. Canon law–Anglican Communion.   3. Canon law–Orthodox Eastern Church.   4. Ecclesiastical law.   I. Title.
KB170.D64A325 2013
262.9–dc23   2013003683

ISBN 978-1-107-00692-8 Hardback
ISBN 978-1-316-50065-1 Paperback

Cambridge University Press has no responsibility for the persistence or accuracy of URLs for external or third-party internet websites referred to in this publication, and does not guarantee that any content on such websites is, or will remain, accurate or appropriate.

CONTENTS

Preface vii
List of abbreviations ix

Introduction *page* 1
1 The sources and purposes of ecclesiastical regulation   11
2 The faithful – the laity and lay ministry   46
3 The ordained ministers of the church   77
4 The institutions of ecclesiastical governance   118
5 Ecclesiastical discipline and conflict resolution   154
6 Doctrine and worship   188
7 The rites of passage   233
8 Ecumenical relations   274
9 Church property and finance   310
10 Church, State and society   346
   General conclusion   384

Appendix The principles of law common to Christian churches   388
Bibliography   399
Index   415

PREFACE

John Witte, the great American scholar of law and religion, invited me in 2007 to write an essay for a book he was editing, with his colleague Frank Alexander, on Christianity and law. The title he gave me was 'Christian Law'. I explained to John that I felt unable to write this essay as I did not consider that such a category existed. As a result I wrote an extremely rudimentary piece, 'Modern Church Law', which duly appeared in J. Witte and F.S. Alexander (eds.), *Christianity and Law* (Cambridge University Press, 2008) pp. 271-291. However, the essay persuaded me that from a comparative study of the contemporary regulatory systems of churches of different ecclesiastical traditions worldwide, and (amongst profound differences) any similarities that might exist between them, it may indeed be possible to construct the category of principles of Christian law. John has encouraged me ever since in this venture into juridical Christianity. Another key stimulus for this book has been the curiosity of and the thirst for comparative church law amongst students at Cardiff Law School on two courses that I teach – the undergraduate module in Law and Religion and the postgraduate LLM in Canon Law. These students, over the years, have all in their own ways advocated the need for a study of the laws of a wider group of Christian traditions and churches across the world than those customarily studied on these two courses at Cardiff – that is, the canon law of Anglican churches and its relation to the canon law of the Roman Catholic Church. This book is the result of several years in gestation, and of staring at and reflecting legally and theologically on the laws and other regulatory systems of approaching one hundred different churches globally across ten Christian traditions of the twenty-two 'church families' recognised as such by the World Council of Churches.

I have enjoyed the support of a great many people in the process of writing this book. To my colleagues at the Centre for Law and Religion at Cardiff Law School I owe a particular debt of gratitude: Professor Mark Hill QC, Anthony Jeremy, Dr Russell Sandberg, Eithne D'Auria, and Frank Cranmer particularly. The same applies to all those from various traditions studied here who have provided help. These include colleagues in the Colloquium of Anglican and Roman Catholic Canon Lawyers: on the Anglican side, as well as Mark Hill and Anthony Jeremy, Gregory Cameron (Bishop of St Asaph, Church in Wales), Stephen Slack (Director of Legal Services at the Archbishops' Council, Church of England), and Paul Colton (Bishop of Cork, Cloyne and Ross, Church of Ireland); and on the Catholic side, Professor James Conn SJ (Pontifical Gregorian University, Rome), Dr. Robert Ombres OP (Blackfriars, Oxford), Revd. Dr. Fintan Gavin (Dublin), Aidan McGrath OFM (Secretary General of the Franciscans and based in Rome); along with many others who have been involved in the work of the Colloquium over the years such as the Revd. Gareth Powell (Deputy Secretary to the British Methodist Conference). A key influence on the method used in this book has been the work of the Anglican Communion Legal Advisers Network. I had the privilege (2002–2007) to work on a draft for the Network of a statement of principles induced from the laws of the forty-four churches of the worldwide Anglican Communion. These were refined and adopted by the Network and launched at the Lambeth Conference in 2008: *The Principles of Canon Law Common to the Churches of the Anglican Communion* (Anglican Communion Office, London, 2008). This also taught me a great deal about the possibilities involved in a comparative study of ecclesiastical legal systems. To the convenor of the Network, Canon John Rees (Legal Adviser to the Anglican Consultative Council), I owe an equally large measure of gratitude. A similar influence was the conference on Protestant Church Polity in Changing Contexts, comparing the polity systems of the Reformed tradition, held in Utrecht in November 2011. I thank Professor Leo Koffeman (Utrecht) especially for the kind invitation to speak about the Anglican project and its possible usefulness in the context of shared principles of polity amongst the Reformed churches worldwide.

Cardiff Law School, under its then head Professor Gillian Douglas, was kind enough to grant me study leave for 2010–2011 to work on the book. During the year, I enjoyed the benefit of a visiting fellowship at Trinity College, Oxford for the Hilary term 2011. I am very grateful to the President and Fellows of the college not least for the warmth of their welcome and hospitality. The fellowship allowed me access to several Oxford libraries and to library staff at the Bodleian, Mansfield College, Blackfriars, and Regent's Park College I owe a special debt of gratitude. Research assistance from Felicity Powell, a Cardiff law graduate, was especially helpful in the summer of 2011, as was that of Wanda Kauffmann for her help with translations of some texts. The current head of Cardiff Law School, Professor Nigel Lowe, has likewise supported and cheered me over the last eight months or so to complete the book, as have those who provide so much invaluable assistance to me as Chancellor of the Diocese of Bangor, in my own ecclesial community, the Church in Wales. At the postgraduate office at Cardiff, Sharron Alldred, Sarah Kennedy and Helen Calvert have, as always, provided first-class support, as have latterly, in the research directorate, Rhian Griffiths, Sharon Willicombe and Rose Cundill. At Cambridge University Press, to which I have returned after 22 years, I am especially grateful to Finola O'Sullivan, Editorial Director, Law, for her continued faith in the project and her infinite patience, as well as to her colleagues.

Finally, I should like to thank my long-suffering family – my wife Heather, our children Rachel, Elizabeth and Edward, brother Martin, my mother Julia, and, before his sad passing in 2011 (just a few months before his hundredth birthday), my father James – for their constant and unfailing support. I make no apology for the density of the footnotes, which some may find tedious – as my doctoral supervisors Professors Ullmann and Milsom at Cambridge used to suggest, more often than not it is there that we find the legal evidence – but any errors in these, and the text, are needless to say my sole responsibility.

ABBREVIATIONS

ABCUSA	American Baptist Churches in the USA
ABF	Asian Baptist Federation
ABL	Administrative Bylaws
AC	Augsburg Confession 1530 (Lutheran)
ACC	Anglican Consultative Council
ACCT	Australian Churches Covenanting Together (2004)
ACROD	American Carpatho-Russian Orthodox Diocese of the USA
ACSA	Anglican Church of Southern Africa
Acts	Acts of the General Assembly of the Church of Scotland
ALATW	A Lutheran Approach to the Theology of Worship (Lutheran Church of Australia, prepared in 1990 by the Commission on Worship, and reviewed by the Commission on Theology and Inter-Church Relations and by the College of Presidents; this version was adopted by the Commission on Worship in 1998 and edited in 2001)
Apol.	Apology to the Augsburg Confession 1531 (Lutheran)
App.	Appendix
AR	Articles of Religion (e.g. UMCNEAE)
Art.	Article
ATGB	Archdiocese of Thyateira and Great Britain (Greek Orthodox)
Australia	Anglican Church of Australia
BC	Book of Concord 1580 (Lutheran)
BCO	Book of Church Order (e.g. RCA; PCA)
BCP	Book of Common Prayer (Anglican)
Bermuda	Anglican Church of Bermuda
Bk.	Book (e.g. MCGB: CPD, Bk. I)
BL	Bylaws (e.g. LWF; BUSA)
BMPP	N.H. Maring and W.S. Hudson, *A Baptist Manual of Polity and Practice* (Judson Press, Valley Forge, PA, 1963)
BO	Book of Order (e.g. PCANZ; PC (USA))
BOD	Book of Discipline (e.g. UMCNEAE)
Brazil	Episcopal Anglican Church of Brazil
BU	Basis of Union
BUGB	Baptist Union of Great Britain
BUNZ	Baptist Union of New Zealand
Burundi	Church of the Province of Burundi (Anglican)
BUS	Baptist Union of Scotland
BUSA	Baptist Union of Southern Africa

ABBREVIATIONS

BWA	Baptist World Alliance
c.	Canon (Catholic, Orthodox)
Can(s).	Canon(s) (Anglican)
CARCCL	Colloquium of Anglican and Roman Catholic Canon Lawyers
Catechism	Catechism: the Christian Doctrine of the Evangelical Church of Finland, approved by the General Synod 1999 (Helsinki, 2000)
CCC	Catechism of the Catholic Church (Geoffrey Chapman, London, 1994)
CCEO	*Codex Canonum Ecclesiarum Orientalium* (1990) (Oriental Catholic Churches)
CD	*Christus Dominus* (Catholic Church, Vatican II, Decree, 1965)
CDC	Constitution Document for Congregations (NALC, 2011)
Central Africa	Church of the Province of Central Africa (Anglican)
Ch.	Chapter
Chile	Anglican Church of Chile
CIC	*Codex Iuris Canonici* (1983) (Roman or Latin Catholic Church)
cl.	Clause
CLAC	N. Doe, *Canon Law in the Anglican Communion* (Oxford, 1998)
CLCS	*The Constitution and Laws of the Church of Scotland*, edited by J.L. Weatherhead (Church of Scotland, Board of Practice and Procedure, Edinburgh, 1997)
CLLS	*The Canon Law: Letter and Spirit – A Practical Guide to the Code of Canon Law*, The Canon Law Society of Great Britain and Ireland (Dublin, 1995)
CNBC	Canadian National Baptist Convention
Code	The Code: The Book of the Constitution and Government of the Presbyterian Church in Ireland
Const.	Constitution
COS	Council of State (Greece)
COTN	Church of the Nazarene
CPC	Code of Pastoral Conduct (Ukrainian Orthodox Church in America)
CPD	Constitutional Practice and Discipline (Methodist Church (Great Britain))
CPP	Code of Pastoral Practice (MCI)
CTIR	Commission on Theology and Inter-Church Relations (Lutheran Church of Australia)
DH	*Dignitas Humanae* (Catholic Church, Vatican II, Decree, 1965)
Dioc.	Diocese
Div.	Division
DOW	Directory of Worship (e.g. PCA, PCANZ)
DU	Deed of Union (e.g. MCGB)
ECHR	European Convention of Human Rights
ED	Directory for the Application of Norms and Principles of Ecumenism 1993 (Catholic Church)
EELC	Estonian Evangelical Lutheran Church
EJCSR	European Journal for Church and State Research

EKD	Evangelische Kirche Deutschland
ELCA	Evangelical Lutheran Church in America
ELCF	Evangelical Lutheran Church of Finland
ELCIC	Evangelical Lutheran Church in Canada
ELCIRE	Evangelical Lutheran Church in Ireland
ELCSA	Evangelical Lutheran Church of Southern Africa
England	Church of England (Anglican)
EPGP	Ethical Principles and Guidelines for Pastors (BUNZ)
ESMP	Ethical Standards and Standards of Practice for Ministry Personnel (UCC)
FC	Formula of Concord 1577 (Lutheran)
FMCNA	Free Methodist Church of North America
G	Guidelines
GC	Guidelines for Clergy (OCIA)
GE	*Gravissimum Educationis* (Catholic Church, Vatican II, Declaration, 1965)
GOAA	Greek Orthodox Archdiocese of America
GOA(AUS)	Greek Orthodox Archdiocese of Australia
GOCER	Guidelines for Orthodox Christians in Ecumenical Relations (SCOBA)
GS	*Gaudium et Spes* (Catholic Church, Vatican II, Pastoral Constitution, 1966)
HOR	Handbook of Order and Rules (PCW)
ICLARS	International Consortium for Law and Religion Studies
Indian Ocean	Church of the Province of the Indian Ocean (Anglican)
Instructions	Instructions (ATGB); Practical Instructions for Diocesan Faithful, Living the Sacramental Life of the Church (UOCIA)
Ireland	Church of Ireland (Anglican)
Japan	Holy Catholic Church in Japan (Nippon Sei Ko Kai) (Anglican)
JBU	Jamaica Baptist Union
Kenya	Church of the Province of Kenya (Anglican)
Korea	Anglican Church of Korea
LAR	Laws and Regulations (MCNZ)
LC	Lambeth Conference (Anglican)
LCA	Lutheran Church of Australia (Incorporated)
LCGB	Lutheran Church in Great Britain
LCMS	Lutheran Church Missouri Synod
LG	*Lumen Gentium* (Catholic Church, Vatican II, Dogmatic Constitution, 1965)
LLC	Luther's Large Catechism (1529)
LSC	Luther's Small Catechism (1529)
LWF	Lutheran World Federation
Man.	Manual (e.g. MCI, Manual of Laws)
MCGB	Methodist Church in Great Britain
MCI	Methodist Church in Ireland
MCLC	Model Constitution for Local Churches (UCCSA, URC)
MCNZ	Methodist Church of New Zealand (Te Haahi Weteriana o Aotearoa)

MCSA	Methodist Church of South Africa
Melanesia	Church of the Province of Melanesia (Anglican)
Mexico	Anglican Church of Mexico
ML	Manual of Laws (MCI)
MOCL	L.J. Patsavos, *Manual for the Course in Orthodox Canon Law* (Hellenic College, Holy Cross Orthodox School of Theology, 1975)
MOSC	Malankara Orthodox Syrian Church
MPP	Manual of Practice and Procedure (UFCS)
MT	Model Trusts (Methodist Church in Great Britain)
MTC	Baptist Model Trusts for Churches 2003 (BUGB: Baptist Union Corporation)
NABC	North American Baptist Conference
NALC	North American Lutheran Church
NAOCC	North American Old Catholic Church
NBC	Nigerian Baptist Convention
NBCUSA	National Baptist Convention USA
NCCC	J.P. Beal, J.A. Coriden and T.J. Green (eds.), *New Commentary on the Code of Canon Law* (Paulist Press, New York, 2000)
Nedungatt	G. Nedungatt SJ (ed.), *A Guide to the Eastern Code: A Commentary on the Code of Canons of the Eastern Churches* (Pontificio Istituto Orientale, Rome, 2002)
New Zealand	Anglican Church in Aotearoa, New Zealand and Polynesia
Nigeria	Church of the Province of Nigeria (Anglican)
North India	(United) Church of North India
NT	New Testament
OCBUU	Old Catholic Bishops United in the Union of Utrecht
OCIA	Orthodox Church in America
OOCL	P. Rodopoulos, *An Overview of Orthodox Canon Law* (Orthodox Research Institute, Rollinsford, NH, 2007)
OT	Old Testament
PACLM	Pastors and Church Leaders Manual (FMCNA)
PAP	Policies and Practices (NBC)
par.	paragraph
PCA	Presbyterian Church in America
PCANZ	Presbyterian Church of Aotearoa New Zealand
PCI	Presbyterian Church in Ireland
PCLCCAC	*The Principles of Canon Law Common to the Churches of the Anglican Communion* (Anglican Communion Office, London, 2008)
PC (USA)	Presbyterian Church (U.S.A.)
PCW	Presbyterian Church of Wales
Pedalion	*The Rudder (Pedalion) of the Orthodox Christians or All the Sacred and Divine Canons*, edited by C. Cummings (Orthodox Christian Educational Society, Chicago, Illinois, 1957)
PG	Pastoral Guidelines
Philippines	Episcopal Church in the Philippines (Anglican Communion)
PNG	Anglican Church of Papua New Guinea

Portugal	Lusitanian Church (Portuguese Episcopal Church) (Anglican Communion)
Pt.	Part
Puerto Rico	Episcopal Church of Puerto Rico
RACCL	*The Canon Law of the Church of England*, Report of the Archbishops' Commission on Canon Law [Church of England] (SPCK, London, 1947)
RAR	Rules and Regulations
RCA	Reformed Church in America
RDG	Regulations, Discipline and Government (MCI)
REC	Reformed Ecumenical Council
Reg(s).	Regulation(s) (e.g. UCA)
Res(s).	Resolution(s) (e.g. Lambeth Conference)
ROC	Russian Orthodox Church
ROMOC	Romanian Orthodox Church
Rwanda	Church of the Province of Rwanda (Anglican)
s.	Section
SBC	Southern Baptist Convention
SC	*Sacrosanctum Consilium* (Catholic Church, Vatican II, Constitution, 1964)
SCBC	Suggested Constitutions for Baptist Churches (BMPP)
Sch.	Schedule
SCOBA	Standing Conference of the Canonical Orthodox Bishops in the Americas
Scotland	Scottish Episcopal Church (Anglican Communion)
SD	Solid Declaration (Lutheran)
SEA	Church of the Province of South East Asia (Anglican)
SFPM	Standards for Pastoral Ministry (NALC)
SO	Standing Order (e.g. MCGB)
SOCA	Syriac Orthodox Church of Antioch
South India	(United) Church of South India
SPGRCP	Some Pastoral Guidelines for Responsible Communion Practice (2011) (Lutheran)
SR	Standing Rules (ABCUSA)
Sudan	Church of the Province of the Sudan (Anglican)
TACC	*The Anglican Communion Covenant* (2009)
Tanzania	Church of the Province of Tanzania (Anglican)
TCCG	*The Church Constitution Guide*, North American Mission Board, An Agency of the Southern Baptist Convention
TCOR	The Covenant of Relationships and its Agreements among the General, National, and Regional Boards of the American Baptist Churches (ABCUSA)
TEC	The Episcopal Church USA (Anglican)
UCA	Uniting Church in Australia
UCC	United Church of Canada
UCCP	United Church of Christ in the Philippines

UCCSA	United Congregational Church of Southern Africa
UCOC	United Church of Christ
UFCS	United Free Church of Scotland
Uganda	Church of the Province of Uganda (Anglican)
UMCNEAE	United Methodist Church in Northern Europe and Eurasia
UMCUSA	United Methodist Church – United States of America
UOCIA	Ukrainian Orthodox Church in America
UR	*Unitatis Redintegratio* (Catholic Church, Vatican II, Decree on Ecumenism 1964)
URC	United Reformed Church
Wales	Church in Wales (Anglican)
WARC	World Alliance of Reformed Churches (now WCRC)
WCC	World Council of Churches
WCRC	World Communion of Reformed Churches
West Africa	Church of the Province of West Africa (Anglican)
WMC	World Methodist Council

Introduction

There is no global system of Christian law, humanly created, applicable to all of the followers of Jesus Christ. Each church or ecclesial community has its own laws or other regulatory instruments consisting of binding norms. These norms are as wide in scope as the visible activities of the churches themselves, though they by no means prescribe the fullness of faith and life enjoyed by Christians worldwide. This book provides a detailed comparative examination of the juridical systems of churches in ten different global Christian traditions: Catholic; Orthodox; Anglican; Lutheran; Methodist; Presbyterian; Reformed; Congregational; United; and Baptist. It proposes three observations. First, despite the different doctrinal or confessional postures of these separate Christian traditions, there are profound similarities between their contemporary regulatory instruments. These similarities encapsulate a theological conception of Christianity and its global identity in juridical form. This juridical unity is based in part on the practices of the different churches to use common sources in shaping their laws (chiefly the Bible) and to adapt the regulatory fundamentals of their mother church, in the case of those within one tradition, or at least elements of them, in the case of churches which have broken away from that tradition. Secondly, the dominant teaching of Christians is that salvation through Christ is fundamentally a matter of human faith and divine grace. This book suggests that Christianity is also a religion of law. Whilst churches have developed different doctrinal reasons for particular juridical arrangements, the similarities between their laws actually serve to link Christians in common norms of conduct. Indeed, the laws of the different ecclesiastical traditions express Christian faith itself in the form of common norms of action. Above all, on the fundamental assumption that Christians broadly obey the laws they make, the juridical unity between the traditions indicates that Christians are engaged in much the same actions in life regardless of their actual denominational affiliation. In short, whilst doctrines divide, laws link Christians in common action. Thirdly, from the profound similarities between the laws of churches it is possible to induce shared principles of the laws of Christians. This book seeks to articulate these contemporary principles of Christian law common to followers of Christ worldwide.[1]

The reasons for this book may be stated simply. In 1974 the Faith and Order Commission of the World Council of Churches recommended – but this was never

---

[1] For discussion of the Jewish inheritance in Christianity, the understanding that Jesus did not abolish but fulfilled the divine law, and the Pauline approach to law, see e.g. B. Lindars (ed.), *Law and Religion: Essays on the Place of Law in Israel and Early Christianity* (Clarke, Cambridge, 1988).

pursued – that the divided churches of Christianity should engage in an ecumenical discussion of 'church law' in order to explore its role in the movement towards greater visible ecclesial unity. It suggested that, *inter alia*: (1) 'The churches differ in their order and their constitution'; (2) 'differences in the structures and legal systems of the churches have their roots in different confessional traditions'; and (3) these differences concern 'not only the actual order which the churches have, but also the general orientation by which their legislation is inspired'.[2] However, there has been no study thus far to test (and challenge) these propositions (focussing on difference) by comparing at global level the legal systems of churches, nor one which proposes the category of principles of Christian law common to those churches. Rather, there is a growing body of scholarly and practitioner literature on the regulatory systems of separate and individual churches such as Roman Catholic canon law, the law of the Church of England, Orthodox canon law and Presbyterian law.[3] Yet, studies which compare the laws of churches generally do so as between either two churches of different traditions, such as Roman Catholic and Anglican canon laws, or else the laws of several churches within the same tradition (such as those of Anglicanism, or the Reformed tradition).[4] Indeed, there is very little on the rules of other churches, such as those of the Methodist and Baptist traditions.[5] Moreover, studies comparing churches of different traditions usually do so in relation to a single issue, such as authority or discipline.[6] Comparative church law beyond such studies as these, like the category Christian law, is still virtually unknown.[7] This book fills this gap.

To this end, this book introduces the key areas addressed by the laws of Christians in their separate institutional churches. The subjects indicate well the pervasiveness of law in the life of the church. Broadly, Chapters 1 to 5 deal with the internal life of the churches, and Chapters 6 to 10 with their external relations. The study opens with an examination of the institutional church and its objects, the forms and purposes of regulation, and the relaxation and interpretation of laws (Chapter 1). Then follow the laws of persons: the faithful, membership, and the functions of the laity, lay officers and associations of the faithful (Chapter 2); and the nature and process of ordination, the appointment, tenure and termination of

---

[2] World Council of Churches, Faith and Order Commission, 'The Ecumenical Movement and Church Law', Document IV.8 (1974).

[3] See e.g. G. Sheehy et al., *The Canon Law: Letter and Spirit* (Veritas, Dublin, 1995); M. Hill, *Ecclesiastical Law* (3rd edn., Oxford University Press, 2007); P. Rodopoulos, *An Overview of Orthodox Canon Law* (Orthodox Research Institute, Rollinsford, New Hampshire, 2007); J.L. Weatherhead (ed.), *The Constitution and Laws of the Church of Scotland* (Board of Practice and Procedure, Edinburgh, 1997).

[4] See e.g. N. Doe, *The Legal Framework of the Church of England* (Clarendon Press, Oxford, 1996): this compares the law of the Church of England with that of the Roman Catholic Church; N. Doe, *Canon Law in the Anglican Communion: A Worldwide Perspective* (Clarendon Press, Oxford, 1998); P. Coertzen, *Church and Order: A Reformed Perspective* (Peeters, Leuven, 1998).

[5] See e.g. D.C. Sparkes, *The Constitutions of the Baptist Union of Great Britain* (BUGB, London, 1996).

[6] See e.g. G. Arthur, *Law, Liberty and Church* (Ashgate, Aldershot, 2006); M.A. MacLean (ed.), *Legal Systems of Scottish Churches* (Dundee University Press, 2009).

[7] The Colloquium of Anglican and Roman Catholic Canon Lawyers founded in 1999 is an exception; see its 'A decade of ecumenical dialogue in canon law' (2009) 11 *Ecclesiastical Law Journal* 284.

ordained ministry, and the functions and grades of ordained minister (Chapter 3). The institutions of church governance are treated in Chapter 4, at the international, national, regional and local levels, including their composition, functions and interrelationships. Next discussed are church discipline, its nature and purpose, mechanisms for its informal application (for example, visitation), systems of courts and tribunals for formal dispute resolution, judicial processes, ecclesiastical offences and sanctions (Chapter 5). Public doctrine and worship are explored in Chapter 6: the lawful doctrines, proclamation of the faith, doctrinal discipline, and the nature, forms and administration of public worship. The study then addresses ritual: baptism, confirmation or profession, the Eucharist, Holy Communion, or Lord's Supper, marriage and funerals (Chapter 7). Next, ecumenical relations, duties and structures, which facilitate or frustrate these, are discussed in Chapter 8. Church property and finance are explored in Chapter 9: the ownership and stewardship of property, sacred places and objects, controlling finance, and income and expenditure. Chapter 10 examines church, State and society: juridical understandings of church–State relations, the position of churches under civil law (taking Europe as an example), the concepts of religious freedom and social responsibility, and ministry in the public institutions of the State. Each chapter also suggests areas for further research. The book concludes with a summary of findings, evaluates the utility of the category Christian law, and, in the Appendix, offers the principles induced from the similarities between the laws of the churches studied.

The book studies the regulatory systems of one hundred churches worldwide spread across the ten Christian traditions (of the twenty-two global 'church families').[8] The Catholic Church, composed of the Roman or Latin Church and the Oriental Churches, is a global communion with the papacy in Rome at its institutional centre.[9] Orthodox Christianity arose in part due to doctrinal disagreement between the undivided church of the east and west which eventually culminated in the Great Schism between the Latin and Byzantine churches in 1054.[10] Today, Orthodox Christians are a family of distinct institutional churches worldwide but with no central system of government.[11] A dozen Orthodox communities are

---

[8] World Council of Churches (*Handbook of Churches and Councils* (WCC, Geneva, 2006)); those not considered here include: Friends (Quakers); Mennonite Churches; Moravian Churches; Pentecostal Churches; Salvation Army; 7th Day Adventists; and Free and Independent Churches.

[9] Catholicism denotes the faith and practice of Christians in communion with the Pope. The Catholic Church (Latin and Oriental) has a hierarchy of bishops and priests, with the Pope at its head, who are regarded as having authority entrusted by Christ to the Apostles (Jn. 20.23) and to St Peter in particular (Matt. 16.18), whose successor is conceived to be the Pope. Doctrinally it adheres to tradition and the teaching authority (*magisterium*) of the church. According to the Vatican's *Annuarium Statisticum Ecclesiae* (2005), the church numbers 1,085,557,000 persons (17.2% of the world's population).

[10] See e.g. H. Chadwick, *East and West: The Making of a Rift in the Church* (Oxford University Press, 2003).

[11] (Eastern) Orthodoxy consists of autocephalous (self-governing) churches: the four ancient patriarchates (Constantinople, Alexandria, Antioch and Jerusalem) and the more recent patriarchates (e.g. Russia, Serbia, Romania and Bulgaria). It has diaspora churches across the globe, and holds the faith of the seven ecumenical councils. It has c. 300 million members worldwide. 'Oriental' Orthodoxy comprises, e.g. the Ethiopian, Coptic, Armenian and Syrian Churches with 60 million members.

studied here.[12] Similarly, the worldwide Anglican Communion is a fellowship of autonomous churches most of which, institutionally, are historical derivatives of the Church of England which separated from Rome in the 1530s.[13] Thirty Anglican churches globally are studied here and what they share legally is summed up in *The Principles of Canon Law Common to the Churches of the Anglican Communion*.[14] The Protestant traditions are generally products of the Reformation of the sixteenth century and the resultant religious conflicts and intolerance stimulated by it.[15] Within the Lutheran World Federation,[16] the Lutheran Churches studied include those in Australia, Canada, Great Britain, Ireland, Denmark, Finland and the United States of America.[17] Originally an eighteenth-century development (inspired by John and Charles Wesley and others) within but today separate from Anglicanism, Methodism is also a global tradition.[18] The Methodist Churches examined are those in Great Britain, Ireland and New Zealand, as well as the United Methodist Church in America and in Northern Europe and Eurasia, the Free Methodist Church of North America, and, also in the Methodist tradition, the Church of the Nazarene.[19] As well as the World Communion of Reformed Churches itself,[20] next

[12] The Russian Orthodox Church; Romanian Orthodox Church; Ecumenical Patriarchate of Constantinople; Church of Greece; Archdiocese of Thyateira and Great Britain (Greek); Greek Orthodox Archdiocese of America; Greek Orthodox Archdiocese of Australia; American Carpatho-Russian Orthodox Diocese of the USA; Syrian Orthodox Church of Antioch; Malankara Orthodox Syrian Church; Orthodox Church in America; and Ukrainian Orthodox Church in America. The book also examines the Standing Conference of the Canonical Orthodox Bishops in the Americas.

[13] The Anglican Communion has forty-four churches (or provinces) worldwide in communion with the See of Canterbury. Churches studied here include those in England, Wales, Scotland, Ireland, USA, Canada and Southern Africa. Anglicanism claims to be reformed and catholic with c. 80 million followers.

[14] *The Principles of Canon Law Common to the Churches of the Anglican Communion* (Anglican Communion Office, London, 2008). The study also includes the Old Catholic Churches in the Union of Utrecht, and reference is made particularly to the North American Old Catholic Church and the Polish National Catholic Church.

[15] See e.g. E. Cameron, *The European Reformation* (Oxford University Press, 1991).

[16] Central to Lutheranism, which began with Martin Luther (16th century), are justification by faith, preaching the gospel and administration of the sacraments, received in faith without any human merit. It has c. 75 million followers worldwide. The LWF (founded 1947) consists of c. 140 churches.

[17] The Lutheran Church of Australia; Lutheran Church in Great Britain; Evangelical Lutheran Church in Ireland; Estonian Evangelical Lutheran Church; Evangelical Lutheran Church in America; Evangelical Lutheran Church of Finland; Evangelical Lutheran Church of Denmark; Evangelical Lutheran Church in Canada; Evangelical Lutheran Church of Southern Africa; Lutheran Church Missouri Synod; and North American Lutheran Church.

[18] The Wesley brothers held the Arminian view that salvation, by God's grace, was possible for all. American Methodists in 1784 constituted themselves as the Methodist Episcopal Church. Methodism is found in over 130 countries. The World Methodist Conference today meets every 5 years.

[19] The Methodist Church in Great Britain; Methodist Church in Ireland; Methodist Church of New Zealand; United Methodist Church – USA; United Methodist Church in Northern Europe and Eurasia; Free Methodist Church of North America; and the Church of the Nazarene.

[20] The term 'Reformed' refers here to bodies with historical roots in the French and Swiss-led Reformation (Calvin, Zwingli, et al.). The World Communion of Reformed Churches (WCRC) brings together 80 million Christians worldwide. Its 230 member churches in 108 countries are

come the Reformed Churches,[21] and those of the Presbyterian tradition – the Presbyterian Churches examined here are those in Scotland, Wales, Ireland, New Zealand and the United States of America.[22] The book also explores the regulatory instruments of the Congregational tradition and United and Uniting Churches (which are themselves the result of ecumenical initiatives and of constitutional unions of Christian churches from two or more different ecclesial traditions) – in India, Australia, Canada, Southern Africa and the Philippines.[23] For the Baptist tradition (which also holds that the local church is the primary expression of Christianity), within and beyond the Baptist World Alliance,[24] ten national Baptist Unions and Conventions worldwide are studied,[25] along with three local churches, two of which are in the USA and one in South Africa.[26]

The expressions 'juridical instrument' and 'regulatory instrument' are used throughout this book. They are used here to embrace a variety of normative or prescriptive entities used by the churches of the different Christian traditions which contain rules of conduct. These range from law – such as the Catholic Codes of Canon Law, Orthodox Charters and Statutes, and Anglican Constitutions and Canons – to systems of church order and polity in the Protestant traditions – such as a Manual of Laws, a Book of Order or a Book of Discipline. However, like Catholics, Orthodox and Anglicans, as we shall see, the Lutheran, Methodist, Presbyterian, United, Congregational and Baptist traditions equally use the term 'law' for their own regulatory instruments. Doctrinal or confessional texts (such as Articles of Religion or a Confession of Faith) are also prescriptive in character when

Congregational, Presbyterian, Reformed and United churches. The WCRC is a merger of the World Alliance of Reformed Churches (WARC) and the Reformed Ecumenical Council (REC) in 2010.

[21] The Reformed Church in America; United Reformed Church in Great Britain; Reformed churches hold, e.g., that Christ is the only head of the church, there is no special elite person/group with extraordinary authority, and salvation is by grace through faith in Christ. Worship is usually simple, orderly and dignified and emphasises the hearing and preaching of God's word.

[22] The Church of Scotland; Presbyterian Church in America; Presbyterian Church of Aotearoa New Zealand; Presbyterian Church in Ireland; Presbyterian Church of Wales. The book also covers the United Free Church of Scotland and the Presbyterian Church (USA).

[23] The United Congregational Church of Southern Africa; (United) Church of North India; (United) Church of South India; United Church of Canada; United Church of Christ; United Church of Christ in the Philippines; and the Uniting Church in Australia.

[24] The modern Baptist tradition was founded in the Netherlands in 1609 by John Smyth, a cleric who left the (Anglican) Church of England and taught that the church should receive its members by baptism after they have consciously acknowledged their faith; he opposed infant baptism. A Baptist church was set up in London in 1612 with Thomas Helwys as its pastor, believing in religious toleration for all. The first Baptist world congress was held in 1905 (London). The Baptist World Alliance (BWA) holds a world congress every 5 years. The Southern Baptist Convention withdrew from the BWA in 2004 and does not participate in ecumenical organizations; it has 16 million adult members, the largest Protestant group in the USA. There are also four African American Baptist Conventions (c. 15 million members).

[25] The Baptist Union of Great Britain; Baptist Union of New Zealand; Baptist Union of Scotland; Baptist Union of Southern Africa; Jamaica Baptist Union; American Baptist Churches in the USA; Canadian National Baptist Convention; North American Baptist Conference; Nigerian Baptist Convention; National Baptist Convention USA; and Southern Baptist Convention.

[26] Riverside Baptist Church, Baltimore, USA; Bethel Baptist Church, Choctaw, Oklahoma, USA; Central Baptist Church, Pretoria, South Africa.

they contain norms of conduct. In addition to these instruments, the study examines less formal but nevertheless prescriptive norms found in what might be styled 'ecclesiastical quasi-legislation' – that is, informal administrative rules designed to complement formal legal and doctrinal texts, such as Guidelines, Codes of Practice and Ethical Standards. Moreover, identifying juridical 'principles' is not problematic in Catholicism, Orthodoxy or Anglicanism.[27] The Catholic Church uses principles and *regulae iuris* to shape its codes of canon law. The Orthodox tradition has its universal (and ancient) Holy Canons (though there has to date been no obvious comparison of the modern regulatory instruments of all the individual Orthodox churches globally), and worldwide Anglicanism has *The Principles of Canon Law Common to the Churches of the Anglican Communion*. By way of contrast, the churches within each Protestant tradition have not officially compared their own laws globally, nor have they produced a statement of principles common to each of them worldwide.[28] However, it is evident from the comparisons undertaken here that each Protestant tradition, too, has its common principles, sometimes derived from doctrinal texts, which either shape or may be induced from their laws and thereby stimulate juridical unity between them. In turn, for the purposes of this study, a 'principle of law' common to the Christian traditions studied here is understood as a foundational proposition or maxim of general applicability which has a strong dimension of weight, is induced from the similarities of the regulatory systems of the churches, derives from their juridical tradition or the practices of the church universal, expresses a basic theological truth or ethical value, and is implicit in, or underlies, the juridical systems of the churches.[29]

Five further methodological issues faced in the preparation of this book are worthy of note. First, as between the chapters, subjects are treated thematically. The topics of chapters (if not their sequence) and the sections within them are not constructed *de novo* but are shaped broadly by the systematisation of subjects appearing in the regulatory instruments of the churches themselves. The regulatory instruments generally deal separately with the institutional church, persons, government, doctrine, worship, rites and property. Secondly, as with any comparative legal study, a particular challenge was the presentation of material; for example, whether to: (1) devote a chapter to each of the traditions (this would provide a broad picture of each tradition but it would not sufficiently juxtapose the laws for the purpose of identifying shared principles); (2) address all the traditions in a single paragraph on a particular topic (this would enable identification of principles but produce too fragmentary a picture of each tradition); or (3) within a section, devote a paragraph to each tradition. Whilst each had its merits, after some experimentation and discussion with colleagues from several of the traditions, option (3) was chosen: generally, each tradition is treated *seriatim* on the topic of

---

[27] See e.g. N. Doe, 'The principles of canon law: a focus of legal unity in Anglican-Roman Catholic relations', *Ecclesiastical Law Journal* (1999) 221.

[28] Such a process is recommended in N. Doe, 'The contribution of common principles of canon law to ecclesial communion in Anglicanism', *The Principles of Canon Law Common to the Churches of the Anglican Communion* (Anglican Communion Office, London, 2008) 97 at 110.

[29] This basic method and a similar definition of a principle of law were employed in N. Doe, *Canon Law in the Anglican Communion: A Worldwide Perspective* (Clarendon Press, Oxford, 1998) and, in the context of secular law, N. Doe, *Law and Religion in Europe: A Comparative Introduction* (Oxford University Press, 2011).

each chapter section, and sometimes a paragraph is devoted exclusively to an individual church. This method provides a reasonably broad picture for each tradition on a cluster of matters within a discrete area, and it eases the articulation of principles on a topic-by-topic basis. Thirdly, in each section, the traditions are generally taken in an order shaped by their theological stance on church polity, and this order also roughly corresponds (with the exception of the Methodist and Baptist traditions) to the sequence of their historical emergence, namely: Catholic, Orthodox and Anglican (all three traditions have bishops); and in the Protestant traditions: Lutheran (most have bishops, some do not) and Methodist (some have bishops, most do not); Reformed and Presbyterian – in the tradition of Calvin (which rejects a separate grade of bishops); the United Churches and the Congregational Churches (most of which locate ultimate authority in the local church); and the Baptist tradition (which locates authority in the local church but assigns some functions to national Unions and Conventions). Fourthly, it is axiomatic that context is critical to understand law. As we shall see, there is a close relationship between theology and the regulatory instruments. The latter often seek to implement theological ideas as norms of conduct. Throughout the study, reference is made where appropriate to the theological foundations of particular juridical arrangements. Fifthly, whilst the juridical history of Christianity has not yet been written, and this book does not offer one, where relevant, brief reference is sometimes made to the historical texts and formularies of these traditions in order to elucidate rules.[30]

Articulation of the principles of Christian law is designed to stimulate debate in two sectors: academic and practical. On the one hand, academic lawyers and theologians need to understand the persistent interaction of theology and law. Each feeds off the other: church law is reliant on theological reflection for its creation, and practical theology is often reliant on law for its implementation in norms of conduct. Moreover, given the Christian genius for doctrinal divisions, it is a particular challenge for both theologians and lawyers to justify the continued significance of doctrinal disagreements when the laws of churches converge so profoundly around norms of conduct shared by all Christians. For lawyers, too, it is increasingly recognised that an understanding of religious laws, such as those of Christians, is useful to identify and evaluate the acceptable scope of State law on religion,[31] but there is generally a lack of studies on the relationship between religious law and the religion law of the State.[32] In its development of the category

---

[30] See also R.H. Helmholz, *The Spirit of Classical Canon Law* (University of Georgia Press, Athens and London, 1996); J.A. Brundage, *Medieval Canon Law* (Longman, London, 1995); J. Witte, *Law and Protestantism: The Legal Teachings of the Protestant Reformation* (Cambridge University Press, 2002). See also the historical studies in J. Witte and F.S. Alexander (eds.), *Christianity and Law* (Cambridge University Press, 2008), but the latter does not seek the category principles of Christian law. For a history of the faith, see D. MacCulloch, *A History of Christianity: The First Three Thousand Years* (Viking, New York, 2009).

[31] See e.g. C. Hamilton, *Family, Law and Religion* (Sweet and Maxwell, London, 1995); P. Edge, *Religion and Law* (Ashgate, Aldershot, 2006); P. Cane, C. Evans and Z. Robinson (eds.), *Law and Religion in Theoretical and Historical Context* (Cambridge University Press 2008); P.M. Taylor, *Freedom of Religion* (Cambridge University Press, 2005).

[32] See e.g. R. Ahdar and I. Leigh, *Religious Freedom in the Liberal State* (Oxford University Press, 2005); J. Rivers, *The Law of Organized Religions* (Oxford University Press, 2011); R. Sandberg,

of Christian law, this book enables debate about this relationship when it involves Christians. The same applies to scholarship in comparative religious law, though coverage of Christianity in this field is sometimes very narrow.[33] The category will certainly provide a point of comparison for those who study the religious law of other single world faiths, such as Jewish law, Islamic law and Hindu law.[34] Islamic law and Jewish law, for example, have themselves been compared.[35] However, because Christian law has not been articulated hitherto in the way proposed here, meaningful comparisons have not been made between Christian law and, for example, Islamic law or Jewish law.[36] This book is designed to facilitate such comparative studies on the basis of its global and interdenominational reach. The book may also be of interest to sociologists of religion. Whilst little attention to date has been given to religious law in the sociology of religion, some scholars are increasingly but briefly recognising the importance of religious 'self-regulation'.[37] In short, it is hoped that presenting the principles of the laws of Christian churches together, and comparatively, in a single volume will be of benefit to academic lawyers, theologians and those who study religious law.[38]

On the other hand, the book is intended as a resource for practitioners, namely, church officers engaged in Christian dialogue with the State and society, interfaith dialogue and ecumenical dialogue. At such moments when a church faces pressure from its host State(s) to adopt secular standards in its ecclesial life and practice, a statement of Christian law might provide support to that church and reinforce or underpin its position on a given matter. For the same reason, the study may assist lawyers in the practice of human rights law and discrimination law, for example, when they need to explain the juridical approaches of Christians in these contexts. Equally, access to a statement of Christian laws enables government to understand what opportunities and constraints the rules of a church place on that church in its dealings with the State and society. State courts often deal with Christian obligations in religious freedom cases, the State legislates on matters which concern Christians, and in the field of charity law, for example, State administrative bodies need to

---

Law and Religion (Cambridge University Press, 2011); N. Doe, *Law and Religion in Europe: A Comparative Introduction* (Oxford University Press, 2011): the latter proposes the need for such a study.

[33] See e.g. A. Huxley (ed.), *Religion, Law and Tradition* (Routledge, Abingdon, 2002): of Christian laws, this covers only Roman Catholic law: 49 (S. Ferrari, 'Canon law as a religious legal system').

[34] See e.g. J. Schacht, *An Introduction to Islamic Law* (Clarendon Press, Oxford, 1982); N.S. Hecht et al. (eds.), *An Introduction to the History and Sources of Jewish Law* (Oxford University Press, 1996); W.F. Menski, *Hindu Law* (Oxford University Press, 2003).

[35] See e.g. J. Neusner and T. Sonn, *Comparing Religions Through Law: Judaism and Islam* (Routledge, London, 1999).

[36] *The First Roman Consultation on Jewish and Canon Law* (Gregorian University, Rome, 2006), *Periodica de re canonica*, XCVI (2007) is a rarity but only compares Jewish law and Roman Catholic canon law.

[37] See e.g. J.A. Beckford and J.T. Richardson, 'Religion and regulation' in J.A. Beckford and N.J. Demerath (eds.), *The Sage Handbook of the Sociology of Religion* (Sage, London, 2007) 396.

[38] National and international societies which study law and religion include the Ecclesiastical Law Society; European Consortium for Church and State Research; International Consortium for Law and Religion Studies (ICLARS); and Colloquium of Anglican and Roman Catholic Canon Lawyers.

understand the juridical standards of accountability prevailing within the churches. Indeed, the Archbishop of Canterbury in 2008 explored the significance of religious law in society today and possible frameworks for the State and religions to accommodate each other's legal systems. This led some commentators to identify as problematic the low levels of knowledge of religious laws, including Christianity, in the pronouncements of government and the courts.[39] The book seeks to improve knowledge about juridical Christianity in this secular context. It is also designed to enable other world faiths to understand the opportunities and constraints which ecclesiastical laws place on a church in its dealings with and policy decisions about their relations and collaboration with Christians, not least in seeing how much those faiths share normatively with Christianity.[40]

Above all, the study is relevant to ecumenism. The Great Schism between east and west (in the eleventh century) and the Reformation (in the sixteenth century and beyond) represent landmarks which stimulated the fragmentation of the undivided Christian church into a proliferation today of different institutional churches or denominations. The ecumenical movement (maturing in the twentieth century) seeks the recovery of Christian unity through the development of greater visible communion between the separated (or divided) institutional churches of Christianity worldwide.[41] The principal focus of this movement, in the practice of ecumenism (through inter-church dialogues and institutional structures like the World Council of Churches) and in ecumenical theology (the study of ecumenism), has been the quest for agreement at the level of doctrine achieved through theological debate. The juridical instruments of churches have not thus far featured as part of the staple diet of ecumenical discourse. In point of fact, church law and its equivalents are seen by some distinguished scholars, both Catholic and Protestant,[42]

---

[39] R. Williams, 'Civil and religious law in England: a religious perspective' (2008) *Ecclesiastical Law Journal* 262. See generally, e.g. R. Sandberg, *Law and Religion* (Cambridge University Press, 2011) esp. Ch. 10.

[40] This study may also be fed into the work of the Interfaith Legal Advisers Network which has representatives from over fifteen religious groups (including Muslim, Jewish, Sikh and Hindu groups).

[41] See generally e.g. N. Lossky, J.M. Bonino, J. Pobee, T.F. Stransky, G. Wainwright and P. Webb (eds.), *Dictionary of the Ecumenical Movement* (WCC Publications, Geneva, 2002).

[42] Catholic scholars include Robert Ombres OP: see Colloquium of Anglican and Roman Catholic Canon Lawyers (CARCCL), 'A decade of ecumenical dialogue in canon law' (2009) 11 *Ecclesiastical Law Journal* 284; see also J. Conn, N. Doe and J. Fox (eds.), *Initiation, Membership and Authority in Anglican and Roman Catholic Canon Law* (Centre for Law and Religion, Cardiff, and Pontifical Gregorian University and Pontifical University of St Thomas Aquinas, Rome, 2005) 317, Statement on Authority (Cardiff, 2003): 'The role of canon law in ecumenical dialogue' is e.g. to provide a stable ecumenical methodology; concrete data which embody theology; a detailed guide to practical action for Christian life; definition of the degree of achieved communion and opportunities for and limits of future progress; a description of identity; order and freedom in decision-making; and information for ecumenical partners as to the binding nature of Christian truth. See also B. Leahy, 'The role of canon law in the ecumenical venture: a Roman Catholic perspective' (2011) 15 *Ecclesiastical Law Journal* 15 and N. Sagovsky, 'The contribution of canon law to Anglican-Roman Catholic ecumenism', ibid., 4. See also the work of the Protestant scholar Leo J. Koffeman, *Het goed recht van de kerk: Een theologische inleiding op het kerkrecht* (Kok, Kampen, 2009); and H. Dombois, 'Ökumenisches Kirchenrecht heute', 24 *Zeitschrift für Evangelisches Kirchenrecht* (1979) 225: this proposes that church law is ecumenical in nature (as churches are united in their use of juridical forms to express their place in the church universal).

as the 'missing link' in ecumenism. As has already been mentioned, the World Council of Churches acknowledged in 1974 the potential of the study of 'church law' as an instrument of ecumenism, but no action was taken to promote this.[43] Yet, these instruments should have a more prominent place in ecumenical practice and theology. They tell us much about the opportunities which laws provide for churches to participate in the ecumenical enterprise. They define what ecclesial communion is possible or not. The book, therefore, proposes the concept of 'juridical ecumenism' which facilitates exploration of the ways in which ecclesial regulatory instruments enable or restrict the development of greater visible communion between separated churches. Juridical ecumenism offers both a theoretical and a practical framework for the global transformation of ecumenism – one designed to complement but not to replace the current (and dominant) doctrinal and theological focus in contemporary ecumenical method and practice: after all, church regulatory systems are applied theology.

Needless to say, with its global reach, each chapter that follows surveys a vast amount of material from a hundred separate legal systems. In consequence, the chapters carry extensive quotations from and footnotes which refer to the primary legal materials of the churches. These are designed not only to provide the legal evidence for propositions which appear in the text, but also to allow the regulatory instruments of churches to speak for themselves. Unless the text or context provide otherwise, references to regulatory instruments in the footnotes are merely examples – when legal provisions are unique to a tradition or a church within it, this is indicated. Secondary literature is listed in the Bibliography, which also carries studies for further reading as to the individual traditions. An Appendix of the principles of Christian law is included towards the end of the book. These, it is argued, are what emerge from a comparative study of the laws and other regulatory instruments of churches worldwide across the ten ecclesiastical traditions studied. The principles indicate, above all, that dogmas divide but laws link Christians in common norms of action.

---

[43] WCC, Faith and Order Commission, Document IV.8 (1974), 'The Ecumenical Movement and Church Law' – the starting point of this document is that church law is an ecumenical problem: see M. Reuver, *Faith and Law: Juridical Perspectives for the Ecumenical Movement* (WCC, Geneva, 2000) 5.

1

The sources and purposes of ecclesiastical regulation

The regulatory instruments of each church in all of the Christian traditions studied in this book provide clearly defined ideas about the nature and purposes of the institutional church. The ideas are essentially theological in origin and substance but juridical in form. Moreover, to a lesser or greater extent all the churches studied here claim to have systems of 'law': the churches across the traditions employ the expression 'law' to signify the general character of at least some species of their regulatory instruments. Within this broad category of 'law', individual written instruments have particular titles, such as constitutions, canons and covenants; unwritten customs also have the force of law in some churches. However, alongside these formal sources of law which have binding force, churches in each of the traditions also employ ecclesiastical quasi-legislation in the shape of guidelines or other types of informal and usually persuasive but nevertheless normative instrument. Not only does the whole regulatory system of a church serve general purposes linked to the mission of that particular ecclesial community, but, depending on its type, each instrument has its own specific objects. In this regard, humanly created juridical norms of conduct have an intimate relationship with theology and are, generally, subject to or operate within the context of the superior law of God. Taking each tradition *seriatim*, this chapter examines these matters as well as facilities for the enforcement, relaxation and interpretation of church regulatory instruments. In so doing, it elucidates from the similarities between the juridical instruments of the churches, of all the Christian traditions examined, contemporary principles of Christian law about the nature of the institutional church and its regulatory systems – their plurality of forms, the subjects which they address, and their enforcement, relaxation and interpretation.

The institutional church

Each of the churches in the Christian traditions studied here presents in its regulatory instruments an understanding of itself – its nature and purposes as 'a church'.[1] What emerges from a comparison of these instruments is that a church

---

[1] The New Testament employs the Greek *ekklesia* (commonly understood to translate the Hebrew *qahal*, assembly) to refer to Christian communities in geographical places (1 Cor. 1.2), a house (Rom. 16.3–5), a city (Acts 8.1) or a region (Acts 9.31), as distinct from the church universal (Eph. 1.22). The English word 'church' (Old English *cirice*, Teutonic *kirika*) derives from the Greek *kuriake*, 'belonging to the Lord', and over time was used for both the church universal and particular local communities of Christians with a visible outward organisation distinct from other communities or 'churches': see the Oxford English Dictionary: 'church'.

is a community of Christians in a particular geographical area with defined objects and a distinct membership, institutional organisation and autonomous polity; moreover, a church may be, or be part of, a local, regional, national or international ecclesial community and at the same time claim its place in the church universal.[2] Indeed, for the World Council of Churches,[3] 'church' may include an association, convention or federation of 'churches',[4] and to be 'churches' for membership of the Council, applicants must satisfy two tests, theological and organisational. To satisfy the theological test, the community must profess faith in the Triune God, maintain a ministry to proclaim the Gospel and administer the Sacraments (as understood by its doctrines), baptise in the name of God, recognise the presence and activity of Christ and the Holy Spirit outside its boundaries, and acknowledge the marks of the church universal in other member churches. To satisfy the organisational test, the church must have a 'sustained autonomous life and organization' and at least 50,000 members (which rule may be waived), recognise the 'essential interdependence' of member churches, and make 'every effort to practise constructive ecumenical relations with other churches'.[5]

The Catholic Church – the Latin Church and the Oriental Churches – is a 'universal church' (with an international organisation) composed of 'particular churches'. It conceives of itself theologically and canonically as a single complex reality, a mystery which is both a spiritual and a human society, composed of 'the people of God', Christ's faithful (*christifideles*), and ordered hierarchically; moreover: 'This Church, established and ordered in this world as a society, subsists (*subsistit*) in the catholic Church, governed by the successor of Peter and the Bishops in communion with him.'[6] The 'teaching office' of the Latin Church is 'to preach the Gospel to all people' and 'to proclaim moral principles' about

---

[2] Whilst ecclesiology is the theological study of the church universal, the Body of Christ or communion of all Christians over space and time, juridical definitions of an institutional church are about its 'ecclesiality' (e.g. its territoriality, sociality and polity). See Chapter 8 for juridical expressions of the church universal.

[3] WCC: Const., Art. I (Basis): the WCC is not itself a church but 'a fellowship of churches which confess the Lord Jesus Christ as God and Saviour according to the scriptures and therefore seek to fulfil together their common calling to the glory of the one God, Father, Son and Holy Spirit'; Art. III (Functions and Purposes): 'to call the churches to the goal of visible unity in one faith and in one Eucharistic fellowship expressed in worship and in common life in Christ, and to advance towards that unity in order that the world may believe'.

[4] WCC: Rules, I.3: a group of churches in the same region or confession may join 'as one church ... to respond to their common calling, to strengthen their joint participation and/or to satisfy the requirement of ... size'.

[5] WCC: Central Committee, Minutes, 52nd Meeting, Geneva (2002) 210; Const., Art. II: 'Applicant churches' must 'express their agreement with the Basis ... and confirm their commitment to [its] Purposes and Functions'.

[6] CIC, cc. 204–205; CCEO, cc. 7–8. LG, 1, 8, 10–11, 48: 'The Church ... is in the nature of a sacrament ... a sign and instrument of communion with God and union among all people', 'a visible organization through which [Christ] communicates truth and grace to all'; yet, 'the society structured with hierarchical organs and the mystical body of Christ, the visible society and the spiritual community ... are not ... two realities', but 'form one complex reality' with 'a human and a divine element'; 'Christ sent his life-giving Spirit upon his disciples and through them set up his body which is the Church as the universal sacrament of salvation.'

'the social order', 'fundamental human rights', and 'the salvation of souls';[7] its 'sanctifying office' is carried out principally in worship and the administration of the sacraments;[8] and its 'governing office' vests primarily in the Pontiff (or Pope) who has 'supreme authority' in 'the universal church here on earth'.[9] Particular churches, those in which 'the one and only catholic Church exists, are principally dioceses', i.e. a portion of the people of God in a defined territory entrusted to and governed by a bishop around whom the faithful are gathered 'through the Gospel and the Eucharist'.[10] Similarly, the Church of Christ is 'truly present in all legitimate local congregations ... where the faithful are gathered together (*congregantur*) in the preaching of the Gospel and in the celebration of the mystery of the Lord's Supper'.[11] Each Oriental church is *sui iuris*, autonomous (but subject to the Pope) and has its own 'rite' or spiritual heritage, and may be within a single territory or dispersed across territories.[12]

Orthodox Christians speak of 'The Orthodox Church' variously as 'the one true church of Christ', 'the Church of the Seven Ecumenical Councils', and, globally, as 'a family of self-governing Churches', held together 'not by a centralized organization', but 'by the double bond of unity in the faith and communion in the sacraments'.[13] Individually, therefore, Orthodox churches are 'local Churches, each having its own jurisdiction'; each local church is either 'autocephalous' (it elects its own primate), or 'autonomous' (it elects its primate with the participation of an autocephalous church), in communion with its 'sister Churches', and 'catholic in its composition and structure'; and, gathered around its bishop, 'the Church is fully present in a local Eucharistic gathering' – 'the local Church is the Church universal' with 'fullness of ecclesial reality'.[14] Legally, like the Catholic Church, an individual Orthodox church may be an international patriarchate (with its headquarters in a nation) or a unit within a patriarchate in a particular territory.[15] For example, the

---

[7] CIC, Bk. III: 'The Teaching Office of the Church'; c. 747: the duty to preach the Gospel.
[8] CIC, Bk. IV: 'The Sanctifying Office'; c. 834: worship; cc. 840–848; the administration of the sacraments.
[9] CIC, Bk. II: 'People of God', Pt. II, 'Hierarchical Constitution'; cc. 330–331: pontiff; CCEO, cc. 42 and 43.
[10] CIC, cc. 368–374: particular churches; LG 23, 27; CCEO, cc. 55–150: patriarchal churches; cc. 151–154: major archiepiscopal churches; cc. 155–176: metropolitan churches and other churches *sui iuris*.
[11] LG, 26; CIC, c. 374: the parish.
[12] CCEO, c. 27: each church is 'a community of the Christian faithful ... joined together by a hierarchy according to ... law and ... recognised as *sui iuris* by the supreme authority'; cc. 39–40: each church preserves its rite as a 'heritage' (c. 28); c. 57: the Pope erects and suppresses a church which is (c. 921) a juridical person.
[13] N. Lossky, 'The Orthodox Churches', in P. Avis (ed.), *The Christian Church: An Introduction to the Major Traditions* (SPCK, London, 2002) 1, at 9 and 13; G. Limouris (ed.), *Orthodox Visions of Ecumenism* (WCC, Geneva, 1994) 29; T. Ware, *The Orthodox Church* (Penguin Books, London, 1963, Reprint 1991) 15.
[14] Limouris, *Orthodox Visions of Ecumenism*, 66; E.J. Stormon (ed.), *Towards the Healing of Schism* (Paulist Press, New York, 1987) 239; J. Zizioulas, *Being as Communion* (St Vladimir's Seminary Press, New York, 1985) 257: 'a local Church, in order to be not just local but also Church, must be in full communion with the rest of the local Churches in the world'.
[15] See e.g. SOCA: Const., Preamble: the Syrian Orthodox Church of Antioch has its headquarters in Damascus and promotes 'Christian teachings', preserves the 'Holy Sacraments' and achieves

Russian Orthodox Church, or the Moscow Patriarchate, defines itself as 'a multi-national Local Autocephalous Church' in 'doctrinal unity and canonical communion with other Local Orthodox Churches' and it consists of 'canonical units' including self-governing churches, dioceses and parishes;[16] it has jurisdiction over Orthodox Christians living within its 'canonical territory', a system of government, doctrine, ritual and property.[17] Similarly, the Romanian Orthodox Church is 'the community of the Orthodox Christians, clergy, monks and lay [people], canonically constituted in parishes and monasteries in the eparchies of the Romanian Patriarchy inside and outside the Romanian frontiers, which witness God in the Holy Trinity, Father, Son and Holy Spirit, based on the Holy Scripture, liturgical services and canonical order'; of 'apostolic origin', the church is 'in communion and dogmatic, liturgical and canonical unity with the universal Orthodox Church' and is 'autocephalous'.[18] Juridical definitions may also include a statement of the objects of a church. For instance, within the Ecumenical Patriarchate of Constantinople (based in Istanbul),[19] the mission of the Greek Orthodox Archdiocese of America, an eparchy of the Ecumenical Patriarchate,[20] is 'to proclaim the Gospel of Christ, to teach and spread the Orthodox Christian Faith, to energize, cultivate and guide the life of the Church ... according to the Orthodox Christian Faith and the Sacred Tradition'; to sanctify 'the faithful through the Divine Worship, especially the Eucharist and other Sacraments'; to build up 'the spiritual and ethical life of the faithful'; and to serve as 'a beacon, carrier and witness of the message of Christ to all persons who live in the [USA]'.[21] Different national Orthodox churches may also associate in an alliance, such as the Standing Conference of the Canonical Orthodox Bishops in the Americas.[22]

'justice for all mankind'; Art. 4: territorial scope; it has archdioceses in e.g. Jerusalem, Canada, Brazil, Germany and New Zealand. E.g. the Malankara Orthodox Syrian Church: MOSC: Const., e.g. Art. 1: foundation, membership, and doctrine; Arts. 2–4: parish, diocese, and archdiocese; Art. 5: Catholicos; Art. 6: Patriarch; Art. 7: Episcopal Synod.

[16] ROC: Statute, I.1-2; see e.g. Diocese of Sourozh: Statutes, I.2: 'The Diocese ... is a canonical unit' of ROC.

[17] ROC: Statute, I.3; e.g. I.7: its governing bodies include the Local Council, Bishops' Council and Holy Synod.

[18] ROMOC: Statutes, Arts. 1 and 2.

[19] OOCL, 213–221; e.g. the (Orthodox) Church of Greece is autocephalous and 'united ... to the Great Church of Constantinople': Constitution of Greece 1975, Art. 3.

[20] GOAA: Charter, Art. 1(a),(c) and (d): the church 'is an Eparchy of the most Holy, Apostolic and Patriarchal Ecumenical Throne of Constantinople (Ecumenical Patriarchate), which is the first-ranking see of the one, holy, Catholic and Apostolic Church whose head is Christ'; the Archdiocese consists of Orthodox Christians 'who either as individuals or as organized groups in Dioceses and Parishes have voluntarily come to it and which acknowledge the supreme spiritual ecclesiastical and canonical jurisdiction of the Ecumenical Patriarchate'.

[21] GOAA: Charter, Art. 2; Arts. 3–4: governance; Art. 9: courts. Also UOCIA: Const., Art. I: a 'canonical entity with territorial jurisdiction' in the USA, its doctrine etc. are those 'as taught by the Holy Scriptures, Holy Tradition ... [and] Holy Fathers'; Arts. II–III: Holy Synod; Art. IV: Major Archbishops; Art. V: Prime Bishop's Council; Art. VI: Archdiocese; Arts. VII–IX: Diocese; Art. X: Deanery; Art. XI: Parish; Art. XII: Courts.

[22] SCOBA: Const., Preamble, Arts I and V.1: the Conference brings together e.g. Greek, Antiochian, Serbian, Romanian, Bulgarian, Carpatho-Russian, Ukrainian and Albanian Orthodox hierarchs.

The worldwide Anglican Communion is 'a fellowship of churches within the One, Holy, Catholic and Apostolic Church, characterised by their historic relationship of communion with the See of Canterbury'.[23] Individually, the churches are 'duly constituted national, regional, provincial churches and dioceses'.[24] As such: '"A church" means an autonomous member church, national, regional, provincial, or extra-provincial, of the Anglican Communion'.[25] Each church is 'an autonomous territorial unit of ecclesiastical jurisdiction' – a national or a regional church may consist of more than one province; a province consists of dioceses and a diocese consists of parishes or other localised ecclesiastical units; an extra-provincial church is organised on a diocesan basis and is not part of a province but may come under metropolitical jurisdiction in another church.[26] Each church has a system of membership, ministry, episcopal-synodical government, doctrine, worship, ritual, and property.[27] The purposes of an institutional church include: '[t]o give glory to God through united and common witness and proclamation of the Gospel of our Lord Jesus Christ'; to 'strengthen and further the Church's fellowship' and 'make disciples of all nations';[28] 'to minister the doctrine and sacraments and discipline of Christ';[29] and to promote justice in the world, responding to human needs by service, and seeking 'to transform unjust structures of society, caring for God's creation and establishing the values of the Kingdom' of God.[30]

Turning to the Protestant traditions, the Lutheran World Federation (like the Anglican Communion) is a global communion of autonomous churches.[31]

---

[23] PCLCCAC, Principle 10.1. See also Thirty-Nine Articles of Religion, Art. 19: 'The visible Church of Christ is a congregation of faithful men, in the which the ... Word of God is preached, and ... Sacraments ... ministered according to Christ's ordinance'; TACC, 1.1.1: each church affirms 'its communion in' the church universal.

[24] PCLCCAC, Principle 10.2: they 'propagate the historic faith and order as typified in the Book of Common Prayer 1662 and its derivatives'; 10.4: 'ecclesial communion' is based on communion with one or more of: the See of Canterbury; Church of England; all Communion churches; all churches in communion with Canterbury; or all churches professing the apostolic faith as received within the Anglican tradition. See e.g. TEC: Const., Preamble: the church is 'a constituent member of the Anglican Communion'. See also LC 1930, Res. 49: provinces 'promote within each of their territories a national expression of Christian faith, life and worship'.

[25] PCLCCAC, Definitions.

[26] PCLCCAC, Principle 15.1–5. E.g.: 'The Episcopal Church in the United States of America'; 'The Anglican Church of Australia'; 'The Anglican Church of Southern Africa' (a single province straddling several States including South Africa); 'The Lusitanian Catholic and Apostolic and Evangelical Church', 'an Extra-Provincial Diocese of the Anglican Communion' with metropolitical authority vested in the Archbishop of Canterbury.

[27] PCLCCAC, Pt. III: Ecclesiastical Government; Pt. IV: Ministry (including membership); Pt. V: Doctrine and Liturgy; Pt. VI: Ecclesiastical Rites; Pt. VII: Church Property; Pt. VIII: Ecumenical Relations.

[28] South East Asia: Const., Preamble. See also Sudan: Const., Preamble.

[29] Ireland: Const., Preamble, I.3.

[30] New Zealand: Const., Preamble. See also Philippines: Const., Art. I.1.

[31] LWF: Const., Art. II: 'the Lutheran Church'; Art. III: the LWF is 'a communion of churches which confess the triune God, agree in the proclamation of the Word of God and are united in pulpit and altar fellowship'; it is e.g. to witness to the Gospel, alleviate human need, promote human rights, and assist its members 'to act jointly in common tasks'; Art. IV: it is 'an instrument of its autonomous member churches'.

Alongside their understandings of the church universal,[32] for Lutherans a church is understood as a national or local assembly of the faithful.[33] Its identity is shaped fundamentally by its confession as set out in the authoritative Reformation texts.[34] For example, the Evangelical Lutheran Church of America sees itself as 'a church body', its roots 'deep in the soil of the Lutheran Confessions and ... [its] biblical foundations', which accepts, *inter alia*, 'the Augsburg Confession as a witness to the Gospel';[35] moreover, the church is 'a particular gathering of people' and 'part of the whole Church of Christ'; its objects include to 'declare the teachings of the prophets and apostles and seek to confess in our time the faith once delivered to the saints'; indeed, 'gathered for worship and Christian service', its congregations 'find their fulfilment in the universal community of the Church, and the Church universal exists in and through congregations'.[36] Similarly, the Lutheran Church of Australia is autonomous and 'consists of congregations voluntarily joined together';[37] its objects include: to 'fulfil the mission of the Christian Church in the world by proclaiming the Word of God and administering the Sacraments'; to unite congregations for the more effective work of the Church; to maintain true Christian unity in the bond of peace; to ensure that preaching and practice conform with the Confession of the Church; to provide pastors and others for service in the Church and its congregations; to encourage every congregation to carry out its mission to its local community; and to minister to human need in the name of Christ and the spirit of Christian love and service.[38] To these ends, a Lutheran church has a system of membership, government (with or without bishops), doctrine, worship, ritual, pastoral care and social activity,[39] and may also assert its own membership of the Lutheran World Federation.[40]

---

[32] AC, Arts. 4, 7, 10, 11: 'the church is the assembly of all believers in which the gospel is preached purely and sacraments are administered rightly', these being 'the means the Holy Spirit employs to create the church as the community of faith' of 'justified sinners [in] communion' with God and each other.

[33] Apol., 7.5, 7.14: 'a group of persons', a society (*societas*), a people (*populus*); see e.g. the Danish Constitution, Art. 4: 'The Evangelical Lutheran Church is the Danish National Church.'

[34] E.g. the Augsburg Confession (1530) (AC), Luther's Small Catechism (1529) (LSC), Formula of Concord (1577) (FC) and the confessions in the Book of Concord (1580) (BC) containing e.g. the Apostles', Nicene and Athanasian Creeds.

[35] ELCA: Constitution and Foundational Texts (2003) Chs. 1 and 2.

[36] ELCA: Const., Ch. 4: it is to proclaim the gospel, carry on outreach, meet human need, engage in worship, administer the sacraments, nurture its members and manifest unity with other Christians.

[37] LCA: Const., Art. VI.3: the church has authority to regulate 'the administration of its own affairs'; Art. VII.1: General Synod is 'the highest constitutional authority of the Church'; Art. VI.7: congregational autonomy.

[38] LCA: Const., Art. III. See also ELCSA: G., 10.10: the church is 'to serve the Gospel of Jesus Christ by Word and Sacrament, to promote brotherly fellowship in prayer and in the following of Jesus Christ, to fulfil the missionary command, to bear public witness, to live a life of charity and to promote Christian upbringing and education'; for similar formulae see LCGB: RAR: Statement of Faith, 7–9; ELCIC: Const., Art. IV.2.

[39] LCA: Const., Art. IV: members; for governance, ELCA: Articles of Incorporation, Art. I, ELCSA: G., 5.1.

[40] ELCA: Const., Ch. 8.73. See also ELCSA: G., 10.11: the church is 'in community with' e.g. Evangelical Lutheran churches 'throughout the world'.

Methodist churches also define themselves by reference to their place in the church universal,[41] and in the World Methodist Council,[42] their institutional formation and territorial compass, and their objects, membership, government, doctrine and rituals.[43] For example, the Methodist Church in Great Britain is a union of the Wesleyan Methodist Church, Primitive Methodist Church and United Methodist Church, by which it became 'a united church or denomination under the name of the Methodist Church'; the purposes of the church are the advancement of 'the Christian faith in accordance with the doctrinal standards and the discipline of the Methodist Church' and any charitable purpose, *inter alia*, of any Connexional, district, circuit, local or other organisation of the church; also, the church 'cherishes its place' in the church universal as well as its membership of the World Methodist Council.[44] Similarly, churches of the Reformed tradition may belong to the World Communion of Reformed Churches, which includes Presbyterian, Reformed, Congregational and United Churches; its churches are 'called together in the name of the one God, Father, Son and Holy Spirit. Under the sovereign God, with Christ's followers across the globe, sharing one baptism, the members of the communion belong to the one holy catholic and apostolic church'.[45] In turn, typically, a Presbyterian church defines itself by reference to its place in the church universal, its doctrinal inheritance from the Reformed tradition, its autonomy, membership and officers, and its system of government by church courts in local church councils, regional presbyteries and a General Assembly.[46] The functions of a

---

[41] UMCNEAE: BOD, par. 103: 'The visible Church of Christ is a congregation of faithful men in which the pure Word of God is preached, and the Sacraments duly administered according to Christ's ordinance.'

[42] It exists e.g. to 'deepen the fellowship of the Methodist people across race, nationality, colour and language', 'advance unity of theological and moral standards', encourage evangelism, promote Christian education, and 'uphold and relieve persecuted Christian minorities'. UMCNEAE: BOD, par. 2403: membership of the WMC; MCGB: CPD, Book VI, Part 4; and SO 335: delegations to the WMC.

[43] See e.g. UMCUSA: Const., Div. 1; the church, a union of the Evangelical United Brethren and the Methodist Church and 'part of the church universal', is autonomous and exists to proclaim the Word of God, worship, administer the sacraments, exercise pastoral care to its members, and engage in social responsibility; the General Conference has jurisdiction over 'the entire Church' (this is mirrored in UMCNEAE: BOD pars. 2–26 and 122). See also e.g. MCI: Const., s. 3: membership; s. 5: Courts of the Church; MCNZ: LAR, Historical Note (on the unions which formed the church); MCGB: CPD, DU 1: Courts (e.g. Conference, Synods, and Circuit Meetings).

[44] MCGB: DU s. 2.3 and Methodist Church Act 1976 s. 4; CPD, DU 4: church universal. See also MCI: RDG, 1.01: 'the Methodist Church has been raised up to spread scriptural holiness through the land by the proclamation of the evangelical faith and experience'; UMCNEAE: BOD, par. 140: it is a 'denomination'.

[45] WCRC: Const., Preamble; Art. II: basis: e.g. 'the Word of ... God, incarnate in ... Christ and revealed in ... Scriptures'; it has 'a Reformed identity as articulated in the Ecumenical Creeds of the early church, in the historic confessions of the Reformation, and as continued in the life ... of the reformed community'; Art. V: mission: e.g. to widen the community, support its churches, and engage in ecumenism; Art. VI: membership.

[46] PCANZ: BO, 1.1; 1.2(1): 'The Church is part of the reformed tradition and derives from the Presbyterian heritage within that tradition' and (1.4) is 'ever requiring reformation'; 'Government ... is vested in local church councils, synods ... and ... General Assembly'; 1.6: it is a union formed in 1901. See also PCA: BCO, 10.1; PCI: Code, I.1; RCA: BCO, Preamble: it

Presbyterian church and its units include sharing in the mission of God to the world and proclaiming the good news of God.[47] Similar definitions are found in the juridical instruments of a United church – a union of churches from, for example, the Reformed and Congregational traditions and consisting of 'Local Churches, Associations, Conferences and [a] General Synod'; its juridical objects include 'to make [the] faith its own in reality of worship, in honesty of thought and expression, and in purity of heart before God'.[48]

The Baptist tradition is at the other end of the definitional spectrum. For Baptists a church is defined as the local church and congregation. The Baptist World Alliance consists of autonomous member churches and other bodies, such as Baptist Unions and Conventions of local churches: 'extending over every part of the world, [it] exists as an expression of the essential oneness of Baptist people in . . . Christ, to impart inspiration to the fellowship, and to provide channels for sharing concerns and skills in witness and ministry'.[49] The Baptist Union of Great Britain, for instance, is composed of 'the Churches, Associations of Churches, Colleges, and other Baptist organizations and persons who are for the time being in membership with the Union'; the object of the Union is 'the advancement of the Christian religion, especially by the means of and in accordance with the principles of the Baptist Denomination' in order, for example, '[t]o cultivate among its own members respect and love for one another, and to all who love the Lord Jesus Christ', to spread the Gospel (e.g. by ministers and evangelists and by establishing churches), to afford opportunities for 'united action on questions affecting the welfare of the member churches', and to promote good relations between Baptists at home and abroad.[50] Accordingly, a Baptist Church means a local church which

ministers 'by preaching, teaching, and proclamation of the gospel . . . and by all Christian good works'; Ch. 1, Pts. I–IV: it has Consistories, Classes, Regional Synods and a General Synod.

[47] PCW: HOR, 1.1: e.g. establishing fellowships, preaching the Gospel, administering the sacraments, providing pastoral care, religious education, mission, community service and 'taking a stand for justice and peace'; s. 1: Governance; 2: Members; 3: Courts; 4: Ministry; 5-7: Property; 8: Procedure; 9: Declarations; 10: Services.

[48] UCC: Man., Declarations: the church is a 'union of the Presbyterian, Methodist, and Congregational Churches in Canada'; UCOC: Const., Preamble, 1: a union (1957) of the Evangelical and Reformed Church and General Council of the Congregational Christian Churches (US) 'to express more fully the oneness in Christ . . . to make more effective their common witness in [Christ], and to serve His kingdom in the world'; Art. V.18: 'autonomy of the Local Church'; UCCSA: Const., Preamble: 'constantly to be reformed according to His Word'; Art. 1: it is a union of e.g. the Congregational Union, London Missionary Society of Southern Africa, and Bantu Congregational Church of Southern Africa and (Art. 2) 'is composed of local churches, Regional Councils, Synods and an Assembly'; Art. 3: local church autonomy; the United Reformed Church in Great Britain is a union (1972) of the Congregational Church in England and Wales and Presbyterian Church of England; it united in 1981 with the Reformed Churches of Christ and in 2000 with the Congregational Union of Scotland.

[49] BWA: Const., Preamble: 'This Alliance recognizes the traditional autonomy and interdependence of Baptist churches and member bodies'; Art. II: it is e.g. to promote 'cooperation', witness to the Gospel, assist members 'in their divine task of bringing all people to God' through Christ, and act as an agency for 'Baptist principles'.

[50] BUGB: Const., Arts. 1–4: the basis of Union is the authority of Christ, baptism by immersion and the duty to evangelise; Art. 5: it acts by the Assembly through a Council; Art. 6: admission of a (local) Baptist church. See also BUSA: Const., 3: the Union has 'member churches' and 'territorial associations' of churches; 5: its objects include advancing 'the kingdom of God',

understands itself as a manifestation of the church universal – it is defined by its members and its functions, for example, to 'glorify God', to 'proclaim the Gospel' and to provide 'instruction and fellowship for believers'; importantly, the congregation is autonomous and free from control by the Union (or Convention) to which it may belong, save to the extent provided in its own constitution or other such instrument.[51]

The forms of ecclesiastical regulation

The churches and other ecclesial communities of the Christian traditions studied here employ laws and other regulatory instruments at international, national, regional and local levels. These instruments represent the formal sources of ecclesiastical regulation. They exist under a variety of titles appropriate to the tradition in question – from codes and canons through charters and statutes to constitutions, books of order or discipline and covenants. All of these instruments contain binding norms of conduct. Importantly, all the traditions use the word 'law' to describe at least some of these written and formal instruments, though unwritten customs are also a source of law in some churches. Ecclesiastical quasi-legislation, in the form of guidelines, policies, codes of practice and ethical standards, is also a common means by which the churches regulate themselves. Ecclesiastical quasi-legislation consists of informal administrative norms which are designed to complement actual laws.

The international level

The instruments of global ecclesial communities fall into three basic categories: codes of canon law (Roman Catholic and Oriental Catholic); canons and covenants

---

promoting 'unity ... amongst its member churches' and establishing churches; 6: it is e.g. to 'engage in medical, educational, relief and other benevolent work'; NBCUSA: Const., Art. II–III: it is e.g. to 'fulfil the Great Commission' of Christ 'through preaching, teaching, and healing', and unite National Baptist Churches, district associations and state conventions in evangelism; CNBC: Const., 1: 'Denomination'; 2: it is e.g. 'to provide an entity for cooperating churches to work together to carry out Christ's mission of preaching, teaching, healing and ministering to all persons throughout the world'; 3: Statement of Belief, VI: 'This church is an autonomous body operating through democratic processes under ... Christ.'

[51] BUSA: MCLC, Arts. 2–4: the local church, as 'a manifestation of the universal church, is a community of believers in a particular place where the Word of God is preached and the ordinances of Believers' Baptism and the Lord's Supper are observed. It is fully autonomous and remains so notwithstanding responsibilities it may accept by voluntary association' (e.g. with the Union); Arts. 5–7: individual members; Art. 9: discipline; Art. 10: ordinances of baptism and Lord's Supper; Arts. 11–16: institutions, deacons, elders and pastors; Arts. 17–21: finance and property; Arts. 22–25: dissolution, constitutional change and resolution of disputes. See also BUGB: MTC, 2.6: membership; JBU: Const., Art. V: autonomy; Riverside Baptist Church (Baltimore): Const., Preamble: this local church is affiliated with the Baptist Convention of Maryland-Delaware and the Southern Baptist Convention and is 'to provide regular opportunities for public worship [and] sustain the ordinances [of baptism and Lord's Supper], doctrines and ethics set forth in the New Testament'; SBC: Const., Art. IV: 'While independent and sovereign in its own sphere, the Convention does not claim and will never attempt to exercise any authority over any Baptist body, whether church, auxiliary organizations, associations, or conventions'.

(Orthodox and Anglican); and constitutions (Lutheran, Reformed, Methodist and Baptist). First, the twentieth century was one of *codification* for the Catholic Church. Its principal sources of law are the Code of Canon Law (1983) for the Latin Church and the Code of Canons of the Oriental Churches (1990). In the Latin or Roman Catholic Church, the Code of Canon Law 1983, replacing that of 1917, was promulgated by Pope John Paul II after revision following the Second Vatican Council in the 1960s. The Code distinguishes 'universal law' and 'particular law' (see below). Universal law is applicable to the Latin Church in all parts of the world; it includes the Code itself, papal decrees and authentic interpretations of a legislator (judicial decisions do not generate law).[52] Similarly, the twenty-one Oriental Catholic churches, reunited with and acknowledging the supremacy of the Roman Pontiff, have their Code of Canons of the Eastern Churches promulgated by Pope John Paul II in 1990.[53] This 1990 code, in which 'the ancient law of the Eastern Churches has been mostly received or adapted', represents their 'common law'; it embraces 'the laws and legitimate customs' of the entire Church and those common to all the Oriental Churches across the world.[54] Pope John Paul II saw the two Codes as 'one *Corpus Iuris Canonici*' for the Catholic Church.[55] Ecclesiastical quasi-legislation is also a notable feature of Catholic governance.[56]

Secondly, in contrast, being a family of self-governing churches with no centralised organisation,[57] the Orthodox Church has no universal code (though whether Orthodox law should be codified is the subject of debate).[58] The 'law of the church' globally is, rather, 'her canonical tradition', that is, 'an outgrowth of the holy canons'.[59] The holy canons stem from three main sources: ecumenical synods (representing the universal church); local synods (subsequently ratified by the ecumenical synods as representing the tradition of the universal church); and the Fathers of the church. These are contained in several collections; the most widely used today in Greek-speaking Orthodoxy is the *Pedalion*.[60] Custom is also a source of law if it has 'enjoyed a long and steady practice', 'consensus of opinion' considers that 'it has the force of law' and it is 'in full harmony with the holy tradition and scripture, as well as doctrine.[61] Moreover, Orthodox churches with an international

---

[52] CIC, cc. 12, 16, 29; LG 27: 'bishops have the sacred right and duty ... to make laws for their subjects, to pass judgment on them, and to moderate pertaining to the ordering of worship and the apostolate'.
[53] A code is a 'comprehensive and systematic arrangement' of laws: Nedungatt 49.
[54] CCEO, cc. 1, 1493; D. Motiuk, 'The code of canons of the Eastern Churches: some ten years later', 36 *Studia Canonica* (2002) 189.
[55] *Acta Apostolicae Sedis*, 83 (1991) 490: along with *Pastor Bonus* 1988 on the Roman Curia.
[56] F. Morrisey, 'Papal and curial pronouncements: their canonical significance in the light of the 1983 code of canon law', 50 *The Jurist* (1990) 102.
[57] T. Ware, *The Orthodox Church* (London, 1963, reprinted 1991) 15.
[58] B. Archondonis, 'A common code for the Orthodox churches', 1 *Kanon* (1973) 45–53.
[59] L. Patsavos, 'The canonical tradition of the Orthodox Church', in F.K. Litsas (ed.), *A Companion to the Greek Orthodox Church* (Orthodox Archdiocese of North and South America, New York, 1984) 137: Synod of Trullo, c. 39: the right of a local church to its own laws.
[60] *The Rudder (Pedalion) of the Orthodox Christians or All the Sacred and Divine Canons*, ed. C. Cummings (Orthodox Christian Educational Society, Chicago, Illinois, 1957), from the metaphor of the church as a ship, 'the members of the Church [are] guided on their voyage through life by means of the holy canons'.
[61] Patsavos, 'The canonical tradition of the Orthodox Church', 137 at 141.

organisation regulate themselves with, typically, a set of 'statutes' based on the canonical tradition and its 'principles'; for example, the multinational Russian Orthodox Church has a Statute which regulates its activities by adherence to: 'the Holy Scriptures and Holy Tradition; the canons and rules of the Holy Apostles, the Holy Ecumenical and Local Councils, and the Holy Fathers; the resolutions of its Local and Bishops' Councils and the Holy Synod and the decrees of the Patriarch of Moscow and All Russia; and the present Statute'.[62] By way of contrast, alliances of Orthodox churches may organise themselves on the basis of a *constitution*, such as that of the Standing Conference of the Canonical Orthodox Bishops in the Americas which preserves the jurisdictional autonomy of the member churches.[63]

Like Orthodoxy, the Anglican Communion has no formal body of law applicable globally to its forty-four member churches; each church is autonomous with its own legal system. The Communion is held together by 'bonds of affection': shared loyalty to scripture, creeds, baptism, eucharist, historic episcopate and its institutional instruments of communion (Archbishop of Canterbury, Primates' Meeting, Lambeth Conference and Anglican Consultative Council); but these institutions cannot make decisions binding on churches.[64] However, *The Principles of Canon Law Common to the Churches of the Anglican Communion* was launched at the Lambeth Conference in 2008. This document is not a system of international canon law but a statement of principles of canon law which articulate the common ground between the legal systems of each of the churches of the global Communion; the document defines a 'principle of canon law' as 'a foundational proposition or maxim of general applicability which has a strong dimension of weight, is induced from the similarities of churches, derives from the canonical tradition or other practices of the church, expresses a basic theological truth or ethical value, and is about, is implicit in, or underlies canon law'.[65] Moreover, the Communion is currently debating adoption by each church of a common and solemn Anglican Communion Covenant to regulate relationships between the churches and to strike a balance between the theological category of ecclesial communion and the juridical category of provincial autonomy.[66]

By way of contrast, global Protestant communities have *constitutions* for collaboration in matters of common concern between, but preserving the juridical autonomy of, member churches. The Lutheran World Federation, 'a communion

---

[62] ROC: Statute, I.4. See also ROMOC: Statutes, Art. 201: these statutes were approved by the Holy Synod 'on the basis of the general principles and stipulations of the Holy Canons of the Orthodox Church'.

[63] SCOBA, Const., Art. II: 'No decision of the Conference shall interfere with the ecclesiastical jurisdiction of any of the Canonical Orthodox Churches, or any of the member Hierarchs.'

[64] N. Doe, *Canon Law in the Anglican Communion* (Clarendon Press, Oxford, 1998) 338, 349: only the Anglican Consultative Council has a formal Constitution (Art. 10: amendment is ratified by two-thirds of the member churches).

[65] PCLCCAC (Anglican Communion Office, London, 2008), Definitions; for background to the project, see N. Doe, 'The contribution of common principles of canon law to ecclesial communion in Anglicanism' in Doe, ibid., 97.

[66] TACC 2009: it has a Preamble, Sections and a Declaration; its Sections, composed of 'affirmations' and 'commitments', are: 1: Our Inheritance of Faith; 2: The Life We Share with Others; Our Anglican Vocation; 3: Our Unity and Common Life; 4: Our Covenanted Life Together. See N. Doe, *An Anglican Covenant: Theological and Legal Considerations for a Global Debate* (Canterbury Press, Norwich, 2008).

of churches which confess the triune God, agree in the proclamation of the Word of God and are united in pulpit and altar fellowship', is 'organized under' its Constitution (and supplementary Bylaws) as an 'instrument of its autonomous member churches'.[67] The World Communion of Reformed Churches, which includes Presbyterian, Congregational, Reformed, United and Uniting churches, has a Constitution (and Bylaws) which enables their participation in common action – but 'Membership in the [WCRC] does not limit the autonomy of any member church or restrict its relationships with other churches or with other ecumenical organizations'.[68] The World Methodist Council, a manifestation of a 'fellowship' of Methodists worldwide, has a Constitution but the Council has no legislative authority over member churches.[69] Likewise, the Baptist World Alliance, 'extending over every part of the world, [is] an expression of the essential oneness of Baptist people in ... Christ'; its Constitution 'recognizes the traditional autonomy and interdependence of Baptist churches and member bodies'.[70]

The national, regional and local levels

Within these global ecclesial communities, each institutional church has its own regulatory system. It is at these levels – national, regional and local – that the word 'law' is most commonly used amongst all the Christian traditions in relation to some of their regulatory instruments. These instruments fall into three broad categories: canon law; constitutions; and instruments of church order. Within these legal systems, instruments may be ordered hierarchically in terms of the authority which each enjoys. The Code of Canon Law of the Roman Catholic Church provides that whereas universal law applies to the whole church, 'particular laws' apply to a specific territory (a particular church,[71] such as a diocese) or a group of people (such as a religious community); particular laws include diocesan legislation (made by a bishop in consultation with the diocesan synod), laws promulgated by national Episcopal Conferences, or the special or proper laws created for and by religious communities; particular laws are abrogated by universal law only by express repeal; custom also has the force of law.[72] A similar position pertains in the Oriental Catholic Churches. Each church is *sui juris* with its own juridical system operative within the common law of the 1990 Code.[73] The churches differ in

---

[67] LWF: Constitution (adopted 1990 by the LWF Eighth Assembly, as amended since) and Bylaws; Const., Arts. I–IV. See also the International Lutheran Council: Constitution and Guiding Principles.

[68] WCRC: Constitution and Bylaws (adopted 2010); Const., Preamble, Art. VI.F: autonomy; VI.A: suspension; VI.J.6: the 'rights' and 'privileges' of member churches.

[69] WMC: Constitution: Constitutional Practice and Discipline of the Methodist Church (Great Britain), 782–3.

[70] BWA: Const., Preamble.

[71] CIC, c. 373; bishops govern as vicars of Christ (not of the Pontiff) and 'in their own right': LG 27.

[72] CIC, cc. 13, 20, 23–26: custom is law if it is: approved by the relevant legislator; not contrary to divine law; reasonable; and observed for continuous years by a community capable of receiving and intending to make law.

[73] Particular churches include patriarchal churches (c. 25), major archiepiscopal churches (c. 151) and metropolitan churches (c. 155). The Episcopal Synod of a patriarchal church may legislate for it: c. 1101.

terms of 'rite' – their liturgical, theological, spiritual and disciplinary heritage – and custom has the force of law; moreover, the common law of the churches does not derogate from particular laws unless it expressly provides for this.[74]

Local Orthodox churches have canon law,[75] charters,[76] constitutions,[77] and statutes,[78] as well as instruments made under these applicable to units within the church (such as 'monastic law').[79] For example, the Greek Orthodox Archdiocese of America, under the canonical jurisdiction of the Ecumenical Patriarchate of Constantinople, is governed by 'the Holy Scriptures, Sacred Tradition, the Holy Canons, this Charter, Regulations promulgated pursuant hereto' and, 'as to canonical ecclesiastical matters not provided herein, by the decisions of the Holy and Sacred Synod of the Ecumenical Patriarchate';[80] the Holy Canons include the 'canons of the Ecumenical and Local Synods, the canons of the Holy Apostles and Fathers of the Church and of all other Synods recognized by the Orthodox Church, as interpreted by the Great Church of Christ in Constantinople'.[81] All Regulations designed to implement the Charter 'shall be in conformity with the Holy Canons, Sacred Tradition and the long established life and practice of the Holy Orthodox Church'.[82] Orthodox instruments also make reference to the 'canonical tradition',[83] and to 'custom'.[84] Furthermore, Orthodox churches may have 'guidelines' which

---

[74] CCEO, c. 28.1: rites; cc. 1506–1509: custom; c. 1502: derogation; see also cc. 1488–1505: these deal with 'ecclesiastical laws', and e.g. their promulgation, obligatory nature and prospective character.

[75] MOCL: 8: 'Canon Law is the sum of laws deriving from the *Ekklesia* on its own authority'.

[76] The Church of Greece has a Statutory Charter 1977 approved by the Greek Parliament: see Chapter 10.

[77] See e.g. UOCIA: Const: it was approved by the All-Church Sobor in 2005 at Kiev; SOCA: the Constitution (approved by Holy Synod in 1998) contains 'General Statutes'; Art. 59: 'canons, bylaws, [and] traditions'.

[78] ROMOC: Statutes (approved by Holy Synod); ROC: Statute, I: the statute was adopted in 1988; II: the church regulates its activities by adherence to e.g. the 'canons and rules' of the Holy Apostles, Councils and Fathers, 'resolutions of its Local and Bishops' Councils and the Holy Synod' and 'decrees of the Patriarch'.

[79] ROC: Statute, II.2: 'rules of procedure'; V.31: 'the statutes of the monasteries'; VII.7: Regulations on Ecclesiastical Courts; VII.1: Patriarchal Tomos; GOAA: Charter, Art. 21(d): monasteries operate under 'the prevailing Monastic Law and ... the regulations that define their operation'; ROMOC: Statutes, Art. 74: the 'canonical statutes of a monastery'; UOCIA: Const., Art. VI: 'the common law or particular law'.

[80] GOAA: Charter (granted by the Holy Synod of the Ecumenical Patriarchate in 2003), Art. 2; see also Art. 9(g): court procedures are in regulations of the Eparchial Synod approved by the Ecumenical Patriarchate.

[81] GOAA: Charter, Arts. 1(b) and 2(b).

[82] GOAA: Charter, Art. 22; Regulations must be approved by the Ecumenical Patriarchate.

[83] GOAA: Charter, Art. 21(a): 'Monasteries ... function according to the long established canonical tradition and practice of the Church'; ROC: Statute, X18(z): the bishop approves church repairs under 'the Orthodox church tradition'; MOSC: Const., Art. 1: members have 'the obligation to observe' the Holy Traditions; ROMOC: Statutes, Art. 26(s): the Patriarch may '[a]ccording to the Orthodox tradition' set up branches in dioceses.

[84] SOCA: Const., Art. 51: a Metropolitan has 'all his pastoral dues in accordance with established custom'; GOAA: Regs., Art. 4.17: in accord with the 'custom and practice of our prior Congresses, Robert's Rules of Order ... shall be the official parliamentary authority for the Plenary Sessions of the [Clergy–Laity] Congress'.

are often declaratory of the holy canons, obligatory in form and addressed to both the clergy and the laity;[85] they may also have 'instructions',[86] and 'codes' of pastoral conduct to which 'adherence' is required.[87]

Like the Orthodox, each autonomous Anglican church has its own central system of 'general law' (typically provincial law created by a synod or other assembly representative of bishops, clergy and laity) and laws made at more localised levels (e.g. diocesan law created by the diocesan synod of bishop, clergy and laity), which to be operative must be consistent with the general law.[88] In terms of general law, while some churches have a code of canons only, most have a constitution, canons and other regulatory instruments, including rules and regulations, ordinances, resolutions and liturgical rubrics found in the service books.[89] Alongside written laws are less formal and sometimes unwritten sources: customs or tradition, the decisions of church courts, the English Canons Ecclesiastical 1603 or pre-Reformation Roman canon law.[90] In sum, the principles of canon law state: 'The laws of churches exist in a variety of formal sources which should be

---

[85] OCIA: Guidelines for Clergy (Holy Synod): Archbishop of Washington, Letter, 1998: 'Not intended to be an all-embracing pastoral handbook, these guidelines ... are a limited compilation addressing significant aspects of a pastor's ministry' and 'contemporary issues'; they often cite the holy canons (e.g. A Selection of Clergy Disciplines, 1: 'clergy are strictly to observe the teachings of the Church, [on] Christ, the Sacred Scriptures and Holy Traditions (Ephesus c. 6, 7; Trullo, c. 1; Carthage, c. 2)'; SCOBA: Guidelines for Orthodox Christians in Ecumenical Relations (1973): its 'directives' supplement 'ecumenical policy'; UOCIA: Const., Art. IV.2: the Major Archbishop may issue pastoral 'guidance'; ACROD: Spiritual-Sacramental Guidelines.

[86] UOCIA: Joint Statement of Hierarchs, Living the Sacramental Life of the Church, Practical Instructions for Diocesan Faithful (undated): these contain e.g. a 'Policy on Marriages' and are often prescriptive (e.g. 'No more than a total of three valid marriages are permitted by the Church'); ROC: Statute, X.47: the activities of the diocese may be subject to 'the Bishop's instructions'; X.52: the Diocesan Assembly may issue 'instructions'.

[87] UOCIA: Code of Pastoral Conduct, Joint Statement of Hierarchs: this is 'a set of standards for conduct in certain pastoral situations'; 'Responsibility for adherence to the Code ... rests with the individual' but those 'who disregard this Code ... will be subject to remedial action by the local Archbishop/Bishop, parish priest' etc; Const., Art. II.6: the Holy Synod may establish 'general policies' as to relations with other Orthodox Churches and non-Orthodox 'religious bodies'; Archdiocese of Thyateira and Great Britain: Instructions.

[88] PCLCCAC, Definitions: 'The expression "general law of a church" means the law of that body which has competent jurisdiction over that church, as distinct from laws of units within a church such as a diocese.'

[89] E.g. the Scottish Episcopal Church has a Code supplemented by synod resolutions; the Anglican Church of Southern Africa has a constitution, code of canons and e.g. acts of the provincial synod; Wales: Const. I.1.1: 'rules and regulations' of the Governing Body; Central Africa: Const., Definitions: 'resolution' is a 'judgment or opinion of Synod, which is intended to have an appreciative, hortatory or advisory and not a mandatory effect'.

[90] E.g. Canada: Book of Alternative Services (1985): 'local custom may be established and followed'; Scotland: Can. 1.1: ordinations occur in accordance with 'the law and custom of the ancient church'; South East Asia: Const., Preamble: dioceses associate as a province 'in accordance with the accepted traditions and usages of the Anglican Communion'; Australia: Can. 11 1992, 4: the canons of 1603 have 'no operation or effect in a diocese which adopts this canon', but a diocese may adopt them; England: Submission of the Clergy Act 1533: pre-Reformation (Roman) canon law applies unless inconsistent with post-1533 statute and common law.

identifiable, including constitutions, canons, rules, regulations, and other instruments. Historical sources recognised as such in the canonical tradition, including custom, have such status within a church as may be prescribed by its law.'[91] Quasi-legislation is also a feature of Anglican governance.[92]

Moving along the spectrum to the Protestant traditions, many Lutheran churches have 'church laws', 'constitutions', 'bylaws' and other regulatory instruments.[93] The Lutheran Church of Australia has a central constitution, bylaws, rules and regulations (which may be amended by its General Synod).[94] In turn, each district of the church,[95] as well as each congregation within a district, has its own constitution and bylaws which must be consistent with the central constitution and bylaws.[96] Lutheran churches also have normative doctrinal texts to which compliance is due.[97] Whilst the decisions of judicial bodies may have no 'precedential value',[98] norms of conduct are also found in 'ecclesiastical practices and customs',[99] guidance,[100] which may contain 'regulations' and 'instructions for the practical performance of official duties',[101]

---

[91] PCLCCAC, Principle 4.1-3: 'Scripture, tradition and reason are fundamental authoritative sources of law'; 4.5. 'Laws should be short, clear and simple to the extent ... consistent with their purpose, meaning' etc.

[92] See CLAC, 23.

[93] ELCSA: G., 10.6: 'church laws'; LCGB: Constitution (2011) and Rules and Regulations (2011); ELCIC: Constitution and Administrative Bylaws; ELCA: Constitution, Bylaws and Continuing Resolutions (2011).

[94] LCA: Const. (1966), Preamble; Art. XII.2: it may be amended with the exception of Arts. II and XII.1; Art. XI.1: General Synod bylaws, rules and regulations must not be inconsistent with the constitution.

[95] LCA: Const., Art. IX.2, BL XI.3, and Bylaws Part A of the Districts: a district constitution and bylaws must be consistent with the constitution and bylaws of the LCA.

[96] LCA, Const., Art. XII; Art. IV.1: a congregation must have 'a Constitution and By-laws acceptable to the Church'; BL, Art. IV.1: the District Church Council approves amendments. See also NALC: Constitution Document for Congregations; LCMS: Const., Art. VI and BL, 2.1-2.4: a constitution must accord with the scriptures or confessions; ELCIC: Approved Model Constitution for Congregations.

[97] For e.g. the Augsburg Confession, LCA: Const., Art. II.2; LCGB: RAR, Statement of Faith, 3; ELCA: Const., Ch. 2; Ch. 5.01: church units 'shall act in accordance with the Confession of Faith'; ELCIC: Const., Art. II.

[98] LCMS: BL, 1.10.7: a Dispute Resolution Panel decision binds the parties but 'has no precedential value'.

[99] LCA: Const., Art. III(k): the church is 'to cultivate uniformity in ... ecclesiastical practices and customs ... in accord with the principles laid down in the Formula of Concord'; LCMS: BL, 1.1.1: congregations should 'strive for uniformity in church practice [and] an appreciation of a variety of responsible practices and customs which are in harmony with our common profession of faith'.

[100] LCA: BL, V.F.1: the General Pastors' Conference issues 'guidance' on doctrine; see e.g. Some Pastoral Guidelines for Responsible Communion Practice (adopted by the Conference 1990, edited 2001); see also Pastoral Practice in Reference to Holy Baptism, adopted by General Synod 1984 (Pts. I and II) and Commission on Theology and Inter-Church Relations, 1986 (Pt. III), and edited 2001: this offers 'advice' to pastors and laity but is cast in prescriptive terms (e.g. the congregation 'should be directly involved in the celebration of baptism'; 'The normal practice should be ... ').

[101] ELCSA (N-T): Guidelines, Introduction: 'These Guidelines offer all congregational members ... a general outline of the regulations concerning church life. They contain instructions for the practical performance of official duties. They are not to be understood legally, but rather

'standards',[102] and 'binding policies'.[103] Methodists too commonly use the terms 'Methodist Law', 'Church law', 'the laws of the Church', 'law' and 'legislation' to describe prescribed regulatory instruments.[104] An individual Methodist church normally has a constitution, which may be contained in a Book of Discipline (with *inter alia* 'laws'), 'Manual of Law', 'Law Book' or 'Code' (with 'Laws and Regulations'),[105] or 'Standing Orders'.[106] As well as the 'General Rules of the Methodist Church',[107] a church may have 'bylaws' which must be consistent with the general law of the church.[108] Also, adherence is often required to 'customs', 'usages', 'laws and usages', 'practices',[109] judicial decisions, and Articles of Religion which, with their 'rules of doctrine' and 'doctrinal standards', are 'legislative enactments'.[110] Again, 'agreements', 'covenants'[111] and 'guidelines', which may present 'obligations', 'expectations' and

in the freedom according to the Gospel'; ELCA: Const., Ch. 20.70–71: 'guidelines' to 'enable clear and uniform application of the grounds for discipline'.

[102] NALC: Standards for Pastoral Ministry; ELCIC: ABL, Pt. III.2: Standards for Acceptance.

[103] ELCA: Const., Ch. 7.31: as to ordination in 'unusual circumstances', the decision of the bishop 'shall be in accordance with policy developed by the appropriate churchwide unit, reviewed by the Conference of Bishops, and adopted by the Church Council'; Ch. 15.20–21: 'policies' on staff employment 'shall be binding'.

[104] MCGB: CPD, DU 25(b): 'Methodist law'; UMCNEAE: BOD, par. 2609: 'Church law'; par. 7: 'laws'; UMCUSA: Const., Div. 2.2, Art. IV.16: 'legislation'; MCI: Const., s. 6: 'Manual of Laws' with 'legislation'; s. 5: Conference 'Rules and Regulations'; RDG, 10.06: 'laws of the Church' (and MCNZ: LAR, s. 9.12); MCGB: CPD, DU 33–36: 'legislation'; COTN: Man., Part II, Church Const., Preamble: 'the fundamental law or Constitution of the Church of the Nazarene' which accords with 'the principles of constitutional legislation'.

[105] UMCNEAE: Book of Discipline, par. 2546: the 'laws and procedures outlined in the [Book of] Discipline'; MCI: Const., s. 5: 'the constitution of the Courts of the Church'; MCNZ: Laws and Regulations (revised 2007); LAR, s. 2.1.2: 'this Law Book'; see also 8.1: 'Code' of disciplinary regulations.

[106] MCGB: CPD, DU 19: Conference may 'make, amend or revoke Standing Orders or other rules and regulations for the constitution and procedure of the Conference', but 'no such Standing Order, rule, regulation or means may be contrary to law or to this Deed or to the purposes of the Methodist Church'; Methodist Church Act 1976, s. 5: the Deed of Union may be altered only in accordance with the procedure prescribed in s. 5.

[107] MCI: RDG, 1.03: 'General Rules of the Society of the People called Methodists' (John Wesley 1743) 'all of which we are taught of God to observe' (they are entrenched: LAR, s. 7.1); Manual of Laws, App. I: Twelve Rules of a Helper; UMCNEAE: BOD, par. 103, General Rules (protected by Restrictive Rules, 5 (par. 21)).

[108] UMCNEAE: BOD, pars. 207–211, 1011.

[109] UMCNEAE: BOD, par. 2503: 'customs'; MCI: RDG, 4A.04: 'rules and usage'; 10.68: 'the usage of the Church'; MCNZ: LAR s. 2.26.1: no activity may take place on Methodist property 'not in accordance with the laws and usages of the Church'; MCGB: CPD, MT 1: 'Methodist practice' which is 'the constitutional practice, usage and discipline of the Church as regulated from time to time by the Deed of Union and Standing Orders'; CPD, DU 6: 'According to Methodist usage the sacrament of baptism is administered to infants.'

[110] UMCUSA: Const., Div. I, Art. III: Articles of Religion; Div. 2.3, Art. I: 'rules of doctrine'; UMCNEAE: BOD, par. 101 and Judicial Decision 358 (1972): Doctrinal Standards are 'legislative enactments [but] neither part of the Constitution nor under the Restrictive Rules'.

[111] MCI: RDG: 4C.12: Conference must ensure that a 'Working Agreement' is in place in a local church which receives a non-stipendiary minister; MCNZ: LAR s. 2.13: lay ministers enter a 'Lay Ministry Covenant'.

'policies',[112] and 'social principles', for the life of the faithful in wider society, are commonplace in Methodist governance; for example: 'The Social Principles, while not to be considered church law ... are a call to faithfulness and are intended to be instructive and persuasive in the best of the prophetic spirit', as a 'studied dialogue of faith and practice'; they deal, for example with the family, marriage, human sexuality, human rights and politics.[113]

Reformed and Presbyterian churches employ, for example, a system of 'law' (e.g. Scotland),[114] a 'code' (e.g. Ireland),[115] a 'book of church order' (America),[116] or a 'book of order' which contains 'legislation' (New Zealand).[117] These instruments may in turn contain a constitution,[118] bylaws[119] and normative doctrinal texts for the church and its units.[120] The church may also provide a model constitution for a local church,[121] recognise the operation of customs[122] and regulate conduct by means of soft-law in the shape of quasi-legislation.[123] United

---

[112] UMCNEAE: BOD, par. 806: General Council 'investment policies and guidelines'; par. 1107; the General Board of Discipleship 'shall adhere to' these; MCNZ: LAR s. 2.23: Conference 'guidelines' on 'supervision' of ministers; Introductory Documents, III Ethical Standards for Ministry: 'standards of conduct for people, clergy and lay', their 'commitments' and 'responsibilities'; MCI: RDG, 10.06: 'guidelines' for working groups.

[113] UMCNEAE: BOD, Pt. IV: Social Principles. See also MCNZ: LAR, Introductory Documents, V, Some Social Principles (based on John Wesley's An Earnest Appeal to Men of Reason and Religion (1743)).

[114] J.L. Weatherhead (ed.), *The Constitution and Laws of the Church of Scotland* (Board of Practice and Procedure, Edinburgh, 1997) 16; A. Herron, *The Law and Practice of the Kirk: A Practical Guide and Commentary* (Bell and Bain Ltd, Glasgow, 1995); see also the *Manual of Practice and Procedure* in the United Free Church of Scotland (2011).

[115] PCI: The Code: The Book of the Constitution and Government of the Presbyterian Church in Ireland; Pt. I: Basic Code (e.g. the Courts); Pt. II: Rules (e.g. on Business in Church Courts, Elections, Ordinations, Records and Reports, Disciplinary Proceedings); Pt. III: Appendix (e.g. General Assembly Standing Orders).

[116] The Book of Church Order, including the Government, Disciplinary and Judicial Procedures, Bylaws and Special Rules of Order of the General Synod, and Formularies of the Reformed Church in America (2010).

[117] PCANZ: Book of Order; 3.1: General Assembly may add 'supplementary provisions' by means of Resolution 'to implement and give effect to any provision of the Book of Order'; 14.8: 'Proposals for legislation'. The Presbyterian Church of Wales has *The Handbook of Order and Rules* (2010).

[118] PCA: The Book of Church Order contains a Preface (e.g. 'Preliminary Principles') and Parts: Form of Government (Pt. I), Rules of Discipline (Pt. II), Directory for the Worship of God (Pt. III).

[119] PCI: Code, Pt. III.15: Trustees' Bylaws.

[120] For e.g. the Westminster Confession of Faith, see e.g. PCANZ: BO, 1.1(3)-(4); PCA: BCO, Preface III; CLCS 24; PCI: Code I.I.III.13; see also PCW: HOR, 9: Declarations and Short Confession; RCA: BCO, Preamble: the Doctrinal Standards include the Heidelberg Catechism 1608 and the Canons of the Synod of Dort 1619.

[121] PCW: Constitution for a Local Church; URC: Model Constitution for Local Churches (Mission Council, 2010): 'There is an ever increasing expectation that Local Churches will have a written Constitution.'

[122] CLCS 9–10: 'custom is a significant source of church law. A custom may acquire the force and status of law by consuetude, and a law may be amended by consuetude, or may lose its force by desuetude'; see also PCA, BCO, III.58.8: the use of custom as to spiritual preparation for the Lord's Supper.

[123] PCW: Employee Safety Handbook (undated): this summarises civil law on health and safety.

28   THE SOURCES AND PURPOSES OF ECCLESIASTICAL REGULATION

Churches, too, have constitutions, bylaws,[124] customs,[125] statements of faith[126] and quasi-legislation with 'ethical standards', 'standards of practice', 'values' and 'norms'.[127]

At the other end of the spectrum lies the Baptist tradition. A national Baptist Union or Convention normally has a constitution, the provisions of which may be classified as 'laws' and, sometimes, bylaws.[128] It may also have normative doctrinal standards (such as a Confession of Faith),[129] as well as guidelines, policies and codes.[130] Within a Union or Convention, a regional Association of churches may have its own constitution.[131] Similarly, a local church may have a constitution and trust instrument,[132] a 'covenant' which sets out the commitments of members both to Christ and to the local church itself, and which operates either alongside or as part of the constitution of the local church,[133]

---

[124] UCOC: Const., Art. III: 'Covenantal Relationships'; Bylaws, Preamble: these are 'consistent with the Constitution'; UCCSA: Constitution (2007) and Model Constitution for Local Churches; UCCP: Constitution and Bylaws (on e.g. Constitutional Amendment); UCC: Manual 2010 (Declarations, Basis of Union, Bylaws, and Model Trust Deed); URC: Manual: e.g. Basis of Union, Church Structure, and Rules of Procedure.

[125] UCOC: Const., Art. V.11: admission in accord with 'the custom and usage of a Local Church'; URC: Model Const. for Local Churches, Notes: 'once adopted, [this] will prevail over any inconsistent unwritten custom'.

[126] UCCP: Statement of Faith.

[127] URC: Man., E: Guidance [on] Baptism and the Basis of Union; UCC: Ethical Standards and Standards of Practice for Ministry Personnel (2008): this is 'a common set of values' and 'a set of norms for the education and formation of ministry personnel' to 'enable [them] to be accountable to self, church, and community'.

[128] JBU: the Constitution was adopted by the Assembly in 1981 (and amended since); BUGB: Const., 1.9 and 2.12: e.g. amendment of the constitution by the Assembly; BUS: Constitution and Bylaws; NBCUSA: Const. (approved by Annual Session, 2002), Preamble: the Convention has 'constitutions' and 'laws'; ABCUSA: Bylaws; BUSA: Const., adopted by Annual Assembly 1933 (and amended since); its Bylaws deal with e.g. Union membership; CNBC: Society Act, Constitution and Bylaws; Bylaws, par. 137: amendment.

[129] CNBC: Const., 3: Statement of Faith: e.g. VIII: the Lord's Day 'should be employed in exercises of worship and spiritual devotion'; BUSA: Model Const., 4: Statement of Faith, 4.2.4: each member must 'participate fully in the life of the church'; NABC: Statement of Faith: 'a doctrinal guide for new churches'.

[130] BUNZ: Ethical Principles and Guidelines for Pastors (Assembly Council 2000, amended 2008): this has undertakings (e.g. 1.5: 'I will seek to develop leadership in others'); Dedication: a 'code of ethics'; NBC: Policies and Practices; NBCUSA: Common Budget Covenant: an 'operating guidelines manual'.

[131] BMPP, 231, App. IV, Suggested Constitutions for an Association.

[132] BUGB: MTC 2003, 2.12 (Church Constitution); Riverside Baptist Church (Baltimore): Bylaws: Art. 1: membership; Art. II: staff and officers; Art. III: committees; Art. IV: meetings; Art. V: amendments.

[133] Riverside Baptist Church (Baltimore): Const., Art. IV: 'Church Covenant': members 'most solemnly and joyfully enter into covenant with one another, as one body in Christ'; BMPP, 213, App. II: Church Covenants; 216, App. III, SCBC, Type A, Art. IV: 'This church has ... adopted the ... covenant ... by which its members may express their intent to accept the lordship of Jesus Christ in the life of the church and ... daily life'; ABCUSA: The Covenant of Relationships and its Agreements among the General, National and Regional Boards (1984); C.W. Deweese, *Baptist Church Covenants* (Broadman Press, Nashville, Tennessee, 1990) viii: 'A church covenant is a series of written pledges based on the Bible which church members

and doctrinal texts.¹³⁴ In short, all ten Christian traditions studied here are familiar with and use the category 'law' in the regulation of the affairs of each of their institutional churches, alongside more informal sources such as long-established customs and ecclesiastical quasi-legislation. All these instruments contain norms of conduct – laws bind but there is also an expectation of compliance with ecclesiastical quasi-legislation. The main differences are terminological – codes, canons, charters, statutes, constitutions, bylaws, books of church order and covenants represent the diversity of regulatory vehicles employed in the laws of Christians.

The purposes of ecclesiastical regulation

The purposes of the regulatory instruments of churches are articulated in the commentaries of jurists and the provisions of the instruments themselves. They are shaped fundamentally by the understanding each church has about the nature of the church (its ecclesiology) and about itself as an institution (its ecclesiality). Both the jurists and the instruments present a distinct relationship between church law and theology. In turn, a concept of the law of God is one which surfaces in various ways in the juridical instruments of all the traditions.¹³⁵

Facility and order

The purposes of juridical instruments are to facilitate and to order the life and mission of the particular church. In the Catholic Church, for Pope John Paul II, canon law 'facilitates ... an orderly development in the life of both the ecclesial society and of the individual persons who belong to it'; laws do not replace faith, grace and charity;¹³⁶ rather, the 'salvation of souls [is] the supreme law'.¹³⁷ Catholic canonists stress the spiritual, pastoral, educative and protective purposes of canon law.¹³⁸ Likewise, for the Orthodox tradition, canon law is 'at the service of the Church ... to guide her members on the way to salvation'; its main function is 'the spiritual growth of the faithful'; moreover, canon law exists 'to guarantee freedom' and 'to safeguard particular interests from the arbitrary intervention of superior

---

voluntarily make to God and to one another regarding their basic moral and spiritual commitments and the practices of their faith.'

[134] BMPP, 216, App. III, SCBC, Type A: Art. IV: 'The confession of faith drawn up and adopted by this church is ... an expression of the essential doctrines of grace as set forth in the Scriptures' and is 'subject to revision ... as new insights from the Word of God ... indicate ways in which faith and life may' reflect scriptural teaching.

[135] At global level: Old Catholic Bishops in the Union of Utrecht: Statute B. Order, Art. 1: the statute seeks 'to promote and to realize' communion; it requires churches e.g. to 'maintain the catholicity, doctrine, and worship in apostolic succession'; SCOBA: Const., Preamble, Arts. I and V.1: the constitution enables the churches 'to actualize ... unity in all those fields in which a common effort is required'; much the same applies to e.g. LWF: Const., Arts. I–III; WCRC: Const., Arts. I.3 and III (1–9); WMC: Const., CPD, pp. 782–783; BWA: Const., II.

[136] *Sacrae Disciplinae Leges* (1983); CCC: par. 1950ff: a definition of 'law' and 'moral law'.

[137] CIC, c. 1752.

[138] J.P. Beal, J.A. Coriden and T.J. Green (eds.), *New Commentary on the Code of Canon Law* (Paulist Press, New York, 2000) 1–8.

interests'; its principal object is the salvation of humanity.¹³⁹ In turn, Orthodox legal instruments reflect these ideas and focus on the 'necessity of canon law' in terms of both order and facility.¹⁴⁰ Anglicans echo these ideas: 'Law exists to assist a church in its mission and witness to Jesus Christ'; a church needs laws 'to order, and so facilitate, its public life and to regulate its own affairs for the common good': 'Law is not an end in itself' but exists 'to uphold the integrity of the faith, sacraments and mission, to provide good order, to support communion amongst the faithful, to put into action Christian values, and to prevent and resolve conflict'.¹⁴¹

Facility and order are equally key concepts in Protestant jurisprudence. Lutheran laws 'provide necessary organizational principles, structures, and policies for good order'; they 'reflect the organic whole of [the] church in its interdependent relationships and as part of the one holy, catholic, and apostolic Church'; and they provide 'organizational flexibility', 'facilitate ministry, not inhibit it', and 'guide, direct, and assist [the church] in mission and ministry'.¹⁴² Similar ideas appear in Methodist laws which may be designed for 'the good of the entire community' and represent the 'minimum' required of the faithful.¹⁴³ One Methodist Book of Discipline is presented as 'the instrument for setting forth the laws, plan, polity, and process by which United Methodists govern themselves' – whilst it is not 'sacrosanct or infallible' it represents a 'statement of how United Methodists agree to live their lives together'; moreover, 'it reflects our understanding of the Church and articulates [its] mission to make disciples of Jesus Christ for the transformation of the world'; in short, the Book of Discipline 'defines what is expected of [the] laity and clergy as they seek to be effective witnesses in the world as part of the whole

---

[139] MOCL: Patsavos, 'The canonical tradition of the Orthodox Church', at 141.

[140] See e.g. GOAA: Regs., Letter of the Ecumenical Patriarch of Constantinople 16 Feb. 2005: the church 'incorporates in herself the necessity of a canon law'; the letter cites the text 'all things should be done decently and in order' (1 Cor. 14.40), so that 'the mystery of the salvation of each one of us is worked in peace and with the presuppositions of the basic principles of the rights and duties that derive from the fact that we are members of Christ'; Preamble: the regulations 'address contemporary issues and needs', 'reflect the true spirit of the Gospel and our mission' and 'promote effective governance of Church activities at all levels'; ROMOC: Statutes, Art. 201: the Statutes 'establish the ways in which [the] Patriarchy regulates, leads and manages its religious, pastoral-missionary, cultural-educational, social-philanthropic, foundational and patrimonial activity'.

[141] PCLCAC, Principles 1 and 2.5. See e.g. Wales: Const., Prefatory Note: law exists 'to serve the sacramental integrity and good order of the Church and to assist its mission and its witness to the Lord Jesus Christ'.

[142] ELCIC: Const., Introduction; Preamble: the church adopts the 'constitution to govern our life and witness in our country and throughout the world'; LCA: Const., Arts. III, VI.3: rules enable a church to 'fulfil the mission of the Christian Church by proclaiming the Word of God and administering the Sacraments in accordance with the Confession of the Church'; they unite the congregations and ensure that preaching, teaching and practice conform to the Confession; and they protect the performance of duties and maintenance of rights.

[143] MCSA: *Laws and Discipline* (2000), Foreword, Presiding Bishop Dandala. See also COTN: Man., Pt. II, Const., Preamble: the constitution is to 'preserve our God-given heritage, the faith once delivered to the saints, especially the doctrine and experience of entire sanctification as a second work of grace'; FMCNA: BOD, Const., Preamble, par. 1: the constitution is designed to 'preserve and pass on to posterity the heritage of doctrine and principles of Christian living', 'ensure church order by sound principles and ecclesiastical polity', and 'prepare the way for evangelization [and] cooperation with other branches of the church of Christ'.

body of Christ' as a 'book of covenant' which sets out the 'theological grounding of the [church] in biblical faith'.[144]

Fundamentally the same ideas appear in the Reformed tradition:[145] 'Law is a necessary part of the structure of the Church as an institution. It serves to define the institution ... and it regulates the way in which its office-bearers and members relate to each other and the institution as a whole and its constituent parts'; also: 'Its purpose is to declare the corporate identity of the Church, and to ensure that all things are done decently and in order within it (1 Cor. 14.40).'[146] Actual laws reflect these ideas: the purpose of the Book of Order of the Presbyterian Church of Aotearoa New Zealand is: 'to order the life and mission of the Church consistently with its standards; to define the membership and provide for individuals to become members of congregations of the Church; and to provide for the government (including administrative, financial, legislative and judicial functions) of the Church'.[147] Again, for one United Church: 'The purpose of law within the church is to order procedures and to provide for the consistent resolution of differences, and so to help to achieve order and justice.'[148] Likewise, a local Baptist church has a constitution to 'govern', 'regulate' and 'enable' church life;[149] a constitution is established, typically: 'For the purpose of preserving and making secure the principles of our faith' so that 'this body be governed in an orderly manner'; 'for the purpose of preserving the liberties inherent in each individual member of the church'; and in order to present 'this body to other bodies of the same faith'.[150] In other words, it is a principle of Christian law that regulatory instruments are servants of the church.

Church law and theology

There is considerable but not complete agreement between the churches that there is an intimate connection between church law and theology. This takes a variety of forms. For some Roman Catholic canonists, theology is a direct

---

[144] UMCNEAE: BOD, par. 7.
[145] PCW: HOR 1.2: 'to safeguard the unity of the Church, and to secure uniformity in the procedures of its courts ... any changes in the constitution and rules' are subject to special procedures prior to adoption by General Assembly; URC: Model Const. for Local Churches, Notes: it is to signify 'collective identity', 'satisfy the outside world', 'make the Church's working transparent' and 'obviate later disagreement within the fellowship'.
[146] CLCS, 1: it also defines relations of the church to 'other institutions, especially the State'; Calvin, Institutes, Bk. IV, Ch. X: 'if in every human society ... government is necessary to ensure the common peace ... this ought specially to be observed in churches, which are best sustained by a constitution in all respects well ordered'.
[147] PCANZ: BO, 2.1. See also PCA: BCO, Preface II.8: 'ecclesiastical discipline must be purely moral or spiritual in its object'; Preface II.2; I.10-11: the protection of doctrinal standards.
[148] UCC: Man., Introduction: this represents the 'need' for the Manual; law is 'an acknowledgement of our human limitations, both individual and corporate, and of our desire to point to God's dominion in our interactions with others'; also, law strikes a balance between 'freedom and responsibility'; UCOC: Const., Preamble, 3: rules 'define and regulate' and 'describe the free and voluntary relationships' of the churches.
[149] BUGB: MTC 2003, Sch., 4.1-4.6.
[150] Riverside Baptist Church (Baltimore): Const., Preamble.

(material) source for canon law.[151] Theology concerns judgment based on knowledge obtained through revelation and canon law imposes a norm of conduct based on that judgment: thus, 'every single piece of law in the church must be in the service of values either defined or at least controlled by theological reflection'.[152] Others see canon law as *ordinatio fidei*, a legal system born of faith.[153] This is echoed by Orthodox jurists: 'Canons are a kind of canonical interpretation of the dogmas for a particular moment of the Church's historical existence ... They express the truth about the order of Church life, but rather than expressing this truth in absolute forms, they conform to historical existence'.[154] Similarly, it is a principle of Anglican canon law that as 'law is the servant of the church', so it has 'a theological foundation, rationale and end' and 'is intended to express publicly the theological self-understanding and practical policies of a church'.[155]

That church laws implement theological propositions as norms of conduct is a fundamental of the Protestant tradition. For instance, for the Evangelical Lutheran Church in America (ELCA): 'The Constitutions, Bylaws, and Continuing Resolutions of the [ELCA] reflect both the underlying theology of this church as well as its organizational principles and governance structures. They are both ecclesial and legal documents.'[156] Indeed, in the Reformed tradition: 'the external juridical order of the church should be at the service of the proclamation of the word'; consequently, 'the external order must be tested ever anew by the confession of faith, and on no level of legal church life can juridical questions be solved without relation to the church's confession'; church law is not a 'constitutive', but a 'consecutive' and 'regulative' element of the reality of a church.[157] As a result, theological propositions are used by church legislators in the creation of regulatory instruments – perhaps also to enhance their legitimacy – and they often surface explicitly in norms of the Latin and Oriental Catholic,[158]

---

[151] T. Urresti, 'Canon law and theology: two different sciences', 8 *Concilium* (1967) 10.
[152] L. Örsy, *Theology and Canon Law: New Horizons for Legislation and Interpretation* (Collegeville, Minnesota, 1992) 137, 165: theology 'contains a body of organised knowledge obtained through revelation and reflection of what was revealed; [canon law] consists of a system of norms of action issued by an ecclesiastical authority'; this study also reviews other schools of thought.
[153] E. Corecco, *The Theology of Canon Law: A Methodological Question* (Duquesne UP, Pittsburgh, Pennsylvania, 1992).
[154] N. Afanasiev, 'The canons of the church: changeable or unchangeable?', 11 *St Vladimir's Theological Quarterly* (1967) 54, at 60. See also J. Meyendorff, 'Contemporary problems of Orthodox canon law', 17 *Greek Orthodox Theological Review* (1972) 41. For the idea of canons as 'pastoral guidelines', see Patsavos, 'The canonical tradition of the Orthodox Church' at 144.
[155] PCLCCAC, Principle 2: law as servant.
[156] ELCA: Const., Introduction (by the Secretary, 4 Sept. 2009).
[157] Statement made at the Barmen Synod 31 May 1934 on the German Evangelical Church: quoted by M. Reuver, *Faith and Law: Juridical Perspectives for the Ecumenical Movement* (WCC, Geneva, 2000) 4; RCA: BCO, Preamble: the purposes of the church are 'achieved most effectively when good order and proper discipline are maintained by means of certain offices, government agencies, and theological and liturgical standards'.
[158] CIC, c. 834: 'In the liturgy ... our sanctification is symbolised and ... brought about.'

Old Catholic,[159] Orthodox,[160] Anglican,[161] Lutheran,[162] Presbyterian[163] and Baptist churches.[164]

The law of God

All the traditions understand their laws to have a relationship with the law of God, which is conceived to be revealed in Holy Scripture. This relationship surfaces in regulatory instruments in several ways: divine law is the foundation of church law; church law must conform to divine law; church laws may incorporate divine law; and church law in conflict with divine law may be invalid. For the Catholic Church 'the highest norm of human life is the divine law itself – eternal, objective and universal'; and it is ascertained by the teaching authority of the church.[165] The Code often presents canons as derived from divine law, and 'no custom which is contrary to divine law can acquire the force of law'.[166] For Orthodox jurists: 'the original source of canon law is found in the will of God' and 'its authority stems from the will of God'.[167] In turn, Orthodox laws provide that a church is 'governed by the Holy Scriptures' or that the church must edify the faithful 'in accordance with the Holy Scriptures'.[168] Moreover, some Orthodox churches demand preservation of 'the norms of Christian morals',[169] require clergy to act 'conscientiously',[170] or provide that a person ceases to be a parishioner in good standing if that person disregards or transgresses 'the moral law of the Church'.[171] Anglicanism, too, recognises that 'human law [is] distinct from the will or law of God'; above all: 'Law should reflect the revealed will of God';[172] and the laws of churches present Holy Scripture as the ultimate standard and rule in matters of faith;[173] but there is no obvious legal evidence from Anglican churches which indicates a general practice that divine law binds directly in a juridical sense, nor that divine law vitiates contrary canon law.[174]

---

[159] OCBUU: Statute (2000), A.3: each local church is 'a representation' of the church universal.
[160] GOAA: Charter, Art. 2: the mission of the archdiocese is to proclaim the gospel.
[161] England: Can. B30.1: marriage is 'in its nature a union permanent and lifelong'.
[162] ELCIC: Const. II.2: 'Congregations find their fulfilment in the universal community of the Church, and the universal Church exists in and through congregations.'
[163] PCA: BCO, I.16: 'Ordinary vocation to office in the Church is the calling of God by the Spirit.'
[164] The Church Constitution Guide, North American Mission Board, A Southern Baptist Convention Agency: a local church covenant should include the 'one another passages' of scripture.
[165] *Dignitatis Humanae* (Vatican II, Decree, 1965) I.3.
[166] CIC, c. 331: papal office; c. 1249: *ex lege divine tenentur* the faithful do penance; c. 207: *ex divina institutione*, among Christ's faithful there are sacred ministers and lay people; c. 24: custom.
[167] MOCL: Patsavos, 'The canonical tradition of the Orthodox Church', at 141.
[168] GOAA: Charter, Art. 1(b) and Art. 2(b): the archdiocese; Regs., Art. 15.3: the parish.
[169] ROC: Statute III.4(a); see also X.18: the diocesan bishop is to preserve 'Christian morality'.
[170] ROC: Statute XI.19: the rector must discharge his responsibilities 'conscientiously'.
[171] GOAA: Regs., Art. 18.3. See also ROMOC: Statutes, Art. 123(9): clergy must not act 'contrary to the Christian morals'; OCIA: Best Practice Principles and Policies for Financial Accountability, 2008 (Mark 4.22).
[172] PCLCCAC, Definitions, 'Law'; and Principle 2: law as servant.
[173] CLAC: 198ff; Thirty-Nine Articles of Religion, Art. 20: 'it is not lawful for the Church to ordain any thing which is contrary to God's Word written'.
[174] M. Hill, 'Gospel and order', 4 *Ecclesiastical Law Journal* (1996) 659.

Protestantism also distinguishes *ius divinum* and *ius humanum*; thus: '[b]ecause divine Church law is a law of the Spirit, a law of grace and love, the ecclesiastical lawgiver has a corresponding legal obligation to mirror this material structure in his human Church law in so far as he can', to provide 'a model for the world'.[175] As such, Lutheranism classifies baptism and preaching, for example, as divinely instituted, whereas forms of ministry, church organisation or worship are of human institution.[176] In turn, laws of Lutheran churches recognise, typically, 'the Holy Scriptures ... as the only infallible source and norm for all matters of faith, doctrine and life',[177] or that the Constitution and bylaws of a church 'are rooted in Scripture'.[178] They also classify entities (such as the office of ministry) as of divine institution,[179] or provide that a rule must not contradict the Word of God and that if it does it may lose its binding force: 'no resolution of the Synod imposing anything upon the individual congregation is of binding force if it is not in accordance with the Word of God or if it appears to be inexpedient as far as the condition of a congregation is concerned'.[180] Indeed, Lutherans commonly refer in their laws to passages from Holy Scripture,[181] 'scriptural principles', 'equity', 'conscience' and 'justice'.[182] Similarly, Methodist laws recognise 'God's Law', require 'obedience to the will of our Lord' and see Holy Scripture as the record of divine revelation in Christ and as containing all things necessary for salvation;[183] others classify the 'law of Christ' as 'the law of love', subject

---

[175] W. Steinmuller, 'Divine law and its dynamism in Protestant theology of law', 8 *Concilium* (1969) 13 at 20.

[176] AC, Art. V.

[177] LCA: Const., Art. II.1: the church accepts the Holy Scriptures as 'the Word of God' and 'norm for all matters of faith, doctrine, and life' or else the 'Word of God always meets man as Law and Gospel'; ELCSA: G., 12.3: 'Law and Gospel'; LCGB: RAR, Statement of Faith, 5: 'the Gospel is transmitted by the Holy Scriptures'; ELCA: Const., Ch. 2; ELCIC, Const., II.3; VII.1: the divine institution of ordained ministry.

[178] ELCA: Const., Introduction. ELCIC: Const., Preamble: the constitution is adopted in the name of God.

[179] NALC: SFPM (2011) 1; citing AC, Arts. IV and V.

[180] LCMS: Const., Art. VII; BL, 1.7: the Synod expects every congregation to respect its resolutions and 'consider them of binding force if they are in accordance with the Word of God', but 'recognizes the right of a congregation to be the judge of the applicability of these to its local condition'; in exercising such judgment, it must not act arbitrarily, 'but in accordance with the principles of Christian love and charity'.

[181] LCA: Const., Art. IV.1: disputes must be resolved 'in keeping with 1 Corinthians 6'; LCA: BL, Sect. V.D., Preamble: 'the office of the ministry is not a human institution but ... instituted by God' (Acts 20.28); ELCSA: G., 4.2: absolution (Matt. 18.15–18; John 20.21–23).

[182] LCA: BL, X.A.1; also Const., Art. X.1; BL IV.3: in disputes 'the question of any equitable distribution of property rights must be referred to the judicial system of the church'; BL, VII. C.28: in General Synod '[m]atters of conscience and doctrine' take precedence; BL, X.C.32–42: the tribunal must observe 'natural justice'; ELCA: Const., Ch. 8.16: decisions 'shall be guided by the biblical and confessional commitments of this church'.

[183] FMCNA: BOD, par. 112: 'God's law for all human life, personal and social, is expressed in two divine commands: Love the Lord God with all your heart, and love your neighbour as yourself'; UMCUSA: Const., Preamble: the will of the Lord; MCI: Const., 2: Statement of Belief: 'divine revelation [is] recorded in the Holy Scriptures'; MCNZ: LAR, s. 7.1: Conference is 'to interpret the mind and will of God'; MCGB: CPD, DU 4: 'the divine revelation recorded in the Holy Scriptures' which is 'the supreme rule of faith and practice'.

members to 'moral obligations' and require discipline to conform to the 'principles of natural justice'.[184]

Moving along the Protestant spectrum, it is commonplace for Presbyterian laws to acknowledge that the church receives its authority from Christ,[185] that 'the Word of God' is the supreme 'rule of faith and life',[186] and that church courts and officers must 'uphold the laws of Scripture' or 'the rules contained in the Word of God', and have 'the right to require obedience to the laws of Christ', and hear cases involving 'violations of the divine law'.[187] Indeed, it is 'the duty of everyone to accept and obey' the will of God as revealed in Scripture.[188] Presbyterian laws also invoke large moral ideas such as 'the principles of natural justice'.[189] United Churches also recognise Christ as Head of the Church, 'the moral law of God',[190] and equity.[191] Presbyterian and United churches both deploy scriptural texts in their legal instruments.[192] In much the same vein, for Baptist norms, Christ is 'the sole and absolute authority in all matters pertaining to faith and practice'; and '[e]ach Church has liberty, under the guidance of the Holy Spirit, to interpret and administer His Laws'.[193] As such, Baptist norms recognise the authority of Holy Scripture as a revelation of God,[194] classify the Holy Bible as part of 'the constitutions and laws' of

---

[184] MCNZ: RDG, 1.01; LAR, s. 7.2.1: exercising 'a moral obligation' in Conference voting; 8.1. the 'forgiveness of the Conference' in discipline; MCGB: SO 053: a sanction may be lifted on the basis of 'repentance and forgiveness'; COTN: Man., Pt. III: the Covenant of Christian Conduct uses scripture to justify its norms, e.g. par. 33.4: 'Test everything. Hold on to the good. Avoid every kind of evil' (1 Thess. 5.21–22).

[185] CLCS 1: 'The Church ... receives the right and power to regulate its own affairs from Christ'; PCI: Code, I.I.IV.15: 'Christ is the sole King and Head of the Church'; RCA: BCO, Preamble.

[186] PCANZ: BO, 1.1(2): 'The supreme rule of faith and life and the supreme standard of the Church is the Word of God contained in the Scriptures of the Old and New Testaments'; CLCS: 2; RCA: BCO, Preamble.

[187] PCA: BCO, Preface, II.3; also II.7: 'laws of Scripture'; BCO, 1.3: members profess Christ and 'promise submission to His laws'; 11.2: laws of Christ; 29.3: violations of divine law; 59.6: 'laws of God'.

[188] PCI: Code, I.I.III.11.

[189] PCANZ: BO, 15.1: disciplinary process incorporates 'principles of natural justice'.

[190] UCOC: Const., Preamble, 2: 'the Word of God in the Scriptures'; URC: Man., A: BU, 12: Scripture is 'the supreme authority for the faith and conduct of all God's people'; UCC: Man., BU 2.14: 'the moral law of God, summarized in the Ten Commandments, testified to by the prophets, and unfolded in the life and teachings of Jesus Christ, stands for ever in truth and equity'; God requires e.g. 'every man to do justly'.

[191] UCCP: Const., Art. II.5: 'justice' is at the heart of its witness to the world; II.6: the church must ensure 'equitable representation' of its general membership in terms of e.g. gender and age.

[192] CLCS: 2; PCI: Code I.IX, par. 132: 1 Cor. 5.9-11; UFCS: MPP VI.II.7: Matt. 18.15–17; UCCSA: Const., Procedure 15: Sacraments are 'remedies for sin (Rom. 6.4 and Matt. 26.29)'; UCC: ESMP, Introduction: when 'one suffers, all suffer together (1 Cor. 12.26)'; UCCP: Const., Art. II.3: the churches unite on the basis of John 17.21; constitutional amendment reflects the theology that 'the church must ... be "always reformed"'.

[193] BUGB: Const., 1.3.1; MTC 2003, 2.8.1. For an identical formula, see e.g. BUSA: Const., 4.1, and BUS: Const., III: Declaration of Principle, 1; for a similar formula, see JBU: Const., Art. III.

[194] BUGB: MTC 2003, 2.8.1 and 6.1, Const., 1.3; Bethel Baptist Church (Choctaw): Const., Art. VI: 'In all issues, the decision of the congregation shall be final, and there is no appeal to a higher authority, the authority of the church being the court of final appeal and the New Testament being the rule of church law.'

a Convention, or as 'the rule of church law',[195] and require a congregation to ascertain and obey 'the will of our Lord in all matters of faith and practice'.[196] Baptist instruments also often cite scriptural texts,[197] and, in one Baptist Union, pastors are required to undertake to support 'biblical morality'.[198]

The structure, effect and relaxation of norms

There is substantial but not exact convergence between churches as to the subjects treated by their regulatory instruments. As we shall see in the coming chapters, the regulatory instruments of national, regional and local churches deal with, typically, governance and ministry, doctrine and worship, rites and property.[199] Moreover, there is very profound agreement amongst the churches in terms of the structure of juridical instruments – these consist of a wide range of preceptive, prohibitive and permissive juristic forms. The instruments of all of the Christian traditions also provide in one way or another for both the enforcement and, in prescribed circumstances, the relaxation of juridical norms.

First, the laws of churches employ standard juridical formulae. Like Catholic canon law,[200] Orthodox laws consist of 'principles', 'policies', 'rules' and 'procedures';[201] institutions have 'canonical jurisdiction', 'responsibilities', 'duties', 'rights' and 'privileges';[202] and individuals have 'rights' and 'duties'.[203] Also, Anglican laws

---

[195] NBCUSA: Const., Art. X.5: the Bible as part of the constitution; ABCUSA: BL, Prologue: it is 'the inspired Word of God [and] final written authority'; each body is 'to order its life in accordance with the Scriptures'; CNBC: Const., 3: Statement of Faith: the Bible 'reveals the principles by which God judges us' and is 'the supreme standard by which all human conduct, creeds, and religious opinions should be tried'.

[196] BMPP, 216, App. III, SCBC, Type A: Art. III.

[197] Riverside Baptist Church (Baltimore): BL, Art. II: qualifications for pastors (1 Tim. 3.1–7; Titus 1.7–9).

[198] BUNZ: EPGP, 6.4: 'I will support biblical morality ... through prophetic witness and social action'.

[199] Globally: the Latin Code has seven 'Books': general norms; people of God; teaching; sanctifying; goods; sanctions; and processes. The Oriental Code has thirty 'Titles' on equivalent subjects. The Orthodox 'canonical tradition' has a similarly wide compass, as has the Anglican PCLCCAC (2008): Pt. I: Church Order; Pt. II: Anglican Communion; Pt. III: Ecclesiastical Government; Pt. IV: Ministry; Pt. V: Doctrine and Liturgy; Pt. VI: Ecclesiastical Rites; Pt. VII: Church Property; Pt. VIII: Ecumenical Relations. The LWF, WCRC and BWA constitutions have a more limited scope (e.g. Objects, Membership and Institutions).

[200] See e.g. CIC, Bk. I: general norms; c. 19: 'principles of law'; cc. 208–223: obligations and rights of the faithful; CCEO, c. 1501: 'principles of canon law'; cc. 1531–1535: privileges.

[201] ROC: Statute, II.5: 'the principles' of church–State relations; GOAA: Regs., Preamble: 'the policies, rules, operation procedures and controls to promote effective governance'; UOCIA: Const., Art. VII.9: 'the requirements of the Holy Canons'; Art. XI.1: a parish must 'comply with the discipline and rules of the Church'; ROMOC: Statutes, Art. 201: the statutes were approved by Holy Synod 'on the basis of the general principles and stipulations of the Holy Canons'; Art. 52(4): clergy 'rights and duties stipulated in the Holy Canons'.

[202] ROC: Statute, III: Bishops' Council's 'jurisdiction' and 'responsibilities'; GOAA: Charter, Art. 13(a): Holy Synod's 'privilege and canonical right' to elect an archbishop; Regs., Art. 29: Parish Council 'duties'.

[203] ROMOC: Statutes, Art. 45: members' 'rights' and 'duties'; ROC: Statute, X.24: 'Bishops shall have the right to leave their dioceses for valid reasons'; SOCA: Const., Art. 105: 'deacons and

contain 'principles, norms, standards, policies, directions, rules, precepts, prohibitions, powers, freedoms, discretions, rights, entitlements, duties, obligations, privileges and other juridical concepts'.[204] Much the same applies in instruments of Lutherans,[205] Methodists,[206] Presbyterians[207] and Baptists.[208]

Secondly, all the traditions agree that juridical norms are binding and enforceable. However, the extent to which, and the ways in which, they are varies as between the different churches. At international level, for the Roman Catholic Church, the Code of 1983 affects only the Latin Church, but its provisions bind all the faithful directly in the particular churches, bishops, clergy and laity alike; the Oriental Catholic code is similar.[209] In the Orthodox Church there is a lively debate as to whether the canonical tradition binds in the sense of letter or spirit,[210] but within an individual church, laws and court decisions are 'binding for all clergymen and laymen without any exception'.[211] Whilst the principles of canon law common to the churches of the Anglican Communion do not bind those churches internationally but are of persuasive authority, in some churches the laws bind only

---

their Duties'; MOSC: Const., Art. 3: rights of the Diocesan Metropolitan; UOCIA: Const., Art. II.6: the 'pastoral duties' of bishops.

[204] PCLCCAC, Principle 4.5.

[205] LCA: Const., Art. III(k): 'the principles ... in the Formula of Concord'; ELCSA: G., 6.1: a congregation has 'responsibility' to nurture children; LCGB: RAR, Responsibilities and Duties of Pastors; ELCA: Const., Ch. 15.31: 'responsibilities' of the Conference of Bishops; Ch. 8.72.14: ministers from a church in communion with ELCA may have 'the privilege' of voice and vote at Synod Assembly; LCMS: BL, 1.3.5: members' 'privileges'.

[206] UMCUSA: Const., Div. 2.2, Art. IV.2: 'privileges and duties' of church membership; Div. 2.3, Art. I: 'standards'; Div. 2.4, Art. V: 'rules and regulations' of a jurisdictional conference; UMCNEAE: BOD, par. 142 'principles set forth in the Constitution or the Book of Discipline'; MCI: Const., s. 2: 'standards of preaching and belief'; RDG, 6.51: 'rules of debate'; 13.01: 'It is a principle in Methodism' that each circuit raises funds; MCNZ: LAR, Nature of New Zealand Methodism: 'the duties and privileges of the Methodist Church under its discipline'; MCGB: CPD, DU 9: 'the privilege and duty of members'; DU 18–21: 'the powers, authorities, rights and duties' of the Conference; CPD, SO 1102: the 'principle of fairness'.

[207] PCANZ: BO, 4.4-6: members' 'rights and privileges' and 'responsibilities'; PCI: Code, par. 138: '"shall" shall be construed as imperative and ... "may" as permissive and empowering'; PCA: BCO, Preface II.5: 'the duty both of private Christians and societies to exercise mutual forbearance'; PCW: HOR, 4.3: 'the responsibility of the elders'; PCANZ: BO, 7.2: Church Council 'functions'; 14.3-4: 'powers' and 'duties' of General Assembly; PCA: BCO, Preface II.11.3: church courts are 'possessed inherently' of 'rights and powers'; PCI: Code, I.IV.II: Presbytery 'Duties and Rights'. PCW: HOR, 2.3: 'Rules of Church Membership'; PCI: Code I.1: General Principles (on e.g. government); RCA: BCO, Preamble: 'The Representative Principle' in church governance.

[208] BUGB: MTC 2003, 2.8.3: 'the duty of every disciple to ... witness to ... Christ'; 3.1: 'the powers, discretions and authorities ... vested in the Union'; NBCUSA: Const., Art. I.8: 'membership rights, privileges, and procedures'; BUSA: Const., 5.3: 'Baptist Principles'; Model Const., Art. 4.2: e.g. 'principle of religious liberty'; Central Baptist Church (Pretoria): Const., 8: 'Privileges and Obligations of Membership'.

[209] CIC, c.1; cc. 11–12; CCEO, cc. 1489–1491.

[210] J.H. Erickson, *The Challenge of Our Past: Studies in Orthodox Canon Law and Church History* (Crestwood, New York, 1991) Ch. 1.

[211] ROC: Statute, VII.8. See also GOAA: Regs., Art. 4.15: the decisions of the Clergy–Laity Congress 'must be faithfully and firmly adhered to by the Archdiocesan District/Metropolises as well as all Parishes'.

ordained ministers, but in others they bind both ordained and lay persons; and often laws provide for undertakings to be made by church members to assent to or comply with the law.[212] For some Lutheran churches, a precondition to membership is acceptance of the constitution and bylaws,[213] or else classes of member 'covenant' compliance.[214] The position is similar in some Presbyterian churches; for example: 'All members of congregations and any other person affected by any provision in the Book of Order must comply with the Book of Order';[215] again: 'All baptised persons, being members of the Church, are subject to its discipline and entitled to the benefits thereof'; however: 'No judicatory may make laws to bind the conscience.'[216] Equally, Methodists are 'accountable for faithfulness to their covenant in baptism', and for church discipline;[217] and judicial decisions are 'binding' on the parties but may have 'persuasive' precedential value.[218] Likewise, Baptist instruments sometimes explicitly require 'strict adherence' to the 'rules and regulations'.[219]

The administration and enforcement of law is assigned to a variety of institutions within churches. Two approaches surface. On the one hand, compliance is effected by means of executive or quasi-judicial authority. In the Roman Catholic Church enforcement is possible through hierarchical administrative recourse, or oaths of fidelity.[220] Orthodox archbishops may enjoy executive authority to implement laws.[221] Anglican clergy owe canonical obedience and undertake to obey the lawful and honest directions of their bishops.[222] Lutheran pastors may administer discipline in their congregations;[223] and in some Presbyterian churches compliance may be effected by visitation.[224] On the other hand, as we shall see more fully in Chapter 5, churches provide for formal judicial law enforcement and resolution of

---

[212] See e.g. Scotland: Can. 58: 'I will give all due obedience to the Code of Canons.'
[213] LCGB: RAR, Congregations, 1: a congregation must 'accept and uphold the Governing Documents (Constitutions and Rules and Regulations)'.
[214] ELCIC, Const. X.3: 'Each lay diaconal minister shall covenant to abide loyally by the constitution, administrative bylaws and enactments of this church and of the [regional] synod.'
[215] PCANZ: BO, 2.2; PCA: BCO 5.8: members 'solemnly promise and covenant' to work together 'on the principles of the faith and order'; CLCS 10: undertaking at ordination to observe the order of worship.
[216] PCA: BCO, Preface, II.8.
[217] UMCNEAE: BOD, par. 221; MCNZ: LAR, 2.3: ministry candidates 'accept [church] polity and discipline'.
[218] UMCNEAE: BOD, par. 2610–2611: Judicial Council decisions are 'binding' on the parties but 'persuasive as precedents, except where their basis has been changed by ... Church law'.
[219] JBU: Const., Art. V: whilst the Union recognises 'the autonomous character of each Church', 'strict adherence shall be given to such Rules and Regulations as are now in force or as may be adopted from time to time' by the Union which, in the case of acts 'in contravention' of these in 'a manner injurious' to its interests, the Union may act in accordance with the rules and regulations relative to 'its discipline and powers'.
[220] CIC, cc. 1732–1755: administrative recourse; c. 380: episcopal oath of fidelity to the Apostolic See.
[221] GOAA: Charter, Art. 6.13: and must 'support' his hierarchs in 'a brotherly manner'.
[222] E.g. England: Can. C14: 'I will pay true and canonical obedience to the Lord Bishop of C and his successors in all things lawful and honest.'
[223] ELCIC: Approved Model Constitution for Congregations, Art. VII.
[224] PCA: BCO, I.13: the Presbytery may visit churches 'for the purpose of inquiring into and redressing the evils that may have arisen in them'.

THE STRUCTURE, EFFECT AND RELAXATION OF NORMS 39

conflict: church courts and tribunals are ordered hierarchically and their subject-matter jurisdictions are prescribed in the Roman Catholic,[225] Orthodox,[226] Anglican,[227] Lutheran,[228] Presbyterian[229] and Methodist churches.[230] Failure to comply with law may result in proceedings for offences and the imposition of sanctions. Elaborate systems of offences, sanctions and restoration operate in the Roman Catholic,[231] Orthodox,[232] Anglican,[233] Lutheran[234] and Presbyterian churches.[235] At the international level, too, the instruments of global ecclesial communities commonly contain disciplinary provisions: the Assembly of the Lutheran World Federation may suspend or terminate the membership of a church by a two-thirds vote of the delegates.[236] The Federation suspended the memberships of two churches in 1977 (which have since been restored), as did the World Alliance of Reformed Churches (as it then was) in 1982 (though it was lifted conditionally in 1997). In the Old Catholic Union of Utrecht, the Bishops' Conference may ascertain whether a bishop has 'gravely harmed' the Declaration of Utrecht, the catholicity of ministry, doctrine, and worship, its Statute or the 'moral order'; it may then deprive the bishop of membership.[237]

Thirdly, however, an important feature of some Christian traditions is that juridical norms may be relaxed in special circumstances: a range of devices is employed to achieve relaxation of norms – dispensation, economy and equity are amongst the most common; though, as we shall see throughout this book, often exceptions or exemptions accompany general rules. In the Catholic Church, canon law may be relaxed by means of dispensation, and laws do not bind, for example, if they have not been promulgated or if there a doubt about the law.[238] Dispensation is 'the relaxation of a merely ecclesiastical law in a particular case'; it may be granted 'within the limits of their competence, by those who have executive power, and by those who either explicitly or implicitly have the power of dispensing, whether by virtue of the law itself or by lawful delegation': however, laws which define what constitutes juridical institutions or acts cannot be the subject of dispensation.[239] The Pontiff enjoys extensive powers of dispensation and a diocesan bishop may dispense with both universal and particular law when this is for the good of the faithful, but cannot dispense from procedural laws, penal laws or in those cases reserved to the Apostolic See. Dispensation must not be granted without 'a just and reasonable cause'; the dispensing authority must consider the circumstances of the case and the gravity of the law from which dispensation is sought; otherwise, the dispensation is illicit and (unless given by the legislator) invalid. The power to

---

[225] CIC, cc. 1417–1475: from courts of first instance through to tribunals of the Apostolic See.
[226] GOAA: Charter, Art. 9: Spiritual Courts (family matters, and moral and disciplinary offences).
[227] CLAC: 80–88.
[228] ELCIC: Const., Art. XVIII: Court of Adjudication: its interpretations of law bind.
[229] PCA: BCO, I: the courts of Session, Presbytery, and General Assembly.
[230] UMCUSA: Const., Div. 4, Art. I: the judicial Council; par. 228: 'just resolution'; par. 416: 'fair process'.
[231] CIC, cc. 1311–1399.   [232] GOAA: Charter, Art. 9.   [233] CLAC: 80–85.
[234] LCA: Const., Art. X.   [235] PCA: BCO, II.27ff.   [236] LWF: Const., Art. V; BL, 2.
[237] OCBUU: Statute B. Order, Art. 3(a)–(k).
[238] CIC, c. 7: promulgation; c. 14: *dubium legis*; c. 221: the law must be applied with equity (*cum aequitate*). See also CCEO, c. 1488: promulgation; c. 1496: doubt of law.
[239] CIC, cc. 87–88. See also CCEO, cc. 1536–1539.

dispense must be construed restrictively and a dispensation ends when the reasons for it cease.[240] Anglican churches also recognised the power of dispensation, to the extent this is authorised by the law of a church,[241] on the basis that laws cannot encompass all facets of ecclesial life.[242]

An equivalent in the Orthodox canonical tradition is the principle of 'economy': 'Mere application of the letter of the law is replaced by a sense for the spirit of the law, and adherence to its principles.' This spirit of the law is the 'spirit of love' – and a 'commitment to the spiritual perfection of the individual, must always prevail in the application of the law'. Economy involves the 'abolition of the letter of the law by the spirit of the law'. Through economy, 'which is always an exception to the general rule, the legal consequences following the violation of a law are lifted'.[243] Economy is granted by a competent authority to provide 'compassion for human frailty' and 'for the general welfare of all concerned' – it is characterised by 'compassion, pastoral sensitivity, and forgiveness'. But it has limitations: 'exception from a law that has been endowed with universal recognition and validity is not possible'; the right to exercise economy belongs only to the legislator (e.g. a Holy Synod of bishops) which may delegate this right to a bishop; and the exercise of economy 'does not set a precedent'.[244] Orthodox laws sometimes refer explicitly to economy (e.g. to tolerate mixed marriages between Orthodox and non-Orthodox, or remarriage after a civil dissolution).[245]

Dispensation and economy are less evident in Protestant juridical traditions, though the concept of moderation in discipline does occasionally surface in laws, as does the idea that church laws should be applied 'with pastoral prudence and Christian love'.[246] However, in Presbyterianism, for example in the United Free Church of Scotland, the General Assembly has a *nobile officium*: 'the power of the General Assembly, as Supreme Court to act in special circumstances beyond or even against its own rules or forms of procedures' as 'shall seem to the General Assembly

---

[240] CIC, cc. 87–93; pastors may sometimes dispense: see e.g. cc. 1079, 1196, 1245.
[241] PCLCCAC, Principle 7: the applicability of law; 1: later laws abrogate earlier laws; 2: laws are prospective and should not be retrospective in effect unless this is clearly provided for in the laws themselves; 3: laws cannot oblige a person to do the impossible; 4: persons cannot give what they do not have; 5: laws should be applied in the service of truth, justice and equity; 6: laws may be dispensed with in their application to particular cases on the basis of legitimate necessity provided authority to dispense is clearly given by the law.
[242] PCLCCAC, Principle 3: the limits of law; 1: laws should reflect but cannot change Christian truths; 2: laws cannot encompass all facets of ecclesial life; 3: laws cannot prescribe the fullness of ecclesial life, ministry and mission; 4: laws function predominantly in the public sphere of church life; 5: the principal subjects with which laws deal are ecclesiastical government, ministry, discipline, doctrine, liturgy, rites, property, and ecumenical relations; 6: some laws articulate immutable truths and values.
[243] Patsavos, 'The canonical tradition of the Orthodox Church', at 144–145.
[244] Ibid., at 145; Synod of Ancyra, c. 2: for indiscipline, 'if any of the bishops shall observe in [a deacon] ... meek humiliation, it shall be lawful to the bishops to grant more indulgence, or to take away [what has been granted]'.
[245] UOCIA: Instructions, Policy Regarding Mixed Marriages, 1: 'dispensations'; ROMOC: Statutes, Art. 88: 'exemptions' for remarriage; GOAA: Charter Art. 21(c): 'the letter and spirit of the Regulations' define the operation of monasteries; Art. 22: Regulations must conform to 'the letter and the spirit of this Charter'.
[246] PCA: BCO, Preface, II; see also 8.3: 'the law of love'.

right and needful for doing justice in the particular case'.[247] This power of suspension is echoed in the laws of other traditions, including the Baptist, at least in relation to the relaxation of rules of procedure applicable to ecclesiastical assemblies.[248]

The interpretation of law

The juridical instruments of all the churches studied here deal with the interpretation of church law. Churches may have general norms on the subject and assign the function of authoritative interpretation to prescribed institutions. Roman Catholic canon law has a set of basic norms about the interpretation of law: laws are 'to be understood in accord with the proper meaning of the words ... in their text and context'; if the meaning remains doubtful, recourse is to be taken to parallel passages, to the circumstances of the law and to the mind of the legislator.[249] However, there is no system of binding judicial precedent in Catholic canon law: a judicial decision does not have the status or force of law: it binds only the parties to it and it affects only the matter for which it was given. The only authentic and binding interpretation of a law which itself possesses the quality of law is that as promulgated by the legislator, and this is treated merely as a descriptive, declaratory or confirmatory statement of existing law; judicial decisions may be consulted as persuasive authorities and (unless it is a penal matter) 'the case is to be decided in the light of ... the jurisprudence and praxis of the Roman Curia'.[250] Under the Oriental Code, the power to interpret the law authentically is given to a range of ecclesiastical institutions: for example, in a patriarchal church, the patriarch issues authentic interpretations of synodal legislation;[251] the interpretation has the same authority as the law itself but this may be overridden by synodal legislation.[252]

Orthodox jurists have developed several norms for the interpretation of law.[253] However, the juridical instruments of some Orthodox churches have definition

---

[247] UFCS: MPP, Glossary of Latin Terms and V.II.8. Compare CLCS: 53: *nobile officium* 'cannot override law, but [can provide] only the want of it when necessary'. See also UCCSA: Standing Orders of the Assembly, 14: 'Any one or more of the Standing Orders, in any case of urgency, may be suspended at any meeting ... provided that three-fourths of the members of the Assembly present and voting shall so decide.'

[248] See e.g. BUS: BL, SO 12: 'Standing Orders [of the Assembly] may be suspended in the interests of considering the subject then before the meeting'. Compare MCNZ: LAR, s. 3.2: the Conference may not suspend the Laws and Regulations in the conduct of meetings.

[249] CIC, c. 17; Örsy, *Theology and Canon Law*. CCEO, c. 1501: interpretation of law and recourse to e.g. 'the principles of canon law applied with equity'.

[250] CIC, cc. 16, 17, 19. The Pontifical Council for Legislative Texts gives authentic interpretations with papal authority; the tribunals commonly consult, adopt and follow the decisions of the Roman Rota – and decisions of the Rota and Apostolic Signatura are regularly published for the guidance of the lower courts: see generally, N. Doe, 'Canonical doctrines of judicial precedent: a comparative study', 54 *The Jurist* (1994) 205.

[251] CCEO, c. 56.   [252] CCEO, c. 112.2; c. 1498.2: it has the force of law on promulgation.

[253] MOCL: 39: the grammatical focuses on 'the letter of the law'; logical, the relation of 'the various component parts of the law to each other'; historical, 'the origin of the law and the situation which led to its promulgation'; and systematic, 'the inner relationship of the law with other laws' and the mind of the legislator; the Holy Spirit is invoked because 'the holy canons constitute an expression of the Holy Spirit'.

sections,²⁵⁴ whilst others provide that norms are to be 'broadly interpreted' to achieve their objectives.²⁵⁵ Generally, the task of interpretation is assigned to the assemblies of a church. For example, the Bishops' Council of the Russian Orthodox Church is responsible for the 'interpretation of the holy canons and other church regulations';²⁵⁶ the Archdiocesan Council of the Greek Orthodox Archdiocese of America interprets the decisions of the Congress and the regulations made under the Charter;²⁵⁷ and the Holy Synod of the Romanian Orthodox Church is responsible for interpretation of the statutes and regulations of the church 'in final and compulsory form for all the church bodies'.²⁵⁸ For Anglicans, '[l]aws should be interpreted by reference to their text and context' and 'according to the proper meaning of their words'; 'Authoritative interpretations of law may be issued by church courts or tribunals, or by commissions or other bodies designated to interpret the law, in such cases, in such manner and with such effect as may be prescribed by the law.'²⁵⁹ However, if 'the meaning of laws remains in doubt recourse may be had to analogous texts, the purposes and circumstances of the law, the mind of the legislator, the jurisprudence of church courts and tribunals, the opinion of jurists, the principles of canon law and theology, the common good, and the practice and tradition of that church and of the church universal'.²⁶⁰ It is common for laws to have interpretation sections.²⁶¹ Moreover: 'The decision of a church court or tribunal has such binding or persuasive authority for other church courts or tribunals as may be provided in the law.'²⁶²

Unlike the Catholic, Orthodox and Anglican traditions, the laws of Protestant churches rarely have general norms applicable to interpretation, but they use

---

²⁵⁴ GOAA: Regs., Definition of Terms (which follows the Preamble).
²⁵⁵ OCIA: Policies, Standards and Procedures on Sexual Misconduct, Holy Synod 2003: these 'should be broadly interpreted and applied to achieve ... preventing sexual misconduct, effectively dealing with it if it occurs, providing appropriate pastoral care, and ensuring that justice and fairness are achieved'.
²⁵⁶ ROC: Statute, III.4; V.32: the Holy Synod is responsible for resolving disputes about interpretation.
²⁵⁷ GOAA: Charter, Art. 17: the Council itself makes regulations as to its own function, but regulations as to its composition are promulgated by the Congress; see also Regs., Definition of Terms; Art. 2.
²⁵⁸ ROMOC: Statutes, Arts. 11–16; see also Arts. 201–205: the Holy Synod may amend the Statutes.
²⁵⁹ PCLCCAC, Principle 8.1–3. See e.g. Burundi, Const. Art. 18: disputes about interpretation of the constitution must be referred by e.g. the House of Bishops to 'a Constitutional Interpretation Committee' whose decision 'shall be final'; South East Asia: Const. Art. XVII: the House of Bishops' decision after consulting the Provincial Chancellor is 'final and binding'; New Zealand: Cans. C.IV.4: the Judicial Committee.
²⁶⁰ PCLCCAC, Principle 8.4.
²⁶¹ Southern Africa: Can. 50: 'It is hereby declared that if any question should arise as to the interpretation of the Canon Law of this Church, or of any part thereof, the interpretation shall be governed by the general principles of Canon Law thereto applicable'; Australia, Const. XII.74.7: the constitution must be construed 'as if the Interpretation Acts 1901–1948 of the Parliament ... of Australia applied to this Constitution'.
²⁶² PCLCCAC, Principle 24.14. See e.g. New Zealand, Cans. D.II.5.3: the courts 'shall not have regard to precedent of sentences inflicted ... before ... 1925 ... but they may have regard to precedents of sentences inflicted under this Canon'; TEC: *Stanton (Bishop of Dallas) and Others v Righter* (1996): the Court for the Trial of a Bishop considered that the case of *Bishop Brown* (1924) 'sets precedent for this Court'.

definition sections and provide for the determination of questions of legal interpretation by prescribed institutions. This applies to Lutheran churches.²⁶³ For example, in the Lutheran Church Missouri Synod, the Commission on Constitutional Matters interprets the constitution, bylaws and resolutions on written request of, *inter alia*, a member, board or commission; appeal lies against an interpretation to a panel of the Commission whose decision 'shall be binding' unless overruled by a convention of the Synod.²⁶⁴ Similarly, in the Evangelical Lutheran Church in Canada, the Court of Adjudication settles questions of 'principle, practice, interpretation, doctrine or conscience'; its decisions are binding (until reversed by the Convention).²⁶⁵ Methodists have much the same approach: alongside definition sections,²⁶⁶ the President of Conference may have authority to issue binding interpretations by means of a 'ruling';²⁶⁷ or a Committee on Methodist Law and Polity advises Conference as to 'the interpretation and application of its laws and Standing Orders'.²⁶⁸ In the Reformed tradition, too, the authority to interpret laws vests in church assemblies,²⁶⁹ though laws may carry definition sections and provide that terms be interpreted according to their text and context.²⁷⁰ Likewise, Baptist instruments commonly contain definition sections or

---

²⁶³ LCA: Const., Interpretation; BL V.D.2: disciplinary norms must be 'interpreted and carried out in an evangelical spirit'; X.C.3: interpretation 'according to the principles' which govern the church; Const. of Districts, X: the district 'has authority to adjudicate on interpretations of its constitution, rules or regulations'.
²⁶⁴ LCMS: BL, 3.9. See also ELCA: Const., Ch. 13.40-42: the Secretary of the Churchwide Assembly 'shall prepare interpretations, as necessary, of the Constitution, Bylaws and Continuing Resolutions' of the church; if a board, committee, or synod disagrees with the interpretation, it may appeal to the Church Council; LCA: BL V.D.2; X.C.3: the General Synod, District Synods and Congregations may submit questions of interpretation (and the facts which underlie them) to the Standing Committee on Constitutions of the Church.
²⁶⁵ ELCIC: Const., Art. XVIII: it has four lay and three ordained members elected by the Convention.
²⁶⁶ MCGB: CPD, DU 1; SO 008: laws should be interpreted according to their text and context.
²⁶⁷ MCNZ: LAR, s. 7.5: 'Should any question arise in the interval between two Conferences as to the meaning or intention of any Resolution of the Conference, or as to the interpretation of any Law or Regulation of the Church', the matter may be referred to the President, 'whose ruling thereon shall be binding until the next Conference'. See also MCNZ: LAR, s. 5.7.8: the Law Revision Committee 'shall monitor all resolutions of the Conference, and if any ... require alteration or deletion of existing law, or promulgation of new law, [it] shall prepare the consequent changes to the Law Book, and present them for approval by the subsequent Conference'; s. 7.10.4.3: it is appointed annually by the Conference with the President's Legal Adviser as *ex officio* member.
²⁶⁸ MCGB: CPD, SO 338; see also SO 123(3), 126(1)(*b*) and 131(19), (25): the committee proposes amendments and scrutinises all new legislative proposals as to their coherence with existing usage.
²⁶⁹ URC: Man., B.2.6: General Assembly has 'final authority ... to interpret all forms and expressions of the polity practice and doctrinal formulations' of the church.
²⁷⁰ PCI: Code, X: e.g. par. 137: definitions listed must be employed 'unless the context otherwise requires'; PCANZ: BO, 2.4: words are defined in App. I which 'is to be regarded as part of this Book of Order'; 2.6: the headings contained in the BO 'are intended only to facilitate use of the [BO] and must not be used for the purposes of interpreting any of its provisions'; PCW: Const. for a Local Church, Art. 1: Interpretation.

44   THE SOURCES AND PURPOSES OF ECCLESIASTICAL REGULATION

else require ascertainment of the intent of the legislator.[271] Indeed, the Baptist Union of Great Britain may settle disputes on 'any issue as to the meaning, construction, or effect' of the provisions of a Baptist trust instrument and its decision 'shall be binding and conclusive'; but: 'The Union may not override any validly made determination of a duly convened Church Meeting or ... Association in regard to the subject matter at issue, when it shall appear to the Union that such determination was within the powers of the Church Meeting or Association [as] to the subject matter at issue.'[272]

Conclusion

A comparison of the juridical instruments of churches reveals a high degree of similarity as to the nature and objects of the institutional church, the forms of ecclesiastical regulation, and the purposes, structure, effect, relaxation and interpretation of church law. Theological ideas are most evident in provisions about the nature and objects of the institutional church and the purposes of its juridical instruments, which themselves indicate that Christians in all the traditions share in the common action of making, justifying, relaxing and interpreting laws. From the similarities between these laws of Christians it is possible to articulate shared principles of Christian law. Each church defines itself legally by reference to its territoriality, polity and objects. An institutional church is an ecclesial community with a defined geographical compass (international, national, regional or local), a distinct membership organised on the basis of ecclesiastical units (such as provinces, districts or congregations), an autonomous and distinctive system of government, and whose objects include proclaiming the Gospel, administering the sacraments and serving the wider community. All the churches employ the term 'law' to describe many of their regulatory instruments. Laws are found in codes of canon law, charters and statutes, constitutions and bylaws, books of church order, covenants and, occasionally, customs. All of the churches also operate systems of ecclesiastical quasi-legislation – informal rules that are nevertheless prescriptive in form and generate the expectation of compliance. It is a principle of Christian law that juridical instruments serve the objects and mission of the church, implement theological propositions, and are subject ultimately to the law of God, as revealed in Holy Scripture. These regulatory instruments are composed of a variety of juridical formulae, including precepts, prohibitions and permissions cast as principles and rules, rights and duties, functions and powers. In turn, regulatory instruments are binding and/or exhortatory, and various devices (such as undertakings) are employed to ensure compliance by those to whom they are addressed. Provision

---

[271] BUSA: Const., 2: 'definitions' (e.g. 'church', 'member', 'minister'); CNBC: BL, Pt. 1: Interpretation; NBCUSA: BL 7.4: 'These Bylaws are to be read in conformity with, are subject to, and shall be governed by the ... Constitution'; 'the provisions and intent' of the constitution 'shall be deemed the superior authority'.

[272] BUGB: MTC 2003, 14.1; 14.3: the rule against overriding a Church Meeting 'protects the autonomy of a properly constituted Church Meeting' (marginal note); parties include the church, its members, an Association or the Union; 14.2: 'The Union may, in its discretion, decline to entertain any referral ... if it does not consider the subject matter ... to be of a sufficiently serious or relevant nature as to call for its intervention.'

is sometimes made for the relaxation of laws, by means of dispensation, economy or other form of equity, but this is more evident in the Catholic, Orthodox, Anglican and Presbyterian juristic traditions. It is a principle of Christian law that juridical instruments should be interpreted by reference to their text and context, and that the church itself has the authority to interpret its own laws through a wide range of institutions competent to do so.

2

The faithful – the laity and lay ministry

The juridical instruments of churches serve not only the wider objects of those churches but also the Christian faithful within them. One traditional and significant element of Christian thought is the classification of the faithful into two broad categories of ecclesiastical person: lay and ordained. Historically, the distinction has been the subject of intense theological debate, and is today more marked in some traditions than in others. However, there is broad ecumenical agreement around the notion that all the faithful (both lay and ordained) comprise the whole 'people of God' sharing in the ministry which Christ envisioned for his followers on earth. The juridical instruments of all the traditions studied here provide for the admission of people to the institutional church and they define what it means to belong to it. Definitions of a church member or other similar category, and the conditions used for admission, vary as between the churches, as does the employment and maintenance of rolls or other registers of church members. Moreover, all the traditions spell out the functions of members. Several provide for the enjoyment and discharge of prescribed rights and duties by all the faithful, regardless of whether they have lay or ordained status. At the same time, all the traditions articulate the duties and to a lesser extent the rights applicable only to the laity. They also enable the appointment of eligible people to a range of lay ministries the functions of which are prescribed by law. This chapter examines these matters as well as the opportunities afforded in a small number of traditions for the faithful to enter religious communities (such as monasteries and convents) and other forms of religious association. In addition to exposing key legal differences, the chapter also induces common principles of Christian law from the profound similarities between the juridical instruments of the various ecclesial traditions and institutional churches studied as to the place of the faithful in the church. Each section of the following deals with the traditions and their juridical instruments *seriatim*.

The people of God

All the Christian traditions studied here distinguish between the laity and the ordained ministers of the church – though the vast majority also assert the essential interconnectedness and equality of lay and ordained persons who together constitute 'the people of God'.[1] According to the canon law of the Catholic Church, Christ's faithful (*christifideles*) are 'incorporated into the Church of Christ through baptism'. The faithful constitute the 'people of God' and each of them 'participates

---

[1] For ecumenical approaches to the church universal as the Body of Christ, see E. Fahlbusch et al. (eds.), *Encyclopedia of Christianity* (Eerdmans, Cambridge, 1997) 487–497.

in their own way in the priestly, prophetic and kingly office of Christ'; moreover, each is called according to his/her own condition 'to exercise the mission which God entrusted to the Church to fulfil in the world'.[2] However, by 'divine institution, among Christ's faithful there are in the Church sacred ministers, who are in law also called clerics; the others are called lay people'.[3] Nevertheless, it is by virtue of baptism that all Christ's faithful (lay and ordained) enjoy within the church 'a genuine equality of dignity and action' to contribute 'each according to his or her own condition and office, to the building up of the Body of Christ'.[4] The Oriental Catholic Churches employ the same outlook and provide that: 'The designation of "lay persons" is applied ... to the Christian faithful whose proper and special quality is secularity and who, living in the world participate in the mission of the Church, but are not in sacred orders nor ascribed in the religious state.'[5]

The same distinction between the lay and ordained faithful is pivotal in Orthodox canon law. Some jurists define *ekklesia* as 'the new people of God living in hierarchical order for the purpose of realizing the Kingdom of God on earth': 'It is composed of all who correctly believe in Christ as God and Saviour of the world and are united organically by the same Orthodox faith and the same sacraments'; and it is 'distinguished into clergy who are consecrated through the sacrament of the priesthood, and the laity'.[6] However, there is a basic equality between clergy and laity: 'Church organization consists of two parts, of the order of the clergy and that of the laity. The distinction does not carry the sense of division or opposition between the faithful, nor that of the formation of privileged classes, in the sense of greater rights or fewer responsibilities, nor that of a difference in worth or quality being created amongst the faithful.' Nevertheless, 'the laity does not have the special property of the priesthood, even though they participate through baptism in the triple office of the Lord. Everyone, however, clergy and laity, partakes of one and the same Spirit'. Importantly, the distinction 'is external and in no way eliminates the fundamental principle of the equality of all the faithful toward the gifts of the grace of the Spirit'; indeed: 'The order of the laity also has by divine law the duty and right to be governed by the clergy.'[7] Anglican laws are similar: 'the *laos* is the whole people of God, but for the purposes of law, a lay person is a person who is not in holy orders'.[8] Yet, all persons are 'equal in dignity before God' and 'as human beings created in the image and likeness of God [are] called to salvation

---

[2] CIC, c. 204; c. 96: 'By baptism one is incorporated into the Church of Christ and constituted a person in it'; see also A. Gauthier, 'Juridical persons in the code of canon law', 25 *Studia Canonica* (1991) 77; LG 10, 11, 32.

[3] CIC, c. 207: 'Their state, although it does not belong to the hierarchical structure of the Church, does pertain to its life and holiness'; see also cc. 96–112 for the canonical status of physical persons.

[4] CIC, c. 208; see also CCC, pars. 871–873.

[5] CCEO, c. 7: the people of God; c. 11: equality; c. 399: lay persons.

[6] MOCL: 5–6; see also OOCL: 115: 'its members are divided into two orders, clergy and laity'.

[7] OOCL: 117; see also MOCL: 59–63: 'the threefold office of our Lord (king, priest, prophet)'.

[8] PCLCCAC, Principle 25.1. See e.g. Sudan: Const., Art. 1: the 'laity' is 'the body of Christians, both men and women, other than those ordained'. See also LC 1958, Res. 94: 'the laity, as baptized members of the Body of Christ, share in the priestly ministry of the Church'; LC 1988, Res. 45: the Conference acknowledges 'that God through the Holy Spirit is bringing about a revolution in terms of the total ministry of all the baptized'.

through Jesus Christ'.[9] Moreover, a church should provide for 'the affirmation and development of the ministry of all the baptized and should have, at the appropriate level, a commission or other body to promote these'.[10]

There is a remarkable degree of juridical unity between these Catholic, Orthodox and Anglican approaches and those that appear in the legal texts of churches at the Protestant end of the ecclesiastical spectrum. According to Lutheran legal texts, the category 'people of God' embraces the priesthood of all believers,[11] but there is a distinction between the lay and ordained faithful: lay persons are those other than ordained ministers and pastors;[12] for example, the Evangelical Lutheran Church of America speaks of the baptised 'people of God' and 'the universal priesthood of all of its baptized members' to whom it has the duty to equip and support in their ministries in the church and the world.[13] Methodist laws recognise the common ministry of Christian service through baptism and the priesthood of all believers,[14] distinguish lay and ordained persons,[15] and embrace the equality of the faithful: for instance, for the Methodist Church in Ireland: 'every member of the Church is equal in spiritual privilege, has the same access to God through Christ, and is charged with the duty of establishing His Kingdom upon earth. The acknowledgment of this spiritual equality in the Methodist Church has led to the recognition of laypersons as being of an equal status with ministers in all the Courts of the Church.'[16] Much the same applies in the Reformed churches; for the United Reformed Church in

---

[9] PCLCCAC, Principle 26. See e.g. Papua New Guinea: Const., Art. 3: 'all persons are of equal value in the sight of God'; Melanesia: Const., Art. 4: the church cares for the needs of 'all people committed to its charge'.

[10] PCLCCAC, Principle 26.11.

[11] LCA: The Ministry of the People of God and the Public Ministry, CTIR 1992 (edited 2001) 1: Introduction; for the category 'Christian', see ELCSA: G., 11.6; LCGB: RAR, Statement of Faith, 6: 'as baptized Christians we are all children of God, at once sinners and saints . . . We encourage all Christian people, having thus been incorporated into the priesthood of all believers, to express their faith in the Church and in daily life.'

[12] LCA: Const., Interpretation: 'lay member' means 'any member . . . other than a pastor'; Theses on the Church, 2 (citing e.g. Col. 1.13): 'The Church is the communion of believers . . . those who . . . have been led to faith in Jesus Christ . . . The Church therefore comprises only believers and all believers at all times and places'; ELCIC: Corporate Bylaws, 1: '"lay person" is a baptized member who has not been ordained or consecrated'.

[13] ELCA: Const., Ch. 7.10-11; see also 5.01 for the principle of inclusivity in terms e.g. of colour.

[14] MCGB: CPD, DU 4: the church holds 'the doctrine of the priesthood of all believers and . . . believes that no priesthood exists which belongs exclusively to a particular order or class . . . but [for] corporate life and worship special qualifications for . . . special duties are required' for ordained ministry; MCNZ: LAR, s. 2, Introduction: 'all those who are "in Christ" by virtue of their baptism, share in this ministry' of Christ; UMCNEAE: BOD, par. 125: 'All Christians are called through their baptism to this ministry of servanthood in the world to the glory of God and for human fulfilment'; see also UMCUSA: Const., Div. I, Art. IV.

[15] MCGB: CPD, DU 1(xiv.A): 'lay' means 'a person who is neither a minister nor a deacon'; MCNZ: LAR, Nature of New Zealand Methodism: ordained presbyters and deacons; UMC-NEAE: BOD, par. 126: 'The ministry of the laity flows from a commitment to Christ's outreaching love. Lay members [are] advocates of the Gospel of Jesus Christ [and] called to carry out the Great Commission (Matthew 28.18-20)'; par. 133: ordained ministry; 137: lay and ordained service; COTN: Man., II, IV.I.B. 112: 'ordained minister' and 'lay member'.

[16] MCI: Const., s. 1; see also RDG, 1.01: 'all believers in Christ may know their sins forgiven, live day by day with the peace of God in their souls and . . . may be enriched with all the privileges

Britain: 'The Lord Jesus Christ continues his ministry in and through the Church, the whole people of God called and committed to his service and equipped for it';[17] and Presbyterian churches also recognise the ministry of all the believers,[18] and they distinguish lay and ordained persons.[19] By way of contrast, whilst the juridical instruments of a local Baptist church present the congregation as a manifestation of the Body of Christ, for some the congregation is composed of 'members' and 'ministers' and for others it is composed of 'members' and 'ordained ministers'; but these instruments do not yield a full juridical treatment of the equality of each category of ecclesiastical person.[20] These rules, across the church families, are direct reflections of essentially the same theological ideas; and they generate common action regardless of denominational affiliation – namely, the practice of distinguishing lay people and ordained people. Moreover, from the details of these shared rules emerges the principle of the laws of Christians that the church is the 'people of God' composed of both lay people and ordained ministers who share a fundamental equality of dignity and mission.

The concept of church membership

All the churches of the Christian traditions studied here present in their juridical instruments an understanding of what constitutes belonging to the institutional church. They do so by means of rules on admission to membership, the conditions applicable to admission, and the use and maintenance of rolls or other registers of church membership to enable, for example, the pastoral care of members. Admission to an institutional church is effected through and administered within the local church rather than at regional, national or international levels.

Catholic canon law does not have a precise concept of membership of the institutional church: the term 'member' is not generally used to designate a person who belongs to the church; rather, as we have seen, as a result of the ecclesiology of the Second Vatican Council, the fundamental category is that of 'Christ's faithful' who constitute the people of God.[21] In any event, baptised persons 'are in full communion with the catholic Church here on earth who are joined with Christ in his visible body, through the bonds of profession of faith, the sacraments and

---

that belong to the children of God'; 'here and now ... Christians [may be] made perfect in love through the obedience of faith'.

[17] URC: Man., A.16 and A.19: 'This service is given by worship, prayer, proclamation of the gospel, and Christian witness; by mutual and outgoing care and responsibility; and by obedient discipleship in the whole of daily life, according to the gifts and opportunities given to each one. The preparation and strengthening of its members for such ministry and discipleship shall always be a major concern of the United Reformed Church.'

[18] PCANZ: BO, 1.4: 'members' and 'ministers'.   [19] PCA: BCO, Preface, II.3.

[20] See e.g. BUSA: MCLC, Art. 4.2: 'the local church, being a manifestation of the universal church, is a community of believers in a particular place'; BUGB: Baptists in Local Ecumenical Partnerships, s. 3: 'Most Baptists appoint members to serve as Deacons and/or Elders to work with a minister'; Bethel Baptist Church (Choctaw): Const., Art. III: 'professing members'; IV: 'ordained officers': see more fully Chapter 3.

[21] See, however, CIC, c. 111: 'Through the reception of baptism a child becomes a member of the Latin Church if the parents belong to that Church'; the word 'member' (*sodalis*) is often used but with a narrow signification, such as being a member of a religious institute.

ecclesiastical governance'.[22] At the local level, a parish, for example, is a 'community of Christ's faithful established within a particular church'.[23] Nevertheless, catechumens, who are not yet admitted into full communion with the Catholic Church, are 'linked with the Church in a special way since, moved by the Holy Spirit, they are expressing an explicit desire to be incorporated in the Church'; it is by this desire and the life of faith, hope and charity that they 'are joined to the Church which already cherishes them as its own'; as a result, the church has 'a special care for catechumens' and while the church 'invites them to lead an evangelical life, and introduces them to the celebration of the sacred rites, it already accords them various prerogatives which are proper to Christians'.[24] The Catholic Church also records in registers the names of those incorporated into the church by baptism: the parish priest of the place in which the baptism was conferred must carefully and without delay record in the register of baptism the names of baptised persons, the date and place of their birth, and the date and place of the baptism; there are also confirmation registers.[25]

The legal instruments of Orthodox churches have a range of styles for the laity, including the 'faithful', 'members' and 'parishioners'.[26] The latter is very common. Various definitions are employed: parishioners are 'persons of the Orthodox confession, who maintain living contacts with their parish';[27] or else: 'Every person who is baptized and chrismated according to the rites of the Orthodox Church is a parishioner';[28] and again: 'Parishioners are those who, by virtue of their Baptism and Chrismation, are members of the Body of Christ and strive to live in accordance with their high calling (Eph. 4.1) as Orthodox Christians.'[29] Some Orthodox churches also require a parish to maintain a record or roll of its parishioners and this must be revised periodically.[30] Anglican laws employ the concept of a church 'member'. Whilst each Anglican Church 'should serve all who seek its ministry, membership in a church' may be based on any or all of the following: baptism;

---

[22] CIC, c. 205; CCEO, cc. 9, 587–588.

[23] CIC, c. 515; SC 42: Vatican II saw a shift from the previous territorial definition of a parish to the notion that it is the people who constitute the parish community. For the parish, see below, Chapter 4.

[24] CIC, c. 206. This canon was inspired by LG 14; for admission to the catechumenate by liturgical rite see c. 788; for their privileges see c. 1170 (blessings) and c. 1183.1 (funerals).

[25] CIC, c. 877; see also c. 895: those baptised persons who have been confirmed are to be recorded in the confirmation register of the diocesan curia or, when prescribed by the Bishops' Conference or the diocesan bishop, in the register to be kept in the parish archive. See below Chapters 7 and 9.

[26] See e.g. GOAA: Charter, Art. 2(b): 'the faithful'; OCIA: GC, Membership in the Body of Christ: 'Membership in the Body of Christ, His Holy Church, is defined by participation in the Holy Eucharist' and is incumbent on 'parishioners'; see also OOCL: 115: both laity and clergy constitute the 'members' of the church.

[27] ROC: Statute, XI.3; see also XI.1: a parish is 'a community of Orthodox Christians', lay and ordained.

[28] GOAA: Regs., Art. 18.1. For chrismation see below, Chapter 7.

[29] UOCIA: Statutes, Art. XI.5: no one may join a parish who 'openly betrays the teaching of the Christian Church', or 'leads a life or acts in a manner condemned by the Holy Canons as incompatible with the name of Orthodox Christian'; OCIA: GC, The Reception of Converts, 1–6: after catechetical instruction.

[30] GOAA: Regs., Art. 18.7: e.g. name, occupation and date of baptism and/or chrismation and marriage.

baptism and confirmation; baptism, confirmation and communicant status; or regular attendance at public worship.[31] In turn, there are various classes of church member: a communicant is a person who has received Holy Communion at such frequency and on such occasions as may be prescribed by law; and a communicant in good standing is a communicant who for a prescribed period has been faithful in worship and has supported the work and mission of the church.[32] Names of persons may be entered on a parish roll or other register of membership, subject to such conditions as may be prescribed by law, enabling eligibility for selection to participate in governance and other functions and offices; but names may be removed from the roll in accordance with the law, justice and equity.[33] Membership of a church implicitly involves profession of the faith, acceptance of its doctrine, government, law and discipline, and the enjoyment of the fundamental and other rights and duties of the faithful.[34]

Lutheran instruments define the membership of a church and the conditions which must be satisfied to acquire it,[35] and they prescribe for the inclusion of the names of members on a church roll.[36] The Evangelical Lutheran Church in America is typical: members of a congregation are those baptised persons on the roll of the congregation, namely: baptised members, those who have been received by baptism or baptised persons received by transfer from another Lutheran congregation; confirmed members, baptised persons confirmed in the congregation (or transferred to it); voting members, that is, confirmed members; and associate members, who hold membership in another congregation but desire to participate in the life of the congregation in which they enrolled.[37] There is little to distinguish Lutheran

---

[31] PCLCCAC, Principle 27.1-2; 3: a church may receive as a member any person who qualifies under its law. See e.g. West Indies: Can. 26.1: 'Any person ... baptised [or] received into this Church, shall be deemed a Lay member'; Central Africa: Can. 182: 'The laity, by virtue of their Baptism and Confirmation, share with the clergy in responsibility' for mission; Australia: Const. XII.74.1: '"Member of this Church" means a baptized person who attends the public worship of this Church and who declares that he is a member of this Church.'

[32] PCLCCAC, Principle 27.4-5. See e.g. Southern Africa: Const., Art. XXIV.6: a communicant is one who has received Holy Communion at least three times in the preceding year; for reception, see e.g. TEC: Cans. I.1.17.

[33] PCLCCAC, Principle 27.6-7. See e.g. Wales: Const., VI.2: entry on the parish roll confers 'eligibility to exercise voting rights'; New Zealand: Cans. B.V.4: the roll has the names of those members over 16.

[34] PCLCCAC, Principle 27.8; 25.1: all the faithful, in a manner appropriate to their state, participate in the tasks of teaching, governing and sanctifying; 25.3: lay persons exercise authority in church life and governance according to law; 25.4: the laity are subject to discipline to the extent and in the manner prescribed by law.

[35] ELCSA: G., 9: belonging to the Body of Christ is based on baptism and congregation membership on baptism, confirmation, written application, transfer or reception (following instruction) decided by the Church Committee of the Congregational Council; LCGB: RAR, Individual Membership in a Congregation, 1: a voting member is a baptised person aged 18 or over who has publicly confessed the faith after instruction in the teachings of the Lutheran Church and is duly received into congregation membership by its council; ELCIRE: Const., Art. 4: membership is based on baptism or by admission of a baptised person; ELCIC: Const., Art. XI.

[36] ELCIRE: Const., Art. 4: the roll contains the name, address, date and place of birth and baptism; members are baptised persons of 18 years of age or more; LCGB: RAR, Individual Membership in a Congregation, 2.

[37] ELCA: Model Constitution for Congregations, Ch. 8.01-02; see also 6.01.

and Methodist laws on these subjects. Methodists also define membership and the conditions for it,[38] including a prohibition against discrimination in this regard,[39] and they require entry of names on a roll or register.[40] By way of illustration, the law of the Methodist Church in Great Britain provides that: 'All those who confess Jesus Christ as Lord and Saviour and accept the obligation to serve him in the life of the Church and the world are welcome as members of the Methodist Church'; a candidate must be approved by the Church Council and publicly received (and baptised and confirmed if not already baptised and confirmed) at a service which includes the Lord's Supper; the Church Council must maintain various registers of the church members.[41] However, the members of the Methodist Church in Ireland are 'those who, desiring to be saved from their sins through faith in our Lord Jesus Christ, and to associate themselves with the people of God in Christian fellowship, have been received into full membership in accordance with the Rules and Regulations of the Conference'.[42] As such, the church welcomes into membership those who have committed their lives to Christ, show evidence of that commitment in life, conduct and service, and formally accept the discipline of the Methodist Church and the obligations of membership. Such persons, after appropriate training under the oversight of a suitable leader, and approval of the Church Council, may be admitted into the privileges and obligations of membership and their names placed on the Membership Register.[43] The register is reviewed annually.[44]

---

[38] MCNZ: LAR, s. 1 Introduction and UMCNEAE: BOD, pars. 215-217: baptism and profession of faith; FMCNA: BOD, Ch. 151: full membership is by baptism, confession of a personal experience in regeneration, 'a pledge to seek diligently until sanctified wholly if that experience has not been attained', acceptance of e.g. the Membership Covenant, approval by the local board and a public declaration of membership vows.

[39] UMCUSA: Const., Div. 1, Art. IV: 'all persons are of sacred worth. All persons without regard to race, colour, national origin, status, or economic condition, shall be eligible to attend its worship services, participate in its programs, receive the sacraments, upon baptism be admitted as baptized members, and upon taking the vows declaring the Christian faith, become professing members in any local church'; UMCNEAE: BOD, par. 4.

[40] MCNZ: LAR, s. 1.7: 'A person ... received as a Member ... and who evidences Christian commitment through regular participation in the worship and mission of the congregation shall be entitled to ... the responsibilities of full membership, and shall be recorded in the ... Electoral Roll of the parish'; s. 1.8: the Pastoral Roll of those 'associated' with the church – e.g. baptised infants and their families, children and young people, and 'persons with peripheral contact'; UMCNEAE: BOD, pars. 226-232: annual membership report and audit.

[41] MCGB: CPD, DU 8(a)-(c); SO 050; CPD, DU 9: Class Book; SO 054: the Membership Roll is kept by the Pastoral Committee of the Church Council; the Community Roll lists non-members under pastoral care.

[42] MCI: Const., s. 3: baptised children of members are 'junior members' and 'it is their duty and privilege when they reach the age of discretion to enter into full membership'; RDG, 1.01: 'Membership ... is not conditional upon the acceptance of any theological tests, nor dependent upon any traditional authority or ecclesiastical ritual'; moreover: 'the spirit and practice of Christian love is the supreme test of membership'.

[43] MCI: RDG, 2.03; also, 1.01; if not yet baptised, they are received through baptism either before or at this service; names are entered in a class book and placed under the care of a class leader; 2.16: classes to prepare people for their 'intelligent acceptance' of membership must be regularly held in each circuit.

[44] MCI: RDG 2.04-2.07: the Membership Register is reviewed annually; 2.15: the Junior Register lists those under 16 who have not yet accepted the membership but may receive pastoral care;

Churches of the Reformed tradition,[45] within the context of the church as the people of God,[46] also define membership of the institutional church, impose conditions for admission to it[47] and provide for membership rolls.[48] The Presbyterian Church of Wales (PCW) is typical: 'The meaning and standards of membership are based on our doctrine regarding the nature and purpose of the Church of God on earth.' Accordingly, the admission of a new member is 'a responsible act on the part of all members of a local church under the guidance of the Minister and/or the Elders'. In turn: 'Membership is open to any individual interested in promoting the Objects who is accepted as a new member of the [PCW] according to the Rules [or] is a member transferring from another Denomination according to the discretion of the Trustees'; the Trustees 'must keep a register of the names and addresses of members which must be made available to any Member upon request'. To be admitted, a new member must make 'a profession of faith in God and belief in Christ, and vows to be loyal to them and faithful to all the ordinances of the church'.[49] In Presbyterian law, the name of a member may be removed from the membership register on the occasion of, for instance, death, transfer or failure to comply with the responsibilities of membership.[50] Similar legal provisions are found in, for example, the Uniting Church in Australia,[51] United Church of

---

2.17: the Conference Connexional Membership Secretary ensures Membership, Congregational and Junior Registers are maintained.

[45] RCA: BCO, Preamble: confessing members are those who have been baptised, received by the board of elders through profession of faith, or transfer, and make 'faithful use of the means of grace'; baptised members, those who participate/not at the Lord's Table but not yet received as confessing members; inactive members, those removed from the confessing members' list; adherents are non-members participating in work and worship.

[46] URC: Man., A.16: 'the people of God, being members one of another, are called to love and serve one another and all people'; Sch. A: the Church Meeting admits persons, if assured of 'the sincerity of their intention' and 'adequate preparation'; admission 'may include the laying on of hands' and 'the giving and receiving of the right hand of fellowship', and shall include a 'public profession of faith and commitment to the Church'.

[47] PCA: BCO, 1.3: 'The members of this visible Church catholic are all those persons in every nation, together with their children, who make profession of their faith in the Lord Jesus Christ and promise submission to His laws'; 6.1: 'The children of believers are, through the covenant and by right of birth, non-communing members'; 6.2: 'Communing members are those who have made a profession of faith in Christ, have been baptized, and have been admitted by the Session to the Lord's Table'; 6.4: associate members; for a similar approach see PCI: Code, I.I, pars. 5–9; PCANZ: BO, 4.2; UFCS: MPP, Ch. I, s. III: the Session must be satisfied of a candidate's profession of faith, knowledge of the cardinal doctrines of Christian belief and ordinances, whose 'outward life is consistent with their profession'; the Session cannot admit the 'ignorant or scandalous' without repentance; if not baptised, 'admission to the fellowship ... must be by baptism'.

[48] PCANZ: BO, 4.10: a Church Council must maintain and review annually a roll of members; this must be submitted when requested to the Presbytery; UFCS: MPP, Ch. I, s. III: for spiritual oversight, the Session must keep a roll of church members in full communion to be revised annually with a copy to the Presbytery.

[49] PCW: HOR, II: Membership and Model Const., Art. 4.

[50] PCANZ: BO, 4.4–4.10; 4.10: the council must give notice to the person and an opportunity to be heard.

[51] UCA: Const., 3: members and adherents; a congregation, 'the embodiment in one place' of the church universal, means 'those people (members and adherents) who worship, witness and

Canada,[52] United Church of Christ in the Philippines[53] and the United Congregational Church in Southern Africa, in which the conditions of membership include confession of faith in Christ, belief in the one God and acceptance of the Bible (as the record of the Word of God) and the church constitution; applications for membership are decided by the Church Meeting and members are subsequently received at a Communion service and their names are recorded on the Church Roll.[54] These churches also provide for the entry and removal of names from the membership register in the event, for example, of death, transfer or expulsion.[55] Much the same juridical approach is used in local Baptist churches; typically, membership is open to individuals who provide evidence to the satisfaction of the local church of their personal experience of salvation by Christ and make 'a public profession of faith in Jesus Christ as Saviour and have undergone believers' baptism by immersion' and are in agreement with the church's Statement of Faith and Covenant; the names of those admitted are recorded on a register of church members,[56] and provision exists for removal of names on the occasion of, for example, death, withdrawal, transfer or breach of the church covenant by way of failure to fulfil the obligations of church membership.[57] In short, it is a principle of Christian law that an institutional church consists of lay members or other category (such as parishioner) which denotes belonging, admitted to membership through the local church on satisfaction of conditions which include baptism or other demonstration of faith in Christ, and whose names are to be entered on a roll or register of members which may be revised periodically.

serve as a fellowship of the Spirit in Christ'; 10: the Church Council is responsible for the Roll of Members, its review and revision.

[52] UCC: Man., 5.8: 'Admission to full membership and ... transfer or removal shall be by ... the Session or ... those in full membership when desired by the Pastoral Charge'; BL 010–014: admission by baptism, confirmation, profession; the membership roll is revised by the Session, Church Board or Church Council.

[53] UCCP: Const., Art. III: 'Membership ... shall be through one of its local churches or congregations' by baptism or dedication, confirmation, transfer and reception, public profession of the faith or affiliation; members have 'rights and privileges' and 'obligations and commitments'.

[54] UCCSA: MCLC: Art. 3; UCOC: Const., Art. IV: persons become members by baptism and either confirmation or profession of faith, re-affirmation or re-profession of faith, or transfer.

[55] UCA: Regs., 1.1.14; UCC: Man., 5.8: see above n. 52; UCCSA: MCLC: Art. 3: no name may be removed from the Church Roll except by vote of the Church Meeting.

[56] Riverside Baptist Church (Baltimore): BL, Art. I: candidates must publicly request membership at a service, complete a class, be recommended by pastor and deacons, and be accepted by majority vote at a business meeting. See also Bethel Baptist Church (Choctaw): Const., Art. III: 'professedly born-again believers' baptised by immersion must give 'creditable evidence of their conversion', are examined in their 'spiritual qualifications' and are received by 'a unanimous vote of the church into the full rights and privileges of church membership'; Central Baptist Church (Pretoria): Const., Art. 6: persons who evidence 'personal salvation through faith' in Christ and confess that faith by Believers Baptism may be entered on the register.

[57] Riverside Baptist Church (Baltimore): BL, Art. I: it may be terminated voluntarily, on joining another church, by death or exclusion (e.g. for persistent breach of the covenant vows); Bethel Baptist Church (Choctaw): Const., Art. III; Central Baptist Church (Pretoria): Const., Art. 7.

The duties and rights of the faithful

The juridical instruments of churches in all of our Christian traditions contain elaborate provisions on the functions of the faithful. In some churches, the instruments present duties and rights applicable to all the faithful, whether lay or ordained, but in others they spell out duties and, more rarely, rights applicable specifically to the lay members of the institutional church. Sometimes, laws identify or conflate duties with rights: a member of the faithful has the duty 'and' the right to perform one and the same act. Moreover, needless to say, duties imposed on an individual may generate correlative rights for another, and, *mutatis mutandis*, rights vested in one may generate duties for another. This indicates the profound interdependence of ecclesiastical rights and duties. Nevertheless, the dominant juridical regime across the Christian traditions is that of responsibilities, and these are both operative within the institutional church and exercisable in relation to wider society beyond. Failure to fulfil these ecclesial responsibilities may result in the suspension and termination of membership (which is explored more fully in Chapter 5 on ecclesiastical discipline).[58]

Catholic canon law distinguishes the duties and rights of all the faithful, lay and ordained, as well as those specifically applicable to the laity. When incorporated by baptism into the Church of Christ, and constituted a person within it, each one of the faithful has 'such duties and rights which, in accordance with each one's status, are proper to Christians, in so far as they are in ecclesiastical communion and unless a lawfully issued sanction intervenes'.[59] The duties of all the faithful include: to preserve their communion with the church; to lead a holy life; to show Christian obedience to what sacred pastors (who represent Christ) declare as teachers of the faith and rulers of the church; to provide for the needs of the church; and to promote social justice and help the poor. Their rights include: to make known their needs and wishes to the pastors; to be assisted by their pastors; to worship God; to establish and direct associations (for e.g. charitable purposes); to have access to a Christian education; and to vindicate and defend their rights.[60] The laity have specific obligations and rights: to strive so that the divine message may be known throughout the world; to permeate the temporal order with the spirit of the gospel; to build up the people of God through marriage and the family; and to acquire knowledge of and proclaim Christian teaching. They are also capable of admission to ecclesiastical offices open to them and of acting as experts and advisors.[61] These

---

[58] In Christianity, the pattern of ministry as set by Christ is one of service or *diaconia* (Matt. 20.28; Mk. 10.45; Luke 22.27); in teaching, healing and prayer, and culminating in his crucifixion as a priestly and sacrificial act of atonement for human sin (Heb. 10.5–14) and reconciliation for the world (2 Cor 5.18–19).

[59] CIC, c. 96; each physical person has duties and rights: as well as the laity (cc. 224–231), there are those attaching to e.g. clergy (cc. 273–289), religious (cc. 662–672), married couples and parents (cc. 1135–1136).

[60] CIC, cc. 208–223: 'obligations and rights of all the faithful'; sometimes, they have both a duty and a right to do one and the same thing: e.g. c. 211: 'All the Christian faithful have the obligation (*officium*) and the right (*ius*) to strive so that the divine message of salvation may ... reach all people of all times and all places'; see C. Lara, 'Some general reflections on the rights and duties of the Christian faithful', 20 *Studia Canonica* (1986) 7.

[61] CIC, cc. 224–231: the 'obligations and rights of the lay members of Christ's faithful'; c. 231: in wider society the laity also have the right to have their 'insurance, social security and medical benefits duly safeguarded'.

duties and rights derive from the fundamental dignity of the individual as a human person and as such are inalienable and inviolable.[62] Moreover, '[i]n exercising their rights, [the] faithful, both individually and in association, must take account of the common good of the church, as well as the rights of others and their own duties to others': the appropriate ecclesiastical authority is entitled 'to regulate, in view of the common good, the exercise of rights which are proper to Christ's faithful'.[63] All the faithful are subject to the discipline of the church but there is no provision for formal defection from the Catholic Church.[64] The Oriental Catholic Code provides similarly for the rights, obligations and discipline of all the faithful, as well as rights and duties specific to lay persons: these broadly mirror those in the Latin Code; but: 'It is for lay persons, according to their own vocation, in the first place to seek the kingdom of God; they do this by dealing with and regulating temporal matters in conformity with God' as 'witnesses to Christ' (in private and socio-political life).[65]

In Orthodox canon law, parishioners are bearers of prescribed duties and rights,[66] and the former commonly include the duty to 'uphold Christian values and conduct',[67] as well as respect for the clergy.[68] However, unlike Catholic canon law, the laws of Orthodox churches do not include explicitly the principle that rights must be exercised for the common good or with respect for the rights of others; though some duties may generate correlative rights, and *vice versa*. For example, in the Russian Orthodox Church all parishioners are 'obliged to take part in the divine services, make Confession and take holy Communion regularly, observe the canons and church prescriptions, carry out deeds of faith, strive for religious and moral perfection and contribute to the well-being of the parish' and 'the material maintenance of the clergy and the church building'. As to rights, parishioners may participate in the Parish Meeting provided they regularly join in parish liturgical life, are over 18 and have sufficient moral standing and experience

---

[62] CIC, c. 208.
[63] CIC, c. 223; see J. Coriden, 'A challenge: make rights real', 45 *The Jurist* (1986) 1. The exercise of conscience is important here: CCC, pars. 1776–1802: 'Conscience is a law of the mind' or 'a judgment of reason whereby the human person recognizes the moral quality of a concrete act that he is about to perform, is in the process of performing, or has already performed'; humans have an obligation to follow the conscience.
[64] CIC, c. 11: canon law binds those baptised or received into the church who enjoy the sufficient use of reason and have completed 7 years of age; for discipline (cc. 1311, 1321–1323, 1341) see Chapter 5.
[65] CCEO, cc. 7–26: rights and obligations; c. 909: juridical persons; cc. 399–409: lay persons; c. 401: vocation, private, family and socio-political life (which includes the right 'to defend just legislation in society').
[66] ROMOC: Statutes, Art. 45: 'the faithful ... have rights to [e.g.] charitable assistance, to elect and be elected in the parochial bodies ... and duties ... to sustain, strengthen and witness the faith of the Orthodox Church; to live according to [its] teaching ... to participate in religious services; to have the Holy Sacraments; to fulfil acts of Christian mercy; [and] to maintain and to help the Church and her servants'; OOCL: 119; MOCL: 63–65.
[67] UOCIA: CPC, I, Preamble; also: II, Responsibility: 'public and private conduct' has the potential to 'scandalize and undermine the people's faith'; responsibility 'rests with the individual'.
[68] OCIA: GC, Priests and Deacons, 2 and Laity, 1–2: 'every parishioner ought to respect' the priest as 'spiritual father'; Members of Masonic and Other Secret Fraternal Societies, 1–3: 'incompatibility' with Orthodoxy.

of life; they are also subject to discipline and may be removed from the Parish Meeting.[69] A similar approach is found in the Greek Orthodox Archdiocese of America: 'The religious, moral and social duties of a parishioner' are to: 'adhere to and live according to the tenets of the Orthodox faith; faithfully attend the Divine Liturgy' and other services; participate regularly in the holy sacraments; respect all ecclesiastical authority and all governing bodies of the Church; be obedient in matters of faith, practice and ecclesiastical order; contribute towards the progress of the Church's sacred mission; and be 'an effective witness and example of the Orthodox faith and Traditions to all people'. A parishioner who is in 'good standing' may attend, participate in and vote at parish elections and assemblies, represent the parish at a Local Assembly or Congress and act as a sponsor – a parishioner in 'good standing' is one who fulfils the duties of a parishioner, is 18 years of age or more, has discharged the requisite financial obligations owed to the parish, abides by all the regulations and 'cooperates in every way towards the welfare and well being of the Parish'. Parishioners wishing to transfer to another parish must present a letter from the priest stating that he/she is in good standing.[70]

By way of contrast, in Anglicanism, the principles of canon law common to the churches of the Anglican Communion do not specify duties and rights applicable only to lay persons. Rather, all the faithful, lay and ordained, by virtue of baptism, are responsible for church life and witness, and should: (1) regularly attend public worship, especially at Holy Communion; (2) practise daily devotion, private prayer, Bible reading and self-discipline; (3) bring the teaching and example of Christ into everyday life; (4) uphold Christian values; (5) be of personal service to church and community; and (6) assist the church financially in its work and mission.[71] Two types of right are envisioned by the principles of canon law: inherent rights and acquired rights. As to the former: 'all persons, equal in dignity before God, have inherent rights and duties inseparable from their dignity as human beings created in the image and likeness of God and called to salvation through Jesus Christ; however, baptism is the foundation of Christian rights and duties, and a church should respect both sets of rights and duties'.[72] In addition, all the faithful, ordained and lay, enjoy such rights to government, ministry, teaching, worship, sacraments, rites and property as may flow from their human dignity, baptism, the duties of others 'and the law of that church'; indeed, in a church there is to be no unlawful denial of equal rights, status or access to the life, membership, government, ministry,

---

[69] ROC: Statute, XI.3.
[70] GOAA: Regs., Art. 18. See also UOCIA: Statutes, Art. XI.5: a voting member is one who is at least 18, partakes of confession and holy communion at least once annually, has belonged to the parish for a period fixed by the parish and fulfils the financial duties fixed by the General Sobor, Diocesan Assembly and parish.
[71] PCLCCAC, Principle 26.6; for 'duties of church membership', see LC 1948, Res. 37, Chile: Cans. A.2.
[72] PCLCCAC, Principle 26.1–3; 4: a church should respect rights and duties founded on the dignity of the human person and on baptism and those afforded by ecclesiastical authority; 5: the church is concerned with the welfare of people in all its aspects, physical, mental and spiritual, and should as far as possible respond to the needs of all. See e.g. Papua New Guinea: Const., Art. 3: 'all persons are of equal value in the sight of God'; Melanesia: Const., Art. 4: the church 'will take care to provide for the needs of all people committed to its charge'.

worship, rites and property of that church on grounds of race, colour, ethnic, tribal or national origin, marital status, sex, sexual orientation, disability or age.[73]

Whereas Catholic, Orthodox and Anglican laws begin with duties and move to rights, in the Protestant traditions the reverse is often the case, and sometimes the two juridical categories are conflated. Lutheran churches commonly distribute 'rights and duties',[74] and provide for the termination of membership.[75] For example, in the Evangelical Lutheran Church in America (ELCA), it is the 'privilege and duty' of members to 'make regular use of the means of grace, both Word and Sacraments', 'live a Christian life in accordance with the Word of God and the teachings of the Lutheran church', and 'support the work of [the] congregation, the synod, and the church-wide organization of the [ELCA] through contributions of their time, abilities, and financial support as biblical stewards'. Membership in the congregation is terminated by death, resignation, transfer or release, disciplinary action by the Congregation Council or removal from the roll due to inactivity – however, persons removed from the roll 'shall remain persons for whom the Church has a continuing pastoral concern'.[76] The Evangelical Lutheran Church in Canada provides a particularly fulsome treatment of the ministry of the laity: 'the members of this church are to be constant in worship and in the study of the Holy Scriptures, regularly nourishing their life in Christ in the Sacrament of the Altar, presenting their children for Holy Baptism and providing for their Christian instruction'; they are 'called by the Spirit to lead godly lives, to promote the unity and welfare of the church in the bond of peace, to proclaim the gospel and to renounce the evil one'; the commitment of each baptised member to this call is 'to be expressed through this church, its synods and its congregations by a life of repentance, faith, prayer and the sharing of resources'.[77]

Methodists also provide for the 'privileges and obligations of membership' (particularly holy living and participation in the sacraments and worship),[78] and

---

[73] PCLCCAC, Principle 26.7–8. See e.g. Indian Ocean: Const., Art. 3 and TEC: Cans. I.17.5: non-discrimination. PCLCCAC: 26.10: 'All the faithful should recognise the unique status and needs of children and young people ... and a church should make such provision ... to ensure their special protection. Mistreatment of children, especially their sexual abuse, offends their humanity and the teaching of Christ.'

[74] See LCA: The Ministry of the People of God and the Public Ministry, CTIR 1992 (edited 2001) 2: e.g. prayer (1 Peter 2.9); proclaiming reconciliation (2 Cor. 5.19); and working together (1 Cor. 12.25–26); ELCSA: G., 2: participation in divine service; 3: Holy Communion; 4: confession; ELCIRE: Const., 6: the rights and obligations of members who are 'accountable to God', 'should testify [to this] through words and deeds in public as in private life', 'respect each person' and 'preserve the natural habitat as created by God'; each has the right e.g. to 'use of the sacraments', pastoral support, Christian instruction, participate in elections, vote and stand in elections; LCMS: Const., BL, 1.3.5; LCGB: RAR, Statement of Faith, 7.

[75] ELCSA: G., 9.5: it ends on e.g. resignation, transfer to another congregation, failure to observe the duties of or renunciation of membership, but may be resumed by readmission; LCGB: RAR, Individual Membership in a Congregation, 2: the congregation council may remove from the register e.g. those who have not supported the life or worship of the church 'over a significant period'; ELCIRE: Const., 7; LCMS: Const., Art. XIII.

[76] ELCA: Model Const. for Congregations, Ch. 8.04–8.05. [77] ELCIC: Const., Art. V.

[78] The General Rules of Societies (1743): duties include 'doing no harm' (e.g. profaning the Lord's Day), 'doing good' (e.g. feeding the hungry, visiting and helping the sick) and

enable discipline and termination of membership.[79] The Methodist Church of Ireland is once again typical: 'Every member shall have their name recorded in the Membership Register and should receive pastoral support and encouragement in their discipleship from the local minister and lay leaders'; but only those whose names are recorded in the Membership Register are entitled to be members of the Church Council, Circuit Executive, District Synod or Conference.[80] As to the obligations of membership: 'All members are expected to (a) attend the means of grace, especially the ministry of the Word, united prayer, and the Sacrament of the Lord's Supper, (b) join with others in Christian fellowship, (c) engage in some form of Christian service, [and] (d) financially support the ongoing work and mission of the church through regular giving, so far as can reasonably be expected.'[81] These rules of church membership are designed on the classical Methodist principle that the faithful are 'helpers one of another', a system which clearly expresses the interdependence inherent in the exercise of right and duties.[82] Moreover, 'a member, who in the judgment of the Church Council, has persistently failed to fulfil the Obligations of Membership, despite being reminded of those obligations, shall be regarded as having withdrawn from membership of the church and their name shall be removed from the Membership Register'.[83] The dual membership of different circuits in the church is forbidden, but there is provision for the transfer of members from

---

attending the ordinances, private prayer, searching Scriptures, fasting and abstinence – habitual failure to observe these 'rules' may lead to admonition and exclusion; UMCNEAE: BOD, par. 134-136: 'The ministry of all Christians consists of privileges and obligations. The privilege is a relationship with God that is deeply spiritual. The obligation is to respond to God's call to holy living'; 204 and 228.1: the church ministers 'to all its members'; 217: covenantal duties; 218: private and public prayer, worship, study, Christian action, systematic giving and holy discipline; 219-220: a member must be 'a servant of Christ'; MCNZ: LAR, Introductory Documents, IV: General Standards for the Guidance of Members and LAR, s. 1.1: 'Responsible membership ... through ... worship and financial support'; MCGB: CPD, DU 9: privileges and duties; FMCNA: BOD, par. 151: 'rights' are e.g. participation in the ordinances and eligibility to vote and hold office on reaching the age fixed by General Conference; par. 154: Membership Covenant; also, Ch. 6, pars. 6100–6150; COTN: Man., III: The Covenant of Christian Conduct.

[79] MCNZ: LAR, s. 1.9; UMCNEAE: BOD, par. 221: 'All members are to be held accountable for faithfulness to their covenant of baptism' (see Chapter 5); MCGB: CPD, SO 057: resigning membership; FMCNA: BOD, par. 151: termination by voluntary withdrawal, joining another denomination, sect or secret order, expulsion summarily or after trial; COTN: Man., III: Covenant of Christian Conduct, E: e.g. joining another church.

[80] MCI: RDG, 2.04 and 2.05; 2.07.   [81] MCI: RDG, 2.06.

[82] MCI: RDG, 1.03: The General Rules of Our Societies; 1.01: 'As union in Christian fellowship is the natural expression of Christian love, the distinctive Methodist institutions, and especially the Covenant Service, are based upon the assumption that those who love the Lord ... will become helpers one of another ... None may be counted as discharged from the debt of love, save those who are debarred, or physically unable to attend at the means of grace'; members must e.g. 'engage in some form of Christian service'; 'partake reverently and in faith of the Lord's Supper'; and practise 'Christian love' and the social obligations which flow from this.

[83] MCI: RDG, 2.08.

one circuit to another, as well as for those who no longer accept the privileges and obligations of membership.[84]

In turn, churches of the Reformed tradition speak of the 'rights and privileges' and 'privileges and responsibilities' of church membership. These clearly reflect the interconnectedness of the faithful, their responsibility for mutual assistance, and the interplay of both duties and correlative rights, and rights and correlative duties.[85] They may also include (like the Catholics and Orthodox) a duty on members to respect the ordained ministers.[86] Presbyterian churches have particularly well-developed compendia of the rights and duties of members,[87] on the basis that, for example, '[t]o be a member of the Church of God is a great privilege and involves a corresponding responsibility and duty'.[88] The Presbyterian Church in New Zealand is typical: (1) as to recognition of membership status, a member of the congregation has 'rights and privileges' to have the church council record their name on the roll of members, to receive baptism for their children, and to receive a certificate recording their own or child's baptism; (2) as to the sacraments, to participate in communion, to have any child participate in communion; (3) as to governance, members have the right to attend, participate and vote at any meeting of the congregation on any matter brought before it, to stand for election to congregational office, to present a proposal to the church council or through the church council to the presbytery on matters affecting his or her interests or those of the congregation, and to receive, on leaving a congregation, a letter of introduction to another congregation. The responsibilities of members are: to lead a life consistent with their profession of the Christian faith; as far as they are able, to join in the

---

[84] MCI: RDG, 2.10–2.14: the Congregational Register lists those (aged 16 or over) who no longer accept members' privileges/duties but are under the pastoral care of Congregational Visitors appointed by the Church Council.

[85] E.g. URC: Man., A.19: Christian service implies 'mutual and outgoing care and responsibility', worship, prayer, proclamation of the gospel, witness and 'obedient discipleship in the whole of daily life'; PCA: BCO, 6.4: 'All baptised persons are entitled to the watchful care, instruction and government of the church, even [without] profession'; but: 'Those only who have made a profession of faith in Christ, have been baptized, and admitted by the Session to the Lord's Table, are entitled to all the rights and privileges of the church.'

[86] UFCS: MPP, Ch. 3, s. 1: 'It is the duty of members to give faithful attendance on Gospel ordinances; to give their minister all dutiful respect, encouragement and obedience in the Lord; to submit to the Session'; 'to promote the peace and prosperity of the congregation'; 'to take a lively interest in ... the welfare of the whole Church'; 'Members in full communion, and they only, have a right to take part in the business of congregational meetings'; and: 'Any member ... in full communion shall be eligible to hold any office within the Church.'

[87] PCI: Code, I.I, pars. 5–9: 'All who profess [Christ] are called to be members of the visible Church in the fellowship of a congregation, with all the rights and responsibilities attached'; members must e.g. make diligent use of the means of grace, share in the worship and work of the Church, 'render whole-hearted service to Christ'; their children are entitled to e.g. baptism, nurture and pastoral care, so 'they may personally embrace Christ and claim the benefits of the covenant'; 'All baptised persons, even [without] personal profession of their faith ... are entitled to the pastoral care and instruction of the Church and are subject to its discipline.'

[88] PCW: HOR, II: members have 'a responsibility for the worship and whole work of the church, and a duty to take part in that work ... in terms of money, time and talents'; their 'regular use' of the means of grace is 'a duty owed to God and a necessity of the Christian life'; other duties are e.g. showing church unity (by neighbourly love, a forgiving spirit and sympathy for fellow-members), and living the Gospel in personal and public life.

worship, life and mission of the congregation, to seek to lead a life consistent with the Christian faith, and to accept the spiritual oversight and discipline of the church; the Church Council is under a fundamental obligation to secure the implementation of these personal rights.[89] Sets of similar rights and duties, to engage fully in the life of the congregation (its worship, work and witness) and to build up its members, as well as provision for termination of membership, appear in the juridical instruments of the Uniting Church in Australia,[90] the United Church of Canada,[91] the United Church of Christ,[92] and the United Congregational Church of Southern Africa.[93]

The instruments of Baptist Unions and local Baptist churches also provide for the 'privileges and obligations of membership', which include attendance at meetings and worship, maintaining the unity and fellowship of the church and supporting the ministry of the church.[94] In the local church, these rights and duties are commonly spelt out in a church covenant under which the faithful 'intentionally define their covenant with God and with each other', an agreement or set of mutual obligations entered voluntarily and with solemnity.[95] The so-called 'one another passages' from Scripture are a key foundation for the statement of the rights and duties of members in a church covenant.[96] Importantly, 'it is the duty of every Disciple to bear personal witness to the Gospel of Jesus Christ, in Family and Public Worship, in the observance of the ordinance of Baptism and the Lord's Supper, in

---

[89] PCANZ: BO, 4.4–4.10; see also 1.4: 'the responsibility . . . guided by the Holy Spirit, to study the Scriptures'.

[90] UCA: Const., 3: members must worship, witness and serve, meet regularly to hear God's Word, celebrate the sacraments, build one another up in love, share wider church responsibilities and serve the world; 10: the Congregation, Ministers and Church Council must provide 'the spiritual oversight and pastoral care of its members and adherents'; Regs., 1: all confirmed members may vote at congregational meetings; see 1.1.14 for removal of names from membership rolls e.g. if the member dies, resigns (there are also rights of appeal).

[91] UCC: Man., 5.8.1–5.8.2 'The members . . . entitled to all church privileges are those who, on a profession of their faith in Jesus Christ and obedience to Him, have been received into full membership'; it is the 'duty and privilege' of children, at 'the age of discretion', to enter full membership; enrolled members are entitled to vote.

[92] UCOC: Const., Art. VI: 'God calls the whole Church and every member to participate in and extend the ministry of Jesus Christ by witnessing to the Gospel in church and society.'

[93] UCCSA: MCLC: Art. 3: for removal from the register, see above n. 55.

[94] Central Baptist Church (Pretoria): Const., Art. 8: privileges and obligations (e.g. attendance at meetings and worship, maintaining unity and fellowship, and support for ministry); Riverside Baptist Church (Baltimore): BL, Art. I: e.g. exclusion from membership (e.g. for persistent breach of the covenant vows); Bethel Baptist Church (Choctaw): Const., Art. III: the 'full rights and privileges of church membership'.

[95] TCCG, p. 6.

[96] TCCG, p.7–8; R. Stanton Norman, *The Baptist Way: Distinctiveness of a Baptist Church* (Broadman and Holman, Nashville, Tennessee, 2005) 118: the 'one another' passages from Scripture express the New Testament characteristics of Christian relationships; they include: to love one another, as Christ loves us (John 13.34); to submit one to another (Eph 5.21); to exhort one another (Heb 3.13; 10.25); to comfort one another (2 Cor. 1.4); to consider others as more important than ourselves (Phil 2.3); to suffer when one suffers and rejoice when another is honoured (1 Cor. 12.25-26); to instruct one another (Rom. 15.14); to admonish one another (Col. 3.16); to nurture one another toward spiritual maturity measured by the life and ministry of Jesus (Eph. 4.13); and to restore gently those who sin (Gal. 6.1).

conduct and in the Evangelisation of the world'.[97] Baptist approaches to the rights and duties of the faithful are not exceptional. As we have seen, a comparative study of the juridical instruments of all these church families reveals contemporary principles of Christian law about the rights and duties of the faithful in general and the laity in particular: the laity has a key function in the mission of the church; the members of the laity, as such or as part of the faithful in general, have clearly defined rights and duties, privileges and obligations; the faithful must engage in the collective ecclesial life, including hearing the Word, celebration of the Sacraments and other corporate rituals of worship, and they must respect church governance; the faithful should in their private lives engage in prayer and reading of Scripture, and in their public life witness to the Gospel in wider society; particularly through admission to full membership, the faithful are entitled to certain ecclesial benefits, which include participation in church governance and receiving the ministrations provided by the ordained ministers of the church; the faithful must exercise their rights responsibly with due regard for the fundamental interaction between the rights and duties of others; and any failure on the part of the faithful to fulfil ecclesial responsibilities may result in the termination of ecclesial benefits, membership or other disciplinary process. On the assumption that there is broad compliance with these laws, this juridical unity means that Christians engage in many of the same actions regardless of their own particular denominational affiliations.

Ecclesiastical offices and ministries open to the laity

The theological development of the notion in contemporary Christianity of the visible church as a community of believers (all of whom have a part to play in the service of Christ on the basis of their baptism and equality), and the juridical implementation of this theology across the traditions, have resulted in an enhanced role for the laity in the institutional life of the church. As we have seen in the previous section, the juridical instruments of most churches commonly list amongst the rights of persons with full church membership the entitlement not only to elect representatives but also to be elected to and hold positions in the corporate assemblies and other institutions of ecclesiastical governance (see more fully in Chapter 4). Moreover, in addition to their eligibility in accordance with law to offer themselves for ordained ministry (dealt with in Chapter 3), all the churches studied here make provision for the lay faithful, *qua* laity, to hold prescribed offices or ministries in the institutional church. The juridical instruments provide in varying degrees a wide range of offices and other positions open to the members of the laity – these instruments deal with the qualifications required for admission, the admission process, the functions attached to the office or ministry, accountability in its exercise and the termination of the lay office or ministry. Whilst there is extensive juridical symmetry, across the traditions, in the absence of an inherent right in the laity to admission to lay offices and ministries, and in the functions which attach to them, there is considerable divergence in the appointing body and mode of admission, from appointment by ordained ministers to election by the assemblies of the church.

---

[97] JBU: Const., Art. III; for a similar formula, see BUS: Const., III.3 and BUSA: Const., 4.3.

The Catholic Church provides, as a result of the Second Vatican Council, for the admission of lay persons to a small number of ecclesiastical offices. In Roman Catholic canon law, an ecclesiastical office is 'any post which by divine or ecclesiastical disposition is established in a stable manner to further a spiritual purpose', and duties and rights proper to an office are defined either by the law, under which the office is established, or by decree of a competent authority.[98] Lay people 'who are found to be suitable are capable of being admitted by the sacred pastors to those ecclesiastical offices and functions which, in accordance with the provisions of law, they can discharge'.[99] Thus, in the spheres of liturgy and education, lay men (if they meet the requirements prescribed by the Episcopal Conference) may be given 'the stable ministry of lector and acolyte' and all lay people may serve as commentator, cantor and, where the needs of the church require this and when ministers are not available, they may 'exercise the ministry of the word, preside over liturgical prayers, confer baptism and distribute holy communion'.[100] They may also serve as catechists (to assist the parish priest) and teach the sacred sciences at educational institutions.[101] Moreover, whilst the laity do not possess the power of governance (which is reserved to those in orders), they may co-operate in its exercise through service, for example, in administrative capacities at provincial and diocesan level: as secretary general of the Episcopal Conference; as diocesan finance officer; as members of diocesan synods and pastoral and finance councils; as members of parish councils; and as parish finance officers.[102] Whilst judicial office is generally reserved to ordained clergy, the Episcopal Conference may permit lay persons to be appointed as diocesan judges (if they possess a doctorate or at least a licentiate in canon law) to assist in a collegial tribunal; the laity may also serve on tribunals as auditors, assessors, promoters of justice and defenders of the bond in matrimonial proceedings.[103] Furthermore, those lay people 'who are outstanding in the requisite knowledge, prudence and integrity, are capable of being experts and advisors, even in councils in accordance with the law, in order to provide assistance to the pastors of the church'.[104] Similar provisions applicable to lay ministry and its regulation are to be found in the Oriental Catholic Code of Canons.[105]

Likewise, a range of offices and ministries is open to lay people under Orthodox canon law. Lay persons may function, for example, as 'Sunday school teachers,

---

[98] CIC, c. 145; see also c. 129.2: 'Lay members of Christ's faithful can cooperate in the exercise of [the power of governance] in accordance with the law'; see generally: S.A. Euart, 'Council, code and laity: implications for lay ministry', 47 *The Jurist* (1987) 492.

[99] CIC, c. 228.1; lay people may hold ecclesiastical office or co-operate in the power of governance if they are appropriately qualified: see e.g. cc. 483.2, 517.2, 1421.2, 1428.2 and 1435.

[100] CIC, c. 230; also cc. 910: minister of Holy Communion; 1128: the administration of sacramentals; c. 231: lay people are entitled to formation for their roles; see also: H. Witte, 'The local bishop and lay pastoral workers: a newly created function in the church and its impact on Episcopal collegiality', 69 *The Jurist* (2009) 84.

[101] CIC, cc. 776, 785; c. 229.3: teaching sacred sciences (for which they must have a mandate: c. 812).

[102] See, respectively, CIC, cc. 494, 451, 443, 463, 512, 492, 470, and 536; see more fully Chapter 4.

[103] CIC, c. 1421. See Chapter 5.

[104] CIC, c. 228.2; see also c. 811.1: the church must provide opportunities to the laity to exercise this.

[105] E.g. CCEO, c. 404.3: mandates to teach; c. 408: experts; c. 409: training; c. 143: laity from each eparchy at the patriarchal assembly; c. 238: laity at an eparchial assembly; c. 273: laity in the pastoral council.

64   THE FAITHFUL — THE LAITY AND LAY MINISTRY

lay theologians, and lay preachers',[106] provided they are suitably qualified and authorised to exercise these ministries by the relevant ecclesiastical authority; their functions are sometimes conceived as providing 'assistance' to the clerical hierarchy.[107] Thus, the juridical instruments of Orthodox churches provide that suitably qualified lay persons (typically parishioners in good standing) may be elected to (and removed from) the assemblies of the local church,[108] and the offices of parish churchwarden,[109] steward, treasurer, chanter, choir member, acolyte and catechist,[110] or to serve as officers of regional or national ecclesiastical institutions (such as secretary or treasurer).[111] Moreover, the laws of some churches enable lay people to establish associations of the faithful to fulfil prescribed functions. For example, in the Russian Orthodox Church, parishioners may form 'brotherhoods and sisterhoods' with the consent of the Rector and the blessing of the bishop. Their function is to maintain the churches in the appropriate state, and to participate in works of charity, social ministry and religious and moral education; they are under the supervision of the rector. The statutes of such associations must be approved by the diocesan bishop and the associations will be guided by the resolutions of the Local and Bishops' Councils and the decrees of the patriarch – but they must comply with the decisions of the rector and the relevant diocesan authority. These parochial lay brotherhoods and sisterhoods may raise funds for parish and diocesan purposes, and in their religious, administrative, financial and economic activities they are ultimately accountable to the diocesan bishop. If members withdraw they are not entitled to claim any rights over the property and assets of the brotherhood or sisterhood.[112]

Anglicanism treats ministry as 'a gift of God exercised by persons, called by God and recognised as such by lawful authority, to serve the church in its mission and witness to the gospel', and public ministry is assigned formally to an

---

[106] MOCL: 65.
[107] OOCL: 119; this cites Quinsext Ecumenical Council, c. 64: 'It does not befit a layman to dispute or teach publicly, thus claiming for himself authority to teach, but he should yield to the order appointed by the Lord, and to open his ears to those who have received the grace to teach, and be taught by them the things divine.'
[108] ROC: Statute, XI.4: the Parish Meeting is open to 'laymen who regularly participate in the liturgical life of the parish and who are worthy to take part ... due to their commitment to Orthodoxy, their moral standing and experience of life'; they must be over 18, not under suspension or standing trial by a church or civil court; the decision to admit is made by the Meeting; removal may occur if the conditions for admission are not met.
[109] ROC: Statute, XI.45–47: the churchwarden (who is chair unless the rector is elected), his assistant, and treasurer are all members of the Parish Council; the bishop may remove members for breach of the canons and statute; the warden represents the parish in administrative, economic and financial matters in civil proceedings.
[110] GOAA: Regs., Art. 19; MOSC: Const., 2.C, pars. 32–37: every parish assembly must elect a lay steward (*kaikaran*) who acts jointly with the vicar as to the assets of the parish to maintain correct accounts of income and expenditure; the lay steward may be removed with the approval of the diocesan metropolitan.
[111] GOAA: Regs., Art. 5.3: officers of the Archdiocesan Council include the vice-president (an elected lay person who presides as directed by the Archbishop), secretary and treasurer; Art. 27: parish council officers; Art. 33: auditors; UOCIA: Statutes, VIII.10: laity may be elected vice-chairman of the Diocesan Assembly.
[112] ROC: Statute, XI.11–17.

'ecclesiastical office'[113] or other official position, exercised normally under episcopal authority.[114] Lay persons may exercise public ministry in prescribed offices.[115] To be eligible for admission to lay ministry or office, a person must satisfy such qualifications and other requirements as may be provided by law and appointment is by lawful selective process, not as of right. Lay ministers and officers are called to a public and representative ministry within and on behalf of a church with such functions as may be prescribed under its law.[116] Tenure terminates on expiry of its term, the death, resignation, retirement or removal of, or withdrawal of authority from, the lay person or as otherwise prescribed by law; moreover, the authority to discipline, dismiss or reappoint a lay minister or officer is dependent on, and its exercise must comply with, the law.[117] As well as admission to such national, regional, provincial and diocesan offices as chairperson, chancellor, secretary, registrar or treasurer,[118] eligible lay persons in a parish may be admitted to such ministries or offices as: warden or steward (selected in the parish to represent the laity) to provide the necessities for and keep order at public worship, and to assist in parish mission, ministry and the administration and management of church property; reader (who assists at public worship by reading, preaching, receiving and

---

[113] PCLCCAC, Principle 28.1; Principle 29: 2: an 'ecclesiastical office' is a 'stable substantive position constituted by law, exists independently of the person who occupies it, enables the discharge of functions of the particular public ministry attaching to it, and may be held in succession by its holders'; 3: it is held by qualified persons (ordained or lay); 4: admission is with the free consent of the candidate, by competent authority and in accord with lawful process; 5: jurisdiction or authority attached to it is determined by the authority which established it, the character of the office and the law; 6: the exercise of office is regulated by e.g. law and the professional ethic of public ministry; 7: office is lost by its dissolution, expiration of the stated term, attainment of the prescribed age limit, or the death, resignation, transfer, retirement or removal of its holder.

[114] PCLCCAC, Principle 28.2: 'Public ministry, ordained and lay, is the fulfilment of a function assigned formally in a church to an office or other position exercised under episcopal authority on behalf of that church'; 3: it is exercised in a church as a structured community and institution, with organisation and standards, to promote the communion of the faithful and the mission of the church to the world; 4: it must be duly authorised in a church, to sanctify, teach and oversee the community of faith, and is exercised on behalf of that church in a representative capacity. See also e.g. LC 1930, Res. 65; LC 1958, Res. 90, 91.

[115] PCLCCAC: Principle 30.1: the law should prescribe: qualifications necessary for a person to be authorised to exercise lay ministry or office; the procedure for, body giving and form of such authorisation; the functions and the manner in which they may be performed; and a fair process and authority competent to review, renew or terminate the exercise of such ministry or office. See e.g. Australia: Authorised Lay Ministry Canon 1992.

[116] PCLCCAC: Principle 30.2–4; 30.5: authority to minister may be limited by: the nature of the functions authorised to be performed; the person or body at whose request or by whose authority the functions may be performed; and the place at which and the period during which the functions may be performed.

[117] PCLCCAC: Principle 30.6–7.

[118] PCLCCAC: Principle 30.8; e.g. South East Asia: Const., Art. IX: the Provincial Chancellor is a communicant and qualified lawyer appointed by the archbishop consulting the Provincial Standing Committee, acts as legal adviser, and holds office for such period as the Provincial Synod approves; the Provincial Secretary is appointed by the Provincial Synod to e.g. assist the archbishop with official correspondence, and to keep minutes of synod proceedings; Scotland: Can. 61, Res. 4: the Diocesan Chancellor must be a lay person; Kenya: Const., Art. XV: the Diocesan Registrar maintains diocesan legal records.

presenting the offerings of the people); lay eucharistic assistant (authorised to distribute the Holy Communion in church and, in the absence of clergy, to the sick); catechist (authorised to prepare persons for baptism, confirmation, reception and the reaffirmation of baptismal vows); and lector (authorised by a member of the clergy in charge of a congregation to read the Word of God and to lead prayers). A register of lay ministers and other officers should be maintained by the appropriate ecclesiastical authority, and usually this is done at the level of the diocese.[119]

Protestant legal approaches to the assumption of office by lay people seem to be rather more complex than those appearing in the Catholic, Orthodox and Anglican churches. As well as the election or other appointment of the laity to the institutions of ecclesiastical governance,[120] Lutheran churches enable lay persons to use 'different talents' for 'different tasks',[121] such as proclamation of the Gospel, spiritual care and other services; for these tasks they serve, for example, as churchwardens, lay preachers, choir leaders, organists, leaders of working groups and 'other co-workers'; admission to such positions is usually at divine service and functions are carried out 'in close co-operation with the minister'.[122] For example, in the Lutheran Church in Australia a 'Church Worker' is any person whose name is listed on the Register of Church Workers provided for in the bylaws of the church; a 'Teacher' includes any lay member called or appointed by the church, districts or congregations to serve on the teaching staff of a school or educational institution established and maintained by the church, district or congregation;[123] a 'Lay Worker' is a person whose name is entered on the Roll of Lay Workers – for entry on the roll the person must be a practising member of the church and meet the minimum requirements set by the Department for Lay Ministry, they may be full-time or part-time and have such responsibilities as are determined by the church, a board, a district or a congregation;[124] and 'Pastoral Assistants' may be appointed by congregations, as may 'Lay Servers' who assist the presiding minister at Holy Communion.[125] Lay preacher is an office in the Lutheran Church in Great Britain: if an ordained minister is unavailable to preach, a lay person may be authorised to do so by the bishop or by the pastor responsible for the congregation. To be

---

[119] PCLCCAC, Principle 30.12–16. See e.g. TEC: Cans. III.3; Mexico: Cans. 17–18; England: Cans. E4–6.

[120] ELCA: Const., Ch. 13: the secretary and treasurer; LCA: Const., Art. VII.3, BL, VII.A: lay delegates elected to church assemblies; LCGB: RAR, Individual Membership in a Congregation, 1: voting members.

[121] ELCSA: G., 11.3–4: 'dependent upon each other, each one [serves] the other with the gift ... he has received'; 'diaconic service' involves responsibility for each other and the sick, aged, needy, disabled and troubled; 10.3: 'All the individual services within the congregation share the same aim, namely that the Word of God may bring about faith, awaken love and build up the congregation.' See also e.g. ELCA: Model Const. for Congregations, Ch. 11: officers; NALC: Const., Ch. 14: congregation officers (e.g. secretary and treasurer).

[122] ELCSA: G., 10.3; LCMS: Guidelines for Constitutions and Bylaws of Congregations, 6.0: 'church workers' include teachers, directors of Christian outreach, directors of parish music and parish assistants.

[123] LCA: Const., Interpretation. See also ELCA: Const., Ch. 7.52: 'lay diaconal ministers' include deaconesses.

[124] LCA: BL, VIII.I.

[125] LCA: Distribution of the Sacrament at the Altar, prepared by the Department of Liturgics and adopted by the Commission on Worship 1995 (edited 2001): 1 Cor. 14.40; AC XV, 1–4.

admitted, the candidate must satisfy a series of questions about, *inter alia*, faith, Scripture, Holy Communion, baptism and sermons.[126]

The Methodist tradition has an abundance of positions open to lay people called to 'lay servant leadership'.[127] In classical Methodism, in addition to helpers,[128] the class leader in the local church is, for example, to see each of the twelve persons in his class at least once a week (to inquire how their souls prosper, advise, reprove, comfort or exhort, as occasion may require, and to receive their gifts towards the relief of the poor), and meet weekly the ministers and stewards of the Society to inform the minister about the sick and disorderly, and the accounts.[129] Today the Methodist Church in Great Britain in the local church has pastoral visitors, class leaders and church stewards. First, a pastoral visitor is 'a person appointed by the Church Council to exercise pastoral care over those committed to his or her charge',[130] namely, all those whose names are on the Community Roll of the Local Church. To be eligible for appointment as pastoral visitor or class leader, a person must be a member in the local church of 18 years of age or more; a minister, deacon or probationer may also be appointed. Pastoral visitors are publicly recognised and commissioned at a service arranged for that purpose.[131] A class leader is: to (1) exercise pastoral care over those committed to his or her charge; (2) meet the class regularly; (3) visit those on his/her pastoral list regularly; (4) encourage members to fulfil their financial commitments as set out on the ticket of membership, and where appropriate encourage others to consider membership; (5) inform the minister, deacon or probationer having pastoral responsibility of any special need or change of address; and (6) pray regularly for those on the pastoral list. Pastoral visitors undertake the duties of a class leader, but are not expected to meet a class.[132]

---

[126] LCGB: RAR, App. A, Inviting Non-Ordained Persons to Preach in LCGB Congregations (2011): questions are on e.g. the meaning of Law and Gospel, presence of Christ in Holy Communion, benefits of baptism, infant baptism, purposes of a sermon in worship and interpretation of the Bible; a Lector may read a sermon from those approved by the LCGB. Lay Ministers may also be licensed by the Church and these meet twice a year for mutual counselling, continuing education and fellowship; they may also meet with ordained ministers.

[127] UMCNEAE: BOD, par. 137: 'servant leadership'; COTN: Man., IIII.F: local churches are 'to elect as church officers active members ... who profess the experience of entire sanctification and whose lives bear public witness to the grace of God ... who are in harmony with the doctrines, polity, and practices of the Church ... and who support the local church faithfully in attendance ... tithes and offerings'; FMCNA: BOD, Ch. 1, par. 152.

[128] For Wesley's Twelve Rules of a Helper see e.g. MCI: Man., App. 1: a helper must e.g. be diligent, serious and punctual, seeking 'to save souls' by e.g. visiting, reading, meditation and prayer.

[129] MCI: RDG, 1.03 (The General Rules of Our Societies 1743); MCGB: CPD, DU 19(vii): the Class Leader is 'a person appointed by the Church Council or by a responsible committee under its authority to meet a class and exercise pastoral care over those committed to his or her charge, and to fulfil such other duties as may be prescribed by this Deed or by Standing Orders'; see also SO 630. See also UMCNEAE: BOD, par. 103.

[130] MCGB: CPD, DU 1(xxvii); see also SO 327: the Connexional Team is responsible for training, support, and promoting lay ministry; for the Local Preachers' Meeting, see SO 560–567.

[131] MCGB: CPD, SO 630: this also applies to Class Leaders; see also DU 9 and SO 631(3) and 050(3).

[132] MCGB: CPD, SO 631: the Pastoral Committee allocates pastoral responsibility among the Class Leaders and Pastoral Visitors; also, the Conference 'recognises that there may be variation in local procedure, but the spirit of the above clauses of this Standing Order is to be observed'; SO 526: circuit ministers must visit Classes.

Secondly, there is the office of church steward (equivalent to the Orthodox, Anglican and Lutheran churchwarden). The General Church Meeting must appoint annually as church stewards two or more persons who are members of the local church. Since the appointment gives a seat on the Pastoral Committee, they should normally be at least 18 years old.[133] The church stewards are corporately responsible with the minister (or probationer) for 'giving leadership and help over the whole range of the church's life and activity', particularly holding together 'in unity the variety of concerns that are contained within the one ministry of the Church'; to this end, they must 'uphold and act upon the decisions and policies of the Church Council'. In the discharge of their responsibilities, church stewards are 'encouraged wherever possible to draw other members with appropriate gifts and skills into a leadership team to be appointed by the Church Council'; they are entitled to appoint one of their number to any official meetings connected with the local church.[134] The church stewards must: (1) ensure that all services, meetings and other engagements appointed on the circuit plan as to the local church are duly held; (2) welcome and attend upon the preacher before and after the service, if necessary, arrange for hospitality and payment of expenses and, if the preacher fails to keep the appointment, ensure that a service or meeting suitable to the occasion is actually held; (3) before each Sunday service for public worship, prepare, for example, for announcement by the preacher written notices of all services, meetings and other engagements appointed on the circuit plan, and see that no announcement is made save such as is in accord with 'the general usage of the Methodist Church'; (4) give due notice of all public collections, arrange for the taking of the collections, enter the amounts in a book kept for this purpose and without delay remit them to the treasurer or other persons authorised to receive them; and (5) ensure that all necessary arrangements are made for the administration of the sacrament of baptism after due notice has been given to the minister (or probationer), in the case of children by the parents or guardians, in other cases by the candidate for baptism.[135] Lay people may also be appointed to the offices of treasurer,[136] and auditor.[137]

Other Methodist churches have, for example, lay workers, to help maintain an environment in the church in which the dignity of all individuals is respected (such as discouraging bullying and harassment) and to report cases to the superintendent of the circuit;[138] lay pastors; lay pastoral assistants; circuit evangelists; and church

---

[133] MCGB: CPD, SO 632; SO 607 and 620: re-appointments and casual vacancies.

[134] MCGB: CPD, SO 633.

[135] MCGB: CPD, SO 634. See also COTN: Man., III.L: the local church must have no fewer than three or more than thirteen Stewards elected by the Church Meeting; their 'duties' are e.g. to serve as a church growth committee; to provide assistance for the needy and distressed (Acts 6:1–3; Rom. 12:6–8); to serve as the Evangelism and Church Membership Committee; to assist the pastor in pastoral care, public worship and Christian nurture; to provide the elements for the Lord's Supper and, if asked by the pastor, to assist in their distribution; and to serve as the Stewardship Committee in co-operation with the pastor and Stewardship Ministries office of the treasurer.

[136] MCGB: CPD, SO 635.   [137] MCGB: CPD, SO 636.

[138] MCI: Dignity in the Church Policy (Man., App. 13) 5.2; see also RDG, 11.01: all persons must be 'spiritually and otherwise fitted' for appointment; nor must they be e.g. persons with

ECCLESIASTICAL OFFICES AND MINISTRIES 69

community workers.[139] Moreover, in the United Methodist Church, a lay speaker is 'a professing member of a local church or charge who is ready and desirous to serve the Church and who is well informed on and committed to the Scriptures and the doctrine, heritage, organization, and life of the United Methodist Church'. Lay speakers serve the local church 'in any way in which their witness or leadership and service inspires the laity to deeper commitment to Christ and more effective discipleship, including the interpretation of the Scriptures, doctrine, organization, and ministries of the church' through, for example: (1) giving leadership, assistance, and support to the programme emphases of the church; (2) leading meetings for prayer, training, study and discussion when requested by the pastor, district superintendent or committee on lay speaking; (3) conducting, or assisting in, services of worship, and presenting sermons and addresses when requested by the pastor, district superintendent or committee on lay speaking; (4) fostering care-giving ministries; and (5) assisting in the distribution of the elements of Holy Communion. A service of commitment is recommended for persons recognised as lay speakers.[140] Lay missioners are committed lay persons, mostly volunteers, willing to be trained and to work in a team with a pastor-mentor to develop faith communities, to establish community ministries, to develop church school extension programmes and to engage in congregational development.[141] Finally, certified lay ministers may be appointed to enhance ministry, for example to small membership churches; they may preach the Word, provide a care ministry to the congregation, assist in programme leadership and be a witness in the community for the growth, mission and connectional thrust of the United Methodist Church as part of a ministry team with the supervision and support of a clergy person.[142]

Equivalent local lay ministries are not difficult to find in the juridical instruments of the Reformed tradition. Like Methodism, but in contrast to the Catholic, Orthodox and Anglican traditions, appointment generally vests in the corporate assemblies of the church. Lay ministries may be in the wider community, governmental and liturgical. First, for work beyond the church in the wider community, the United Reformed Church in Great Britain has 'church related community workers'; these are prepared, trained, called and commissioned to the 'office' and inducted to serve in a particular post for a designated period, namely: to care for, to challenge and to pray for the community; to discern with others God's will for the well-being of the community; and to endeavour to enable the church to live out its calling to proclaim the love and mercy of God through working with others in both church and community for 'peace and justice in the world' - they may be

---

unspent criminal convictions; MCNZ: LAR, Introductory Documents, III, Ethical Standards for Ministry: these also apply to 'lay' public ministry.

[139] MCI: RDG, 4H.01-03: these may be employed and function within the framework of contracts of employment under civil law; Superintendents ensure that all persons employed in such positions are properly vetted, sign all contracts of employment on behalf of the circuit, and report annually to Synod on all employees with a significant vocational element in their work; these must be remunerated in accordance with scales of salaries and expenses determined by the Conference; the church has an Employment Advisory Group.

[140] UMCNEAE: BOD, pars. 266-267.
[141] UMCNEAE: BOD, par. 270   [142] UMCNEAE: BOD, par. 271.

stipendiary or non-stipendiary.[143] Secondly, in Presbyterianism,[144] the presbytery clerk is a key position in the system of church governance: elected for a renewable term of 5 years, the clerk is, *inter alia*, to: keep a record of all presbytery proceedings; keep a presbytery roll; advise all affected parties of presbytery decisions; attend to presbytery correspondence; have custody of the books and records of the presbytery; provide information and reports to the General Assembly and other bodies as required; and prepare the agenda for presbytery meetings.[145]

Thirdly, as to liturgical roles, a lay preacher may be 'authorised to conduct services of worship in the Congregation in which such Lay Preacher holds membership and in any other Congregation to which the Lay Preacher may be invited by the Minister thereof'; candidates must be accredited in accordance with procedures prescribed by the Assembly, and, for selection, the candidate must satisfy the Presbytery as to church membership (confirmed status) and suitability (in character, personality, spiritual maturity and capacity). Written application is made to the Presbytery through the minister of the congregation. The Church Council interviews the applicant and reports and recommends to the Presbytery, which, with a two-thirds majority, may accept the applicant for training and examination to a standard determined by the Ministerial Education Committee. The candidate then applies to the Presbytery for accreditation, acknowledged at a service of worship, and is certified. The Presbytery exercises oversight and may withdraw accreditation (by two-thirds vote) from those 'whom it determines to be no longer acceptable to the Church as Lay Preachers'.[146] Lay persons may also be admitted as youth workers,[147] community ministers[148] and lay pastors.[149] Particularly relevant in

---

[143] URC: Man., A.22; Schedule for their duties; see also Man., K: lay preachers.

[144] Lay people may also elect or be elected to church assemblies and offices: see e.g. PCANZ: BO, 4.4; UFCS: MPP, Ch. 3, s. 1; UCCSA: MCLC, Art. 7: secretary and treasurer; UCA: Regs., 1: confirmed members may vote at congregational meetings.

[145] PCANZ: BO, 8.12. See also e.g. CLCS: 90: Principal Clerk of the General Assembly; 98: Presbytery Clerk; 105: Kirk Session Clerk; PCW: HOR, 3.3: the Clerk and the Treasurer of an Association.

[146] UCA: Regs., 2.8: appeal lies to Synod on withdrawal of accreditation; UFCS: MPP, Ch. 1, s. III: a Leader of Praise must be of 'Christian character', is under the direction of the minister, and may be dismissed by the Session; UCCSA: Const., 6.3: Assembly officers; UCOC: Const., Art. IX: General Synod officers.

[147] UCA: Regs., 2.9: the Presbytery, Synod or Assembly may place these in a congregation for a 3-year renewable term which may be terminated at any time; UCCP: Const., Art. V.13: 'Christian educators'.

[148] UCA: Regs., 2.12: the minister is a member of the Church Council and Presbytery and may be dismissed for no longer living within the faith, inability to fulfil the ministry or indiscipline.

[149] UCA: Regs., 2.13: (1) this is a 'specified lay ministry' within a 'local setting' – it is full time and a stipend attaches to it; (2) an applicant must be a confirmed member of at least 12 months' standing, accept church doctrine, polity and discipline, have church leadership experience and satisfy the Synod as to their profession of faith, sense of call and capacity; (3) application is to the Synod through the Minister of the Congregation; (4) Synod certifies the Lay Pastor; (5) the Presbytery is responsible for placement after consulting the Congregation and Synod; (6) a service marks commencement of the placement which is normally for 3 years but extensions are possible; (7) the Presbytery may terminate a placement at the request of the Lay Pastor, Church Council, Presbytery (after consulting the congregation and pastor) and Placements Committee of Synod – appeal lies to Synod; (8) a Lay Pastor is on the roll of confirmed members of the congregation, a member of the Church Council, and a member of and under

those Baptist communities with a system of ordained ministry, lay people may act as officers in Baptist Unions and Conventions,[150] as well as, for instance, secretaries, treasurers, teachers and musicians in a local Baptist Church.[151]

In sum, the juridical instruments of all of the churches studied here, from Catholic to Protestant, enable lay persons to participate in a wide range of ecclesiastical offices and ministries. However, there is no inherent right to admission to an office or ministry. To engage in public ministry, they must be suitable, qualified, selected and admitted by the appropriate ecclesiastical authority; in some churches they are appointed by the ordained ministers, in others by election of a church assembly and in some by a mixture of the two. Their functions are shaped by the particular office or ministry to which they are assigned; at the local level, these functions range from administration of the temporal affairs of the church (such as record-keeping and accounting) to delivery of spiritual goods (such as preaching, teaching and assistance in other liturgical functions). Lay officers and ministers are subject to the authority of the appointing body and their tenure in office may be for a renewable fixed term, though provision is made for their removal in accordance with due legal process.

Associations of the faithful and religious communities

As we have already seen, the laws of some Orthodox churches enable the laity of a parish to associate in brotherhoods and sisterhoods to carry out, for example, religious, charitable and educational work. This is not unique: many Protestant churches have, for instance, national equivalents.[152] The juridical instruments of several traditions enable lay people (as well as ordained) to come together outside the ordinary local units of the parish, congregation or other pastoral charge, in a range of associations and other groupings, including monasteries and convents. Three traditions are examined here: Catholic, Orthodox and Anglican.

---

the oversight of the Presbytery. See also UCC: BL 343: Lay Ministers (licensed to administer the sacraments); and 344: Licensed Lay Worship Leaders; see also Community Ministry Standards and Best Practices: Administrative Standards for Community and Social Justice Ministries (2007).

[150] For secretaries, treasurers, etc, see e.g. BUGB: Const., 1.8; BUSA: Const., 8; NBCUSA: BL Art. V.

[151] Central Baptist Church (Pretoria): Const., Art. 18: Bible teachers; Bethel Baptist Church (Choctaw): Const., Art. IV: as well as the 'ordained officers' (pastor and deacons), 'other offices' include those of church clerk and church treasurer (elected by the church); Riverside Baptist Church (Baltimore): BL Art. II: 'church staff and officers' include the trustees, treasurer, clerk, youth ministries officer and music director.

[152] ELCIC: Const., Art. XVII.1 and ABL, XVII: the Evangelical Lutheran Women of the ELCIC is 'an official women's organization' and a composite of congregational organisations; it has 'authority, in conformity with the personnel policies of this church, to employ an executive staff person and additional staff as needed to carry out its purpose'; it is responsible for its own financial affairs and is 'an integral part of this church'; MCI: RDG 17: Methodist Women in Ireland: this is an 'organizing body' to enable fellowship and mission; CLCS: 132: the Woman's Guild has a national structure but its congregational branch is subject to the 'spiritual supervision' of the Kirk Session of the local Presbyterian Church; similarly, UFCS: MPP, Ch. I, s. III: 'All societies or associations of members or adherents . . . are under the supervision of the Session and no society or association can be sanctioned as congregational without . . . the approval of the Session.'

The Roman Catholic Church has a very complex and large body of law applicable to communities of the faithful composed of lay, clerical, or both lay and clerical members. These are: the institutes of consecrated life; societies of apostolic life; and associations of the faithful. Institutes of consecrated life are established by competent ecclesiastical authority to enable the faithful (lay or clerical) to engage in 'a stable form of living, in which [they] follow Christ more closely under the action of the Holy Spirit, and are totally dedicated to God'; in these institutes, by vows or other sacred bonds, the faithful freely profess the evangelical counsels of poverty, chastity and obedience.[153] Whilst, in itself, 'the state of consecrated life is neither clerical nor lay', religious institutes may be clerical or lay. A 'lay institute' is one recognised as such by ecclesiastical authority because 'by its nature, character and purpose, its proper role, defined by its founder or by lawful tradition, does not include the exercise of sacred orders'.[154] There are norms common to all institutes of consecrated life,[155] and special provisions on 'religious institutes' (a society in which the members make public vows and live life in common and involving 'separation from the world' proper to each institute), their governance and membership in terms of admission, rights and duties and dismissal,[156] and 'secular institutes' (in which the faithful live in the world and at the same time 'strive for the perfection of charity and endeavour to contribute to the sanctification of the world').[157] The Code of Canons of the Oriental Churches also contains a large body of equivalent norms on the religious life and its various forms.[158]

In addition, Catholic 'societies of apostolic life' enable their members (lay or clerical or both) to live a common fraternal life and 'pursue the apostolic purpose proper to each society' but members do not take religious vows. A house is established and a local community is constituted by the competent authority of the society and with the written consent of the diocesan bishop (who must also be consulted prior to suppression). The society is governed in accordance with its own constitution and there is provision for the admission, probation, incorporation, formation and dismissal of the members, as well as for the juridical personality of the society – the members are subject to the authority of the moderator of the society in relation to its internal life and discipline, but to the diocesan bishop as to public worship, the care of souls and other works of the apostolate.[159] In turn, 'associations of the faithful' may be clerical or lay, or both clerical and lay, public or private, and may include initiatives to promote public worship, Christian teaching

---

[153] CIC, c. 573; see also LG 43-44; CCC pars. 944-945.
[154] CIC, c. 588.1-3; a clerical institute is one governed by clerics.   [155] CIC, cc. 573-606.
[156] CIC, c. 607: definitions of religious life and religious institute; cc. 608-616: establishment and suppression; cc. 617-640: governance (superiors, councils, chapters, temporal goods and their administration); cc. 641-661: admission and formation (admission to the novitiate, the novitiate and the formation of novices, religious profession, and formation of religious); cc. 662-672: obligations and rights of institutes and their members; cc. 673-683: the apostolate of institutes; cc. 684-704: separation of members from the institute (transfer, departure, and dismissal); cc. 705-707: religious raised to the episcopate; cc. 708-709: conferences of major superiors.
[157] CIC, cc. 710-730.
[158] CCEO, cc. 410-553: monks; cc. 433-503: monasteries; cc. 504-553: orders and congregations.
[159] CIC, cc. 731-746; under c. 732, cc. 578-597 and 606 on institutes of consecrated life apply to societies of apostolic life; c. 734: cc. 617-633 apply *mutatis mutandis*.

and other works of the apostolate such as evangelisation, piety or charity.¹⁶⁰ The faithful may constitute an association by 'private agreement' and, to be recognised in the church, its statutes must be approved by competent ecclesiastical authority.¹⁶¹ However, 'public associations of the faithful' are those established by competent ecclesiastical authority to impart Christian teaching or to promote public worship or other spiritual ends not adequately provided for by private associations.¹⁶² Every association of the faithful, lay or clerical or mixed, public or private, must have its own statutes which must define its name, purposes, centre, governance and conditions of membership; and each one is subject to the supervision of the Holy See.¹⁶³ Moreover: 'Lay members of the faithful must hold in high esteem associations established' for spiritual purposes, especially those whose aim is 'to animate the temporal order with the Christian spirit, and thus greatly foster an intimate union between faith and life'; and moderators of lay associations must ensure that 'the members receive due formation so that they may carry out the apostolate which is proper to the laity'.¹⁶⁴ The Oriental Catholic Churches have similar arrangements for shared life and activity under their Code of Canons.¹⁶⁵

Monasticism is also an important feature of Orthodox Christianity and is treated extensively in the canonical tradition, which sees the monastic as an order between the clergy and the laity; this life is open to both women (nuns) and men (monks).¹⁶⁶ The contemporary juridical instruments of Orthodox churches provide for the definition,¹⁶⁷ establishment (and dissolution) and governance of monasteries (including their own statutes),¹⁶⁸ the admission, vows, transfer and withdrawal of

---

¹⁶⁰ CIC, c. 298; c. 300: it may call itself 'catholic' with consent of ecclesiastical authority (under c. 312).
¹⁶¹ CIC, c. 299: private associations; see also cc. 321–326.
¹⁶² CIC, c. 301: public associations; c. 302: clerical associations are those under the direction of clergy; c. 303: 'Associations whose members live in the world but share in the spirit of some religious institute' under its 'overall direction', and who lead an apostolic life and strive for Christian perfection, are e.g. 'third orders'.
¹⁶³ CIC, c. 304: statutes; c. 305: supervision by the Holy See and/or the local ordinary; cc. 306–308: admission and dismissal; c. 309: it may make its own norms for e.g. holding meetings and the appointment of officers.
¹⁶⁴ CIC, cc. 327–329.
¹⁶⁵ CCEO, cc. 554–562: societies for common life; cc. 563–569: secular institutes; cc. 570–572: other forms of consecrated life and societies of apostolic life; cc. 573–583: associations of the faithful.
¹⁶⁶ OOCL: 115, 129.
¹⁶⁷ See e.g. ROMOC: Statutes, Art. 74: 'The Monastery is a community of monks or nuns who [have] decided of their own accord, to live their life in chastity, poverty and obedience'; Art. 76: it is 'a place of distinguished spiritual life, of Christian virtues, of pious participation in religious services, of spiritual edification, both for the inhabitants ... and for those who come to pray there'; Art. 77: if the bishop approves, it may host courses e.g. in 'spiritual guidance' and iconography; GOAA: Regs., Definition of Terms: monasteries are 'Communities of monastics ... organised and functioning in accordance with the canons of the Church and the Special Regulations pertaining to Monastic Communities'.
¹⁶⁸ GOAA: Charter, Art. 21: a monastery is under the supervision of the hierarch in whose jurisdiction it is located; it is founded by the hierarch after approval by the Eparchial Synod; it functions in accordance with 'Monastic Law' and Synod regulations approved by the Ecumenical Patriarchate; MOSC: Const., 11, 124–125: establishment with approval of the Episcopal Synod; ROMOC: Statutes, Arts. 74–75: establishment or dissolution is approved by the Metropolitan Synod on the proposal of hierarchs; SOCA: Const., Art. 137: the Patriarch

men and women,[169] the monastic hierarchy[170] and the administration of monastic property.[171] For example, in the Russian Orthodox Church a monastery is defined as 'a community of men or women, consisting of Orthodox Christians, who voluntarily have chosen the monastic way of life for spiritual and moral perfection and the common confession of the Orthodox faith'. Establishing a monastery belongs to the Patriarch of Moscow and All Russia and to the Holy Synod on the petition of a diocesan bishop. A stavropegic monastery is under the supervision and canonical administration of the Patriarch of Moscow and a diocesan monastery is under the supervision of the diocesan bishop. Admission to and withdrawal from a monastery are executed by the decrees of a diocesan bishop on the petition of the father/mother superior or abbot/abbess. The monastery is governed in accordance with the Statute of the Russian Orthodox Church, the Regulations on Monasteries and its own statutes which must be approved by the diocesan bishop. If a monastery decides to withdraw from the hierarchic structure and jurisdiction of the church, then its recognition as belonging to the church, its activities as a religious organization of the church, its right to property and its use of the name and symbols of the Russian Orthodox Church cease.[172]

In Anglicanism,[173] the practice of lay (and ordained) people entering religious communities led the Lambeth Conference in 1930 to advise 'the establishment, by canon law or other means, of closer co-operation between the episcopate and the

---

is Supreme Head of all monasteries, establishes them and appoints and dismisses abbots, and transfers monks and nuns from one to another; Art. 139: 'Every monastery or monastic order has its own internal regulations, approved by H.H. the Patriarch, and observed by all who will join males or females.'

[169] SOCA: Const., Art. 132: the vows are 'celibacy (chastity), obedience and voluntary poverty'; 133: candidates must be of 'good conduct and reputation'; 134: no one under 20 'shall wear the monastic habit'; 135–136: attire; 138: no monastic may travel unless the Patriarch permits; ROMOC: Statutes, Art. 78: the minimum age is 18 (and with parental consent 16); tonsuring occurs with approval of the diocesan bishop after 3 years' 'canonical examination and living in the monastery'; monks may be ordained if the diocesan bishop approves; Art. 123.9: the dignity of a monk is not compatible with 'the practice of any personal (private) activity' of an 'economic, financial and commercial character contrary to the Christian morals and [the] interests of the Church'.

[170] ROMOC: Statutes, Art. 79: the diocesan bishop is 'canonical leader of a monastery' and delegates authority to an abbot/abbess chosen from 'among the more remarkable monks [or nuns], with a good monastic life, intense spiritual activity, [and] theological' education; the abbot/abbess is assisted by the Spiritual and Teaching Council, Economic Council and Disciplinary Council; Art. 80: retired hierarchs may become abbots if the bishop approves; Art. 81: the monastic ranks are: for men, brother (novice), *rasophor* and monk; and for women, sister, *rasophor* and nun; Art. 82: the bishop makes an annual *synax* (consultation) into the monastic life and takes steps to improve this; and a metropolitan *synax* is made every 3 years.

[171] ROMOC: Statutes, Art. 170: alienation of monastic property must be approved by the Eparchial Council; Art. 193: 'All the goods the monks and nuns brought with them or donated [on entry], as well as those acquired [whilst there], remain in the possession of the monastery and cannot be claimed later on'; MOSC: Const., par. 125: if any monastery leaves the church, 'their assets shall remain ... in the ownership of this Church'.

[172] ROC: Statute, XII.1–10: a monastery may be registered as a legal entity under State law; any monastic who withdraws has no claim on monastic property; a monastery may be represented in the assemblies of the church.

[173] For the revival of monasticism in Anglicanism, see A.M. Allchin, *The Silent Rebellion: Anglican Religious Communities 1845–1900* (SCM Press, London, 1958).

communities'.¹⁷⁴ Today, according to the principles of canon law common to the churches of the Anglican Communion, the faithful may freely associate in a religious order or other society which enjoys autonomy to establish and administer for its life in community its own rule, statutes or other constitution. The relationship between an order or society and a church is governed by the mutual acceptance of their respective regulatory systems.¹⁷⁵ For example, according to the law of the Episcopal Church in the USA, a religious order is 'a society of Christians (in communion with the See of Canterbury) who voluntarily commit themselves for life, or a term of years: to holding their possessions in common or in trust; to a celibate life in community; and to obedience to their Rule and Constitution'. To be recognised as such, a religious order must have at least six professed members, and it must be approved by and registered with the Standing Committee of the House of Bishops on Religious Orders. Each order must have a bishop visitor or a protector who may, but need not, be the diocesan bishop; if not the bishop of the diocese in which the mother house of the order is located, the appointment of the visitor or protector must be approved by the diocesan bishop. The visitor or protector acts as 'the guardian of the Constitution of the Order' and serves as an arbiter in matters which the order or its members cannot resolve through its normal processes. A person wishing to be released from vows who has exhausted the processes of the order may petition the bishop visitor or protector for dispensation; a right of appeal lies to the presiding bishop of the church who must institute a board of three bishops to review the petition and to recommend to the presiding bishop 'who shall have the highest dispensing power for Religious Orders'. A religious order may establish a house in any diocese only with the permission of the diocesan bishop. The constitution of the order must provide for, *inter alia*, the legal ownership and administration of property and the disposition of its assets in the event of dissolution.¹⁷⁶ Similar provisions apply to Christian communities, societies of Christians (in communion with the See of Canterbury) who voluntarily commit themselves for life, or for a term of years, in obedience to their rule and constitution; members of such Christian communities do not hold possessions in common nor do they commit themselves to celibacy.¹⁷⁷

Conclusion

All the churches studied here have legal rules which deal with all the faithful. The church itself is conceived as the people of God, the community of the Christian faithful. It is composed of both lay and ordained persons and all are equal, having been created in the image and likeness of God and sharing in the threefold ministry

---

[174] LC 1930, Res. 74. [175] PCLCCAC, Principle 26.
[176] TEC: Cans. III.30.1: a religious order is not, canonically, a parish, mission, congregation or institution of the diocese; on dissolution, disposition of assets must be in accordance with the laws governing non-profit-making religious organisations in the State in which the order is incorporated civilly.
[177] TEC: Cans. 30.2; for similar provisions, see e.g. Papua New Guinea, Can. No. 1 of 1995; Melanesia, Cans., E.10; Philippines, Cans. III.4; England: *A Directory of the Religious Life* (Advisory Council on the Relations of Bishops and Religious Communities, 1990) issued by the Advisory Council on the Relations of Bishops and Religious Communities, 5; Scotland: Can. 56: the College of Bishops may release a person from religious vows.

of Christ – king, prophet and priest. The churches define membership of the institutional church in various ways but all share the concept that admission to membership is based on the satisfaction of conditions, and the most common amongst these is baptism, profession of the faith and submission to the governance of the church in question. Most churches operate a system of church membership rolls or registers and some have special rolls related to a set of prescribed ecclesial classes (such as full members and children). These rolls and registers are maintained at the level of the local church and provision is made for their periodical revision and for removal of names. The churches share fundamental provisions about the rights and duties, or privileges and responsibilities, of membership. Chief amongst these are participation in the mission of the church, proclamation of and witness to the faith in public and private life, participation in the sacraments or other ordinances of the church and its public worship, and the right to elect members to and to be elected to and hold office in the assemblies of the church at its various levels. All the churches enable lay persons to hold offices or other positions of ministry in the church which are distinct from those held by ordained ministers, who are set apart by virtue of their ordination. Catholic and Orthodox laws are fairly restrictive in the range of positions open to the laity – these include the positions of acolyte, lector and server. By way of contrast, Anglican, Lutheran and Methodist laws and those of the Reformed, Presbyterian and United Churches enable admission of lay persons to a very wide variety of offices and ministries. Typically lay persons may be admitted as lay preachers, lay pastoral workers, stewards or churchwardens. The laws spell out the modes of appointment to these offices, which generally is in the keeping of the ordained ministers and/or representative assemblies of churches, their functions in terms of duties and rights, and the lines of accountability and termination of lay ministry. The laws of Protestant churches do not generally provide for societies for lay people within the church beyond the congregation. However, by way of contrast, Catholic and Orthodox laws, and to a lesser extent Anglican laws, do provide for the establishment of associations of the lay faithful (Catholic), brotherhoods and sisterhoods (Orthodox) or societies (Anglican) to engage in prescribed activities such as charity work. Lay people (along with ordained ministers) may also be members of institutes of consecrated life and associations of the faithful (Catholic), religious communities (Anglican) or monasteries and other institutions of religious order and life (Orthodox). Admission of members to these communities, the distribution and nature of their rights and duties and termination of their membership are subject to complex juridical rules. Alongside these emergent principles of Christian law, it is evident that the juridical unity across these church families indicates how the regulatory systems of churches generate common action amongst Christian lay people worldwide, whatever their actual denominational affiliation may be.

3

The ordained ministers of the church

The juridical instruments of the churches across the Christian traditions studied here contain very large bodies of complicated rules applicable to ordained ministers. Ordained ministers are understood to exercise a special ministry and they are conceived theologically and legally as set apart from the laity. The juridical instruments deal with the nature of ordained status and ministry, and its differences in quality from lay status and ministry. Indeed, the nature of ordained ministry has been the subject of controversy amongst Christians for centuries and disagreements over whether the ordained ministers of different churches enjoy apostolic succession is still a key focus of ecumenical discussion. The special ministry of leadership is sometimes exercised by ordained ministers in different ways. There are also differences in nomenclature and in the many doctrines that underlie it. Churches in the Episcopal tradition generally adopt a threefold ministry of bishop, priest and deacon which stresses broadly the dependence of the laity on the ordained ministers for prescribed spiritual facilities (such as presidency at the Holy Communion). By way of contrast, churches of the Protestant reformed tradition generally stress the mutual interdependence of laity and ordained ministers but at the same time recognise special gifts as belonging to those who are ordained. The juridical instruments of the churches deal with the process of ordination; the appointment of ordained ministers to and their tenure in ecclesiastical offices and other positions; the duties and rights of ordained ministers; and the termination of ministry. This chapter examines these matters in relation to ordained ministers who function at the local, regional, national and, sometimes, international level, namely: priests and deacons (Catholic, Orthodox and Anglican) and pastors, ministers and elders (Lutheran, Methodist, Reformed, Presbyterian, Congregational and Baptist); bishops, presbyters and superintendents; and popes, patriarchs and presidents. The chapter also proposes that principles of Christian law emerge from a study of the juridical instruments of the different traditions in so far as all ordained ministry exists to benefit the church and the world.[1]

Ordained ministers and the process of ordination

The juridical instruments of all the church families studied here contain provisions on five pivotal subjects: (1) the nature of ordained ministry and grades of ordained minister; (2) vocations for ordination; (3) the authorities competent to select

---

[1] For New Testatment (NT) terms used for special ministries, e.g. apostle, prophet, evangelist, overseer, elder, deacon, see F.L. Cross and E.A. Livingstone (eds.), *The Oxford Dictionary of the Christian Church* (Oxford University Press, Revised, 2005).

candidates for ordination and the selection process; (4) the qualities and age required for candidature and formation or other training; and (5) the nature, administration and effects of ordination. Legal provisions on these subjects are generally more detailed and rigorous than those applicable to lay ministers outlined in Chapter 2. Whilst all the churches agree that there is no right to ordination, the principal differences between them concern the bodies competent to decide on matters which relate to ordination. Two models emerge: in the Episcopal tradition, ordination is in the keeping of the bishop, and the laity plays an incidental role; but in the Reformed tradition, the congregation plays a more enhanced role.

The Catholic Church teaches that ordination is a sacrament. For the Latin Church: 'By divine institution some among Christ's faithful are, through the sacrament of order, marked with an indelible character and are thus constituted sacred ministers; thereby they are consecrated and deputed so that, each according to his own grade, they fulfil, in the person of Christ the Head, the offices of teaching, sanctifying and ruling, and so they nourish the people of God'; and: 'The orders are the episcopate, the priesthood and the diaconate'.[2] It is the duty and right of the Church to train persons for sacred ministries and the whole Christian community must foster vocations.[3] Only men may be ordained: and no man is to be ordained unless he has completed the required probation, possesses the requisite qualities, and is free of any irregularity or impediment – there is no right to ordination, but it is absolutely wrong to deny orders to anyone canonically suitable.[4] The minimum interval between diaconate and priesthood is six months, and the right to determine the suitability of candidates for ordination rests with the Ordinary.[5] Baptism is required for valid ordination and confirmation for licit ordination, and candidates must have sound faith, the right intention, requisite knowledge, a good reputation, moral probity, proven virtue and the physical and psychological qualities appropriate to the order received.[6] The age for ordination is 25 for the priesthood and 23 for the diaconate.[7] Clerics must observe continence, and are therefore bound to celibacy; marriage is an impediment to ordination, but there are exceptions.[8] The diocesan bishop may admit to the seminary only those whose human, moral, spiritual and intellectual gifts, physical and psychological health, and right intention, show they are capable of permanent dedication to the sacred ministry.[9] An ordained deacon must make a profession of faith and take the oath of fidelity to the Pontiff.[10] Ordinarily, ordination is celebrated during Mass, on a Sunday or holyday of obligation and in the cathedral church. The minister is a consecrated bishop. Orders are conferred by the laying on of hands and the prayer of consecration which the liturgical books prescribe for each grade; it is absolutely wrong to compel

---

[2] CIC, cc. 1008–1009; c. 207: clerics; c. 266: by admission to the diaconate, a person becomes a cleric.

[3] CIC, c. 232: the right to train; c. 233: families, educators, priests and bishops must foster vocations.

[4] CIC, cc. 1024–1026, 1033–1038 and 1050.

[5] CIC, cc. 1010–1023, 1031: a deacon should not be refused without canonical reason.

[6] CIC, cc. 1024, 1029, 1033; W.H. Woestman, *The Sacrament of Orders and the Clerical State* (St Paul University, Ottawa, 1999).

[7] CIC, c. 1031.   [8] CIC, cc. 277, 291, 1041–1041 and 1087.   [9] CIC, c. 241; cc. 1050-2.

[10] CIC, c. 833; R. Ombres, 'The new profession of faith and oath', 3 *Priests & People* (1989) 339–343.

a man to receive orders.[11] The Code of Canons of the Oriental Catholic Churches on the nature of sacred ministry, the selection of candidates, clerical formation and the rite of ordination itself broadly reflects the Latin Code.[12]

The contemporary juridical instruments of Orthodox churches also deal with the nature of ordained ministry and the process of ordination.[13] According to Greek Orthodox canon law: 'Clerics are the bearers of the spiritual authority in the *Ekklesia*' and the 'major orders' are bishops, presbyters and deacons who are admitted by ordination (*cheirotonia*), which takes place within the sanctuary of a church; as in Catholic canon law, the right to ordain is the exclusive right of the bishop; and ordination occurs through the invocation of the grace of the Holy Spirit upon the candidate and it is administered to a specific position in the church; repetition of ordination is forbidden.[14] Prescribed qualities are required for ordination: the candidate must be of Orthodox faith, male, of sufficient age, educated theologically and free from bodily or mental disorders – lawfully married persons may become candidates (but unmarried priests and deacons cannot marry).[15] Similarly, as in the Syrian Orthodox Church of Antioch,[16] for the Russian Orthodox Church, to be ordained priest or deacon it is necessary to have: membership of the church; the requisite age; the necessary moral qualities; sufficient theological training; and a certificate from his father-confessor of the absence of canonical obstacles to ordination; candidates must also have taken an ecclesiastical oath.[17]

For Anglicanism, the holy orders are bishops, priests and deacons, and this 'threefold ordained ministry accords with the practice and tradition of the church'.[18] No person is to be a priest or deacon unless called, tried, examined and admitted according to the rite of ordination, and the diocesan bishop has a special responsibility, assisted by the faithful, to provide sufficient priests and deacons

---

[11] CIC, cc. 1010–1012, 1026 and 1036.
[12] CCEO, cc. 328–330: clerics; cc. 331–341: seminaries; cc. 342–356: formation; c. 743: ordination; cc. 744–753: the minister; cc. 754–768: candidates; cc. 769–772: preliminaries; cc. 773–775: time, place, and registration; cc. 357–366: ascription to an eparchy; cc. 367–393: clerical rights and duties; cc. 394–398: loss of the clerical state.
[13] For the holy canons, see e.g. Apostles, cc. 29, 30; 7th Ecumenical Council, cc. 3, 5: ordination by simony is forbidden; Carthage, cc. 31, 39: it must be freely consented to, but, to a higher degree, must not be refused.
[14] MOCL: 66–74; GOAA: Charter, Arts. 7 and 9, and Regs., 17: the Metropolitan ordains with the consent of the Eparchial Synod or between its meetings the Archbishop; OCIA: GC, Priests and Deacons, 1.
[15] MOCL: 72–73: 30 for priests, 25 for deacons; see also Nicea, c. 2: faith; Apostles, c. 79: physical and mental qualities; impediments include unlawful marriage (ibid., c. 19) and loss of good reputation (Laodicea, c. 12).
[16] SOCA: Const., Art. 6: episcopate, priesthood and diaconate; Arts. 105–124: a candidate 'must be known for his piety, good conduct, zeal, gentleness, good health, and blamelessness'; MOSC: Const., pars. 110–11: the Parish Assembly recommends a candidate, the Diocesan Metropolitan approves and the Metropolitan confirms examination that the candidate is 'fit for ordination' – the Diocesan Metropolitan ordains the candidate.
[17] ROC: Statute, XI.22–24: 'The Clergy shall be determined in the following composition: a priest, a deacon and a psalm-reader ... a person in holy orders can assume the office of a psalm-reader'; see also ROMOC: Statutes, Art. 52: clergy include priests, deacons and chanters; Arts. 115–121: theological education for clergy.
[18] PCLCCAC, Principle 31. See e.g. England: Can. C1(1); Wales: Book of Common Prayer 1984, v.

and to foster vocations to ordained ministry; the normal age for the diaconate is 23 and that for the priesthood 24.[19] There is no right to ordination: baptism and confirmation are necessary qualifications and the authority to determine suitability of a candidate rests with the bishop, who must be satisfied the candidate has the necessary spiritual, moral, physical and mental qualities – both men and women may be ordained to the extent permitted by law.[20] A candidate must assent to church doctrine, to use only lawful forms of service, to obey the lawful and honest directions of the bishop, and to comply with the law.[21] Progression from diaconate to priesthood is not automatic: normally, a deacon may not be ordained priest for at least 1 year, unless the bishop has good cause to ordain earlier; laws provide for training, and the production of prescribed documents prior to ordination.[22] The ordination must be in accordance with the ordinal or other authorised form of service, and it must be administered episcopally under the authority of the diocesan bishop.[23] Valid ordination consists in fulfilment of what the church universal intends with the free consent of the candidate through the imposition of hands by a validly consecrated bishop with the invocation of the Holy Spirit to give grace for the work of a priest or deacon, whichever particular order is bestowed. Ordination cannot be repeated; orders are indelible.[24]

Lutheran churches also have ordained ministers (or pastors) admitted to 'holy ministry' by way of ordination. The Lutheran Church in Australia is typical: public ordained ministry is 'the special office of teaching the gospel and administering the sacraments' – it is 'the gift of Christ to the church' and one of divine not human institution – 'the church does not create the office of the public ministry, but it does call and ordain persons into that office' who are 'qualified by personal qualities, gifts and training'.[25] For this purpose: 'it shall receive into its Ministry, by ordination or by colloquy of ministers ordained elsewhere, men whose qualifications for the office have been established, and who: (a) accept and hold the Confession of the Church; (b) accept the Constitution and By-laws of the Church; and (c) undertake to participate in the work of the Church and to promote its Objects. Such members of the Ministry shall be recorded in the official Roll of Pastors'.[26] A candidate for

---

[19] PCLCCAC, Principle 32.1-2. See e.g. New Zealand: Cans. G.XIII.1.1; Scotland: Can. 11.5; Philippines: Cans. III.11; Korea: Const. Art. 108; Southern Africa: Can. 18; West Indies: Can. 17.9.

[20] PCLCCAC, Principle 32. See e.g. TEC: Cans. III.4.1: 'No one shall be denied access to the selection process for ordination in this Church because of race, color, ethnic origin, sex, national origin, marital status, sexual orientation, disabilities or age, except as otherwise specified ... No right to ordination is hereby established'; Ireland: Const. IX.22: 'Men and women alike may be ordained to the holy orders' of priest and of deacon.

[21] PCLCCAC, Principle 32.12. See e.g. Wales: Const., VI.10.

[22] See e.g. New Zealand: Cans. G.XIII.3.4; England: Can. C7; West Indies: Cans. 16-17.

[23] PCLCCAC, Principle 32.13-14. See e.g. Ireland: Const. IX.17.

[24] PCLCCAC, Principle 32; CLAC: 136-7.

[25] LCA: The Ministry of the People of God and Public Ministry, CTIR 1992, edited 2001, citing e.g. Acts 6.4; Rom. 10.15; 2 Tim. 1.6; ELCIC: Const., Art. VII.1: 'God instituted the office of the ordained ministry, that is, the Ministry of Word and Sacrament, as a means of creating and nourishing faith within the Church.'

[26] LCA: Const., Art. V.1; see also BL, V.D, Preamble: this cites Matt. 10 and 28.18-20; AC V; FC XI.29: 'the office of the ministry is not a human institution but one instituted by God' (e.g. Acts 20.28). See also NALC: SFPM (2011) 1; ELCA: Const., Ch. 7.23: 'commitment to Christ, soundness in the faith, aptness to preach, teach, and witness, and educational qualifications'; LCMS: BL, 2.10.

ministry must be a person (1) who has indicated willingness for and dedication to this office; (2) who has been found as being of sufficient standard in theological knowledge for this office and of sound confessional standing; and (3) who has indicated willingness to accept a call or appointment.[27] In turn: 'By the rite of ordination the church sets a person apart and says that he is fit and authorised to be a pastor'.[28] The president is responsible for the ordination of an approved candidate and may authorise the president of a district or other deputy to ordain a candidate, assisted where possible by one or more pastors; ordination may take place in home congregations but 'good reasons may suggest ordinations be held elsewhere'.[29]

Much the same approach is found in the instruments of Methodist churches. Ordained ministry is divine in origin.[30] There are grades of ordained minister: deacons, ministers (or elders and presbyters) and (in some Methodist churches) bishops – all are set apart for the ordained ministry of Word and Sacrament.[31] As to vocation, 'all whom the Church ordains shall be conscious of God's call to ordained ministry, and their call shall be acknowledged and authenticated by the Church'.[32] Candidates must have prescribed qualities: they must be a member of the church, of the requisite age and accept the doctrinal standards of the church;[33] or else, they must have 'personal faith', 'spiritual discipline and patterns of holiness',

---

[27] LCA: BL, Sect. V, The Ministry, 1-3: education; NALC: SFPM, 1: a candidate must be baptised, have a 'sense of vocation', 'soundness in the faith, aptness to teach, and educational qualifications', accept the confession, be faithful in its exercise and above reproach; ELCA: Const., 7.31.13; LCGB: RAR, Vocations Committee; ELCIC: Const., VII.3: Synods recruit, approve and supervise 'all candidates for the ordained ministry'.

[28] LCA: What is a Call? CTIR 1978, edited 2000. See also ELCA: Const., Ch. 7.31.13; and LCMS: BL, 2.10: ordination 'shall normally take place in the presence of the congregation' to which the candidate is called.

[29] LCA: BL, Sect. V.A.5-8; V.B.8: Official Roll of Pastors. See also NALC: SFPM, 2: approval by the candidacy committee and ordination by the bishop; ELCA: Ch. 7.31.17: ordination by the bishop or for 'pastoral reasons in unusual circumstances' by a pastor; 7.40-41: roster; LCMS: BL, 2.10: ordination must be 'in accordance with the forms and practices developed by the Synod'; ELCIC: Const., Art. VII.2: synod roster.

[30] MCI: Const., s. 1: 'For ... leadership ... our Lord appointed the Apostles'; 'others were chosen for various offices ... under the guidance of the Holy Spirit and with the concurrence of the local communities' to 'a separated and ordained ministry'; UMCNEAE: BOD, par. 301: 'Ministry ... is derived from the ministry of Christ'; FMCNA: BOD, 5300: 'It is biblical ... to set apart particular persons for special tasks of leadership.'

[31] UMCNEAE: BOD, pars. 304-305: bishops; par. 141: 'clergy [are] ministers, deacons, elders, and local pastors under appointment of a bishop'; FMCNA: Man., II and III; MCNZ: LAR, 2. 1: 'A Presbyter ... is ordained ... to the ... ministry of Word, Sacrament, and Pastoral Care and to leadership'; 2.2: 'A Deacon ... is ordained ... to a ministry shaped by the community [they] serve'; COTN: Man., IV.I.B: 'clergy'; 'ordained minister'.

[32] UMCNEAE: BOD, par. 304; par. 137: 'God's call to servant leadership is inward as it comes to the individual and outward through the discernment and validation of the Church'; FMCNA: BOD, 5300: 'an inward call of the Holy Spirit'; MCGB: CPD, DU 4: 'the call of God who bestows the gifts of the Spirit the grace and the fruit which indicate those whom He has chosen'; MCNZ: LAR, Nature of New Zealand Methodism.

[33] MCI: RDG, 4B: they must normally be under 55; MCNZ: LAR, s. 2.3-2.10: a candidate for presbyter or deacon must be baptised, confirmed, in active membership, 'find general acceptance in the community and in the Church', and committed to the church, with gifts, insight and ability to relate to people.

commitment to lead in loving service, the 'trust and confidence' of the church, belief that Scripture contains all things necessary for salvation, competence in, for example, theology, church history and church polity, and accept the doctrine, discipline and authority of the church.[34] Marriage is no bar to ordination.[35] There is a rigorous selection process and a period of probation;[36] fundamental to the whole process is the principle that: 'a Minister is constituted by the Call of God, the consent of the members of the Church, the election of the Conference, and the ordination to the office and work of a Minister in the Church of God by prayer and the laying on of hands'.[37] Ordination takes place at the Conference; typically, those judged by the Conference Ministerial Session to be fit for admission are presented to the Representative Session and ordained at a service held during the Conference at which the president presides: 'Each ordinand shall be ordained by the laying-on of hands with prayer by the President or a deputy, assisted by two other ministers ... one of whom may be nominated by the ordinand'.[38] Moreover: 'At Ordination each Minister receives, under the hand of the Church, the promise of God's Spirit and is commissioned to proclaim the Gospel, maintain the Faith, build up the Body of Christ and equip God's people for their work of mission. Each Minister is placed at the disposal of Christ and accepts the discipline of His Church.'[39] Ordination cannot be repeated.[40]

In Reformed churches, ordained ministry is conceived as instituted by Christ.[41] Ordained persons are ministers, elders and deacons who 'represent Christ'.[42]

---

[34] UMCNEAE: BOD, par. 304; practising homosexuals cannot be candidates, ordained or appointed to serve: Judicial Council Decisions 984, 985; MCGB: CPD, Bk. VI, Sect. 14: Conference in 2006 affirmed 'the traditional teaching of the Church on human sexuality (chastity outside marriage and fidelity within it)'.

[35] UMCNEAE: BOD, par. 103, AR, Art. XXI: 'The ministers of Christ are not commanded by God's law either to vow the estate of single life, or to abstain from marriage; therefore it is lawful for them ... to marry.'

[36] MCNZ: LAR, 2: the candidate is referred by the parish Superintendent to the Synod Candidates Convenor who reports to the District Ministerial Synod which votes on the report; the candidate attends a national Assessment Event arranged by the Board of Ministry which recommends to the Conference; if accepted, training ensues, after which the candidate is received to full connexion and ordained by the Conference; MCGB: CPD, DU 4, SO 710–729; MCI: RDG, 4B; FMCNA: BOD, 5300: candidates 'are examined and set apart by public ordination, including the laying on of hands after the pattern of the early church'.

[37] MCI: Const., s. 4; MCNZ: LAR, Nature of New Zealand Methodism.

[38] MCGB: CPD, SO 321; see also MCGB: CPD, DU 4.

[39] MCNZ: LAR, s. 2.29. UMCNEAE: BOD, par. 302: this cites e.g. Eph. 4:1–12; COTN: Man., IV. III: General superintendents ordain 'in connection with the ordained ministers present', those duly elected elders or deacons.

[40] UMCNEAE: BOD, par. 303.5; 5310; MCGB: CPD, SO 700: ministers and deacons are ordained to 'a life-long' ministry; MCI: RDG, 4B: the person is entered in the Journal (and/or Minutes) of Conference.

[41] RCA: BCO, Preamble: 'their authority derives from Christ though they are elected by the people'; 'he distributes these functions among those whom he calls to serve'; URC: Man., A.20: 'Christ gives particular gifts for particular ministries and calls some ... to exercise them in offices duly recognised within his Church'; the church 'acknowledges their vocation and gives them authority' to exercise it 'setting them apart with prayer'.

[42] RCA: BCO: Ch. I, Pt. I, Art. 1: 'Ministers are ... men and women ... inducted into that office by ordination.'

The local church recommends candidates who must be eligible, called, trained and examined, and ordained.[43] For Presbyterians, too, ordained ministry is divine in origin.[44] The 'officers of the Church' generally fall into two categories: elders (teaching and ruling) and deacons;[45] and laws provide for the eligibility of candidates,[46] vocation,[47] examination,[48] training[49] and ordination (which is for life) by the Presbytery.[50] The law of the Presbyterian Church in America is typical: 'Our blessed Saviour, for the edification of the visible Church ... has appointed officers not only to preach the Gospel and administer the Sacraments, but also to exercise discipline for the preservation both of truth and duty';[51] moreover: 'Though the character, qualifications and authority of church officers are laid down in the Holy

---

[43] RCA: BCO: Ch. I, Pt. I, Art. 1: elders are 'chosen members of spiritual discernment, exemplary life, charitable spirit, and wisdom grounded in God's Word'; Pt. II, Art. 13: preaching elders are elected by the classis; Pt. I, Art. I: deacons are ordained 'representing Christ through the action of the Holy Spirit'; URC: Man., A.23 and K: candidates must be aged from 25–55; the local Church Meeting and District Council recommend prior to a National Assessment Conference – Synod decides and training follows; Sch. B and C: affirmations at ordination/induction (e.g. belief in the Word and a promise to fulfil the duties of office).

[44] PCI: Code, par. 18.2: 'The authority of any officer ... is derived from Christ and belongs not to the officer'; PCANZ: BO, 6.1: 'Within the ministry of the ... Church ... Christ calls men and women to proclaim the Gospel ... through the ordained ministry of word and sacrament and through ordination to the office of elder.'

[45] PCW: HOR, 2.6: 'An elder ... is a man or woman called to serve the local church through a ballot held prayerfully and under the guidance of the Holy Spirit'; PCANZ: BO, 6.1: 'Ordained ministers'; PCI: Code, I.IV. par. 16: 'permanent officers are the Presbyters (that is, elders) ... in Apostolic times ... also called bishops or overseers, and deacons'; there was 'a plurality of Presbyters ... hence the titles Teaching Elder and Ruling Elder'.

[46] PCW: HOR, 4.21–4.25: 'unimpeachable character'; 'a deep experience of the truth of the Gospel'; ability to lead, heal and deliver 'the Gospel ... with conviction'; PCANZ: BO, 9.2–3: 'appropriate character, qualities and gifts'; hold 'the fundamentals of faith'; be called to a charge or other position; 'good standing'.

[47] PCI: Code, par. 17: 'Calling to office ... is an act of God by ... Christ in the Holy Spirit. This calling is ordinarily made manifest through the inward testimony of a good conscience on the part of the person, the approval of God's people on the part of the Church and the concurring judgment of a court of the Church.'

[48] PCI: Code, pars. 177–182: the Presbytery commission examines the candidate as to 'his acquaintance with divine truth, his personal faith, and his sense of the responsibilities and duties of the office'; PCANZ: BO, 9.4.

[49] PCANZ: BO, 9.5–9.10: General Assembly determines the policies, procedures and training standards; a person must obtain approval from the church council, register interest with the Presbytery, undergo a national assessment and selection process, and is then trained, licensed, ordained and inducted.

[50] PCW: HOR, 4.1. 4.2: 'A minister at ... ordination is set apart'; 3.3.9: at ordination, the Moderator of the Association 'shall lay his hands on the head of each candidate and the Moderator of the General Assembly shall extend to them the right hand of fellowship'; PCANZ: BO, 6.1: 'Ordination to these offices is for life'; 9.7–44: ordination includes 'the laying on of hands, joined by all ministers who are present' and a declaration; PCI: Code, 189–206: ordination and installation of ruling elders is conducted by the Presbytery 'with prayer and the laying on of hands'; the congregation may suggest candidates; UFCS: MPP, Ch. 1.

[51] PCA: BCO, 7.1: 'our Lord ... collected His people ... and united them to the household of faith by the ministry of extraordinary gifts of the Spirit and who were agents by whom God completed His revelation to His Church'.

Scriptures, as well as the proper method of office investiture, the power to elect persons to the exercise of authority in any particular society rests with that society'.[52] The 'officers of the Church, by whom all its powers are administered, are, according to Scriptures, teaching and ruling elders and deacons'; these officers 'represent Christ',[53] and are ordained 'ordinarily by a court'.[54] As to elders, a candidate 'should possess a competency of human learning and be blameless in life, sound in the faith and apt to teach. He should exhibit a sobriety and holiness of life becoming the Gospel. He should rule his own house well and should have a good report of them that are outside the Church'.[55] As to deacons, the office is ordinary and perpetual, one of sympathy and service, and only men of 'spiritual character, honest repute, exemplary lives, brotherly spirit, warm sympathies, and sound judgment' may be admitted as deacons.[56] The Presbytery receives, examines, ordains and licenses candidates for 'the holy ministry'.[57] Vocation is 'the calling of God by the Spirit, through the inward testimony of a good conscience, the manifest approbation of God's people, and the concurring judgment of a lawful court of the Church'.[58] Ordination is 'the authoritative admission of one duly called to an office in the Church of God, accompanied with prayer and the laying on of hands, to which it is proper to add the giving of the right hand of fellowship'.[59] To become a teaching elder, a person must be a member of the church 'who, believing himself to be called to preach the Gospel, submits himself to the care and guidance of the Presbytery in his course of study and of practical training to prepare himself for this office' in, for example, conducting worship, expounding Scripture and Christian work.[60] At ordination, candidates make various undertakings as to the Bible, Confession of Faith and government and discipline.[61] The ordination of ruling elders and deacons is similar.[62] Parallel arrangements are found in the juridical instruments of the United Churches.[63]

---

[52] PCA: BCO, Preface, II.6; BCO, 1.1.
[53] PCA: BCO, 1.4 and 7.2: the 'two orders ... jointly have the government and spiritual oversight of the Church'; 'elders ... gifted, called and trained ... may serve as teaching elder. The office of deacon is not one of rule, but ... service'; in 'accord with Scripture', these offices are open to men only'; 16.2: they represent Christ.
[54] PCA: BCO, 3.1–3.2, 4.2.
[55] PCA: BCO, 8.2; 8.1: 'in Scripture ... As he has the oversight of the flock of Christ, he is termed bishop or pastor ... These titles do not indicate different grades of office, but all describe one and the same office.'
[56] PCA: BCO, 9.2–9.3.   [57] PCA: BCO, 13.
[58] PCA: BCO, 16.1: vocation; 16.2: the right of the people to call is 'inalienable'; 16.3: approval of a court.
[59] PCA: BCO, 17.1–3.
[60] PCA: BCO, 18; 19: examination is on e.g. experiential religion, Greek and Hebrew, Bible, theology.
[61] PCA: BCO, 20: a person is called to 'definite work'; 21: ordination (and installation).
[62] PCA: BCO, 24.
[63] UCC: Man., BU, 2.17: divine origin; 9: 'The Order of Ministry shall be open to both men and women'; UCOC: Const., Art. VI: 'Ordination is the rite whereby the [UCOC] through an Association ... recognizes ... [a] member whom God has called to ordained ministry, and sets that person apart by prayer and the laying on of hands. By this rite ordained ministerial standing and status ... is conferred and authorization given to perform the duties and exercise the prerogatives of ordained ministry'; BL, Art. I: process; UCCSA: Const., 7, Procedures 1; UCA: Const., 3 and 14: 'Ordination (being the setting apart of persons for ministry as Ministers of the Word or deacons) shall be conducted by the Presbytery by prayer and laying on of hands.'

In the Baptist tradition, whether a local church subscribes to ordination is a matter for that church – some churches have ordination,[64] others do not.[65] Thus, a local church may have 'ordained officers', the pastor and deacons, and elders 'whether ordained or not' – the qualifications for pastors and deacons are those required by Scripture (1 Timothy 3.1-13 and Titus 1.5-9).[66] For example, the Nigerian Baptist Convention provides that ordination is 'the prerogative of the local congregation'; but it is 'the duty of the local church' to make a request for the ordination of its pastor to the Conference and to interview the candidate in accordance with criteria set by the Ministerial Board of the Convention. Ordinations take place at the Conference as to candidates approved by the Convention without 'elaborate ceremonies' – those aged 65 or more 'should not be recommended for ordination'; 'No homosexual, polygamist, drunkard, member of secret societies, divorcees or person of questionable character should be ordained'. The candidate must have completed a recognized theological course and produce evidence of Christian character (in accordance with 1 Timothy 3.1-7), 'conviction of divine call to the ministry', 'spiritual maturity' and service as a pastor for at least 1 year before being recommended.[67] Similarly, for the North American Baptist Conference: 'The current practice of ordination ... is the result of the blending of biblical precedent with historical developments';[68] the 'act of ordination' confirms the call of God, commissions the person for service and declares ministerial status.[69]

---

[64] R.V. Pierard (ed.), *Baptists Together in Christ 1905-2005: A Hundred-Year History of the Baptist World Alliance* (BWA, Falls Church, Virginia, 2005) 310 (18th Baptist World Convention, Melbourne, 2000): 'Ordination is an issue decided by Baptist bodies and local congregations'; W.H. Brackney, *Historical Dictionary of the Baptists* (The Scarecrow Press, Lanham, Maryland, and London, 1999) 313: ordination sets a person apart for lifelong 'professional church leadership'; BMPP, 87.

[65] BUGB: Baptists in Local Ecumenical Partnerships, Sect. 3: 'Most Baptist churches appoint members to serve as Deacons and/or Elders to work with a minister or ministers in the oversight of the church. This is a shared ministry, though Deacons are not normally ordained, and ordination, commission or recognition of Elders is a matter for each local church and not normally the wider Baptist community.' Compare: *Orders and Prayers for Church Worship: A Manual for Ministers*, compiled by E.A. Payne and S.F. Winward (Baptist Union of Great Britain and Ireland, London, 1960, reprinted 1972) 217: 'Ordination to this holy ministry rests upon the call of God, acknowledged and confirmed by the Church' to a position of 'sacred office'.

[66] Bethel Baptist Church (Choctaw): Const., Art. IV: ordained officers; Riverside Baptist Church (Baltimore): BL, Art. II: a candidate to be a pastor must satisfy 1 Tim. 3.1-7 and Titus 1.7-9; 'A pastor shall be chosen and called by the church'; deacons are elected; Central Baptist Church (Pretoria): Const., 15: elders (who assist the pastor) are 'gifted by the holy Spirit for such office' and elected; 16: deacons (who assist the elders); BUSA: Const., 4.2.4; CNBC: Const., VI: 'Its Scriptural officers are pastors and deacons.'

[67] NBC: Policies and Practices, Ordination, 1-2.

[68] NABC: Ordination Guidelines (2004), I: Biblical Background: this traces e.g. delegation of the priestly roles (Num. 8.10); consecration for the office of prophet (1 Kings 19.16); laying on of hands by Peter and John at reception of the Holy Spirit (Acts 8.17-19), commissioning of Paul (Acts 13.3), imposition of hands (1 Tim. 4.14) and the appointment of elders (Titus 1.5); see also II: Historical Development and Practice (amongst Baptists).

[69] NABC: ibid., III: Purpose of Ordination, A: an act of ordination is 'necessary in order that the community may publicly and in an official manner acknowledge the special role' fulfilled; B: 'laying on of hands is a bestowing or imparting of a blessing' and 'commissioning entails

To be ordained, the candidate must be: called of God; gifted and prepared for ministry; sound in doctrine; exemplary in lifestyle; and affirmed by a body of believers as to both the gifts and call of the person.[70] The Association recommends its view on whether a candidate should be examined and trained for ordination before the local church decides.[71] In sum, denominationally separated Christians share much in terms of action associated with ordained ministry. On the basis of a belief that ordained ministry is of divine origin and that it exists in grades of minister, they all: foster and discern the call of the laity to ordained ministry; decide on whether to ordain a suitably qualified individual; train that person; ordain or otherwise ritually set apart a person for ordained ministry; and lay hands on the candidate in the rite of ordination; and the lay faithful contribute in various ways in this process.

The tenure of ministerial office

Most ordained ministers exercise their ministry in the local church (such as a parish in the Episcopal traditions or a congregation in the Reformed traditions). The juridical instruments of all the Christian traditions studied here deal with the tenure of ordained ministers who hold offices or other positions in the local church in terms of both appointment to office and termination of tenure in accordance with prescribed processes. Whilst there are profound similarities as to the procedures involved, the rules on these matters have different ecclesiological foundations as between the traditions. The required juridical actions are the much same, but the authorities performing them differ: needless to say, in the Episcopal tradition, the bishop plays a central role with or without prior consultation with the parish; and in the Protestant traditions, generally, the local church nominates or is consulted and a wider authority appoints or else the local church elects and a wider authority is either consulted or confirms the election. Termination of ministry is subject to similar processes.

In the Roman Catholic Church, only clerics may obtain offices the exercise of which requires the power of order and governance. Clerics do not have a right to an ecclesiastical office, but, unless excused by a lawful impediment, they are obliged to accept and faithfully discharge the office committed to them by their Ordinary.[72] Every cleric must be incardinated in (or tied to) a particular church

---

entrusting the person with a specific task'; C: 'Ordination is the public declaration that a specific person has been entrusted with ministerial status.'

[70] NABC: ibid., IV, A: 'the candidate for ordination must be one who has heard and answered the divine call, first to personal salvation, and then, to the Gospel ministry'; B: ministry requires 'a divine endowment (ministry gifts) and personal diligence'; C: 'ability as a teacher ... ought to be tested before ordination'; D: exemplary lifestyle includes the person being 'a model of Christian maturity'; E: affirmation by the body of believers.

[71] NABC: ibid., VI: the candidate is introduced to the local church Ordination Council by a representative of the local church who presents the evidence in support; the candidate presents statements on Christian conversion, call to ministry, preparation for it, Christian service and doctrinal beliefs; after public cross-examination, the council withdraws to executive session for voting delegates; plans are then made for an ordination service.

[72] CIC, c. 274; see also cc. 129, 228.

(generally a diocese) – 'wandering' clergy are not allowed.[73] There are extensive provisions on the free conferral of ecclesiastical offices.[74] Appointment to the office of parish priest belongs to the diocesan bishop who may confer it on whomsoever he wishes, unless someone else has a right of presentation or election. To assess the suitability of a priest for office, the bishop must consult the vicar forane (or dean), conduct suitable enquiries and, if appropriate, seek the views of priests and laity.[75] To achieve stability, appointment is for an indeterminate period, but a specified period may be permitted by the Bishops' Conference.[76] The bishop may appoint an assistant priest, if he judges it opportune, after consulting the parish priest and vicar forane.[77] Ecclesiastical office is lost on expiry of a predetermined time, reaching the age limit defined by law, resignation, transfer, removal and deprivation.[78] The parish priest must offer his resignation at the age of 75.[79] There is no right to relinquish the clerical state for the lay state, or to be reinstated (except by the Apostolic See).[80] Similar rules apply to the Oriental Catholic Churches; however, unlike the Latin Church, a cleric has a right to be given an ecclesiastical office.[81]

Orthodox laws similarly provide for appointment to parish ministry and for termination of parish ministry. Four short examples illustrate how the authority to appoint, transfer and dismiss a parish priest vests in the bishop with only occasional provision for participation of the laity in the process of appointment; but the exercise of episcopal authority is subject to due process. The Russian Orthodox Church is typical: 'Every parish shall be headed by the Rector of the church appointed by the Diocesan Bishop for spiritual guidance of the believers and the administration of the clergy and the parish. The Rector shall be accountable to the Diocesan Bishop for his activity.'[82] Clergy may be transferred and dismissed from their ministerial positions by the bishop at their personal request, according to the ruling of the ecclesiastical court or 'in accordance with ecclesiastical

---

[73] CIC, cc. 265–272; c. 269: the diocesan bishop is not to incardinate a cleric unless e.g. 'the need or advantage of his particular Church requires it'; c. 270: excardination may be granted for a 'just reason'.

[74] CIC, cc. 145–196; c. 147: free conferral; c. 149: the cleric 'must be in communion with the Church, and be suitable, that is, possessed of ... qualities ... required for that office by universal or particular law'; simony invalidates tenure; c. 150: only priests have the cure of souls; c. 153: vacancy; c. 156: written appointment.

[75] CIC, cc. 523–4; c. 521: to be a parish priest, the candidate must be outstanding in sound doctrine and uprightness of character, endowed with zeal for souls and other virtues.

[76] CIC, cc. 520–522; c. 527: the priest is put in 'canonical possession' of the parish under procedures of particular law or lawful custom but the ordinary may dispense from this.

[77] CIC, c. 547; c. 548: the vicar forane is also known as the dean or archpriest.

[78] CIC, cc. 184–189: a person may resign for 'just cause'; resignation from 'grave fear unjustly inflicted' is invalid; c. 189: resignation may be accepted for 'a just and proportionate reason'; cc. 190–191: 'a grave reason' is needed to transfer against the will of the office-holder; cc. 192–195: removal is by a decree for 'grave reason'; c. 194: a person who loses the clerical state is removed from office by law; c. 196: 'Deprivation of office [is] a punishment'; cc. 1740–1752: R. Ombres, 'The removal of parish priests', 1 *Priests & People* (1987) 9–12.

[79] CIC, c. 538.   [80] CIC, c. 293.

[81] CCEO, c. 371.1: 'clerics have the right to obtain from their eparchial bishop an office, ministry or function to be exercised in the service of the Church'; c. 284–310: appointment; cc. 285: qualities; if the cleric is married, good morals are required in his wife and children; cc. 394–398: the loss of the clerical state.

[82] ROC: Statute, XI.18–21; 49. See also UOCIA: Statutes, Art. XI.4: the rector is appointed by the bishop.

expediency'.[83] Deposition and excommunication may be imposed by the diocesan bishop or the patriarch only on presentation by an Ecclesiastical Court.[84] Likewise, in the Greek Orthodox Archdiocese of America, the placement and transfer of clergy are 'the exclusive right and privilege of the respective Hierarch', but initial placement is made by the archbishop in consultation with the metropolitan; the transfer of clergy between metropolises is the right of the hierarchs involved.[85] Clergy of the Orthodox Church in America are 'sent to serve the Church, the Body of Christ, in a specific community'.[86] For the Romanian Orthodox Church, the parish priest has the status of a 'delegate of the Hierarch' and it is the hierarch who appoints and removes parish priests at a meeting of the Standing Committee of the Eparchial Council.[87]

In Anglicanism, to exercise public ordained ministry within a diocese prior authorisation must be obtained from the diocesan bishop or other designated authority.[88] The bishop may confer authority to minister publicly by means of appointment to a particular office or public ministry (such as that of parish priest), by licence, by written permission or by such other process as may be prescribed by law. The laity, or their representatives, may participate in the appointment of clergy to an office or other public ministry in such manner, and to such extent, as may be prescribed by law. Authorisation to exercise public ministry in a diocese may be refused only on grounds provided for in the law. No bishop, priest or deacon coming from another diocese may exercise public ministry in the host diocese without the prior permission of the host diocesan bishop. Before they may be permitted by the bishop to minister in the diocese, clergy from another diocese must produce to the host bishop such satisfactory evidence of ordination and good standing as may be lawfully required.[89] The withdrawal or termination of authority to exercise public ministry must be carried out in accordance with the grounds and procedures prescribed by law.[90] Clergy may tender a resignation to the bishop but must resign or may be removed if their incapacity or unfitness to discharge ministry is lawfully established. Clergy must retire from office at such age as is fixed by law but may continue in public ministry with the approval of the bishop or other competent authority in the manner and to the extent prescribed by law. A person may voluntarily relinquish the exercise of holy orders. Relinquishment may be reversed in such circumstances as may be allowed under the law. A person may be deposed from holy orders by lawful pronouncement of a competent ecclesiastical authority. Deposition disables the exercise of holy orders, either irreversibly or reversibly, as the case may be, according to the law.[91]

---

[83] ROC: Statute, XI.25.   [84] ROC: Statute, II.4 and VII.3.
[85] GOAA: Charter, Arts. 7.2; Regs., Definition of Terms, 'Priest'; 17.6–7: transfer and removal.
[86] OCIA: GC, Priests and Deacons, 1: this cites Luke 22.27; John 13.13.
[87] ROMOC: Statutes, Art. 49: status and appointment; 51: assistant clergy.
[88] PCLCCAC, Principle 42.1; 34.1: charge of a parish; 34.2: assistant clergy.
[89] PCLCCAC, Principle 42.1–6. See e.g. England: Can. C10 and Patronage (Benefices) Measure 1986: appointment is by (1) presentation/nomination by the patron (e.g. bishop) consulting parish representatives (with appeal against refusal to the archbishop); (2) admission/institution by the bishop; and (3) induction. Compare TEC: Cans. III.14, 17, and 33: a rector is elected by the parish but this must be confirmed by the bishop.
[90] PCLCCAC: Principle 42.7.
[91] PCLCCAC, Principle 47. See e.g. Southern Africa: Can. 25: revocation by the bishop if 'the work of God in a Pastoral Charge demands ... a change of Incumbent'; Canada: Can. XIX:

On the Protestant side, there are equally elaborate provisions for the appointment of ordained ministers to office and for the termination of their ministry. For Lutheranism, generally, the process of appointment commences with a call from the local, district or national church.[92] The procedure which governs the right to call may involve meetings between representatives of the parish in question and the officers of the district in which the parish is situated.[93] The call may be issued only to qualified candidates who are both suitable and eligible under rules created by the central assembly of the wider church.[94] This is followed by installation at the local church administered by a senior ordained minister.[95] Tenure of office may be for a determinate period.[96] The ministry terminates typically on the death, resignation,[97] retirement,[98] transfer,[99] incapacity or dismissal of the pastor or by mutual agreement with the congregation.[100] Provision also exists to appoint interim pastors in the event that there is a pastoral vacancy in the local church.[101]

abandonment of ministry is 'presumed' on e.g. 'public renunciation of its doctrine or discipline' and 'formal admission into another religious body' not in communion with the church. For relinquishment of orders, see CLAC: 88–92,157.

[92] LCA: BL, V.D. (AC, Art. 14): the 'right of call shall be exercised by (a) the congregation ... as a parish, and (b) the Church or any regularly constituted body of the Church, or of its Districts, to which such authority has been delegated'; ELCA: Const., Ch. 7.44.A05: 'A "call" is an action ... through which a person is asked to serve in a specified ministry ... attested in a "letter of call" ... A call expresses a relationship between this church and the person called involving mutual service, support, accountability, supervision, and discipline'; ELCIC: Const., Art. VII.6–7; NALC: SFPM (2011) p.3; LCMS: BL, 2.5.

[93] LCA: BL, V.D: the district president meets parish representatives to consider candidates proposed by the district president on behalf of the District Church Council and by the parish representatives; the Parish Meeting (convened by the district president) then votes to accept or reject the nomination(s) emerging.

[94] LCA: BL, V.E: pastors called to parish ministry must normally be members of the congregation where they reside; ELCIC: ABL, Pt. III.1: to be included on the roster of ministers, the candidate must have accepted a call; LCMS: BL, 2.5: good standing; ELCA: Const., Ch. 7.40–41.

[95] LCA: BL, V.A: the district president is responsible for the installation of a pastor called by a parish.

[96] LCA: BL, V.D.11: 'Generally a pastor shall remain in a parish for at least three years unless it is the first call or appointment [when it is] four years'; ELCA: Const., Ch. 7.41.11–12: the letter of call may prescribe service for a specified period but initial service of at least 3 years should be in parish ministry.

[97] ELCIC: ABL, Pt. III.8: a minister may voluntarily resign by written notice to the synod bishop and may be reinstated; ELCA: Ch. 7.41.17: retirement at 60; 7.42: transfer; 7.46: termination of call.

[98] ELCIC: ABL, Pt. III.11: on application, the status of retired is granted to an ordained minister who attains the age of 55 or who has 30 years of service; LCA: Const., Art. V.3; NALC: SFPM (2011) p.3.

[99] LCA: BL, V.D. 12–13; ELCIC: ABL, Pt. III.6–7.

[100] LCA: BL, V.D: 'A pastor shall not arbitrarily leave a pastorate and neither shall a pastor be arbitrarily dismissed by a parish. The regular call of a parish when accepted by a pastor shall constitute a permanent relationship terminated only' on: (a) the death of the pastor or dissolution of the parish; (b) the acceptance of another office by the pastor or his resignation; (c) dismissal of the pastor through disciplinary action; (d) a major reorganisation of the parish; (e) the physical or mental disability of the pastor; (f) persistent or continued neglect of duty; or (g) inability to conduct the pastoral office efficiently in that parish. See also LCGB: RAR, Disciplinary Procedures for Pastors of the Church; ELCA: Model Const. for Congregations, Ch. 9.05.

[101] ELCIC: ABL, Pt. II.3–6: 'At the time of a pastoral vacancy, the congregation or its council in consultation with the bishop of the synod shall appoint an interim pastor'; ELCA: Const., 7.61.

Key concepts for appointment to ministry in Methodist law are those of itinerancy (the yearly appointment of ministers to fill vacancies),[102] and stationing,[103] which is carried out by the Conference.[104] The tenure of a minister terminates on expiry of the term, death, resignation (normally offered to the district superintendent),[105] transfer[106] and retirement (at a fixed age);[107] there is also provision for interim ministry on the occurrence of these events.[108] For example, in the Methodist Church in Great Britain, ministers are stationed by the Conference and 'stations' means 'the comprehensive list adopted annually by the Conference for the ensuing connexional year of ministers, deacons, probationers, arranged according to circuits, institutions, offices and other spheres of work to which they are appointed or in which they are authorised to serve'.[109] A connexional Stationing Committee is appointed annually by the Conference to recommend to the Conference the stations, for the ensuing year, of ministers, deacons and probationers.[110] Ministers in 'active work exercise their ministry ... primarily in the setting in which they are stationed' (i.e. a pastoral charge in a circuit); probationers serve in a circuit under the oversight of a circuit superintendent and do not have a pastoral charge in a circuit.[111] Similar rules apply to deacons.[112] Any minister or deacon wishing to resign from full connexion must notify the Conference President who refers the notice to an advisory committee for consideration; the minister or deacon is present at the committee. The committee advises the president as to whether the resignation should be accepted and, if so, the date from which it should take effect. The committee also advises the president, circuit superintendent and district chair whether a public announcement should be made and, if so, to whom and in what

---

[102] See e.g. MCI: Const., 7.4.1: 'The principle of the Itinerancy, being essential to the life and wellbeing of the Church, is maintained by the yearly appointment of Ministers.'

[103] MCI: CPP (Man., App. 11); COTN: Man., V.I: call; V.II.F: retirement; G: transfer; I: resignation/removal.

[104] MCI: RDG, 6.52-64: the Conference is advised by its Stationing Committee; MCNZ: LAR, s. 2. Compare UMCNEAE: BOD, par. 331: e.g. the bishop appoints deacons but may refuse in 'the best interest of the Church' and consulting the deacon and the board of ordained ministry; par. 337: appointing elders by the bishop.

[105] MCI: RDG, 4E: a minister may offer resignation to the district superintendent who consults the president.

[106] MCI: RDG, 4C: transfer may be approved by the Ministerial Session of the Conference.

[107] MCI: RDG, 4F: ministers seeking to retire at the next Conference apply to the district superintendent; the minimum age is 65; retired ministers may by arrangement with the Circuit Executive take charge of stations; UMCNEAE: BOD, par. 358: retirement is mandatory at 72, or voluntary (with 20, 30, 40 years service); involuntary retirement is by two-thirds vote of clergy members; FMCNA: BOD, 5300.

[108] MCI: RDG. 4E.

[109] MCGB: CPD, DU 1(xxxi), SO 770-783; CPD, DU lxxviii: 'Probationer means a person ... admitted by the Conference ... for the ministry or diaconate and is stationed by [it] but ... not yet ... admitted into full connexion.'

[110] MCGB: CPD, SO: 322-323: it also advises on stationing policy; discussions about particular ministers etc. are 'absolutely confidential'; SO 323: the Stationing Advisory Committee advises e.g. on movement of ministers. See also Guidance on the Stationing of Ministers and Deacons: MCGB: CPD, Bk. VI, Pt. 2, Sect. 1.

[111] MCGB: CPD, SO 700: this is the case whether the minister is full-time or part-time.

[112] MCGB: CPD, SO 701: deacons in active work exercise ministry primarily where they are appointed.

terms.[113] There are also provisions which deal with the death, retirement, transfer and dismissal of ministers from their charges.[114]

The Reformed traditions have equivalent rules on appointment to and termination of local ministry. Reformed churches base appointment on a call by the local church, approval by the Consistory and induction at a service;[115] they also provide for resignation, retirement and removal.[116] Much the same applies in Presbyterianism: the people have 'the choice of those officers whom He has appointed in His Church', and the Presbytery licenses, installs, removes and judges ministers; the local congregation nominates candidates to the Presbytery for appointment,[117] and it advises on resignation.[118] For example, in the Presbyterian Church of Scotland, a congregation may call its own minister after the Presbytery has given permission, and if a congregation fails to do so the right passes to the Presbytery.[119] When the vacancy of a charge is anticipated, the congregation's vacancy committee nominates a candidate to the Kirk Session and the candidate must then be approved by the Presbytery – prior to induction, an edict is read to the congregation to provide an opportunity to object on the grounds of the life or doctrine of the minister to be inducted and to state these to the Presbytery for determination; the Presbytery then proceeds to induction.[120] Ministers may withdraw from a charge (by written demission) or from status as a minister, but only with the consent of the Presbytery.[121] Ministers are required to retire at the age of 65.[122] Also, a minister's pastoral tie may be severed by disciplinary process or

---

[113] MCGB: CPD, SO 760; 761: for reinstatement the person must apply to the President.

[114] See below, Chapter 5.

[115] RCA: BCO: Ch. I, Pt. I, Art.2: the consistory consults the congregation whose judgment is of 'significant weight, but not binding'; the call is approved by the consistory, candidate and classis; if there are no 'lawful objections', the classis installs at a service; Art. 1: the election of elders and deacons is for 5 years but re-election is permitted; URC: Man., L: a minister is called to a pastorate if 'concurred with' by the District Council; A.23: elders are elected by the church meeting and are inducted for such period as the church determines.

[116] RCA: BCO, Ch. I, Pt. II, Art. 1: no one who relinquishes ministry or is deposed may exercise office; Art. 12: termination, retirement at 60 or 70, and relinquishment with the classis' consent; URC: Man., A.21 and Sch. C.

[117] PCA: BCO, 3.1: choice; 13: Presbytery; 20–21: 'No minister, licentiate or candidate shall receive a call from a church but by the permission of the Presbytery'; a local church, Presbytery or General Assembly may call and elect; locally, the Session recommends candidates, the congregation votes, and Presbytery approves and installs.

[118] PCA: BCO, 23: a minister tenders resignation to the Presbytery and the local church recommends as to whether it should be accepted; the Presbytery may also designate a minister as honourably retired if unable by reason of infirmity to continue as pastor; 24.8: installation of ruling elders and deacons.

[119] CLCS: 113; Act IV, 1984. See also UFCS: MPP, Ch. 1, s. 1 and Ch. 5, s. 3: Kirk Session elects elders; a congregation calls a minister and Presbytery approves and inducts; a minister offers resignation to Presbytery.

[120] CLCS: 113; Act V, 1984. See also PCI: Code, 193–196: Presbytery receives and sustains/refuses calls from congregations; 204–206: it installs/inducts ministers to charges; App. 4: it receives resignations of ministers, and (220) determines whether they have abandoned their charges.

[121] CLCS: 118. See also PCANZ: BO, 10: a ministry settlement terminates on e.g. death, resignation, retirement, incapacity, dissolution of the pastoral tie, inability of the congregation to meet its financial obligations to the minister or disciplinary process; PCI: Code, 189–192.

[122] CLCS: 121: Act IV, 1995.

due to the mental incapacity of the minister.[123] A slightly different approach is found in the Presbyterian Church of Wales: 'It is the responsibility of the elders to inform Presbytery that a church/pastorate wishes to call a minister'; the Presbytery will 'take the voice of the churches' in a general meeting and if the vote is favourable the Presbytery will seek the permission of the Association for the Presbytery to visit the pastorate and establish a Pastorate Committee to consider candidates whose names are submitted to the church for election and then the Presbytery confirms the election – all the arrangements regarding the ministry are to be made with the consent of the Presbytery. The minister must retire at 67, and a resignation is to be tendered to the Presbytery.[124] Similar arrangements are to be found in United Churches and Congregational Churches.[125]

In the Baptist tradition, it is the local church which extends a call to a minister or pastor,[126] inducts the pastor[127] and receives their resignation or terminates their ministry.[128] By way of illustration, for the appointment to a pastorate in the Baptist Union of Southern Africa, the General Meeting of a local church appoints its Executive Committee as a Call Committee, the function of which is to recommend one name to a Special General Meeting of the church. An invitation is contingent on: at least two-thirds of the members present voting in favour by ballot; the prospective pastor must have been baptised by immersion and must accept in writing the constitution; and the name of the prospective pastor shall be on one of the Ministerial Lists of the Baptist Union of Southern Africa. Any engagement between the church and the pastor is terminable by three months' notice on either side unless otherwise mutually agreed. The Code of Pastoral Ethics of the Union

---

[123] CLCS: 121; 65: discipline; Act I, 1988: severance due to changed circumstances. See also PCANZ: BO, 6.1; see 9.21–22: transfer to other local or national ordained ministry; 9.43–44: induction of elders and deacons.

[124] PCW: HOR, 4.3–4.8; also: 2.6: an elder is called through a ballot held, 'prayerfully and under the guidance of the Holy Spirit', every 7 years but a Presbytery may authorise one earlier; an elder wishing to resign informs the minister and elders and the Presbytery decides; 4.17: part-time and non-stipendiary ministry.

[125] UCCSA: Const., 7.7–7.9: the local church calls its minister and this is confirmed by Regional Council; a pastoral charge is vacant on death, resignation etc.; ministers retire at 55; UCA: Const., 18: placement and induction by the congregation is affirmed by the Presbytery; placements may be by General Assembly and a Presbytery; Regs., 2.7: tenure is 10 years; UCC: Man., 9: the Conference Settlement Committee (on which a Presbytery is represented) considers applications from local churches; UCOC: Const., Art. VI: licensing.

[126] BUGB: Baptists in Local Ecumenical Partnerships, s. 2: 'ministers ... are usually called to a pastorate without a fixed term and move in response to a call to another pastorate' with advice from the Regional Minister; MTC 2003, 6.1: a church appoints its own ministers 'who have been baptised, who affirm the Declaration of Belief, who hold to the authority of the Holy Scriptures', 'who ... practise ... baptism and whose name appears in the register' of Union ministers; the minister may be removed by the church; BMPP: 216, App. III, SCBC, Type A, Art. VIII.1: 'When a pastorate is vacant, the advisory council [or board of deacons] shall select a ... pulpit committee ... to secure ... prospective pastors, working ... with the Area Minister'; when a suitable candidate is found, a vote of three-quarters at a church meeting 'shall be necessary to extend a call'; ABCUSA: TCOR, II.A.4.

[127] NBC: PAP: 'formal transfer of both physical and spiritual authority ... of a local Church to the Pastor.'

[128] BMPP: 216, App. III, SCBC, Type A, Art. VIII.2: 'The term of office may be ended upon ninety days' notice on the part of the pastor or the church' or by majority vote at a business meeting.

must be accepted and signed by the pastor. A Letter of Call including the duties of the pastor and the conditions of service must be prepared and upon acceptance signed by the pastor. Only a properly constituted Church Meeting has power to dismiss the pastor. The retirement age is 65 but the church may extend the ministry of the pastor on an annual basis.[129] The constitution of a local Baptist church may also address the call to and induction of a pastor, as well as termination of ministry.[130]

The functions of ordained ministers

In terms of action, there is profound juridical convergence between the churches as to the functions, duties and rights of ordained ministers in the local church. Three functions come to the fore: the ministry of word; the administration of ritual; and pastoral care of the faithful and perhaps those in wider society. Ordained ministers also owe duties to church authorities.

Catholic canon law provides a set of duties and rights applicable to all clerics, as well as specific functions applicable to parish clergy. First, since they all work to build up the body of Christ, Roman Catholic clerics are united with one another 'in the bond of brotherhood and prayer' and must 'seek to cooperate with one another', promote the mission of the laity, and show reverence and obedience to the Supreme Pontiff and their own Ordinary.[131] All clerics must, *inter alia*: seek holiness in their lives; fulfil their pastoral ministry; nourish their own spiritual life with Scripture and Eucharist, prayer and spiritual retreats; observe 'perfect and perpetual continence' and celibacy; refrain from associations inconsistent with the clerical state; hold the doctrine of the church; reside in their diocese unless permitted otherwise by the Ordinary (or to take 'a rightful and sufficient holiday'); wear suitable ecclesiastical dress; and do their utmost to foster peace and harmony based on justice – they are forbidden everything 'unbecoming to their state' (e.g. to assume public office involving the exercise of civil power, and to practise commerce or trade except with the permission of ecclesiastical authority).[132] Secondly, deacons are the ordinary

---

[129] BUSA: Model Const., 11–16: a Pastoral Committee draws up the Letter of Call for vote at the Annual General Meeting; Const., 2: the Union operates a system of accredited ministers.

[130] Riverside Baptist Church (Baltimore): BL, Art. II.2: 'A pastor shall be chosen and called by the church whenever a vacancy occurs' (by vote of 70% of members), serves until termination by the pastor or church, and gives at least 2 weeks' notice to resign; II.4: deacons are elected at regular business meetings by secret ballot; Bethel Baptist Church (Choctaw): Const., Art. IV: election and: 'Termination of his pastorate shall occur when he believes the Lord is leading him elsewhere, when his health prevents his continuing in that office, or when he forfeits his right to the office ... by immoral and unbecoming conduct'; Central Baptist Church (Pretoria): Const., 15.1: 'The choice and appointment of a Called Elder (Pastor) is vested in the membership of the Church.'

[131] CIC, cc. 273, 275; c. 274: only clerics exercise governance; c. 384: the bishop is to care for priests, defend their rights, ensure that they fulfil their duties and have an adequate means of livelihood and social welfare.

[132] CIC, c. 276: holiness, etc; c. 277: continence and celibacy; c. 278: secular clergy have the right to associate; c. 279: studies; c. 280: common life; c. 281: remuneration; c. 282: a simple way of life avoiding worldliness; c. 283: residence etc.; c. 284: dress; c. 285: conduct inconsistent with their state; c. 286: commerce; c. 287: justice. See also Congregation for the Clergy, *Directory for the Ministry and Life of Priests* (Vatican, 1994).

ministers of baptism, have various roles at the Eucharist, may celebrate marriages if delegated and may act as minister of the Word.[133] Thirdly, the 'care of souls' (*cura animarum*) is reserved to priests who are co-operators of the bishops; the functions of a parish priest (from the moment he takes possession of the parish) include: administration of baptism; assistance at marriages; conducting funerals; celebrating the Eucharist on Sundays and holydays; instructing and prudently correcting the faithful; preaching; and visiting the faithful entrusted to his care.[134] The parish priest acts on behalf of the parish, must ensure that parish goods are administered in accordance with law and must reside in the parochial house (or elsewhere if the bishop permits).[135] As well as parish clergy, within the diocese the bishop appoints a vicar general, episcopal vicars and vicars forane to assist in the governance of the diocese and oversight of clergy.[136] Similar functions are performed by parish and other clergy in the Code of the Oriental Catholic Churches.[137]

Like the Catholic Church, the Orthodox Church distinguishes between the common ministry of all clergy (priests and deacons) and the specific ministry of parish clergy.[138] The Orthodox Church in America is typical. Clergy are: 'strictly to observe the teachings of the Church, regarding Christ, the Sacred Scriptures and Holy Traditions'; under the 'complete authority' of the diocesan hierarch 'without whose blessing they cannot function' and 'to whom they must show proper respect'; to 'show respect and concern for other members of the clergy'; to be examples 'through prayer and fasting' and 'not abstain from the Eucharist'; not to run for 'political office' or accept 'secular appointments or engage in business without the permission of the diocesan hierarch'.[139] Moreover, ordained ministry is 'to serve the Church, the Body of Christ, in a specific community'.[140] The priest is 'the spiritual father of his parish' and must 'treat his parishioners, his parochial family, as a father

---

[133] See e.g. CIC, c. 757: ministry of the Word; see generally post Chapter 7; c. 288: permanent deacons.

[134] CIC, cc. 150 and 149: cures; c. 757: co-operators; c. 527: possession; cc. 528–530: rights and duties. See also Congregation for the Clergy, *The Priest, Pastor and Leader of the Parish Community* (Vatican, 2002).

[135] CIC, c. 532: temporal goods; c. 533: residence; c. 535: registers; cc. 540–552: cover in cases of absence.

[136] CIC, cc. 475–481: a vicar general helps to govern the whole diocese; an episcopal vicar assists in a specific area or activity; cc. 553–555: a vicar forane oversees clergy, visits parishes, and oversees property in a district.

[137] CCEO, cc. 367–393: clerics; cc. 288–303: parish pastors.

[138] MOCL: 67–68, 76–78: e.g. a parish cleric administers the sacraments, preaches the Word of God and has the right to be supported by the church he serves; clerics must behave publicly in a manner 'becoming of the priesthood', wear the 'proper dress' and must not exercise any occupation unbecoming the priesthood (e.g. managing another's property for payment) or exercise a political office; OOCL: 128: once ordained, a cleric cannot marry, engage in matters which conflict with the priestly state or resign without permission.

[139] OCIA: GC, A Selection of Clergy Disciplines, 1–8: observing teaching (Ephesus, c. 6; Carthage, c. 2); authority of the hierarch (Holy Apostles, c. 31, 39, 55); respect other clergy (Holy Apostles, c. 56, 59); godliness (Holy Apostles, c. 58); example to the flock (Carthage, c. 41); eucharist (Trullo, c. 80); pious repentance (Holy Apostles, c. 52); 8: political office (Carthage, c. 16; Holy Apostles, c. 81, 83); secular work (Holy Apostles, c. 39; Chalcedon, c. 3); right to a hearing before a Church Court (Chalcedon, c. 9; OCIA Statutes, Art. XI).

[140] OCIA: GC, Priests and Deacons, 1 (Luke 22.27; John 13.13).

treats his children, i.e. with love, kindness, patience and understanding' – the priest is 'their true guide along the path of salvation', the 'builder of souls'.[141] As such, the parish priest must deliver homilies, provide liturgy, instruct the faithful, have personal contact with and visit parishioners (especially the sick), direct parish life, activities and administration, and work with the parish council; priests must not be absent from the parish without the permission of the diocesan hierarch (except for holidays), nor minister in another parish unless invited by its priest.[142] The same functions are performed by parish clergy under the regulatory instruments of the Greek, Russian, Ukrainian, Romanian and Syrian Orthodox churches.[143] Orthodox laws also provide for offices within the diocese beyond the parish, such as that of dean.[144]

In Anglicanism, ministry is service, a gift of God, and the public ministry of ordained persons is exercised under episcopal authority in various forms, including parish ministry,[145] to which, like all offices, prescribed functions attach.[146] First, all clergy: (1) should fashion themselves after the example of Christ and should not engage in any occupations, habits or recreations inconsistent with their sacred calling but lead a disciplined way of life appropriate to their clerical state; (2) must be diligent in liturgical life, particularly the Eucharist, personal prayer, self-examination and study, especially of Holy Scripture; (3) must not engage in any secular employment or other occupation without permission from the diocesan bishop; (4) must reside within the territory of the ecclesiastical unit to which they are assigned unless the bishop permits otherwise; (5) are subject to the jurisdiction of their diocesan bishop and must comply with that bishop's lawful and honest directions; and (6) should dress in a manner suitable to the performance of their ministry as may be a sign and mark of their calling both to those within their charge

---

[141] OCIA: GC, Priests and Deacons, 2. See also UOCIA: CPC, III: Pastoral Standards.

[142] OCIA: GC, Priests and Deacons, 3–6: liturgy and instruction; 7–10: visits; 11–12: parish meetings; 13–14: absence and holidays; 15: ministry in another parish; 16–18: property and contracts; 19: secular employment.

[143] ROC: Statute, XI.18–21; the rector is responsible for the doctrinal, canonical, liturgical, catechetical, pastoral and administrative life of the parish subject to the authority of the bishop; UOCIA: Statutes, Art. XI.4: the rector; ROMOC: Statutes, Arts. 48–52, 122–125: the parish priest (who is 'delegate of the Hierarch'); SOCA: Const., Arts. 10–11: priests, deacons; 105–124: parish priests must minister 'church mysteries', preach, visit, reconcile, be a good example to the faithful, and remain unmarried unless allowed by the metropolitan.

[144] ROC: Statute, X. 50–58: the Dean (appointed by the bishop) oversees the parishes in his area by means of e.g. visits; UOCIA: Statutes, Art. X: the district dean, head of the deanery, is appointed after election from the deanery rectors confirmed by the bishop; he is subject to the instructions of the bishop, directs deanery affairs, supervises, directs, counsels and admonishes clergy, investigates complaints against clergy and parish bodies, convokes deanery meetings, and reports to the bishop; ROMOC: Statutes, Art. 70–71: the Archpriest, appointed by the bishop, e.g. guides, co-ordinates and supervises deanery activities, inspects the parishes annually, reports to the diocese, oversees catechesis and makes suggestions as to vacant parishes.

[145] PCLCCAC, Principle 28: the exercise of ministry is structured, authorised, representative and accountable.

[146] PCLCCAC, Principle 29; 29.1: ecclesiastical offices include the offices of primate, archbishop, bishop, dean, archdeacon and parish priest; for ecclesiastical office (its meaning and admission to it) see Chapter 2 n. 113.

and to society at large.¹⁴⁷ Secondly, a deacon must care for people in need and assist the priest (subject to the priest's direction), but must not exercise functions reserved to the order of priests.¹⁴⁸ Thirdly, working with the bishop, a priest is to (1) proclaim the Gospel through preaching and teaching, administer the sacraments and provide pastoral care; (2) preside at the Eucharist, pronounce the absolution; (3) visit those within their charge for spiritual consultation and advice, prepare candidates for baptism, confirmation and reception, and instruct children within their care in the Christian faith.¹⁴⁹ Fourthly, a parish priest has the primary authority and responsibility for the care of souls exercised under the general authority, oversight and pastoral direction of the diocesan bishop.¹⁵⁰ Fifthly, in the exercise of their ministry, clergy must uphold the professional ethic of public ministry (e.g. honesty, integrity and efficiency) and standards in the delivery of pastoral care, respect for colleagues and confidentiality.¹⁵¹ A cleric may be authorised to function in non-parochial ministry. In some churches, a bishop may be empowered to appoint: a vicar general to act whenever the bishop is outside the diocese or incapacitated; an archdeacon who assists the bishop with governance within the archdeaconries of a diocese; and an area dean who must report to the bishop any matter in a parish within the deanery which it may be necessary or useful for the bishop to know (e.g. illness amongst the clergy).¹⁵²

Moving to the Protestant side of the ecclesiastical spectrum, the functions of clergy in Catholicism, Orthodoxy and Anglicanism find direct parallels in the responsibilities of Protestant ordained ministers. On the basis of the evangelical spirit of interdependence,¹⁵³ Lutheran pastors serve the whole congregation,¹⁵⁴ preach the Gospel, administer the sacraments, provide pastoral care,¹⁵⁵ engage only

---

[147] PCLCCAC, Principle 41: clerical discipleship. See e.g.: Southern Africa: Can. 24.1: diligence in liturgical life; England: Can. C26(1): personal prayer, self-examination and study; Ireland: Const. IX.33: occupations, habits or recreations; Scotland: Can. 19: secular employment without the permission of the diocesan bishop; Wales: Const., VI.19: residence; England: Can. C14(3): 'I swear by Almighty God that I will pay true and canonical obedience to the Lord Bishop of C and his successors in all things lawful and honest.'

[148] PCLCCAC, Principle 33.1–3. See e.g. Brazil: Cans. III.11.   [149] PCLCCAC, Principle 33.4–6.

[150] PCLCCAC, Principle 34. See e.g. TEC: Cans. III.14.1: 'The authority of and responsibility for the conduct of the worship and the spiritual jurisdiction of the Parish are vested in the Rector, subject to the Rubrics of the Book of Common Prayer, the Constitution and Canons of the Church, and the pastoral direction of the Bishop'; West Indies: Can. 15.1: 'the spiritual jurisdiction of a Parish is vested in the Incumbent or Priest-in-Charge subject to Canons and Regulations of the Diocese and the authority of the Bishop'; Scotland: Cans. 17.3, 38.4.

[151] PCLCCAC, Principle 43: trust; 44: compassion and accessibility; 45: respect for diversity and custom; 46: disclosure of confidential information received outside confession may be subject to disciplinary process.

[152] PCLCCAC, Principle 33.6. See in turn Melanesia: Can. C.8; Ireland: Const., II.38–42: Wales: Const. VI.2.

[153] LCA: BL, Sect. V.D–F: the General Pastors' Conference provides mutual support.

[154] ELCSA: G., 10.4: also, 'the Congregation members assist their minister with advice and every support ... The congregation is not lord over the minister, nor is the minister lord over the congregation'; ELCIC: Const., Art. VII.4–5: as well as preaching: 'Each ordained minister ... shall lead a life befitting the office. No ordained minister shall belong to any organization, which in its ... rites or practices contradicts the gospel.'

[155] ELCIRE: Const., Art. 9; NALC: CDC, Ch. 9.

in occupations consistent with ordained ministry,[156] maintain standards in personal life,[157] honour confidentiality[158] and reside in the pastorate.[159] By way of example, for the Evangelical Lutheran Church in America: 'Leaders in this church should demonstrate that they are servants by their words, life-style, and manner of leadership', recognising 'their accountability to the Triune God, to the whole Church, to each other, and to the [church] ... in which they have been asked to serve'.[160] Every ordained minister must: (1) preach the Word; (2) administer the sacraments; (3) conduct public worship; (4) provide pastoral care; and (5) speak publicly to the world in solidarity with the poor and oppressed, calling for justice and proclaiming God's love for the world. Moreover, each minister with a congregational call shall, within the congregation: (1) offer instruction, confirm, marry, visit the sick and distressed and bury the dead; (2) supervise all schools and organisations of the congregation; (3) install regularly elected members of the Congregation Council; and (4) with the council, administer discipline. Every pastor must: (1) strive to extend the Kingdom of God in the community, in the nation and abroad; (2) seek out and encourage qualified persons to prepare for the Gospel ministry; (3) impart knowledge of this church and its wider ministry through distribution of its publications; and (4) endeavour to increase the support given by the congregation to the work of the church-wide organisation of the Evangelical Lutheran Church of America (ELCA) and its own Synod.[161] Like those of the Catholic, Orthodox and Anglican traditions, Lutheran officers may be appointed to assist in oversight of districts in the church; for instance, in the Estonian Evangelical Lutheran Church, the dean is subordinate to the bishop and exercises functions of oversight in the Deanery.[162]

---

[156] LCGB: RAR, Responsibilities and Duties of Pastors, 1–24: e.g. refrain from any actions that could bring the church into disrepute e.g. Freemasonry; ELCIC: ABL, Pt. III.9: no engagement in other occupations without approval of the calling authority and synod bishop; Const., Art. VIII.2 and 3: diaconal duties.
[157] NALC: SFPM, p.2: 'A pastor shall be a person, whose personal life and morality shall be above reproach, in accordance with Biblical standards', a 'model of the godly life', a 'faithful user of the means of grace, Word and Sacrament', 'diligently engage in personal prayer, devotions, and other spiritual disciplines', 'personally believe and publicly profess the Christian faith', and comply with the law of the church.
[158] ELCIC: ABL, Pt. III.4 and IV.4: confidentiality in the exercise of ministry.
[159] LCA: BL, V.D.4: 'A pastor shall not arbitrarily leave a pastorate '; but BL, V.C.1–5: they may apply to the District Church Council on e.g. health, family or personal grounds for up to 3 years' leave; ELCA: Const., 7.31.16: leave of absence; ELCIC: ABL, Pt. III.10: leave from the bishop for up to 3 years; Pt. IV.5: if a diaconal minister resides at too great a distance from the congregation to sustain a living relationship, the bishop may grant permission to hold membership in a congregation of another church.
[160] ELCA: Const., Ch. 5.01; 7.42: every pastor is related to the synod where the calling congregation resides.
[161] ELCA: Const., 7.31.12; Model Const., Ch. 9.04: the duties, remuneration, etc., of the pastor are in a letter of call attested by the synod bishop; Const., 7.31.10–11: 'standards, policies, and procedures' applicable to pastors.
[162] EELC: Const., Art. 6; LCGB: RAR, The Role of the Dean, 1–2: a Dean is elected at Synod for a 5-year term to exercise the functions of the bishop (except ordinations) in the event of e.g. incapacity.

Many of the same functions are found in the laws of Methodism: whether as presbyters or deacons, ordained ministers are to preach the Word, administer the sacraments and provide pastoral care.[163] These essentials form the basis of ministerial responsibilities in the local church.[164] For example, the Methodist Church in Ireland provides: 'Christ's Ministers in the Church are Stewards in the Household of God and Shepherds of His Flock'.[165] A minister is ordained to the ministry of Word and Sacrament, in full connexion with the Conference and answerable to Synod and Conference in matters of discipline and doctrine.[166] As such, the office of a minister is to: (1) win and watch over souls as one who must give account; (2) feed and guide the congregation by regular and faithful preaching, teaching and pastoral visitation; (3) recognise that the quality of her/his life and witness will determine her/his effectiveness under God; (4) exercise such self-discipline that no offence or occasion to stumble is given to anyone; and (5) act with particular responsibility when her/his actions may be the cause of physical or moral harm to others. Moreover, ministers must: obey reverently the ministers placed in authority over them; attend to all matters of Methodist discipline; meet and confer with the Church Council; regard ministerial colleagues as co-workers in the Gospel and when necessary defend each other's character and reputation; engage in further study, training and professional development as directed by the Board of Examiners;[167] and dress publicly in a manner appropriate to their representation of Christ.[168] Each minister undertakes an appraisal of their work once every 2 years.[169]

---

[163] MCNZ: LAR 3.6: 'A Presbyter shall: (a) exercise a ministry of Word, Sacrament and Pastoral Care; (b) share with the members ... in making disciples, preparing people for membership, Christian ministry, mission and evangelism; (c) enable and ensure that all Leaders' Meeting functions are effectively implemented ... ; (d) [ensure] the keeping of adequate pastoral records; (e) give oversight to person(s) leading worship'; 'A Deacon shall: (a) exercise the particular serving ministry which has been set out in the form of a covenant; (b) [act] under the guidance and oversight of the Parish Superintendent and the Parish Stewards; (c) carry out a ministry ... shaped by the community [they] serve'; 3.7: a Presbyter is Superintendent of the Parish; MCGB: CPD, SO 701.7: deacons share in leadership of pastoral care, worship and mission of the circuit and its churches, collaborating with others, ordained and lay; SO 701.8: deacons account for their servant ministry and support one another in the Convocation of the Methodist Diaconal Order; SO 740–745: presbyters and deacons must uphold the authority of the Conference, attend synod and 'confer together, encourage and watch over one another'; SO 750–754: the Order of Deacons is a 'religious order' reflecting 'the service ministry of Christ'; CPD, Bk. VI, Pt. 10: Rule of Life of the Methodist Diaconal Order; CPD, Bk. VI, Pt. 1, Resolutions on Pastoral Work. See also UMCNEAE: BOD, pars. 132–138, 332–328: elders and deacons; 303–304: living the Gospel; 228: pastors; FMCNA: Man., III: the duties of ordained ministers and pastors; COTN: Man. II and V.II.
[164] MCGB: CPD, SO 700: a pastoral charge in a circuit; MCNZ: LAR, 3.6: 'Ministers appointed by the Conference to a Parish shall carry out ... duties and responsibilities with the local congregation(s).'
[165] MCI: Const., s. 1.   [166] MCI: RDG, 4A.01.   [167] MCI: RDG, 4A.03; CPP (Man., App. 11).
[168] Ibid: 'The Minister has a representative role in the wider community ... It is vital that when in the public eye, Ministers conduct themselves in a manner appropriate to the occasion in terms of behaviour, public speaking and dress code, especially dress for funerals and the conduct of worship.'
[169] MCI: RDG, 4A.05: Accompanied Self Appraisal Scheme (1999); each District Synod must appoint a district appraisal officer and group to conduct appraisals and report annually to the district superintendent.

THE FUNCTIONS OF ORDAINED MINISTERS   99

Any minister appointed to a circuit is responsible to the superintendent of the circuit and must not be involved with another circuit without the invitation of its superintendent.[170] Beyond the local church in the circuit,[171] the circuit superintendent must, typically, oversee circuit discipline, confer with circuit colleagues (as co-pastors) on the affairs of the circuit, instruct and supervise probationers, and admit to and exclude people from church membership (with the local Church Council). The circuit superintendent must also arrange for regular ministerial visitations, keep lists of members received from or removed to other circuits, arrange Congregational and Circuit Meetings and their proper conduct, nominate and oversee local preachers, and ensure that the Baptismal Register, Circuit Schedule Book, Furniture Book and Circuit Register of Members and Classes are maintained, and that collections for Connexional Funds are made at the proper times.[172]

Likewise, in the Reformed churches ordained persons are to preach the Word, administer the Sacraments, provide pastoral care and conduct their lives in a manner compatible with their calling, either as ministers,[173] or as elders and deacons.[174] For example, in the Reformed Church in America, ministers, elders and deacons exercise their 'service representing Christ through the action of the Holy Spirit'. In the local church, the minister: (1) serves as pastor and teacher of the congregation; (2) preaches and teaches the Word of God and administers the Sacraments; (3) shares responsibility with the elders, deacons, and congregation members for their mutual Christian growth; (4) exercises Christian love and discipline with the elders; and (5) endeavours that everything be done in a proper and orderly way; the minister is under the supervision of the classis. Elders have 'supervision of the church entrusted to them': they must study God's Word, oversee the household of faith, encourage spiritual growth, maintain loving discipline, provide for proclamation of the Gospel and celebration of the Sacraments, and oversee the conduct of one another, the deacons and the minister (ensuring e.g. that what is taught accords with Holy Scripture); and they may administer the

---

[170] MCI: Code of Pastoral Practice (Man., App. 11).
[171] MCGB: CPD, SO 522–523; SO 700.9: Superintendent ministers share with other ministers appointed to the circuit the pastoral charge of the circuit and have oversight of all ministers, deacons and probationers.
[172] MCI: RDG, 4A.04; see also Dignity in the Church Policy (Man., App. 13).
[173] URC: Man., A.21: local ministers are ordained and inducted 'to conduct public worship, to preach the Word and to administer the Sacraments, to exercise pastoral care and oversight, and to give leadership to the church in its mission to the world' (stipendiary or non-stipendiary); Sch. F: 'Ministers must conduct themselves and exercise all aspects of their ministries in a manner which is compatible with the unity and peace' of the URC and the affirmation made at ordination and induction; Man., G: the Ministries Committee of the General Assembly is responsible for their pastoral support (including supervision, appraisal, self-evaluation and counselling); Man., K: ministers must have: a 'total commitment to [Christ] and a growing experience of shared life in the Spirit so that worship and service of God becomes the minister's central and controlling passion'; L: 'A minister is called to serve a pastorate, the call being concurred with by the District Council.'
[174] URC: Man., A.23: elders 'share with ministers of the Word and sacrament in the pastoral oversight and leadership of the local churches, taking counsel together in the leaders' meeting for the whole church and having severally groups of members particularly entrusted to their pastoral care'; Schedule B: affirmations made by elders at ordination and induction include acceptance of office and a promise to perform the duties faithfully.

Sacraments. Deacons exercise a particular ministry of service: they receive the contributions of the congregation and distribute them under the direction of the Consistory, attend to the benevolence programme of the church, distribute gifts to the poor, and visit and comfort those in material need.[175]

Presbyterian ministers are also charged to preach the Gospel, administer the Ordinances, provide pastoral care, exercise discipline and give leadership in mission and worship, subject to oversight by the Presbytery; elders and deacons assist in these tasks.[176] The Presbyterian Church of Wales is typical: 'A minister at his/her ordination is set apart by the Church to lead it in this varied ministry by entrusting him/her especially with the preaching of the Word, the administration of the Sacraments, the pastoral care of members and their instruction in the Christian faith and with leading the Church in its work (both missionary and humanitarian) in the local community, the nation and the world.'[177] Elders, along with the minister, have responsibility 'as a team for the life, worship and witness of the local congregation'; they are 'to visit the sick, to teach the young, to guide and support those who are seeking Christ, and to train and encourage believers', and 'to work with their fellow elders and the ministers to build up the body of Christ through all the courts of the Church'.[178] Similar rules operate in the Presbyterian Church of Ireland, with its ministers,[179] teaching elders, ruling elders and deacons (who may function as a committee or board),[180] and, with the same offices, the Presbyterian Church in America.[181] Parallel arrangements exist in the United and

---

[175] RCA: BCO, Ch. I., Pt. I, Art.1; Pt. II, Art. 7: the Classis President oversees minister, elders and deacons.

[176] PCANZ: BO, 8.1–9; 6.9–6.15: an elder exercises a spiritual office, leadership in mission, pastoral oversight of a congregation, participates in church government and is responsible to the church council for these duties.

[177] PCW: HOR, 4.2–4.21: 'There are three particular aspects to the work of the Ministry, the preaching of the Word, the administration of the Sacraments, pastoral work and mission. A Minister is required ... to be of unimpeachable character; to possess a deep experience of the truth of the Gospel.'

[178] PCW: HOR, 2.6; 4.1–4.2: 'those who are ordained are maintained by the whole Church and responsible to it'. See also UFCS: MPP, Ch. 1, s. 1: ruling elders (ordained and inducted by the Presbytery and accountable to it).

[179] PCI: Code, par. 80: 'The special calling of the minister is the ministry of the Word, in public and in private, the conduct of public worship, the administration of the Sacraments, the instruction of the young and the pastoral care of souls'; 82: a minister must not function in another charge without the authority of its minister.

[180] PCI: Code, I.IV, par. 16: 'The Teaching Elder ... preacher, evangelist, teacher, pastor or minister ... is commissioned to preach God's Word, to administer the sacraments ... and to instruct the people, and is set for the defence of the Gospel'; 'The Ruling Elder is ... to watch for souls and to exercise government and discipline in conjunction with the Teaching Elder'; 'Deacons are ... to care for those in need and to manage the temporal affairs of the congregation'; 18: these are entitled to the support and 'esteem' of the congregation which is 'to obey them that have rule over them'; 27: the Moderator is a minister who presides at the Kirk Session.

[181] PCA: BCO, 7: a (male) elder has 'the oversight of the flock of Christ, he is termed bishop or pastor', must be 'grave and prudent, an example to the flock', 'watch diligently over [it] ... that no corruption of doctrine or of morals enter therein', exercise government and discipline, visit (especially the sick), instruct, comfort the mourner, nourish and guard the children, and 'set a worthy example ... by zeal to evangelize ... and make disciples'; 8: a teaching elder expounds the Word, administers Sacraments and reports to Presbytery annually.

Congregational Churches, such as the United Church of Canada,[182] the United Church of Christ[183] and the Uniting Church in Australia.[184]

In Baptist polity, too, the minister is 'pastoral overseer' of a local church, preacher, teacher and administrator, and must ensure that their public and private lives are consistent within their call and prescribed standards: these duties are to be found in the instruments of Unions and Conventions,[185] as well as those of the local church, in which ministerial duties may form part of a church covenant, which itself may present such responsibilities as requirements of Holy Scripture; the minister may also be assisted in these functions by elders, deacons and other officers.[186] In short, the juridical instruments of churches across the Christian traditions indicate clearly the profound theological nexus between separated denominations in terms of the functions of ordained ministers. They also reveal a fundamental convergence in the actions of ordained ministers, not least in terms of common principles of Christian law. All ordained ministers must preach the Word of God, administer the Sacraments and other Ordinances, provide pastoral care and nurture the faithful in the mission of Christ, and lead lives which are consistent with their sacred calling and the standards imposed by the church.

---

[182] UCC: Man., BU, 2.17: 'Every member of the order of Ministry duly settled in a Pastoral Charge shall have the right to conduct services in the church, churches, or other places of worship in connection with the Pastoral Charge; and the right of occupancy of a manse'; BL 061: 'It shall be the duty of the Presbytery to provide an Act of Covenant through which a new relationship is established between an individual and a Pastoral Charge.'

[183] UCOC: Const., Art. VI: 'An Ordained Minister ... has been called by God and ordained to preach and teach the gospel, to administer the sacraments and rites of the Church, and to exercise pastoral care and leadership'; there is 'a covenantal relationship among the Ordained Minister ... the Local Church, and the [UCOC].'

[184] UCA: Const., 15: ministers are 'responsible to a Presbytery and Synod in ... faith and doctrine and to the Presbytery or other appointing body for ... their ministry'; 19: elders 'share with the Minister in oversight'; Regs., 2.4: ministers must preach the Word, preside at the sacraments, witness to the Gospel, equip members, nurture candidates for baptism and confirmation, give pastoral counsel, serve the disadvantaged, attend to administration and report annually to Presbytery; Const., 3: deacons and deaconesses.

[185] BUGB: MTC 2003, 6.1: 'pastoral overseers'; BUNZ: EPGP 2008: the pastor is a preacher, teacher and administrator and must e.g. develop leadership in others, engage in personal study, not engage in paid work (if full-time) without the consent of the church leadership and maintain confidentiality; NABC: Code of Ministerial Ethics 2004: ministers undertake to e.g. live honestly, not seek financial privileges and balance 'family commitments and church duties properly'; BUSA: Model Const., 4.2.4: 'Overseers (who are called Pastors or Elders)' are 'to lead in a spirit of servanthood, to equip and provide spiritual oversight, and Deacons [are] to facilitate the smooth functioning of the Church'; CNBC: Const., VI: pastors and deacons.

[186] Riverside Baptist Church (Baltimore): BL Art. II.1: 'The pastor shall seek to perform with fidelity the ministries of evangelism, stewardship, missions, and teaching; administer the ordinances; and exercise leadership in the church', and is *ex officio* member of all church boards and committees; Bethel Baptist Church (Choctaw): Const., Art. IV.2: 'The duties of pastors and elders shall be those assigned by our Lord and the inspired writers of the New Testament in the following passages' e.g. John 21:15–17; Acts 20:17–35; IV.3: deacons 'assist the pastor by overseeing the temporal affairs of the church according to the example of Acts 6:1–7'; deacons may also function as elders; Central Baptist Church (Pretoria): Const., 15: elders; 16: deacons.

Bishops and archbishops – superintendents and presidents

All the Christian traditions studied here employ an office at regional level in which juridical instruments recognise a ministry of oversight (or *episcope*). In the Catholic, Orthodox and Anglican churches, and in various Lutheran and Methodist churches, the function of oversight vests in the bishop of a diocese or equivalent regional unit. In turn, bishops may be subject to oversight by archbishops or other senior ordained ministers. In Protestant traditions, for some Lutheran and most Methodist churches, and in the Reformed and Presbyterian churches, superintendents and equivalents also function in regional church units beyond the local congregation – and presidents exercise a wider ministry at national level. Such senior ministries beyond the local church are less prominent in Congregational and Baptist churches. What follows proposes that there is juridical equivalence – not exactitude – as between the churches in terms of shared systems of appointment, tenure, and functions.

Bishops: appointment, tenure and functions

In Catholicism, Orthodoxy and Anglicanism, a priest is admitted to the order of bishop by means of election and/or confirmation and consecration; the function of a bishop is to provide oversight of a diocese. For the Roman Catholic Church: 'By divine institution, bishops succeed the apostles through the Holy Spirit who is given to them. They are constituted pastors in the church, to be teachers of doctrine, priests of sacred worship, and the ministers of governance' (if in hierarchical communion with the Pontiff and the other bishops). Bishops entrusted with a diocese are 'diocesan bishops' and others are 'titular bishops', i.e. auxiliary bishops (requested by the diocesan) or coadjutor bishops (imposed), both of whom assist the diocesan.[187] The Supreme Pontiff 'freely appoints bishops or confirms those lawfully elected': candidates may be nominated, for example by the national Episcopal Conference, and there is provision for consultation, for example, with clergy and laity 'outstanding for their wisdom'. The diocesan bishop may propose priests for appointment as an auxiliary bishop.[188] To become a bishop, a person must be at least 35, a priest for at least 5 years, outstanding in faith, good morals, piety, zeal for souls, wisdom and human virtues, and of good esteem – 'the definitive judgment on the suitability of the person' rests with the Apostolic See. Valid consecration is effected by a consecrated bishop who is assisted by at least two other bishops; it confers an indelible character and expresses the fullness of the sacrament of orders.[189] The diocesan bishop is to govern, teach and sanctify: (1) the bishop has all the ordinary, proper and immediate power required for his pastoral office, legislative, executive and judicial; he oversees clerical and lay discipline and the administration of property, and represents the diocese; (2) the bishop must protect and explain the doctrine of the faith, preach frequently and oversee the ministry of Word and catechesis; (3) the bishop must set a personal example of holiness, promote that of the faithful (through e.g. celebration of the sacraments),

---

[187] CIC, cc. 375, 376; c. 403: auxiliaries and coadjutors; c. 409: the latter succeed on a vacancy in see.
[188] CIC, c. 377: every 3 years, the Conference draws up a list of potential candidates.
[189] CIC, cc. 378–380, 1012–1014; LG 21.

celebrate mass regularly, ordain candidates to the priesthood and diaconate, reside in the diocese (for at least 11 months a year), conduct a visitation every 5 years and report on the diocese to the Pope similarly.[190] The diocese is vacated when the bishop dies, resigns or is transferred or deprived; he may resign with papal consent, and at 75 should do so, or if he cannot fulfil his office due to ill health or other serious reason.[191] There are similar provisions applicable to eparchial and other bishops in the Code of Canons of the Oriental Catholic Churches.[192]

Orthodox churches also elect their bishops.[193] They serve to oversee the diocese,[194] may be assisted by assistant bishops,[195] and are subject to ecclesiastical discipline.[196] For example, in the Russian Orthodox Church, in which bishops enjoy apostolic succession,[197] the Holy Synod elects and appoints a bishop to a diocese after confirmation by the patriarch.[198] A candidate must be a monk or unmarried cleric, no less than 30, and distinguished by his 'moral qualification' and theological education.[199] A diocesan bishop is 'the Primate of the Local Church – the diocese – and shall canonically rule it with the conciliar assistance of the clergymen and

---

[190] CIC, cc. 273, 375, 380, 381–399: the bishop visits the Pope in the year of the report.
[191] CIC, cc. 401–402.
[192] CCEO, cc. 178–180; cc. 181–189: election and enthronement; cc. 190–209: functions; cc. 210–211: the patriarch may accept a resignation with the consent of the synod of bishops; cc. 212–218: coadjutors and auxiliaries; cc. 219–233: vacancies; c. 234: the Pontiff may for 'grave and special reasons' commit the governance of an eparchy (occupied or vacant) to apostolic administrators.
[193] UOCIA: Statutes, VII.7–11: the Holy Synod declares the see vacant on the death, retirement, incapacity, transfer or deposition of the bishop; the Prime Bishop appoints a *locum tenens*; consecration/installation (Holy Apostles, c. 1: ordination is by two or three bishops); the candidate must be 35, meet e.g. the requirements of the Holy Canons and may be nominated from monastic or celibate clergy or the laity; the Diocesan Assembly nominates, the Holy Synod elects (with a two-thirds majority); GOAA: Charter, Art. 15; ROMOC: Statutes, Arts. 126–134.
[194] OCIA: GC, Some Considerations on Authority etc – Episcopacy, 1–5: 'The hierarch has direct supervision over all matters in his diocese involving canon law and the spiritual function, rights and duties of the clergy'; UOCIA: Statutes, Art. VII: the bishop has 'full hierarchical authority within his Diocese' to e.g. expound Orthodox faith and morals, issue pastoral letters, ordain, exercise 'pastoral action and discipline over clergy and laity in cases not requiring the action of a Church Court' and visit parishes.
[195] UOCIA: Statutes, Art. VII.5: the bishop nominates a candidate (with agreement of the Diocesan Council) who is elected by Holy Synod; GOAA: Regs., Definition of Terms and Art. 5.6: an auxiliary bishop is 'a hierarch who serves under the authority of the Archbishop or a Metropolitan'; he is nominated by the Eparchial Synod and elected by the Holy Synod of the Ecumenical Patriarchate; ROMOC: Statutes, Art. 131.
[196] ROMOC: Statutes, Arts. 86–89, 126, 130–134: the bishop (elected by Holy Synod after consulting clergy and laity) serves in communion with Holy Synod (as teacher, servant of the sacraments and shepherd), governs in accord with the Holy canons, church statutes and regulations, supervises church life, convenes and presides at eparchial assemblies, represents the eparchy, makes visitations, submits an annual report to Holy Synod, proposes assistant bishops, ordains, fills parish vacancies, and approves sentences of the Eparchial Consistory.
[197] ROC: Statute, X.6: bishops are 'in succession of the authority from the holy apostles'.
[198] ROC: Statute, V.26: election; VIII.9: bishops of self-governing churches are elected by Synod from candidates confirmed by the Patriarch and Synod; see also e.g. Dioc. of Sourozh: Statutes, V.
[199] ROC: Statute, X.7–10.

laymen'; the Holy Synod may also appoint an assistant bishop.[200] The diocesan bishop, *inter alia*: enjoys 'the fullness of hierarchical authority in matters of doctrine, religious rites and pastoral care'; ordains clergy and appoints them to the place of their ministry; consents to decisions of the bodies of diocesan administration; issues pastoral letters to clergy and laity; and submits an annual report about 'the religious, administrative, financial and economic state of the diocese and his own activities to the Patriarch'.[201] In 'governing the diocese' the bishop must: ensure 'the preservation of the faith, Christian morality and piety'; supervise the celebration of the divine services and preserve 'divine beauty'; ensure implementation of decisions of the Councils and Holy Synod; convene and preside over the Diocesan Assembly and Diocesan Council; supervise diocesan institutions, monasteries and clergy; and approve the establishment of new parishes and construction of new churches.[202] The bishop supervises the 'canonical order and church discipline' and exercises 'the right of fatherly influence' over the clergy and laity.[203] A bishop may leave the diocese for a valid reason for not more than 14 days each year without permission from 'the highest church authorities'.[204] The Holy Synod may in exceptional circumstances transfer and retire bishops,[205] and they must retire at 75 by petition to the patriarch.[206] Bishops are also involved in the life of the wider church, for example through membership of its assemblies.[207]

Under Anglican canon law, whilst bishops, clergy and laity share in synodical government, leadership by bishops is fundamental to the polity of a church.[208] Admission to the episcopate is reserved to priests who satisfy such requirements of age, eligibility, suitability, learning, sound mind and good morals as are prescribed by law. A priest enters the order of bishops by consecration administered by three validly consecrated bishops.[209] Election as a diocesan bishop is carried out by an electoral body consisting of representatives of the episcopate, clergy and laity; the election may be challenged to the extent provided by law. The authority to confirm the election of a bishop vests in an archbishop, episcopal assembly or other competent authority. Confirmation is followed by installation in the diocese.[210]

---

[200] ROC: Statute, X: 'If need be, the Holy Synod shall appoint vicar bishops to assist the Diocesan Bishop.'
[201] ROC: Statute, X.11: authority; 12–16: oversight; 16: report; 17: the bishop represents the diocese.
[202] ROC: Statute, X.18; see e.g. Dioc. of Sourozh: Statutes, V.21. See also MOSC: Const., pars. 63–69.
[203] ROC: Statute, X.19; see 27–33: Assembly; 34–44: Council; 45–49: Administration and Institutions.
[204] ROC: Statute, X.23–24.   [205] ROC: Statute, V.26.   [206] ROC: Statute, X.25–26.
[207] ROC: Statute, II.3. See below, Chapter 5.   [208] PCLCCAC, Principle 15.10.
[209] PCLCCAC, Principle 35. See e.g. Melanesia: Cans. A.7.C: a candidate must be a priest over 29; Philippines: Const. Art. V.3: 35 years old; for qualities, e.g. 'competent learning', 'sound mind' and 'good morals', see e.g. Papua New Guinea: Const. Art. 14 and Southern Africa, Can. 7.2; for female bishops, see e.g. Ireland: Const., IX.22: 'Men and women alike may be ordained to the holy orders of deacons, of priests and of bishops.'
[210] PCLCCAC, Principle 36: See e.g. Melanesia: Const., Art. 13: nomination; Wales: Const., V.10–14: Electoral College; TEC: Cans. III.22: the bishops and diocesan standing committees consent to the election; Papua New Guinea: Const., Art. 14: the House of Bishops confirms; Southern Africa: Can. 7: an objection in the Court of Confirmation (episcopal); West Indies: Can. 8.8: consecration; Scotland: Can. 4.41: installation.

BISHOPS, ARCHBISHOPS, SUPERINTENDENTS, PRESIDENTS 105

The diocesan bishop is the chief pastor, minister and teacher of the diocese, a governor and guardian of discipline, and exercises ministry in accordance with law. For example, the bishop must foster the spiritual welfare and unity of the diocese; minister the Word and Sacraments; ensure the worthiness of public worship; preside at the Eucharist; administer ordination and confirmation; and uphold the faith and doctrine of the church. The bishop is also president of the diocesan assembly and must reside in the diocese. A see is vacated on the death, retirement, resignation or removal of the bishop.[211] A designated ecclesiastical authority may appoint a coadjutor bishop to the diocese (with a right of succession on vacancy), and a diocesan bishop may have an assistant bishop (with no right of succession), if this is approved by the designated authority, who may be authorised by the diocesan bishop to undertake such ministry as may be lawfully required or permitted by that diocesan bishop; an assistant bishop is subject to the ordinary jurisdiction of the diocesan.[212] Laws also stress collegiality among bishops and provide for their collective action in episcopal assemblies.[213]

Similarly, Lutheran bishops are elected, set apart and installed, provide oversight of the clergy and laity in a diocese or synod, and their ministry may be terminated on death, incapacity, resignation, retirement or removal.[214] For example, in the Evangelical Lutheran Church in America, the bishop of a synod is elected by the Synod Assembly and installed in office by the (national) Presiding Bishop;[215] election is for a term of 6 years but re-election is possible.[216] A candidate must be 'an ordained minister'. The bishop is to 'preach, teach, and administer the sacraments in accord with the Confession of Faith'. To this end, the bishop: (1) has 'primary responsibility for the ministry of Word and Sacrament in [the]

---

[211] PCLCCAC, Principle 37. See e.g. Papua New Guinea: Const., Art. 14.1: 'the servant of Christ and the servant of all' and 'chief shepherd of souls'; Scotland: Can. 6: the bishop, 'Chief Pastor' with 'charge of the diocese', in which he must reside, is 'to teach and uphold sound and wholesome doctrine', and act as 'principal minister of the Word and Sacraments'; TEC: Cans. III.24.5 and West Indies, Can. 9.3: issuing pastoral letters on doctrine, worship and discipline. For retirement, resignation and removal, e.g. Southern Africa: Can. 14.3: retirement at 70; Scotland: Can. 7.1: resignation is offered to the primate; Ireland: Const. VI.30: removal for incapacity after enquiry by the General Synod; Nigeria: Const. Ch. VIII: removal for indiscipline (e.g. heresy).

[212] PCLCCAC, Principle 38. See e.g. TEC: Cans. III.25: a coadjutor with right of succession; Canada: Can. XVII.2: a coadjutor is 'subject to the jurisdiction of the bishop of the diocese'; Southern Africa: Cans. 8.3 and 10: the Synod of Bishops may grant or withhold their permission for appointment of a suffragan who holds the commission of the diocesan bishop; for assistant and auxiliary bishops, see e.g. Wales: Const., V.15.

[213] PCLCCAC, Principle 15.11: 'Collegiality amongst bishops is fundamental to ecclesiastical polity.' See e.g. TEC: Cans. III.14.2: the House of Bishops may issue pastoral letters to be read by clergy in their congregations.

[214] LCGB: RAR, Role of the Bishop, 1–3: the bishop (elected by simple majority at Synod, consecrated by other bishops, and in office for 6 years) is to e.g. ordain, ensure clergy are appointed to pastoral vacancies and maintain collegiality with other Lutheran bishops; ELCIC: ABL, Pt. V.4.

[215] ELCA: Const., Ch. 10.31; Const. for Synods, Ch. 9: the process includes the use of special majorities.

[216] ELCA: Const., Ch. 10.31; Const. for Synods, Ch. 8.50–57: the bishop may be re-elected. If absent for an 'extended period', the bishop may, with the consent of the Synod Council, appoint an acting bishop.

synod and its congregations'; (2) provides 'pastoral care and leadership' for the synod, its congregations and ordained ministers; (3) ordains, commissions (as ministry associates) and consecrates (as deacons and deaconesses) approved candidates, and attests letters of call from congregations and installs pastors; (4) leads in mission and unity, presides at the Synod Assembly and administers processes as to the discipline of ordained ministers and congregations; and (5) consults with fellow bishops, liaises with the Lutheran World Federation and acts as chief ecumenical officer of the synod. The bishop may have such assistants as the synod authorises.[217] Ministry is terminated by death, resignation, retirement or removal.[218] There are provisions to prevent conflicts of interest arising in episcopal ministry,[219] and for synodical bishops to confer together in the Conference of Bishops.[220] Similar arrangements apply in relation to the bishops of the United Methodist Church.[221]

District presidents, superintendents and moderators

Protestant churches have broadly equivalent offices, to provide oversight of their own regional church units beyond the local church, in the form of, for example, district presidents, superintendents and moderators. The churches differ to the extent that in some these officers perform exclusively governmental and pastoral functions, and in others they perform these functions as well as 'sacramental' functions (such as ordination). For example, the Lutheran Church Missouri Synod is divided into districts with geographical boundaries determined by the Synod.[222] The officers of the district include the district president and vice-presidents elected by the district.[223] District presidents exercise 'supervision over the doctrine, life, and administration of office of the ordained and commissioned ministers of their

---

[217] ELCA: Const., Ch. 10; Const. for Synods, Ch. 8.01–16.01.
[218] ELCA: Const. for Synods, Ch. 8.22–23: on the death, resignation or disability of the bishop, the Synod Council arranges cover until, with temporary disability, the bishop resumes duties or a new bishop is elected.
[219] ELCA: Const., Ch. 10.32: these deal with e.g. personal nexus between the bishop and others.
[220] ELCA: Const., Ch. 15.31.A07.a-I: the Conference of Bishops provides 'opportunities for worship, spiritual renewal, and theological enrichment for those elected to the office of bishop of a synod, the presiding bishop' (and other designated offices); ELCIC: ABL, Pts. X–XII: the Conference of Bishops (the national bishop (convenor) and synod bishops) meets annually e.g. to attend to the spiritual and collegial nurture of its members, develop strategies for pastoral leadership, and recommend policy and practice to the National Church Council.
[221] UMCUSA: Const., Div. 3, Art. I, Div. III, Art. II; see also UMCNEAE: BOD, par. 45, 401–413: e.g. election by Conference, the ministry of oversight, termination of ministry. See also FMCNA: BOD, par. 200, 220: the General Conference elects bishops; 4100–4420: bishops function as 'overseers'.
[222] LCMS: Const., Art. XII.1; XII.2: 2. This Constitution is also the constitution of each district of the Synod; however, each district is at liberty to adopt such bylaws and resolutions as it deems expedient for its conditions, provided that such bylaws and resolutions do not conflict with the Constitution and Bylaws of the Synod.
[223] LCMS: Const., Art. XII.5: the election and time of service of the district officers is determined by the Constitution and Bylaws of the Synod; 6: all officers of the districts have the same rights and duties as those outlined in the Constitution for the officers of the Synod but only insofar as these apply to the district.

district and acquaint themselves with the religious conditions of the congregations of their district'; to this end, 'they shall visit and, according as they deem it necessary, hold investigations in the congregations'.[224] They may 'suspend from membership ordained and commissioned ministers for persistently adhering to false doctrine or for having given offense by an ungodly life'.[225] They must ensure that 'all resolutions of the Synod which concern the districts are made known to the districts and are carried out by them'; they must also submit an annual report of their administration to the president of the Synod and permit him to obtain all necessary insight into their official activities. District presidents perform, either in person or by proxy, 'the ecclesiastical ordination of candidates for the ministry assigned to their districts and their installation', as well as the installation of candidates to the office of schoolteacher and of all ministers and teachers called by the congregations in their districts, and sign examination papers, certificates of ordination and 'all official papers and documents of their district'.[226]

Methodism employs the concept of 'superintendence' for the oversight of a district (which consists of circuits of local churches). The Methodist Church in Ireland is typical. The district superintendent must: (1) exercise 'pastoral responsibility for the ministers and their families' within the district, and, when a situation arises which might lead to the resignation or dismissal of a minister, appoint another person with appropriate skills to undertake the pastoral role of that minister; (2) arrange for the holding of the Synods of the district, preside over their deliberations, and ensure that their business is duly transacted; and (3) exercise careful supervision of the circuits under their 'jurisdiction' and visit the circuits for 'the promotion of peace and order, and to the faithful and judicious execution of the Church's discipline' – where the case is sufficiently serious, the district superintendent is to confer with the District Advisory Committee, and decide what action is necessary, which includes reporting the matter to the President's Advisory Committee to obtain its sanction for such action as may be considered necessary. District superintendents meet annually for mutual consultation.[227] Similarly, in the Methodist Church in Great Britain, each district has a chair who is a minister in active service, elected by the Conference and appointed for a renewable term of 6 years 'to further the work of God in the District'. The district chair must use 'all the gifts and graces [he] has received' in order 'to be a pastor to the ministers, deacons and probationers and to lead all the people of the District in the work of preaching and worship, evangelism, pastoral care, teaching and administration'. The chair presides over the District Synod, and, with its members, is responsible to the Conference for 'the observance within the District of Methodist order and discipline'. It is also 'the duty of the Chair to exercise oversight of the character

---

[224] LCMS: Const., Art. XII.7: their assistants in this work are the circuit counsellors.
[225] LCMS: Const., Art. XII.8: in accordance with the procedure in the Bylaws of the Synod.
[226] LCMS: Const., Art. XII.9.
[227] MCI: RDG, 9.15–9.19. See also COTN: Man., IV.II.E: the District Assembly elects the district superintendent who is e.g. to: 'organize, recognize and superintend local churches' as to 'spiritual, financial, and pastoral matters'; advise churches in 'an unhealthy, declining situation' and address this with the approval of the District Advisory Board and general superintendent; schedule regular church–pastoral review; consult the church board on nomination of an elder or licensed minister and approve this with the consent of the District Advisory Board; approve licences; investigate complaints against ministers; and appoint interim pastors.

and fidelity of the ministers and . . . probationers in the District', and to visit annually the circuits of the district or arrange for a circuit superintendent to do so.[228]

By way of contrast, in the Presbyterian tradition, the Presbytery exercises oversight ('similar in some ways to that exercised by a bishop'), spiritual leadership and encouragement to the ministers, office-holders and congregations within the bounds of the Presbytery; normally, the Presbytery elects a moderator from amongst the ministers, elders and deacons of the Presbytery to hold office for 1 year and to call the meetings of the Presbytery.[229] For example, in the Presbyterian Church in New Zealand, the Presbytery elects the moderator (and terminates the term of office) to constitute, preside over and generally direct the business of the meetings of the Presbytery, to ensure due order and efficiency, to 'exercise pastoral oversight over members of the presbytery' and to perform such other functions as prescribed in the Book of Order. If the position of moderator falls vacant (through death, transfer or other reason), the most recent former moderator assumes the duties, and if that person is unavailable, the functions are assumed by the Moderator of the General Assembly. If the moderator is an elder, the Presbytery may authorise the moderator to administer the sacrament of Holy Communion, and officiate at ordinations and inductions (including laying-on-of-hands); the elder moderator must be trained.[230] Similar functions are performed by presidents in Reformed Churches,[231] moderators in Congregational Churches (e.g. in the United Congregational Church in Southern Africa, the Moderator of the Regional Council

---

[228] MCGB: CPD, DU 42(a); SO 420–426; see also SO 545(4)(*a*) and 574: the involvement of the chair in various appointments; SO 1110(4): the chair may act as 'local complaints officer'. See also SO 754: the Warden of the Methodist Diaconal Order, acting in conjunction with the Convocation, is responsible for the oversight of the character and fidelity of the deacons and diaconal probationers.

[229] CSCL: 97–99; see Act VIII 1996; PCA: BCO, 13: the Presbytery receives, examines and licenses candidates for 'holy ministry', and receives, dismisses, ordains, installs, removes and judges ministers; PCI: Code, 64: the Presbytery elects its moderator; 72: has oversight and election of ministers (189–195); receives, sustains or refuses calls from congregations (196); ordains and installs/inducts and appoints ministers to charges (204–206); commissions/appoints deaconesses, lay agents and missionaries (201–203); receives resignations of ministers (App. 4); determines whether a minister has abandoned a charge (220); and receives resignations of ruling elders (33); see also 73: it ensures that ministers preach the word faithfully, visit families and the sick, promote peace, ruling elders discharge their duties, ministers do not accept paid appointment (unless occasional) without its consent; 74: enquires into and deals with complaints; PCW: HOR, 3.3: the moderator of an Association of churches is elected by the Association (by secret ballot) from the elders every 3 years and holds office for 1 year; UFCS: MPP, Ch. 4: the Presbytery provides oversight of the local church and elects its moderator to constitute, preside and have a casting vote at, and conclude its meetings, and administers discipline.

[230] PCANZ: BO, 8: the Presbytery oversees worship and mission and provides the link between congregations.

[231] URC: Man., B.2 and C.7: the moderator of a Synod (a minister appointed by General Assembly for a 7-year term) must 'stimulate and encourage the work of the [URC] within the province or nation', preside over Synod meetings, 'exercise a pastoral office towards the ministers', nominate ministers to vacant pastorates, preside at ordinations and/or inductions of ministers and commissioning and/or inductions of church-related community workers, and submit an annual report to General Assembly; RCA: BCO, Ch. I, Pt. II, Art. 12: the Classis provides 'supervision' of local ministers; see also Art. 7: the President of the Classis.

is responsible for the 'general spiritual well-being of the Council', counsellor to local churches, presides at ordinations and inductions held at local churches, and has a right of access to local churches)[232] and to a lesser extent presidents of associations in some Baptist Unions.[233]

Metropolitans and archbishops

As we have already seen, Catholic, Orthodox and Anglican dioceses are gathered in provinces or other similar territorial units, usually at national level. Each such unit has a senior bishop, typically a metropolitan or archbishop to exercise a general oversight of that unit. Their particular style, appointment and functions depend on the tradition and polity in question. Nevertheless, the similarities between the laws are a unifying force across the traditions in terms of common action. In the Roman Catholic Church, the metropolitan or archbishop (designated as such by the Pope) presides over an ecclesiastical province to ensure that the faith and discipline of the dioceses in the province entrusted to him are preserved and to inform the Pontiff of abuses. The metropolitan: must visit a diocese if the diocesan bishop neglects to do so; may suggest candidates to become bishops; convokes, presides at and dissolves the provincial council; and makes arrangements for a diocese if the bishop is impeded or prohibited from exercising office.[234] Similarly, in the Oriental Catholic Churches, the patriarch presides over a province within a patriarchal church; he is obliged to: ordain and enthrone bishops of the province; convoke the metropolitan synod (at times fixed by the patriarchal synod of bishops) and preside over, suspend or dissolve it; erect the metropolitan tribunal; exercise vigilance over the faith and discipline; conduct a canonical visitation (if the eparchial bishop neglects to do so); and represent the province in all its legal affairs.[235]

Parallel arrangements are found in Orthodox churches. Three examples may be offered. In the Romanian Orthodox Church, the metropolitan is elected by the Holy Synod as 'the canonical leader of a metropolitan See' to: convene and chair the Metropolitan Synod and chair the Holy Synod when it elects bishops; ordain (with other hierarchs) bishops; appoint bishops *locum tenens*; and pay brotherly visits to bishops.[236] In the Russian Orthodox Church, the primate of a self-governing

---

[232] UCA: Const., 14: the Presbytery oversees ministers; Regs., 3.5.13–17: the Moderator of Synod (a regional body which oversees Presbyteries) is elected by Synod for up to 3 years e.g. to: 'give general and pastoral leadership to the Ministers and people within [its] bounds'; assist and encourage mission and witness; counsel so that 'the life of the Church expresses the faith, the policies, standards and procedures to which it is committed'; preside at Synod; fill vacancies in offices between Synod meetings, interpret Synod decisions; speak on public issues on behalf of Synod; administer discipline and enquire into any grievance which 'adversely affects the good name of the Church, or the order and peace of its Congregations or the progress of the work of God, and to seek a remedy for such situations'; see also UCCSA: Const., 4.4.5.

[233] BMPP: 233: Suggested Const. for an Association, Art. VI: Association officers include the Moderator, elected to preside at Association meetings, report annually on its affairs and supervise its work.

[234] CIC, cc. 415, 435–438, 442, 467.

[235] CCEO, c. 133; cc. 134–139: commemorating metropolitans; cc. 151–154: major archbishops (metropolitans of archiepiscopal churches); cc. 155–163: metropolitans of metropolitan churches.

[236] ROMOC: Statutes, Art. 114: functions; 129: election by the Holy Synod; 133: enthronement; 134: vacancy.

church is elected by its Council from a list of candidates approved by the patriarch and the Holy Synod and takes office on confirmation of the election by the patriarch; the primate is bishop of his own diocese and head of the Council in the rank of metropolitan or archbishop.[237] In the Greek Archdiocese of America,[238] election of the archbishop is 'the exclusive privilege and the canonical right of the Holy Synod'; the Eparchial Synod nominates a candidate who must be, for example, a Greek Orthodox Christian of 'deep faith and ethos', able in administration and pastoral work, committed to unity within the Archdiocese and its unity with the Ecumenical Patriarchate, and not less than 40 years old.[239] The archbishop is Primate of the Archdiocese, President of the Eparchial Synod and Exarch of the Ecumenical Patriarch of Constantinople; his 'rights and responsibilities' include: to exercise 'the rights and duties designated for his office by the Holy Canons'; with the Eparchial Synod, to oversee the 'canonical and orderly functioning, life, governance and activities' of the Archdiocese; to report annually to the Ecumenical Patriarchate; to oversee his own Archdiocesan district and the metropolises; to ordain metropolitans and install them in their eparchies; to support fellow hierarchs 'in a brotherly manner'; and to represent the Archdiocese and Ecumenical Patriarchate *vis-à-vis* ecclesiastical and civil authorities. On a vacancy, the member of the Eparchial Synod first in order of seniority of episcopal ordination acts as *locum tenens* by designation of the Ecumenical Patriarchate until the election of a new archbishop.[240]

Within Anglicanism, the principal office in a province is that of archbishop or presiding bishop, an office to which metropolitical authority customarily attaches and to which a person is admitted by election or other process involving the representative participation of that church. A vacancy in the office occurs on death, resignation, completion of the term, retirement or removal. A principal bishop: exercises authority and leadership over the province; convenes and presides at its legislative and episcopal assemblies; oversees the episcopacy; exercises visitatorial and judicial functions assigned to that office; represents the province in its external relations; and enjoys precedence over the bishops of the province.[241] In turn, an archbishop or bishop may also be assigned to the office of primate or other such

---

[237] ROC: Statute, VIII.4–7; V.4: prescribed metropolitans are members of the Holy Synod; IX: an exarch (of dioceses in an exarchate) is elected by Holy Synod and appointed by the patriarch.

[238] GOAA: Regs., Definition of Terms, 'Hierarch': 'The Archbishop for the Direct Archdiocesan District, Metropolitan for a local Metropolis, or Auxiliary Bishop who serves under the authority of either.'

[239] GOAA: Charter, Art. 13; Regs. Art. 5.6.

[240] GOAA: Charter, Art. 4–5; Regs., Definition of Terms and Art. 3. See also UOCIA: Statutes, Art. IV. 1–2: Major archbishops have 'shared primacy, being equals among equals'; they are: 'the Chief Shepherds of the Church'; with the prime bishop they 'supervise the internal and external welfare of the Church' and represent it; they consecrate and distribute Holy Chrism; convene their Sobor, Holy Synod and Council; issue pastoral letters to bishops, clergy and laity; report to the General Sobor; advise brother bishops and if necessary submit their cases to the Holy Synod; and provide pastoral guidance and 'where necessary pastoral intervention'; Art. IV.3–4: the office is vacated by vote of the Holy Synod on death, retirement, medically certified incapacity or 'deposition by due canonical process' for e.g. heresy or 'proven immorality'; a new major archbishop is elected by the Holy Synod: the Sobor nominates by secret ballot; the prime bishop approves the election.

[241] PCLCCAC, Principle 39. See e.g. Uganda: Const., Art. 10: candidates must be at least 50; South East Asia: Const., Art. 1: the central assembly elects; Sudan: Const. Art. 18: the archbishop is

presiding office in a national, regional or provincial church. Again, this is by election or other lawful process which involves the representative participation of that church. A primate is responsible for general leadership in initiating, developing and implementing the policy and strategy of a church, represents it in its dealings with other churches, and national and international bodies, and has such other functions and jurisdiction as are prescribed by law. A primate holds office for such term as is prescribed by law.[242]

Lutheran churches also have archbishops or presiding bishops.[243] For example, the Evangelical Lutheran Church in America has a presiding bishop elected by the Churchwide Assembly (to a 6-year term) who 'shall be a teacher of the faith of this church and shall provide leadership for the life and witness of this church'. The presiding bishop, who must be an ordained minister, male or female, is *inter alia*: (1) to be the president, chief executive officer and 'primary representative' of the church; (2) to prepare the agenda for and preside at the Churchwide Assembly, Conference of Bishops and other bodies; (3) to provide leadership and care for the bishops of the synods; (4) to direct the work of the executive and appoint members to and advise prescribed committees; and (5) to preside at the installation to office of bishops.[244] Provision exists for the death, inability, resignation, retirement[245] and discipline of the presiding bishop.[246] There is also a vice-president who must be a lay person.[247] Ordained ministers who function as president of the Lutheran Church in Australia are similarly elected: (1) to provide spiritual leadership for

---

elected for 10 years but must retire at 70 and may resign or be removed e.g. for 'inability' or 'misbehaviour'; England: Can. C17: the archbishop has throughout the province 'metropolitical jurisdiction', acts as 'superintendent of all ecclesiastical matters', must 'correct and supply the defects of other bishops', is 'principal minister', presides over the provincial convocation, is chief consecrator at episcopal consecrations and on a vacancy in a diocese acts as 'the guardian of the spiritualities'; West Indies: Const. Art. 2: the archbishop is 'the focus of Provincial unity' and exercises 'Metropolitical authority as determined by this Constitutions and Canons'.

[242] PCLCCAC, Principle 40. See e.g. TEC: Const., Art. 1, Cans. I.2: the General Convention elects a presiding bishop for 9 years to act as 'the Chief Pastor and Primate', responsible to: lead in initiating, developing and implementing the policy and strategy of the church; 'speak God's Word to the Church and to the world' as the representative of the church 'and its episcopate in its corporate capacity'; ensure adequate episcopal services are provided when a diocese is vacant; take order for the consecration of bishops; convene and preside over the House of Bishops, preside over the General Convention, recommend legislation, visit every diocese and issue pastoral letters; Scotland: Can. 3.1: the Primus is elected by the Episcopal Synod; England: Can. C17: 'the Archbishop of Canterbury is styled Primate of All England and Metropolitan': the Crown appoints.

[243] EELC: Const., Art. 6: 'The archbishop as the highest ranking pastor governs the whole [EELC]'; the subordinate bishop carries out orders of the archbishop.

[244] ELCA: Const., Ch. 13.21–22 and Ch. 10.80–81; ELCIC: Const., Art. XIII.1–5: 'This church shall be served by a [national] bishop ... its chief pastor and chief executive officer' and (for a 4-year term) e.g. serves as its leader and counsellor; preserves its peace and order; convenes and presides at its conventions and National Church Council; speaks publicly on its behalf; oversees its officers; and convenes meetings of synod bishops.

[245] ELCA: Const., Ch. 13.60–61: if the presiding bishop dies, resigns, or is unable to serve, the vice-president must convene the Church Council to arrange for discharge of the duties of the presiding bishop until the election of a new one at a special meeting of the Churchwide Assembly or until the incapacity ceases.

[246] ELCA: Const., Ch. 20.53.   [247] ELCA: Const., Ch. 13.30–32.

the national church, to preach, teach and administer the Sacraments (consulting the congregation and pastor concerned) and to promote spiritual welfare and preserve peace and order; (2) to exercise oversight over the doctrine and practice of district presidents, pastors, congregations and their officers, ensure the pastoral care of pastors (with or through the district presidents), ordain candidates, and install district presidents and all those elected or called to spiritual offices; and (3) to represent the church, preside over and report to the General Synod, supervise execution of its resolutions, attend District Synods, and preside at the General Church Council and its Executive.[248]

Presidents and moderators

Oversight beyond regional level is performed in the Methodist, Reformed, and Baptist traditions by presidents and moderators. In Methodism, each Conference has a president with general functions of oversight.[249] For example, in the Methodist Church in Great Britain, the president of the Conference must be a minister and is elected by the Conference (designated at the previous Conference by ballot and by a clear majority of the votes cast) to hold office for one year.[250] The presidency 'plays a significant part in the oversight and leadership of the Church in responding to God's Spirit and developing prophetic vision'. The president presides at the Conference; stations ministers on the death etc. of a minister or probationer;[251] exercises 'a ministry through visits to and encouragement of the constituent parts of the Connexion and beyond';[252] may assist at any Synod, if requested to do so by the Chair or by a majority of the superintendents in the district; and, if requested to do so, visit any circuit, to inquire into its affairs and to take any steps judged beneficial.[253] However, in the Methodist Church in New Zealand, the president of the church exercises 'leadership through service, and as the chief Pastor of the Church guards its faith and discipline, supports its work and mission, has a prophetic voice in its pursuit of justice, and shares in the administrative work of the Church as authorised'; the president presides at Conference. A candidate must be a church member (presbyter, deacon or lay person) familiar with its polity and discipline and is elected at the Conference to hold office until he resigns or dies, is incapable of acting or is succeeded in office. The president functions as 'a focus of service and leadership throughout the Church, exercising prophetic,

---

[248] LCA: Const., Art. VIII.1: election and qualifications; BL, VIII.B and F: functions; BL VIII.B.2: Vice-President; Const., Art. VIII.4: the College of Presidents consists of the president, vice-president and district presidents 'to provide leadership, oversight and guidance to the Church', and e.g. to: give special attention to doctrine, worship and life; support the president; encourage mission and 'strive for unity, harmony and good order in the Church'. See also LCMS: Const. Arts. X–XI: the president provides 'ecclesiastical supervision'.

[249] MCI: RDG, 6.14-22. See also COTN: Man., IV.III: G: the general superintendents are elected by General Assembly e.g. to: 'have general supervision of the Church of the Nazarene, subject to the law and order as adopted by the General Assembly'; preside over General Assembly; 'ordain, or appoint others to ordain, in connection with the ordained ministers present, those who have been duly elected to be elders or deacons'; and appoint district superintendents between district assemblies; I: The Board of General Superintendents.

[250] MCGB: CPD, DU 26. The vice-president is a lay member and is elected similarly (ibid., 27).
[251] MCGB: CPD, DU 28-29.   [252] MCGB: CPD, SO 110.   [253] MCGB: CPD, SO 111.

priestly and pastoral functions, and carrying out administrative tasks' as are required by the instruments of the church.[254]

Each Presbyterian Church has a moderator elected by and appointed to preside over its central assembly and perform such functions as are prescribed by the regulatory instruments of the church in question; generally, the functions of the moderator are in the sphere of church governance.[255] Similar arrangements are to be found in Reformed Churches: for example, in the United Reformed Church in Great Britain, two moderators of the General Assembly are elected by secret ballot on the nomination of a synod – one is a minister or church-related community worker and the other is an elder.[256] Furthermore, in the Uniting Church in Australia, the president of the Assembly is elected by it and installed in an act of worship: 'The responsibilities of the president shall be to give spiritual leadership and encouragement to the Church generally, to represent the Church as appropriate, to give counsel as occasion requires and to do such other things as may be requested or advised by the Assembly'; Presidential Rulings issued on request from any member of the Assembly or Synod moderator (e.g. as to the interpretation of an Assembly resolution) are binding until confirmed, varied, modified, rescinded or overruled by the Assembly; there is no duty to give a ruling if the president considers this not in the interests of the church, the ruling is requested as to hypothetical circumstances or there is a genuine dispute as to the material facts of which the ruling is sought; if unavailable the ex-president functions as president.[257] Baptist Unions, Conventions or analogous entities also have presidents, directors or moderators with limited functions due to the autonomy of each member church.[258] In short, whatever title is applied to the office, all traditions have senior ministers within and beyond their regional units who exercise a general oversight of the life of the regional or wider unit.

---

[254] MCNZ: LAR, s. 7: the President's Legal Adviser is a barrister or solicitor.

[255] PCW: HOR, 3.4.3.5: the moderator is elected from the association in three provinces and admitted at a service for installation at which the person is given the Assembly Bible 'as sign of [his] authority'; App. A: the moderator holds office for 1 year; chairs meetings of the General Assembly and directs its proceedings; is member of every Board; and visits Presbyteries and Associations by invitation; see also PCI: Code, pars. 99–100; UFCS: MPP, Ch. 5, s. 2; PCANZ: BO 14: the 'duties' of the moderator are to preside over all meetings of the Assembly, preserve order, open sittings with prayer, take votes and announce results.

[256] URC: Man., C.3; see C.4 for the General Secretary and c. 5 for the Clerk of Assembly.

[257] UCA: Regs., 3.6.9–3.6.15; see also UCC: BL 430–431.

[258] BUGB: Const., 2.3: the vice-president is elected annually, becomes the president elect for 1 year and takes office as president at the annual Assembly; JBU: Const., Art. VI: the president, vice-president and general secretary; BUS: Const., IX: core leaders include the general director, ministry advisor and mission advisor; BL VIII: their functions are agreed by Council; CNBC: BL 25: the president, first vice-president and second vice-president and national ministry leader are elected by Annual Convention for one year; 37: the president chairs the meetings of the Convention, is (94) *ex officio* member of Convention boards, and may be removed by the Board by a 75% vote; ABCUSA: SR 15: President; TCOR, VIII.11: the general secretary is 'chief administrative officer' and implements General Board 'policy decisions'; NABC: Const., 5: the moderator chairs the Triennial Conference, General Council and Executive Committee; NBC: Const., Art. V: the president is elected by Convention as (BL 5) 'chief executive officer'; BUSA: BL 4.

Pontiffs, patriarchs, primates and presidents

At the international level, Christians may have offices to which attach either a coercive or a persuasive authority over churches within the particular tradition. In Catholicism, the Pope exercises coercive jurisdiction and acts as a governor, teacher and sanctifier. Supreme authority in the Catholic Church vests in the Roman Pontiff (successor of Peter) and College of Bishops (successors of the apostles) united together in one.[259] He is head of the College of Bishops, Vicar of Christ and pastor of the universal church on earth; by virtue of his office, the Pope has 'supreme, full, immediate and universal ordinary power in the Church, and he can always freely exercise this power'.[260] As supreme pastor, the Pontiff 'is always joined in full communion with the other bishops and indeed with the whole Church'.[261] The College of Cardinals elects the Roman Pontiff in accordance with norms of special law and may be called upon to assist the Pontiff in the care of the universal church.[262] Whilst subject to the authority of the Pontiff, the patriarchs of the Oriental Catholic Churches may also exercise an international jurisdiction over the faithful of each church dispersed around the world; a patriarch is 'a bishop who has power over all the bishops including metropolitans and other Christian faithful of the Church over which he presides';[263] he is elected in the synod of bishops of the patriarchal church.[264] Amongst the powers of a patriarch are: to issue decrees, encyclicals and other orders; to explain doctrine, foster piety, and correct abuses; to carry out pastoral visitation of eparchies; to erect and suppress provinces, exarchies and eparchies (with the consent of the synod of bishops and after consulting Rome); to ordain and enthrone metropolitans and other bishops; to receive 'due obedience' from bishops to whom he is to show 'due reverence' and 'fraternal charity'; and to manifest hierarchical communion with the Pontiff through fidelity, reverence and obedience.[265] The patriarchal see is vacant on the death or

---

[259] CIC, c. 330: 'Just as, by the decree of the Lord, Saint Peter and the rest of the Apostles form one College, so for a like reason the Roman Pontiff, the successor of Peter, and the Bishops, the successors of the Apostles, are united together in one'; see also CCEO, cc. 43–49: these deal, *inter alia*, with the attributes of the Pontiff (c. 43); the origin, extent and exercise of papal power (c. 45); vacancy of the see and election (cc. 44, 47); sharing in the exercise of primacy (c. 46); names applied to the Roman See (c. 46).

[260] CIC, c. 331: 'The office uniquely committed by the Lord to Peter, the first of the Apostles, and to be transmitted to his successors, abides in the Bishop of the Church of Rome'; c. 332.1: the Pontiff 'acquires full and supreme power in the Church when, together with Episcopal consecration, he has been lawfully elected and has accepted the election'; c. 332.2 deals with resignation. For papal governance, see Chapter 4.

[261] CIC, c. 333.

[262] CIC, cc. 349–359: it has three orders – bishops, priests and deacons appointed freely by the Pontiff.

[263] CCEO, cc. 55 and 56; c. 57: permanent see for the residence of the patriarch, if possible in a principal city from which the patriarch takes his title; c. 58: patriarchs precede all bishops (except the Roman Pontiff); c. 59: all patriarchs are equal but with due regard for the precedence of honour among them.

[264] CCEO, cc. 63–77; c. 67: in the election cc. 947–957 must be observed; c. 71: secrecy must be observed; c. 77: the patriarch exercises his office only after enthronement and the (new) patriarch must not convoke the synod of bishops nor ordain bishops 'before he receives ecclesiastical communion from the Roman Pontiff'.

[265] CCEO, cc. 78–101.

resignation of the patriarch – the synod of bishops may accept the resignation after consulting with the Pontiff unless the patriarch approaches the Pontiff directly.[266]

In the Orthodox tradition, a patriarch may exercise an international jurisdiction.[267] For example, in the Russian Orthodox Church, the Patriarch of Moscow and All Russia is elected by the Local Council, and functions as the head of the Holy Synod, president of the Local Council and convenor (with the Holy Synod) and president of the Bishops' Council. The Patriarch governs the Moscow Patriarchate; approves decisions of the General Ecclesiastical Court and the Holy Synod (subject to referral to the Bishops' Council for final ruling); approves nominations for admission to the office of bishop; receives annual reports from each bishop; appoints a *locum tenens* on a vacancy in See; confers awards; approves the establishment of monasteries (with the Holy Synod); supervises patriarchal administration; and manages the general church funds. The Patriarch may be disciplined by the Bishops' Council for 'dogmatic and canonical deviations'.[268] Similarly, the Ecumenical Patriarchate of Constantinople (to which Greek Orthodox churches worldwide may belong) is presided over by the Ecumenical Patriarch (considered as 'first among equals').[269] However, in the Syrian Orthodox Church of Antioch, 'the Patriarch is the legitimate successor of St. Peter ... the Pontiff who is lawfully elected by', for example, the Catholicos and metropolitans, 'the Supreme Head of the [SOCA], defender of its faith, doctrine, and apostolic traditions, symbol of its unity, its representative ... everywhere ... general supervisor of its affairs, and the spiritual father of all Syrian Orthodox people worldwide. He must be obeyed by the Catholicos, Metropolitans, priests, monks, nuns, deacons and all laity ... His title is Supreme Pontiff'.[270]

By way of contrast, the officers of the global Anglican, Lutheran and Reformed communions exercise no coercive jurisdiction. The Archbishop of Canterbury has no general jurisdiction exercisable over the autonomous churches of the Anglican Communion; he has 'a primacy of honour and respect among the college of bishops

---

[266] CCEO, c. 126; c. 127–131: during a vacancy the senior bishop becomes its administrator.

[267] MOSC: Const., pars. 99–100: the powers of the Catholicos include consecration of Prelates, presiding over the Episcopal Synod, declaring and implementing its decisions, and conducting administration as representative of Synod; 101: the patriarch is 'canonically consecrated with the co-operation of the Catholicos'.

[268] ROC: Statute, I.4, II.2, II.5–6, II.18, III.2, IV.5, V.20, VI.1, VII.23, VIII.9, VIII.17, IX.11, X.16, X.18, X.20, XII.2–3, XIII.2, XV.3. See also ROMOC: Statutes, Art. 24: Primate: 'The Patriarch is the Primate among the Hierarchs' and President of the central deliberative and executive church bodies; 25: title; 26: he convenes and chairs the central bodies; consecrates the Holy Myrrh; represents the patriarchy; addresses pastoral letters; visits hierarchs; ordains with the other hierarchs and enthrones metropolitans; appoints metropolitans *locum tenens* in vacancy of sees; gives 'brotherly advice' to the hierarchs; examines within the Standing Committee complaints against hierarchs; and proposes candidates for assistant bishop; 126–128: election is by secret vote in the Holy Synod after consultation with clergy and laity; 133: enthronement; 134: vacancy.

[269] OOCL: 213–221: the Patriarch (whose titles include Archbishop of Constantinople and of New Rome and Ecumenical Patriarch), has pastoral jurisdiction over the Archdiocese of Constantinople, is elected by the Endemousa Holy Synod (composed of metropolitans) to which is also sent the vote of the *sympsephon*, the Hierarchy of the Throne Abroad (metropolitans outside Turkey).

[270] SOCA: Const., 7, 12–49.

in the Anglican Communion as first among equals (*primus inter pares*)'; thus: 'As a focus and means of unity, the Archbishop gathers and works with the Lambeth Conference and Primates' Meeting, and presides in the Anglican Consultative Council.'[271] The President of the Lutheran World Federation is elected by its Assembly and holds office until the close of the next Assembly (normally 6 years) and is not eligible for a second term – the President is 'the chief official representative and spokesperson of the Federation', presides at the Assembly, Council and Executive Committee, and must 'oversee the life and work of the Federation', in consultation with the Treasurer and General Secretary; the Assembly must act on reports of the President.[272] In the World Communion of Reformed Churches, the General Council elects the president and four vice-presidents; they may approve the agendas for the meetings of the Executive Committee, ensure coherence in the interdepartmental work of the Communion, report for review to the Executive Committee actions which have been taken and oversee the assets of the Communion. The General Secretary is the 'chief executive officer' of the Communion, serves for a term of 7 years (renewable for like term) and is responsible to the General Council and the Executive Committee 'to direct and coordinate the work' of the Communion, and to convene, report, and ensure the proper conduct of the General Council, and supervise the personnel of the Communion and the proper functioning of the secretariat.[273] The President of the Baptist World Alliance has similar international functions.[274]

Conclusion

A comparative study of the juridical instruments of churches in these Christian traditions yields a wide range of principles of Christian law. Ordained ministry is divine in origin. Ordained ministers exist in a variety of grades, from priest to pastor. Candidates for ordination must be called by God and their vocation is tested by the church through a process of selection, examination and training. Candidates must be suitable. They are admitted to their various grades through the rite of ordination administered by competent authority through the laying on of hands and invocation of the Holy Spirit. Ordination cannot be repeated. Ordained ministers are admitted to particular offices either by appointment or other election by competent ecclesiastical authority (such as a bishop or a local church). Their tenure is terminated by death, resignation, retirement or removal. The core functions of ordained ministers in the local church are to preach the Word, administer the

---

[271] TACC: 3.1.4.1; PCLCCAC, 11.4: 'focus of unity'; the Archbishop has limited metropolitical authority in e.g. the extra-provincial dioceses of Puerto Rico, Const., II.5, the Lusitanian Catholic Apostolic and Evangelical Church, Const., Preamble, 7: see CLAC: 344–345.

[272] LWF: Const., Art. VII.1; VIII.1: the President is a member of the Council; VIII.3: the Council elects the general secretary (see also XII) and treasurer (see also X.2); VIII.4: on the death or incapacity of the President, the Council elects a president within three months; X.1: the election and functions.

[273] WCRC: Const., Art. XI; XII: general secretary; XIII: executive secretaries; BL I.B: appointment of Standing Committees; II.D: if the presidency is vacant, the Executive Committee fills it from the vice-presidents.

[274] BWA: Const., VI. See also Asian Baptist Federation: Const., VI: the president elected by General Council.

Sacraments and provide pastoral care. Particular offices may also be held by suitably qualified ordained ministers beyond the local church. Oversight of the regional church is carried out by bishops, superintendents or other ecclesiastical person either elected or otherwise appointed to office with the participation of the laity by means of either consent or consultation. At national level, too, archbishops, metropolitans, presidents and moderators exercise a general oversight over ordained and lay people; in some churches it is jurisdictional and in others it is advisory. Only in the Catholic (Pontiff) and Orthodox (patriarchs) traditions do ordained ministers exercise a coercive international jurisdiction. Within the Anglican, Lutheran and Reformed traditions, archbishops and presidents exercise important global functions of advice, encouragement and admonition, but not coercive jurisdiction. Again, these principles of laws represent unity of action across the Christian traditions irrespective of denominational affiliation with regard to the setting apart, tenure and functions of ordained ministers.

4

The institutions of ecclesiastical governance

The history of Christianity is rich in theological debate about the nature, location and exercise of authority in the church in terms of the forms of ecclesiastical government (or polity). The Reformation in particular stimulated perhaps the most far-reaching doctrinal reappraisal of church polity, largely on the basis of arguments that scripture prescribed patterns of church government different from those rooted in the papacy and bishops of the Church of Rome. With the new institutional churches that emerged from the Reformation, today it is commonly understood that there are three principal forms of church polity – Episcopal, Presbyterian and Congregational – and the merits of each, and whether they fuel Christian disunity, continue to arouse debate amongst contemporary theologians.[1] Certainly, the modern juridical instruments of churches reflect directly different doctrinal postures on church polity arising from distinctive denominational understandings of the nature of the church and the location of institutional authority within it. However, regardless of their particular doctrinal positions on authority and the implications of these for church polity, these juridical instruments also reveal profound similarities between the traditions and denominations within them. All the traditions have four basic levels in their institutional organisation – international, national, regional and local; the traditions differ at each level in terms of the authority to govern vested in these institutions – their jurisdiction (and functions), composition and structures. The instruments also yield shared principles of church governance: the separation of powers; institutional interdependence; subsidiarity (making decisions at the most appropriate level); representation (and the role of the laity in government); and due process (the rule of law). The institutional organisation of legislative and administrative powers is examined here – judicial power, and the courts, tribunals and other institutions which exercise it, is treated in Chapter 5 on ecclesiastical discipline.

An overview of systems of church polity

Each Christian tradition understands that its own system of church polity is either required or permitted by divine law. Across the traditions studied here, governance is exercised through a hierarchical system of international, national, regional and

---

[1] To these, other forms of polity are sometimes added, such as Erastian (churches controlled by the State) and minimalist or non-governmental (such as the Quakers): see C.O. Brand and R.S. Norman (eds.), *Perspectives on Church Government: Five Views of Church Polity* (Boardman and Holman, Nashville, Tennessee, 2004); see also D.A. Boldon, 'Formal church polity and ecumenical activity', 49 *Sociological Analysis* (1988) 293–303.

local institutions. The authority which an institution has at each level varies between the traditions and their doctrinal postures. In some (e.g. Catholicism), the highest authority is an international institution and authority descends to national, regional and local institutions; in others (e.g. the Baptist tradition), authority resides primarily in the local church and ascends to regional, national and international institutions; or else (e.g. Anglicanism) it is located at the national level and ascends to international institutions and descends to regional and local institutions. Nevertheless, whilst they have authority appropriate to their own level, these institutions are interdependent. Also, their composition is determined by theology as to who may possess or participate in the power of governance: an institution may be composed of ordained persons, lay persons or both. However, all the traditions recognise that institutions exercise one or more of three functions in church government: legislative, administrative or executive, and judicial functions which must be exercised according to law. These features of ecclesiastical government are arranged between the traditions as follows.

The Catholic Church has a global 'hierarchical constitution' in which the power of governance (*potestas gubernandi*) belongs to the church by divine institution and vests only in ordained ministers; the laity may co-operate in its exercise but do not possess it.[2] Supreme authority, legislative, executive and judicial, resides in the Pope (and College of Bishops) and is exercisable over the universal church (Latin and Oriental).[3] At national level, the Episcopal Conference (Latin) or Patriarchal Synod (Oriental) may create legislation (which must be approved by the Holy See) and discharge prescribed administrative functions. The particular church, a diocese (Latin) or eparchy (Oriental), is governed by a bishop with legislative, executive and judicial power – legislative power may be exercised in consultation with the diocesan or eparchial synod (composed of ordained and lay people), executive functions are carried out by the diocesan curia (Latin) or eparchial administration (Oriental), with judicial power in a tribunal. A diocese or eparchy consists of parishes, each with its own priest and councils (composed of lay people) which exercise administrative functions.[4] In the Orthodox tradition, no single institution has jurisdiction over all Orthodox churches worldwide. However, there are different

---

[2] CIC, cc. 129–132: it is also called the 'power of jurisdiction'; see also J. Provost, 'The participation of the laity in the governance of the church', 17 *Studia Canonica* (1983) 417; see also CCEO, c. 408.2: lay people are eligible for ecclesiastical *munera* (functions) that do not *per se* 'require sacred orders'.

[3] CIC, c. 135.1–2: 'The power of governance is divided into legislative, executive and judicial power'; legislative power must be exercised in the manner prescribed by law and legislators below the supreme authority may not delegate it unless the law expressly provides; a lower legislator cannot validly make a law contrary to that of a higher legislator; cc. 135–144: executive power may be delegated unless the law expressly provides otherwise; delegation of power includes everything necessary to exercise that power; delegated power lapses on e.g. completion of the mandate, expiry of time, completion of the cases and cessation of the reason for delegation; CCEO, cc. 979–984: the power of governance; cc. 985–987: types of power; cc. 988–990: executive power; cc. 991–993: loss or suspension of power; cc. 994–995: the scope of executive power.

[4] CCEO, c. 11: there are four grades of Oriental church with 'equality in dignity and action'; cc. 55–150: a patriarchal church has a patriarch pre-eminent particularly in executive matters, and a Synod of Bishops with legislative and judicial authority; cc. 151–154: a major archiepiscopal church has a major archbishop and a Synod of Bishops; cc. 155–173: a metropolitan church has a

patriarchates with an international jurisdiction: each is autocephalous (self-governing and with its own head) and consists of autonomous churches (their heads appointed by the patriarchate).[5] Each patriarchate through its patriarch and Holy Synod has such authority over its churches as is consistent with the autocephaly of the patriarchate and the autonomy of those churches. Each church at national level (itself typically divided into metropolises) is governed by a synod of bishops (normally with doctrinal authority) and an assembly representative of bishops, clergy and laity exercising legislative, executive and judicial functions and assisted by various administrative bodies. In turn, a diocese (or eparchy) is governed by a bishop and synod or other assembly (which consists of ordained and elected lay persons) with legislative, administrative and judicial functions. A diocese is composed of parishes each with a priest and council invested with administrative functions.[6]

At international level, the institutions of the worldwide Anglican Communion, Lutheran World Federation, World Methodist Council, World Communion of Reformed Churches and Baptist World Alliance exercise no coercive jurisdiction over their autonomous member churches but co-ordinate their work in matters of common concern on the basis of an authority conferred individually by those member churches. The institutions of the worldwide Anglican Communion (e.g. Anglican Consultative Council) co-ordinate the work of the autonomous churches in matters of common concern but exercise no legislative, executive or judicial power over them – they may guide but cannot oblige.[7] The primary locus of coercive jurisdiction in Anglicanism is the province, typically national and with a metropolitan or archbishop.[8] Leadership and authority are treated as gifts of God and Anglican polity is based on episcopal leadership and synodical government.[9] Each province has a central assembly (General Synod or Council) representative of bishops, clergy and laity, competent to legislate, and assisted by various administrative bodies.[10] In turn, the diocese is governed by an assembly (Diocesan Synod or Council) composed of the bishop, and clerical and lay representatives; it is competent to legislate for the diocese and is assisted by various administrative bodies.[11] A diocese is divided into parishes each with a priest and a council, representing

---

metropolitan and a Council of Hierarchs; cc. 174–176: other churches; cc. 177–310: an eparchy is divided into parishes (cc. 295–296) with a priest and councils.

[5] See Introduction, n. 11.

[6] For a general overview see T. Ware, *The Orthodox Church* (Penguin, London, 1964) 152–199.

[7] PCLCCAC, Principle 11.2: 'the churches ... are bound together, not juridically by a central legislative, executive or judicial authority, but by mutual loyalty sustained through the instruments of Anglican unity'; 11.5: the latter 'enjoy such binding authority within a church as may be prescribed by the law of that church'.

[8] PCLCCAC, Principle 15; see above Chapter 1.

[9] PCLCCAC, Principle 16.1; see also 15.6: 'Each church, province, and diocese has an assembly, namely a synod, council or other body, the function of which is to govern'; 18: 'Representative government is fundamental to church polity, and in matters which touch all, all should have a voice'; 22: 'Lay people are entitled to participate in the governance of a church', subject to conditions as to eligibility and selection.

[10] PCLCCAC, Principle 18.2–4 and 19: the central assembly is organised in 'houses, orders or other cameral systems' (with persons elected/admitted to it); 19: it may legislate for the whole of the church.

[11] PCLCCAC, Principle 20.

the laity, with predominantly administrative functions.[12] Each church also has a system of courts at provincial and diocesan levels but not at parochial level.[13] In Anglican polity, the 'exercise of ecclesiastical governance should be characterised by the Christian virtues, transparency, and the rule of law applied with justice and equity' – and laws should set out clearly the composition and functions of these institutions and the relationship between them.[14]

Lutheran juridical instruments recognise that Christ is the head of the Church and that the exercise of authority is governed by the will of God as revealed in Scripture; moreover, systems of polity are of human not divine institution, and church institutions should be representative and interdependent.[15] At international level, the Lutheran World Federation exercises no legislative authority over the autonomous member churches but simply acts as their 'instrument' and co-ordinates their work in matters of common concern; it does so through an Assembly, Council and Secretariat representative of ordained and lay people.[16] At national level, each Lutheran church has a central legislative assembly (typically a General Synod) composed of ordained ministers and elected lay persons, and assisted by various administrative bodies.[17] At the regional level of dioceses or synods there is an assembly (e.g. Synod Assembly, District Synod or Convention) consisting of the bishop (if the church has bishops), ministers and lay delegates competent to legislate for the region and assisted by administrative bodies. At local level, the regional unit is divided, for example, into parishes and congregations and each has its own autonomy, constitution and assembly (e.g. Church Committee) composed of the minister and lay representatives for the administration of the local unit.[18] Each Lutheran church also has judicial

---

[12] PCLCCAC, Principle 21.   [13] PCLCCAC, Principle 24.
[14] PCLCCAC, Principle 15.12–14; 17: administrative practices must be lawful, competent and courteous, and e.g. consultation and co-operation are key elements of good ecclesiastical administration.
[15] See e.g. LCA: Const., Art. VI.1–3. See also ELCA: Const., Ch. 3: 'This church ... derives its character and powers both from the sanction and representation of its congregations and from its inherent nature as an expression of the broader fellowship of the faithful' (AC, Art. 5); Ch. 4.03, and 5.01ff: the church needs 'structures and decision-making processes ... that foster mutuality and interdependence' and 'involve people in making decisions that affect them'; its institutions act under the 'rule and authority' of Christ in accordance with 'principles' e.g. interdependence, congregational autonomy, lay participation in governance and equality.
[16] LWF: Const., Art. III: 'a communion of churches', it 'helps them to act jointly in common tasks'; IV: it is an 'instrument of its autonomous member churches' which 'may take action in matters committed to it by the member churches'; VI: it exercises 'its functions through' the Assembly, Council, Secretariat and the 'instrumentalities of the member churches'; 'In all these functions ... ordained and lay persons ... shall be eligible to participate'; VII: 'As [its] principal authority', the Assembly is responsible for the constitution and shall 'give general direction to the work' of the LWF; VIII: the Council administers LWF business between Assemblies.
[17] LCA: General Synod; ELCIC: Convention; ELCSA, LCMS, LCGB: Synod. LCA: Const., Art. VI.3: 'The Church ... shall have power and authority to make rules and regulations for the administration of its own affairs' and 'to delegate the exercise of its authority to such persons and in such manner as it may deem advisable'.
[18] LCA: Theses on the Church, 6, 14, 16: a congregation is 'truly *ecclesia*'; Const., Art. VI.7: 'The jurisdiction of the Church over the congregation shall, subject to this Constitution' be used e.g. to uphold the Confession and 'apply discipline'; but 'it shall not include power over the purely internal administration of a congregation'.

bodies.[19] Similarly, the World Methodist Council exercises no legislative authority over its autonomous member churches.[20] Each Methodist church has territorial units at national, regional and local level each with its own representative assembly (or 'court') which exercises 'jurisdiction' and 'oversight', and whose interdependence is expressed in the principle of 'connexionalism'.[21] At local level, typically, classes are grouped into a Society, sometimes styled a 'parish' with a Leaders' Meeting; one or more societies are grouped into a circuit (the administrative body of which may be the Quarterly Meeting of Class and Society officers). Circuits are grouped into districts each administered by a District Synod or other assembly of all ministers and lay representatives of the circuit – the District Synod has no legislative authority but administrative functions and recommends matters to the Conference at national level. The Conference, typically with two Sessions (ministerial and representative) under a president (an ordained minister), has legislative, administrative and judicial authority and is assisted by numerous committees.[22]

Similarly, at international level, the General Council of the World Communion of Reformed Churches co-ordinates the work of the member churches in matters of common concern but exercises no coercive jurisdiction over them by virtue of their autonomy.[23] Each Reformed church has four basic units of government, and each exercises superintendence through legislative, administrative and judicial functions: at the local level the Classis and Consistory (composed of elders), the Regional Synod (ministers and elders) and the General Synod.[24] In turn, the juridical instruments of Presbyterian churches provide that: (1) Christ is the head of the church; (2) Scripture is the only rule of governance; (3) each church has the right to constitute its own form of government; (4) the scriptural form of government is Presbyterian and representative; (5) ecclesiastical 'jurisdiction' is not several but

---

[19] See Chapter 5.
[20] WMC: Const: the Council must convene a World Methodist Conference at least every 10 years; UMCUSA: this church exercises 'global connectionalism and has bishops'.
[21] UMCNEAE: BOD, par. 721: 'Connectionalism', 'a vital web of interactive relations', 'includes the agencies of the church' and 'other units ... within the various levels of Church organization' for 'equipping local churches for ministry and by providing a connection for ministry throughout the world, all to the glory of God'.
[22] MCI: Const., s.5: 'The principal courts of the Church' are Classes, Societies, Circuits, Districts and Conference; MCGB: CPD, DU 1(iv), 40: 'Church Courts' means Conference, Synods, Circuit Meetings, Local Preachers' Meetings, Church Councils and boards appointed by or reporting to them; SO 010: Districts are 'jurisdictions'; COTN: Man., Pt. II: it has 'a representative form of government' and General Assembly.
[23] WCRC: Const., Art. V: the interdependence and participation of all members; Art. VI: membership; Art. VII: the General Council is 'the main governing body' and its decisions are binding on WCRC organisations and activities but those 'involving the life and witness of the member churches are advisory in character'.
[24] RCA: e.g. BCO, Preamble; Ch. 1, Pt. III: government exists 'to aid the church in the development of its own life' and is organised 'according to the presbyteral order'; authority to govern is delegated from Christ and exercised through 'representative governing bodies' at various levels; URC: Man., B.1: Church Meeting and Elders' Meeting (local church); District Council; Provincial or National Synod (e.g. the 'national synod' of the province of Wales); and the General Assembly; each of these four parts has 'consultative, legislative and executive functions' exercisable 'under the Word of God and the promised guidance of the Holy Spirit'.

exercised jointly by the faithful; and (6) no institution may make laws to bind the conscience.[25] Presbyterian churches have a system of courts: typically, the General Assembly (national); Presbytery (regional); and (Kirk) Session (local). The General Assembly consists of representatives from Presbyteries and Sessions and has legislative, administrative and judicial functions. The Presbytery consists of ministers and elders appointed by each (Kirk) Session and it oversees the congregations. A (Kirk) Session, composed of the pastor and (ruling) elders, oversees a congregation (which may also have its own Congregational Meeting or Committee).[26] The United churches, too, have a central Assembly, Synods, Regional Councils, with 'powers and responsibilities', and autonomous congregational assemblies at local level.[27]

The Baptist model of church polity is at the other end of the ecclesiastical spectrum. As the local church is 'the primary expression' of the church universal, so Baptist polity recognises 'Congregational Church Government as the standard Biblical form of government'; it is characterised by 'the independence of the local church, and the advisory nature of all denominational organisations composed of representative churches' above the local level where 'the Church is also expressed in groupings of interdependent congregations in associations, regional units, or national bodies'; these are bound together on the basis of covenants and voluntary co-operation, receiving from each other mutual counsel and correction.[28] The

---

[25] PCA: BCO, Preface, I and 1.5–1.7, and 3.1–3.2: 'every Christian Church ... is entitled to declare ... the whole system of its internal government which Christ has appointed'; 'The scriptural form of church government, which is representative or Presbyterian' consists of the church, members, officers, courts and orders; 'All church power, whether exercised by the body in general, or by representation, is only ministerial and declarative' as Holy Scripture is the ultimate standard; 'No church judicatory may make laws to bind the conscience'; 'Ecclesiastical jurisdiction is not several, but a joint power ... exercised by presbyters in courts. These courts may have jurisdiction over one or many churches, but they sustain such mutual relations as to realize ... the unity of the Church'; the 'scriptural doctrine of Presbytery is necessary to the perfection of the order of the visible Church, but is not essential to its existence'; 'The power ... Christ has committed to His Church vests in the whole body ... rulers and ... ruled ... a spiritual commonwealth'; 'Ecclesiastical power, which is wholly spiritual' is exercised 'severally' (by officers) and 'jointly in church courts' as 'the power of jurisdiction'; PCW: HOR, s. 1: Constitutional Rule; PCI: Code, pars. 10–16: Christ is 'the sole King and Head of the Church' and governs it by his 'Word and Spirit'; church governance is 'both representative and corporate'.

[26] PCANZ: BO, 1.4: Session, Presbytery, and General Assembly; PCA: BCO 10: Church Sessions, Presbyteries, and General Assembly; PCW: HOR, s. III: Courts of the Church: District Meeting, Presbytery, Association, General Assembly; PCI: Code, pars. 19–33, 61–69: a congregation is under the jurisdiction of the Kirk Session, Kirk Session under the Presbytery, and Presbytery under General Assembly; UFCS: MPP, IV.I–III.

[27] UCA: Const., Art. 22: 'The powers and responsibilities of government and administration ... shall be vested in the Congregation, the Presbytery, the Synod and the Assembly'; 25–30: Presbytery; 31–37: Synod; 38–48: Assembly; UCC: Man., s. 3.1: courts; BU, s. 6: presbytery; s. 7: Conference; s. 8: General Council.

[28] ABCUSA: TCOR (1984) Preamble and I: a 'congregation ... to be a faithful witness to the ... universality of the Church, should covenant with other ... congregations regarding cooperative mission and interdependence within the Body of Christ ([to] acknowledge the appropriate limits to its legitimate independence)'; BUS: Const., III.1: 'each Church has liberty, under the guidance of the Holy Spirit, to interpret and administer His laws'.

Congress of the Baptist World Alliance exercises no coercive jurisdiction over the autonomous member unions, conventions and churches.[29] Typically, at national level each Baptist Union or Convention is composed of co-operating churches, associations of churches, and congregations and has a Convention, Assembly or General Assembly which consists of representatives from churches and associations of churches.[30] At regional level an association of local churches has an assembly representative of and competent to make policies for churches in the territory of the association.[31] At local level, the congregation is autonomous – it orders its own affairs but its freedom is not absolute 'since the nature of the body of Christ calls for interdependence between congregations whether in associational, regional, national, denomination-wide, or international expressions of the Church'; it is overseen by pastors and elders and has a general meeting, an executive, and officers.[32]

International ecclesial structures and institutions

The historical migration of Christians from the homelands of their respective traditions to all parts of the world has resulted in the development of international configurations of ecclesial bodies as well as the institutional structures necessary to sustain communion between them. As we have seen, in the Catholic Church (Latin and Oriental) 'supreme authority' vests in the Roman Pontiff and the College of Bishops.[33] The Pontiff, as Vicar of Christ, has 'supreme, full, immediate and universal ordinary power in the Church, and he can always freely exercise this power'.[34] In addition, he has 'the right ... to determine ... whether [his] office is to be exercised in a personal or collegial manner', and '[t]here is neither appeal nor recourse against a judgment or decree of the Roman Pontiff'.[35] The College of

---

[29] BWA: Const., Preamble.
[30] BUGB: Const., I.2: Churches and Associations of Churches; I.7: Assembly; see P. Goodliff, 'Baptist church polity and practice', 168 *Law and Justice* (2012) 5; JBU: Const., Art. VII: General Assembly; NBCUSA: Const., Art. VI: Annual Session of the Convention; BUSA: Const., 8: Assembly; CNBC: BL 3: Convention; ABCUSA: BL Art. 1: National Board, Regional Boards, and Cooperating Churches.
[31] NABC: Const., 3.2: 'Each Association or Region shall establish policies and practices ... in harmony with the Conference Statement of Beliefs' as 'an organisation of Baptist churches in a specific geographic area that have been formally recognised by the Conference'; BUSA: Const., 2: a Territorial Association has ten or more member churches united by a constitution; ABCUSA: BL VI: Regional Organisations and Boards.
[32] ABCUSA: TCOR, I.A-B; JBU: Const., Art. V: the units of the Union are the member churches; the Union recognises 'the autonomous character of each Church in membership'; however, 'strict adherence' must be given to the Rules and Regulations of the Union; Bethel Baptist Church (Choctaw): Const., Art. VI: Congregational Church Government is 'the standard Biblical form of government for the church while acknowledging the oversight of the pastor and the role of elders'; 'In all issues, the decisions of the congregation shall be final, and there is no appeal to a higher authority, the authority of the church being the court of final appeal'; Central Baptist Church (Pretoria): Const., 10-17: General Meeting, Executive, Officers.
[33] CIC, c. 330; CCEO, cc. 43-49: the attributes, origin, extent and exercise of papal power.
[34] CIC, cc. 331-332: see Chapter 3.
[35] CIC, c. 333: papal power is used to reinforce and defend the proper, ordinary and immediate power of bishops in the particular churches; c. 334: the bishops co-operate with the Pontiff in

Bishops exercises power over the universal church in solemn form in an Ecumenical Council: the Pope (as its head) determines how the college exercises its office and he alone summons, presides over, suspends and dissolves, and determines the agenda of, an Ecumenical Council.[36] Council decrees, if confirmed by the Pontiff,[37] are to be observed by all the faithful.[38] The Pontiff also convenes (and presides over) the Synod of Bishops which assists the Pope 'in the defence and development of faith and morals and in the preservation and strengthening of ecclesiastical discipline'; its decisions must be ratified by the Pontiff.[39] In terms of administration, the Pontiff conducts the business of the universal church through the Roman Curia; this is composed of the Secretariat of State or Papal Secretariat, the Council for the public affairs of the church, the congregations, the tribunals and other institutes; their constitutions and competences are defined by special law.[40] Papal legates may also be appointed to represent the Pontiff in particular churches in the various countries and regions of the world or in States.[41]

In Orthodox polity, an autocephalous patriarchate exercises jurisdiction over its local churches across the world.[42] Three examples may be offered. First, the Ecumenical Patriarchate of Constantinople, presided over by the Ecumenical Patriarch ('first among equals'), is governed by a Holy Synod, composed of metropolitans, with jurisdiction over eparchies throughout the world with regard to, for example, the election of bishops and the oversight of monasteries; it also has

---

the exercise of his office; the cardinals also assist the Pope; c. 335: when the Roman See is vacant (or impeded), 'no innovation is to be made in the governance of the universal Church'; special laws enacted for these circumstances must be observed.

[36] CIC, cc. 336–340: the college, in union with and never without its head, has supreme authority in the universal church; bishops are members of it by their consecration and communion with the Pope; CCEO, cc. 49–54.

[37] CIC, c. 341: when the college acts by the united action of its bishops dispersed throughout the world (see c. 337.2), its decrees have binding effect similarly when freely accepted by the Pontiff.

[38] CIC, c. 754: as are all decrees issued by lawful ecclesiastical authority.

[39] CIC, cc. 342–348: the synod must not 'settle matters or to draw up decrees, unless the Roman Pontiff has given it deliberative power in certain cases'; the Pope ratifies synod decisions; the synod has a permanent secretary (appointed by the Pope); see J.G. Johnson, 'The synod of bishops: an exploration of its nature and function', 20 *Studia Canonica* (1986) 275; see also CCEO, c. 46.

[40] CIC, cc. 360–361: the Apostolic or Holy See may denote the Pontiff and/or bodies of the Curia. For norms applicable to these, see the apostolic constitution *Pastor Bonus* (1988).

[41] CIC, cc. 362–367: this also deals with their functions: see Chapter 10.

[42] See e.g. SOCA: Const., Art. 7: the Patriarch (and Pontiff) is 'Supreme Head'; see Chapter 3. Compare SCOBA: Const., Art. I: the Conference consists of hierarchs from various churches (see Chapter 1 n. 22); its purpose is 'the consideration and resolution of common ecclesiastical problems, the co-ordination of effort in matters of common concern, and the strengthening of Orthodox unity'; Art. II: 'All authority in the Conference resides in the member hierarchs and is derived from them'; 'No decision of the Conference shall interfere with the ecclesiastical jurisdiction of any of the Canonical Orthodox Churches, or any of the member Hierarchs. Autocephalous Churches represented ... are recognizing each other as equal sister Orthodox Churches with equal canonical rights'; it has a Presiding Hierarch (passing annually among the hierarchs); Art. IV: it has e.g. an Orthodox Christian Education Commission and a Committee on Standardized Liturgical Texts; Art. V: it meets twice annually; Art. VI: the constitution and bylaws may be amended by two-thirds of the hierarchs.

numerous committees (such as those on finance and audit, canonical matters and inter-Orthodox and ecumenical affairs).[43] Secondly, the Romanian Orthodox Church, with eparchies worldwide, has 'a synodal hierarchic leadership' and is 'administered through ... representative bodies ... of clergy and laity'.[44] Its 'deliberative bodies' include the Holy Synod, its 'executive bodies' the Patriarch, and its 'administrative bodies' the Holy Synod Office and Patriarchal Administration.[45] The Holy Synod is its 'highest authority ... in all fields of activity' and is composed of the Patriarch (who presides at its annual meetings) and all metropolitans, archbishops, bishops and hierarchs. The Holy Synod is, *inter alia*, to: (1) preserve dogmatic, liturgical, and canonical unity and its communion 'with the entire Orthodox Church'; (2) approve the statutes of the church (with a two-thirds majority), rules made under them and eparchial statutes; (3) establish and dissolve eparchies; (4) elect the Patriarch, metropolitans, archbishops and eparchial bishops; (5) adjudicate disciplinary cases; and (6) engage in social and charitable work and oversee its commissions.[46] Thirdly, the Russian Orthodox Church, with jurisdiction over its exarchates, dioceses, deaneries, parishes and monasteries (which 'canonically comprise the Moscow Patriarchate'),[47] has 'a hierarchic structure of governance', and its 'supreme bodies' are the Local Council, Bishops' Council and Holy Synod headed by the Patriarch of Moscow and All Russia.[48] Composed of bishops and clerical, monastic and lay delegates, the Local Council has 'supreme power in the field of doctrine and canonical order'; ordinarily convened by the Bishops' Council and extraordinarily by the Patriarch and Holy Synod, the Patriarch presides.[49] The Bishops' Council is convened by the Patriarch and Holy Synod at least once every 4 years; its functions include: amendment of the church's Statute and 'approval and annulment of the legislative acts of the Holy Synod and ... alterations to them'; 'interpretation of the holy canons and other church regulations'; establishment, reorganisation and dissolution of self-governing churches, exarchates and dioceses; 'the procedure for all church courts'; and supervising implementation of

---

[43] OOCL: 213–221: its Holy Synaxis consists of hierarchs globally and meets every 2 years for mutual counsel and support; its committees are on e.g. finance, auditing, canonical matters, ecumenism; it has a secretariat.

[44] ROMOC: Statutes, Arts. 1–8.

[45] ROMOC: Statutes, Art. 9: its 'deliberative bodies' are the Holy Synod, Standing Synod and Church National Assembly; its 'executive bodies' are the Patriarch, Church National Council and Standing Church National Council; and its 'administrative bodies' are the Holy Synod Office and Patriarchal Administration.

[46] ROMOC: Statutes, Arts. 11–16, 201–205: it amends the Statutes; it has e.g. a Pastoral, Monastic and Social Commission; Theological and Liturgical Commission; Canonical, Juridical and Disciplinary Commission.

[47] ROC: Statute, I.1–3: its canonical territory covers e.g. Russia, Ukraine, Moldavia, Latvia and Lithuania.

[48] ROC: Statute, I.6.

[49] ROC: Statute, II.1–19: its functions are e.g. to interpret Orthodox teaching, maintain doctrinal and canonical unity; resolve canonical, liturgical and pastoral matters; approve decisions of the Bishops' Council on doctrine and canonical order; canonize saints; elect the Patriarch; and express its concern for contemporary problems. The Bishops' Council sets its agenda and procedure for approval by the Local Council. Its lay delegates are elected in accordance with procedures of the Bishops' Council. There are also rules on quorum and voting.

Local Council decisions.[50] The Holy Synod (its head the Patriarch) is 'the governing body of the Russian Orthodox Church in the period between [meetings of the] Bishops' Council' and consists of bishops.[51] The Moscow Patriarchate and its departments are 'the bodies of executive power of the Patriarch [and] Holy Synod'; the regulations of the Patriarchate are confirmed by the Patriarch and approved by the Holy Synod; it has a Chancery, and Departments of, for example, External Church Relations and Mission.[52]

The authority of the institutions of the Anglican Communion, Lutheran World Federation, World Methodist Council, World Communion of Reformed Churches and Baptist World Alliance is more limited than that operative internationally in the Catholic and Orthodox traditions. In the Anglican Communion, as a general principle, no coercive jurisdiction is exercised above the level of the autonomous province; its 'Instruments of Communion' enjoy persuasive but not binding authority.[53] The Archbishop of Canterbury has 'a primacy of honour and respect among the college of bishops in the Anglican Communion as first among equals (*primus inter pares*)'; thus: 'As a focus and means of unity, the Archbishop gathers and works with the Lambeth Conference and Primates' Meeting, and presides in the Anglican Consultative Council'.[54] The Lambeth Conference consists of bishops who meet every 10 years at the invitation of the Archbishop of Canterbury and its resolutions are not binding but enjoy a moral authority: 'The Lambeth Conference expresses episcopal collegiality worldwide, and brings together the bishops for common worship, counsel, consultation and encouragement in their ministry of guarding the faith and unity of the Communion and equipping the saints for the work of ministry (Eph 4.12) and mission'.[55] The Anglican Consultative Council, comprised of lay, clerical and episcopal representatives from the Communion churches, 'facilitates the co-operative work of the [churches], co-ordinates aspects of international Anglican ecumenical and mission work, calls the Churches into mutual responsibility and interdependence, and advises on developing provincial

---

[50] ROC: Statute, III.4: it consists of e.g. diocesan bishops; its functions include: preservation of 'Orthodox doctrine and the norms of moral life'; approval of ownership and disposal of property; financial oversight; there are also provisions on voting and quorum; III.5: it is 'the ecclesiastical court of final appeal'; III.6–15: the Patriarch is chair; the Holy Synod is the Presidium of the Bishops' Council; XVIII: amendment of the statute.

[51] ROC: Statute, V; X: sessions are convened by the Patriarch; it must *inter alia* elect and appoint bishops, consider the reports of bishops on their dioceses and determine the salaries of bishops; the Bishops' Council approves the decisions of the Holy Synod as to the establishment and dissolution of dioceses.

[52] ROC: Statute, VI.

[53] PCLCCAC, Principle 11: see n. 7 above. See also TACC, 3.1.2: the churches are bound together 'not by a central ... authority, but by mutual loyalty sustained through the common counsel of the bishops in conference and of the other instruments'; 3.1.3: the instruments 'assist in the discernment, articulation and exercise of our shared faith and common life'; 3.2.1: each church is 'to have regard for the common good of the Communion in the exercise of its autonomy', support and receive the work of the instruments 'with a readiness to undertake reflection upon their counsels, and to endeavour to accommodate their recommendations'.

[54] TACC: 3.1.4.1; PCLCCAC, 11.4: 'focus of unity'; the Archbishop has limited metropolitical authority in e.g. the extra-provincial dioceses of Puerto Rico, Const., II.5, and Lusitanian Catholic Apostolic and Evangelical Church, Const., Preamble, 7; CLAC: 344–345.

[55] TACC, 3.1.4.II.

structures'.[56] The Primates' Meeting is convened by the Archbishop of Canterbury for mutual support, prayer and counsel: 'the authority that primates bring to the meeting arises from their own positions as the senior bishops of their Provinces' (in conversation with their Houses of Bishops and located within their own synodical structures); its members are called 'to work as representatives of their Provinces in collaboration with one another in mission and in doctrinal, moral and pastoral matters that have Communion-wide implications'.[57] The Communion is currently developing structures for the resolution of conflict between churches and the relational consequences which flow from any resultant impaired communion.[58]

The Lutheran World Federation is a 'communion' and an 'instrument' of its autonomous member churches which, to be admitted to the communion, must accept its doctrinal basis and constitution.[59] It exercises its functions through the Assembly, Council, Secretariat and other 'instrumentalities of the member churches' and in all these functions, 'ordained and lay persons, men, women and youth shall be eligible to participate'.[60] The Assembly consists of representatives of the member churches and is 'the principal authority' of the Federation; it is responsible for the Constitution (and its amendment by a two-thirds majority), the general direction of the work of the Federation, election of the president and the members of the Council, and action on the reports of the president, the general secretary and the treasurer; it normally meets every 6 years with the time, place and programme determined by the Council.[61] The Council, composed of the president, treasurer and persons elected by the Assembly, is responsible for Federation business between ordinary Assemblies, elects its officers, decides on the structure of the Secretariat, presents an annual report to member churches, receives and approves audited accounts and decides on the Federation budget; the Council may amend the Bylaws of the Federation and has an Executive Committee (which also serves as the Board of Trustees) and may appoint other committees.[62] The Assembly may suspend or terminate membership by a two-thirds vote of the delegates; a suspended church may send representatives to the Assembly with a right to speak but not vote or hold

---

[56] TACC, s. 3.1.4; see also ACC Const., Arts. 2 and 3, and Schedule.   [57] TACC, 3.1.4.
[58] TACC, 4.2: this provides for suspension of membership of the Instruments of Communion.
[59] LWF: Const., Art. III: nature and objects; Art. IV: 'As instrument of its autonomous member churches the Lutheran World Federation may take action in matters committed to it by the member churches. It may act on behalf of one or more churches in such specific tasks as they commit to it. It may request individual member churches to assume tasks on behalf of the entire Communion'; Art. V and BL 2: membership.
[60] LWF: Const., Art. VI; see also Art. IX: each member church may constitute a National Committee to co-ordinate its relationships with the LWF, and each church has the right of direct communication with the LWF. Each National Committee must present to the Council an annual report on its activities.
[61] LWF: Const., Art. VII: the Council may call Extraordinary Assemblies and must do so at the request of one-fifth of the member churches; the number of representatives is determined by Council but each member church has the right to at least one representative in the Assembly. Art. XIV.1: amendment of the Constitution.
[62] LWF: Const., Art. VIII: the Executive Committee consists of the President, Vice-Presidents, Treasurer and Program Committee chair; Art. X: officers; Art. XI: secretariat; Art. XII: general secretary; Art. XIII: finances; Art. XIV.2: the Council must adopt bylaws which may be amended or rescinded by a majority of votes.

office and it must be reinstated upon a two-thirds vote of the Assembly that the reasons for suspension no longer exist. Termination may occur voluntarily or, if the Assembly so decides, by a two-thirds majority vote or if the church ceases to exist as an autonomous body.[63]

The World Communion of Reformed Churches, consisting of member churches admitted in accordance with a prescribed procedure,[64] has a General Council: meeting ordinarily every 7 years, it is composed of delegates representative of its member churches and is 'the main governing body' of the Communion; its functions *inter alia* are: to provide leadership in achieving the aims of the Communion; to adopt and amend the Constitution (by a two-thirds majority) and bylaws (simple majority); to make and adopt policies and programmes; to elect officers and members of the Executive Committee; to consider matters brought before it by member churches; and to ratify decisions of the Executive Committee. Decisions of General Council 'concerning its organization and institutional activities shall be binding' but its decisions 'involving the life and witness of the member churches are advisory in character'.[65] The Executive Committee exercises 'general oversight' of the work of the Communion between meetings of the General Council: it may perform all the functions of the General Council; establish departments, commissions and committees; approve financial reports and adopt the annual budget; fill vacancies in offices; and elect a general secretary and executive secretaries. Importantly, it may also admit to and suspend membership in the Communion in consultation with local member churches and subject to ratification by the next General Council, as well as amend the bylaws subject to ratification at the next General Council.[66] The World Methodist Council is similar. It meets in Conference every 5 years and consists of representatives of member churches: 'The functions of the World Methodist Council are not legislative or an invasion of the autonomy of member Churches'; it exists, for example, to deepen Methodist fellowship worldwide, foster Methodist participation in the ecumenical movement, advance unity of theological and moral standards, encourage evangelism, provide consultation and co-operation with 'other world communions' and encourage exchanges of preachers and the study of 'liturgy and forms of worship'. Between Conferences, the functions of the Council are exercised by the Executive Committee composed of members elected by the Council and representing each member church.[67] The Baptist World Alliance, which holds a Congress every 5 years, has similar institutional structures.[68]

---

[63] LWF: BL 2.4.4–2.4.5; the relationship of a suspended church to the LWF is subject to 'periodic review'. The Federation suspended the membership of two churches in 1977 (but they have since been restored).
[64] WCRC: Const., Art. I: nature; Art. II: basis; Art. III: identity; Art. IV: values; Art. V: purposes; Art. VI: membership.
[65] WCRC: Const., Arts. VII–IX: the Executive Committee must convene a special meeting on request by at least 1/5 of the member churches; the Council must adopt 'rules of procedure' to conduct its business.
[66] WCRC: Const., X: Executive Committee; Art. XI: officers; Art. XII: General Secretary; Art. XIII: Executive Secretaries; Art. XIV: finance; Art. XV: departments, committees and commissions; Art. XVI: Regional Councils; see also BL II: Executive Committee.
[67] MCGB: CPD, VI.4.
[68] BWA: Const., Preamble: it 'recognizes the traditional autonomy and independence of Baptist Churches and member bodies'; Art. III: it operates through the Baptist World Congress

Two basic models of international ecclesial polity emerge from the juridical instruments of the ecclesial traditions studied here – and they straddle all three forms of church government: Episcopal, Presbyterian and Congregational. On the one hand, the Catholic and Orthodox churches employ a hierarchical system of global church government. In the Catholic Church (Latin and Oriental) the Pontiff and College of Bishops exercise supreme authority over the universal church. Whilst there is no global institution with jurisdiction exercisable over all Orthodox churches worldwide (and some international Orthodox alliances exercise no coercive jurisdiction over their member churches), an autocephalous patriarchate exercises juridical authority internationally through its patriarch and Holy Synod (and sometimes a Council of ordained and lay persons) over its autonomous member churches. In this model, authority descends to the localities. On the other hand, the institutions of the international Anglican, Lutheran, Reformed, Methodist and Baptist communities exercise moral or advisory authority but not coercive jurisdiction over their autonomous member churches: coercive jurisdiction is retained as a prerogative of the national, regional or local church. In this model, authority ascends to international bodies either *from* the national level (Anglicanism, Lutheranism and Methodism), *through* the national level from an ecclesial source of authority at local level (Reformed and Congregational), or *both* (Baptist). However, both models share fundamentals in terms of the institutions themselves, their functions and their composition. Institutions are composed of persons elected by designated bodies in the associated ecclesial community (from the College of Cardinals in the Catholic Church to a Baptist Union, Convention or local church). They exercise norm-making authority (in the form of law or soft-law), executive authority (in policy-making and administration), and judicial or quasi-judicial authority (in the form of discipline). They must meet at prescribed times, they have procedural norms for the transaction of their business (such as systems of voting), and they establish, or conduct their business through, a variety of interdependent commissions, committees and other administrative bodies. In short, it is a principle of Christian law and order that ecclesial communities may establish institutions at international level with such authority as reflects their doctrinal postures on church polity.

National church structures and institutions

Each tradition has institutions of government which function at national level. Once more, the jurisdiction of national institutions varies as between the three basic systems of church polity. Catholic national institutions enjoy a form of limited competence the exercise of which is subject to superior papal authority. In Latin canon law,[69] the Episcopal Conference (a permanent institution) is 'the assembly of

---

(V: it meets every 5 years for e.g. fellowship, inspiration and information), General Council (VI–VII: 'representative responsibility'), Executive Committee (VIII–IX), Officers (X), 'such committees and ... structures as are provided for in the bylaws or as authorized by the General Council' (XI), and Regional Fellowships or Federations (XII); BL 1–7: membership (each member must promote WBA work 'consistent with its own work' and pay a membership fee).

[69] CIC, cc. 435–446: neighbouring particular churches may be grouped into provinces to promote inter-diocesan relations; provinces are established, altered or suppressed by the Pope; the

the Bishops of a country or of a certain territory, exercising together certain pastoral offices for Christ's faithful of that territory'; it must promote 'that greater good which the Church offers to all people'; it is for the supreme authority of the church alone, after consultation with the bishops concerned, to establish, alter or suppress a national Episcopal Conference.[70] The Episcopal Conference is composed of all diocesan bishops in its territory, and all coadjutor, auxiliary and titular bishops; each Conference is to draw up its own statutes (to be reviewed by the Apostolic See) which must deal with, *inter alia*, its plenary meetings, a permanent committee of bishops, a general secretary and other offices and commissions; each Conference must elect a president who presides over its plenary meetings and permanent committee. Plenary meetings are to be held at least once each year; the diocesan and coadjutor bishops have a deliberative vote at these, and auxiliary and titular bishops have a consultative vote.[71] The Episcopal Conference may issue decrees only in cases where the universal law so prescribes or by special mandate of the Holy See either on its own initiative or at the request of the Conference itself; a proposed decree must receive two-thirds of the votes at a plenary meeting of those with a deliberative vote; moreover: 'These decrees do not oblige until they have been reviewed by the Apostolic See and lawfully promulgated'; the competence of a diocesan bishop is protected.[72]

In Oriental Catholicism, beneath the level of the supreme authority (Pontiff), and jointly with the patriarch,[73] the Synod of Bishops is the highest authority in a Patriarchal Church – the patriarch has executive authority, and the Synod legislative and judicial authority.[74] The Synod is composed of diocesan (eparchial) bishops but the patriarch may invite others to participate (but not vote).[75] The patriarch convokes, prepares the agenda (for approval at the first session), presides over and may suspend or dissolve the synod, which ordinarily meets annually.[76] The Synod may enact particular law for the church inside its territory, constitute a tribunal for prescribed cases, and elect the patriarch, bishops and candidates for office outside its territory – the patriarch promulgates synodal legislation (at a time fixed by the Synod of Bishops) which must be communicated to the Roman Pontiff, and provides an authentic interpretation of this legislation.[77] The Patriarchal Curia assists the patriarch in governance and consists of, for example, bishops of the

provincial council and metropolitan (see Chapter 3) oversee the province; its council may legislate by decrees sent to Rome for approval.

[70] CIC, cc. 447–449; c. 459: relations between Conferences; c. 753: the Conference as teacher; S. Wood, 'The theological foundation of episcopal conferences and collegiality', 22 *Studia Canonica* (1988) 327.

[71] CIC, cc. 450–454; c. 456: the president must send the minutes of plenary meetings to Rome; c. 457: the permanent committee prepares the agenda and ensures decisions are executed; c. 458: general secretary.

[72] CIC, c. 455: the Conference determines the manner of promulgation and the time decrees come into force.

[73] See Chapter 3.

[74] CCEO, c. 110; the patriarch may also authorise administration by the Synod of Bishops.

[75] CCEO, c. 102; a bishop is excluded if e.g. incapacitated or subject to discipline: cc. 953, 1433.

[76] CCEO, cc. 103–111: a synod must be convoked if one-third of the bishops demand this.

[77] CCEO, cc. 110–112; for election see cc. 63–77 (election of the patriarch), 180–189 (bishops); cc. 111–112: promulgation and communication to Rome; c. 1488: a law comes into existence at promulgation.

patriarchal curia, finance officer, chancellor and the ordinary tribunal; the Patriarchal Assembly is a consultative body which advises the patriarch and the Synod of Bishops – it is convoked by the patriarch at least every 5 years and is composed of bishops and representatives of clergy and laity.[78] A Major Archiepiscopal Church is similarly organised.[79] In a Metropolitan Church the metropolitan is assisted by a Council of Hierarchs – it meets at least once a year, has its own statutes which regulate its structure, secretariat and commissions, and its legislation must be reviewed by the Apostolic See. The metropolitan has a superior administrative authority and convokes and presides over a Metropolitan Assembly with functions similar to a Patriarchal Assembly.[80]

Each Orthodox Church has various assemblies at national level amongst which doctrinal, legislative, judicial and administrative functions are distributed; these may be composed of bishops and clerical and lay representatives elected by eparchies or parishes.[81] For instance, the Greek Orthodox Archdiocese of America, an eparchy under the Ecumenical Patriarchate of Constantinople, has an Archdiocesan District (headed by the Archbishop) and eight metropolises (each with a metropolitan).[82] The Eparchial Synod (composed of archbishop and metropolitans) 'constitutes the ecclesiastical instrument of governance' in dogmatic and canonical matters and the archbishop convenes and presides at its biannual sessions.[83] The Charter and Regulations of the Archdiocese may be amended by the Synod with the approval of the Ecumenical Patriarchate.[84] In turn, the Archdiocesan Clergy–Laity Congress is 'the highest legislative body of the Archdiocese in matters other than dogmatic and canonical'; composed of the archbishop, metropolitans, and clerical and lay representatives elected by the parishes, it is convened triennially by the

---

[78] CCEO, c. 114: establishment; cc. 115–121: permanent synod; c. 122: finance officer; c. 123: chancery and archives; c. 124: commissions; c. 125: expenses; cc. 126–132: vacant or impeded patriarchal sees; cc. 133–139: metropolitans; cc. 140–145: patriarchal assembly; c. 146: territory of the patriarchal church.

[79] CCEO. cc. 151–152: these include the Ukrainian Greek Catholic Church and the Syro-Malabar Church.

[80] CCEO, c. 164–171: Council of Hierarchs; c. 172: Metropolitan Assembly; cc. 174–176: other churches.

[81] E.g. ROMOC: Statutes, Art. 19–34: the National Assembly has hierarchs and clergy and laity elected by the eparchies to e.g. legislate, elect bishops and establish dioceses; the National Council attends to 'the administrative, social, cultural, economical and patrimonial fields'; the Patriarch presides, it meets annually and has a Standing Committee; MOSC: Const., 4: the Episcopal Synod has authority over 'faith, order and discipline'; 4.70–77: the Association has bishops, and clerical and lay representatives elected by each parish; 4.78: Managing Committee.

[82] GOAA: Regs., Art. 2. See also UOCIA: Statutes, Art. II: also under Constantinople, Holy Synod is 'the supreme canonical authority in the Church'; composed of the prime bishop, major archbishops and diocesan bishops, it meets annually, acts as the Supreme Church Court of Appeals and appoints the Prime Bishop's Council and its own officers; Art. III: there is also an assembly of the prime bishop (president), major archbishops, diocesan bishops, priests and lay delegates elected by the parishes; this is 'the highest legislative and administrative authority' and meets every 3 years; Art. V: the 'permanent executive'.

[83] GOAA: Charter, Art. 4: a special meeting may also be called by the archbishop or a majority of its members; Art. 13: the Eparchial Synod advises on the election of the archbishop and metropolitans, and has all of 'the authority and responsibility that the Holy Canons and this Charter ascribe to the "Eparchial Synod"'.

[84] GOAA: Charter, Arts. 22, 25.

archbishop (president) to decide all matters which affect 'the life, mission, growth and unity' of the Archdiocese, the administration of the Archdiocesan District, metropolises and parishes, education, finance and charity; Congress decisions must be approved by the Ecumenical Patriarchate and 'faithfully and firmly adhered to by all Parishes'.[85] The Archdiocesan Council has the authority of the Congress between Congresses and advises the archbishop and Eparchial Synod; it consists of the archbishop, metropolitans, auxiliary bishops and clerical and lay parish representatives, and is convened by the archbishop twice a year; it cannot address dogmatic and canonical matters.[86] The Council has an Executive Committee and Standing Committees (such as its Finance Committee).[87] The Archdiocesan Presbyters Council also meets twice a year (under the presidency of the Archbishop) to promote the ministry and spiritual growth of priests.[88]

As we have seen, each Anglican Church consists of one or more province(s) (and within them dioceses).[89] In line with Lambeth Conference calls for the full participation of the laity in the institutions of church governance,[90] the central organ of government is the national, regional or provincial assembly, styled variously the General Synod, General Convention or Synod, or Provincial Synod or Council, and composed either of three Houses (or Orders) – bishops, clergy, and laity – or two – bishops, and clerical and lay – with representatives elected by elaborate systems of electoral law.[91] The primate convenes and presides at meetings which are held annually or at intervals of 2, 3 or 4 years – and there are complex procedures for the transaction of business.[92] The principal functions of central assemblies are law-making, policy-making and, to a lesser extent, administration over a wide range of prescribed subjects of common concern to the whole of the national, regional or provincial church.[93] In those churches with Fundamental Declarations (or Fundamental Principles), these may be altered only in accordance with special procedures or else they are entrenched and incapable of

---

[85] GOAA: Charter, Art. 10.
[86] GOAA: Charter, Art. 17; the Council itself makes regulations as to its own functions; regulations as to the composition of the Council are promulgated by the Congress.
[87] GOAA: Charter, Art. 22; Regs., Art. 5.
[88] GOAA: Regs., Art. 6: it has two priests elected by each Metropolis Clergy Syndesmos.
[89] ACC-4, 1979, Res. B: a province is 'a self-governing Church composed of several dioceses operating under a common Constitution and having one supreme legislative body'; LC 1878, Res. 2: dioceses should 'associate themselves into a province ... in accordance with the ancient laws and usages of the Catholic Church'.
[90] LC 1867, Ress. 4, 5, 8; LC 1897, Res. 24; LC 1920, Ress. 14 and 43; LC 1930, Res. 53.
[91] E.g. England: Synodical Government Measure 1969: General Synod has three Houses: bishops, clergy and laity; cf. TEC: Const., Art. I.1: General Convention has two Houses – House of Bishops and House of Deputies (clergy and laity). Typically a House of Bishops consists of the primate, metropolitans and diocesan bishops: see e.g. Australia: Const., IV.16; a House of Clergy has clergy from the dioceses: e.g. Canada: Declaration of Principles, 3; a House of Laity has lay representatives from the dioceses: e.g. Scotland: Can. 52.
[92] E.g. Wales: Const., II.20: the archbishop presides; Ireland: Standing Orders of General Synod.
[93] E.g. Ireland: Const., Preamble, Declaration IV: General Synod has 'chief legislative power ... and such administrative power as may be necessary for the Church and consistent with its episcopal constitution'; Canada: Declaration of Principles, 6–7: General Synod has 'authority and jurisdiction in all matters affecting in any way the general interest and well-being of the whole Church'.

alteration;[94] the amendment of constitutions is similarly by special majority procedure, sometimes with referral to the diocese for either consultation or consent;[95] procedures for making canons are generally those which apply *mutatis mutandis* to constitutional amendment, though sometimes they are different.[96] Between meetings the business of the central assembly is carried out by a Standing or Executive Committee which must implement the decisions of and act under the direction of the central assembly.[97] The central assembly also has various committees, commissions, boards and other advisory bodies.[98]

In Lutheranism, each church has a superior legislative authority at national level (Convention, Synod or Assembly), which meets annually, biennially or triennially, composed of bishops and/or ministers and lay delegates elected by congregations (or parishes), and is assisted by an executive council similarly composed, which meets at prescribed times each year, and departments for administration and finance.[99] For example, in the Lutheran Church of Australia: 'The power of the Church shall be exercised through the General Synod, which shall be the highest constitutional authority of the Church, with power to direct and control those to whom it has entrusted tasks or delegated authority'.[100] The General Synod consists

---

[94] E.g. Central Africa: Fundamental Declarations, VII and Can. 33: these may be altered by the Provincial Synod only if the Episcopal Synod, a Diocesan Synod, the Provincial Standing Committee or other designated body proposes alteration; the alteration must be confirmed by the Provincial Synod by a two-thirds majority after approval by each diocesan synod; Australia: Const., XI.66: entrenchment of its Fundamental Declaration.

[95] E.g. South East Asia: Const., Art. 19: diocesan consultation; Papua New Guinea: Const., Art. 19: the consent of the diocesan synods; Sudan: Const., Art. 63: referral to the dioceses 'for their agreement'.

[96] E.g. Scotland: Can. 52: canons are made with a two-thirds majority in each of the three Houses of General Synod after considering diocesan views; Australia: Const., V.30: General Synod canons on e.g. order, government and property (not involving ritual, ceremonial or discipline) are operative only on adoption by a Diocesan Synod.

[97] E.g. Canada: Const. of General Synod, VII.35: the Executive Council is responsible for 'overall strategy planning and visioning with the mandate of the General Synod'.

[98] E.g. TEC: Cans. I.1.2: the General Convention may establish Standing Commissions, advisory bodies on e.g. the Constitution and Canons, Health, Human Affairs, Peace with Justice, and Evangelism; Korea: Const., Art. 41: Canons Committee, Liturgical Commission, and Church and Society Committee.

[99] ELCIC: Const., Art. XI: the Convention is: the 'highest legislative authority'; held biennially; and composed of ministers and lay delegates elected by each parish; Art. XII: the National Church Council meets at least twice a year, acts as trustee, encourages, interprets the constitution, and its Department of Finance and Administration has 'general oversight and control of the finance and business management of [the] church'; ELCA: Const., Chs. 8, 11, 12, 15: the Churchwide Assembly is composed e.g. of the presiding bishop, bishops, and elected ministerial and lay persons representative of each Synod; it e.g. amends the constitution and bylaws, establishes policy and reviews the work of churchwide units, synods and congregations; the Church Council has the 'management and direction' of the church between Assembly meetings and elects the Executive for Administration; LCMS: Const., Arts. VIII–XV: the Synod meets every 3 years, is the legislative assembly for policy and programmes, and amends the constitution (with a two-thirds majority); LCGB: RAR, Annual Synod.

[100] LCA: Const., Art. VII.1; Art. V.2; BL V.F: The General Pastors' Conference is held in conjunction with the regular convention of the General Synod to give guidance in matters of doctrine, confession and ministry.

of the lay delegates of the congregations (and the unit of representation is the parish), pastor delegates, the members of the General Church Council, its executive officers and chairs of boards.[101] It meets every 3 years and has a president who must be a pastor elected by it to function as 'the spiritual leader of the church'.[102] The General Synod may amend the constitution (except for its 'fundamental and unalterable' articles) and bylaws of the church,[103] and delegate any of its powers, authorities and duties to such persons or bodies as it sees fit.[104] The General Church Council, consisting *inter alia* of the president and representatives of the General Synod and districts, has the authority of General Synod between its conventions to implement General Synod policies, ensure the mission of the church is carried out, submit the budget for approval by General Synod and discipline its members – the council has an executive. In turn, the College of Presidents consists of the president, vice-president and district presidents; its function is 'to provide leadership, oversight and guidance to the Church', encourage unity and good order, attend to doctrine and worship, oversee ministry, and give leadership in the resolution of conflict. Moreover, the church may appoint such Boards and Standing Committees as necessary to carry out its objects; there are boards and committees on education, mission, youth, the family, salaries, social issues and constitutions – these are responsible to General Synod and between its sessions to the General Church Council.[105]

A Reformed church has a central assembly composed of ministers and lay representatives with legislative authority.[106] For instance, the Reformed Church in America has a General Synod, 'the highest assembly and judicatory', which consists of ministers and elder delegates from the classes and regional synods. It meets annually to exercise 'a general superintendence over the interests and concerns of the whole church'; its specific functions include appellate supervision over lower assemblies, the establishment of regional synods, determination of policy, legal custodianship of funds, original authority over doctrine, oversight of ministerial standards, and the establishment of agencies, boards and other bodies. The General Synod Council is the Executive Committee and administers the affairs of the General Synod between sessions, in relation, for example, to

---

[101] LCA: Const., Art. VII; BL, VII.A: there are rules on tenure, re-election and filling vacancies.
[102] LCA: Const., Art. VII: it also has a vice-president and officers (the secretary is the 'executive officer').
[103] LCA: Const., Art. XI.1–2: bylaws; Art. XII.1–2: constitution (except Arts. II and XII.1). See also ELCIC: Const., Art. XX: the constitution is altered by Convention with a two-thirds majority, but Art. II on the Confession of Faith is unalterable; Art. XIX: administrative bylaws are amended by the Convention with a two-thirds majority.
[104] LCA: Const., Art. VII.13.   [105] LCA: Const., Art. VIII; BL VIII.D–H.
[106] URC: Man. B.2.6; 3.1: General Assembly is 'the central organ [and] final authority, under the Word of God and ... guidance of the Holy Spirit in ... doctrine and order and in all other concerns of its common life'; it has representatives of synods (equal ministerial and lay); it is to e.g. oversee the work of the church and 'alter, add to, modify or supersede the Basis, Structure and any other form ... of the polity and doctrinal formulations of the [URC]'; constitutional amendment is proposed by a two-thirds majority, referred to the provinces, and effected by majority vote; C: Rules of Procedure; G: Committees: e.g. Mission Council and Ministries Committee.

property and finance, and works through various committees.[107] Similarly, each Presbyterian Church has a General Assembly, its highest court composed typically of teaching elders from Presbyteries and ruling elders from the (Kirk) Sessions. It meets annually under the supervision of a moderator to legislate on government, discipline, worship and mission, to adjudicate on disputes about doctrine, order and discipline, for example, and to establish bodies for national administration.[108] For example, the General Assembly of the Presbyterian Church in Ireland is composed *inter alia* of ministers in active duty of the congregations, ruling elders appointed by Kirk Session and officers which include the Moderator; it meets at least once annually as 'the supreme court' with jurisdiction to superintend doctrine, worship, witness, discipline and government, 'declare the mind of the Church thereupon', decide the general policy of the church and issue directions for the welfare of the church. Its decisions are 'final and binding' (but a member may dissent); only the General Assembly may 'enact, alter or abrogate a law of the Church' and amend, rescind or reverse its own sentences, decisions or resolutions. It may delegate to a commission its power to regulate the number and extent of presbyteries, remove congregations and ministers from one presbytery to another, sanction new congregations and create Standing Orders to transact its business. It has various Commissions and Boards.[109] Much the same applies to many United and Congregational Churches: a representative Assembly is the 'highest court' with authority, for example, to approve the constitutions of local churches, to refer matters to Regional Councils, Synods and Committees for consideration and action (and co-ordinate their work) and to oversee the work of its committees.[110]

---

[107] RCA: BCO, Ch. 1, Pt. IV. Arts. 1–7; see also Ch. 3, Pt. I: bylaws, special rules of order and General Synod Council; there are General Synod commissions on e.g. Christian Unity, Judicial Business, Race and Ethnicity.

[108] PCA: BCO, 10: General Assembly has moral/spiritual jurisdiction and may make 'rules for the government, discipline, worship, and extension of the Church' consistent with its doctrine; it has 'all the administrative authority necessary to give effect to these powers'; 11: as 'the highest court' it 'represents . . . all the churches' of PCA; 14: it meets annually and consists of teaching elders from Presbyteries and ruling elders from Sessions; 26: it may amend the Book of Church Order – it approves a proposal by simple majority, obtains the consent of two-thirds of the Presbyteries, and approves amendment at a subsequent Assembly; it may amend the Confession of Faith and Larger and Shorter Catechisms with consent of three-quarters of the Presbyteries by a three-quarters vote at a subsequent Assembly; CLCS: 88–96; PCW: HOR, 3.4–5; PCANZ: BO, 14; UFCS: MPP, V.I–V: I: 'The General Assembly, the Supreme Court of the Church, is a representative body consisting of ministers and elders elected by Presbyteries'; its 'functions . . . are legislative as well as judicial and administrative' as to doctrine, worship, discipline and government; when it legislates by Act of Assembly, it must submit the proposal as an overture to the Presbyteries for approval by a majority of them; III: Committees (e.g. Administration and Finance Committee); IV: Assembly Commission; Appeal Commission; App. 3: Standing Orders.

[109] PCI: Code, pars. 97–103: composition; 104–109: powers and duties; 110–112: legislation; 126–130, 268–288: commissions and boards (e.g. Judicial Commission, Commission on Trusts, Business Board); 141–147: ordering of business; 148–155: rules of debate; 156–160: voting; Appendix 1 (Standing Orders).

[110] UCCSA: Const., 6: 'The Assembly is the governing body of the Church and its highest court' with officers, ministers and lay delegates from each Synod; it has e.g. an Executive Committee, Ministerial Committee and Mission Council; it is to: refer matters to Regional Councils,

In Methodist polity, too, the Conference is a 'court' with the power to bind: it meets annually under a president and consists of a Ministerial Session, with authority primarily over the admission, probation, appointment and discipline of ministers, and a Representative Session (composed of lay delegates) with authority over the government and management of the church. The Conference may amend the constitution with a three-quarters majority vote of all its members. Its General Committee (appointed by the Representative Session) has such authority as the Conference may delegate to it to carry on its business between Conferences.[111] For example, the Conference of the Methodist Church in Great Britain (one of its 'Church Courts and Jurisdictions') meets annually and consists of ministers (in the Ministerial Session) and lay representatives (in the Representative Session). It is responsible for 'the government and discipline of the [church] and the management and administration of its affairs' and has 'all the powers, authorities, rights and duties necessary or desirable in its discretion for such government, discipline, management and administration'; as such, it may: (1) make, amend and repeal Standing Orders or other rules and regulations for the constitution of the Conference consistent with the Deed of Union; (2) found connexional funds for the promulgation of the Gospel and for circuits and local churches and manage connexional property; (3) conduct ordinations; and (4) appoint boards, committees and officers, including its president and the Methodist Council and Executive to act on its behalf between Conferences and ensure that 'the decisions of the Conference are fully implemented'; the Council also has a Committee on Methodist Law and Polity to advise on Methodist 'legislation and administration', changes to law and their 'coherence with existing usage' – it reports annually to the Conference.[112] The United Methodist Church in the USA, which has bishops, also has a General Conference which meets every 4 years and is composed of bishops, ministers and

---

Synods, Committees or local churches for consideration and action; co-ordinate the work of Synods; engage in evangelism; and approve constitutions of local churches; 5: the Synod is a court of the Assembly and has 'general oversight of the Regional Councils within its bounds' and consists of representatives from these; UCC: Man., BU s. 7 and BL 500–572: General Council is e.g. 'to legislate'; BU s. 7 and BL 400–470: Conference; UCOC: Const., Art. IX: General Synod has officers and delegates elected by Conferences; it cannot 'invade the autonomy of Conferences, Associations, and Local Churches'; and acts through an Executive Council; UCA: Const., 31–37: Synod.

[111] MCI: Const., s. 6; RDG, 6: Conference composition, functions, constitutional amendment, procedure, quorum, rules of debate and president; RDG, 8: General Committee; MCNZ: LAR, s. 7: Conference decisions are 'final and binding on both Ministry and Laity'; it may legislate but 'cannot stand above or apart from these Laws and Regulations'; members are not delegates instructed on how to vote; COTN: Man., Pt. II, Art. IV: with ministerial and lay delegates elected by each district, 'General Assembly shall have power to legislate ... but not in conflict with this Constitution' (which is amended by a two-thirds vote with the consent of two-thirds of the district assemblies); Pt. IV, Ch. III: it is 'the supreme doctrine-formulating, lawmaking, and elective authority'.

[112] MCGB: CPD, SO 003: Church Courts and Jurisdictions; DU 18–21: powers; DU 11, 13–14: membership; DU 19: Standing Orders; 21: officers and committees; 23: ordination; DU 26–29 and SO 110–111: President; SO 210–216: Methodist Council and Executive (and Audit Committee); SO 230–232: other committees; SO 302: General Secretary or 'executive officer'; SO 338 for the Committee on Methodist Law and Polity.

lay delegates with 'full legislative power over matters distinctively connexional' and Jurisdictional Conferences.[113]

By way of contrast, the national institutions of Baptist Unions, Conventions and Conferences have more limited jurisdictions. Typically, a Union of Baptist Churches has an Assembly composed of representatives of its members (its associations and its congregations) – policies are formulated by a Council for approval by the Assembly which may also amend the constitution of the Union but not interfere with the autonomy of congregations.[114] Likewise, the National Convention of Baptist Churches in the USA has an Annual Session composed *inter alia* of representatives from the regional units of the Convention and its officers (including its president, vice-president, regional vice-presidents, treasurer and general secretary). Provision is made to amend the constitution of the Convention – the Board of Directors examines a proposed constitutional amendment and may submit this to the Annual Session for its approval on the basis of a two-thirds vote in favour; the Board is also to 'enforce the orders' and exercise corporate oversight of all the business and operations of the Convention. The subsidiary bodies of the Convention include the National Baptist Congress of Christian Education, Music Auxiliary and Commission on Evangelism – their charters must reflect that 'they are subordinate and subject to the governance, jurisdiction, and control of the Convention'; the Convention appoints their officers and they must submit annual reports to the Convention.[115] Similarly, the North American Baptist Conference consists of the

---

[113] UMCUSA: Const., Div. 2; for constitutional amendment see Div. 5, Art. I (two-thirds majority). See also FMCNA: BOD, Ch.2: General Conference has 'general organizational, legislative, judicial promotional and supervisory powers over the activities of the church', is 'the primary legislative body', is composed of ministerial and lay delegates elected by Annual Conference; the bishops preside; Ch. 5: Annual Conference has ministers and lay delegates elected from each society, officers (its presiding officer is a bishop), but it 'cannot enact laws'.

[114] BUGB: Const., I.5: the Union acts by the Assembly through a Council; I.7: the Assembly includes all registered ministers as well as delegates from churches and associations; I.9: the constitution may be amended by Assembly resolution approved by two-thirds vote with notice at the previous Assembly; II.1–10: 'The general policy of the Union, subject to any directions of the Assembly, shall be decided by a Council' which meets twice a year and consists e.g. of representatives of Associations and the officers and past presidents; Council may appoint committees and working groups; JBU: Const., Arts. VIII, XIV: General Assembly departments are e.g. Board of Mission and Evangelism; BUSA: Const., 8–14: the Assembly may amend the constitution and bylaws by two-thirds majority vote; but amendment of the Declaration of Principle requires approval by 'all members of the Union'; Model Const., 4: Principles of Governance: e.g. 'Each individual member has the responsibility and right to participate fully in the Church's life and government, including the appointment of its leadership'; and: 'Any change [to local] church structure or organisation ... in conflict directly or indirectly with one or more of the stated Baptist Principles will be invalid unless approved by at least 90% of the members present and entitled to vote at a duly constituted Special Meeting of which at least three months' notice has been given.'

[115] NBCUSA: Const., Art. VI: Annual Session and Board of Directors; Art. X: constitutional amendment; Art. VII: subsidiary bodies; BL Art. V: officers; Art. VI: Directors; Art. VII: bylaws. See also: CNBC: BL 3, 10–16: an annual Convention consists of messengers who are members of Cooperating Baptist Churches and elected by them; if a church ceases to co-operate with the Convention or becomes corrupt in doctrine or practice it is no longer in fellowship with it; 17: 'The Convention shall respect the autonomy of each Baptist body and shall not exercise ecclesiastical authority or control over any Cooperating Baptist Church'; 25–37: the Convention

members of all Baptist churches belonging to the Associations or Regions of the Conference; its Triennial Conference is to motivate the member bodies to fulfil the Great Commission, cultivate a sense of unity, develop a deeper dimension of caring and outreach, elect its officers (e.g. moderator and executive director) and approve resolutions. A General Council, 'the governing body' between Triennial Conferences, formulates policies, approves its own bylaws and the Conference budget, oversees property and appoints the Council Executive Committee (which carries on its work between biannual General Council meetings). Proposed amendments to the constitution must be submitted to the Constitutional Change Committee, which in turn submits them to the General Council for subsequent approval by the Triennial Conference.[116] Finally, the General Board of the American Baptist Churches in the USA is composed of representatives from the co-operating churches and is to 'serve as the legislative body' with 'oversight and direction' in relation to policy-making, determination of membership, election of officers, establishment of committees and commissions and review of finances; it may 'formulate, adopt, promulgate, review, amend, rescind and implement American Baptist Policy Statements and Resolutions'.[117]

In sum, all the ecclesial traditions have a national manifestation and organisation with such institutions as are prescribed by the regulatory instrument applicable to it. The autonomy and functions of a national ecclesial entity, and its conference, synod, council or other form of central assembly, may include the authority to legislate, administer and adjudicate on matters within its competence. A national ecclesial assembly or other such institution is composed of such members of the faithful as are elected or otherwise appointed to it in accordance with law.

Regional church structures and institutions

Within the national structures of churches, each Christian tradition studied here has a territorial unit at the regional or district level between the national and local structures. Catholics, Orthodox and Anglicans have dioceses or other form of episcopal see. In the Protestant traditions, Lutheran churches have dioceses or synods and, within these, districts or circuits; Methodists too have districts and circuits; Reformed and Presbyterian churches have synods, presbyteries and districts; and, typically, Baptist Unions or Conventions have associations and regions. Each territorial unit has its own institutions of government.

According to Roman Catholic canon law, a diocese is a portion of the people of God entrusted to a bishop and nurtured by him with the co-operation of the *presbyterum*; remaining close to the bishop, and by him through the Gospel and

---

President is elected by it; 38–59; General Meetings are governed by Robert's Rules of Order; 60–75: Directors; 76–85: proceedings, 86–93: committees; 137: the constitution and bylaws are altered by special resolution.

[116] NABC: Const., 1–11: Robert's Rules of Order govern proceedings of the Conference.

[117] ABCUSA: BL Art. 1 (and SR 1): constituencies; II (and SR 2): members; III (and SR 3): regional representatives; IV (and SR 4): Biennial Meeting; V (and SR 5): Cooperating Churches (e.g. admitted by a Regional Board); VI (and SR 6): Regional Organisations; VII (and SR 7): Affiliating Organisations; VIII (and SR 8): Covenants of the Denomination; IX (and SR 9): meetings; X (and SR 10): General Board and American Baptist Policy Statements and Resolutions (under XII); XIX: Standing Rules.

Eucharist, 'it constitutes a particular church' in which 'the one, holy, catholic and apostolic Church of Christ truly exists and functions'; a diocese has a defined territory and juridical personality, and may only be established by the supreme authority.[118] The diocesan bishop 'governs the particular church ... with legislative, executive and judicial power, in accordance with the law'; the bishop exercises legislative power himself (it cannot be delegated), executive power personally or through vicars general or episcopal vicars, and judicial power personally or through a judicial vicar.[119] The Diocesan Synod assists the bishop and consists of prescribed classes of clergy and lay members elected by the Diocesan Pastoral Council. The bishop convenes, presides at and dissolves the Synod. He is its sole legislator (members have only a consultative vote), and signs and publishes synodal decrees which he must communicate to the metropolitan and the Episcopal Conference.[120] The Diocesan Curia consists of those institutions and persons who assist the bishop in the governance of the diocese 'especially in directing pastoral action, in providing for the administration of the diocese, and in exercising judicial power'.[121] The bishop is also assisted by a Presbyteral Council,[122] Finance Committee[123] and Pastoral Council (which consists of clergy and laity and meets at least once a year).[124] Similar arrangements are found in an Oriental Catholic eparchy (equivalent to a Latin diocese): the eparchial bishop has legislative, executive and judicial powers and may convene an Eparchial Assembly which has a consultative vote in the making of eparchial legislation by the bishop; the eparchial curia assists with administration.[125]

In the Orthodox model, beneath the national level each church is typically composed of metropolises, archdioceses and eparchies (or dioceses).[126] Each has its own regional Synod or Assembly,[127] which is representative of clergy and

---

[118] CIC, cc. 368–369; see also cc. 370–371 for e.g. territorial prelatures and vicariates.

[119] CIC, c. 391; c. 381: a bishop has 'all the ordinary, proper and immediate power required for the exercise of his pastoral office, except in matters which the law or a decree of the Supreme Pontiff reserves to the supreme or to some other ecclesiastical authority'; c. 134: an 'ordinary' is e.g. a diocesan bishop.

[120] CIC, cc. 460–468: the bishop determines the manner of election and number of lay members.

[121] CIC, cc. 469–494: the officers include the vicar general, episcopal vicar and chancellor.

[122] CIC, cc. 495–502: he must consult the Council as to matters prescribed under e.g. cc. 461, 515, 1263 and 1742; the College of Consultors has prescribed functions when the diocese is impeded or vacant.

[123] CIC, cc. 492–494: its members (clerical or lay) must be persons of outstanding integrity and skilled in finance and civil law; the bishop must also appoint a financial administrator: see below, Chapter 9.

[124] CIC, cc. 511–514: those 'outstanding in firm faith, high moral standards and prudence' are appointed.

[125] CCEO, cc. 177–178: the eparchy and its bishop; cc. 235–242: assembly; cc. 243–263: curia; cc. 262–263: finance administrator; cc. 264–271: presbyteral council and college of consultors; cc. 272–275: pastoral council.

[126] MOSC: Const., 45–55: the Diocesan Assembly is composed of parish clergy and laity elected by the parish assembly; the diocesan metropolitan convenes and presides; it meets once per annum and is assisted by a Diocesan Council; the Assembly has no authority as to 'faith, order or discipline'; the diocesan metropolitan carries out 'the administration' of the diocese subject to supervision by the metropolitan.

[127] ROC: Statute, X.1–5: a diocese is established by Holy Synod with approval of the Bishops' Council; the Diocesan Assembly is its 'governing body' with clergy and laity 'representing [its]

laity, and convened and presided over by the bishop.[128] This assembly exercises prescribed legislative, administrative and judicial functions,[129] and may be assisted by a council which is involved in the administration of the unit in question.[130] The assembly may also have its own committees,[131] and other bodies. [132] The Romanian Orthodox Church is not untypical: a Metropolitan See consists of eparchies (archdioceses and dioceses) and has a Metropolitan Synod composed of the metropolitan, archbishops and bishops – and the metropolitan convenes and presides. Its functions may include proposing to the Holy Synod the establishment of new eparchies, entertaining appeals for the deposition of clergy, approving the decrees of eparchial assemblies and approving the establishment and dissolution of monasteries.[133] In turn, an eparchy (an archdiocese or diocese) is composed of parishes, deaneries and monasteries, and is overseen by an archbishop or diocesan bishop; the Eparchial Assembly is the deliberative body for administrative, cultural, social, economic and patrimonial matters, composed of representatives of clergy and laity elected by the parishes; the Eparchial Council is 'the executive body of the Eparchial Assembly' and is elected by it; the council has a standing council, to carry on council business between meetings, and an eparchial administration.[134]

---

canonical units'; convened by the bishop, it meets annually to e.g. elect persons to the Local Council, Diocesan Council and Diocesan Court, and create 'diocesan rules and regulations'; a diocese may establish 'bodies of diocesan administration'.

[128] GOAA: Charter, Art. 11: the Archdiocesan District and each metropolis has a Local Clergy-Laity Assembly; convened and presided over by the local hierarch it meets annually and is composed of priests and parish lay representatives; it cannot address dogmatic or canonical issues but may address e.g. the uniform governance of parishes, education, finance and charity; Art. 18: the Local Council administers between Assembly meetings.

[129] UOCIA: Statutes, Arts. VII–VIII: a Diocese is the 'basic church body', comprises the parishes and is 'governed by the Diocesan Bishop with the assistance of a Diocesan Assembly and a Diocesan Council'; a diocese is established by Holy Synod; the Diocesan Assembly is composed of the bishop (president), priests and deacons (*ex officio*), and lay delegates elected by parishes; it is e.g. to elect members of the Diocesan Council, authorise property transactions, and implement General Sobor decisions; no Assembly resolution is valid without approval of the bishop; it has its own procedures, officers and committees.

[130] ROC: Statute, X.34–44: the Diocesan Council consists of the bishop (chair) and at least four others; it must meet every 6 months to e.g. establish the procedure for elections to the Diocesan Assembly, submit annual reports to the Diocesan Assembly, determine deanery and parish boundaries, and supervise Parish Councils.

[131] UOCIA: Statutes, Art. IX: the Diocesan Council is 'the permanent body of diocesan administration' (e.g. to effect Diocesan Assembly decisions and 'the directives of the Diocesan Bishop') and has a Diocesan Chancery.

[132] ROC: Statute, 45–49: the Diocesan Administration is the 'executive and managerial body of the diocese under the guidance of the Diocesan Bishop, and together with other Diocesan institutions shall assist the Bishop in exercising his executive authority'; it is regulated by statutes approved by Holy Synod and 'instructions' of the bishop; it has a chancery, accounting and other departments (e.g. for social and charitable work).

[133] ROMOC: Statutes, Arts. 111–113; 114: the Metropolitan.

[134] ROMOC: Statutes, Arts. 84–106: 84: Eparchy; 86–89: Eparchial Archbishop or Diocesan Bishop; 90–94: Assembly; 95–99: Council; 100–102: Standing Council; 103–108: Eparchial Administration and Office.

The territory of each Anglican Church is divided into dioceses; a diocese is a territory under the spiritual leadership and oversight of a bishop and governed by a representative assembly,[135] styled, variously, Diocesan Synod, Convention or Conference; some laws recognise the diocese as the primary unit of the church.[136] The creation, division, amalgamation and dissolution of a diocese are usually in the keeping of the central assembly of the national, regional or provincial church.[137] The diocesan assembly consists of houses composed of the bishop and elected representatives of the clergy and laity; meetings are convened and presided over by the bishop and are usually annual.[138] The diocese is autonomous: 'the Diocesan Synods should be free to dispose of matters of local interest and to manage the affairs of the Dioceses'; the central assembly is not competent to interfere in the internal affairs of a diocese unless this is permitted by law.[139] In most churches the diocesan assembly has competence to legislate for the diocese in relation to prescribed matters, as well as jurisdiction over its more localised ecclesiastical units (such as parishes); the diocesan assembly must also consider any matter referred by the central assembly and implement the lawful directions of the latter to which it must make an annual report.[140] Diocesan legislation, in the form of a constitution, canons or other instruments, must not be inconsistent with the general law of a national, regional or provincial church; as with provincial law, special procedures commonly apply to the enactment of diocesan legislation.[141] The diocesan assembly has an executive organ (its Standing or Executive Committee) which acts with the authority of the assembly between sessions, advises the bishop and discharges other functions assigned to it by the assembly; the diocesan assembly may also establish a variety of committees, boards,

---

[135] PCLCCAC, Principle 20: a diocese consists of the faithful in a particular territory overseen by a bishop; the bishop may give/withhold consent to proposed diocesan legislation if allowed by law, but may not legislate unilaterally; Korea: Const., Art. 57: a diocese is 'an independent evangelistic organisation administered by a bishop'; South East Asia: Const., Art. XIV: 'A Diocese shall be governed by the Bishop and a Synod.'

[136] England: Synodical Government Measure 1969, s. 5: Diocesan Synod; TEC: Cans. I.9: Diocesan Convention; Wales: Const., IV: Diocesan Conference; Australia: Const. III.1: 'A diocese shall in accordance with the historic custom of the ... Church continue to be the unit of organisation [and] ... see of a bishop.'

[137] PCLCCAC, Principle 20. See e.g. West Indies: Can. 12.1: Provincial Synod.

[138] See e.g. Scotland: Can. 50; Wales: Const., IV; New Zealand: Cans. B.II.1.

[139] LC 1867, Report 1; e.g. South East Asia: Const., Art. XVI: Provincial Synod deals with matters of 'concern to the whole Province and ... the Communion of the Dioceses ... and of the province with other Provinces'; it must give dioceses 'the greatest possible liberty compatible with the unity and good order of the Church'.

[140] E.g. Melanesia: Const., Art. 16: composition; Philippines: Const., VII.2: annual meetings; England: Synodical Government Measure 1969: the bishop must consult the Diocesan Synod on matters of importance to the diocese; TEC: Cans. I.6.2: report to General Convention; Wales: Const., IV.A.21: control of lower units.

[141] E.g. Uganda: Const., Art. 14: 'the [Diocesan] Synod shall make a Constitution for the government and administration of the Diocese, provided that a constitution of a Diocese shall be approved by the Provincial Synod'; where 'there is any conflict between the Diocesan Constitution and the provisions of this Constitution, the Provincial Constitution shall prevail, at any rate to the extent of the inconsistency'; for diocesan canons, see e.g. New Zealand: Const., D-F; for Acts of a Diocesan Synod, see e.g. Ireland: Const., II.I.28-33.

commissions and other bodies, such as on ministry, liturgy and finance, under the control of the diocesan assembly.[142]

Typically, Lutheran churches are divided into units styled dioceses or synods, or districts and circuits, with defined boundaries, functions and a constitution and bylaws.[143] Each unit has an assembly, variously styled a Diocesan Synod or Synod Assembly, or District Synod or Circuit Synod, which is composed of ordained ministers and lay representatives who are elected from the congregations within it. The assembly meets at prescribed intervals to discharge such legislative, executive and judicial functions as are prescribed by its own constitution and bylaws or the national constitution and bylaws (such as co-ordinating the work of and disciplining congregations, and establishing both administrative and advisory bodies).[144] For example, the Evangelical Lutheran Church in America is divided into Synods,[145] each with a Synod Assembly which meets biennially and consists of the bishop (president), its officers (e.g. secretary), and ministerial and lay members elected by the congregations (and 60 per cent of its voting members must be lay people); the Synod Assembly is the 'highest legislative authority' in the Synod and may amend the synod constitution and bylaws.[146] Moreover, each synod must have a Synod Council which acts as the board of directors with 'interim legislative authority' between meetings of the Synod Assembly, as well as an Executive Committee.[147] Methodism too, has a system of districts, which consists of circuits, subject to the jurisdiction of the Conference.[148] For instance, in the Methodist Church in Ireland,

---

[142] For executive committees, see e.g. Wales: Const., IV.A.23–28; TEC: Const., Art. IV; for boards, etc., see e.g. England: Diocesan Boards of Finance Measure 1925, s. 1–3: the Board must comply with synod directions.

[143] ELCIC: Const., Art. X: a synod is e.g. to shepherd congregations, advance church mission, conserve unity, develop resources and co-operate with the National Church Council; Church of Norway: General Synod and Diocesan Councils; Church of Sweden: General Synod and Diocesan Synods; EKD-Central Germany: synod.

[144] LCA: Const., Art. IX; BL, IX: each district has a constitution and bylaws and exercises 'general supervision over the members of the Ministry and the congregations' within it and collaborates with the wider church; the District Synod, 'the highest authority of the District', consists of ministers and lay delegates elected by congregations; it may amend the district constitution and bylaws if approved by General Synod or General Church Council; its Church Council implements the Synod programme and policies; Synod may also establish boards, commissions and tribunals. Compare LCMS: Const., Art. XII; BL, 1.4 and 4; 5: the Synod is divided into districts (set by Synod); a District Convention is 'the principal legislative assembly' for the district and its circuits and makes its own constitution and bylaws; Synod is 'not an ecclesiastical government exercising legislative or coercive powers' over a congregation (with its 'right of self-government') but 'an advisory body'; ELCSA (N–T): G., 10.7: this has circuits, each with a synod and committee under the oversight of a dean.

[145] ELCA: Const., Ch. 8.13, 10.20–21: a Synod (as partner of the churchwide organisation) has 'primary responsibility for the oversight of the life and mission of [ELCA] in its territory', the pastoral care of congregations and ministers, leadership, discipline, mission and interdependence of congregations.

[146] ELCA: Const., Ch. 10.31 and 41; see also Const. for Synods, Ch. 18.

[147] ELCA: Const., Ch. 10.50–22: Synod Council; 60–63: Executive Committee.

[148] MCGB: CPD, SO 400: the Conference designates a district 'to advance the mission of the Church in a region, by providing opportunities for Circuits to work together and support each other, by offering them resources of finance, personnel and expertise which may not be available locally and by enabling them to engage with the wider society of the region as a whole'; MCNZ:

the circuits are grouped into districts administered by a District Synod (a committee of the Conference) which consists of 'all the Ministers in the area, together with Lay Representatives appointed in accordance with the Rules and Regulations of the Conference' – these sit respectively in a Ministerial Session and a Representative Session. The District Synod normally assembles twice a year. The powers, duties and privileges of a District Synod are set out in the Rules and Regulations of the Conference – its function is to give effect to the rules and regulations of the Conference within its own area, and to prepare business for the ensuing Conference with the power of recommendation and suggestion; the District Synod is assisted between its sessions by a District Advisory Committee.[149]

Regional units are also a feature of the Reformed tradition. Reformed churches are divided into regions or districts each with an assembly, such as a Regional Synod or District Council, composed of ministers and elders delegated by each of the classes within its bounds, meeting at prescribed intervals (typically annually) to exercise a general superintendence, an appellate supervisory power, and an administrative authority over its classes (such as the creation and dissolution of classes); it has prescribed officers (including a president) and may establish other offices and bodies for its administration.[150] In Presbyterian polity, the Presbytery is a court which gives spiritual leadership to the ministers, officers and congregations within its bounds; it appoints a moderator (an elder or deacon responsible for order) and a clerk (to record its proceedings), has a membership of representative elders elected by the Kirk Sessions and meets at prescribed times to legislate, adjudicate on disputes and administer its affairs.[151] For example, an Irish Presbytery is 'the body

---

LAR, s. 4: the 'regional courts responsible to the Conference and ... Parishes ... exercise governance on behalf of the Conference ... and exercise a corporate episcopacy of the people ... in their districts and regions'; a District Synod promotes e.g. evangelism; it has an Executive Committee and committees on e.g. Discipleship and Evangelism; Synod is composed of its officers (e.g. Synod superintendent, convenor), presbyters, deacons, lay workers and parish lay representatives; it meets quarterly; UMCNEAE: BOD, pars. 657–668; COTN: Man., Part II, Art. III: District Assemblies.

[149] MCI: Const., s.5; RDG, 9: the District Advisory Committee is composed of the district superintendent (who presides), two ministers and two lay persons; other committees include the District Property Committee. See also MCGB: CPD, SO 412: the District Synod is a link between Conference, circuits and local churches; it oversees district affairs, formulates policies through its officers and committees, inspires church leaders, and acts as forum for issues of public concern; 401: committees; 414: officers; 417: elections to Conference.

[150] RCA: BCO, Ch. I, Pt. III, Arts. 1–7: a Regional Synod is 'an assembly and judicatory ... of ministers and elders delegated by each of the classes within the bounds determined for it by the General Synod'; it exercises 'a general superintendence over the interests and concerns of the classes within its bounds', e.g. forms/disbands classes, meets annually, has prescribed officers, and reports annually and appoints a delegate to General Synod; URC: Man., B.2.3: the District Council (moderator and representatives of local churches) meets annually to discharge tasks under the URC Acts 1972, 1981, 2000; see also B.2.4: the Provincial (or National) Synod.

[151] CLCS: 97: Act VIII, 1996: moderator; Act III, 1992: membership; PCA: BCO, 10: officers; 11: it may make 'rules for the government, discipline, worship, and extension of the Church', resolve questions of doctrine and discipline, and refer disputes to the higher courts; 12: it consists of teaching and ruling elders elected by each Session; 13: it may consider appeals, complaints, and references; receive, examine and license candidates for ministry; review records of Sessions and redress their acts contrary to church order; ensure obedience to the higher courts; administer

primarily responsible for corporate oversight of the congregations and causes assigned to it by the General Assembly'; it may issue 'ordinances' but must observe 'the laws and directions of the Assembly'; and it 'superintends' the 'spiritual and temporal affairs of its congregations'.[152] By way of contrast, in New Zealand: 'A presbytery may exercise executive, judicial and administrative functions, but has no legislative powers' over members, congregations and ministers as to matters committed to it by the General Assembly; its primary role is to 'facilitate and resource the life, worship, spiritual nurture and mission of the congregations for which it has responsibility', ordain ministers and ensure the administration of word and sacrament; it may suggest legislative proposals to General Assembly and consider legislative proposals of the latter; it is independent and it must not interfere in the operations of another presbytery.[153]

In Congregational polity, authority vests in a regional assembly by virtue of conferral by local congregations. For instance, the United Congregational Church of Southern Africa 'is divided into regions whose bounds and designation are determined by the Assembly': a region consists of local churches. The Regional Council is a court with representative members elected by local churches (on a basis determined by the Regional Council), its officers (including moderator, president and secretary) and co-opted members. The functions of the Regional Council are: (1) to be concerned with the welfare of all local churches; (2) to receive and act on business submitted to it by the local churches, Synod and Assembly; (3) to raise and administer funds; (4) to investigate and adjudicate in any matter referred to it by a local church, Synodical Committee or the Assembly Executive Committee; and (5) to approve calls to ministry in local churches, place ministers in them and 'issue directives/instructions to local churches within its bounds'. The Administrative Committee transacts the business of the Council between sessions and the Council's Standing Committees (e.g. the Ministerial Committee, Finance Committee and Mission Council) report to the Council or its Administrative Committee. Amendments to the constitution of the Regional Council must be approved by the Synod (a court of the Assembly).[154] Similarly, in Baptist polity, a region is 'a formal partnership of Associations that have been recognized by the [national] Conference',[155] and an Association is 'an organization of Baptist churches in a specific geographic area that have been formally recognized by the Conference',[156] which is

---

discipline; visit, unite, divide or form churches; dismiss churches with their consent; and propose measures to General Assembly; it records its proceedings and meets twice a year.

[152] PCI: Code, pars. 61–79: it consists of ministers and ruling elders appointed by each Kirk Session, has officers (moderator, clerk), meets four times per annum, forms new congregations if authorised by General Assembly, approves calls from congregations, ordains, installs and oversees ministers (e.g. in preaching, doctrine), and inquires into the work of Kirk Sessions and Congregational Meetings; 141–147: transaction of business; 148–155: rules of debate; 156–160: voting; 227–234: new congregations; 256: annual report to the General Assembly.

[153] PCANZ: BO, 8: it meets at least once a year. See also PCW: HOR, 3.2; UFCS: MPP, IV.I–III.

[154] UCCSA: Const., 4.4; UCOC: Const., Art. VIII: Associations (of local churches) are Conference members; UCA: Const., Arts. 25–30 and Regs., 3.4: Presbytery; UCC: Man., BU, s. 6 and BL 300–393: Presbytery.

[155] NABC: Const., 3.3.

[156] NABC: Const., 3.2: also: 'Each Association or Region shall establish policies and practices that are in harmony with the Conference Statement of Beliefs.'

united by way of a constitution.[157] The assembly of the regional association may issue policy statements and resolutions which may be freely adopted by its autonomous local churches.[158] In short, a diocese, synod, district, presbytery, association or other regional unit is governed by a bishop and/or an assembly whose jurisdiction is derived either from an international or national authority or from the local church, whose membership is representative of ordained ministers and lay people, and whose functions may be legislative, administrative and judicial.

The local church: institutions and structures

Regional units are further composed of local units. Catholic, Orthodox and Anglican dioceses are divided into parishes. Lutherans and Methodists have congregations and, sometimes, parishes. In the Reformed, Presbyterian, Congregational and Baptist models, regions and districts are typically composed of circuits, congregations and local churches. Each unit has its own assembly. Common to all traditions is their mixed ordained and lay composition and the autonomy they enjoy to the extent prescribed by law. Differences are found in their titles, authority and functions. For instance, Catholics, Orthodox and Anglicans have Parish Councils; Lutherans have Church Committees; Methodists have Circuit Meetings, Church Councils and Classes; Reformed have a Consistory and Classis; Presbyterians have (Kirk) Sessions and Congregational Meetings; Congregationalists have Church Meetings; and Baptists have Meetings and other assemblies.

In Catholic canon law (Latin and Oriental) each diocese or eparchy is divided into parishes.[159] In the Latin Church, a parish is 'a certain community of Christ's faithful stably established within a particular church, whose pastoral care, under the authority of the diocesan bishop, is entrusted to a parish priest as its proper pastor'. A parish has juridical personality and the bishop alone is competent to erect, suppress or alter parishes.[160] After the bishop has consulted the Presbyteral Council, and if he judges it expedient, a pastoral council is to be established in each parish; the pastor presides, and through the council the faithful assist in fostering pastoral activity; the council has a consultative (not determinative) vote and is governed by norms determined by the bishop.[161] Each parish must also have a finance committee to assist the parish priest in the administration of the parish; it must act in accordance with universal law and norms issued by the diocesan bishop (who determines the mode of selecting its members).[162] The pastor is the administrator of the parish property and must keep and preserve parish sacramental

---

[157] BUSA: Const., 2: a Territorial Association 'includes 10 or more member churches in a district ... united by ... a formal constitution ... for ... fellowship and service and admitted ... to the ... Union by a 75% vote of the Assembly'; a General Association 'comprises individuals, churches or groups united ... by ... a constitution acceptable to the Union' and recognised by it.

[158] ABCUSA: Const., XIII (and SR 13): see also TCOR, V.

[159] CIC, c. 374: for common action, neighbouring parishes may be grouped (e.g. in vicariates forane).

[160] CIC, c. 515; c. 518: personal parishes may also be established according to rite, language or nationality.

[161] CIC, c. 536; W. Dalton, 'Parish councils or parish pastoral councils', 22 *Studia Canonica* (1988) 169.

[162] CIC, c. 537.

records and archives.[163] Similar arrangements exist in the Oriental Catholic Churches: an eparchy consists of parishes each with its own priest and two councils, one which assists in pastoral matters and the other financial matters – both are regulated by statutes in accordance with the norms of particular law.[164]

Whilst some Orthodox churches have intermediate deaneries,[165] each diocese or eparchy is divided into parishes established by the diocesan assembly: the most local 'canonical unit' is the parish, 'a community of Orthodox Christians under the supervision of the diocesan bishop and guided by a rector; parish boundaries are determined by the Diocesan Council'.[166] Each parish has a parish assembly which elects lay representatives to a parish council which with the parish priest carries out parish administration as to mission, property and finance – but it has no authority over doctrine.[167] For example, a Russian Orthodox parish 'in its religious, administrative, financial and economic activities shall be subordinate and accountable to the Diocesan Bishop'; the administration of the parish is in the hands of the Rector, Parish Meeting, Parish Council and the Auditing Commission. The Parish Meeting is composed of the clergy and laity who regularly participate in the life of the parish and are in good standing; it meets annually *inter alia*: to elect the Parish Council; preserve and promote the spiritual and moral life of the parish; plan parish finances and economic activities; safeguard parish property; and consider complaints against members of the Parish Council. The Parish Council is 'an executive and managerial body of the parish meeting' and is accountable to the rector and Parish Meeting – its principal function is to implement the decisions of the Parish Meeting; the Auditing Commission carries out regular audits and administers donations.[168] Similar arrangements are found in parishes of the Greek Archdiocese of America.[169]

---

[163] CIC, cc. 532, 535, 1220, 1279, 1281–1288.
[164] CCEO, c. 279: 'the parish is a community of Christian faithful established on a stable basis in an eparchy, whose pastoral care is entrusted to a parish priest'; cc. 295–296: the councils.
[165] See e.g. UOCIA: Statutes, Art. X: deaneries are districts within a diocese established by the Diocesan Council; each one has a District Dean; ROMOC: Statutes, Arts. 40, 69–70; 40: the 'local organisation' of ROMOC is composed of the following 'units: the parish, monastery, deanery, eparchy and metropolitan see', each one 'entitled to lead and administer itself autonomously' and through its clerical and lay representatives to participate in 'the life of the church above these units'; GOAA: Charter, Arts. 21–22.
[166] ROMOC: Statutes, Arts. 43–68; see also UOCIA: Statutes, Art. XI; GOAA: Regs., Definitions: parish: the 'local organised Eucharistic Orthodox Christian body of Communicants within the Archdiocese headed by a Priest'.
[167] UOCIA: Statutes, Art. XI: a parish meeting elects a parish council to assist the priest in 'administration of the parish and to execute the decisions of the parish meeting'; it is chaired by a lay person and responsible 'not only for the spiritual and material needs ... but also for the parish's unity and connection with the Diocese'; MOSC: Const., 2.6-31: 'Every Parish Church shall have a Parish Assembly'; it meets twice yearly and has a Managing Committee; ROMOC: Statutes, Arts. 43–68: the Parochial Assembly elects the Parochial Council (executive).
[168] ROC: Statute, XI: XI.8: a parish may withdraw from the church.
[169] GOAA: Regs. 24–33: a Parish Assembly is 'the general meeting of the Parishioners in good standing ... and the general policymaking and appropriating body of the Parish'; convened by the priest and Parish Assembly, which meets at least twice yearly, the Council is responsible to the Parish Assembly and hierarch; Council members are elected from parishioners and ratified by the hierarch; the Council meets at least once a month to: 'assist the priest in the administration of the affairs and ministries of the Parish'; establish committees (e.g. on finance, planning and property); administer finances; and submit an annual report as required by the

An Anglican diocese also consists of more localised ecclesiastical units: in some there are intermediate archdeaconries and deaneries; in the vast majority of churches, however, the diocese is directly divided into parishes,[170] or other forms of pastorate, the territorial organisation of which is usually in the keeping of the diocesan assembly.[171] Each parish is governed by an assembly which consists of clergy and representatives of the laity elected at an annual meeting of the ecclesiastical unit; the assembly (variously styled a Council, Vestry or Committee) is usually under the presidency of the minister in charge of the unit and elaborate rules cover meetings, quorum and decision-making.[172] The local assembly and minister must co-operate in the governance of the parish (or other unit) in the exercise of its spiritual, governmental and administrative functions; typically, the assembly must promote the whole mission of the church, pastoral, evangelistic, social and ecumenical; it must submit reports to the standing committee of the diocesan assembly (e.g. with data on baptisms, confirmations, marriages and the state of the unit), elect officers to the diocesan assembly, consider and implement matters referred to it by the diocesan bishop or assembly, provide for the administration of property and finance and co-operate at visitations.[173]

According to Lutheran polity, each synod, diocese or district consists of congregations or parishes in which the church universal is present.[174] Each unit enjoys such autonomy as is prescribed by law and is administered by its own elected assembly (Council or Committee) representative of the faithful.[175] The Lutheran Church in Australia is typical: a congregation is 'a group of persons adhering to

Archdiocese, Archdiocesan District and Metropolis: 'Each Parish shall be administered by the priest and Parish Council cooperatively.'

[170] PCLCCAC, Principle 21.

[171] For archdeaconries and deaneries see e.g. Ireland: Const., II.42; England: Synodical Government Measure 1969, s. 3: a deanery has a synod (an archdeaconry, divided into deaneries, does not); for parishes, see e.g. Brazil: Cans. I.1; for pastorates, see e.g. South India: Const., VII.I: 'A pastorate is an organised congregation or group recognised as such by the Diocesan Council, under the superintendence of a presbyter.'

[172] E.g. Papua New Guinea: Can., No. 5 of 1977, 19: representation; Southern Africa: Can. 27: the annual vestry elects the representatives; Wales: Const., IV.C: meetings etc. of the Parochial Church Council.

[173] E.g. Wales: Const., VI.22: mission; TEC: Cans. I.6: report to the diocesan convention; Scotland: Can. 60: administration of property and finance; Papua New Guinea: Can. 5 of 1977, 18: co-operation at visitations.

[174] LCGB: RAR, Definition of a Congregation, 1–2: 'a community of baptised Christians who meet regularly for the proclamation of the Gospel and the administration of the Sacraments'; ELCA: Const., Ch. 3: 'the universal Church exists in and through the congregations'; Ch. 9.10–11: its purpose is 'to worship God, to nurture its members, and to reach out in witness and service to the world'; thus: 'it assembles regularly for worship and nurture, organizes and carries out ministry to its people and neighbourhood, and cooperates with and supports the wider church'; ELCIC: Const., Arts. III and VI, ABL, Pt. II.2; LCMS: BL, 1.3.1.

[175] ELCSA: G., 10: a Congregation (as Body of Christ), directed by the minister and Church Committee, 'administers its own affairs' e.g. instruction, discipline, spiritual care and mission; the Church Committee is the pastor, churchwardens and others elected by the congregation; ELCIC: Const., Art. 11–18: the annual Church Assembly elects the Parish Council; ELCA: Const., Ch. 9.31: a congregation has 'authority in all matters that are not assigned by the constitution and bylaws of [ELCA] to synods' and wider church; 50–52: members.

the Lutheran Faith who regularly meet for the administration of the means of Grace and who have constituted themselves as an organised body by the adoption of a constitution' – a congregation acts 'in association as a parish'.[176] A congregation is subject to the jurisdiction of the church as to its adherence to the Confession, doctrinal discipline and any 'persistent disregard of the resolutions of the Church' – but the jurisdiction of the church does not extend to 'the purely internal administration of a congregation'.[177] A congregation (seeking membership) must accept the Church Confession, Constitution and Bylaws, submit its own constitution and bylaws, and undertake to participate in the objects of the church; church membership and amendments to its (congregational) constitution must be approved by the District Church Council to be operative.[178] Congregational membership of the church may be terminated by the congregation itself (by a resolution passed with a two-thirds majority) or by the church.[179]

At local level, Methodist churches are divided into circuits and these into societies, classes and congregations.[180] In the Methodist Church in Great Britain the circuit is a unit of one or more local churches and 'the primary unit in which Local Churches express and experience their interconnexion in the Body of Christ'. The purposes of the circuit include the deployment of resources for ministry (people, property and finance), and promoting and supporting the work of the society 'to the end that every member may share actively in world mission'. The circuit meeting, composed of the circuit superintendent (who presides), ministers and elected representatives from each local church, is 'the principal meeting responsible for the affairs of a Circuit' and 'the development of circuit policy'; it exercises a 'combination of spiritual leadership and administrative efficiency' and is the focal point of 'the working fellowship of the churches in the Circuit, overseeing their pastoral, training and evangelistic work' and the encouragement of leadership.[181] The Church Council is 'the principal meeting responsible for the affairs of a Local

---

[176] LCA: Const., Interpretation: 'congregation'; Arts. III–IV, and BL, V.D; Const., 4.03: one object of the LCA is to 'encourage every congregation to carry out its mission to its local community' and to 'establish, develop and support new congregations where it is not possible for individual congregations to do so'.

[177] LCA: Const., Art. VI.7. See also ELCIC: ABL, Pt. VI: a parish consists of baptised persons served by a common pastoral ministry in one/more congregations; ELCIRE: Const., Art. 9: parish.

[178] LCA: Const., IV.1; BL IV.1–2. See also LCGB: RAR, Congregations, 1: a congregation must accept the Statement of Faith, Constitution, Rules and Regulations, and have its own constitution; ELCA: Const., Ch. 9.20–21, 9.60–62: admission and termination; LCMS: Const., Art. VI.

[179] LCA: Const., Art. IV.3, BL IV.3. See also ELCIC: Administrative Bylaws, Pt. II.3–6: expulsion; ELCSA: G., 89.2: the Church Committee (or Congregational Council) decides on applications for individual membership.

[180] MCI: General Rules of the Society (1743): a Society is 'a company of men having the form, and seeking the power, of Godliness; united in order to pray together, to receive the word of exhortation, and to watch over one another in love, that they may help each other to work out their salvation'; each Society is divided into smaller companies, Classes, of about twelve persons and a Leader (see Chapter 3); RDG, 10: Circuit Meeting, Congregational Meeting (which elects the Church Council) and Circuit Executive.

[181] MCGB: CPD, DU 1(v)–(vi); SO 500–517; 501: changes to circuits are in the keeping of the Conference.

150   THE INSTITUTIONS OF ECCLESIASTICAL GOVERNANCE

Church' or 'Society'.[182] It is composed of ministers and lay representatives elected by the annual General Church Meeting and has 'authority and oversight over the whole area of the ministry of the church'; it may appoint committees to discharge its functions.[183] Some Methodist churches with bishops have parishes,[184] governed by a Congregational Meeting,[185] a Leaders' Meeting[186] and a Parish Meeting,[187] and others, in their 'connectional societies',[188] have pastoral charges with a Charge Conference and a Church Council (the executive agency of the Charge Conference).[189]

In the Reformed tradition the local church is governed by an assembly composed of the minister and representatives of the congregation.[190] For example, in the Reformed Church in America, a congregation is 'a body of baptized Christians meeting regularly in a particular place of worship'; a local church is a congregation properly organised and governed by a Consistory, namely: 'the governing body of a local church' consisting of ministers, elders and deacons. The Consistory must, for

---

[182] MCGB: CPD, DU 1(iii); see also SO 61: church council; DU 1(xv): 'Local church and society are equivalents and mean "the whole body of members of the Methodist Church connected with and attending one particular place of worship"'; SO 600(1): it 'exercises ... worship, fellowship, pastoral care, mission and service'; SO 602: 'In the government of the Local Church the several responsibilities must be exercised without the loss of the unity of the one ministry. The Church Council is constituted to unite those who hold responsibility in the church in one working community. It has the authority to take decisions for the church and to manage its affairs to this same end. The General Church Meeting has a responsibility to consider the whole ministry of the church and every part of it and in making appointments to ensure the co-operation of the whole church in that ministry.'

[183] MCGB: CPD, SO 603: duties; 604: committees; 605: formation; 610: members; 621: Church Meeting.

[184] MCNZ: LAR, s. 3, 1–2: 'The Parish is a visible expression of the body of Christ in a particular place' and comprises 'one or more congregations situated in an area and in a relationship with each other as from time to time determined by the Conference'.

[185] MCNZ: LAR, s. 3, 3.1–4: this meets at least annually to e.g. consider the life and mission of the congregation.

[186] MCNZ: LAR, s. 3, 4.1–4.8: the Leaders' Meeting (of those appointed from the Electoral Roll) normally meets monthly to e.g. give leadership to and in the congregation.

[187] MCNZ: LAR, s. 3, 5.1–5.9: Parish Meeting members are appointed by the Leaders' Meeting e.g. 'to co-ordinate congregational life within its area and give oversight to the life and work of the congregations'.

[188] UMCNEAE: BOD, pars. 201–203: 'The local church provides the most significant arena through which disciple-making occurs. It is a community of true believers under the Lordship of Christ.'

[189] UMCNEAE: BOD, par. 206: pastoral charge; 243: organisation; 244: administration and planning; 251: Charge Conference; 252: the pastor is the 'administrative officer'; 246–251: membership and functions; 252: Church Council; 259: formation of a new church with the consent of the bishop; FMCNA: BOD, Ch. 6.

[190] URC: Man., B.1: a local church consists of members associated in a locality for worship, witness and service; the Church Meeting is presided over by the minister and meets quarterly to e.g. further the church's mission, offer ministry in the locality, call ministers with the consent of Synod, elect elders and officers and admit and transfer members; B.2.1: the Elders' Meeting (the minister and elders) has 'spiritual oversight'; it is presided over by the minister e.g. to foster concern for witness and service to the community, evangelism, Christian education, ensure that public worship is regularly offered and the sacraments duly administered, provide for the pastoral welfare of the congregation and arrange for pulpit supply in a vacancy.

example, provide a minister and services of worship, oversee property and finance, supervise the election of elders and deacons, and appoint a president (minister), vice-president (elder) and clerk. Its Board of Elders meets at least four times a year to admit persons to membership and maintain a roll; and its Board of Deacons serves those in distress and need. Above the Consistory is the Classis: 'an assembly and judicatory' consisting of all enrolled ministers and the elder delegates who represent the churches within its bounds; it exercises 'a general superintendence' over the ministers and churches in its territory; it must not interfere in the affairs of other classes, consistories or synods; it has original and appellate supervisory power over the acts, proceedings and decisions of the Board of Elders and Consistories in temporal and disciplinary matters; it also forms and dissolves churches, ordains, installs, suspends and deposes ministers, and meets annually.[191]

Presbyterian government at local level is based on the congregation which functions under the authority of the Presbytery: 'A particular church consists of a number of professing Christians, with their children, associated together for divine worship and godly living, agreeable to the Scriptures, and submitting to the lawful government of Christ's kingdom.'[192] The Session (Kirk Session or Council) is the court of the local church.[193] For example, in the Presbyterian Church in Ireland, the Kirk Session consists of the ordained minister(s) and ruling elders of the congregation and has a moderator (minister) and a clerk; it meets at least twice a year to provide for 'the oversight and government of the congregation'. The Kirk Session is 'the governing body of a congregation' and must watch over and promote the spiritual interest of the congregation, contribute to Christian witness and service in the local community, and authorise co-operation with other churches. It calls meetings of the congregation, provides for the administration of the ordinances of sacrament and word, appoints officers, exercises authority over the congregation as to doctrine and conduct (including adjudication in disciplinary cases), keeps a roll of members, promotes stewardship and appoints representatives to the Presbytery and General Assembly.[194] The Kirk Session may call such Congregational Meetings as the Presbytery or a superior court may determine to consider the state of religion and the needs of the community, promote mission, foster fellowship, authorise transactions (e.g. as to property), appoint and remove trustees, appoint auditors and contribute to and raise funds.[195] Congregationalism is not dissimilar.[196]

[191] RCA: BCO, Ch. 1, Pt. I, Arts. 1-6: these may also be styled 'parishes'; Ch. 1, Pt. II, Arts. 1-7: classis; president; officers; transaction of business; the classis president exercises superintendence over the churches.
[192] PCA: BCO, 4-5. See also UFCS: MPP, III.I-III: a congregation is 'a company of persons, together with their children, associated in a particular locality for Christian worship, instruction, fellowship, and work'.
[193] CLCS, 103, Act XVII, 1931: Kirk Session; PCA: BCO, 10-12: Session.
[194] PCI: Code, pars. 25-44; 141-147: transaction of business; 148-155: rules of debate; 156-160: voting; see also PCW: HOR, 3.1: District Meeting; PCANZ: BO, 5: Church Council.
[195] PCI: Code, pars. 45-52.
[196] UCCSA: Const., 3: the local church is 'a fellowship of members of the Church gathered in a particular locality for worship, witness and service' and may consist of one or more congregations; its autonomy is 'recognised'; it is formed by the Regional Council and has its own constitution (complying with the Model Constitution approved by the Assembly); its functions are e.g. to provide for the pastoral care of its members and witness to Christ in the local community; it belongs to a circuit and has a Congregational Meeting to e.g. provide worship,

In Baptist polity the local church is the primary location of authority with its own institutions of governance.[197] For example, in the Baptist Union of Southern Africa: 'the local church, being a manifestation of the universal church, is a community of believers in a particular place where the Word of God is preached and the ordinances of Believers' Baptism and the Lord's Supper are observed. It is fully autonomous and remains so notwithstanding responsibilities it may accept by voluntary association'; however, it 'shall seek and maintain membership with [BUSA] but shall be independent of any control by it save as hereinafter provided'; the local church is 'to manage its affairs according to the New Testament, believing that as the Body of Christ it is equipped by His Spirit to act, decide and direct', to glorify the Lord, proclaim the Gospel and provide instruction and fellowship for believers. The local church must hold an Annual General Meeting to receive reports from church departments, elect deacons, consider audited financial statements and elect the ordinary quarterly General Meeting which has an Executive: the pastors, deacons and elders constitute the executive to act as directed by the General Meeting.[198] The constitutions of local Baptist churches provide for their own organisation on the basis of a church covenant, with a council, officers and standing committees (such as on ministry, education, administration, finance).[199]

---

receive members, maintain property and elect deacons and officers; the Church Meeting consists of all congregations in the local church, is presided over by the minister and oversees discipline and doctrine; UCOC: Const., Art. V: the local church is the 'basic unit' for worship, fellowship and witness – its autonomy is 'inherent and modifiable only by its own action' and the General Synod has no power 'to abridge or impair the autonomy of any local Church in the management of its own affairs' (e.g. covenants, confession of faith, discipline, property and finance) but decisions of the General Synod, a Conference or an Association 'should be held in the highest regard by every Local Church'; UCC: Man., BU.3 and BL 101–295.

[197] ABCUSA: TCOR, I.A-B: 'A local congregation, as a company of believers covenanting together to maintain a worshipping, caring, and witnessing fellowship in the name of Jesus Christ, is endowed by the Holy Spirit and is free and capable of ordering its inner life', e.g. determining its membership, maintaining discipline, selecting officers, fixing its relations with other congregations and/or ecclesiastical bodies and its own confessional position: 'The freedom of the congregation is genuine, but not absolute, since the nature of the body of Christ calls for interdependence between congregations whether in associational, regional, national, denomination-wide, or international expressions of the Church'; self-government must be balanced by an affirmation of the biblical imperative for Christian unity; local congregations covenant together to form broader manifestations of the Church to strengthen local congregations in their fidelity to the gospel: 'Denominational structures are established to facilitate dialogue, debate, and even dissent in dealing openly with our disagreements.'

[198] BUSA: Model Const., Art. 4: the 'congregational principle' of oversight by pastors and elders; Art. 3: it may withdraw by resolution on a 90% vote at a meeting of members; Art. 11: the pastors, deacons and elders are the executive which acts as directed by the General Meeting and is responsible for the administration of e.g. funds: Art. 13; dissolution of the church: Art. 23; modification of the constitution by the General Meeting: Art. 24.

[199] Central Baptist Church (Pretoria): Const., Arts. 10 and 17: Executive; 11: General Meeting (which may frame regulations: Art. 19); Art. 27: constitutional amendment; Riverside Baptist Church (Baltimore): Const., Art. III: committees (e.g. worship, ministry, education, administration, finance, church council); IV: meetings; V: amendments to the constitution and bylaws; Bethel Baptist Church (Choctaw): Const., Art. VI.

Conclusion

Despite their historical and doctrinal differences about the nature, origin and location of ecclesiastical authority, the regulatory instruments of churches generate a high degree of commonality amongst Christians worldwide in terms of convergent action. This is the case irrespective of actual denominational affiliation. All the Christian traditions studied here use international, national, regional and local structures of ecclesiastical polity. However, their institutions at these levels enjoy very different degrees of legislative, executive and judicial authority. At international level, the Catholic Church (Latin and Oriental) has a system of global polity with papal jurisdiction exercisable over the universal church; Orthodox patriarchates also exercise international authority. But the institutions of the worldwide Anglican Communion, Lutheran World Federation, World Communion of Reformed Churches, World Methodist Council and Baptist World Alliance have no general jurisdiction over their autonomous member churches. At the national level, the Catholic Episcopal Conference is subject to papal authority, and national Orthodox assemblies may be subject to the superior authority of the patriarchate. The role of the laity at this level in Orthodoxy is greater than that in Catholicism, where the laity possess no power of governance. By way of contrast, at the national level the central assemblies of Anglican, Lutheran, Methodist, Reformed and Presbyterian churches exercise coercive jurisdiction over the ecclesiastical units within them – and the laity participates directly in these assemblies – but the national Baptist Unions and Conventions exercise a much more limited authority over the local Baptist church. Regional government is also carried out subject to national or international authorities in some of the ecclesial traditions: the diocesan assemblies of Orthodox, Anglicans and Lutherans, and the assemblies of Protestant districts and presbyteries, all have authority to govern at that level; but in the Catholic Church the diocesan synod merely assists the bishop to govern; and in the Baptist tradition regional or associational bodies may guide but not direct the local church, which is autonomous. At the most localised ecclesiastical level, the local church is a manifestation of the church universal. It is configured as between traditions under a range of titles. However, these parishes, circuits and congregations have their own assemblies of governance – in all the traditions except the Congregational and Baptist, these are subject to the authority of the higher bodies or courts. It is a principle of Christian constitutional law that legislative, administrative (or executive) and judicial functions in church government are shaped by subsidiarity and the rule of law and enjoyed by such members of the faithful as are lawfully elected or otherwise appointed to exercise them.

5

Ecclesiastical discipline and conflict resolution

The study of religious courts is commonplace in contemporary scholarship. However, to date, there has been no comparative study of the tribunals and other dispute resolution structures within Christianity. The juridical instruments of Christian churches provide a very wide range of mechanisms to enforce ecclesiastical discipline and to resolve internally disputes between church members. Whilst the governance of ecclesiastical discipline is sometimes within the jurisdictional competence of central legislatures either at international or national level, generally these instruments reserve to the regional or local church institutions the responsibility of resolving disputes involving both ordained clergy and lay persons. The use of visitation, an ancient Christian institution preserved in the juridical systems of the vast majority of churches, is another important means by which quasi-judicial power may be applied to ecclesiastical conflict. In addition, most of the traditions studied operate a hierarchical court or tribunal system to deal with instances of ecclesiastical indiscipline of the clergy and, often, of the laity. Elaborate provision is made for due process. The concept of an ecclesiastical offence is a common and fundamental feature of all the ecclesiastical disciplinary systems, as is the provision of sanctions. This chapter proposes that from the profound similarities between the juridical instruments of churches emerge shared principles of modern Christian laws on church discipline and conflict resolution which exist regardless of the system of church polity operative within the particular ecclesial tradition.

The nature and purposes of ecclesiastical discipline

There is considerable juridical unity between Christian churches in terms of recognition of the need and right both to enforce discipline and to resolve conflicts amongst the faithful. This need is implicit in the presence of judicial power (or the function of adjudication) in the institutional polity of churches. Theological justifications for discipline are also commonly woven into legal texts which address this matter. For the Catholic Church 'the integral development of the human and Christian person ... positively includes penal discipline' as a means of 'fostering communion'; the existence of 'judicial power' to sustain discipline is fundamental to governance in the Catholic Church and is recognised as such in both Latin and Oriental canon law – the church has 'its own and exclusive right to judge' in spiritual and disciplinary matters and this belongs to the church by divine institution;[1] but judicial process is treated as the last resort – disputants are under a duty

---

[1] Pope John Paul II, First Address to the Roman Rota, 'The Church and Protection of Fundamental Human Rights', in W.H. Woestman (ed.), *Papal Allocutions to the Roman Rota (1939–1994)*

to settle amicably, promptly and equitably out of court – and the Episcopal Conference (at national level) is encouraged to establish permanent offices in every diocese to resolve disputes without going to the tribunals of the church.[2] The categories of 'discipline' and 'adjudication' also appear in Orthodox and Anglican laws: in the former, discipline is understood as founded on divine authority and exercised through church judicial authority;[3] and in the latter discipline exists to enable the church to fulfil its mission, to preserve unity and peace, and to cure the failings of the faithful amongst whom '[t]he laity are subject to discipline to the extent and in the manner prescribed by law'; however, as in Catholicism, recourse to the church courts is a last resort.[4]

By way of contrast, Protestant juridical instruments contain far richer statements about the attributes of discipline and adjudication in terms of their importance, underlying authority and ecclesial purpose. First, some Protestant churches across the traditions assert their own right to 'apply discipline',[5] as well as their own authority to adjudicate on disputes between their units and ordained and lay members.[6] The competence to discipline is based on the idea that the church is under the 'rule and authority' of Christ,[7] or 'the discipline of the Holy Spirit'.[8]

(St Paul University, Ottawa, 1994) 153–158 at 156; CIC, c. 135.1-2: the power of governance includes 'judicial power'; c. 1401: the right of the church to judge in spiritual matters and in cases of 'the violation of ecclesiastical law and whatever contains an element of sin, to determine guilt and impose ecclesiastical penalties'; c. 129.1: divine institution; CCEO, cc. 979–984: governance; cc. 985–987: powers (including judicial); cc. 988–995: the scope, suspension and loss of power.

[2] CIC, c. 1446: 'All Christ's faithful ... are ... to ensure that disputes among the people of God are as far as possible avoided, and are settled promptly and without rancour.'

[3] MOCL: 111: 'According to the authority granted by our Lord to the Apostles, and through them to their successors the bishops (Mt. 18,18: "Whatsoever ye shall bind on earth shall be bound in heaven; and whatsoever ye shall loose on earth shall be loosed in heaven."), the bishops are those who exercise true judiciary authority in the Church.' See also e.g. ROC: Statute X: Diocesan Bishops, 18: 'In supervising canonical order and church discipline' the bishop shall (e.g.) 'admonish laymen and, if need be, impose punishments upon or temporarily excommunicate them; submit grave misdemeanours to the consideration of the ecclesiastical court'.

[4] RACCL, 3, 4: discipline is needed to 'prevent anything creeping into [the church's] life that may hinder it from performing its proper functions'; 'the Church is for the most part made up of ordinary frail human beings'; PCLCCAC: Principle 6.6: 'Persons who exercise ecclesiastical governance, as agents of healing and reconciliation, are to be a visible sign of unity and should not jeopardise that unity or be the cause or focus of division and strife by the exercise of their leadership'; 3.5: laws deal with e.g. 'discipline'; 24.1: jurisdiction in matters of discipline; 25.4: lay discipline; 26.6: self-discipline; 37.1: the bishop is 'guardian of discipline' and (38.6): is to 'maintain ecclesiastical discipline to the extent and in the manner prescribed by law'; 41.2: clergy should lead a 'disciplined way of life' and (48.8) follow the 'discipline of Christ'; 50.1: the discipline of the church universal; 24: 'Due judicial process'; 24.2: amicable resolution; and 25.4: the laity.

[5] LCA: Const., Art. VI.7: i.e. 'when departure from ... doctrine ... is evident' or for 'persistent disregard of the resolutions of the Church'; but not 'over the purely internal administration of a congregation'.

[6] LCA: Const., Art. X.1–3; Const. of the Districts, X; BL, X.A.1–3: 'The Church shall establish a judicial system to deal with discipline and adjudication. The rules governing such judicial system shall be laid down in the By-laws'; 'Ecclesiastical discipline shall be exercised in a District by a congregation against any one of its members who evidently departs from the confession of the church or manifestly leads an ungodly life'; a district may adjudicate disputes between congregations and must establish judicial procedure to deal with discipline.

[7] ELCA: Const., Ch. 4.03, and 5.01ff.   [8] UMCNEAE: BOD, par. 201.

Secondly, therefore, for many churches, disciplinary competence is based on scriptural,[9] or divine,[10] authority; typically: 'Discipline is an ordinance appointed by the Lord Jesus Christ as King and head of the Church, to be administered by the Church in His name and under His authority by methods in harmony with the constitution of the Church as a spiritual community'.[11] Sometimes discipline is seen as 'the process by which the Church seeks to exercise the authority given by Christ, both in the guidance, control and nurture of its members, and in the correction of offenders'.[12] Discipline covers 'the whole government, inspection, training, guardianship and control which the church maintains over its members, its officers and its courts', or it may apply (technically) only to the 'judicial process' (that is, to the resolution of disputes).[13]

Thirdly, the aims of discipline are divine, corporate and personal: discipline is 'directed to the glory of God, the purity of the Church and the spiritual benefit of members';[14] it seeks to preserve truth and duty,[15] and 'to foster and protect ... the objectives of the Church'.[16] For some churches, discipline is an aspect of individual discipleship – 'to sustain and strengthen the members to obey the word of God, to protect them from sin, to uplift those who have fallen and guide them back into the fellowship of the congregation'.[17] As such, discipline is restorative: 'Ecclesiastical discipline shall be carried out in an evangelical manner in accordance with scriptural principles and upholding the rules of natural justice. At all stages of the procedure the purpose of all ecclesiastical discipline, to gain a member, is to be observed.'[18] Again: 'The objectives of church discipline are to sustain the integrity of the church, to protect the innocent from harm, to protect the effectiveness of the witness of the church, to warn and correct the careless, to bring the guilty to salvation, to restore to effective service those who are rehabilitated, and to protect the reputation and resources of the church.'[19] The need for discipline 'stems from the imperfect nature of human beings', from the fact that '[t]he Church is a fallible

---

[9] PCI: Code, par. 131: 'Discipline ... is of Scriptural authority'; PCA: BCO, 27.1: 'scriptural law' on discipline.

[10] RCA: BCO, Ch. 2, Pt. I, Art. 1: 'Discipline is the exercise of the authority which ... Christ has given to the church to promote purity, to benefit the offender, and to vindicate [His] honour'; PCW: HOR, s. 1: 'Discipline in the Church is an exercise of that spiritual authority which the Lord Jesus has appointed in His Church.'

[11] UFCS: MPP, VI.I–VI: I: discipline is for 'the maintenance of the Church's purity, the spiritual benefit of her members, and the glory of the Redeemer'.

[12] PCANZ: BO, 15.1.   [13] PCA: BCO, 27.1.   [14] PCI: Code, par. 131.

[15] PCA: BCO, Preface, I: 'discipline for the preservation both of truth and duty'; 'All church courts may err through human frailty, yet it rests upon them to uphold the laws of Scripture though this obligation be lodged with fallible men'; BCO, 11.4: courts oversee discipline to maintain truth and righteousness, 'condemning erroneous opinions and practices which tend to injure the peace, purity or progress of the church'.

[16] PCW: HOR, s. 2.4: 'The purpose of church discipline is to foster and protect, to deepen and to strengthen, the Christian life and objectives of the Church.'

[17] ELCSA: G., 5: each person is 'to be commended in intercession to the mercy of God'; LCMS: BL, 1.10: this justifies discipline by citing scripture; URC: Man., O: '"disciple" and "discipline" have obvious common roots.'

[18] LCA: Const., Art. X.1–3; BL, X.A.1–3; ELCSA: G., 5: its aim is 'to bring back the brother or the sister to renewed faith and into the full communion of the congregation'; LCMS: BL, 1.10.

[19] COTN: Man., Part VI.I: Judicial Administration.

community' and because the behaviour of its members may not only be 'damaging to themselves and others' but also 'undermine the credibility of the Church's witness'; in short, discipline seeks 'to enable healing and reconciliation to take place through ... accountability', responding to 'the call through Christ for justice, openness and honesty, and the need for each of us to accept responsibility for our own acts'.[20]

Fourthly, discipline is moral or spiritual and not temporal or secular: 'Since ecclesiastical discipline must be purely moral or spiritual in its object, and not attended with any civil effects, it can derive no force whatever, but from its own justice, the approbation of an impartial public, and the countenance and blessing of the great Head of the Church.'[21] Consequently, discipline is to be administered with mercy and gentleness: it is to be exercised under 'the dispensation of mercy' and in faithfulness, meekness, love and tenderness for 'the condemnation of offences and the recovery of offenders'.[22] Lastly, in Protestant churches all the faithful – ordained and lay persons – are subject to church discipline: this applies under the polity of Presbyterian,[23] Reformed,[24] Congregational[25] and Baptist churches.[26]

It may at this point be useful to present in outline the position of a single church in order to draw together the principles of church discipline outlined above; the law of the Methodist Church in Ireland provides: 'Discipline in the Church is an exercise of that spiritual authority which the Lord Jesus has appointed in His Church. The ends contemplated by discipline are the maintenance of the purity of the Church, the spiritual benefit of the members and the honour of our Lord'; moreover: 'All Members and Ministers of the Church are subject to its government and discipline, and are under the jurisdiction and care of the appropriate Courts of

---

[20] MCGB: CPD, SO 1100–1156.   [21] PCA: BCO, Preface, II.8.
[22] PCI: Code, par. 131; PCA: BCO, 27: it is exercised under 'a dispensation of mercy and not of wrath'; PCNZ: BO, 15.1: disciplinary 'proceedings must be distinguished by Christian gentleness, impartiality and faithfulness'; MCNZ: LAR, 8.1: in discipline 'the Church expects all parties to seek to exercise Christian grace, forgiveness and reconciliation'; LCA: Const., Art. X.1 and BL, X.C: 'the prerogative of mercy'.
[23] PCANZ: BO, 15.1; 15.3–4: ministers, elders, other office bearers, church workers and members are subject to discipline exercised by the church courts; PCI: Code, par. 131: all the baptised members are subject to it.
[24] RCA: BCO, Ch. 2, Pt. I, Art. 3: all members, ministers and elders are subject to discipline as administered by the Board of Elders; the Classis may discipline both ministers of word and sacrament and a consistory.
[25] UCCSA: Procedure 15: 'As people in covenant with the Lord, the Church is called to be holy, to live according to the Spirit of Christ and to share in Christ's saving mission' – as such 'it must live a disciplined life within the covenant'; its members must recognise their own weaknesses and 'encourage one another in Christian obedience'; 'It requires each congregation to be under the discipline of the Lord'; as authority is 'ministerial, not magisterial; pastoral, not punitive' and based on 'Scripture and the Spirit', so discipline is 'remedial, not punitive' and exercised by the Church Meeting, Regional Council, Synod and Assembly; 'Every member of this Church is subject to discipline'; the pattern of discipline is based on Matt. 18.15–17.
[26] Bethel Baptist Church (Choctaw): Const., Art. VII: when a member ceases to meet the standards of the New Testament 'that member will be subject to the discipline of the church'; Riverside Baptist Church (Baltimore): BL, Art. I: 'Membership may terminate through exclusion by action of this church ... after faithful efforts have been made to bring such member to repentance and amendment' (e.g. for 'persistent breach of the covenant vows'); Central Baptist Church (Pretoria): Const., Art. 9: discipline.

the Church in all matters of Doctrine, Worship, Discipline, and Order in accordance with the Rules and Regulations from time to time made by the Conference.'[27]

Quasi-judicial discipline and dispute settlement

The juridical instruments of Christian churches often provide for the settlement of disputes by means of an administrative process which necessitates the making of quasi-judicial decisions. Churches differ in terms of the institution which possesses authority to settle disputes quasi-judicially: in churches with an Episcopal form of government, the bishop plays a central role in the informal resolution of disputes; in churches with a Presbyterian system of government it is the regional presbytery and its officers; and in a church with a Congregational polity it is the local congregation and its officers. Two common mechanisms for the informal resolution of disputes are hierarchical recourse and visitation – both have an adjudicative dimension.

Hierarchical recourse

With hierarchical recourse, procedural rules allow a complainant to appeal against a decision or conduct of a person or body to the superior of that person or body: this process is predominantly administrative without recourse to a church court or tribunal, though the determination by the superior has a quasi-judicial element in the establishment of facts and the application of norms. There is a discrete body of canon law in the Roman Catholic Church on hierarchical recourse. This is a process which enables an aggrieved party to challenge an administrative act by way of an appeal to the administrator who performed that act, or to the hierarchical superior of that administrator; it takes three forms: conciliation (a mediation between the aggrieved party and the administrator to reach an amicable solution without recourse to the superior); a request for reconsideration (when the aggrieved party petitions the administrator to modify or revoke the act, which may be made during both a conciliation and recourse to the superior); and recourse to the hierarchical superior – this may be made directly to the superior for any just reason without having sought a conciliation or a request for reconsideration (for example, recourse is available against a diocesan bishop to the Congregation for the Clergy). The superior has power to confirm, rescind or modify the original executive act.[28] The Oriental Catholic churches have a similar system.[29]

Norms in Orthodox churches on hierarchical recourse are scattered rather than drawn together under a separate title. Various forms of hierarchical recourse are possible; for example: the diocesan bishop may exercise 'the right of pastoral act and discipline in reference to the diocesan clergy and laity in all cases not requiring the action of a Church Court';[30] a dean must resolve 'misunderstandings' among

---

[27] MCI: Const., s. 5; and RDG, 5: for members, Church Council; for local preachers, Circuit Executive, District Disciplinary Committee, District Synod and Conference; for ministers, District Pastoral Committee, District Disciplinary Committee, District Synod and Conference.

[28] CIC, cc. 1732–1739; see K. Matthews, 'Extra-judicial appeal and hierarchical recourse', 18 *Studia Canonica* (1984) 95; administrative acts cannot be challenged in the church courts: CIC, c. 1400.2; administrative acts cover a spectrum of decisions, orders, policies and decrees issued by those with executive authority.

[29] CCEO, cc. 996–1006; see also Nedungatt, 675–687.   [30] UOCIA: Statutes, VII.4.f.

parish clergy and laity 'without formal legal proceedings';[31] and an appeal may be made against the decision of a Parish Assembly to the diocesan metropolitan.[32] In the Greek Orthodox Archdiocese of America, a dispute between a priest and a parishioner is under the direct jurisdiction of the hierarch whose determination is final – however, in a dispute between a parishioner and a Parish Council or Assembly, the parties must initially meet in good faith with the priest to resolve the matter in a pastoral manner but, if this fails, the matter must be submitted to the Chancellor of the Archdiocesan District or Metropolis for a first level review and determination with a right of appeal to the Local Council Dispute Resolution Panel, whose recommendation is sent to the hierarch for review and approval – all those involved in these processes are 'fervently charged to invoke the guidance of the Holy Spirit and pray for spiritual resolution and healing'.[33] Some Anglican churches also provide for the referral of complaints and disagreements to the bishop or other diocesan authority for quasi-judicial determination over a variety of different matters; for example: the removal of a name from a roll of church members; a churchwarden's complaint of a minister's conduct; or the refusal by a cleric to provide liturgical facilities.[34] Indeed, the Scottish Episcopal Church has a canon 'Of Differences and Disputes and Appeals'; this applies to all appeals allowed under the canons to the diocesan bishop or to the Episcopal Synod, as well as 'to any disputes between clergy or other members of this Church as to questions affecting Congregations, Dioceses or the Province'. The decision of the bishop or of the Episcopal Synod is final; moreover, 'the Bishop in dealing with disputes shall have full power and absolute discretion' to regulate the procedure, hear parties or dispense with a hearing, require oral or written

---

[31] ROC: Statute, X: 5, Deaneries, par. 52; XI: a Parish Meeting considers complaints against Parish Council members; OCIA: GC., Matters of Appeal, 1–2: 'The first instance of appeal for priest and parish alike is the district dean'; the diocesan hierarch may appoint other clergy to assist the dean 'in determining action'.

[32] MOSC: Const., 2.19–21: an 'appeal' lies against 'any decision' of the Parish Assembly to the diocesan metropolitan to determine whether it is beyond its authority; 3.62: an appeal to the Malankara Metropolitan against a decision of a diocesan metropolitan is decided by the Advisory Council of the former; 9.115–119: complaints lie against laity/clergy to diocesan metropolitans with appeal to the Malankara Metropolitan who must bring the case before the Episcopal Synod.

[33] GOAA: Regs., Art. 35; Addendum B, I–VII: ecclesiastical, theological or canonical disputes, or those about governance, property and parish life, are governed by dispute resolution procedures; but these do not limit or prohibit a hierarch or Eparchial Synod from convening a Spiritual Court to address the dispute; the procedure governs e.g. requests for review, evidence, representation, confidentiality, enforcement and costs; disputes involving hierarchs come to the Eparchial Synod; these provisions do not apply to sexual misconduct, which is governed by the Statement of Policy Regarding Sexual Misconduct by Clergy. See also UOCIA: Statutes, IV.2: the right of 'pastoral intervention' vests in a major archbishop; Art. X: the district dean may investigate complaints against clergy and 'parish bodies' and submit these to the bishop; Sexual Abuse Policy: this deals with forms of abuse; criminal records checks; process; the Review Board; and procedure.

[34] E.g. Wales: Const. IV.C.6: appeal lies to the archdeacon; Southern Africa: Can. 28: churchwardens; England: Can. B3(4): refusal of a cleric to provide liturgical facilities; Canada: Can. XXI.26: when re-married persons seek holy communion, the bishop issues a 'judgment' for their 'spiritual welfare'; New Zealand: Cans. B.V.5.2.2: refusal of a Vestry to allow use of the parish hall is referred to the diocesan Standing Committee.

contentions, take evidence formally or informally and generally control the process. All parties may be represented.[35]

There are equivalent mechanisms in Protestant churches. For example, in Lutheran churches, a Synod is to decide on the termination of the membership of congregations wishing to withdraw;[36] a College of Presidents is to give leadership in the resolution of conflict;[37] and a congregation is to settle its own disputes.[38] Similarly, under Presbyterian polity, an inferior court may refer a matter to a superior court for advice or determination and complain to a superior court about the proceedings of any co-ordinate or lower authority;[39] and the Session may refer disputes of doctrine and order to the higher courts for decision.[40] Parallel mechanisms are to be found in United and Congregational churches. For example, in the United Congregational Church of Southern Africa (UCCSA), when fifteen members of a local church complain or the secretary of a Synod or Regional Council believes there is 'serious trouble' in a local church, a report is made to the Administrative Committee of the Synod or Region to institute a full investigation by a commission. The local church must receive the commission. The grounds for the complaint must be in writing and the investigation takes place in the presence of the church and witnesses. The commission reports to the Administrative Committee which, if satisfied that there is serious trouble, reports its finding to the local church, the complainants and the Assembly Executive Committee. The decision of the Administrative Committee is final but any person directly concerned may appeal to the (central) Assembly Executive Committee which hears the appeal through a Special Committee which reports to the Assembly Executive Committee for a final decision; if the local church does not comply with the decision it may be disassociated from UCCSA.[41]

Churches may also employ explicitly a system of arbitration. For example, under the constitution of the (United) Church of South India: '[a]ll disputes of any nature whatsoever, concerning the affairs of the Synod and/or any matter in relation to the Synod and/or any of its institutions shall be resolved only by Arbitration'. The Synod is obliged to appoint a panel of arbitrators consisting of five bishops, ten presbyters and fifteen lay people. Any member of the church may submit a complaint in writing which may be resolved 'in a pastoral way'. If this fails, the General Secretary must 'call upon both the parties to the dispute to select from out of the panel of Arbitrators, any one person for each side who he/she/they desire to have as his/her/their Arbitrator'. Two arbitrators, 'one on the side of the person raising the dispute, and the other on the side of the person against whom the

---

[35] Scotland: Can. 55: if the bishop is 'so personally concerned that it is expedient that another should act', the bishop or the parties may apply to the College of Bishops to appoint one of its members to resolve the case.
[36] LCGB: RAR, Termination of Membership. [37] LCA: Const., Art. VIII and BL VIII.F.
[38] ELCSA: G., 10; ELCIRE: Const., Arts. 11–14: cases on Parish Council 'jurisdiction', elections and acts.
[39] PCI: Code, par. 21. [40] PCA: BCO, 11.1–11.3.
[41] UCCSA: Procedure, 14. See also (United) Church of North India: Const. II.III.IX.34: any 'memoranda, representations, complaints, references, petitions, and appeals related to administrative matters in the Pastorates or the diocese' must be referred to the Diocesan Council; the Diocesan Council is under a duty to submit complaints or appeals by any aggrieved party against its own decisions to the central Synod.

dispute is raised shall be Arbitrators for resolving the dispute'; the award of the arbitrators 'shall be binding on all parties to the dispute'. If the award is not acceptable to any party, such party is deemed to be 'ineligible to participate in the Government of the Church at all levels'. The dioceses must incorporate similar provisions in their respective constitutions.[42] Some Baptist Unions also use systems of arbitration to resolve disagreements amongst the membership of a church.[43] In short, it is a principle of Christian law that ecclesiastical disputes may be settled by means of administrative and/or quasi-judicial process in such manner as may be prescribed by law.

Visitation and the maintenance of discipline

Whilst hierarchical recourse involves an appeal which ascends to a superior ecclesial authority or an arbitrator, visitation is a process by which an institutional authority descends to a lower unit to investigate, maintain and improve its discipline. There is profound juridical unity across Christian traditions with regard to visitation. The mechanism is particularly well developed in Catholic polity. According to Roman Catholic canon law, the bishop is bound 'to visit his diocese in whole or in part each year, so that at least every five years he will have visited the whole diocese, either personally or, if he is lawfully impeded, through the coadjutor or auxiliary bishop, the vicar general, an Episcopal vicar or some other priest'. Persons, catholic institutes, pious objects and places within the diocese are subject to episcopal visitation (but the bishop may visit the members of religious institutes of pontifical right and their houses only in cases stated in the law); the bishop must carry out his pastoral visitation with due diligence, ensuring it is not a burden to anyone on grounds of undue expense; every 5 years the diocesan bishop must submit to the Pontiff a report on the state of the diocese in a form and at a time determined by the Apostolic See.[44] Similar provisions exist in the Code of Canons of the Oriental Catholic Churches; for example, in each patriarchal church, visitation enables maintenance of the bonds between the patriarch and the faithful residing outside the patriarchal territory; a report is made to the Synod of Bishops, which may in turn make appropriate recommendations to the Roman Pontiff.[45]

Visitation is also provided for under Orthodox canon law. Typically: the bishop must 'in accordance with the canons visit the parishes in his diocese and exercise control over their activities directly or through plenipotentiary

---

[42] South India: Const. XI(a). See also ELCIRE: Const., 12.3: when disagreements arise between the parish council and the pastor, both sides can ask a person they trust to mediate. The other side shall agree.

[43] BUSA: Const., 10: 'It is desired and expected that every member of the Union shall submit all grave differences, which tend to create divisions, to the Executive for arbitration and shall abide by the award therein subject to a right of appeal to the next meeting of the Assembly'; see also BL 6: the Executive appoints arbitrators and it may remove accredited ministers on complaint and a finding of guilt of misconduct.

[44] CIC, cc. 396–399; c. 400: in the same year as the report, the bishop must visit the Pontiff in Rome.

[45] CCEO, c. 83: if an eparchial bishop fails to carry out a visitation, the metropolitan is to make the visitation, and the patriarch must if there is no metropolitan; see also c. 148.

representatives';[46] and, if necessary, the bishop may convene the parish assembly at a visitation.[47] Also, the bishop must 'at least once a year' organise 'the synaxes (consultations) of the abbots and abbesses' of monasteries 'in order to analyse the specific problems, to promote the exchange of spiritual and administrative experience and to adopt adequate steps for improving the monastic life and discipline'.[48] In turn, a major archbishop has 'the right of pastoral initiative and guidance, and when necessary the right of pastoral intervention';[49] and laws may enable an archpriest to inspect annually the parishes of the deanery to learn about 'the quality of the religious, moral and social life of the parishioners' and the state of parochial property.[50] There are three forms of visitation in Anglican canon law.[51] In several churches, the law imposes a duty on the primate, metropolitan or archbishop to visit the dioceses of the province regularly: in the Episcopal Church in the USA, for example, the presiding bishop must visit every diocese for the purpose of '[h]olding pastoral consultations with the Bishop or Bishops ... and, with their advice, with the Lay and Clerical Leaders of the jurisdiction', preaching the Word and celebrating Holy Communion.[52] In some churches the diocesan bishop has a right and in others a duty of visitation over the parishes and congregations of the diocese at prescribed times (usually at intervals of every 3 years); the pastoral and liturgical side of visitation is stressed as well as an examination of the life and ministry of clergy and laity and the administration of the parish or other unit in question; some laws require an episcopal report following the visitation to the diocesan assembly.[53] Other churches provide for a visitation by the archdeacon who is required to

---

[46] ROC: Statute, X.18(g); UOCIA: Statutes, Art. VII.4: the bishop 'shall make canonical visits to the parishes'; ROMOC: Statutes, Art. 88: the bishop is to make 'often canonical and pastoral visits within the Eparchy'.

[47] MOSC: Const., 3 par. 67 and 4 par. 98: the Malankara Metropolitan and diocesan metropolitans may officially visit and if necessary convene the Parish Assembly or (after informing the diocesan metropolitan) the Diocesan Assembly; visitation expenses are borne by the units visited; see also UOCIA: Statutes, IV.2: the right of 'pastoral intervention' vested in a major archbishop.

[48] ROMOC: Statutes, Art. 82; see also Art. 83: metropolitan synaxes are held at least every 3 years.

[49] UOCIA: Statutes, Art. IV.2.

[50] ROMOC: Statutes, Art. 71; see also ROC: Statute X.53: the dean is to visit all the parishes at least once a year 'to inspect the liturgical life, interior and exterior of the churches and other church buildings as well as the regularity of the conduct of church affairs and ... archives and to study the moral state of the parishioners'.

[51] PCLCCAC, Principle 23: visitation enables the exercise of a supervisory jurisdiction or a pastoral ministry, including enquiry into and assessment of the condition of an ecclesiastical entity; it may be exercised by the primate, archbishop, bishop or other ecclesiastical person to the extent authorised by the law; only those ecclesiastical entities may be visited which are prescribed by law; visitations may be held at such intervals, in such form and with such consequences as may be prescribed under the law.

[52] TEC: Cans. I.2.4; for metropolitical and archiepiscopal visitation see e.g. England: Can. G5; Uganda: Const., Art. 9; West Africa: Const., Art. V; Indian Ocean: Const., Art. 11; cf. Southern Africa: Can. 2.1: with or without invitation; Korea: Const. Ch. 2, Art. 6: a primatial visitation is 'at the request of a diocesan bishop'.

[53] See e.g. Southern Africa: Can. 39 and England: Can. C18: discretion; Wales: Const., IX.43: duty; Scotland: Can. 6.1: congregations; Philippines: Cans. III.15.5: report to the diocesan assembly; West Indies: Can. 92: examination of conditions.

examine prescribed matters.[54] Anglican laws also provide procedures to address the breakdown of pastoral relations in a local church unit.[55]

By way of contrast, in Protestant churches visitation is normally carried out under the authority of assemblies. This applies in Lutheran and Reformed churches.[56] In Presbyterian polity, the Presbytery must carry out visitations for 'the purpose of inquiring into and redressing the evils that may have arisen' in the local church;[57] it may involve examination of people, activities, places and documents and with 'all fidelity and affection deal with them as the justice of the case and the interests of the congregation may require'.[58] For example, under the law of the Presbyterian Church in Ireland, the Presbytery (as part of its 'continuing oversight') must visit each congregation at least once every 10 years or sooner when the Presbytery considers it necessary. Its purpose is 'to seek the improvement of Church life and work in the congregation and area concerned, by inquiry into all matters affecting the congregation, by the encouragement of members in their Christian witness and service, and by advice or correction in anything found amiss'. The procedure requires formal notice and examination of documents (e.g. the minute books of the Kirk Session and Congregational Committee, communicants' roll, baptism and marriage registers and inventory of church property). The inquiry involves preparatory meetings held separately and privately by the Presbytery with the minister, Kirk Session and Congregational Committee. This public visitation should address the challenges and opportunities of the congregation – it also includes an act of worship. The findings of the Presbytery are read publicly to the congregation, which itself must report after 12 months to the Presbytery as to how recommendations made as a result of the visitation have been addressed.[59]

---

[54] England: Can. C22(5); Southern Africa: Can. 15.4; Wales: Const., IX.43.
[55] TEC: Cans. III.20; England: Incumbents (Vacation of Benefices) Measure 1977 (as amended 1993).
[56] ELCSA: G., 109: the Church Synod, Bishop and Church Council may carry out visitations of congregations; URC: Man., B.2.4: the Provincial Synod is to arrange for regular visitations to local churches for consultation concerning their life and work; see also RCA: BCO, Ch. 1, Pt. II, Arts. 1–7.
[57] PCA: BCO, 13.9; see also: PCANZ: BO, 8.4: the Presbytery may carry out visitations of congregations.
[58] UFCS: MPP, IV.III.I: the quinquennial visitation is designed 'to strengthen the hands of the ministers, elders, deacons, and managers, and to give such counsel and encouragement as may be suitable, as well as to satisfy the Presbytery that the congregations under its charge are in a satisfactory state'; it is carried out by a Visitation Committee of no less than one minister and one elder who should conduct public worship and counsel and encourage the congregation; they must examine bible classes, Sunday schools and minute books; a report is transmitted to the General Assembly Arrangements Committee; 'When a Presbytery finds the unsatisfactory state of a congregation to be due largely to faults on the part of the office bearers, or the people, or any of them, it shall with all fidelity and affection deal with them as the justice of the case and the interests of the congregation may require' – congregation members may also bring grievances to the Presbytery which may make 'a special Presbyterial visitation of the congregation at any time, to call Sessions before them, examine minutes, inquire as to arrears of stipend, or deal with any matter affecting the welfare of the congregation'.
[59] PCI: Code, par. 70; pars. 246–251: guidelines on visitation are authorised by the General Board.

Elaborate rules on visitation are also found in the Methodist tradition.[60] The president of a Conference may have 'the right if requested to do so to visit any Circuit, to inquire into its affairs, and to take any steps open to him or her which he or she judges beneficial'.[61] Moreover, a district superintendent 'shall visit any Circuit in the District when he/she considers it desirable'; but: 'Every Circuit in a District shall be officially visited by a District Superintendent at least once in three years'. On all such official visits, a meeting of the members of the Circuit Executive must be held at which the district superintendent presides. At this meeting the working of the circuit comes under review and special attention is given to the state of the work of God, including openings for evangelistic effort. The district superintendents must report to the Conference, through the General Committee, as to the circuits officially visited by them during the year.[62] A special Connexional Visitation Commission may also make visitations (organised by the Visitation Secretary) to enquire into the state of church property and mission in the circuit.[63] In short, it is a principle of Christian law that regional authorities within the church may to the extent permitted by the polity of a church carry out visitations to the local church to enquire into, to encourage and to correct or recommend the correction of the life and the maintenance of discipline at that level.

Church courts and tribunals

All the traditions have mechanisms for the formal enforcement of discipline and the judicial resolution of ecclesiastical disputes. Such mechanisms are normally found in a system of courts or tribunals, usually ordered hierarchically. The juridical instruments of the churches deal with church courts and tribunals in terms of their establishment, composition and jurisdiction (original and appellate), and sometimes explicit provision is made for their independence and the binding effect of their decisions on the parties involved in a case.[64] The court of first instance in churches with an episcopal polity is that at the regional level of the diocese with appellate jurisdiction exercised at national level only (as in Anglicanism), or at both national level and international level (as in Catholicism and some Orthodox

---

[60] MCNZ: LAR, 4.8: the Synod superintendent makes annual visits of 'an inspirational and advisory character'; he has 'the right after due notice to the Parish Superintendent to visit any Parish within the boundaries of the region and in sole discretion, to inquire into the affairs of the Parish ... to confer with the Parish officials', and inspect 'all Parish records and books'; s. 3.5.6: the parish may invite the Synod superintendent to visit; s. 5.8: every fifth year of a ministerial appointment there is normally a consultation to review the life, work and future of the parish; this is initiated by the Synod (4.12.4) and conducted in accord with prescribed guidelines.

[61] MCGB: CPD, SO 111: the president may delegate this power e.g. to the chair of the district concerned, and may refer any matter to be dealt with by a connexional complaints team (unless the relevant request to the president came from such a team). See also SO 425: the district chair must visit each circuit annually.

[62] MCI: RDG, 9.17.

[63] MCI: RDG, 29.15: 'All Circuits shall be visited from time to time by a Connexional Visitation Commission which shall inquire into the work of the Circuit and the condition of all trust property on the Circuit'; this is in addition to an annual visual inspection.

[64] See Chapter 1 for the creative force of judicial decisions and limited use of doctrines of binding precedent.

systems). The court of first instance in those churches with a Presbyterian or Congregational polity is generally at the local level of the congregation, with appellate jurisdiction exercisable in a tiered form at the regional and the national levels (but not beyond, at the international level). However, there is little obvious theological content to rules on church courts and tribunals.

The tribunals of the Roman Catholic Church are established on the basis of the Code of Canon Law promulgated by the Pontiff. The tribunals are ordered hierarchically and exercise jurisdiction over cases concerning spiritual matters, the violation of ecclesiastical laws and all those cases in which there is a question of sin in respect to the determination of culpability and the imposition of ecclesiastical penalties.[65] Whilst in the diocese there is no strict separation of powers (as judicial, legislative and executive power vests in the bishop),[66] the forum of first instance is the diocesan tribunal, presided over by the bishop exercising judicial power either personally or through a judicial vicar (with ordinary and not delegated power) who may be assisted by adjutant judicial vicars. The judicial vicar and adjutants must be priests, but lay judges may be appointed to assist. The tribunal deals in the main with matrimonial cases – with contentious marriage cases reserved to a collegiate tribunal of three judges – and specified cases concerning dismissal from the clerical state.[67] The tribunal of second instance is the metropolitan tribunal (the archdiocesan tribunal of a province) or a regional tribunal which entertains appeals from the diocesan tribunal.[68] The Pontiff is the supreme judge for the universal church and may judge personally or through the tribunals of the Apostolic See.[69] The Apostolic See has two tribunals: the Roman Rota is 'the ordinary tribunal constituted by the Roman Pontiff to receive appeals' (e.g. as a tribunal of third instance) and the Apostolic Signatura is 'the supreme tribunal' of the Apostolic See which hears appeals against Rotal judgments, for example – it also functions as the supreme administrative tribunal in disputes about administrative acts and the competence of the inferior tribunals.[70] Importantly, any of the faithful may refer a case directly to the Pope; moreover: 'There is neither appeal nor recourse against a judgment or decree of the Roman Pontiff'.[71] The tribunals of the Oriental Catholic churches are constituted similarly.[72] For example, in a patriarchal church, the eparchial bishop exercises judicial power over all cases either personally or through judicial officers (vicars and judges) and appeal lies against a decision of an eparchial

---

[65] CIC, cc. 1401–1416: competent forum; cc. 1417–1418: tribunal grades; cc. 1446–1457: judges and officers.
[66] CIC, c. 391; see also c. 469: the diocesan curia assists the bishop 'in exercising judicial power'.
[67] CIC, cc. 1419–1427, 1453, 1601–1618: officers include promoter of justice and defenders of the bond.
[68] CIC, cc. 1438–1441: the metropolitan tribunal may also be a first instance tribunal in prescribed cases.
[69] CIC, c. 1442; c. 1405: cases reserved to the Pope (e.g. judging cardinals and bishops in contentious cases).
[70] CIC, cc. 1443–1444: the Rota also acts as a first instance tribunal in e.g. contentious cases involving bishops; 1445: the Apostolic Signatura hears e.g. recourses against rotal judgments; see also cc. 1645–1648.
[71] CIC, c. 1417: referral to the Pope; c. 333: no appeal against a papal judgment.
[72] CCEO, c. 24: the right to judge subjects according to law and to impose penalties; cc. 1055–1057: basic norms; cc. 1058–1085: competent forum; cc. 1086–1093: tribunal personnel; cc. 1103–1116: judges' duties.

tribunal to the Synod of Bishops of the patriarchal church.[73] The Synod of Bishops elects an 'ordinary tribunal' of three bishops for a 5-year term to hear appeals from the eparchial tribunal, as well as a 'special tribunal' to entertain appeals against an administrative decree of the patriarch. Appeals lie ultimately to the Apostolic See.[74]

The courts of Orthodox churches are also ordered hierarchically and there are rules on their establishment,[75] composition (which may include laity)[76] and original and appellate jurisdiction (which may be exercised over both clergy and laity).[77] The number of tiers in the judicial hierarchy depends on the status of the church within its wider international affiliation. At international level, in the Moscow Patriarchate: 'Judicial authority in the Russian Orthodox Church shall be exercised by the Ecclesiastical Courts through ecclesiastical proceedings'; no other church bodies may assume the functions of these courts. The decisions of the courts are 'binding for all clergymen and laymen without exception'. The Diocesan Court consists of priests – with a chair appointed by the bishop and two others by the Diocesan Assembly – and its decisions are executed on approval by the bishop; if the bishop disagrees with a decision there is a reference to the General Ecclesiastical Court for a final judgment. The General Ecclesiastical Court is the court of second instance; its decisions are operative on approval by the Patriarch of Moscow and the Holy Synod; if these disagree with the decision, the case is referred to the Court of the Bishops' Council as 'the ecclesiastical court of final appeal'.[78] Nationally, the Greek Orthodox Archdiocese of America (under the Ecumenical Patriarchate of

---

[73] CCEO, cc. 1066 and 1086.

[74] CCEO, cc. 110, 1062: whilst crimes involving patriarchs and bishops are reserved to the Pontiff, the tribunal of the Synod of Bishops is competent in non-criminal cases involving bishops and must establish a 'special tribunal' for appeals against administrative decrees of the patriarch; the special tribunal is constituted in accordance with particular law: c. 1006; see also c. 11: legislative and judicial powers vest in the Synod.

[75] OOCL: 170ff: the bishop's court, synodal courts (first instance and appeal), courts of the hierarchy (first instance and appeal) and the court for members of the Synod; MOSC: Const., 7.102–109: Episcopal Synod.

[76] UOCIA: Statutes, Art. XII: the Diocesan Court consists of two clergy and two lay persons appointed by the bishop from members of the Diocesan Council; the bishop presides as a non-voting member; in clergy cases it is composed only of clergy; it acts as a court of first instance in cases involving a priest, deacon, deaconess or 'member of the laity'; it judges cases of 'allegations of unorthodox belief, breaches of canonical or moral discipline, marital problems, disputes involving clergy and parish officers, disputes over parish institutions, and any other matter involving the good order of the Church'; either party may appeal to the Holy Synod as Supreme Court of Appeals; deposition of clergy requires confirmation by the Holy Synod; the decision of the Holy Synod is final; Art. II: the Holy Synod has original jurisdiction in cases involving bishops.

[77] ROMOC: Statutes, Arts. 11–16: the Holy Synod adjudicates on members 'accused of infringing the church discipline and teaching', on deposition of clergy and 'their requests for forgiveness', on interpretation of church statutes and regulations 'in final and compulsory form for all the church bodies'; see also Arts. 148–160: the Archpriest Disciplinary Consistory and Eparchial Consistory with appeals to the Metropolitan Consistory.

[78] ROC: Statute, I.8; VII: the judicial system is established on the foundation of the Holy Canons, the Statute and Regulations on Ecclesiastical Courts; there is provision for the staffing and funding of the courts; XI: the Diocesan Assembly appoints the judges to the Diocesan Court; VIII.12: the General Ecclesiastical Court and the Court of the Bishops' Council are the appellate courts for a self-governing church and an exarchate.

Constantinople) has Spiritual Courts – the 'judicial bodies of the Archdiocese having jurisdiction over spiritual and canonical matters'. The Archdiocesan District and each metropolis have a 'Spiritual Court of First Instance' with four clergy selected by the hierarch (who presides) to hear cases involving 'family problems, divorce, and moral and disciplinary offences of clergy and lay persons'. The Spiritual Court of Second Instance (Appeals) consists of the archbishop (president), members of the Eparchial Synod and archdiocesan chancellor (secretary); it convenes when the Eparchial Synod meets and hears all appeals from first instance and has original jurisdiction in cases involving metropolitans and bishops. Appeals from second instance (as to bishops, clergy and laity) may be submitted to the Ecumenical Patriarchate for final and irrevocable decision; as to deposition of clergy, the Eparchial Synod submits the case for trial to the Holy and Sacred Synod of the Ecumenical Patriarchate.[79]

According to the principles of canon law common to the churches of the Anglican Communion, 'ordinary jurisdiction in matters of discipline rests either with the bishop or with such other ecclesiastical person, court or tribunal as may be prescribed by law'. The relationship between courts or tribunals of original and appellate jurisdiction in the judicial hierarchy is to be clearly prescribed by law, as is their subject-matter jurisdiction in disciplinary and other causes. The judges are to be duly qualified, selected and appointed by a designated ecclesiastical authority in accordance with a prescribed procedure, and are to exercise their office impartially, without fear or favour. Church courts and tribunals are to enjoy independence from external interference and uphold the rule of law in the church.[80] The power to establish courts and tribunals is generally reserved to the central assembly of a national, regional or provincial church;[81] and some laws expressly forbid the exercise of judicial power by the central assembly.[82] Broadly, Anglican churches fall into two groups: those with a three-tier hierarchy of courts, with the diocesan court as the tribunal of first instance, the provincial court as an appellate tribunal and a further final court of appeal; and those with a two-tier system, a diocesan court and an appellate provincial court.[83] The diocesan tribunal is in some churches styled the Court of the Bishop (and the bishop presides, assisted typically by an appointee of the diocesan assembly) and in others the Diocesan Court or Tribunal, sometimes presided over by the bishop or by a judge elected by the diocesan

---

[79] GOAA: Charter, Art. 9; Art. 22: the courts are governed by Regulations of the Eparchial Synod approved by the Ecumenical Patriarchate; a hierarch who judges at first instance cannot participate in an appeal.
[80] PCLCCAC, Principle 24: church courts and tribunals are to be available as necessary to resolve disputes.
[81] See e.g. Uganda: Const., Art. 16; Canada: Declaration of Principles, 7A.
[82] See e.g. Scotland: Can. 52.16: 'General Synod shall have no judicial power, either primary or on appeal'; West Indies: Const., Art. 3.4: Provincial Synod cannot determine 'such matters as lie within the jurisdiction of the Ecclesiastical Courts'.
[83] See e.g. West Indies: Can. 22: the Diocesan Court (to try priests and deacons), Provincial Court of Appeal (for appeals from the diocese) and Provincial Court (to try bishops); Australia: Const. IX.53–57: the Court of the Bishop (to try priests and deacons), Special Court (with original jurisdiction over bishops) and Provincial Tribunal (an appeal court which also has jurisdiction in matters of faith, ritual and ceremonial). For the two-tier system, e.g. TEC: Cans. IV.4: Diocesan Court (to try clergy with appeal to the provincial Commission of Review) and Court for the Trial of a Bishop (appeal is to the Commission of Review for the Trial of a Bishop).

assembly.[84] Diocesan courts usually have original jurisdiction over the discipline of priests and deacons and in several churches over the laity (and the commission of ecclesiastical offences by them).[85] With respect to appeals, the laws provide for: limitation periods; grounds of appeal; leave to appeal; and powers of the appellate tribunal.[86] The superior tribunals have an original jurisdiction over, typically, the trial of bishops, and constitutional, doctrinal and liturgical matters.[87]

The judicial bodies of Protestant churches are ordered similarly. However, the court of first instance is generally at local rather than the regional level of the diocesan courts in the Episcopal tradition – with the exception, that is, of Protestant churches with bishops.[88] In Lutheranism, typically, juridical instruments provide for the establishment of tribunals organised on the basis of a tiered system of original and appellate jurisdictions over both ordained ministerial and lay discipline.[89] For instance, in the Lutheran Church in Australia: 'The Church shall establish a judicial system to deal with discipline and adjudication. The rules governing such judicial system shall be laid down in the By-laws'; in turn, the district must establish a judicial procedure to deal with discipline, adjudication and appeals.[90] The Evangelical Lutheran Church in Canada has a Court of Adjudication, with four lay and three ordained members elected by the Convention, to hear appeals as to discipline from the Synods; its decisions are binding (until they are reversed by the Convention) and it may make rules as to procedure to supplement those in the Constitution.[91] In Reformed churches there are usually three tiers of judicial authority: the Classis, the Regional Synod and the General Synod 'exercise judicial as well as legislative powers'; when each exercises judicial powers it acts as a

---

[84] See e.g. Scotland: Can. 54: the bishop is assisted by the diocesan chancellor; Ireland: Const., VIII.5–6: the bishop is 'the judge in the Diocesan Court' with the chancellor acting as assessor; TEC: Const., Art. X, Cans. IV.4: the Diocesan Court for the trial of clergy has a presiding judge elected by the Diocesan Convention.

[85] See e.g. New Zealand: Cans. D.I.1.1: the Bishops' Court has jurisdiction over clergy and lay members who have assented to the authority of the General Synod; Wales: Const., IX.8: the Disciplinary Tribunal is a provincial body.

[86] See e.g. Tanzania: Const., IV.20: the court consists of two bishops, two clergy and two lay persons; West Indies: Can. XVII.4: limitation periods; Central Africa; Can. 26.9: appeal on a matter of law and fact.

[87] See e.g. Wales: Const. XI: Special Provincial Court (bishops); Australia: Const., V.29: Appellate Tribunal (constitutionality of legislation); England: Ecclesiastical Jurisdiction Measure 1963, ss. 38, 42, 45: Court of Ecclesiastical Causes Reserved (doctrine, ritual and ceremonial).

[88] N. Doe, *Law and Religion in Europe: A Comparative Introduction* (Oxford University Press, 2011), 132: Denmark and Lutheran Courts.

[89] LCGB: RAR, Disciplinary Procedure for Pastors of the Church: Episcopal Committee, Council Tribunal, with appeal to the Board of Appeal; LCA: BL, X.C: the General Church Council must appoint a Tribunal (with appellate jurisdiction); ELCA: Const., Ch. 20–21: a disciplinary hearing before the synod's Committee on Discipline; a right of appeal lies to the Committee on Appeals; 20.53: trial of the presiding bishop (General Church Council).

[90] LCA: Const., Art. X.1–3; see also VII; Const. of the Districts, X; BL, X.A.1–3.

[91] ELCIC: Const., Art. XVIII; see also: LCMS: BL, 1.10.8: a decision of the Dispute Resolution Panel is 'binding on the parties to the dispute' but shall 'have no precedential value'; also: BL, 3.9: the Commission on Constitutional Matters interprets the constitution, bylaws and resolutions on written request of a member (congregation or ordained minister), board, commission etc. of the Synod; an appeal lies against an interpretation to a panel of the Commission whose decision 'shall be binding' unless overruled by a convention of the Synod.

'judicatory'. The Classis acting as a judicatory has original and appellate authority over the acts, proceedings and decisions of the board of elders and consistories in temporal and disciplinary matters, including the suspension and deposition of ministers. The Regional Synod acting as a judicatory of ministers and elders has an appellate supervisory power over the Classis. The General Synod is 'the highest judicatory' with appellate supervisory power over lower judicatories. All church members, ministers and elders are subject to discipline.[92]

In Presbyterian churches there are three tiers of judicial forum: the Kirk Session (which adjudicates on disciplinary charges against members);[93] the Presbytery (with authority over ministers and elders and appeals in cases of lay members);[94] and the General Assembly (which may exercise its judicial functions through a Judicial Commission), the decisions of which are 'final and binding'.[95] For example, in the Presbyterian Church in America: the 'courts are not separate and independent tribunals, but they have a mutual relation, and every act of jurisdiction is the act of the whole Church performed by it through the appropriate organ'. The Session possesses 'the right to require obedience to the laws of Christ' and may resolve questions of discipline; disputes of order may be referred to the higher courts for decision. In turn, the Presbytery oversees discipline and may consider appeals, complaints and references brought before it and review the records of Sessions and redress whatever is done contrary to church order, as well as ensure compliance with the decisions of higher courts: 'A Presbytery as a whole may try a judicial case within its jurisdiction' or 'commit any judicial case to a commission' appointed by the Presbytery; the commission must resolve the case in accordance with the Rules of Discipline and submit to the Presbytery its judgment for approval; the Moderator of the Presbytery oversees judicial cases.[96] Appeal lies to the General Assembly: this elects a Standing Judicial Commission to hear all cases committed to it within its jurisdiction and is governed by the judicial procedures of the General Assembly – there is no

---

[92] RCA: BCO, Preamble: the tiers; Ch. 1, Pt. II, Arts. 1–7 and Ch. 2, Pt. I, Art. 3: Classis; Ch. 1, Pt. III, Arts. 1–7: Regional Synod; Ch. 1, Pt. IV. Arts. 1–2: General Synod. See also URC: Man., B.2.6 and B.5: the General Assembly determines references and appeals, questions as to the inclusion of ministers on the roll of ministers, and it is to set up an Appeals Commission; see also Man. C.8: appeals against the decision of any council.

[93] PCI: Code, pars. 34–44. See also UFCS: MPP, VI.I: the primary courts for discipline are the Session for elders, deacons, members and adherents and the Presbytery for ministers; cases may be brought by protest and appeal, or by dissent and complaint by a member of the court from the Session to the Presbytery and from the Presbytery to the General Assembly; PCANZ: BO, 7.7–7.26: Deacons' Court (but this cannot depose).

[94] PCANZ: BO, 8.1–8.18: 'A presbytery may exercise ... judicial ... powers' over members, church councils, congregations and ministers in matters committed to it by the General Assembly; BO, 15: Pastoral Resolution Committee; Disciplinary Commission (hearing); appeal to the Assembly Judicial Commission. Compare: PCW: HOR, 2.5.1: 'It is the church that administers discipline in the case of a member; the Presbytery in the case of a candidate for ministry, an elder, a preacher and a lay preacher, and the Association in the case of a minister.'

[95] PCI: Code, pars. 104–109: the General Assembly is 'the supreme court' of the church with jurisdiction to superintend discipline; its decisions are 'final and binding'; 268–288: its commissions include the Judicial Commission which (par. 127) has the power of the Assembly; PCW: HOR, 3.4–5: General Assembly; UFCS: MPP, V: the General Assembly is the Supreme Court of the Church and its decisions are final as to discipline.

[96] PCA: BCO, 11: Session; 13: Presbytery; 12.3: Moderator; 15.3: Presbytery and its commission.

appeal against the commission decision but the General Assembly may order a re-trial; the commission must issue a summary of the facts, a statement of the issues and its judgment and reasoning (together with any dissenting opinion – minority decisions may also be approved by the General Assembly).[97] Much the same arrangements are to be found in the regulatory instruments of Congregational and United churches,[98] as well as in Baptist Unions and Conventions.[99] With regard to the latter, provision may exist for a regional Baptist Association to be involved in the resolution of conflict which arises in the local church.[100]

All of the elements of a tiered system of judicial authority shared by the Protestant churches studied here are found in the juridical instruments of Methodism.[101] In Methodist polity, the Class and Local Society are responsible for the discipline of members. For example, according to the law of the Methodist Church in Ireland, whilst at local level the members of the Society are to 'help each other to work out their salvation', the class leader is to 'reprove [them] ... as occasion may require' and must meet the ministers and the stewards of the Society weekly 'to inform the Minister ... of any that walk disorderly, and will not be reproved'.[102] Church members are subject to the disciplinary authority of the Church Council. Cases which involve local preachers are heard by the Circuit Executive (at which the district superintendent presides), with appeal to the District Disciplinary Committee (convened by the district superintendent with seven members from the district), and further appeal to the Conference which is to appoint a committee to hear the appeal (presided over by the president of the Conference). As to ministers, if the District

---

[97] PCA: BCO, 15.4–15.6.
[98] UCCSA: Const., 3–5 and Procedure 15: 'Every member ... is subject to discipline'; the Congregational Meeting decides matters of dispute and discipline with appeal to the Regional Council (the latter is also to investigate and adjudicate any matter referred to it by a local church); the Synod is a court of the Assembly with 'general oversight of the Regional Councils'; UCOC: Const., Art. V: the local church has authority over discipline but decisions of the General Synod, a Conference or an Association 'should be held in the highest regard by every Local Church'; see also UCA: Const., 31–37; Regs., 3.5; UCC: Man., BU, s. 7 and BL 400–470.
[99] NBCUSA: Const., Art. IV: 'The Convention ... is the sole and final arbiter of any question regarding membership rights, privileges, and obligations' and 'shall adjudicate such disputes and questions ... in accordance with Biblical principles and procedures established by the Board of Directors'; the Board makes a 'binding' decision, subject to review and ratification by Convention, but a two-thirds majority vote of the Board is required for removal from office or expulsion from the Convention subject also to review and ratification by Convention. See also ABCUSA: TCOR, I.A: 'A local congregation ... is ... capable of ordering its inner life' through 'maintaining a disciplined life'; Bethel Baptist Church (Choctaw): Const., Art. VII: 'the church' disciplines.
[100] BUSA: Model Const., Art. 9: the Executive Committee of the local church enquires into breaches of membership and reports to the General Meeting for action; in listed disputes (e.g. between members, or pastor and members), the Pastor or four members of the Executive Committee or ten church members may call a special meeting of the Executive Committee to resolve differences; the meeting includes nominees of the Association; if this process fails, the Association representatives must recommend an independent person to lead the church through a conflict resolution process (set out in Art. 25); see e.g. Central Baptist Church (Pretoria): Const., 9: the Executive inquires and the General Meeting decides on an appropriate sanction.
[101] Ultimately, discipline vests in Conference: MCGB: CPD, DU 18–21; MCNZ: LAR, s. 7.1.1–4.
[102] MCI: General Rules of the Society of the People called Methodists (1743) 1.

Pastoral Committee decides there is a case to answer the case is sent to the District Disciplinary Committee (convened and presided over by the district superintendent) which reports to the District Synod for decision; there is a right of appeal to the Conference. Moreover, only the Ministerial Session of the Conference has the final decision as to 'Discipline and Expulsion of Ministers'.[103]

There is a similar system in those Methodist churches with bishops. For example, in the United Methodist Church in the USA, the General Conference is 'to provide a judicial system' and a 'judicial procedure'.[104] This 'judicial system . . . shall guarantee to our clergy a right to trial by a committee and an appeal and to our members a right to trial before the Church, or by a committee, and an appeal'; the Annual Conference may also 'make inquiry into the moral and official conduct of its clergy members' and 'hear complaints' against these.[105] Moreover: 'There shall be a Judicial Council. The General Conference shall determine the number and qualifications of its members, their terms of office, and the method of election and the filling of vacancies.'[106] The Judicial Council has authority *inter alia*: to determine 'the constitutionality of any act of the General Conference' and 'the legality' of acts of a board of the General Conference, jurisdictional conference or central conference; and it is to hear and determine any appeal from the decision of a bishop on a question of law made in the annual conferences.[107] All decisions of the Judicial Council shall be final.[108] The legal evidence, from across the church families, indicates that a church or other ecclesial community may establish courts or tribunals for the judicial resolution of disputes and the enforcement of its discipline. These judicial bodies may exist at international, national, regional and/or local level to the extent permitted by ecclesial polity, are composed of qualified personnel, may be tiered as to their original and their appellate jurisdiction, and exercise such authority over lay and ordained persons as is conferred upon them by law. Once again, all Christians, regardless of their denominational affiliation, provide for the adjudication of disputes amongst the faithful by means of church courts and tribunals.

Judicial procedure – due process

The juridical instruments of many churches, particularly Protestant, expressly invoke scriptural processes for the resolution of disputes, notably those contained in Matthew 18.[109] These instruments often provide that recourse to the courts is a

---

[103] MCI: RDG, 5: the three tiers; Const., s. 6.4: Ministerial Session; RDG, 10.0.1: the Church Council is responsible for the 'discipline and exclusion of members as required by the laws of the Church'.
[104] UMCUSA: Const., Div. 2.1–2.3; UMCNEAE: BOD, pars. 8, 13, 14, 15, 16, 17, 501–511.
[105] UMCUSA: Const., Div. 4, Art. IV; see also UMCNEAE: BOD, par. 58. See also: FMCNA: BOD, Ch. 4: General Conference has 'judicial promotional and supervisory powers over the activities of the church'.
[106] UMCUSA: Const., Div. 4, Art I; see also UMCNEAE: BOD, par. 55.
[107] UMCUSA: Const., Div. 4, Art. II; see also UMCNEAE: BOD, par. 56.
[108] UMCUSA: Const., Div. 4, Art. III: if the Judicial Council declares unconstitutional any act of the General Conference, its decision is reported to that Conference immediately; see also UMCNEAE: BOD, par. 57.
[109] See e.g. UCCSA: Procedure 15.1: the pattern of discipline is based on Matt. 18.15–17; BUSA: Model Const., Art. 9: 'In purely personal matters, members shall be expected to act in

last resort and that other means of settlement should be pursued initially. They set down elaborate procedures for due process which deal with, *inter alia*, the object of trials, rights of access to courts and tribunals, preliminary examination, presentation of charges, rights to a hearing, judicial impartiality and, sometimes, legal representation. These provisions on due process, shared across the Christian traditions studied here, underscore the applicability of the principle of the rule of law in the church.

According to Catholic canon law, in the Latin Church, judicial process is treated very much as the last resort: disputants are under a duty to settle amicably, promptly and equitably out of court – and the Episcopal Conference is encouraged to establish permanent offices in every diocese to resolve disputes without going to trial.[110] The object of a trial is to prosecute or to vindicate the rights of physical or juridical persons, to declare juridical facts and to pronounce the penalty for offences; judicial power – possessed by judges or judicial colleges – must be exercised in the manner prescribed by law; it cannot be delegated, except to carry out acts which are preparatory to a decree or a decision. Once jurisdiction is established, anyone (whether baptised or not) may bring an action before a tribunal. The faithful have access to the courts to vindicate or defend their rights and there is a legal action to defend every right. Provision is made for oral hearings, but proceedings are generally in writing; cases must be concluded within a year.[111] There are special provisions on contentious trials,[112] matrimonial cases[113] and penal cases.[114] The ordinary (e.g. a bishop) initiates penal processes when all other pastoral means have failed to repair scandal, restore justice and reform the offender; after a preliminary investigation, the accused must be given the opportunity to be heard in their own defence and be given canonical counsel; if a violation is established, but the person is truly sorry for the offence and

---

accordance with the Lord's injunction in Matthew 18.15–17'; this is implicit in e.g. LCA: BL, X.C: see below n. 126; see also: PCA: BCO, 31: initial 'gentle spiritual restoration' rests on Gal. 6.1; COTN: Man. IV.I.I, par. 122 cites both Matt. 18 and Gal. 6: the pastor and congregation should seek to resolve differences by discussing them face to face; if this fails, to seek the assistance of one or two others; if this fails, to bring the matter to the church board.

[110] CIC, c. 1446: 'All Christ's faithful, and especially bishops, are to strive earnestly, with due regard for justice, to ensure that disputes among the people of God are as far as possible avoided, and are settled promptly and without rancour'; the judge must exhort the parties to seek an 'equitable solution' by mediation or arbitration and determine whether these (cc. 1717–1720) serve to resolve the matter; c. 1733: the Episcopal Conference.

[111] CIC, cc. 135, 1400; c. 1476: right to bring an action; c. 221: vindicating rights; c. 1453: first instance process must not exceed a year, and second instance, 6 months; c. 1455: confidentiality; c. 1456: judicial impartiality; c. 1457: process against judges acting unlawfully; cc. 1458–1462: hearing; cc. 1465–1467: time limits and postponements; cc. 1468–1469: place of trial; cc. 1470–1475: admission to hearings; cc. 1476–1480: plaintiff and respondent; cc. 1481–1490: procurators and advocates; cc. 1491–1500: actions and exceptions.

[112] CIC, cc. 1501–1655: e.g. petitions; summons; joinder of issue; trial; proofs; inspection (e.g. places); publication of acts; pronouncement of the judge (who must have 'moral certainty' and weigh the evidence 'conscientiously'); appeals; expenses and free legal aid; execution of the judgment.

[113] CIC, cc. 1671–1707: the competent forum, proofs, documentary process, judgment and appeal.

[114] CIC, cc. 1717–1719: investigation; cc. 1720–1728: process; cc. 1729–1731: compensation for harm.

promises to make amends, there can be no penalty.[115] These provisions are mirrored in Oriental Catholic canon law.[116]

Anglican procedures in disciplinary and other trials make provision for: the right to bring a complaint; notice; the charge; a preliminary enquiry (usually by the bishop or an appointee of the bishop); interim suspension of the accused; the trial; the right to be heard; legal representation; holding the hearing in public or private; and the right to appeal.[117] These procedural elements have been summed up in the principles of canon law common to the churches of the Anglican Communion. Ordinary jurisdiction in matters of discipline rests either with the bishop or with such other ecclesiastical person, court or tribunal as may be prescribed by law. Church disputes should be resolved equitably and, in the first instance, the parties should seek to resolve their differences amicably. Courts and tribunals are to be available as necessary to resolve disputes and accessible to such of the faithful, ordained or lay, as may be prescribed by law. Judicial officers are to exercise their office impartially, without fear or favour. In disciplinary and other cases, the procedure is at all times to be fair and just, and is to protect rights of the parties to notice of proceedings, to adequate time for preparation of defence, to a presumption of innocence, to be heard within a reasonable time, to question evidence, to representation and to appeal in appropriate cases on a matter of fact or law. Church courts and tribunals must give their decisions, and the reasons for them, in writing, and both decisions and reasons must be based on fact and law.[118] Similar procedural patterns are found in Orthodox churches in which there is provision for both preliminary investigation and formal trial.[119] For example, in the Ukrainian Orthodox Church in America: 'Every member of the Church is entitled to due canonical procedure in the courts of the Church'; accusations of indiscipline must be presented in writing to the bishop; a preliminary process determines whether there is a case to answer; the bishop may impose temporary suspension on a cleric and temporary excommunication on the laity prior to trial; the decision at trial must be unanimous; penalties may be imposed subject to approval by the bishop; there is a right of appeal in either party to the Holy Synod as Supreme Court of Appeals; deposition of clergy requires confirmation by the Holy Synod; and the decision of the Holy Synod is final.[120]

---

[115] CIC, cc. 1341–1349, 1717–1732.
[116] CCEO, cc. 1117–1123: order of adjudication; cc. 1124–1128: time limits, delays and place of trial; cc. 1129–1133: persons admitted to trial and tribunal acts; cc. 1134–1138: petitioner and respondent; cc. 1139–1148: procurators and advocates; cc. 1149–1163: the right of action; cc. 1164–1184: avoiding trials (e.g. settlements and arbitration); cc. 1185–1356: contentious trials; cc. 1357–1400: special processes: cc. 1401–1487: sanctions.
[117] E.g. Canada: Principles and General Procedures, 16–24: 'natural justice'; Scotland: Can. 54: at least 3 communicants must bring a complaint; Southern Africa: Can. 37: charge; Ireland: Const., VIII.15: preliminary enquiry; TEC: Cans. IV.1: suspension pending trial; Kenya: Can. V: assessors; West Indies: Can 24.11: public and private hearings; Nigeria: Can. V: witnesses; South East Asia: Const., Art. II: appeals (on fact and law).
[118] PCLCCAC, Principle 24: due judicial process.
[119] OCIA: GC, A Selection of Clergy Disciplines, 10: 'Clergy have the right to a hearing before a Church Court (Chalcedon, c. 9, Statutes of the OCIA, Art. XI)'; UOCIA: Statutes, Art. VIII; ROC: Statute, X.35.
[120] UOCIA: Statutes, Art. XII; there are special provisions on marital problems: see Chapter 7; e.g. Holy Apostles, c. IX: 'All the faithful who come in and hear the Scriptures, but do not

Protestant churches employ both general principles and detailed procedural rules in the governance of disciplinary process. This is the case in some Lutheran churches: it is a fundamental principle that parties in dispute should seek an informal resolution of the matter;[121] also: 'Ecclesiastical discipline shall be carried out in an evangelical manner in accordance with scriptural principles and upholding the rules of natural justice ... process must be initiated and completed where possible at first instance within the congregation or district'.[122] Typically, provision is made for a preliminary enquiry into accusations as well as for the temporary suspension of a person.[123] At trial, 'due process' requires written notice of charges, testimony in person (and the right to remain silent at the election of the accused), witnesses, cross-examination and a written decision; moreover, the accused has the right 'to be treated with fundamental procedural fairness', which includes the right to be heard.[124] Procedures may vary as between ordained and lay persons. As to process against clergy, the Lutheran Church in Great Britain may be offered as an example – it provides for three stages. First, informal settlement: the bishop (with others) determines whether a pastor's performance, behaviour, practices or beliefs are of sufficient concern as to merit discussion with the pastor; there follows an informal meeting with the pastor. If concerns remain, an action plan may be instituted to resolve the issue. If unsuccessful, the bishop recommends to the Council withdrawal of the pastor's authority to minister and an interim suspension may be imposed pending investigation by the bishop: reasons must be given. Secondly, there is an investigation. Thirdly, if formal disciplinary action is decided upon there is a hearing before a panel of Council members chosen by the bishop – the pastor is given notice and a right to a hearing (which may be in private). If the bishop and the Council decide to withdraw the pastor's authority to minister, there is a right of appeal to a Board of Appeal appointed by the Council.[125]

Process against lay people is not dissimilar. For example, the Lutheran Church in Australia provides that, in the case of complaints, a person alleging 'fault against a member' must first in personal admonition endeavour to convince the member of such fault and, if unsuccessful, make the same endeavour in the presence of witnesses. If this fails, the matter must be submitted to the congregation with the errant member attending the meeting and responding to the allegation. The

---

stay for the prayers and the Holy Communion, are to be excommunicated, as causing disorder in the Church.'

[121] ELCSA: G., 5: discipline within the congregation should start with 'a brotherly consultation' with the minister; if this fails, the person concerned is called before the church committee to render an account; if this fails, the congregation may deny 'some or all church rights'; ELCA: Const., Ch. 20: consultation and informal resolution by the bishop.

[122] See e.g. LCA: Const., Art. X.

[123] ELCA: Const., Ch. 7.46; see also Ch. 20: when allegations of physical or mental incapacity or 'ineffective conduct' of a pastor come to the attention of the Bishop of the Synod, the bishop may investigate personally or with a committee of two ministers and one layperson; provision is made for interim suspension by the bishop.

[124] ELCA: Const., Ch. 20: fundamental procedural fairness means e.g. allowing the accused to present their cases without unnecessary interruptions and to be accompanied by a representative.

[125] LCGB: RAR, Disciplinary Procedure for Pastors of the Church: the bishop acts with the dean and council chair; if the bishop is the subject of allegations, similar processes apply with the dean and deputy chair.

congregation may admonish the member but if the member remains impenitent, the final step of exclusion (or excommunication) is pronounced by the pastor; if the errant member fails to submit to the discipline, the congregation may declare such person to be no longer a member. An appeal lies to the district president, who must seek informal resolution (and may exercise 'the prerogative of mercy'), but if this fails may submit the case to the Tribunal; a further appeal may overturn the decision if it is manifestly against the evidence, in breach of natural justice or the sanction was excessive or inadequate in severity.[126] The General Church Council must appoint a Tribunal (of pastors and lay members from each district) to hear and to determine matters referred to it.[127] In point of fact, analogous procedures apply to complaints against the pastors; there are, once again, three basic stages: an informal meeting; investigation by the Church Council; and referral to the Tribunal of the General Church Council (with appeal to the College of Presidents).[128]

Parallel arrangements exist in Reformed and Presbyterian churches. For the former, a typical pattern is pastoral resolution, investigation (and if necessary a caution) and hearing (which may be subject to an appeal).[129] The same applies, broadly, in Presbyterian churches.[130] Thus, under the Book of Church Order of the Presbyterian Church in America, if pastoral measures fail, an investigation follows, and, if this results in 'a strong presumption of guilt', there is a trial – the trial of ministers is by the Presbytery (or a commission appointed by it) and the trial of lay members by the Session. An appeal lies (on grounds of procedural irregularity) to the General Assembly. A judicial commission of the General Assembly deals with the matter – it must deliver a summary of the facts, a statement of the issues and a judgment which may affirm or reverse the decision or order a re-trial – this must include the reasoning upon which the decision is based (together with any

---

[126] LCA: Const., Art. X.1: process may occur e.g. for departure from the confession and leading an ungodly life; BL, X.C: there is provision for interim suspension of a pastor; BL, X.C.4: submission of disputes to the Tribunal; BL, X.C10: process may also be made against a congregation for failure to uphold discipline resulting in censure by the district president or public censure before the District Synod.

[127] LCA: BL, X.C.14–18; 27–58: this sets out the procedure.

[128] LCA: BL, V.D: a pastor must not 'be arbitrarily dismissed by a parish'; there must first be 'fraternal discussion' between the pastor and the parish committee to seek 'a peaceable resolution' and the endeavour must be 'genuine'; if this fails, the matter is sent to the Church Council which in its 'absolute discretion' may submit the matter to the Tribunal which recommends to the Church Council which may e.g. direct further discussions or that the pastor takes leave, or recommend to the College of Presidents termination of the call; there is a right to be heard either in person or in writing; the decision of the College of Presidents is final.

[129] RCA: Ch. 2, Pt. I, Arts. 4–6: a charge (written accusation); consideration by a committee to determine whether there is a case; citation; trial by the judicatory; right to a hearing; representation; record; sanction; see also Pt. II: nature of and process for complaints; Pt. III: appeals; see also URC: Man., O: Ministerial Disciplinary Process: the hearing is by an Assembly Commission and there are Guidelines on Appeals.

[130] PCANZ: BO, 15: the Pastoral Resolution Committee investigates; the Disciplinary Commission hears the case – there are rules on the right to a hearing, the hearing, records, witnesses and the decision; there is an appeal to the Assembly Judicial Commission; PCW: HOR, 2.5: complaint; unbiased investigation; a hearing; and appeals (to Presbytery or Association); UFCS: MPP, VI.I: if private admonition and counsel fail, the Session tries elders, deacons and members, and the Presbytery tries ministers; VI.II: rules common to Sessions and Presbyteries (Primary Courts of Discipline); VII: appeals/complaints heard by General Assembly.

dissenting opinion, if there is one).[131] In the trial process, the accuser is always the church and the court may appoint a committee to converse privately with the offender to establish guilt before instituting full process by means of an indictment stating the particulars of the case. At the trial, the accused may be represented by a communing church member, the moderator charges the court, the indictment is read, witnesses and the accused are examined, and the parties must be heard; the court members express their opinion, a vote is taken and the verdict announced and recorded – the decision itself must be 'equitable' and it must promote 'the welfare of the church'.[132]

These elements of judicial process shared by Christian churches are also found in the juridical instruments of the Methodist tradition.[133] Such instruments often spell out general principles applicable to the disciplinary process: for instance, the Methodist Church in New Zealand has 'a responsibility to exercise discipline' and it recognises the need for 'adequate processes and procedures for the receipt and dealing with complaints in accordance with the principles of natural justice'; moreover, throughout the process, 'the church expects all parties to seek to exercise Christian grace, forgiveness and reconciliation'.[134] Methodist procedures are designed to uphold 'the laws of the Church', to encourage 'responsible membership' within the church, to ensure that complaints are dealt with 'adequately, promptly, and with attention to procedural fairness', to ensure 'appropriate confidentiality and privacy' and to achieve 'an appropriate resolution of each matter'. The complaints procedure applies to all members of the church (ministers and those on an electoral roll), but process may be suspended if the case is before the civil or criminal courts of the State.[135] Mediation or other form of reconciliation is a first step.[136] Resource

---

[131] PCA: BCO, 15: 'A Presbytery as a whole may try a judicial case within its jurisdiction' or 'commit any judicial case to a commission' appointed by it to resolve the case under the Rules of Discipline and submit to the Presbytery its judgment for approval. See also PCI: Code, par. 127: Judicial Commission of General Assembly.

[132] PCA: BCO, 31-42.

[133] COTN: Man., Pt. VI.II-III: resolution by agreement; IV-V: contested lay and clergy discipline; VI: procedure; VII: District Court of Appeals; VIII: General Court of Appeals; IX: Regional Court of Appeals; X: Guarantee of Rights (e.g. 'to a fair and impartial hearing of charges pending against an accused minister or layperson'; written charges must be given; there is a presumption of innocence and a right to present orally).

[134] MCNZ: LAR, 8.1; see also LAR, 2.18: in cases involving ministers, the Code of Disciplinary Regulations must be followed; interim suspension is permitted; the President's primary role is 'pastoral'; the Board of Administration administers the Complaints Procedures, and must report on them to Conference.

[135] UMCNEAE: BOD, par. 228ff and Complaints Procedures: in a complaint against a 'professing' member, the pastor and district superintendent must attempt 'just resolution' through mediation (par. 361); if this fails, a charge follows; pars. 362-363: fair process; 2702: the complainant has rights to be heard, to be accompanied and to be informed of the resolution; the respondent has the same rights and a right against double jeopardy.

[136] MCNZ: LAR, 8: as to ministers, the Conference Complaints Officer arranges 'a mediation if appropriate'. If this fails, the officer arranges an investigation and reports to the Conference Complaints Review Panel to decide if a charge be brought (or further mediation). The charge is determined by a Conference Disciplinary Tribunal. There is no appeal from its finding, but with leave of the president (consulting his Committee of Advice). A person against whom a charge is proved may seek 'forgiveness' of Conference. See also FMCNA: BOD, Ch. 7.

JUDICIAL PROCEDURE – DUE PROCESS 177

to the formal process is a last resort.[137] Formal process is thus threefold: informal resolution; investigation; and determination (and appeal).[138]

This approach is employed by the Methodist Church in Great Britain. First, the complaints and discipline process seeks to embody several 'principles', namely: the initiation of complaints should not be limited to members of the Church; there should be no difference of principle between ordained and lay people in the way in which complaints against them are dealt with; the possibility of reconciliation should be explored carefully in every case in which that is appropriate; help and support should be offered both to the person making the complaint and the one complained against at every stage; the process should be fair; the person or body making the decision at each stage should be competent to do so; there should be a means of correcting any errors which may be made and a means of ensuring compliance with any decision; and there should be appropriate requirements as to confidentiality and record-keeping.[139] In turn, a respondent should have an adequate opportunity of responding to the complaint and meeting any charge and dealing with the evidence, be treated fairly by the complaints team and receive 'a fair hearing from any church court which is to decide whether any charge is established'.[140] Secondly, provision is made for Local Complaints Officers, Complaints Support Groups, District Reconciliation Groups and Connexional Complaints Panels (and Connexional Advocates), as well as for interim suspension. Thirdly, if at district level a reconciliation fails, the complaint is investigated at connexional level, and if a case is made out a charge is formulated for a hearing by the Connexional Discipline Committee which is to produce a finding that the charge is established (or not) on the balance of probabilities. A penalty is imposed but there is an appeal to the Connexional Appeal Committee and a further appeal to the Conference (and its Ministerial Session).[141]

A similar threefold process of informal resolution, formal investigation and a hearing (with the rights and duties of parties clearly set out) is found in the regulatory instruments of Congregational churches,[142] United

---

[137] UMCNEAE: BOD, par. 2707: 'Church trials are ... an expedient of last resort ... after every reasonable effort has been made to correct any wrong'; 'No such trial ... shall be construed to deprive the respondent or the Church of legal civil rights, except to the extent ... provided in [par.] 2701.9'; pars. 2709–2719: process.

[138] MCI: RDG, 9.18–19 and Man., Ch. 5: if informal resolution (initiated by the district superintendent) fails, and a complaint is made, the District Pastoral Committee investigates and offers counsel or decides to submit the case to the District Disciplinary Committee on the basis of a charge. The Synod or the Conference considers the report of the District Disciplinary Committee and issues final judgment.

[139] MCGB: CPD, SO 1100.   [140] MCGB: CPD, SO 1102.

[141] MCGB: CPD, SO 1105–1155.

[142] UCCSA: Procedure 13 and 15: in the case of a complaint or charge (which must be specific and written) against a minister, the local Church Council reports the matter to the Regional Ministerial Committee whose officers meet the accused privately and in a brotherly way for a preliminary enquiry; if this fails and the committee considers 'the charge has substance', the minister may be suspended prior to a full investigation; at this, the complainant is heard in the presence of the minister, who has the right to reply; witnesses are examined and cross-examined; a record is kept and a report submitted to the Regional Ministerial Committee which then submits its recommendation to the Synod, which in turn makes a recommendation to the Executive Committee for decision and action; an appeal lies to the Assembly Ministerial

178   ECCLESIASTICAL DISCIPLINE AND CONFLICT RESOLUTION

churches[143] and Baptist Unions and Conventions.[144] In other words, it is a principle of Christian law that disciplinary process is composed of informal resolution (and the faithful must make every effort to settle their disputes amicably, with recourse to courts and tribunals a last resort), formal investigation by competent authority, a judicial hearing or trial (which must satisfy the principles of natural justice) and such other stages as may be prescribed by law, including the opportunity for an appeal.

Ecclesiastical offences and sanctions

There is remarkable juridical unity between the Christian traditions studied here as to the ecclesiastical offences and sanctions which lie at the heart of church discipline. Prohibitions against the commission of ecclesiastical offences may apply to both ordained and lay people. What is striking is the level of generality with which ecclesiastical offences are defined. The enumeration of ecclesiastical sanctions is a straightforward task. However, it is rather more difficult to generalise about approaches to the location of authority to impose sanctions, the applicability of specific sanctions to specific offences and the reversibility of censures.

Ecclesiastical offences

Christian churches are in general agreement about the nature of an ecclesiastical offence, the definitional elements of the offence and the classes within the church to which offences apply. However, there is juridical diversity in terms of the defences available to excuse an offender or justify their conduct. For the Roman Catholic Church a canonical offence is an external violation, which is gravely imputable to the person by reason of deliberate intent or culpable negligence, of a law or precept to which a penalty attaches; it is committed in the public life (external forum) of the church and not in the forum of conscience (internal forum); penal laws (which may be made at various ecclesial levels) must be interpreted strictly or narrowly.[145]

Committee, which appoints a Reference Committee to review the case; the Reference Committee reports its findings to the Assembly Ministerial Committee, which submits them to the Executive Committee for final decision and action.

[143] See e.g. (United) Church of North India: Const., II.V.IX.3: the bishop must 'if possible, settle the matter by personal inquiry and advice ... But if the bishop shall direct or the accused minister demands' the case must be referred to the Court of the Diocesan Council; South India: Const., XI.11: interim suspension.

[144] BUSA: Model Const., Art. 9: the Executive (of the local church) makes enquiry, and if there is no 'satisfactory response' it may submit a recommendation to the General Meeting which is to sanction 'only if all efforts at restoration prove unsuccessful'; Const., Art. 25: mediation on the initiative of the Association. See also NBCUSA: Const., Art. IV; NBC: Policies and Practices, Conflict: 'Any conflict between the pastor and his church should be resolved internally'; if this fails, 'the matter should be referred to the association' and if that fails to resolve it, the matter should be referred to the Conference and subsequently to the Convention.

[145] CIC, cc. 1311-12: the punishment of offences in general; cc. 1313-1320: penal laws and precepts; those with legislative authority may also make penal laws and may attach penalties to the laws of higher authorities; see c. 18 for the narrow interpretation of penal laws; c. 49: those with executive authority may issue precepts.

These include offences against religion and the unity of the church (such as apostasy, heresy, schism, blasphemy, perjury and harm to public morals); offences against church authorities (such as the use of physical force against the Roman Pontiff, teaching doctrine condemned by the Pope, incitement to hatred against the Apostolic See and profanation of a sacred object); the usurpation of ecclesiastical offices (attempting to celebrate Mass when not a priest, simony and the unlawful exercise of sacred ministry); falsehood (such as falsely denouncing an offence to a confessor); offences against special obligations (such as unlawful clerical engagement in a trade or business); and offences against human life and liberty (such as murder, the infliction of bodily harm and procurement of an abortion).[146] When an external violation occurs, imputability is presumed – but this may be rebutted; however, an external violation will not be penalised if the person has a recognised defence – for example, the person is under 16 years of age, is unaware that the action was a violation, acted accidentally, lacked the use of reason, acted under duress or acted in self-defence or the defence of another.[147] Similar offences are punishable in the Oriental Catholic Churches.[148]

Juridical lists in Orthodox, Anglican and Lutheran churches contain fewer offences than those appearing in Catholic canon law – and the offences listed are spelt out with a far higher level of generality, not least in terms of the *mens rea* required for liability. One canonist of the Orthodox tradition defines an ecclesiastical offence as 'any transgression by an external action or omission against the ecclesiastical law in force': serious offences include apostasy, heresy, schism, simony, sacrilege, violation of graves and perjury.[149] Some offences are common to both clergy and laity and others are confined to either the clergy or the laity.[150] Across the Orthodox churches studied here, offences applicable to all the faithful include: 'infringing the church discipline and teaching';[151] the violation of 'the doctrinal, canonical or moral norms of the Orthodox Church';[152] 'unorthodox belief, [and] breaches of canonical or moral discipline';[153] the violation of moral standards and the commission of more specified actions.[154] According to the Holy Canons, offences for which only the clergy may be liable include: repetition of a valid ordination, the performance of priestly actions by a deposed cleric, the exercise of ministry outside the jurisdiction and conspiracy against canonical authorities; and those for which both clergy and laity may be liable include:

---

[146] CIC, cc. 1364–1399: simony is the receipt of payment for conferral of a spiritual benefit (such as administration of the sacraments).
[147] CIC, cc. 1321–1330: those who are liable to penal sanctions.
[148] CCEO, e.g. c. 1436–1437: heresy, apostasy and schism; c. 1446: disobedience to lawful orders of a superior.
[149] OOCL: 173: definition of offence; MOCL: 116–117: the offences.
[150] GOAA: Charter, Art. 9: the 'moral and disciplinary offences of clergy and lay persons'.
[151] ROMOC: Statutes, Art. 14; see also Arts. 148–160: doctrinal, moral and canonical offences.
[152] ROC: Statute, X.35: if the members of the Diocesan Council 'violate the doctrinal, canonical or moral norms of the Orthodox Church and if they stand trial in the ecclesiastical court or are under investigation, they shall be dismissed from their office by the decision of the Diocesan Bishop'.
[153] UOCIA: Statutes, Art. XII; there are special provisions on marital problems: see Chapter 7.
[154] UOCIA: Statutes, Art. VIII.

apostasy, heresy, schism, simony and sacrilege.[155] Anglicanism, too, is notable for the lack of juridical precision in the definitional elements of its ecclesiastical offences – though *The Principles of Canon Law Common to the Churches of the Anglican Communion* provide: 'In disciplinary cases, ecclesiastical offences and defences to them are to be clearly defined and set out in writing.'[156] Thus, under the laws of provincial churches, bishops, clergy and (in some churches) the laity may be tried for a number of ecclesiastical offences. Typically these include: the commission of a crime under State law; 'immorality' or immoral conduct; teaching doctrines contrary to those of the church; violation of the law of the church or of ordination vows; habitual or wilful neglect of duty; conduct unbecoming the office and work of an ordained minister; and disobedience to the lawful directions of a bishop.[157] These are mirrored, broadly, in some Lutheran lists of ecclesiastical offences for which pastors may be disciplined: preaching or teaching contrary to the faith confessed by the church; conduct incompatible with the character of ministerial office; wilful disregard or violation of the constitution and bylaws; wilful disregard or violation of the ministerial standards of the church; unlawful disclosure of confidential communications; sexual misconduct; fiscal mismanagement; and divorce and remarriage.[158] Moreover, the lay faithful may be disciplined for prescribed ecclesiastical offences to the extent authorised by law.[159]

The concept of sin as the core of ecclesiastical offences is more prominent in the juridical instruments of the Reformed and Presbyterian traditions. However, like Anglican, Orthodox and Lutheran churches, and unlike the Catholic Church, juridical instruments do not provide for explicit defences. The juridical instruments of some Presbyterian churches address the nature of an ecclesiastical offence. The Presbyterian Church in America has a particularly well-developed juridical definition of an ecclesiastical offence – an 'offence' is defined as 'anything in the

---

[155] Apostolic Canon 68, Canon 48 of the Synod in Cartagena: re-ordination; Apostolic Canon 28, Canon 6 of the Second Ecumenical Synod, Canon 4 of the Synod in Antioch: actions by a deposed cleric; Apostolic Canon 35, Canon 15 of the First Ecumenical Synod: ministry outside the jurisdiction; Canon 18 of the Fourth Ecumenical Synod: conspiracy; Apostolic Canon 31: schism, etc; Canon 2 of the Fourth Ecumenical Synod: simony.

[156] PCLCCAC, Principle 24.9. For a criticism of the Anglican approach, see Doe, *Canon Law in the Anglican Communion: A Worldwide Perspective* (Clarendon Press, Oxford, 1998), 83.

[157] See e.g. West Africa: Const., Art. XXII.6: crime; Ireland: Const. VIII.53: immorality; West Indies: Can. 25: doctrine; Wales: Const., IX.9: disobedience to law; Canada: Can. XVIII.8: neglect of duty; Scotland: Can. 54.2: conduct unbecoming; New Zealand: Can. D.II.4: disobedience of lawful episcopal directions.

[158] NALC: SFPM (2011); see also LCGB: RAR, Disciplinary Procedure for Pastors of the Church: failure to observe the rules 'in a serious and persistent manner'; ELCA: Const., Ch. 20.20–21: preaching and teaching in conflict with the faith; conduct incompatible with the character of ministerial office; wilful violation of the constitution and bylaws; LCA: Const., Art. X.1: departure from the confession and leading an ungodly life; BL, V.D: a pastor's 'persistent or continued neglect of duty'.

[159] ELCA: Const., Ch. 20.21: all members may be disciplined for e.g. denial of the faith, 'conduct grossly unbecoming a member of the Church of Christ', 'persistent trouble-making' and wilful disregard of the constitution and bylaws; ELCSA: G., 5: 'brotherly discipline' applies if 'a person publicly despises or insults the Christian faith, by word and deed, if he continually and consciously trespasses God's commandments or if he defames the glory of God'; see also LCMS: BL, 1.10.

doctrines or practice of a Church member professing faith in Christ which is contrary to the Word of God'; offences are either personal or general, private or public; being sins against God, their commission is a ground for discipline; personal offences are violations of divine law involving wrongs to particular individuals, and general offences are heresies or immoralities; private offences are those known to a few people, and public offences those which are notorious.[160] By way of contrast, the Presbyterian Church in Wales provides: 'It is not practicable to draw up a list of transgressions and specify the appropriate discipline for each one. This must be left to the conscience and judgement of the church and it must administer judgement in accordance with the nature of the transgression, taking into consideration on the one hand the age, experience, history and circumstances of the transgressor, and on the other the discipline which would be appropriate. Every act of discipline should be an opportunity for the church to examine itself, to bring its conscience to the light and to strengthen its life and unity.'[161] Nevertheless, across Presbyterian churches, offences include: anything in teaching or conduct of a person under its jurisdiction which has been declared censurable by the Word of God or 'by the law and practice of the Church'; anything among the members which gives rise to 'scandal injurious to the purity or peace of the Church' (such as disobedience to the courts of the church);[162] 'conduct unbecoming a minister';[163] 'gross crime or heresy';[164] prolonged absence from the gospel ordinances; and a sin or offence of 'doctrinal error or grave impropriety of conduct' especially on account of its public and scandalous nature.[165] The instruments of Congregational churches also carry lists of ecclesiastical offences; for instance, the United Congregational Church of Southern Africa provides for judicial process in the event that ministers engage in: 'wilful and persistent neglect of the duties of a minister'; 'the breach of or non-compliance with any constitutional requirements or procedures of the Church or any competent court of the Church'; 'grave moral misconduct unworthy of a minister'; conviction of a minister in a secular court for 'any grave criminal charge'; and teaching contrary to scripture and church doctrine.[166]

Methodist lists of offences are generally more extensive than those of other Protestant churches, and often separate lists operate for ministers and lay members.[167] Offences may include: neglect of the vows of the baptismal covenant and regular absence from the worship of the church without valid reason; immorality including but not limited to not being celibate in singleness or not faithful in a

---

[160] PCA: BCO, 29.1-4; see also 36: infliction of censures.   [161] PCW: HOR, 2.5.2.
[162] PCI: Code, pars. 131-132: (e.g. 1 Cor. 5.9-11).   [163] PCANZ: BO, 15.2.
[164] PCA: BCO, 30.1-5.   [165] UFCS: MPP, VI.I-VI: I.
[166] UCCSA: Procedure 13 and 15: offences committed more than 5 years previously cannot be disciplined.
[167] MCNZ: LAR, 8.4: complaints may be made against a minister who has 'breached the Laws', failed 'to adhere to the General Standards for the Guidance of Members, and the Ethical Standards for Ministry', or 'to carry out … ordination vows', brought the church 'into disrepute', failed 'to uphold the doctrinal standards' of the church or has been convicted of 'a criminal or quasi-criminal offence'; complaints may be brought against a person on an electoral roll (other than a minister) who has 'breached the Laws', failed to adhere to the General Standards for the Guidance of Members, brought the church into disrepute or 'by words or actions refused to accept the discipline of the Conference or otherwise repudiated their membership of the Church'.

heterosexual marriage; practices declared incompatible with Christian teachings (such as being a self-avowed practising homosexual, conducting ceremonies which celebrate homosexual unions or performing same-sex wedding ceremonies); crime; failure to perform the work of the ministry; disobedience to the order and discipline of the church; dissemination of doctrines contrary to the established standards of doctrine of the church; relationships and/or behaviour that undermines the ministry of another pastor; child abuse; sexual abuse; sexual misconduct or harassment, including, but not limited to racial and/or sexual harassment; or racial or gender discrimination. Moreover, any professing member may be charged with the same offences as well as conduct which undermines the ministry of those serving in a church appointment.[168] Disciplinary processes may also be undertaken in Baptist churches for misconduct,[169] such as when a member becomes 'an offence to the church and to its good name by reason of immoral or unchristian conduct, or by persistent breach of covenant vows, or non-support of the church',[170] or: 'If any member is absent from services of the Church and/or neglects to comply with any of the privileges and obligations of membership for a prolonged period without apparent good reason'; the same applies to members engaged in 'unworthy conduct or erroneous belief'.[171]

Disciplinary sanctions

As we have seen, one of the purposes of ecclesiastical discipline is the correction of the faithful. Across the Christian traditions studied here penalties, sanctions or censures are understood to be medicinal. Juridical instruments contain lists of penalties, which are sometimes prescribed for particular offences, and they also provide for the cessation of penalties. Roman Catholic penal law is designed to repair scandal, to restore justice and to reform the offender; however, if by due process a violation of the law is established, but the person is truly sorry for the offence and seriously promises to make amends, that person cannot be penalised.[172] Penalties may be imposed by a sentence (*ferendae sententiae*) or they may be incurred automatically (*latae sententiae*).[173] The penalties are: penal remedies (used to prevent future violations, such as admonition and rebuke); penances (such as a retreat, alms or fast); expiatory penalties which may be permanent or for a determinate period (to make satisfaction, such as deprivation of office); and

---

[168] UMCNEAE: BOD, par. 228(b) and par. 2702. See also MCI: RDG, 5.15: complaints may be made as to e.g. the 'moral and religious character' of a minister, failure to believe and preach church doctrine and failure to fulfil 'the duties of ministerial office'; COTN: Man., Part VI.I: e.g. 'violence to the Covenant of Christian Character or the Covenant of Christian Conduct' and wilful and continuous violation of membership vows.

[169] JBU: Const., Art. V: disciplinary action may follow if members act 'in contravention of the Rules and Regulations of the Union' and 'in a manner injurious or calculated to be injurious to its interests'.

[170] Riverside Baptist Church (Baltimore): BL Art. I. See also Bethel Baptist Church (Choctaw): Const., Art. VII: 'moral offence against the Lord and the church', 'doctrinal offence', and 'personal offence against another member'.

[171] BUSA: Model Const., Arts. 9 and 25.   [172] CIC, cc. 1341–1349, 1717–1732.

[173] CIC, c. 1314; the latter includes e.g. procuring an abortion and a clerical attempt at marriage; penalties may be suspended while under appeal.

medicinal penalties or censures (such as excommunication); provision also exists for the cessation of penalties (and all who may dispense from a law which is supported by a penalty may also remit the penalty itself).[174] Different penalties attach to difference offences: for example, apostasy, heresy and schism attract a *latae sententiae* excommunication; participation in prohibited rites attracts a 'just penalty'; simony attracts suspension; and clerics or religious who engage in unlawful trading or business are 'to be punished according to the gravity of the offence'.[175] Likewise, under the Oriental Code: 'Since God employs every means to bring back the erring sheep, those who have received from Him the power to loose and bind are to apply suitable medicine to the sickness of those who have committed delicts, reproving, imploring and rebuking them with the greatest patience and teaching'. However, authority exists in the church 'to impose penalties in order to heal the wounds caused by the delict, so that those who commit delicts are not driven to the depth of despair nor are restraints relaxed unto a dissoluteness of life and contempt of the law'; penalties should not be imposed if the offender (not yet brought to trial) and moved by sincere repentance has confessed his delict to the hierarch in the external forum and has appropriately provided for the reparation of the scandal and harm; as is the case under the Latin Code, so too Oriental canon law prescribes particular penalties for individual delicts and for the cessation of penalties.[176]

By way of contrast, Orthodox and Anglican laws on sanctions are generally less elaborate. The former often attach prescribed penalties to particular offences; the latter, sometimes. According to Greek Orthodox canon law, ecclesiastical penalties are generally divided into four categories. Penalties which may be imposed on all the faithful include acts of penance or *epitimia* (such as fasting, works of charity and pilgrimages); major excommunication (or *anathema*), total expulsion from the church; and forfeiture of a church burial. Penalties which may be imposed on clerics include defrocking (*kathairesis*), degradation or demotion (*hypovivasmos*), suspension (*argia*), loss of seniority, and a fine. Penalties which may be imposed on clerics and monks include transfer, removal from administrative office, corporal confinement and reproach (*epiplexis*). Penalties imposed only on monks include: expulsion from the monastery, denial of daily ration and penance.[177] In the Russian Orthodox Church, lay people who are members of church institutions may also be dismissed from office.[178] As an overarching principle, in the Ukrainian Orthodox

---

[174] CIC, cc. 1331–1340: forms of penalty; cc. 1341–1352: application of penalties; 1354–1361: cessation of penalties; cc. 1369–1398: the offences which attract special penalties.

[175] CIC, c. 1364: apostasy, heresy, schism; c. 1365: prohibited rites; c. 1380: simony; c. 1392: trade.

[176] CCEO, c. 1401: the justification for penalties; c. 1403: non-imposition of penalties; c. 1409: the judge may defer, abstain from imposing, moderate and suspend penalties; c. 1414: a person is only subject to penalties for a deliberate or seriously culpable violation of the law; c. 1427: public rebuke; c. 1428: supervision; c. 1429: prohibition; c. 1430: privation; c. 1431: minor excommunication; c. 1432: suspension; c. 1434: major excommunication; c. 1436–1437: major excommunication for apostasy, heresy and schism.

[177] OOCL: 176–178; MOCL: 112: this cites e.g. Matt. 12.31–32 and 1 Cor 5.1–5; denial of a church burial is imposed on those under major excommunication, those who have died in a duel (or from wounds as a result) and suicides.

[178] ROC: Statute, X.35: 'If the members of the Diocesan Council violate the doctrinal, canonical or moral norms of the Orthodox Church and if they stand trial in the ecclesiastical court or are under investigation, they shall be dismissed from their office by the decision of the Diocesan Bishop.'

Church in America penalties that may be imposed by the court are as 'prescribed by the canons of the ecumenical and local councils and the holy fathers and their application is subject to approval by the bishop': the bishop may impose temporary suspension on a cleric and temporary excommunication on the laity prior to trial.[179] Moreover, in the case of deposition of clerics (for example), requests for forgiveness may also be entertained (as is the case in the Romanian Orthodox Church).[180]

According to *The Principles of Canon Law Common to the Churches of the Anglican Communion*, penalties or other forms of censure which may be imposed following proceedings in church courts or tribunals are to be clearly set out in the written law of a church; 'Customary censures include deposition, deprivation, suspension, inhibition, admonition and rebuke'.[181] The provincial laws of churches often define these sanctions: deposition from holy orders is the permanent taking away of the right to perform holy orders; deprivation, a permanent removal of the right to hold an office or appointment; suspension, a temporary taking away of the right to perform prescribed functions; inhibition, a prohibition against prescribed acts; admonition, a formal warning; and rebuke, a severe censure; excommunication may also be imposed in the case of both clergy and laity.[182]

By way of contrast, Protestant juridical instruments provide a wide range of disciplinary sanctions applicable to both congregations (corporately) and individual members of the faithful (both ministers and laity). Some Lutheran churches enable the bishop to impose a public censure and admonition upon a congregation, for example for wilful violation of the constitution and bylaws,[183] and most allow for termination of the corporate membership of a congregation in the church.[184] As to individual members generally, in the Lutheran Church in Australia, a complainant may issue a 'personal admonition' when alleging 'fault against a member', or (if this fails) the congregation may admonish that member; if the member remains impenitent, the pastor may pronounce excommunication; and if the errant member fails to submit to this, the congregation may declare such person to be no longer a member.[185] Similarly, in the Evangelical Lutheran Church in Southern Africa, if 'a brotherly consultation' with the minister fails, the church committee may require

---

[179] UOCIA: Statutes, Art. XII: deposition of clergy must be confirmed by Holy Synod, whose decision is final.

[180] ROMOC: Statutes, Art. 14: Holy Synod adjudicates on deposition of clergy and 'requests for forgiveness'.

[181] PCLCCAC, Principle 24.9, 11 and 15.

[182] E.g. New Zealand: Can. D.II.1: deposition; Nigeria: Can. XL(c): deprivation; TEC: Cans. IV.12: suspension; West Indies: Can. 25: inhibition; Southern Africa: Can. 40: admonition; Canada: Can. XVIII.15: rebuke.

[183] ELCA: Const., Ch. 20.18: 'The authority to administer private censure and admonition upon an individual or public censure and admonition upon a congregation is inherent in the office of bishop'; Ch. 20.21, 41: for the members of congregations, public censure and admonition by the bishop, and suspension from the church.

[184] LCA: Const., Art. IV.3; BL, IV.3 and BL, X.C10: process may also be made against a congregation for failure to uphold discipline resulting in censure by the district president or public censure before the District Synod; ELCIC: ABL, Pt. II.3–6: expulsion of a congregation; ELCSA: G., 89.2: termination by action of the congregation or by action of the church; ELCA: Const., Ch. 7 and Ch. 20.

[185] LCA: Const., Art. X.1: e.g. for departure from the confession and leading an ungodly life.

the person to render an account and if this is unsatisfactory the congregation may deny 'some or all church rights' (such as deprivation of admission to office, rights to vote or church burial, postponing the baptism of children and denial of the Lord's Supper).[186] With regard to pastors, in the Evangelical Lutheran Church in America, as well as suspension pending the outcome of a formal investigation or disciplinary hearing,[187] the bishop may impose private censure and admonition, suspension from office and ultimately removal from ordained ministry.[188]

Equivalent arrangements are found in Reformed and Presbyterian churches.[189] Once more, the medicinal quality of sanctions is prominent. For instance, in the United Free Church of Scotland: 'censures are not in the nature of penance or satisfaction ... [nor] punishments or the exercise of retributive justice' but are 'the means of grace used for the recovery of the erring from sin and peril, for the protection of Christ's people from occasions of stumbling, and for the edification of the Church' – and the church should seek to manifest 'a forgiving spirit in its own community'; moreover, sins or offences not publicly known may be addressed by private admonition, counsel and reproof, and the public censures are admonition, rebuke, suspension, deposition from office and excommunication.[190] In other Presbyterian churches, a congregation may be censured or dissolved, or its membership in the church terminated.[191] As to the individual members, one church asserts 'the right to require obedience to the laws of Christ', to impose 'spiritual penalties', to 'censure the delinquent' and to 'remove members for just cause'.[192] As well as removal of officers (such as trustees),[193] Presbyterian churches provide for the admonition, suspension, removal and deposition of pastors and other ministers.[194] The Presbyterian Church in America provides a list of censures with definitions of each: 'The censures, which may be inflicted by church courts, are admonition, suspension from the Sacraments, excommunication, suspension from office, and deposition from office.' Admonition is imposed on those who, on conviction, show repentance and make restitution as appropriate. Suspension or excommunication is imposed on persons who, on conviction, remain impenitent. Admonition is 'the formal reproof of an offender by a church court, warning him of his guilt and danger, and exhorting him to be more circumspect and watchful in the future'. Suspension from the sacraments is 'the temporary exclusion from those ordinances, and is

---

[186] ELCSA: G., 5; ELCA: Const., Ch. 20; ELCIC: Const., Art. 7: expulsion by a parish council.
[187] ELCA: Ch. 20: for e.g. 'ineffective conduct' a pastor may be dismissed by the congregation after consultation with the synodical bishop; or disciplinary action may ensue (interim suspension by the bishop).
[188] ELCA: Const., Ch. 20; ELCIC: ABL, Pt. III: suspension and expulsion of ordained ministers (and restoration on evidence of 'repentance and amendment of life'); LCMS: Const., Art. XIII; BL, 2: expulsion of a member from synod; ELCIRE: Const., Art. 7: expulsion of a member by a parish council.
[189] RCA: BCO, Ch. 2, Pt. I, Art. 1: admonition and rebuke, suspension from the privileges of membership, deposition from office, and excommunication; Ch. 1, Pt. II, Arts. 1–7: the classis suspends and deposes ministers; PCW: HOR, 2.5: censure may be imposed with 'meekness and love'.
[190] UFCS: MPP, V.II: censures generally; VI: private reproof etc.
[191] PCANZ: BO, 5.1: dissolution of a congregation; 5.10A: appeals against dissolution.
[192] PCA: BCO, 11–12.
[193] PCI: Code, pars. 45–46; 46–52: the Congregational Meeting may remove trustees.
[194] PCANZ: BO, 7.7–7.26: the Deacons' Court cannot depose ministers.

indefinite as to its duration', and suspension from office may be definite or indefinite (if the offender is impenitent). Excommunication is the excision of an offender from the communion of the church for 'gross crime or heresy'. Deposition is 'the degradation of an officer from his office' and may be accompanied with another censure. Provision also exists for the removal of censures.[195] Admonition, reproof, suspension, excommunication and removal from membership or office are also found in instruments of Congregational churches,[196] Methodist churches[197] and Baptist Unions and Conventions.[198]

From an examination of the legal instruments of the churches studied here, clear principles of Christian law emerge with regard to ecclesiastical offences and sanctions. A church may institute a system of ecclesiastical offences on the basis of its inherent right to impose spiritual censures, penalties and sanctions upon the faithful provided a breach of ecclesiastical discipline has been established objectively. Sanctions must be lawful and just and may include admonition, rebuke, suspension, excommunication and ultimately removal from office or membership. They are imposed for the remedial or medicinal purpose of the reform of the offender and the welfare of the church. These sanctions may be removed on the basis of forgiveness and the person restored to the full benefits of ecclesial association.

Conclusion

There is profound juridical unity between the Christian traditions studied here with regard to ecclesiastical discipline and the resolution of church conflict. The similarities outweigh the differences between the churches within these traditions, and from these similarities emerge common principles of Christian law on this subject.

---

[195] PCA: BCO, 30.1–5; 36: infliction of censures; 37: removal of censures. See also PCI: Code, par. 133: admonition, rebuke, suspension from rights and privileges of church membership, suspension from office and deposition from office; UFCS: MPP, V.II: restoration of persons under church censure.

[196] UCCSA: Procedure 15, Church Discipline: discipline is 'pastoral ... [and] remedial, not punitive'; suspension from participation in the Lord's Supper excludes a person from Christian fellowship and the means of grace; admonition exhorts repentance; rebuke is a 'solemn reproof' and is administered to a person guilty of 'a more serious offence'; suspension prevents a person from exercising 'the rights and privileges of membership or office' for a specified or indefinite period; deposition may be from office or membership; removal means dismissal from membership; Procedure 13.1: a minister convicted in a secular court for 'any grave criminal charge' may be suspended at the discretion of the Synod or Regional Council.

[197] MCI: RDG, 5.03–05: if a charge is sustained, the Meeting has power to admonish, rebuke, suspend or remove a person from office; suspension from office may be for a definite or indefinite period, or subject to any condition as to its duration or removal; 2.08: a member, whom the Church Council judges has persistently failed to fulfil the Obligations of Membership, despite being reminded of those obligations, shall be regarded as having withdrawn from membership and their name removed from the Membership Register; MCNZ: LAR, s. 2.29: suspension and expulsion of ministers; UMCNEAE: BOD, par. 361: interim suspension.

[198] NBCUSA: Const., Art. IV: removal from office or expulsion from the Convention; CNBC: BL 10–16: if a church ceases to co-operate with the Convention or becomes corrupt in doctrine or practice it is no longer in fellowship with the Convention; Riverside Baptist Church (Baltimore): BL Art. I: membership may be terminated by 80% vote 'but only after due notice and hearing, and after faithful efforts have been made to bring such member to repentance and amendment'.

All the traditions accept and justify theologically the need and the right to enforce discipline and to resolve conflicts amongst the faithful. Moreover, all the churches, but in varying degrees and ways, apply discipline to both ordained ministers and the lay faithful. Whilst justifications for ecclesiastical discipline in the juridical instruments of Protestant churches are more elaborate than those in the texts of Catholic, Orthodox and Anglican canon law, there is broad agreement that the right to discipline is based on divine or spiritual authority and that the purpose of discipline is to glorify God, to protect the integrity of the church, to safeguard the vulnerable from harm and to promote the spiritual benefit of its members through just structures. The juridical instruments of churches often provide for the settlement of disputes by means of administrative processes and the use of quasi-judicial powers. Hierarchical recourse and its equivalents enable a complainant to challenge decisions by means of appeal to a superior authority – either to an ecclesiastical person (such as the bishop in canonical systems) or to an ecclesiastical person and/or an assembly (in the case of most Protestant churches). This mechanism is usually available with complaints arising in the local church and a regional authority exercises a quasi-judicial function to settle the matter in a process short of formal judicial process. In this respect it is assumed by Christians that disputes may be settled by means of informal hierarchical recourse. Visitation is also used across traditions. Whereas hierarchical recourse involves complaints ascending the ecclesiastical hierarchy, visitation is a mechanism by which (typically) a regional institutional authority descends to the local church to monitor, affirm and improve the life and discipline of that church (i.e. a parish or congregation).

All the traditions have a hierarchical system of courts or tribunals to provide for the enforcement of discipline and the formal resolution of ecclesiastical disputes. Each church studied here has norms on the establishment, composition and jurisdiction of these judicial bodies. These bodies are established by the highest legislative authority in each church, manned by qualified personnel, and tiered in terms of original and appellate jurisdiction to exercise authority over ministers, or the laity or both. First instance jurisdiction in Episcopal churches is normally at the regional level (the diocese) with a right to appeal to a national (Anglicanism) or international (Catholicism and some Orthodox churches) authority, or in many Protestant traditions at the regional level or the congregational level with appeal to a regional body and/or national body (but not beyond). In all the church families, recourse to the courts and tribunals is a last resort. Judicial process is in the vast majority of the churches a threefold procedure, with movement from each stage to the next in the event of failure in the prior stage: informal resolution; formal investigation; a hearing (with appeal beyond). Disciplinary procedures at trial particularly seek to secure fair and due process on the basis of natural justice – with rights to notice, to be heard, to question evidence, to silence, to an unbiased hearing and to appeal being commonplace among the rights of the accused. A substantive law of ecclesiastical offences is employed in all the churches studied here, but generally offences are expressed with a high degree of generality – offences shared by all traditions include immoral conduct, teaching contrary to the doctrine of the church, and wilful neglect of duty. All the church families have disciplinary sanctions, censures or penalties which include withdrawal from spiritual privileges for the remedial or medicinal purpose of the reform of the offender and the welfare of the church. Typical are admonition, rebuke, suspension, excommunication and ultimately removal from office or membership.

6

Doctrine and worship

The proclamation of the faith and the worship of God are fundamental actions of the Christian church. They are also inseparable: doctrine shapes worship and *vice versa*. Needless to say, Christian faith and worship, their expression in teaching or doctrine and in forms of service, and the encounter of the faithful with these, represent a moment of great sensitivity not only for the individual at the personal level but also for the churches as communities in the public sphere of their corporate lives. However, the regulation of Christian belief and its doctrinal manifestation in public teaching and worship has posed particular problems in the history of the church. On the one hand, there is an assumption that rules should not intrude in belief and worship in so far as these are intimate to the relationship between the individual and God. On the other hand, there is the desire for order – for maintenance of fidelity to the historic Christian message and for decorum in the worship as a public event which goes to the heart of the corporate identity of Christians. Nevertheless, the juridical instruments of all the Christian traditions studied here deal with doctrine and worship. This chapter explores the extent to which the rules of the separated churches define legitimate belief, manage the development of teaching and doctrine, regulate the proclamation of the faith (in preaching, instruction, Sunday schools and other forms of Christian education) and maintain or enforce doctrinal standards through discipline. The chapter also examines how the churches regulate public worship – the nature and purpose of worship, the formulation of forms of service, the provision and administration of worship, the conduct of services, the celebration of Sunday, and oversight of worship discipline. It draws conclusions about the centrality of teaching and worship as a Christian action, delineates the key theological differences between churches on these subjects, and, from the similarities between their juridical instruments elucidates common principles of Christian law.

The sources, definition and development of doctrine

Doctrine is understood here to embrace not only the creeds shared by churches (the formal and historic statements of Christian belief) but a spectrum of entities which includes both faith and belief and the teaching of churches on morals and Christian practice – the body of faith or teaching that is received and believed by those comprising an ecclesial community. The juridical instruments of churches in all of the ecclesial families studied here deal with the location of doctrine (sources), its continuity from generation to generation, and those ecclesiastical authorities competent to define, interpret and declare it. In the Catholic Church the teaching function (*magisterium*) belongs to the ordained ministers: supreme teaching authority, exercising authentic *magisterium*, vests in the Pontiff and the College of Bishops; these may declare infallible doctrine, by which faith or morals on a matter of truth is solemnly defined, and they may proclaim truth, as contained in the written Word of God or in tradition, which is defined as existing in the deposit of faith entrusted to the church and proposed as divinely revealed.[1] Alternatively, the Pontiff or College of Bishops may proclaim doctrine on faith or morals non-definitively, as might the bishops (while not infallible in their teaching) individually or collectively in matters of faith.[2] Similar norms appear in the canons of the Oriental Catholic Churches.[3] The doctrines of the Catholic Church are found, for example, in the documents of the Second Vatican Council and the Catechism of the Catholic Church (issued by the apostolic constitution *Fidei Depositum*).[4]

There is no exact equivalent to the institutional Catholic *magisterium* for Orthodox Christians worldwide. First, doctrine is found in and inherited from the Apostolic Faith and its 'custodian' is the church.[5] 'Orthodoxy is the wholeness of the people of God sharing in the true Apostolic Faith, proclaiming the mighty works of God in history as fully revealed in the person ... of Jesus Christ and as confirmed by the ... activity of the Holy Spirit who calls us into unity in the one Body of Christ'; thus, 'unity in faith' and loyalty to 'the authentic Christian Tradition' are essential features of Orthodox teaching.[6] For example, the Greek Orthodox Archdiocese of America adheres to 'the Holy Scriptures, Sacred Tradition, the doctrines and canons of Ecumenical and Local Synods, the canons of the Holy Apostles and Fathers of the Church and of all other Synods recognized by the Orthodox Church, as interpreted by the Great Church of Christ in Constantinople';[7] similarly, the doctrines of the

---

[1] CIC, c. 749.1: 'the Supreme Pontiff is infallible in his teaching when, as chief Shepherd and teacher of all Christ's faithful, with the duty of strengthening his brethren in the faith, he proclaims by definitive act a doctrine to be held concerning faith or morals'; c. 749.2: College of Bishops; c. 749.3: 'No doctrine is understood to be infallibly defined unless this is manifestly demonstrated'; c. 750: 'Those things are to be believed by divine and catholic faith which are contained in the word of God as it has been written or handed down by tradition, that is, the single deposit of faith entrusted to the Church, and which are at the same time proposed as divinely revealed by the solemn ... or ordinary and universal *magisterium* ... which is manifested by the common adherence of Christ's faithful under the guidance of the sacred *magisterium*. All are therefore bound to shun any contrary doctrines'; c. 748: all are bound to seek the truth but none to embrace catholic faith against their conscience.

[2] CIC, cc. 752,753,386; the Sacred Congregation for the Doctrine of the Faith is also active in this field.

[3] CCEO, cc. 595–597.

[4] Apostolic Constitution *Fidei Depositum*, on the publication of the Catechism of the Catholic Church, prepared following the Second Vatican Council, Pope John Paul II (1994).

[5] SCOBA: Const., Preamble: the church is 'the inheritor and custodian of the glorious Paradosis of the Apostles, Fathers and the Ecumenical Councils'. The Ecumenical Councils include: Nicea 325: Nicene Creed and divinity of Christ; Constantinople 381: the definition of the Holy Spirit; Ephesus 431: Jesus as the incarnate word of God; Constantinople 553: the Trinity; Constantinople 680: the humanity of Jesus Christ; Penthekti (or Quinisext) 692; Nicea 878: icons. MOSC: this accepts only the first three Ecumenical Synods.

[6] SCOBA: GOCER, Pt. I, 6; 7: 'theology and worship do not express the thought and life of one particular denomination, but of the Church of Christ'; 11: 'The Confessional principle stresses that Christian unity is grounded and expressed in the unity of the Apostolic Tradition.'

[7] GOAA: Charter, Art. 2(b); Regs., Art. 2.1. See also ROC: Statute, General Provisions, 4: the church adheres to 'the Holy Scriptures and Holy Tradition'; ROMOC: Statutes, Art. 2: the church is in 'dogmatic ... unity with the universal Orthodox Church'.

Ukrainian Orthodox Church in America are 'those of the One, Holy, Catholic and Apostolic Church as taught by the Holy Scriptures, Holy Tradition, the Ecumenical and Provincial Sobors, and the Holy Fathers'.[8] Secondly, authority to define doctrine vests in a Holy Synod; for example, the Holy Synod of the Romanian Orthodox Church must maintain its 'dogmatic unity' and resolve any 'dogmatic issue ... according to the teaching of the Orthodox Church';[9] for the Malankara Orthodox Syrian Church: 'No-one shall have the right to alter the faith of the Church. But in case there may arise any dispute as to what is faith, the Episcopal Synod ... may decide the matter and the final decision about this shall vest in the Ecumenical Synod'.[10] Thirdly, therefore, doctrine is interpreted, declared and preserved, not created: for instance, in the Russian Orthodox Church, the Local Council is to 'interpret the teaching of the Orthodox Church on the basis of the Holy Scriptures and Holy Tradition, while maintaining doctrinal and canonical unity with the Local Orthodox Churches' and it is to approve decisions of the Bishops' Council as to 'doctrine and canonical order'; in turn, the Bishops' Council is responsible for: the 'preservation of the purity and steadfastness of the Orthodox doctrine and the norms of Christian morals'; the 'preservation of the dogmatic and canonical unity' of the church; and disciplining (as a court) 'dogmatic ... deviations in the activities' of the Patriarch and the bishops; similarly, the Holy Synod (the governing body between meetings of the Bishops' Council) has a duty to 'care for the sound preservation and interpretation of the Orthodox faith and the norms of Christian morals and piety'.[11]

For Anglicans, doctrine is the teaching of the church on any matter of faith which a church receives, believes and represents afresh from generation to generation by virtue of its belonging to the One, Holy, Catholic and Apostolic Church.[12] 'The faith of Our Lord Jesus Christ is taught in the Holy Scriptures, summed up in the Creeds, and affirmed by the ancient Fathers and undisputed General Councils'; the Holy Scriptures contain 'all things necessary to salvation and are the rule and ultimate standard of faith', the Apostles' Creed represents 'the Baptismal Symbol', and the Nicene Creed is recognised as 'the sufficient statement of the Christian faith'. Moreover, the Thirty-Nine Articles of Religion, the Book of Common Prayer

---

[8] UOCIA: Statutes, Preamble; see also Art. II.6(a): Holy Synod has authority in 'All matters involving doctrine [and] morals'; Art. VIII.3: the Diocesan Assembly 'approves measures to strengthen the Orthodox faith'.

[9] ROMOC: Statutes, Art. 14: it also 'initiates, authorises and supervises the translation, correction and distribution of the Holy Scriptures' and 'manuals of theology and religion'; Art. 111.2: the Metropolitan Synod must protect 'the Orthodox faith'; Art. 140: the Conference of Priests and Deacons is responsible for the 'defence of the teaching of faith and of Orthodox morals' and for improvement of 'theological knowledge'.

[10] MOSC: Const., Art. 108; see also Art. 128: the Parish Assembly and Diocesan Assembly 'shall have no authority to pass any resolution concerning faith'. See also SOCA: Const., Art. 19: the Patriarch has 'the sole right to publish our heritage especially in matters of faith, doctrine and rites'; GOAA: Charter, Arts. 10, 11, and 17: the Clergy–Laity Congress and Assemblies and Archdiocesan Council do not deal with dogmatic matters.

[11] ROC: Statute, II.5: Local Council; II.5, III.4 and 11: Bishops' Council; V.25: Holy Synod.

[12] PCLCCAC, Principle 48.1. See e.g. TEC: *Stanton (Bishop of Dallas) v Righter* (1996) Court for the Trial of a Bishop: 'doctrine involves more than creedal affirmations'; i.e. 'a spectrum which includes not only faith and belief, but morals and practice'; Southern Cone: Const., Art. 1: the church 'professes the historic faith'.

and the Ordinal 1662, all 'grounded in the Holy Scriptures, and in such teachings of the ancient Fathers and Councils of the Church as are agreeable to the Holy Scriptures', represent the historic sources of lawful doctrine for a church in the Anglican Communion.[13] Furthermore, each church must maintain 'the Faith, Doctrine, Sacraments and Discipline of the One, Holy, Catholic and Apostolic Church, and its own doctrinal formularies shall be compatible with the faith revealed in Holy Scripture, summed up in the Creeds, and received, practised and held by the church universal in the light of tradition and reason'. However, a church may draw up its own doctrinal formularies in terms suitable to the present day and needs of its people and circumstances so that the faith may be presented loyally and intelligibly from generation to generation.[14] Competence to develop, reformulate or alter doctrinal formulae vests only in the national, regional or provincial assemblies of a church subject to such substantive limitations and special procedural requirements as may be prescribed by the law of that church to ensure the protection of the faith of the church universal. No new doctrinal formulae may be approved by a central church assembly without the consent of the House of Bishops or equivalent body. A church may also have a doctrine commission or similar body to advise on and propose doctrinal development to the extent and in the manner prescribed by law.[15]

A similar approach is found in Lutheran laws, but with a wider range of historical texts. For Lutheran Churches, doctrine is contained in the Holy Scriptures,[16] and the historic Lutheran Confessions, Catechisms, Theses, Articles of Faith, and other teaching documents of a church.[17] In turn, the power to define doctrine is assigned to the central assemblies of the church.[18] By way of illustration,

---

[13] PCLCCAC, Principle 49.1. See also TACC, 1.1: each church affirms the catholic and apostolic faith revealed in scripture, and it affirms the historic formularies (Thirty-Nine Articles of Religion, Book of Common Prayer, and the Ordinal) and Creeds. See e.g. England: Can. A2-5.

[14] PCLCCAC, Principle 50.1-2. See also TACC 1.2.1. See e.g. West Indies: Declaration of Fundamental Principles (a)-(c): the church maintains 'the faith of Our Lord Jesus Christ as taught in the Holy Scriptures, held in the Primitive Church, summed up in the Creeds, and affirmed in the undisputed General Councils'.

[15] PCLCCAC, Principle 50.3-6. See e.g. Kenya: Const., Art. II: 'The Church ... a wholly ... self-governing part of the Body of Christ, affirms its right to draw up its own formularies of faith'; for procedures, see e.g. Wales: Const., II.27-32: the Governing Body; Melanesia: Cans. E.11: the Commission on Doctrine and Theology.

[16] LCGB: RAR, Statement of Faith, 2: Scripture, 'sole norm for the faith and the life of the Church', is 'the divinely inspired record of God's redemptive act in Christ' and 'God still speaks through' it; ELCA: Const., Ch. 2: 'the inspired Word of God and the authoritative source and norm of its proclamation, faith, and life'; ELCSA: G., 12.2-3: 'We do not understand the Bible as statutory, as a book of many separate laws and regulations'; LCMS: Const., Art. II.1: 'the written Word of God ... the only rule and norm of faith and of practice'.

[17] LCGB: RAR, Statement of Faith, 3-4: the Three Ecumenical Creeds and Lutheran Confessions (e.g. Unaltered Augsburg Confession, Luther's Small Catechism, 'pure expositions of the Word of God'), the symbolical books (e.g. Apology of the Augsburg Confession, Smalcald Articles, Luther's Large Catechism and Formula of Concord, 'further valid interpretations of the confession of this Church'); for similar lists see ELCA: Const., Ch. 2; ELCIRE: Const., Preamble, ELCIC: Const., Art. II; LCMS: Const., Art. II.2.

[18] LCMS: Const., Art. VIII.B: 'All matters of doctrine and of conscience shall be decided only by the Word of God'; BL 1.6.2: the Synod 'in seeking ... to settle doctrinal controversy ... shall have the right to adopt doctrinal resolutions and statements ... in harmony with Scripture and the

the Lutheran Church in Australia 'accepts without reservation the Holy Scriptures of the Old and New Testaments, as a whole and in all their parts, as the divinely inspired, written and inerrant Word of God, and as the only infallible source and norm for all matters of faith, doctrine, and life'.[19] Moreover: 'The Church acknowledges and accepts as true expositions of the Word of God and as its own confession all the Symbolic Books of the Evangelical Lutheran Church contained in the Book of Concord of 1580, namely, the three Ecumenical Creeds: the Apostles' Creed, the Nicene Creed and the Athanasian Creed; the Unaltered Augsburg Confession; the Apology of the Augsburg Confession; the Smalcald Articles; the Small Catechism of Luther; the Large Catechism of Luther; and the Formula of Concord'.[20] In turn, in proceedings of the General Synod, a 'decision on a matter of doctrine shall be deemed to be the official position of the Church only if at least two-thirds of the delegates ... have voted in favour'; however, the exercise of this doctrinal authority is 'governed by the will of Christ as revealed in Scripture' and some provisions on doctrine are unalterable; also: 'Matters of conscience and of doctrine shall have precedence over other questions.'[21] The General Pastors Conference advises General Synod and gives general guidance in matters of doctrine, confession and theology.[22]

Much the same approach is found in the Methodist tradition. Doctrine is contained in the Holy Scriptures,[23] 'the inheritance of the apostolic faith', 'the fundamental principles of the historic creeds and of the Protestant Reformation',[24] and in Articles of Religion, Confessions of Faith, Statements of Belief and the Sermons of Wesley.[25] For example, for the Methodist Church of Great Britain: 'The doctrines of the evangelical faith, which Methodism has held from the beginning, and still holds, are based upon the divine revelation recorded in the Holy Scriptures. The Methodist Church acknowledges this revelation as the supreme rule of faith and practice. These evangelical doctrines to which the preachers of the Methodist Church, ministerial and lay, are pledged are contained in Wesley's Notes on

---

Lutheran Confessions'; also: 'Doctrinal resolutions may be adopted for the information, counsel, and guidance of the membership' and 'shall ordinarily cite the pertinent passages of the Scriptures, the Lutheran Confessions, and any previously adopted official doctrinal statements and resolutions' of Synod; resolutions 'are to be ... upheld until ... the Synod amends or repeals them'; see also ELCIC: Const., Art. XX: Art. II on the Confession of Faith 'shall be unalterable'.

[19] LCA: Const., Art. II.1.   [20] LCA: Const., Art. II.2.
[21] LCA: Const., Arts. VI.1, VII.1, XII.1 and 2: the provisions of Art. II are unalterable; see also BL VII.C.28.
[22] LCA: BL, V.F.1-2; also BL, VIII.F: College of Presidents. See also LCGB: RAR, Terms of Reference of the Theological Committee, 1-3: it reports to Council and provides 'theological input'.
[23] UMCNEAE: AR, Art. IV: the Bible 'reveals the Word of God so far as it is necessary for our salvation' as 'the true rule and guide for faith and practice. Whatever is not revealed in or established by ... Scriptures is not ... an article of faith nor ... to be taught as essential to salvation'; BOD, par. 101: 'the apostolic witness ... is the source and measure of all valid Christian teaching'; the Creeds 'set boundaries for acceptable Christian doctrine, and proclaimed the basic elements of the enduring Christian message' as 'statements of faith'.
[24] MCGB: CPD, DU 4; MCNZ: LAR, Nature of New Zealand Methodism; MCI: Const., s. 2.
[25] MCGB: CPD, Bk. V, Historic Texts, e.g. Wesley's Rules of the Society (1743), Twelve Rules of a Helper (1753), and Liverpool Minutes (1820); UMCNEAE: BOD, par. 3: Articles of Religion and Confession of Faith.

the New Testament and the first four volumes of his sermons'.²⁶ The Conference is 'the final authority within the Church with regard to all questions concerning the interpretation of its doctrines'; it is assisted in this by boards, but it cannot alter the fundamental doctrines of the church.²⁷ Similarly, the General Conference of the United Methodist Church USA 'shall not revoke, alter, or change our Articles of Religion or establish any new standards or rules of doctrine contrary to our present existing and established standards of doctrine'.²⁸ However, the United Methodist Church of Northern Europe and Eurasia encourages 'theological exploration' to express 'the mysterious reality of God's presence ... in the world' and 'by interpreting the world's needs and challenges to the Church and by interpreting the gospel to the world'. The criteria used by the church to assess theological developments are Scripture (the primary source and criterion for doctrine), tradition (which provides a consensus of faith), reason and experience (which are to be interpreted in the light of scriptural norms).²⁹

Moving along the Protestant spectrum, the principal source of Presbyterian doctrine is 'the Word of God as set forth in the Scriptures of the Old and New Testaments', 'the only infallible rule of faith and practice, and the supreme standard of the Church'; doctrine is also located in the 'subordinate standards',³⁰ which 'expound' what is revealed in Scripture,³¹ or set out what a church understands 'the Word of God to teach on certain important points of doctrine and worship' – these include typically the Westminster Confession of Faith and Larger and Shorter Catechisms.³² For example,

---

[26] MCGB: CPD, DU, 4. See also MCNZ: LAR, Introductory Documents, IV, General Standards for the Guidance of Members: a Statement of Beliefs. FMCNA: BOD, 131: 'The doctrines of the [church] are based upon the Holy Scriptures'; scriptural references are given for each Article of Religion.

[27] MCGB: CPD, DU 5. See also MCI: Const., s. 2: Statement of Belief; RDG, 6.37 and 26.01: Conference's Committee on Faith and Order is 'to scrutinize and make recommendations regarding any doctrinal statements and documents ... issued in the name of the Church'; MCNZ: LAR, s. 7: Conference, 'under the judgment of God', has no power 'to revoke, alter or change any doctrines of the Church as contained in the Standard Sermons of John Wesley and his notes on the New Testament, nor to establish any new doctrine contrary thereto'; however (LAR, Nature of New Zealand Methodism) it is 'the final authority ... on all questions concerning the interpretation of its doctrines'; the Faith and Order Committee reports on 'doctrine and polity' to the Synods and Conference; COTN: Man., Pt. IV, Preamble: General Assembly is the supreme 'doctrine-formulating' body.

[28] UMCUSA: Const., Div. 2.2–2.3, Arts. I and II; see also UMCNEAE: BOD, pars. 17 and 18.

[29] UMCNEAE: BOD, par. 104.

[30] Church of Scotland Act 1921, Sch., Articles Declaratory: 'the Word of God ... in the Scriptures' (Art. I), 'as interpreted by the Church' (VIII), is the source of doctrine; the Westminster Confession is 'the principal subordinate standard' (II); PCA: BCO 11.2: 'the doctrines ... contained in the Scriptures'; 19.2: Confession of Faith; Larger and Shorter Catechisms; 4.7.1: 'Holy Scriptures are the only infallible rule of faith and practice'.

[31] PCW: HOR 2.1: 'The Gospel is the standard and inspiration of the life of the Christian'; 9.5: Short Confession; 9.6: Short Declaration of Faith and Practice. PCA: BCO 29.1. 'The Confession of Faith and the Larger and Shorter Catechisms are ... standard expositions of the teachings of Scripture in ... faith and practice.'

[32] PCI: Code, III.12; 10: 'The Word of God ... in the Scriptures ... is the only infallible rule of faith and practice, and the supreme standard of the Church'; 11: 'It is the privilege, right and duty of everyone to examine the Scriptures personally, and ... submit to their authority'; 13: the Confession of Faith (Church of Scotland, 1647) and Larger and Shorter Catechisms (of the Westminster Assembly of Divines) are 'the subordinate standards'.

the Presbyterian Church of Aotearoa New Zealand provides: 'The supreme rule of faith and life and the supreme standard of the church is the Word of God contained in the Scriptures of the Old and New Testaments' and its 'subordinate standards' include the Westminster Confession of Faith (as interpreted by the Declaratory Act 1892-3 of the General Assembly with regard to 'certain doctrine' required from those entering office), the Larger and Shorter Catechisms and, 'as authoritative statements of our Reformed heritage the Scots Confession, the Heidelberg Catechism and the Second Helvetic Confession'; it also accepts the Nicene and Apostles Creeds.[33] In turn, each church, through its General Assembly,[34] has the right to 'deliberate upon', 'superintend',[35] or 'state' the doctrine of the church,[36] and to alter doctrinal formulae, if 'agreeable to the Word of God',[37] and in accordance with the applicable procedures;[38] but nothing may be added to or subtracted from the doctrines of Christ.[39] Once again, for the Presbyterians of New Zealand: 'The Church itself has the right, in dependence on the promised guidance of the Holy Spirit, to formulate, interpret or modify its subordinate standards, always in agreement with its supreme standard and the fundamental doctrines of the Reformed Faith contained in its subordinate standards.' Moreover: 'The Church itself will be the sole judge whether this formulation, interpretation or modification is in agreement with its supreme standard.'[40]

Similar provisions are found in United, Reformed and Congregational churches: these, too, recognise that Holy Scripture is the supreme authority in matters of faith, and they have 'doctrinal standards' or 'statements' of faith.[41] They also assert their

---

[33] PCANZ: BO 1.1.
[34] CLCS: 26-28: e.g. Assembly no longer affirms Westminster Confession statements on the Pope: Act V, 1986.
[35] PCI: Code, 104: General Assembly may 'deliberate upon and superintend matters which concern the whole Church in its doctrine ... and declare the mind of the Church thereupon'.
[36] PCANZ: BO 14.7(3): General Assembly may issue 'statements of doctrine and faith for members'.
[37] PCA: BCO 11.2: the church courts have power as to 'the doctrines and precepts of Christ' and 'to make rules for government [etc] which must be agreeable to the doctrines relating thereto contained in the Scriptures'.
[38] PCA: BCO 26.2-3: e.g. the Westminster Confession may be altered on proposal by three-quarters of General Assembly, consent of three-quarters of Presbyteries and approval by a subsequent General Assembly by three-quarters majority vote.
[39] PCA: BCO, Preface I: 'Christ ... ordained ... a system of doctrine ... either expressly set down in Scripture, or [that] may be deduced therefrom ... to which ... He commands that nothing be added [or] taken away.'
[40] PCANZ: BO 1.1(6). See also PCI: Code, III.14: 'In the Church resides the right to interpret and explain her standards under the guidance of the Spirit of God'; PCW: HOR 3.4.4: General Assembly has a Doctrine and Worship Panel with 'expertise in worship and doctrinal matters' to 'give guidance on ... Doctrine and Worship'.
[41] URC: Man., A.12: Scripture is 'the supreme authority for the faith and conduct of all God's people'; A.17: a 'statement' of its faith; RCA: BCO, Preamble: 'the Doctrinal Standards' are e.g. the Belgic Confession of Faith, Heidelberg Catechism and Canons of the Synod of Dort; UCCP: Const., Art. II.4: its 'doctrines ... are based on the Word of God ... revealed in ... Holy Scriptures ... articulated in the historic ... creeds, expressed in the diverse heritage ... brought into the union by its uniting Churches, and embodied in its Statement of faith'; UCOC: Const, Preamble: Scriptures and 'ancient creeds'; UFCS: MPP, App. 2: 'supreme Standard [of] the Word of God contained in the Scriptures'; 'Subordinate Standard [of] the Westminster Confession of Faith';

own right to declare and interpret the teaching of the church.[42] Similarly, in the instruments of Baptist Conventions, Unions and Churches, the Bible is accepted as 'the divinely inspired Word of God' and 'the final written authority' in matters of doctrine.[43] However, they also have Declarations of Principle, Confessions of Faith and Statements of Belief.[44] The interpretation of these doctrinal instruments belongs to the local church, which has authority to determine its own 'confessional position' in accordance with whatever special procedures are required.[45]

The proclamation of the faith

The theological principle that the church exists to proclaim the Word of God as revealed in Christ finds juridical expression in a variety of forms. As we saw in Chapter 1, the proclamation of the faith is listed in juridical instruments across the Christian traditions as one of the fundamental objects of an institutional church. It is cast variously as a duty, a right or a privilege which resides in a church corporately and in its members individually, both ordained and lay. The function is also particularised in activities such as preaching, the instruction of candidates preparing for particular rites, the teaching of the young in Sunday schools and, within the wider community, in evangelism, mission and outreach. In some churches both ordained ministers and the laity may participate in these functions. All these matters, in each of the church families studied here, are regulated in considerable detail.

The duty to proclaim the Gospel

All of the churches examined in this study recognise that it is a function of the institutional church and each of its members to proclaim the Gospel of Christ. This is a principle of divine law and based on the Great Commission of Christ (Matthew

   UCC: Man., BU 2.0, 'Doctrine': Scripture is 'the primary source and ultimate standard'; the Articles [of Belief] follow.
[42] RCA: BCO, Preamble: 'The church shall declare what is the Word of God and act upon it, and may not properly go beyond this'; Ch. 1, Pt. IV, Art. 2: 'General Synod alone shall have original authority over all matters pertaining to doctrine'; UCOC: Const., Art. V.18: a local church may 'formulate its own ... confessions of faith'; UFCS: MPP, App. 2: the church may 'interpret, add to, modify or change the Subordinate Standards and Formulas, under the promised guidance of the Holy Spirit'; UCC: BL: 505(a): General Council.
[43] ABCUSA: BL, Prologue. See also BUSA: Const., 2: 'the supreme and final authority of Holy Scripture in all matters of faith and practice'; BUS: Const., III.1; JBU: Const., Art. III.1; Riverside Baptist Church (Baltimore): Const., Art. II: the church is 'to sustain the ordinances, doctrines, and ethics set forth in the New Testament'.
[44] BUGB: MTC 2003, 2.8: Declaration of Principle: Christ is 'sole and absolute authority in all matters [of] faith and practice, as revealed in the Holy Scriptures'; BUSA: Const., Arts. 2, 4: Declaration of Principle; CNBC: Const., Art. 3: Statement of Faith; JBU: Const., Art. III: Affirmation; NABC: Statement of Beliefs ('our common doctrinal understandings' and 'a doctrinal guide for new churches'); Riverside Baptist Church (Baltimore): Const., Art. III: 'The Baptist Faith and Message, a Statement Adopted by the Southern Baptist Convention, 1963'; Central Baptist Church (Pretoria): Const., Art. 5: Statement of Belief.
[45] ABCUSA: TCOR II.A.4: a congregation is free in 'determining its own confessional position'; ABCUSA: BL, Prologue: the Bible is 'to be interpreted responsibly under the guidance of the Holy Spirit within the community of faith'; BUSA: Model Const., Art. 4: the Statement of Baptist Principles may be changed only with approval of 90 per cent of members voting at a Special Church Meeting.

28.18–20). The Catholic Church presents this as both a right and a duty of the church corporately and the faithful individually. For the Roman Catholic Church: 'It is the obligation and inherent right of the Church, independent of any human authority, to preach the Gospel to all people, using for this purpose even its own means of social communication; for it is to the Church that Christ the Lord entrusted the deposit of faith, so that by the assistance of the Holy Spirit, it might conscientiously guard revealed truth, more intimately penetrate it, and faithfully proclaim and expound it.'[46] All must seek the truth in the matters which concern God and his Church and 'when they have found it, then by divine law they are bound, and they have the right, to embrace and keep it'; but: 'It is never lawful for anyone to force others to embrace the catholic faith against their conscience.'[47] All the faithful, lay and ordained, have a general duty to present the Christ-given 'deposit of faith' to the world: the church is 'missionary by its nature' and therefore evangelisation is 'a fundamental duty of the people of God' who are 'to work so that the divine message of salvation may increasingly reach the whole of humankind in every age and in every land'.[48] Moreover, the faithful have a duty and a right to acquire knowledge of Christian doctrine in order to live in accordance with it, to announce it, to defend it when necessary and to assume their apostolic role – indeed, parents have a special obligation to proclaim the gospel to their children 'according to the teaching handed down to them by the Church'.[49] Similar norms apply to the Oriental Churches.[50]

Orthodox and Anglican churches employ much the same approach: the proclamation of the faith, witness to it and mission are functions of the church corporately and its members individually, ordained (especially the bishops) and lay. Three examples may be offered from the Orthodox tradition. The Greek Orthodox Archdiocese of America provides: 'The mission of the Archdiocese is to proclaim the Gospel of Christ, to teach and spread the Orthodox Christian faith' and serve as 'a beacon, carrier and witness of the message of Christ to all persons who live in the United States of America, through Divine Worship, preaching, teaching and living the Orthodox Christian faith'; each parish is 'to keep, practice and proclaim the Orthodox Christian Faith pure and undefiled'; the parish priest is to 'proclaim the Gospel and impart knowledge of the doctrines, traditions, canons and disciplines of the Church'; and each parishioner is to be 'an effective witness and example of the Orthodox Faith and Traditions to all people'.[51] For the

---

[46] CIC, c. 747.1; also: 747 2: 'The Church has the right always and everywhere to proclaim moral principles, even in respect of the social order, and to make judgments about any human matter in so far as this is required by fundamental human rights or the salvation of souls'; see also LG 25; CCC, par. 848.

[47] CIC, c. 748; DH 2.

[48] CIC, cc. 211, 781; LG 33; c. 225: the faithful may work in associations to spread the divine message; c. 227: the faithful cannot pass off their own opinions as the teaching of Christ in questions open to various opinions.

[49] CIC, cc. 217, 229; c. 226: parents.

[50] CCEO, cc. 584–594; c. 584: 'Obeying the mandate of Christ to evangelise all people, and moved by the grace and charity of the Holy Spirit, the Church recognises herself to be totally missionary'; the gospel should be 'expressed in the culture of each individual people' (e.g. in catechesis, liturgical rites and sacred art).

[51] GOAA: Charter, Art. 2(a); Regs., Arts. 15.2, 17 and 18.1.

Romanian Orthodox Church, 'Orthodox Christians' must 'witness to God in the Holy Trinity, the Father, Son and Holy Spirit, based on the Holy Scripture', and have a right 'to sustain, strengthen and witness to the faith of the Orthodox Church [and] live according to the teaching of the Orthodox faith'.[52] Bishops have a special teaching function; for instance, in the Ukrainian Orthodox Church in America the Diocesan Bishop 'shall expound Orthodox faith and morals and guide his flock in accordance with the teachings of the Church'.[53] Similarly, the Anglican faithful have a responsibility to proclaim the Word of God revealed in Christ. Bishops have a special responsibility to teach the faith, to state publicly the doctrines of the church and to expound their application to the people and issues of the age; priests and deacons share with the bishop in this function.[54]

There is very little to distinguish between these arrangements and those which appear in Protestant laws. Lutheranism advocates proclamation of the Gospel as a fundamental task of the church,[55] its institutions,[56] its congregations,[57] its members individually[58] and its ordained ministers (including bishops) in particular.[59] Typically, a Lutheran Church is 'called and sent to bear witness to God's creative, redeeming, and sanctifying activity in the world' – it is to proclaim 'God's saving Gospel of justification by grace for Christ's sake through faith alone, according to the apostolic witness in the Holy Scripture, preserving and transmitting the Gospel faithfully to future generations';[60] the bishop and clergy have a special responsibility for proclamation of the faith,[61] and each congregation must 'regularly and faithfully

---

[52] ROMOC: Statutes, Arts. 1 and 45:
[53] UOCIA: Statutes, Art. VII. 4(a). See also ROMOC: Statutes, Art. 88(a).
[54] PCLCCAC, Principle 48.1–4. See also TACC, 1.2: each church is e.g. 'to teach and act in continuity and consonance with Scripture and the catholic and apostolic faith, order and tradition, as received by the Churches' of the Communion; see e.g. England: Can. C18.1: bishops must 'uphold sound and wholesome doctrine'.
[55] LCGB: RAR, Statement of Faith, 7–8: 'This Church affirms the special ministry of proclamation of the Gospel' through which it 'fulfils its divine mission and purpose'; ELCSA: G., 10.10: the church is 'to serve the Gospel of Jesus Christ by Word and Sacrament'; G., 1.1: the church has a divine commission to 'make disciples of all nations' (Matt. 28, 18–20); ELCA: Const., Introduction (4 Sept. 2009).
[56] ELCSA: G., 10.9: the central assembly is responsible for proclamation of the Gospel according to Scripture and the Confessional Books; LCA: Const., Art. III; BL, VIII.D.1 and 2: the General Church Council must ensure 'the mission of the church, the proclamation of the gospel remains central to the work of the church'.
[57] LCGB: RAR, Definition of a Congregation, 2: it 'will participate in the universal mission of God'; ELCSA: G., 10.1: it is 'responsible for the proper proclamation of the Word of God'; ELCA: Const., Ch. 9.10–11.
[58] ELCSA: G., 5.1: 'Every Christian should bear witness ... through ... his life'; ELCIC: Const., Art. IV.2.
[59] ELCIC: Const., Art. XIII.5; ABL, Pt. X: the bishop shall '[s]peak publicly and witness for the gospel on behalf of this church'; LCGB: RAR, Role of the Bishop, 1: ministry of Word; Pastors, 1–24.
[60] ELCA: Const., Ch. 4.01–03.
[61] ELCA: Const., Ch. 10.31; see also Ch. 15.31.A07: the Bishops' Conference supports 'bishops in their role as teachers by being a forum for serious reflections on the theological and ethical implications of issues that affect the life of this church'; for much the same formula, see ELCIC: ABL, Pt. XII; LCA: Const., Art. III; ELCSA: G., 10.2: 'The pastor ... has the duty to properly proclaim the Gospel of Jesus Christ.'

proclaim the Word', cultivate in its members a life of prayer and an awareness of the presence of God, '[e]ducate persons of all ages in the faith ... and in its implications for daily living' and 'encourage and stimulate its members in their witness to Christ'.[62] Methodist laws mirror these principles: a fundamental task of the church is to preach the Word of God (and to administer the sacraments).[63] Typically: 'The mission of the Church is to make disciples of Jesus Christ for the transformation of the world by proclaiming the good news of God's grace'.[64] Ordained ministers have a special responsibility to teach the faith.[65]

In the Presbyterian tradition, juridical instruments identify proclamation of the faith as a fundamental task of the church corporately: this is the Great Commission.[66] For the Presbyterian Church of Wales, for instance: 'Our purpose is to ... spread the Gospel of the Lord Jesus Christ as it is revealed in the Holy Scriptures and expounded in our doctrinal standards' by *inter alia*: 'Preaching the Gospel', 'Religious Biblical education and training in the Faith', 'Missionary work and evangelising at home and abroad' and 'Providing and publishing literature'.[67] Moreover, proclamation of the Word of God is a task assigned to the members of the church individually, its congregations and its officers (ministers and elders).[68] Similar provisions are found in United, Reformed and Congregational churches,[69] as well as in the regulatory instruments of Baptist Unions and Churches: proclamation of the faith is a

---

[62] ELCIC: ABL, Pt. II.2.

[63] MCGB: CPD, DU 4: 'Methodism was raised up to spread scriptural holiness ... by the proclamation of the evangelical faith' and resolves 'to be true to its divinely appointed mission'; MCI: Const., s. 2: Statement of Belief and RDG, 1.01; FMCNA: PACLM, I.1: Matt. 28.19: 'Go therefore and make disciples of all nations'; I.2: the church is 'to make known to all people everywhere God's call'; COTN: Man., Foreword: Matt. 28.19.

[64] UMCUSA: Const., Preamble; see also UMCNEAE: BOD, par. 120–121; see also Preamble.

[65] MCNZ: LAR, s. 2.29: each minister is 'to proclaim the Gospel' and (4A.02) 'feed and guide the congregation by regular and faithful preaching [and] teaching'; UMCNEAE: BOD, par. 329: the 'deacon is to teach and to form disciples'; 414: the bishop; FCMNA: PACLM, II: pastors engage in 'preaching and teaching the Word of God'; the elder is 'to teach the apostolic gospel and to protect the church from error', make 'official statements to the church and the public at large'; and 'must be theologically orthodox and an able preacher of the gospel'.

[66] PCA: BCO 14.1: 'The Church is responsible for carrying out the Great Commission. The initiative for [this] belongs ... at every court level' and the Assembly must 'encourage this'; PCANZ: BO 1.3: the church is 'committed to sharing in God's mission to the world, and seeking to announce, with the promised guidance and power of the Holy Spirit, the good news of God's transforming life in Jesus Christ'; 1.4(2): 'the potential for study, teaching and proclamation of the Word of God to change lives and transform society'.

[67] PCW: HOR, 1.1. See also PCI: Code, II.9: 'The whole Church, in its ministry and membership, is called to proclaim to all people by word and deed the Christian Gospel of salvation.'

[68] PCA: BCO, Preface II.3: 'Our blessed Saviour ... has appointed officers ... to preach the Gospel'; 4.1: the particular church consists of 'professing Christians' and (5.8) must preach the Word; PCW: HOR, 2.1: 'The new member makes a profession of his/her faith in God and belief in Christ, and vows to be loyal to them.'

[69] RCA: BCO, Preamble: 'The Purpose of [RCA] is to minister to the total life of all people by preaching, teaching, and proclamation of the gospel of Jesus Christ'; hearing the Word of God is a 'means of grace'; URC: Man., A.13: 'through preaching and the study of the Scriptures, God makes known in each age his saving love, his will for his people'; UCOC: Const., Preamble: the 'responsibility of the Church in each generation to make the faith its own'; UCA: Const., 4: the church is 'to proclaim the Gospel of the Lord Jesus Christ'.

fundamental task of a church, and 'the duty of every disciple to bear personal witness to the Gospel of Jesus Christ and to take part in the evangelisation of the world'.[70] The juridical instruments of all the traditions, then, require proclamation of the Gospel by the faithful.

Preaching and the delivery of sermons

Christian churches regulate in some detail the teaching functions of ordained ministers, particularly preaching and the delivery of sermons. For the Latin Church, the office of preaching the gospel to the whole church has been committed principally to the Roman Pontiff and to the College of Bishops; for the particular church, this office is exercised by the individual bishops 'who are the moderators of the entire ministry of the word in their churches'.[71] In addition, it belongs to priests, as co-operators with the bishops, 'to proclaim the Gospel of God', especially parish priests, though deacons may also serve in the ministry of the word, as might members of institutes of consecrated life and the lay faithful.[72] The mystery of Christ is 'to be faithfully and fully presented in the ministry of the word, which must be founded upon sacred Scripture, Tradition, liturgy and the *magisterium* of the church'.[73] The faithful are entitled to seek the word of God from their priests: 'For this reason, sacred ministers are to consider the office of preaching as of great importance'; the laity may also be allowed to preach if it is necessary or advantageous according to provisions of the Episcopal Conference.[74] The most important form of preaching is the homily which is part of the liturgy, reserved to a priest or deacon, and delivered on prescribed occasions; a homily must set out 'those things which it is necessary to believe and to practise for the glory of God and the salvation of all'; it must also explain the teaching of the *magisterium* of the church concerning the dignity and freedom of the human person, the unity, stability and duties of the family, the social obligations of people and the ordering of temporal affairs according to the plan of God – and 'Christian teaching is to be explained in a manner that is suited to the condition of the hearers and adapted to the circumstances of the times'.[75]

---

[70] BUGB: Const., 4: the Union is 'to spread the Gospel of Christ by ministers and evangelists, by establishing Churches, forming Sunday schools, distributing the Scriptures' and such other means as the Council determines; MTC 2003, 2.8.3 and JBU: Const., Art. III: 'It is the duty of every Disciple to bear personal witness to the Gospel'; NBC: Const., Art. III: Great Commission; ABCUSA: BL Prologue: the ABCUSA is 'to bear witness to the Gospel ... and to lead persons to Christ'; TCOR, II.A.8: a congregation is 'an agent for proclaiming the gospel'.

[71] CIC, c. 773f; c. 756; CCC, pars. 2033, 2092. See also CCEO, cc.607–616: preaching.

[72] CIC, c. 757; c. 758: members of institutes of consecrated life bear 'a particular witness to the Gospel'; c. 759: 'lay members ... by ... baptism and confirmation, are witnesses to ... the gospel, by their words and ... Christian life. They can also be called upon to cooperate with bishops and priests in ... the ministry of the word'.

[73] CIC, c. 760; CD 14.

[74] CIC, c. 762; c. 763: bishops may preach everywhere unless the local bishop forbids it expressly; the same applies (with the consent of the rector) to priests and deacons: c. 764; c. 765: to preach to religious in their churches or oratories, the permission of the superior is required; c. 766: laity (and c. 767.1).

[75] CIC, cc. 767–770; c. 771: pastors must ensure the Word reaches those without pastoral care and non-believers; c. 772: preachers must observe the norms issued by the bishop, and for radio and TV, Episcopal Conference.

The juridical instruments of Orthodox and Anglican churches also deal in some detail with preaching. In Orthodoxy, typically: 'The sermon or homily [at the Divine Liturgy] is directed to the up-building of the congregation, and is intended to be a clear exposition of the Orthodox teaching'; indeed: 'The preacher is entrusted to proclaim the Apostolic Faith in the name and under the authority of the Bishop.'[76] Thus, as in the Orthodox Church in America: 'The priest must be diligent in preparing homilies for his flock, giving this priority over administrative duties. The homily at the Divine Liturgy should take place immediately after the reading of the Holy Gospel.'[77] Supervision of parish preaching may also be exercised by senior clergy beneath the rank of bishop.[78] In Anglicanism, too, priests and deacons have a responsibility to preach sermons and the laity may be authorised to do so.[79] In sermons or other forms of teaching a minister must 'endeavour with care and sincerity to expound the word of truth according to Holy Scripture, to the glory of God and to the edification of the people'. A sermon should be preached on Sundays and on the major festivals.[80] Preaching should lead people to greater exploration and understanding of the gospel and its challenge to contemporary life within the tradition of faith; and ministers should ensure that biblical texts are treated respectfully and coherently, building on tradition and scholarship, and bring new insights and knowledge to the interpretation and application of scripture, so that the gospel can be proclaimed to this age as the good news that it has been to ages past.[81]

Protestant laws give an equally prominent place to preaching. In Lutheranism, the preaching of the Word is 'a means of grace' (along with administration of the sacraments).[82] Preaching is assigned primarily to ordained ministers.[83] For example, in the Evangelical Lutheran Church in America, an ordained minister is to 'preach the Word', and in so doing ensure that preaching conforms to the Confession of the church.[84] Likewise for Methodism, the congregation is the principal location for

---

[76] SCOBA: GOCER, Pt. I, Preaching on Ecumenical Occasions, 1.

[77] OCIA: GC, Some Considerations on Authority, Responsibility and Accountability in the Church, Priests and Deacons, 3. See also ROMOC: Statutes, Art. 50; SOCA: Const., Art. 108; SCOBA: GOCER, Pt I., Preaching on Ecumenical Occasions, 1: only a duly authorised Orthodox cleric should preach at the Divine Liturgy.

[78] ROC: Statute, X.52(b): the Dean supervises 'the state of church sermons'; ROMOC: Statutes, Art. 71(d).

[79] PCLCCAC, Principle 48.2–5.

[80] PCLCCAC, Principle 48.6–7. See e.g. Australia: Can. P6 1992, 5: '[a] sermon must be preached at least once each Sunday in every cathedral and church ... except for some reasonable cause approved by the bishop'.

[81] PCLCCAC, Principle 51. See also TACC 1.2.3: each church is 'to ensure that biblical texts are received, read and interpreted faithfully, respectfully, comprehensively and coherently'.

[82] LCA: BL, Sect. V.D., Preamble: through these 'the Holy Spirit works saving faith in the ... people' (AC V).

[83] NALC: SFPM (2011), p.1: 'to obtain the faith that justifies by God's grace, God has instituted ... the office of Word and Sacrament'; AC XIV: 'nobody should publicly teach or preach or administer the sacraments in the church without a regular call'; LCGB: RAR, App. A: lay persons may do so if no ordained minister is available.

[84] ELCA: Const., Ch. 7.31.12; ELCIC: Const., Art. VII.4–5: 'Each ordained minister shall conform in preaching ... to the Confession of Faith'; for their 'acceptance' of this, see ABL, Pt. III.2; LCA: Const., Art. III.

preaching by ordained ministers: 'the Word of God is preached by persons divinely called and the sacraments are duly administered according to Christ's own appointment'.[85] Methodist 'standards of preaching' include loyalty to the gospel of redemption and fidelity to the Christian experience of salvation.[86] For instance, in the Methodist Church of Great Britain, the circuit superintendent in consultation with colleagues is responsible to make the circuit plan for preaching responsibilities;[87] the church recognises that: 'There is urgent need that the main doctrines of the Christian faith should be more plainly and systematically set forth in public preaching, so that the Methodist people may be established in the faith and better defended against error and uncertainty. Ministers, deacons and probationers are directed to consider together how this may be arranged.'[88]

The preaching of the Word is also central in the Presbyterian tradition and it is understood as an ordinance of God.[89] There is a particularly full treatment in the Book of Church Order of the Presbyterian Church in America about 'expounding and preaching the Word of God';[90] the Session is to ensure the preaching of the Word by ministers and elders;[91] moreover: 'The preaching of the Word is an ordinance of God for the salvation of men. Serious attention should be paid to the manner in which it is done. The minister should apply himself to it with diligence and prove himself a "worker who does not need to be ashamed, rightly dividing the word of truth" (2 Timothy 2.15)'. Furthermore: 'The subject of a sermon should be some verse or verses of Scripture, and its object, to explain, defend and apply some part of the system of divine truth; or to point out the nature, and state the bounds and obligation, of some duty. A text should not be merely a

---

[85] UMCNEAE: BOD, par. 201; par. 332: elders; MCGB: CPD, DU 1(xvi): a local preacher is 'recommended by the Local Preachers' meeting, approved by the Circuit Meeting and admitted in an act of public worship'; SO 424: a district chair is 'to lead all the people of the District in ... preaching ... evangelism [and] teaching'.

[86] MCGB: CPD, DU 4: 'The Notes on the New Testament and the 44 Sermons are not intended to impose a system of formal or speculative theology on Methodist preachers, but to set up standards of preaching and belief which should secure loyalty to the fundamental truths of the gospel of redemption and ensure the continued witness of the Church to the realities of the Christian experience of salvation.' For an almost identical provision, see MCI: Const., s. 2; RDG, 4A.04: District superintendents must ensure 'only persons duly accredited ... preach in any place of worship under her/his care'; MCNZ: LAR, Introductory Documents, II Pastoral Resolutions: 'in all our preaching, teaching and administering of the Sacraments [we are] at the disposal of the Holy Spirit so that our words and actions may confront men and women with the Risen Christ'; s. 1.10.1–10: lay preachers.

[87] MCGB: CPD, SO 521.   [88] MCGB: CPD, SO 524.

[89] PCW: HOR, 9: Declarations: Preaching the Gospel is an ordinance of the church which 'derives from' Christ during his earthly ministry; 4.14: Preaching Areas; 4.19: Lay Preachers: 'It is the privilege and responsibility of the Church to seek to recognise and guide those who offer themselves to preach the Gospel, and to do all it can to train and equip them for effective performance of their work'; PCANZ: BO, 6.3(1): the minister 'preaches the Word, ensures that the Scriptures are read'; PCI: Code, 81.4: 'No one shall occupy the pulpit ... without the permission of the minister, except by direction of the Presbytery or a superior court.'

[90] PCA: BCO, 4.4; 8.1: the elder is a teacher who 'expounds the Word'.

[91] PCA: BCO, 12.5: the Session is 'to exercise, in accordance with the Directory for Worship, authority over the time and place of the preaching of the Word' by such as are sufficiently qualified (BCO, 4.4; 1 Tim. 2.11–12).

motto, but should fairly contain the doctrine to be handled'; thus, preaching constitutes 'instruction of the people in the meaning and use of the sacred Scriptures'.[92] The Presbyterian Church of Aotearoa New Zealand has analogous rules: 'The preached Word or sermon is to be based upon the written Word'; in it 'through the Holy Spirit Jesus Christ is present to the gathered people, offering grace and calling for obedience'; preaching requires 'diligence and discernment in the study of Scripture, the discipline of daily prayer, cultivated sensitivity to events and issues affecting the lives of the people, and a consistent and personal obedience to Jesus Christ'. A sermon should present the gospel with simplicity and clarity, in language which can be understood by the people.[93] Parallel rules are found in the United, Reformed, Congregational and Baptist traditions: in these, too, ministers must preach the Word of God and sermons must accord with Holy Scripture.[94]

Catechesis and instruction

The laws of churches both facilitate and order the provision of catechesis or instruction in the faith. In the Latin Church, catechesis, the ministry of the word directed to those who have responded to the faith, is the process by which 'through doctrinal formation ... the faith of the people may be living, manifest and active'. The diocesan bishop, Conference of Bishops and pastors have special responsibilities to provide catechetical formation; the diocesan bishop must issue norms on the subject and foster and co-ordinate catechetical initiatives; parish priests must ensure that: adequate catechesis is given for the celebration of the sacraments; children are properly prepared for confession and first holy communion; and, as far as conditions allow, formation is given to the mentally and physically disabled.[95] Orthodox parish priests also have a general duty to instruct the faithful, particularly the young, by way of catechesis and Sunday School: 'The duty of the priest is to instruct the faithful in the way of godliness'; indeed: 'It is the primary responsibility of the parish priest to continue ongoing education of the faithful in matters of dogma, tradition, precepts, and sacred rites of the Church'; also: the priest 'supervises the Church School, gives direction to its instructors, and decides on

---

[92] PCA: BCO, 53.1: diligence; 53.2: subject; 53.3: preaching requires much study, meditation and prayer and ministers should prepare their sermons with care; 53.4: they should not be long; 53.6: 'No person should be invited to preach in any of the churches under our care without the consent of the Session.'

[93] PCANZ: DOW, 2.2.7: for 'reasons of order' preaching is entrusted to a minister of Word and Sacrament but: 'It is appropriate ... for ministers to involve others ... A minister of the Word and Sacrament, lay preacher, or other person may be invited to preach by the minister who out of courtesy advises the Session/Parish Council.'

[94] RCA: BCO, Ch. 1, Pt. I, Art. 1.4: 'The minister preaches and teaches the Word of God'; 1.8: elders ensure 'what is preached and taught by the minister is in accord with ... Holy Scripture'; 2.11: 'points of doctrine in the Heidelberg Catechism shall be explained by the minister at regular services'; UCOC: Const., Art. V.23; UCA: BL 2.4.2; BMPP 216: SCBC, Type A, Art. VI.1: the pastor 'shall preach the gospel'; VI.8: the Board of Deacons co-operates with the pastor 'in providing pulpit supply ... in his absence'; Riverside Baptist Church (Baltimore): Const., Art. II: the church is 'to preach the gospel of the Revelation of God through Jesus Christ'.

[95] CIC, c. 773: duty to catechise; c. 774: care for catechesis extends to all (especially parents); c. 775: diocesan bishop and Episcopal Conference; c. 776: parish priest; c. 777: recipients. See also CCEO, cc. 617–626.

appropriate resources and texts in conformity to diocesan directives'.[96] Parish committees may also assist clergy in 'the spreading and reading of the Holy Scripture and spiritual books on the recommendation of the parish priest' and in 'the organisation of missionary activity, in order to have better knowledge, preservation and consolidation of the Orthodox faith'; this may include the distribution of literature and the establishment of educational programmes.[97] In Anglicanism, too, priests and deacons must provide instruction in the faith for those entrusted to their charge,[98] especially children and young persons, who are to be instructed in the doctrine, sacraments and discipline of Christ, as the Lord has commanded and as found in Holy Scripture, and in the teaching and catechism of a church.[99]

The instruction of the faithful is likewise a key function in Protestant laws. Within a Lutheran congregation, an ordained minister has 'a special duty to instruct the faithful',[100] 'supervise all schools and organizations of the congregation' and 'impart knowledge of this church and its wider ministry through distribution of its periodicals and other publications'.[101] Moreover, the congregation itself must provide for the instruction in the faith of children and young people.[102] The work of the Sunday school is particularly important here. Typically: 'The congregation is responsible before God for the Christian upbringing and education of its children' and parents 'should teach their children to pray and help them lead a Christian life in faith'. Moreover: 'The Christian upbringing at home is supported by Sunday School. The children should be encouraged to attend Sunday school from an early age. There they hear the good news of Jesus Christ and experience the fellowship of Christians.'[103] Churches might also disseminate the faith in wider society through schools and theological institutes.[104]

---

[96] OCIA: GC, A Selection of Clergy Disciplines, 4; Some Considerations on Authority etc, Priests and Deacons, 6; ROMOC: Statutes, Art. 50: a parish priest must catechise children, young people and adults; Art. 98(f), (g): the Eparchial Council must support this; it also supervises theological institutes and confessional schools; ROC: Statute, 20: the Rector organises the 'catechetical . . . and educational activities of the parish'; SOCA: Const., Art. 108: priests must 'visit . . . homes teaching Christian principles'; MOSC: Const., Art. 22: Sunday Schools; UOCIA: Statutes, XI.4: the rector has 'final authority over the church school'.

[97] ROMOC: Statutes, Art. 67: it also 'encourages the community to read Orthodox literature and listen to Orthodox radio and TV programmes, [and] engage in educational activity to promote the Orthodox faith'.

[98] PCLCCAC, Principle 48.2–4.

[99] PCLCCAC, Principle 48.8. See e.g. Ireland: Const., IX.27.   [100] ELCSA: G., 10.2.

[101] ELCA: Const., Ch. 7.31.12; ELCIC: Const., Art. VII.4 and 5.

[102] LCGB: RAR, Congregations, 2: it must 'as far as its resources and abilities make it possible', 'teach both adults and children through Bible studies, Confirmation and Baptism classes and other appropriate media'; ELCA: Const., Ch. 4.03: the church nurtures its members 'in the Word of God so as to grow in faith and hope and love, [and] see daily life as the primary setting for the exercise of their Christian calling'; Ch. 9.41: the congregation shall 'challenge, equip, and support all members in carrying out their calling in their daily life and in their congregation . . . Teach the Word of God . . . Witness to the reconciling Word of God in Christ'.

[103] ELCSA: G., 6.1–6.2; G., 2.7: 'In Sunday School the Gospel is explained to the children according to their age'; 6.4: catechism; ELCF: the Catechism (2000) states in 'a concise and clear format what the Christian faith is . . . to lead us to live . . . in faith to God and in love to one another'; it has e.g. the Ten Commandments, Apostles' Creed and Lord's Prayer; 'the spiritual manual for every home', it conveys the 'essential message of the Bible'.

[104] LCA: Const., Art. III; LCMS: Const., Art. III: the Synod aids congregations to establish schools and must support synodical colleges, universities and seminaries; see also ELCIC: ABL, Pt.

This juridical pattern is shared by Methodists who should engage in their own private and collective reading of the Bible.[105] Typically: 'Within the Societies of the Methodist Church provision shall be made for the Christian nurture of children and young people. The aim shall be to develop faith and commitment to Christ, as they share in worship and learning based on Holy Scripture.'[106] Thus: 'It shall be the duty of the congregation, led by the pastor, to instruct [the young] in the meaning of baptism [and] the meaning of the Christian faith.'[107] Parents, too, have a duty to instruct their children in the faith.[108] There is extensive provision for ministerial training.[109] Rules about Sunday schools are particularly well developed: the local church should set up a Sunday school to build 'knowledge of the Bible [and] the Christian faith'.[110] For example, in the Methodist Church in Ireland, the main object of Methodist Sunday Schools is 'to instruct and train the scholars in the doctrines, privileges, and duties of the Christian religion. The Holy Scriptures and, as far as possible, the Methodist Catechisms shall be used as the means of instruction and training. All the scholars shall be trained in the duty of regular attendance at public worship on the Lord's Day'. Every Sunday school is under the management of a Committee which consists of the minister (who presides) and the officers of the school – a superintendent appointed by the Circuit Executive, a secretary, and if necessary a treasurer, librarian and a missionary secretary. The teachers must be of good moral character, and in sympathy with the doctrines and discipline of Methodism. No person may continue as an officer or teacher who shall at any time be declared by the Committee, or by Church Council or Circuit Executive, to be unfit as to general character or 'religious opinions' to take part in the religious education of the young. The Committee determines the programme of instruction in the school, arranges for examinations, inquires concerning absent scholars and deals with all matters affecting the welfare of the school.[111] A Methodist church may also have wider educational functions.[112]

XIV; ELCA: Const., Ch. 7.31.13 and 51.03–04: theological seminaries; Ch. 8.31–32: 'This church shall sponsor, support, and provide for oversight of seminaries' to prepare persons for ministry and (Ch. 11.20–21) 'oversee and establish policy' for them; for training pastors, see e.g. NALC: SFPM (2011), p.2 and LCGB: RAR, Church Session, 1 and 2.

[105] MCI: RDG, 3.01: 'The means of grace ... include ... Bible study [and] individual Bible study and prayer.'
[106] MCGB: CPD, DU 7; see also SO 050(2).
[107] UMCNEAE: BOD, par. 216. See also MCI: RDG, 11.02: the functions of class leaders.
[108] UMCNEAE: BOD, par. 225: pastors should exhort parents to do so especially in preparation for baptism.
[109] MCI: RDG, 4B.22–29; MCNZ: LAR, s. 2.4: for ministry students (e.g. biblical studies, systematic theology, and homiletics); FMCNA: BOD 5230: Ministerial Education and Guidance Board (of the annual conference).
[110] UMCNEAE: BOD, par. 256: in each local church 'there shall be a church school for the purpose of accomplishing the church's educational ministry'; par. 255: the charge conference may elect 'a superintendent of the church school or Sunday school' to 'supervise the total program for nurturing faith, building Christian community, and equipping people of all ages for ministry in daily life through small groups in the church'.
[111] MCI: RDG, 10.71–74. See also COTN: Man., 33.6: 'Nazarene ... Sunday Schools, schools ... child care centres, adult care centres, colleges and seminaries, are expected to teach children, youth and adults biblical principles and ethical standards' so that 'our doctrines may be known'; 145–146: Sunday Schools.
[112] UMCNEAE: BOD, par. 1109: the General Board of Discipleship oversees 'the educational interests of the Church' as directed by General Conference; MCNZ: LAR, s. 4.3: a Synod

Likewise, Presbyterian ministers are under a duty to instruct children, young people and adults in the elements of Christian doctrine, and some churches impose this duty on parents and offer a right of church members to such instruction or catechism.[113] There are also provisions about the establishment of a Sunday school in the local church. This is the case, for example, in the Presbyterian Church in Ireland, in which the Kirk Session is to 'control the Sunday Schools of the congregation, and approve the teachers employed, the books used, and the regulations of the schools'; above the local church, the Presbytery shall 'foster Sunday School work within its bounds, requiring as far as possible that at least one school be maintained in connection with each congregation, having a programme which embraces study of Scripture, the Shorter Catechism, and the Missions and Agencies of the Church'.[114] Similar provisions are found in United, Reformed, Congregational and Baptist traditions; these, too, have Sunday schools and commissions to study theological issues.[115]

Mission and evangelism

In addition to the provision of preaching and instruction in the setting of the local church, the juridical instruments of churches also enable the proclamation of the faith by means of mission and evangelism beyond the ecclesial community to wider society. The Latin Code of Canon Law has extensive provisions on the missionary activity of the church,[116]

---

oversees 'Christian education and leadership training' with committees on Discipleship, Evangelism, Nurture, and Christian Education.

[113] PCA: BCO, 6.1: the children of believers 'are entitled to ... instruction'; 6.3: 'All baptized persons are entitled to ... instruction'; 28.1: 'instruction and training of the children of the Church are committed by God primarily to their parents ... True discipleship involves learning the Word ... both at home and in the Church'; 28.2: 'The home and the Church should [provide] for instructing ... children in the Bible and ... church catechisms'; Sessions encourage parents 'to guide their children in the catechising and disciplining of them in the Christian religion'.

[114] PCI: Code, 37 and 77. See also PCW: HOR, 3.2.2: the Presbytery supervises 'the work of the Sunday School, young people and children'; 3.4.2: General Assembly. Compare PCA: BCO, 12.5: the Session is 'to establish and control Sunday schools and Bible classes with special reference to the children of the church'; CLCS: 132: 'Sunday School ... is under the supervision of the Kirk Session. The minister is head of the Sunday School.'

[115] UFCS: MPP, I.III.17: the Session must ensure 'that parents attend to the godly upbringing of their children, and to aid them by instituting a Sunday school' under 'the supervision of the Session'; teachers should have 'intelligence and piety'; UCA: BL 2.4.2; BUGB: MTC 2003, 5.1.4: a church is a place 'where children and adults are instructed in the Christian faith'; NBCUSA: Const., Art. III.4: one object of NBC is 'to publish and distribute Sunday school and other Christian literature, music, and other works'; BUSA: Const., Art. 6: the Union is 'to provide for theological education and for training for service'; BUSA: Model Const., Art. 3.2.3: the church is 'to provide instruction' for believers 'to build them up to the measure and stature ... of Christ (Eph. 4.13)'; Riverside Baptist Church (Baltimore): Const., Art. II: the church is 'to nurture its members through a program of Christian education'; Art. IV: each member covenants 'to religiously educate our children'.

[116] CIC, c. 781: 'Because the whole church is of its nature missionary and ... evangelisation is ... a fundamental duty of the people of God, all Christ's faithful must be conscious of the responsibility to play their part in missionary activity'; c. 782: the Pontiff and College of Bishops direct this; c. 783: institutes; c. 784: missionaries (clergy or lay); c. 785: catechists and mission; c. 786: mission where the gospel has not taken root; c. 787: mission and non-believers; c. 788:

Catholic education,[117] in schools, catholic universities and other institutes of higher studies, and the means of social communication (and the publication of books in particular).[118] Indeed: 'While pride of place must always be given to preaching and catechetical instruction, all the available means of proclaiming Christian doctrine are to be used: the exposition of doctrine in schools, in institutes of higher learning, at conferences and meetings of all kinds; public declarations by lawful authority on the occasion of certain events; the printed word and other means of social communication.'[119] Similar norms are found in the Code of the Oriental Catholic Churches.[120] For the churches of the Anglican Communion, too, 'outreach' should seek to ensure that 'scriptural revelation may continue to illuminate, challenge and transform cultures, structures, thinking and doing', though responsibility for mission in any place belongs primarily to a church in that place.[121] Each church may have commissions, boards or other such bodies to lead, advise on and carry out the work of evangelism, mission and teaching at the appropriate levels of and in a manner prescribed by that church.[122]

It is commonly the case that Orthodox churches provide for the establishment of commissions and other bodies engaged in the work of evangelisation and theological education.[123] For example, in the Russian Orthodox Church the Holy Synod may set up commissions or other bodies for: 'the solution of the important theological problems pertaining to the internal and external activity of the Church'; the publication of theological literature; 'the improvement of theological, spiritual and moral training of clergy and the activities of theological educational institutions'; and 'mission, catechisation and religious education'.[124] The oversight of catechesis, theological institutions and seminaries is generally in the keeping of the

---

formation for mission; c. 789: formation of neophytes; c. 790: mission territories; c. 791: fostering vocations to mission; c. 792: the Episcopal Conference and mission.

[117] CIC, cc. 793–795: the parental duty to teach their children; the church has a right to educate by virtue of its divine mission; education must pay regard to 'the formation of the whole person'.

[118] CIC, cc. 796–806: schools; cc. 807–821: universities; cc. 822–832: publishing books (e.g. catechisms).

[119] CIC, c. 761; CD 13.

[120] CCEO, c. 585.1: each church is 'to take care that, through suitably prepared preachers sent by a competent authority in accord with the norms of the common law, the gospel is preached in the whole world under the guidance of the Roman Pontiff'; c. 585.2: the commission on mission of the synod of bishops; c. 586: it is strictly forbidden to coerce and induce through improper practices anyone to join the church; c. 588: catechesis; c. 589–591: missionaries; cc. 627–666: catholic schools, universities and media.

[121] PCLCCAC, Principle 51.2 and 4: mission. See also TACC 2.2: engagement in mission.

[122] PCLCCAC, Principle 48.9. E.g. TEC: Cans. I.1.2 and 11: a Standing Commission on Evangelism develops policy and action on evangelism; New Zealand: Cans. B.IX: the Board of Mission is to 'assist and encourage the church at diocesan and local levels to arouse support among parishioners for the objects of the Board'.

[123] SOCA: Const., Art. 105: ordination candidates must complete 'Theological Studies'; ROMOC: Statutes, Arts. 127, 129, and 130: candidates for patriarch, metropolitan and bishop must be theology graduates.

[124] ROC: Statute, V.28; Dioc. of Sourozh, Statutes, Art. 10: 'religious education', and 'production, acquisition and distribution of religious literature'; GOAA: Regs., Art. 19.3: the parish Outreach and Evangelism Ministry.

Holy Synod.[125] Typically, Mission Commissions are 'to study the needs and opportunities of the jurisdictions in the external and internal mission fields of the Church, at home and abroad, to point out opportunities or failures, and to suggest areas in which necessary resources might be found'.[126] Laws also provide for establishing theological institutions to train clergy and other church officers, as well as rules about their governance, staff appointments and curricula.[127] Indeed, the Ukrainian Orthodox Church in America enables bishops to erect 'missions' and provide financial resources for these: 'The diocesan bishop, by virtue of his Episcopal office, is bound to propagate and expound Orthodox Faith and morals among all people within the diocesan boundaries'; in order to accomplish this, the bishop must: take measures 'to ensure that his clergy make an Orthodox witness in their communities'; 'establish missions for the purpose of propagating the Orthodox faith'; and take measures 'to provide the necessary funds for missionary activity within his diocese'.[128]

Mission is also fundamental in Protestantism. A Lutheran Church has a duty 'to participate in God's mission' and reach out 'to all people to bring them to faith in Christ and by doing all ministry with a global awareness consistent with the understanding of God as Creator, Redeemer, and Sanctifier of all';[129] or else it is 'to fulfil the mission of the Christian Church in the world by proclaiming the Word of God' and supporting and co-operating with churches in other lands as they seek to carry out their mission;[130] it may also be empowered to establish mission centres,[131] and to 'publish, procure, and distribute literature compatible with the Confession and principles of the Church'.[132] As mission beyond the church is a key feature of Lutheranism,[133] so churches have special boards devoted to it.[134] Much the same applies in Methodism: mission and evangelisation are fundamental to each ecclesial component – institutional and ministerial.[135] Therefore, Conferences are

---

[125] ROC: Statute, V.31; VI.7: Education Committee; Department for Catechisation; Mission Department; SCOBA: Const., IV.2: Orthodox Christian Education Commission, and Committee on Theological Education.

[126] SCOBA: Const., Art. IV.2; ROMOC: Statutes, Art. 106: the Eparchial Missionary Department; Arts. 161–166: the Bible and Missionary Institute (with its Printing Press) and Media Institutions (radio, TV and press).

[127] SOCA: Const., Art. 76: a metropolitan may establish schools and seminaries; GOAA: Const., Art. 19 and Regs., Art. 15.5: the Archdiocese establishes and oversees parish schools and publishes materials 'appropriate to ... its mission'; ROMOC: Statutes, Arts. 115–121: institutes to train clergy; Art. 113(c): the Metropolitan Synod approves curricula; MOSC: Const., Art. 109: Mission Work; Art. 111: Theological Seminary.

[128] UOCIA: Statutes, Art. VII.12; see also VII.4(h). [129] ELCA: Const., Ch. 4.01–03.

[130] LCA: Const., Art. III. [131] LCA: BL, Sect. IV.4. [132] LCA: Const., Art. III.

[133] ELCSA: G., 11.5: the 'missionary command ... concerns the whole Church', and includes 'reaching out to those on the outside'; LCGB: RAR, Definition of a Congregation, 2: 'the universal mission of God'; RAR, Church Session, 1 and 2: outreach and missions; ELCA: Const., 8.14: 'the extended mission of the Church'; 8.12: 'The congregation shall include in its mission ... outreach in witness and service to its community.'

[134] LCA: BL, VIII.G and H; ELCA: Const., Ch. 11.20–21: it must 'provide resources to equip members' and 'support and establish policy ... and coordinate planning and evaluation for mission throughout the world'.

[135] MCI: RDG, 10.06: the Church Council oversees 'Evangelism ... in the local community'; 16.02–03: every member belongs to the Methodist Missionary Society (Ireland) overseen by Conference; UMCNEAE: BOD, par. 243–244: local 'outreach programmes' which (252) the Church Council designs and implements; pars. 590–591: establishing a mission; pars. 1101–1103,

to promote evangelistic, educational and missionary activities nationally and globally;[136] the same applies to congregations.[137] Moreover: 'Every layperson is called to carry out the Great Commission (Matthew 28:18-20) ... The witness of the laity, their Christ-like examples of everyday living as well as the sharing of their own faith experiences of the Gospel, is the primary evangelistic ministry through which all people will come to know Christ and ... [the] Church will fulfil its mission.'[138] Ordained ministers, too, must engage in evangelism.[139] There are also institutions devoted to evangelisation. The Methodist Church of New Zealand is typical: 'The Church expresses its commitment to mission, global partnership, and ecumenical relations through the Mission and Ecumenical Committee' which is to 'support and strengthen the worldwide mission' of the church, 'promote an understanding of mission as a joining of evangelism, ministry to human needs, concern for social justice, and ... for the world in which we live'. The functions of the Committee are, for example, to share in one world mission, engage in the mutual sharing of resources with churches overseas, engage in ongoing study of a theology of mission and strengthen those special Partners-in-Mission relationships which already exist.[140] A church may also have extensive provisions on Methodist Schools.[141] Presbyterian engagement in wider mission is incumbent on church members,[142] congregations,[143] ministers[144] and the assemblies of the church, including their boards for mission abroad,[145] publishing and

1113: the General Board of Discipleship is 'to assist annual conferences, districts, and local churches ... in their efforts to win persons to Jesus Christ' and provide for 'special publications directed toward ... outreach'; MCGB: CPD, DU 21: publishing; FMCNA: BOD 4500: Free Methodist World Missions; 4550: Mission Districts; COTN: Man., 338: Nazarene Publishing House.

[136] UMCUSA: Const., Div. 2.4, Art. V; UMCNEAE: BOD, par. 27: jurisdictional conference must promote 'evangelistic, educational, [and] missionary' activities; par. 122: global mission; par. 401 and Judicial Council Decision 524: the bishop is 'to enable the gathered Church to worship and to evangelize faithfully'.

[137] MCI: Const., s. 1: the 'passion for evangelisation'; MCNZ: LAR, s. 3.2-3.3: 'mission of the congregation'; MCGB: CPD, SO 424: the district chair is 'to lead all the people of the District in the work of ... evangelism'.

[138] UMCNEAE: BOD, par. 126.

[139] MCGB: CPD, SO 7000-7001; MCI: RDG, 4A.02; MCNZ: LAR, s. 2.29: ministers must 'equip ... people for their work of mission'; FMCNA: PACLM, II, Responsibilities of Call, 3: elders as evangelists and educators.

[140] MCNZ: LAR, s.5.4.

[141] MCI: RDG, 2012-15: schools under the management of the Methodist Church; the circuit superintendent is the manager of the school; visitation; appointment and discipline of staff; insurance of teachers and pupils.

[142] PCANZ: BO, 4.2(2): a candidate for membership 'will unite in the ... mission of the congregation'.

[143] PCANZ: BO, 5.2(1) and (2): it is 'to participate in God's mission to the world'; 6.1: 'Baptism invites us to share in God's mission through our own vocation and commitment to God's new and coming world.'

[144] PCANZ: BO, 6.3: 'leadership' in mission; PCA: BCO, 8.4.1 and 13.9: Presbytery is to 'set apart evangelists', 'oversee the mission of the congregation' and 'recognise new forms of mission'.

[145] PCA: BCO, 5.1-5.7: a Mission Church is overseen by Presbytery or by Session; PCI: Code, 35: Kirk Session and 'Christian witness ... in the local community'; 113-117: mission home/abroad; 279-280: Boards of Mission.

other media[146] and theological education and training.[147] Similar provisions are found in United, Reformed and Congregational churches,[148] as well as Baptist bodies: all require members and institutions to engage in mission.[149]

The maintenance of doctrinal standards

The maintenance of doctrinal standards is achieved principally by two devices: rules which require subscription or other form of assent to the faith of the church, particularly from ordained ministers; and rules which enable oversight or enforcement of doctrinal discipline by means of executive action or judicial proceedings. Generally, whilst the regulatory instruments of churches do not require disciplinary action for failure to proclaim the Gospel in the daily lives of the faithful, they do provide for the imposition of sanctions in the event that the faithful (especially its ordained ministers) manifest publicly words or deeds which are contrary to the doctrine of a church as enunciated in its own doctrinal or confessional texts.

Within Catholicism, the faithful of the Latin Church are under an absolute duty to give an assent of faith to infallible doctrine, which must be 'held definitively'; i.e. doctrine declared part of the deposit of faith 'must be believed with divine and catholic faith' and the faithful are 'bound to shun any contrary doctrines'.[150] As to non-definitive doctrine: 'While the assent of faith is not required, a religious submission [*obsequium*] of intellect and will is to be given to any doctrine which either the Supreme Pontiff or the College of Bishops, exercising their authentic *magisterium*, declare upon a matter of faith or morals, even though they do not intend to proclaim that doctrine by definitive act. Christ's faithful are therefore to ensure that they avoid whatever does not accord with that doctrine.'[151] Prescribed

---

[146] PCA: BCO, 14.1: General Assembly Mission to North America; World Mission; Publications Committee.

[147] PCW: HOR, 3.4.4: Candidates and Training Panel.

[148] UCCSA: MCLC, Art. 3; UCOC: Const., Art. V.11 and VI.20; UFCS: MPP I.III.19: Session 'oversight of the mission work undertaken by the congregation'; 20: mission stations; UCA: Const., 4 and 25: Presbytery oversees mission; UCA: BL 2.2: Ministerial Education Commission; 3.1.28: parish Mission; UCC: Man., 12: Missions; UCOC: Const., Art. X.65: Boards of Mission; BL, Art. III.212: Mission Planning Council.

[149] BUS: Const., IV.2: the Union is 'to support and extend Christ's mission both at home and overseas through evangelism, church planting and caring ministries'; BMPP 216, SCBC, Type A, Art. VII.7: the Evangelism Committee provides 'practical ways for implementing the evangelistic mission of the church, such as neighbourhood visitation, preaching services, and study groups'; Art. VII.8: Committee on World Mission Support; NABC: Const., III.3: the NABC is 'to promote home and foreign mission efforts'; CNBC: Const., Art. 3: Statement of Faith, XI: 'It is the duty and privilege of every follower of Christ and of every church ... to endeavour to make disciples of all nations ... Missionary effort on the part of all rests thus upon a spiritual necessity of the regenerate life, and is expressly and repeatedly commanded in the teachings of Christ. It is the duty of every child of God ... to win the lost to Christ by personal effort ... in harmony with the gospel'; ABCUSA: TCOR II.A.4: a congregation must maintain a 'witnessing fellowship'; Riverside Baptist Church (Baltimore): BL Art. III.4: Missions Committee; III.6: Education Committee.

[150] CIC, cc. 749, 750.

[151] CIC, c. 752; see F.A. Sullivan, 'The response to the non-definitive exercise of magisterium', 23 *Studia Canonica* (1989) 267: *obsequium* has been translated respectively as 'submission' and 'respect'.

classes are required to make a profession of faith, and soundness in faith is required in ordination candidates;[152] also: 'All the Christian faithful are obliged to observe the constitutions and decrees which the legitimate authority of the Church issues in order to propose doctrine and proscribe erroneous opinions'; nevertheless, they have 'the right and even at times the duty to manifest to the sacred pastors their opinion on matters which pertain to the good of the Church' as well as to the other Christian faithful, but in so doing must have 'due regard for the integrity of faith and morals and reverence towards their pastors, and consideration of the common good and the dignity of persons'.[153] Those engaged in theological study enjoy the right of free enquiry and expression, and public dissent may be permissible if grounded in a 'true respect for the *magisterium* even while disagreeing with it on a particular point'.[154] Heresy is 'the obstinate post-baptismal denial of some truth which must be believed with divine and catholic faith, or it is likewise an obstinate doubt concerning the same'; apostasy is 'the total repudiation of the Christian faith'; schism is 'the refusal of submission to the Roman Pontiff or of communion with the members of the Church subject to him' – the penalties for each are automatic excommunication for lay people, and for clerics excommunication, suspension, deprivation or penal transfer; and blasphemy is committed by a 'person who uses a public show or speech, published writings, or other media of social communication to blaspheme, seriously damage good morals, express wrongs against religion or the church [and] is punished with a just penalty'.[155] Persons who teach a doctrine condemned by the Pontiff or an ecumenical council or who perniciously reject non-definitive doctrine are punished with just penalties unless, after warning by the Apostolic See or by the ordinary, the persons retract.[156] Similar norms are found in the canon law applicable to the Oriental Catholic Churches.[157]

Broad equivalents to these Catholic norms appear in Orthodox laws – but there is no neat compendium of rules about the maintenance of doctrinal standards. First, acceptance of the Orthodox faith is a criterion for admission to membership: baptised persons may be admitted if they 'believe in the divinity of the Holy Trinity, the incarnation of the Son, the procedure of the Holy Spirit, the Holy Church and the application of the Nicene Creed, the divine inspiration of the Holy Traditions, the mediation of the Mother of God and the saints, and the canonical observances'.[158] Secondly, the faithful must shape their lives on the foundation of the Orthodox faith: for instance, 'the spiritual and ethical life of the faithful' is built, *inter alia*, on the 'Holy Scriptures, Sacred Tradition, [and] the doctrines ... of Ecumenical and Local Synods ... as interpreted by the Great Church of Christ in

---

[152] CIC, c. 833; c. 1029: sound faith (ordination); c. 378: strong faith (bishops); c. 865: baptism of adults.

[153] CIC, c. 754 and c. 212.3.

[154] CIC, c. 218; P. Huizing and K. Walf, 'What does the "right to dissent" mean in the Church?', 158 *Concilium* (1982) 3.

[155] CIC, c. 751: the offences; c. 1364: the penalties; cc. 1323–4: baptised persons who have fallen into heresy, apostasy or schism as a matter of conscience do not incur these censures; c. 1369: blasphemy.

[156] CIC, c. 1371.   [157] CCEO, cc. 598–606.

[158] MOSC: Const., 1.2. See also ROC: Statute, XI.31: parishioners are 'persons of the Orthodox confession'.

Constantinople';[159] or else, a parishioner must 'apply the tenets of the Orthodox Faith to his/her life', 'adhere to and live according to ... the Orthodox faith' and be 'obedient in matters of the Faith';[160] and candidates for ordained ministry must satisfy tests about the depth of their faith.[161] Thirdly, doctrinal standards are maintained executively and judicially. The bishop, senior clergy and parish clergy have a particular role to play in this. For example: 'The Diocesan Bishop shall enjoy the fullness of hierarchical authority in matters of doctrine' and shall 'take care of the preservation of the faith, Christian morality and piety';[162] similarly, the dean must care for 'the purity of the Orthodox faith' and the 'moral education of the believers';[163] and in the parish: 'The clergy are strictly to observe the teachings of the Church, regarding Christ, the Sacred Scriptures and Holy Traditions.'[164] Moreover, a Holy Synod may investigate 'heresies and violations of church traditions' and other matters 'concerning the Church's faith',[165] and a church court may entertain 'allegations of unorthodox belief'.[166]

It is a fundamental principle of Anglican canon law that: 'The church has authority in controversies of faith.' Doctrinal discipline applies primarily to ordained and lay ministers rather than to the laity in general. At ordination and consecration, candidates must subscribe, assent or otherwise affirm publicly their belief in or loyalty to the doctrine of their church. Ordained ministers may also be required to subscribe to the doctrine of their church on admission to an office or other appointment; the same applies to lay ministers or lay officers.[167] The width of permissible theological opinion in a church is determined (a) legislatively, by its central assembly; (b) executively, by its bishops (individually or collectively); and (c) judicially, by its courts and tribunals. The bishop has a special responsibility to guard and uphold sound and wholesome doctrine. Moreover, ministers (ordained and lay) must not teach, preach, publish or profess doctrine or belief incompatible with that of their own church.[168] A person who engages in unlawful doctrinal dissent may be subject to disciplinary process in church courts or tribunals in the

---

[159] See e.g. GOAA: Const., Art. 2(b).
[160] GOAA: Regs., Art. 18.1. See also UOCIA: Statutes, Art. XI.1 and 5: parishioners are those 'who live in accordance with the teachings of the Orthodox Church' and a person cannot be a parishioner who 'openly betrays the teaching of the Orthodox Church'; 7: 'all members ... are responsible for the preservation of the faith'. ROMOC: Statutes, Art. 54.2: Parish Assembly members are those 'who prove their affection for the Orthodox Church, for her teaching of faith and her institutions, through their faith, deeds and moral conduct'.
[161] See e.g. GOAA: Const., Art. 14: candidates for the office of archbishop must be persons of 'deep faith'; UOCIA: Statutes, Art. VII.9: a candidate for the office of bishop must be a graduate in theology.
[162] ROC: Statute, X.11; see also 18(a) for the preservation of the faith.   [163] ROC: Statute, X.52.
[164] OCIA: GC, A Selection of Clergy Disciplines; Ephesus, cc. 6, 7; Trullo, c. 1; Carthage, c. 2.
[165] SOCA: Const., Arts. 59 and 103.
[166] UOCA: Statutes, Art. XII.3: the Diocesan Court has competence over such allegations.
[167] PCLCCAC, Principle 53.1-3. AR, Art. 20: 'it is not lawful for the Church to ordain anything that is contrary to God's Word written'. See e.g. England: Can. C15: clergy; E5-6: lay workers.
[168] PCLCCAC, Principle 53.5-7. See e.g. Southern Africa: Can. 37: doctrinal offences include heresy ('false doctrine'), schism ('acceptance of membership in a religious body not in communion' with the church) and apostasy (abandonment of 'the Christian faith'); the accused must have 'taught, published, or otherwise publicly promulgated, some doctrine or opinion repugnant to or at variance with the Faith and Doctrine of the Church'.

manner and to the extent provided by law. However, the courts and tribunals of a church do not declare true doctrine or create new doctrine but only state what the law is with regard to doctrine. The interpretation of the standards and formularies of, and all questions of faith and doctrine arising in, a church must be determined within that church save to the extent that its law permits reference for consultation or determination to a body external to that church.[169]

Protestant churches also have systems for the maintenance of doctrinal standards. It is a fundamental principle of Lutheran law that the institutions of the church must act in conformity with the doctrine of the church.[170] Congregations may be admitted to the church if their members 'accept and hold the Confession of the Church'.[171] The same applies to candidates for ordination.[172] Similarly, ordained ministers must personally hold the faith and faithfully uphold the doctrine of the church in their teaching.[173] Moreover, the church may exercise discipline over its members 'to ensure faithful adherence to the Confession of the Church' and 'to apply discipline when departure from the doctrine of the Church is evident'.[174] Thus, executive doctrinal supervision may be exercised by bishops, presidents and district presidents,[175] and disciplinary process may follow for disobedience to or denial of the Word of God, apostasy, heresy and 'false doctrine'.[176] Some churches deal with lawful doctrinal dissent,[177] and they provide a process to determine

---

[169] PCLCCAC, Principle 53.8-10. See e.g. South East Asia: Fundamental Declarations: in 'the interpretation of the ... standards and formularies and in all questions of faith [and] doctrine ... the Province ... shall ... give due weight to the teaching and traditions of the Communion in the ... decisions of its own ecclesiastical tribunals'.

[170] ELCA: Const., Ch. 5.01: congregations, synods, and the churchwide organization must act 'under His rule', the Confession of Faith (Const., Ch. 2) and Statement of Purpose (Const., Ch. 4).

[171] NALC: SFPM (2011), p.1; LCA: Const., Art. IV.1: membership consists of 'baptised members of congregations which ... accept and hold the Confession of the Church'; ELCA: Model Const. for Congregations, Ch. 3; LCMS: Const., Art. VI; see also BL, 2; ELCIRE: Const., Art. 4 and 6; LCGB: RAR, Congregations, 1.

[172] LCA: BL, Sect. V.1-3: 'sufficient standard in theological knowledge ... and of sound confessional standing'.

[173] NALC: SFPM (2011), p.2: 'A pastor shall personally believe and publicly profess the Christian faith, in accordance with ... the confession of faith and the Common Confession'; LCA: Const., Arts. V.1 and IX.2; LCGB: RAR, Responsibilities and Duties of Pastors, 1-24: pastors must faithfully uphold the Statement of Faith and ensure that the gospel is proclaimed regularly in accordance with the teachings and worship traditions of the church; ELCA: Const., Ch. 7.31.10-11: 'acceptance and adherence to the Confession of Faith'.

[174] LCA: Const., Art. VI.7; also, Const. of the Districts, X: members who 'depart from the confession'.

[175] ELCA: Const. for Synods, Ch. 8.01-16.01: the bishop has 'oversight of the preaching, teaching ... in accord with the Confession of Faith'; LCA: BL, VIII.F.3(b): the president must 'exercise oversight over the doctrine and practice of all pastors and congregations' with district presidents.

[176] NALC: CDC: 4-6: 'Preaching or teaching in conflict with the faith'; ELCA: Const., Ch. 20.20-21, 20.41: 'departing from the faith'; 'denial of the Christian faith'; ELCSA: G., 5.1: 'apostasy'; ELCIC: ABL, Pt. II.3-6: 'turning aside from the faith'; LCMS: Const., Art. III: the Synod must combat 'schism, sectarianism (Rom. 16:17), and heresy'; Art. XII: district presidents may suspend ministers for 'false doctrine'.

[177] LCMS: BL, 1.8: 'Dissent from doctrinal resolutions and statements is ... expressed first within the fellowship of peers and then brought to ... the Commission on Theology and Church

whether statements conform to the church confession.[178] Churches may also distinguish mandatory 'public doctrine' (Scripture and Confessions)[179] and persuasive 'pious opinion'.[180]

Methodist doctrinal discipline is also prospective and retrospective. Members are admitted, *inter alia*, on their profession of the faith.[181] Moreover: 'No person shall be appointed to office in the Church who teaches doctrines contrary to those of the Church, or who holds doctrines likely to injure the peace and welfare of the Church.'[182] Thus, candidates for ordained ministry must accept the doctrinal standards of the church and deacons must engage in 'the careful study of Scripture and its faithful interpretation'.[183] Doctrinal standards are overseen by various officers.[184] In the United Methodist Church, for example, bishops, clergy and deacons may be disciplined for 'practices declared by The United Methodist Church to be incompatible with Christian teachings', including but not limited to 'being a self-avowed practicing homosexual; or conducting ceremonies which celebrate homosexual unions; or performing same-sex wedding ceremonies'. Likewise, a professing member may be charged with 'dissemination of doctrines contrary to the established standards of doctrine' of the church.[185] In some churches a minister

---

Relations before ... an overture to the convention calling for revision or recision. While the conscience of the dissenter shall be respected, the consciences of others, as well as the collective will of the Synod, shall also be respected.'

[178] LCMS: BL, 1.9.: 'Doctrinal review is ... the Synod's responsibility to determine that every doctrinal statement made in its or ... its agencies' ... materials is in accord with the Scriptures and the Lutheran Confessions' (e.g. 'official periodicals and journals of the Synod [and] any material with doctrinal content issued publicly by boards, commissions' etc); the Commission on Doctrinal Review considers cases following BL 3.9.3.2.1; ELCIC: Const., Art. XVIII.5–12: the Court of Adjudication may hear 'questions of doctrine and conscience'.

[179] LCA: Public Doctrine and Pious Opinion, CTIR, 1984, 2001 edn.: public doctrine is that 'established by the Scriptures' or 'laid down in [the] Confessions'; the latter provide 'criteria for measuring public teaching' but do not contain 'everything that could be said on the doctrines they discuss'; 'it is necessary ... to elaborate (positively and negatively) on certain teachings and ... doctrinal statements ... agreed to by the whole church'.

[180] Ibid: i.e. 'the interpretations ... [of] doctrinal statements' on the basis of 'traditional thinking'; AC, Art. 6: for unity 'it is enough to agree [on] the doctrine of the gospel and ... sacraments'; thus, agreement in pious opinions 'is not necessary for the unity of the church'; so 'differences of opinion ... should not be held to in a way which hinders friendly discussion, and makes submission to the Scriptures difficult or ... impossible'; indeed, 'pious opinions can enrich the church [and] have often stimulated thinking and discussion on central matters of faith'.

[181] MCGB: CPD, DU 7; UMCNEAE: BOD, par. 215. Compare MCI: RDG, 101: 'Membership ... is not conditional upon ... theological tests'; MCNZ: LAR, Nature of New Zealand Methodism: admission to 'all who sincerely express their faith in Jesus Christ [and] who give evidence of that in their daily living'.

[182] MCGB: CPD, SO 010(1).

[183] UMCNEAE: BOD, par. 304: candidates must 'accept that Scripture contains all things necessary for salvation through faith in God through Jesus Christ' and 'its Doctrinal Standards'; par. 138: deacons.

[184] MCNZ: LAR, s. 7.5.: the president 'guards its faith'. UMCNEAE: BOD, par. 403: bishops 'are authorized to guard the faith, order, liturgy, doctrine'; MCNZ: LAR, s. 2.29: each minister must 'maintain the Faith'.

[185] UMCNEAE: BOD, par. 2702.

may resign if unable to subscribe to doctrine, and norms expressly provide for the protection of conscience in doctrinal matters.[186]

The enforcement of doctrinal standards is an important aspect of Presbyterian discipline.[187] Christian belief and acceptance of the faith is a pre-condition to admission to, variously, the membership of a church,[188] ordination,[189] and offices and ministries;[190] and ministers may be required to subscribe to doctrine.[191] As to doctrinal supervision, Irish Presbyterianism is typical: 'Each congregation and each member of a congregation (except members of the Kirk Session) in all matters of doctrine ... is under the immediate jurisdiction of the Kirk Session', which itself is under the jurisdiction of the Presbytery, which is in turn under that of General Assembly.[192] Equally, in the Presbyterian Church in America, an elder must ensure that 'no corruption of doctrine or of morals' enters the life of the members and the Presbytery must ensure that the elder has 'full freedom to maintain and teach the doctrine of our Church'.[193] However, for example, in the Presbyterian Church of Scotland: 'A member or office-holder of the Church is free to believe that all the words of the Bible are together literally the Word of God, but that is not required of all members and office-bearers. Likewise a member or office-bearer is free to believe that all the doctrines in the Westminster Confession are fundamental, but again that is not required'; thus: 'The constitutional possibility of different beliefs is what allows the Church to be described as a "broad" Church' – and conscientious objection is allowed in some cases.[194] Above all: 'God alone is Lord of the conscience and has left it free from any doctrines or commandments of men (a) which are in any respect contrary to the Word of God, or (b) which, in regard to matters of faith and worship, are not governed by the Word of God. Therefore, the rights of

---

[186] MCI: RDG, 4E.07: i.e. if 'unable to subscribe to Methodist doctrine'; MCNZ: LAR, s. 2.6.1.2: withdrawal on grounds of 'good faith and conscience'; s. 1.9.1: membership is 'a creative tension between the "General Standards for the Guidance of Members" ... and the freedom to exercise individual conscience'.

[187] PCA: BCO, 13.9: Presbytery is 'to condemn erroneous opinions which injure the purity or peace of the Church'; 4.6: General Assembly must 'bear testimony against error in doctrine and immorality in practice'; PCI: Code, 38, 69: Kirk Session is to 'exercise authority ... [as] ... to both doctrine and conduct'; in turn, the Presbytery ensures the Word is 'faithfully preached' by ministers.

[188] PCANZ: BO, 4.2: a person is admitted who e.g. 'publicly professes his or her faith in Jesus Christ'; PCI: Code, II.5: 'All who profess faith in Jesus Christ ... are called to be members of the visible Church.'

[189] PCI: Code, 205: statements at ordination include belief in the Word of God; PCA: BCO, 19.3, 21.5.

[190] PCANZ: BO, 9.2(1): a minister must 'hold the fundamentals of the faith'.

[191] PCANZ: BO, 1.7: ministers and elders subscribe: 'I believe in the Word of God ... and the fundamental doctrines of Christian faith ... in [e.g.] the Westminster Confession of Faith, and other subordinate standards of this Church. I accept that liberty of conviction is recognised ... on such points as do not enter into the fundamental doctrines ... I acknowledge the Presbyterian government ... to be agreeable to the Word of God and I promise to submit to it [and] observe the order and administration of public worship as allowed in this Church.'

[192] PCI: Code, 19.2.   [193] PCA: BCO, 8.3 and 8.7.

[194] CLCS: 26; see also 27: 'In no case is individual conscience a valid reason for disobedience', but e.g. Act XXVI, 1959 allows ministers to object in conscience to remarriage after divorce; if members consider church law contrary to the Word of God, they may inform the church but must obey it until it is changed.

private judgment in all matters that respect religion are universal and inalienable.'[195] Nevertheless, in a serious case, discipline may follow the commission of a doctrinal offence if this is provable from Scripture.[196] Similar norms for subscription to doctrine, and the supervision and enforcement of doctrinal standards, appear in United, Reformed, Congregational[197] and Baptist instruments.[198]

The nature of worship and the forms of worship

Alongside proclamation of the Word of God, the worship of God is one of the central functions of the Christian church. The laws of churches on worship seek to strike a balance between fidelity to the historic patterns of worship in each tradition and freedom of expression in worship, including the need to adapt to local uses, choices and needs. These two values directly shape the regulation of worship. The following section deals with the juridical understandings of worship and the development of forms of service for use in worship. It also introduces basic norms about the administration of the sacraments.

The nature of worship

The nature of worship is addressed across the traditions mainly in ecclesiastical quasi-legislation rather than laws properly so called, though in some churches the law spells out the rudiments of the character of worship as an essential action of the church involving an interaction between the faithful and God. Some traditions express worship in 'liturgy', but in many Protestant churches 'liturgy' is not a juridical category. In the Roman Catholic Church, worship is 'the first act of the

---

[195] PCA: BCO, Preface II.1; II.8: 'No church judicatory may make laws to bind the conscience.'
[196] PCA: BCO, 29.1: 'An offense ... is anything in the doctrines or practice of a Church member ... contrary to the Word of God'; 'Nothing ... ought to be considered by any court as an offense ... which cannot be proved to be such from Scripture'; 34.5: 'Heresy and schism'; 27.5. See also e.g. PCI: Code, 132: offences include 'anything in the teaching ... of a person ... which has been declared censurable by the Word of God'.
[197] RCA: BCO, Ch. 1, Pt. I, Art. 2.2: a consistory ensures the congregation is 'in obedience to Holy Scripture'; Ch. 1, Pt. II, Art. 7: the Classis president ensures 'the doctrines of the gospel preached [are] in their purity in conformity with' the Word of God and church Standards; App., Formularies: declaration for ministers, e.g. 'I accept the Scriptures as the only rule of faith and life'; URC: Man., A, Sch. B: elders' Declarations of Belief; UFCS: MPP, App. 2: Formula of Subscription: 'I will constantly maintain and defend the doctrine, worship and government of this Church'; MPP I.III.9: the Session is 'to satisfy itself as to their profession of faith in Christ, their knowledge of the cardinal doctrines of Christian belief, and the nature and significance of church ordinances'; MPP VI.3: 'doctrinal error'; see also UCOC: Const., Art. V.10; UCC: BL, 010.
[198] BUSA: Model Const., Art. 5: admitting those who have 'given evidence of their personal salvation through faith in ... Christ'; BMPP 216, SCBC, Type A, Art. V: any person 'who confesses Jesus Christ as Saviour and Lord and who is in essential agreement with the doctrine and practice of this church may be received into the fellowship ... following ... baptism by immersion'; 231: Suggested Const. for an Association, Art. X: the Permanent Council on Ordination examines candidates as to 'their doctrinal beliefs'; BUGB: MTC 2003, 6.1: ministers 'maintain and practise the doctrine' of baptism; Riverside Baptist Church (Baltimore): Const., Art. II: a member covenants to sustain church doctrine; BUSA: Model Const., Art. 9.2: 'erroneous belief'.

virtue of religion' and involves adoration, prayer and the participation of the faithful in the performance of liturgical actions.[199] In turn, liturgy is 'an action of the church' – an expression by the people of their relationship to Christ and to the church: it is a response to God's initiative, a dialogue between the Word and actions of God and his people.[200] The purpose of liturgy is to enable the sanctification of the faithful through worship: the whole church, both clergy and laity, shares in the exercise of the office of sanctifying, and liturgical actions themselves are not private actions but corporate celebrations of the church with the presence and active participation of the faithful; and the faithful have the right to worship God according to the prescriptions of their own rites approved by the legitimate pastors of the church.[201] The detailed liturgical law is found outside the Code of Canon Law in the ritual books (*ordines*) and their preambles (*praenotandae*) and rubrics: 'for the most part the Code does not define the rites which are to be observed in celebrating liturgical actions'; rather: 'current liturgical norms retain their force unless ... contrary to the canons of the Code'.[202] Similar norms apply to the Oriental Catholic churches.[203]

Much the same approach is used in Orthodoxy, for which 'unity in faith and worship' is critical.[204] Worship is a fundamental action of the church and is expressed in the form of liturgy.[205] The purpose of worship is the sanctification of the faithful: typically, the church 'sanctifies the faithful through Divine Worship, especially the Eucharist and other Sacraments' and Divine Worship is a means of witness.[206] Consequently, all Orthodox Christians should participate in 'liturgical worship',[207] and parishioners must 'faithfully attend the Divine Liturgy and other worship services' and 'participate regularly in the holy sacraments'.[208] Moreover, the parish priest is to 'sanctify his parishioners through the administration of the

---

[199] CCC, pars. 2096–2098; 1069: liturgy is a 'public work' or 'service in the name of/on behalf of the people', 'the participation of the People of God in "the work of God"'; 1070: liturgical celebration of divine worship.

[200] SC, 1; CCC, pars. 1076–1109.

[201] CIC, cc. 834–837; SC 26; for offices of sanctification (e.g. prayers) see c. 839; c. 217: the right to worship.

[202] CIC, c. 2; see also J.M. Huels, 'The interpretation of liturgical law', 55 *Worship* (1981) 218.

[203] CCEO, c. 668: the nature of divine worship; c. 673: the Divine Liturgy should be performed with the active participation of the faithful; c. 674: the authorised liturgical books should be observed accurately.

[204] SCOBA: GOCER, Pt. I, Worship with Non-Orthodox, 6; 7: 'theology and worship do not express the thought and life of one particular denomination, but of the Church of Christ'.

[205] Ibid., 1 and 2: 'liturgical prayer ... is the official prayer of the Orthodox Church ... conducted according to the forms, prescriptions and canons'; also: 'Non-liturgical prayer ... is the private prayer or devotions of the faithful.'

[206] GOAA: Const., Art. 2(b); Regs., Art. 15.3: the church is 'sanctifying the faithful through Divine Worship'; ROMOC: Statutes, Art. 1: 'witness to God in ... liturgical services'; ROC: Dioc. of Sourozh, Statutes, Art. 10: witness by 'church services, sacraments, devotions, sacred processions and ceremonies in churches'.

[207] SCOBA: GOCER, Pt. I, Worship with Non-Orthodox, 3: this 'encourages liturgical worship and frequent participation in the sacraments'; ROC: Statute, XI.32: parishioners must 'take part in the divine services'.

[208] GOAA: Regs., Art. 18.1. OCIA: GC, Priests and Deacons, 10: the priest must minister to those 'unable to attend the Divine Services regularly'; ROMOC: Statutes, Art. 45.

THE NATURE OF WORSHIP AND THE FORMS OF WORSHIP 217

sacraments and the performance of all other prescribed services of worship';[209] more particularly: 'In addition to the Vigil, or Vespers and Matins, and the Divine Liturgy celebrated on Sundays and on the prescribed Great Feasts, the priest must strive to enhance the daily liturgical life of his parish by celebrating these services and other devotional services at appropriate times.'[210] Similarly, in the Romanian Orthodox Church, the parish priest 'celebrates the Divine Liturgy and other church services on Sundays, feasts and other days of the week',[211] and a Parochial Committee must encourage the participation of school pupils in the Divine Liturgy and other services.[212] Personal devotion is also important: in the Syrian Orthodox Church of Antioch, for instance, 'prayer is a religious duty for all believers, male and female, in the morning and evening'.[213] Likewise, for Anglicanism, 'the worship of God is a fundamental action and responsibility of the church'.[214] Worship involves praise, adoration, confession, prayer and thanksgiving, and liturgy is 'the work of the faithful through corporate public worship in accordance with the lawful forms of service of a church'. A balance should be struck between the liturgical inheritance and adaptations to local use and the needs of the people and the age. Rubrics and other norms in service books provide for order and decorum in liturgy, enable the community to participate fully in worship and ensure adaptability to meet local circumstances, practices and needs.[215] All the faithful should attend regularly at corporate public worship and keep the Lord's Day, commonly called Sunday, by regular participation in corporate public worship, hearing the Word of God read and taught, acts of devotion and of charity, using all godly and sober conversation, and abstention from all unnecessary labour and business.[216]

The instruments of Lutheran Churches treat the nature and purposes of worship in some detail.[217] The Lutheran Church in Australia has a particularly fulsome treatment of the matter. The church, 'as a divine institution, exists through and for

---

[209] GOAA: Regs., Art. 15.5 and 17.1.   [210] OCIA: GC, Divine Services, 5.
[211] ROMOC: Statutes, Art. 50. See also OCIA: GC, Divine Services, 1: 'Only a canonically ordained clergyman can perform holy services. He must not be under suspension or excommunication by his hierarch or by his own sins. He must be properly prepared, spiritually and physically, for divine worship.'
[212] ROMOC: Statutes, Art. 67.
[213] SOCA: Const., Art. 140: 'Whereas Syriac is the liturgical language in the ... Church, local language in conjunction may be used'; 141: the clergy 'must say the canonical prayers including the common daily prayer in the morning and evening, and whoever neglects this, without an acceptable excuse, falls into iniquity'.
[214] PCLCCAC, Principle 54.1; Chile: Can. D.1: 'adoration of God is the greatest privilege of a Christian'.
[215] PCLCCAC, Principle 54.2-5. See e.g. Southern Africa: Prayer Book 1989, 9: 'liturgy is the public worship of the Church of God'; Ireland: Alternative Prayer Book, 1984: 'liturgy becomes worship when the people ... make the prayers their own prayers, and turn in faith to God'; New Zealand: Prayer Book 1989, xiii–xiv: 'liturgy is not to protect particular linguistic forms. It is ... to provide conditions in which [God's] presence may be experienced'.
[216] PCLCCAC, Principle 54.6: attendance; 7: Sunday. See e.g. TEC: Cans. II.1: '[a]ll ... shall celebrate and keep the Lord's Day, commonly called Sunday, by regular participation in the public worship ... by hearing the Word of God read and taught, and by other acts of devotion and works of charity'.
[217] ELCSA: G., 10.3: 'All individual services within the congregation share the same aim, namely that the Word of God may bring about faith, awaken love and build up the congregation.'

divine worship': 'Worship is the chief ritual activity of the church; it constitutes and identifies the church as a social entity. Worship embodies and communicates those values and beliefs which underlie the existence of the church, and it shapes the corporate character, the way of thinking, and the lifestyle of those who participate in it.' Thus, worship is bilateral. On the one hand, through worship the communion of the saints participates in the life of the Trinity and 'serve God, each other, and the world'. On the other hand, in worship 'the Triune God creates and sustains the faith of his people' and 'establishes and builds up the church as a community on earth'; by worship 'God calls his people to participate in his divine life and in his saving work on earth whose citizenship is in heaven'. Moreover, 'the essence of worship is the proclamation of God's word, the performance of baptism, and the administration of the Lord's Supper'.[218] For Methodism,[219] 'divine worship is essential to the life of the Church', 'necessary to Christian fellowship and spiritual growth' and 'the duty and privilege of man who, in the presence of God, bows in adoration, humility and dedication'; however: 'the order of public worship need not be the same in all places but may be modified ... according to circumstances and the needs of men. It should be in a language and form understood by the people, consistent with the Holy Scriptures to the edification of all, and in accordance with the order and Discipline of the Church.'[220] Worship includes thanksgiving, prayer and praise, and liturgical texts contain essentials and matters recommended.[221] In short: 'the church exists for the maintenance of worship, the edification of believers, and the redemption of the world';[222] it is a 'means of grace'[223] and, so, every congregation should engage in worship.[224]

---

[218] LCA: LATW: this cites e.g. AC, 7 and 28. See also ELCSA: G., 2.1: 'The divine service is central to the faith of the Christian as well as for the life of the congregation. The risen Lord acts within His congregation through Word and Sacrament ... In the assurance of the presence of its Lord (Matt. 18.20) the congregation gives affirmation through praise, prayer, intercession and offering. Through participation in [it] the Christian acknowledges his relationship to his Lord and to the communion ... the Holy Spirit creates amongst believers'; ELCA: Const., Ch. 4.03: prayer, praise, thanksgiving, witness and service; ELCF: Catechism (2000) 84: prayer.

[219] UMCNEAE: BOD, Const., Preamble: 'Under the discipline of the Holy Spirit the church seeks to provide for the maintenance of worship [and] the edification of believers'; MCGB: CPD, SO 332: 'liturgy'.

[220] UMCNEAE: BOD, par. 103, AR, Art. XIII, Public Worship; MCGB: CPD, SO 569: 'creative and culturally appropriate ways ... to meet with God in worship'; FMCNA: BOD, AR, 122: 'According to the Word of God and the custom of the early church, public worship ... should be in a language understood by the people.'

[221] MCI: RDG, 3.02: 'The usual order of public worship' consists of: the Preparation (with prayers of adoration and confession); Ministry of the Word (with OT and NT readings); Sermon; Prayers; Hymns; FMCNA: PACLM, II, Responsibilities of the Call, 2: 'In worship the church gives praise to God, pleads with Him for mercy and receives the grace God mediates to His people. The elder leads [in] adoration and petition of God.'

[222] UMCNEAE: BOD, pars. 201 and 401; FMCNA: PACLM, I.1: the 'central activity of God's people'.

[223] MCI: RDG, 3.01: 'The means of grace ... include: (a) public worship and the Sacraments, (b) meetings for fellowship, prayer and Bible study, (c) family worship, (d) individual Bible study and prayer.'

[224] MCI: RDG, 10.04: 'every congregation is to glorify God through its worship and its witness'.

Presbyterian laws are equally rich on this subject. For example, the Presbyterian Church of Wales holds: 'Our purpose is to worship God and spread the Gospel of the Lord Jesus Christ as it is revealed in the Holy Scriptures and expounded in our doctrinal standards, by establishing and maintaining fellowships of people worshipping God and believing in the Lord Jesus Christ under the guidance of the Holy Spirit.'[225] Thus: 'The means of grace in a worshipping community are the reading of the Scriptures, prayer, the singing of hymns, the preaching and hearing of the Word and the administration and receiving of the sacraments. The regular use of these means is a duty to God and a necessity of the Christian life.'[226] In turn, there are 'principles and elements of public worship' and worship itself must be scriptural.[227] The Presbyterian Church in America is typical: 'Since the Holy Scriptures are the only infallible rule of faith and practice, the principles of public worship must be derived from the Bible, and from no other source'; as such: 'The Scriptures forbid the worshipping of God by images, or in any other way not appointed in His Word, and requires the receiving, observing, and keeping pure and entire all such religious worship and ordinances as God hath appointed in His Word.'[228] Moreover: 'A service of public worship is not merely a gathering of God's children with each other, but before all else, a meeting of the triune God with His chosen people. God is present in publish worship.'[229] Indeed: 'The end of public worship is the glory of God. His people should engage in all its several parts with an eye single to His glory'; it has as its aim 'the building of Christ's Church by the perfecting of the saints and the addition to its membership of such as are being saved – all to the glory of God'; in worship of the Lord's Day Christians 'should learn to serve God all the days of the week'.[230] Moreover: 'The Bible teaches that the following are proper elements of worship: reading of Holy Scripture, singing of psalms and hymns, the offering of prayer, the preaching of the Word, the presentation of offerings, confessing the faith and observing the Sacraments; and on special occasions taking oaths'.[231] Other Reformed churches follow this pattern.[232]

---

[225] PCW: HOR, 1.1. See also PCANZ: Directory of Worship, Preface: this 'reflects the conviction that the life of the Church is one, and that its worship, witness, and service are inseparable'.
[226] PCW: HOR, 2.1.
[227] See e.g. PCANZ: Directory of Worship, 1.1.1: 'The core of worship is God acting to give God's life to humankind and to bring humankind to partake of that life. Christian worship involves God's self-revelation and human response enabled by God. At the centre of both is Jesus Christ who reveals God to us and through whom we make our response'; 1.1.5: in worship: 'The people of God respond with words and deeds of praise and thanksgiving in acts of prayer, proclamation, remembrance, and offering. In the name of Christ, by the power of the Holy Spirit, the Christian community worships and serves God.'
[228] PCA: BCO, 47.1.
[229] PCA: BCO, 47.2: 'The Lord Jesus Christ said: "Where two or three are gathered together in my name there I am in the midst of them" (Matthew 18.20).'
[230] PCA: BCO, 47.3; 47.4: public worship is Christian when worshippers recognise Christ as Mediator by whom alone they can come to God; 47.5: it must be performed 'in spirit and in truth' without 'externalism and hypocrisy'; 47.8: people should come to worship with a deep sense of awe at His perfectness.
[231] PCA: BCO, 47.9; 48.1: the 'sanctification of the Lord's Day'.
[232] URC: Man., A.25: 'worship of the local church is an expression of the worship of the whole people of God'.

The development of forms of service

Given the importance of worship in ecclesial life, and the link between worship and doctrine (in so far as the former expresses the latter), it is not surprising that the development of liturgical texts or other forms of service is a matter regulated by substantial bodies of rules. Once more, there is considerable convergence between the traditions, but differences in terms of the authorities involved in the approval of such texts. Roman Catholic canon law provides for the formation of liturgical texts and authority over these vests in the Pontiff. The local ordinary must attest that reprinting and translation of liturgical books correspond with editions approved by Rome; it is for the Apostolic See to order the sacred liturgy of the universal church and 'publish the liturgical books [and] review their translations into vernacular languages'; the Conference of Bishops may prepare both translations and particular ritual texts adopted to local needs and to publish them with the prior review (*recognitio*) of the Holy See.[233] The Church has a range of texts for use on different occasions, such as celebration of the sacraments; the principal liturgies are in the Roman Missal (1969), Roman Ritual (1969–1984) and Roman Pontifical (1968–1984).[234]

In the Orthodox tradition, as a basic principle, liturgy is as prescribed by the Apostolic Faith; thus, 'worship' is that 'of the One, Holy, Catholic and Apostolic Church as taught by the Holy Scriptures [and] Holy Tradition'.[235] Typically, an assembly of bishops has responsibility for the 'approval of the liturgical offices and rites' of the church,[236] and may set up commissions or other bodies for 'the preservation of the texts of the liturgical books, their amendment, editing and publishing' as well as 'the production of church utilities, candles, vestments and all other necessary items for maintaining the liturgical tradition, beauty and good order of the churches'.[237] For example, the Holy Synod of the Romanian Orthodox Church 'initiates, authorises and supervises the translation, correction and distribution of ... the books of rite'; it has a Theological, Liturgical and Didactical Commission which assists in this regard – however, the Conference of Priests and Deacons may suggest liturgical developments, and the Metropolitan Synod considers requests from the eparchies as to changes in liturgical texts.[238] Similarly, the Standing Conference of the Canonical Orthodox Bishops in the Americas has a Committee on

---

[233] CIC, c. 826: local ordinary; c. 838.2: Apostolic See; 838.3: Conference of Bishops; c. 455.2.

[234] Many liturgies were prepared by the Council for the Implementation of the Constitution on the Liturgy (1964) and promulgated by Pope Paul VI, in the decrees of the Congregation of Sacred Rites (until 1969), subsequently by the Sacred Congregation for Divine Worship (1969–1975) and latterly by the Sacred Congregation for the Sacraments and Divine Worship. See e.g. Rite of Marriage (1969), Rite of Baptism for Children (1969), Rite of Funerals (1969), Rite of Religious Profession (1970), Rite of Anointing and Pastoral Care of the Sick (1972), Holy Communion and Worship of the Eucharist Outside Mass (1973), Rite of Penance (1973), Rite of Ordination (1968), Rite of Institution of Readers and Acolytes etc. (1972): see NCCC 596.

[235] UOCIA: Statutes, Preamble; ROMOC: Statutes, Art. 2: 'liturgical ... unity with the ... Orthodox Church'.

[236] ROC: Statute, II.5(b): Bishops' Council; III.4(d)-(e): Holy Synod.   [237] ROC: Statute, V.28.

[238] ROMOC: Statutes, Art. 14(x): Holy Synod; Art. 15: the Commission; Art. 113(b): the Metropolitan Synod 'analyses and approves requests from the eparchies' as to 'projects of liturgical texts' and submits these to the Holy Synod; Art. 140: Conferences of Priests and Deacons engage in 'improvement in the liturgical' field.

Standardized Liturgical Texts,[239] and the Patriarch of the Syrian Orthodox Church of Antioch has 'the right to examine, correct, scrutinize, eliminate or introduce new church rites', as well as the right to publish liturgical texts.[240]

Liturgical revision and the development of forms of service are the subject of substantial regulation in Anglicanism. Whilst the Book of Common Prayer 1662 is the normative standard for liturgy, a church may make such revisions, adaptations and innovations in the forms of service as are desirable to adapt to particular needs and circumstances. A church may have a commission or other body to prepare, advise on and recommend liturgical adaptation and innovation. However, it belongs to the central church assembly to approve, amend, continue or discontinue forms of service.[241] There are limits on the power of liturgical revision. A form of service must be neither contrary to, nor indicative of a departure from, the doctrine of the church in any essential matter, nor inconsistent with the Word of God and the spirit and teaching of the Book of Common Prayer 1662. It is also for the central church assembly to approve new forms of service for experimental use, during such period and subject to such conditions as may be prescribed by law, which use in a diocese may be authorised by its bishop.[242] The bishop may authorise for a diocese variations, adjustments or substitutes for or additions to any part of a liturgical text under trial use to the extent permitted by law. If permitted by law, a bishop or other ecclesiastical body may also authorise services for use in a diocese, for which no provision already exists. However, no minister in a parish or other local unit may formulate or use a form of service for which no provision exists in authorised service books without lawful authority.[243] Forms of service must be in a language understood by the people. Local customs may be followed in the matter of posture, whether of standing, kneeling or sitting, at the time of public worship. Also, all persons present should pay reverent attention at the time of divine worship, give due reverence to the name of the Lord Jesus and stand at the Creed and reading of the Gospel at the Holy Communion.[244]

There are similarly complex provisions applicable to the development of worship texts in Protestantism. Within Lutheranism, the Lutheran Church in Australia is 'to cultivate uniformity in worship, ecclesiastical practice and customs in accord with the principles ... in the Formula of Concord'.[245] However: 'Christ did not command and establish a particular order or pattern of worship [but] He did ... give clear directives on the constant and essential features of Christian worship', namely, 'baptism, confession and absolution, reading and preaching the word, prayer, and the sacrament of the altar' – these essential elements have been

---

[239] SCOBA: Const., IV.2.   [240] SOCA: Const., Art. 19.
[241] PCLCCAC, Principle 55.1-4. See e.g. Melanesia: Const., Art. 5: the General Synod has 'the power to authorise forms of worship for the whole province' and these must not conflict with the standards of faith.
[242] PCLCCAC, Principle 55.5-6. See e.g. England: Church of England (Worship and Doctrine) Measure 1974: General Synod; Scotland: Can. 22.4: the College of Bishops may authorise services for experimental use.
[243] PCLCCAC, Principle 55.7-9. See e.g. West Indies: Can. 31.2: the diocesan bishop may authorise services not provided for by the Provincial Synod.
[244] PCLCCAC, Principle 54.8-10. E.g. Philippines: Cans. II.4.4: language; England: Can. B6(1): attentiveness.
[245] LCA: Const., Art. III; see also Art. X.

'divinely-instituted'.[246] Thus, Orders of Worship act 'as confessions of the faith' and highlight 'the presence and work of the Triune God in the means of grace'. Therefore, they should: (1) 'be consistent with the truth of God's word and the teaching of the gospel'; (2) 'use the words of the Holy Scriptures'; (3) express 'the teaching of the Lutheran Church, for correct doctrine defines what is correct in worship'; (4) be faithful to 'the catholic tradition of the church';[247] (5) be 'culturally appropriate and ... use ways of communication and expression which people can readily appreciate and understand'; and (6) provide 'a framework for each person to respond to God's presence and grace, as led by the Holy Spirit, in corporate adoration, confession, dedication, thanksgiving, praise, petition, and intercession'.[248] These 'forms for public worship regulate the corporate activity of the congregation', and the approval of new forms of worship vests in the General Convention.[249] Methodist churches also have designated books of worship and hymnals.[250] These are formulated and approved at central level by the Conference,[251] which may be assisted by various boards.[252] Provision is also made for

[246] LCA: ALATW: this cites AC 7, 15, 16:40–45: a distinction is made between the essentials of worship (divinely instituted), and non-essentials (*adiaphora*) which have been neither commanded nor forbidden (AC 28:54ff; FC SD X.8ff). See also ELCSA: G., 2.2: the main components of the divine service are the liturgical prayers, proclamation of the Gospel and Sacraments (Acts 2.42). Through hymns, antiphony and prayers the congregation expresses thanks for the grace with which the Lord accepts the sinner; in the Creed it confesses its faith in God; through Old Testament readings and sermon, it learns what God does and expects; in the Sacrament it participates in the Glory of its Lord; the Lord's Prayer sums up all prayers and unites all Christians; with the blessing it is equipped to witness and sent out into the world (Numbers 6.24–26).
[247] LCA: ALATW; this cites e.g. LLC I, 92ff, FC SD X, 5ff, AC 24:1–3.
[248] LCA: ALATW; this cites e.g. FC SD X.9ff, AC 15, 26:40, 28:53.
[249] LCA: Resolution 269 of the 1987 General Convention, Order with Holy Communion; Service with Communion, The Service – Alternative Form (trial use), Liturgy in Modern Form (Worship Today); Rationale for the Synodical Decision on the Use of Approved Orders with Holy Communion, Commission on Worship, 1987, revised 1998, edited 2001: 'pastors and congregations shall normally use the above ... orders'; this 'does not refer to other acts of worship which congregations ... may wish to conduct. Nor ... to special services and extraordinary situations that may call for adaptation'; Guidelines for Services on Special Occasions, Department of Liturgics, adopted by the Commission on Worship 1993, adopted 1998, edited 2001.
[250] MCI: RDG, 3.02: the Methodist Hymn Book (1933), Hymns and Psalms (1983), Revised Common Lectionary (1992), Book of Offices (1936) and Methodist Service Book (1975) are authorised for use; the Methodist Worship Book (1999) is recommended subject to approval of the Church Council; these 'shall be used for the administration of the Sacraments of Baptism and the Lord's Supper, and for the celebration of marriage'. Services include the Covenant Service on the first Sunday of the year.
[251] UMCNEAE: BOD, par. 1114: United Methodist Book of Worship (1992), United Methodist Hymnal (1989).
[252] MCI: RDG, 26.01: Conference annually appoints a Committee on Faith and Order to 'make recommendations concerning any proposed revisions in orders of worship'; MCNZ: LAR, s. 4.3: each Synod must foster worship; UMCNEAE: BOD, par. 1114: the General Board of Discipleship is to: 'cultivate the fullest possible meaning in ... corporate worship ... to the glory of God, including liturgy, preaching, the sacraments, music, related arts, and the observance of the liturgical seasons of the Christian year'; develop 'standards and resources for the conduct of public worship'; and recommend to General Conference on 'a book of worship and a hymnal'.

THE NATURE OF WORSHIP AND THE FORMS OF WORSHIP   223

experimental services: for instance, the Methodist Church of Great Britain has a Faith and Order Committee which is 'authorised to make proposals to the Conference for the revision from time to time of the forms of service authorised by the Conference for use in the Methodist Church, and forms of worship intended for regular and general use in Methodist public worship shall be submitted to the Conference for approval after a period of experimentation on the recommendation of the committee'.[253]

The Presbyterian approach to worship texts is similar: 'Christ has prescribed no fixed forms for public worship but, in the interest of life and power in worship, has given His Church large measure of liberty in this matter'; but 'the rules of God's Word', decency, order, reverence, beauty, simplicity and dignity should be observed as 'a manifestation of holiness'.[254] The Church of Scotland is typical: 'There is no prescribed liturgy in the Church of Scotland, and ministers enjoy considerable freedom in matters of worship'; rather, the principles of worship are in accordance with the Directory for the Public Worship of God 1645 as that 'has been or may hereafter be modified by Acts of the General Assembly or by consuetude'.[255] It is the General Assembly, therefore, that may commend forms of service – but these are not 'regulative' as such.[256] This is typical: a General Assembly may 'superintend matters which concern ... worship ... [and] declare the mind of the Church thereupon',[257] and 'make rules for ... worship ... which must be agreeable to the doctrines relating thereto contained in the Scriptures'.[258] A Directory of Worship sets out the 'order of worship' – it is not of itself a service book, but suggests possibilities for 'Reformed worship';[259] it is 'an approved guide and should be taken seriously as the mind of the Church agreeable to the Standards. However, it does not have the force of law and is not considered obligatory in all its parts'.[260] Plurality in the forms of

---

[253] MCGB: CPD, SO 330.   [254] PCA: BCO 4.7.6.
[255] CLCS: 29; Church of Scotland Act 1921, Sch., Articles Declaratory, Art. II.
[256] CLCS: 30: however, successive books of Common Order 'have been "authorised" by the Assembly ... In accordance with the principles of the Directory, they are not regulative, although they contain valuable material, worthy of use, with or without modification, in a Church which is both catholic and reformed'. See also PCW: HOR 9: the Book of Services includes e.g. the Lord's Supper, Baptism, Confirmation, Marriage and Funerals.
[257] PCI: Code, 104. See also PCW: HOR 3.4.2: the General Assembly is responsible for 'Praise'; 3.4.4: services at General Assembly meetings; 10: this contains the structure for the services of e.g. ordination and induction.
[258] PCA: BCO, 11.2; 50.1: public reading of the Holy Scriptures is performed by a minister and through it 'God speaks most directly to the congregation, even more directly than through sermons'.
[259] PCANZ: BO, 1.1(5); Directory of Worship (1995) sets out 'the order of worship'; Preface: 'A Directory for Worship is not a service book' but 'describes the theology that underlies Reformed worship and outlines appropriate forms for that worship', 'suggests possibilities for worship, invites development in worship, and encourages continuing reform of worship', 'sets standards and ... norms for the conduct of worship in the life of congregations and the courts'; 'As the constitutional document ordering ... worship ... this Directory ... shall be authoritative'; see also BO, 14.2(1): a primary function of the General Assembly is 'to worship God' and 'to facilitate and resource the life, worship and spiritual nature of the Church'.
[260] PCA: Directory of Worship, Preface. See also CLCS 28: the Directory for the Public Worship of God provides for 'such things as are of divine institution in every ordinance' and 'other things ... set forth according to the rules of Christian prudence, agreeable to the general rules of the word of God; our meaning therein being only, that the general heads, the sense and

service is sometimes explicitly justified: 'it has not been considered necessary for the churches to confine themselves to any one form of service. In the past the Connexion has found that many forms of service have been a source of blessing. But the form of service used should be determined by the minister of the congregation. Let all things be done for love, for edification, with decorum and in order.'[261] Moreover, worship must be in a language which is understood by the participants in it.[262] Similar provisions are found in United, Reformed and Congregational churches.[263]

The administration of worship

The regulatory instruments of all the Christian traditions studied here deal with the provision of worship as a public facility, the conduct of worship and use of authorised forms of service, the duty of Christians to participate in worship (especially on Sunday) and the oversight of worship by a designated authority (from a bishop to a Presbytery); some churches also deal with the use of music in worship. According to Roman Catholic canon law, in order to be considered as liturgy, worship takes place when it is carried out in the name of the church by persons lawfully deputed and through acts approved by the authority of the church; 'the faithful are deputed by the baptismal character to the worship of the Christian religion'; and liturgy is conducted under the presidency of the ordained ministers.[264] The supervision of the sacred liturgy depends solely on the authority of the church: liturgical supervision resides in the Pontiff and, in accord with the law, the diocesan bishop, who has power to issue liturgical norms by which all the faithful are bound.[265] The liturgical books approved by competent authority are to be faithfully observed in the celebration of the sacraments; therefore no one on personal authority may add, remove or change anything in them.[266] However, as liturgical law exists to facilitate worship, it should be applied flexibly, offering choices and options – liturgical norms are treated as 'aesthetic norms' which may be relaxed in order to allow an authentic worship of God according to the community's needs.[267] The diocesan bishop must supervise liturgical discipline and may dispense with the requirements of

---

scope of the prayers, and other parts of public worship ... may be a consent of all the churches in those things that contain the substance of the service and worship of God'.

[261] PCW: HOR, 9.

[262] PCANZ: DOW, 1.2.2; PCA: BCO, 52.3: 'All prayer is to be offered in the language of the people.'

[263] UCOC: Const., Art. V.18: the local church has 'the right to retain or adopt its own methods of ... worship'; UCA: BL 2.12.13: a community minister is commissioned 'according to a form of service authorised by the Assembly'; UCC: B: 505(a): General Council legislates on worship; UCA: Regs., 3.6.5: the Assembly 'may approve orders of service for general use within the Church and make prescriptions in particular cases'.

[264] CIC, c. 834.2; LG 11. See also CCEO c. 656: only approved books may be used in liturgy.

[265] CIC, c. 838; SC 22.   [266] CIC, c. 846.

[267] CCLTC, 595: 'liturgical celebrations ... are matters of the most intimate faith and piety ... The norms that govern them are more aesthetic and artistic than juridic ... The renewed tone and spirit that infuse them ... and the relative weight of their demands in the face of conflicting pastoral expectations have led to a legitimate openness, a recognition of the religious value of diversity, and an invitation to cultural and other adaptation'.

universal and particular liturgical law in this regard; but a minister cannot unilaterally dispense with liturgical laws, though some writers stress that a governing principle is the *de minimis* rule and the directory rather than mandatory nature of liturgical law.[268]

Much the same pertains in the Orthodox Church. Parishioners are to 'faithfully attend the Divine Liturgy and other worship services' and 'participate regularly in the holy sacraments'.[269] Only the ordained clergy may administer the liturgy.[270] Oversight of worship is in the keeping of the bishop. The Russian Orthodox Church is typical: 'The Diocesan Bishop shall enjoy the fullness of hierarchical authority in matters of ... religious rites' and shall 'supervise the correct celebration of the divine services and preservation of church beauty'.[271] Beneath the bishop, the dean has 'supervision over the correct and regular celebration of the divine services'.[272] In the parish, the rector is responsible for: 'the correct celebration of the divine services in accordance with the Statute of the Church'; the availability of 'all objects necessary for the divine services in accordance with the requirements of the liturgical rubrics and instruction of the Church authorities'; the 'correct and reverential reading and singing in the church'; and the maintenance of 'a liturgical journal'.[273] Moreover: 'A clergyman may take part in the celebration of a divine service in another parish with the consent of the Diocesan Bishop of the diocese in which this parish is located, or with the consent of the dean or the rector.'[274] Indeed, the Orthodox Church in America provides: 'No-one may schedule any liturgical service without the approval of the rector of the parish' and 'No-one may invite any clergy to participate in a liturgical service without the approval of the rector'.[275] Within the service, clergy must comply with the rubrics of liturgical books, but may vary the text if permitted by the local hierarch: 'In all holy services, the clergy are to follow the order and rubrics prescribed by the service books approved for use in the Church'; 'Any departure from the usual order or rubrics must meet with the specific approval of the diocesan hierarch.'[276] There are elaborate provisions on sacred objects for divine services,[277] the wearing of clerical vestments,[278] commemoration of hierarchs in

---

[268] CIC, cc. 87–88: dispensation (see also c. 392.2); c. 89: ministerial compliance.
[269] GOAA: Regs., Art. 18.1; ROMOC: Statutes, Art. 45: the faithful are to participate in religious services; Art. 67: a Parish Committee must encourage participation of school pupils in the Divine Liturgy and other services.
[270] OCIA: GC, Divine Services, 1: 'Only a canonically ordained clergyman can perform holy services. He must not be under suspension or excommunication by his hierarch or by his own sins. He must be properly prepared, spiritually and physically, for divine worship.'
[271] ROC: Statute, X.11: hierarchical authority; 18(b): liturgical supervision.
[272] ROC: Statute, X.52(b).
[273] ROC: Statute, XI.19 and 20; see also 27: parish clergy must discharge their liturgical duties.
[274] ROC: Statute, XI.29. See also OCIA: GC, Priests and Deacons, 14.
[275] OCIA: GC, The Laity, 1 and 2; 10: ministry to those 'unable to attend the Divine Services regularly'.
[276] OCIA: GC, Divine Services, 6.
[277] ROC: Statute, XI.43 and 46: the Parish Meeting and Council ensure availability of 'all objects necessary for the canonical celebration of the divine services' and attend to 'church singing'; MOSC: Const., 2.44.
[278] SOCA: Const., Arts. 125–131: vestments of the patriarch, metropolitans, archpriests, priests and monks.

the Divine Liturgy,[279] the consecration of places of worship[280] and the personal preparation of a cleric for the administration of worship.[281] Failure to observe the rules applicable to worship may result in disciplinary proceedings.[282]

Liturgical administration is also regulated in Anglicanism. A minister must use in public worship only those forms of service authorised or otherwise permitted by lawful authority. A church may require uniformity of a single liturgical use throughout that church or conformity with a number of alternative services. However, liturgical life should be characterised by flexibility (as authorised by law). Appropriate patterns of worship may vary from place to place, and time to time, and ministers may use their own sensitivity and discretion to conduct worship so the faithful participate with sincerity and understanding. A minister may make variations in an authorised form of service which are lawful, reverent and seemly and not contrary to the doctrine of the church. Rubrics or other liturgical directions are to be interpreted and applied flexibly to meet local circumstances, practices and needs. Questions of liturgical variation may be referred to the bishop to permit, advise or direct as appropriate. Failure to use the authorised forms of service or otherwise to conduct public worship lawfully may result in disciplinary action.[283] In each parish there should be a place for worship led by the clergy (sharing functions with lay people where lawful) unless hindered by lawful cause. A minister should prepare services thoughtfully, carefully, and collaboratively, considering the needs of the locality and people, especially those who are disabled or disadvantaged.[284] The right to supervise the conduct of public worship in a parish vests in the member of clergy responsible for that parish. No minister, lay or ordained, from another parish or diocese may conduct divine services publicly within a parish without the prior consent of its clergy. The oversight of public worship in the diocese is

---

[279] ROMOC: Statutes, Art. 245.2: 'According to the Holy Canons, the pan-Orthodox tradition and the practice of the [ROMOC], the patriarch is remembered at the religious services by the metropolitans', the metropolitan by hierarchs, and these by priests; GOAA: Const., Art. 8; OCIA: GC, Divine Services, 19: this is a 'custom'.

[280] OCIA: GC, Divine Services, 9: 'Divine Liturgy is normally celebrated in a consecrated temple'; however: 'In the case of a specific necessity, [it] may be celebrated outdoors or in a suitable place ... only with the blessing of the diocesan hierarch. Before the celebration of the Divine Liturgy, the site must be blessed with holy water'; GOAA: Const., Art. 7.3: the metropolitan is to 'consecrate and sanctify for worship churches and chapels'.

[281] OCIA: GC, Divine Services, 2-4: 'At Divine Liturgy the clergyman, like each Christian person, must be at peace with all people' and 'harbour no anger, resentment, or ill will against anyone'; thus, he must fast from the previous evening, and administer the Vigil (or, at least, Vespers) and the other requisite prayers.

[282] See above Chapter 5.

[283] PCLCCAC, Principle 56.1-9. See e.g. England: Can. B1, C15: '[e]very minister shall use only the forms of service authorised'; Burundi: Const., Art. 3: '[t]he aim ... is to have, as far as possible, one single liturgical model for the whole Province'; Australia: Can. P6 1992: '[t]he minister may make and use variations which are not of substantial importance in any form of service ... according to the particular circumstances'.

[284] PCLCCAC, Principle 57.1-4; public worship may be dispensed with for reasonable cause; 58: alternative services; 59: sharing functions with the laity. See e.g. Japan: Const., Art. 2: 'In each Parish there shall be a stated place of worship in which the Priest ... regularly conducts Common Prayer, administers the Sacraments, and performs other Rites and Ceremonies of the Church with the participation of the Laity.'

subject to the general direction of the bishop.[285] The bishop has authority to order liturgy and public worship within the diocese and to prohibit any unlawful practice.[286] Any minister who fails to provide public worship, to administer the sacraments or to use lawful liturgical ritual or ceremonial, according to the order and use of a church, may be the subject of disciplinary proceedings in the church courts or tribunals.[287]

The basic elements of Catholic, Orthodox and Anglican laws are repeated in Lutheranism and Methodism. The congregation is to ensure the provision of public worship,[288] the minister is responsible for the conduct of services in accordance with the forms of service permitted by the church,[289] and the faithful should attend divine service, particularly on Sundays.[290] For example, members of the Evangelical Lutheran Church in Canada are 'to be constant in worship and in the study of the Holy Scriptures, regularly nourishing their life in Christ in the Sacrament of the Altar'.[291] Those who fail to participate in regular worship may be removed from the membership roll.[292] Methodist law is the same.[293] Typically: 'Divine worship shall be held regularly in all Churches and preaching places on the Lord's Day, or as may be otherwise arranged and shall be conducted according to the established forms and usages of Methodism'; moreover: 'The Festivals of the Christian Year, such as the season of Lent and Easter, Ascension Day, Pentecost, Trinity Sunday, the season

---

[285] PCLCCAC, Principle 59. See e.g. Southern Africa: Can. 24: 'Incumbents are recognized as leaders . . . for the oversight of the Pastoral Charges . . . in regard to . . . liturgical worship, under the authority of the bishop.'

[286] PCLCCAC, Principle 60.1-2. See e.g. Ireland: Const., IX.2: '[it] shall be competent for the ordinary to restrain and prohibit in the conduct of public worship any practice not enjoined in the Book of Common Prayer, or in any rubric or canon enacted by lawful authority of the Church of Ireland'.

[287] PCLCCAC, Principle 60.3-6. See e.g. New Zealand: Cans. D.II.2: it is an offence to '[r]efuse or neglect to use' either the Book of Common Prayer or a New Zealand Prayer Book, 'or other services authorised', or to administer the sacraments as authorised 'except so far as shall be otherwise ordered by lawful authority'.

[288] ELCIC: Const., Art. VI.3; ELCA: Const., Ch. 8.12, 9.10-11; LCGB: RAR, Definition of a Congregation, 2: a congregation is to '[p]rovide services of worship at which the Word of God is preached'.

[289] ELCSA: G., 2.6: 'As a rule the service is conducted by an ordained minister' but it may 'be conducted by a lay preacher'; LCA: General Convention, Res. 269, 1987: 'pastors and congregations shall normally use the . . . specified orders for the corporate celebration of the Lord's Supper'.

[290] ELCSA: G., 2.4: one who fails to worship 'forfeits the blessing of the communion with Christ and the congregation'; one prevented due to illness or duties may know he is 'united with the congregation through prayer'; 2.3: 'the main service of the week takes place on a Sunday morning in commemoration of the resurrection of the Lord'; 2.8: week-day and other services; ELCA: Const., Ch. 9.41: the congregation shall 'Provide services of worship at which the Word of God is preached and sacraments . . . administered'.

[291] ELCIC: Const., Art. V.

[292] LCGB: RAR, Individual Membership in a Congregation, 2: the congregation council may remove the names of those 'who have not supported the life and worship of the congregation over a significant period of time'.

[293] MCI: RDG, 10.06: the Church Council oversees the work of God, 'including . . . Arrangements for worship'.

of Advent, and Christmas Day shall be observed.'[294] Ordained ministers are to conduct public worship but lay speakers may be appointed to assist.[295] Also: 'No pastor shall hold a religious service within the bounds of a pastoral charge other than the one to which appointed without the consent of the pastor of the charge, or the district superintendent'.[296] There is provision for an Annual Covenant Service,[297] and for the discontinuance of public worship.[298] Methodists must attend upon all 'the public worship of God', the 'ministry of the Word … read or expounded', the Lord's Supper, and family and private prayer;[299] or else: 'All members are expected to attend the means of grace, especially the ministry of the Word, united prayer, and the Sacrament of the Lord's Supper.'[300] Private family worship is also commended.[301] The Lord's Day is divinely ordained for private and public worship, rest from unnecessary work, spiritual improvement, Christian fellowship and service.[302] Oversight of worship is provided e.g. by district superintendents who must ensure that public worship is conducted properly.[303] Also: 'no person is permitted to preach on or from Church property who maintains, promulgates or teaches any doctrine or practice which is contrary to what is contained in the Standard Sermons of John Wesley and his Notes on the New Testament'.[304]

Whilst a Presbyterian Directory of Worship sets out the forms of services, the Kirk Session is to 'fix the time and place for the administration of the ordinances of the Church';[305] the Minister is responsible for the conduct of services (including

---

[294] MCNZ: LAR, s. 1.5.1–3: 'Suitable mid-week services and prayer meetings shall be arranged … as found practicable. Open-air Services shall be held [if] practicable in order to reach non-attendants.'

[295] MCNZ: LAR, s. 3.4: a Leaders' Meeting is to 'share responsibility with the minister(s) appointed to the Parish serving that congregation for worship'; MCGB: CPD, SO 700–7001; UMCNEAE: BOD, par. 266: lay speakers may 'conduct, or assist in conducting, services of worship, and present sermons and addresses when requested by the pastor, district superintendent, or committee on lay speaking'.

[296] UMCNEAE: BOD, par. 341; MCGB: CPD, SO 631(1): class leaders and worship.

[297] MCGB: CPD, SO 608: 'An annual covenant service shall normally be held in every Local Church.'

[298] MCI: RDG, 4A.04: discontinuance of Sunday services may be permitted by the District Synod.

[299] UMCNEAE: BOD, par. 103, General Rules of the Methodist Church; par. 214: 'All people may attend its worship services [and] receive the sacraments'; par. 218: 'members involve themselves in private and public prayer, worship, the sacraments'; MCI: RDG, 1.01: the duty to attend.

[300] MCI: RDG, 2.06.

[301] MCI: RDG, 3.07: 'Regular and reverent family worship and the saying of grace before meals are encouraged in all homes' and in 'regular reading of and meditation on Scripture and in private prayer'.

[302] UMCNEAE: BOD, par. 103, AR, Art. XIV: 'It is commemorative of our Lord's resurrection and is an emblem of our eternal rest. It is essential to the permanence and growth of the Christian Church, and important to the welfare of the civil community'; MCGB: CPD, SO 609: 'acts of worship' in residential and nursing homes; FMCNA: BOD 3121: 'God makes clear in Scripture by both example and command that one day in seven is to be devoted to worship and rest (Genesis 2.2–3; Exodus 20.8–11).'

[303] MCI: RDG, 4A.04: the District superintendent is 'to see that public worship is conducted … as provided for in the Circuit plan'; UMCNEAE: BOD, par. 403: the bishop guards liturgy.

[304] MCNZ: LAR, s. 3.5.

[305] PCA: BCO, 4.4 and 12.5: the Session exercises 'authority over the time and place of the preaching of the Word and the administration of the Sacraments'; PCANZ: BO, 7.2: the church

the selection of Scripture to be read),[306] and in so doing must 'observe the order and administration of public worship';[307] and the Presbytery oversees the proper administration of worship: 'the supervision of worship being a function of presbyteries, they are to enjoin the discontinuance, or prohibit the introduction of any novel practice in worship which is inconsistent with the laws and usages of the Church, or a cause of division in a congregation, or unfit from any cause to be used in the worship of God'.[308] Presbyterian laws also require the faithful to attend worship, to participate in it fully, and to set aside Sunday particularly. The law of the Presbyterian Church in America has particularly well-developed provisions on these matters: 'When the congregation is to meet for public worship, the people (having before prepared their hearts thereto) ought all to come and join therein; not absenting themselves from the public ordinances through negligence, or upon pretence of private meetings'.[309] Moreover, the people should 'unite with one heart in all parts of public worship' (and not depart until the blessing is pronounced); they should take their seats in 'a decent and reverent manner, and engage in a silent prayer'. All those who attend are expected 'to be present in a spirit of reverence and godly fear, forbearing to engage in any conduct unbecoming to the place and occasion'; it is important that families worship together as 'the basic institution in society'.[310] Congregations without ministers or in remote places must also assemble for worship,[311] and Presbyterian ministers, like their Episcopal counterparts, may confer a benediction.[312]

---

council must 'fix the times and places of public worship' and ensure 'leadership in worship, provide for the celebration of the sacraments [and] that the minister or local ministry team has final authority as to who preaches and conducts worship'.

[306] PCI: Code, 37: 'In the conduct of services and any invitation to occupy the pulpit the minister is responsible to the Presbytery, not to the Kirk Session'; CLCS: 30: a minister must enable participation of the laity in parts of the service; PCANZ: BO, 6.3(1): a minister provides 'leadership in worship' and 'preaches the Word, ensures that the Scriptures are read, presides at the sacraments, conducts public worship, [and] oversees hymns and music'; DOW, 2.2: a minister ensures 'over a period of time the people will hear the full message of Scripture'.

[307] PCANZ: BO, 1.7.

[308] CLCS: 30 and Act VII, 1866; PCANZ: BO, 84.(3): Presbytery must ensure that 'in its primary function of facilitating the worship of the congregations' the Scriptures are read; PCI: Code, 19.2: 'Each congregation and each member ... in all matters of ... worship ... is under the immediate jurisdiction of the Kirk Session.'

[309] PCA: BCO, 49.1. See also PCANZ: BO, 5.2(1): a congregation is 'to worship God'; 4.6: a congregation member must 'as far as he or she is able, join in the worship' (and mission) of the congregation.

[310] PCA: BCO, 49.1–4. See also PCANZ: BO, 4.2(2) and 4.6.

[311] PCA: BCO, 4.5: 'Churches without teaching elders ought not to forsake the assembling of themselves together, but should be convened by the Session on the Lord's Day, and at other times, for prayer, praise, the presenting and expounding of the Holy Scriptures, and exhortation, or the reading of a sermon of some approved minister. In like manner, Christians whose lot is cast in destitute regions ought to meet regularly for the worship of God.' See also PCANZ: DOW, 1.4.3: 'No-one shall be excluded from participation or leadership in public worship' on grounds of colour, disability etc; PCI: Code, II.6: members are 'to share faithfully in ... worship'.

[312] CLCS: 31: only a minister may close worship with a benediction; PCANZ: BO, 1416: the Moderator of the General Assembly is 'to open each sitting of the Assembly with prayer and close it with the benediction'.

Importantly, for American Presbyterianism, Sundays are kept for attendance at public worship (and private devotion) – this is a divine command; thus: 'It is the duty of every person to remember the Lord's Day; and to prepare for it before its approach. All worldly business should be so ordered, and seasonably laid aside, as that they may not be hindered thereby from sanctifying the Sabbath, as the Holy Scriptures require.' The 'whole day is to be kept to the Lord; and ... employed in the public and private exercises of religion', with rest from unnecessary labours and, 'as much as possible, from worldly thoughts and conversation'. Moreover: 'Let the time not used for public worship be spent in prayer, in devotional reading, and especially in the study of the Scriptures, meditation, catechising, religious conversation, the singing of psalms, hymns, or spiritual songs; visiting the sick, relieving the poor, teaching the ignorant, holy resting, and performing such like duties of piety, charity and mercy.'[313] United, Reformed, Congregational and Baptist norms also require the local church to provide for worship,[314] the conduct of services to be in line with the principles applicable to worship or the authorised services of the church,[315] for the faithful to attend worship (especially on the Lord's Day)[316] and for the supervision of worship.[317]

---

[313] PCA: BCO, 48: 'God commanded His ... people to keep holy the last day of the week, but he sanctified the first day of the Sabbath by the resurrection of ... Christ from the dead'; thus: 'the Church ... has from the time of the apostles kept holy the first day of the week as the Lord's Day'; 'Let ... support of the family on that day be so ordered that others be not ... detained from the public worship ... nor hindered from sanctifying the Sabbath'; let every person and family in the morning exercise 'secret and private prayer, for themselves and others' and read Scripture, engage in 'holy meditation' and prepare for 'communion with God in his public ordinances'. See also PCW: HOR, 3.4.4: the Department of Spirituality is to 'promote the various aspects of spirituality within the Church such as meditation, prayer and personal devotions'; PCANZ: DOW, 1.3.1: Sundays.

[314] RCA: BCO, Ch. 1, Pt. I, Art. 2.10: 'The consistory shall provide services of worship ... for the spiritual benefit and growth of Christ's people'; UFCS: MPP, I.III.2: the Session is 'in concurrence with the minister to regulate the hours and forms or modes of public worship'; UCA: Const., 4: the church is 'to provide for the worship of God'; BL 3.1.13: the Church Council assists the minister and determines 'the time and place of services of public worship'; UCC: BL 153: the Session oversees 'the order of public worship'; ABCUSA: TCOR, II.A.4: the congregation must maintain 'a worshipping ... fellowship'; Riverside Baptist Church (Baltimore): Const., Art. II: the church is 'to provide regular opportunities for public worship'.

[315] RCA: BCO, Ch. 1, Pt. I, Art. 2.11: 'worship ... shall be in accordance with the Liturgy ... or with the principles ... in the Directory of Worship, as the consistory may direct'; UCCP: Const., Art. V.4: a local church ensures worship is 'orderly and solemn yet joyful and meaningful'; BL Art. III.1: it must 'conduct its worship life in the light of the Gospel and in accordance with its witness and service to all of God's creation'; BL Art. II.13: a church worker, 'as a priest, [is] to intercede for the people and lead them in interceding before God for others'; BMPP, 219: SCBC, Type A, Art. VI.1: the pastor has 'charge ... of public worship'.

[316] UCCSA: Model Const., Art. 3; UCOC: Const., Art. V.11; UFCS: MPP, III.1.4: 'It is the duty of members to give faithful attendance on Gospel ordinances'. JBU: Const., Art. III: every disciple must engage 'in Family and Public Worship'; Riverside Baptist Church (Baltimore): Const., Art. IV: each member covenants 'to maintain family and secret devotions'; CNBC: Const., Art. 3: Statement of Faith VIII: the Lord's Day is 'a Christian institution for regular observance' commemorating the resurrection of Christ from the dead and 'should be employed in exercises of worship and spiritual devotion, both public and private, and by refraining from worldly amusements, and resting from secular employments, work of necessity and mercy only being expected'.

[317] RCA: BCO, Ch. 1, Pt. II, Art. 7.12: the classis president ensures regular services are held; URC: Man., B.2(2): the Elders' Meeting ensures 'public worship is regularly offered'; UCOC: Const.,

A codetta: all the traditions regulate the performance of music in worship. For the Catholic Church: 'The musical tradition of the universal Church is a treasure of inestimable value, greater even than that of any other art' – a combination of sacred music and words forms 'a necessary or integral part of solemn liturgy'. As such, texts to be sung must always be in conformity with Catholic doctrine and should be drawn chiefly from scripture and liturgical sources.[318] In Orthodoxy, the metropolitan is to have his *pheme* (anthem) chanted during the Divine Liturgy.[319] The bishop has oversight of singing in the parishes[320] and: 'The priest must ensure that the appropriate hymns and responses are sung during Divine Services in accordance with the Orthodox Tradition and by persons trained for the exercise of this ministry.' The choir director or cantor and choristers are directly responsible to the priest who should also encourage congregational singing under the leadership of a qualified cantor or musician.[321] Likewise, in Anglicanism, the officiating minister is responsible for music at public worship, should collaborate in this with the congregation, organist, choirmaster or other director of music, and take account of local custom. Chants, hymns, anthems and other settings must be appropriate, both in words and music, to the acts of worship and prayer as well as to the congregation, and must not be contrary to church doctrine but glorify God and help the people to worship. And disagreements about music may be referred to the bishop for resolution.[322] Lutheran congregations also participate in 'divine service through choir singing';[323] and Methodist Conferences are 'to provide and revise the hymnal and ritual of the Church and to regulate all matters relating to the form and mode of worship'.[324] Singing is equally an essential element in Presbyterian worship, but a choir should not displace the singing of a congregation;[325] and the Session has immediate oversight of it.[326]

Art. VI.28; Riverside Baptist Church (Baltimore): BL Art. III.3: the Worship Committee is 'responsible for oversight of the worship'; BUGB: MTC 2003, 5.1.1: property may be used as 'a place for public worship'.

[318] CCC, pars. 1156–1158.
[319] GOAA: Const., Art. 7.8; Regs., Art. 10.2; ROMOC: Statutes, Art. 52.4: 'church singers have the rights and duties stipulated in the Holy Canons', and e.g. eparchial regulations; Art. 71(g): vacancies in church singers; Art. 116: schools for church singers; Art. 150: the Disciplinary Consistory disciplines 'religious singers'.
[320] ROC: Statute, X.18.
[321] OCIA: GC, Priests and Deacons, 4 and 5. See also GOAA: Regs., Art. 19.2: parish choir.
[322] PCLCCAC, Principle 54.11–13. See e.g. England: Can. B20.
[323] ELCSA: G., 2.6: this also takes place in special youth and family services. LCMS: Const., Art. V. A and B: director of parish music. LCMS: Const., Art. VI; see also BL, 2: there must be an 'exclusive use of doctrinally pure ... hymnbooks, and catechisms in church and school'.
[324] UMCUSA: Const., Div. 2.2, Art. IV.16: the General Conference is to do so subject to the Restrictive Rules.
[325] PCA: BCO 4.4: prayer and singing praises is an ordinance of Christ; 51.1: 'Praising God through ... music is a duty and a privilege'; 'singing of hymns and psalms and the use of musical instruments should have an important part in public worship': PCA: BCO, 51.1; 51.2: the people are to sing 'in the spirit of worship, with understanding in [their] hearts'; 51.3: caution should be observed in hymns so that they are 'true to the Word'.
[326] PCA: BCO, 4.4, 12.5: the Session has authority 'over the music in the services', and 'oversight of the singing in the public worship of God'; 51.4: 'The leadership in song is left to the judgment of the Session, who should give careful thought to the character of those asked to lead in this part of worship, and the singing of a choir should not be allowed to displace congregational

Similar provisions are found in United, Reformed, Congregational and Baptist churches.[327]

Conclusion

The regulatory instruments of churches share much in common in terms of their treatment of doctrine and worship. Whilst differences exist with regard to the authority competent to regulate these matters, the profound similarities between the legal systems reveals the following principles of Christian law. The doctrine of the church is rooted in the revelation of God as recorded in Holy Scripture and expounded in texts and pronouncements issued by those with authority to teach. The doctrines of a church may be developed to the extent and in the manner prescribed by law provided that this accords with the apostolic faith of the church universal. The proclamation of the Word of God is a fundamental action of the church and a divine imperative incumbent on all the faithful. Consequently, the church is responsible for the instruction of the faithful and the evangelisation of the world. Each church should have in place institutions which facilitate mission. The faithful should believe the doctrine of the church and should not publicly manifest, in word or deed, a position which is contrary to the doctrine of the church – if they do so, disciplinary action may ensue. The worship of God is a fundamental action of the church and divinely instituted. Worship involves an intimate encounter between the church corporately and its individual members and the presence of God. Each church is competent to develop liturgical texts or other forms of service for the public worship of the faithful provided these are consistent with the Word of God. The church must provide for public worship. The ministers of the church are responsible for the conduct of public worship in accordance with the authorised forms of service. The faithful must engage in regular attendance at divine worship, particularly on the Lord's Day, Sunday. The administration of worship is subject to supervision by those authorities designated by law to provide this; and the performance of music is an essential feature of Christian worship.

---

singing'; 51.5: 'The proportion of the time of public worship given to praise [in music] is left to the judgment of the minister, and the singing of psalms and hymns by the congregation should be encouraged'; PCANZ: BO, 6.3(1): the minister 'oversees hymns and music for services of worship'; DOW, 2.1.2: 'Song unites the faithful in common prayer whenever they gather for worship'; this also deals with the use of a choir and instruments and supervision over these; PCI: Code, 37: the Kirk Session is responsible for 'the appointment of the organist, choirmaster and members of the choir'.

[327] RCA: BCO, Ch. 1, Pt. I, Art. 2.11: 'The hymns used in public worship shall be in harmony with the Standards' of RCA; Riverside Baptist Church (Baltimore): BL, Art. III.3: the Worship Committee is responsible for 'promotion of special music', and 'repair of all musical instruments'; it must: teach hymnody; provide music and musicians; lead persons to participate in hymn singing; train persons to lead, sing and play music.

7

The rites of passage

The rites of passage are those ceremonies which mark key stages in the spiritual life of the Christian. They are conducted in the context of worship in accordance with the liturgical and other forms of service authorised for use in the churches. Historically, different theological understandings of some of these rituals (especially Holy Communion) have caused division amongst Christians, particularly during the Reformation in the sixteenth century – and in part they continue to do so. This chapter compares the laws of churches with regard to the so-called rites of initiation – baptism and confirmation, and the Eucharist, Holy Communion or Lord's Supper. It also examines marriage (its formation and dissolution), confession and absolution, anointing the sick and dying, and funerals. All churches practise these rites of passage, but private confession and anointing are practised only in the Episcopal churches. What follows deals with: (1) the nature, purpose and effect of the rites; (2) prerequisites for admission to them in terms of rights and duties; (3) the preparation of candidates and others associated with their administration; (4) the conditions required for their valid celebration; and (5) the minister competent and responsible for their lawful administration. The chapter exposes differences and similarities from which it articulates principles of Christian law.

However, before taking each rite in turn, it is important to recognise the differences in approaches between the traditions in terms of the classification of some rites as sacraments. Catholics attribute the character of sacrament to seven rites: baptism, confirmation, Eucharist (the initiatory sacraments), marriage, confession, anointing and ordination. Instituted by Christ, sacraments are actions of the Church and of Christ, participation in them contributes to sanctification, and determining what constitutes valid sacraments rests with the supreme authority of the Church. The faithful have a right to the sacraments provided they seek them at the appropriate time, with the proper disposition, and are not prohibited by law from receiving them.[1] The Orthodox Church also recognises the sacraments as a means of grace,[2] as does Anglicanism, though canonically, only baptism and Eucharist are dominical sacraments ordained by Christ (each a visible sign of a

---

[1] CIC, cc. 840–841; cc. 213, 843: the right to them; c. 842: initiation; c. 845: no repetition; c. 846: sacramental law must be observed strictly; c. 848: no payment for them; cc. 834–839: sanctifying office; CCEO, cc. 667–670.

[2] SOCA: Const., Art. 148: 'Among the graces of God granted to the church are the seven Sacraments': baptism and chrismation, confession, Holy Communion, priesthood, matrimony and anointment of the sick; GOAA: Charter, Art. 2(b): the faithful are sanctified 'through the Eucharist and other sacraments'; SCOBA: GOCER, Pt. I, Sacraments and Other Liturgical Services VI: 'The sacraments are a means of divine grace and a sacred activity of the community of faith, celebrated within the community and symbolising [its] oneness.'

spiritual grace).³ The same approach appears in the Protestant traditions: for Lutheranism, sacraments are a means of grace,⁴ and the sacraments instituted by God are baptism and the Lord's Supper;⁵ in Methodism: 'the Sacraments of Baptism and the Lord's Supper are of divine origin',⁶ 'signs of grace' in which God works invisibly in the faithful;⁷ the church must ensure that 'the Sacraments are duly administered according to Christ's own appointment',⁸ and the faithful should avail themselves of them.⁹ Presbyterianism also holds that baptism and the Lord's Supper, or Holy Communion, are sacraments instituted by Christ;¹⁰ ordinarily, they are administered at a public service,¹¹ and the faithful must give attendance upon these 'gospel ordinances'.¹² Much the same is found in Reformed,¹³ Congregational¹⁴ and Baptist churches.¹⁵

---

³ PCLCCAC, Principles 11.1, 61.1, 66.1. See also Thirty-Nine Articles of Religion, Arts. 25, 27.
⁴ ELCIC: Const., Art. VI.3; LCA: Const., Interpretation; ELCSA: G., 10.1; LCGB: RAR, Statement of Faith, 5: 'In both Word and Sacraments Christ comes to us, and the Holy Spirit creates and sustains Christian faith and life'; ELCIRE: Const., Preamble: God 'works through the Holy Spirit in word and sacrament'.
⁵ ELCF: Catechism: 'Christ himself has instituted Baptism and the Holy Communion'; 'The sacraments are the visible signs of grace'; in them, 'Christ is present ... in a real and discernible manner'; LCA: BL, Sect. V.D., Preamble: in 'the Sacraments ... the Holy Spirit works saving faith in the hearts of people' (2 Cor. 3.5–8; AC V).
⁶ MCI: Const., s. 1; see also RDG, 3.01: 'the means of grace'; 3.03: 'There are two sacraments ordained of Christ, that is to say, Baptism and the Lord's Supper'; MCGB: CPD, DU 4: the two sacraments are 'of divine appointment' and the 'perpetual obligation of which it is the privilege of members ... to avail themselves'.
⁷ UMCNEAE: BOD, par. 103, AR, Art. XVI: 'Sacraments ordained of Christ are not only badges or tokens of Christian men's profession, but ... certain signs of grace, and God's good will toward us, by which he doth work invisibly in us ... There are two Sacraments ordained of Christ ... Baptism and the Supper of the Lord.'
⁸ UMCUSA: Const., Preamble; for an identical formula see UMCNEAE: BOD, Const., Preamble.
⁹ MCGB: CPD, DU 4 and 9; see also SO 054(5) and (6).
¹⁰ CLCS: 31; PCANZ: BO, 6.1; PCW: HOR, 9, Declaration on the Ordinances and Sacraments of the Church; 9.1: 'The grace of God is bestowed ... by mediation' e.g. in 'the ordinances of the Church'; 'Baptism [and] the Lord's Supper' are instituted by Christ as 'sacramental ordinances' and 'symbolic acts' with three aspects: the elements (water, bread and wine), their use ('sprinkling of water in Baptism, the breaking, distributing and eating of the bread, and the pouring, giving and drinking of the wine in the Holy Supper'); the intention: ordained ministers and elders administer them representing 'the priesthood of believers' and act 'on behalf of Christ'; PCA: BCO, 56.4: baptism is instituted by Christ; 58.4: the Lord's Supper is 'an ordinance of Christ'.
¹¹ CLCS 32; Acts XXIII, 1955, and XXI, 1956; PCANZ: BO, 6.11 and 7.2(3); PCW: HOR, 2.6.3.
¹² PCW: HOR, 9, Declaration on the Ordinances and Sacraments of the Church.
¹³ URC: Man., A.21; B.2(4); RCA: BCO, Pt. I, Ch. I, Art. 1.4.
¹⁴ UCCSA: Const., 3.5.1: the church must 'celebrate the sacraments of Baptism and the Lord's Supper'; UCOC: Const., Preamble: two sacraments; UCC: Man., BU 2.16: the two sacraments are 'signs and seals of the covenant ratified in [Christ's] precious blood' and are 'a means of grace' in which Christ works in the faithful.
¹⁵ BUSA: Const., 2: the church 'observes the two ordinances of Believers' Baptism by Immersion and the Lord's Supper'; BUSA: Model Const., Art. 4.1.12: they are to be observed as 'acts of obedience and as perpetual witnesses to the cardinal facts of the Christian faith'; Bethel Baptist Church, Choctaw (Oklahoma): Const., Art. V: 'the Church Ordinances ... are two in number: baptism and the Lord's Supper'.

The rite of baptism

The Christian traditions differ as to whether baptism and confirmation are distinct (but related) rites or whether they represent a single rite of initiation. To a lesser extent, norms also differ as to whether the baptism of infants is permissible, and in some Baptist churches the rite is reserved only to adults who confess the faith by means of Believers' Baptism. However, it is a principle of Christian law that baptism incorporates a person into the church universal through spiritual rebirth. It is validly administered by the application of water and the invocation of the triune God. The candidate and/or their sponsors should be instructed in their responsibilities for the spiritual nurture of their charge. The rite of baptism is normally administered publicly by an ordained minister but may be administered privately in cases of necessity by a lay person. A baptism should be registered. And baptism cannot be repeated.

The Catholic Church separates the two rites of baptism and confirmation. According to Roman Catholic canon law, baptism is the gate to the sacraments, necessary for salvation in fact or at least in intention, freeing individuals from their sins and constituting for them a rebirth as children of God configured to Christ; by baptism, a person is incorporated into the Church and this cannot be repeated.[16] Baptism is conferred either by immersion or pouring; the Episcopal Conference may issue norms on this matter.[17] In the case of infant baptism, parents and sponsors must be suitably instructed so that they 'understand the meaning of this sacrament and the obligations which attach to it'; those who have reached the age of reason (on completion of the 7th year) may also be baptised, and adulthood is attained on completion of the 18th year.[18] In the case of baptism of a person in danger of death, the candidate must have 'some knowledge of the principal truths of the faith'.[19] Parents must bring their children to be baptised, and parental consent is required for celebration to be licit.[20] Whilst there is a right to baptism, if the hope that the infant will be brought up in the catholic religion is 'altogether lacking, the baptism is to be put off according to the prescriptions of particular law'; the parents must be informed of the reason.[21] Ordinarily, a minister baptises only those whose parents reside in his territorial cure of souls. An infant in danger of death is to be baptised without delay, and one of Catholic or non-Catholic parents in danger of death is validly and lawfully baptised 'even against the will of the parents'.[22] Though

---

[16] CIC, cc. 204, 849; LG 16; c. 205: 'The baptised are in full communion with the catholic Church.'
[17] CIC, c. 854; c. 853: outside the case of necessity, the water should be blessed.
[18] CIC, c. 851: preparation; c. 852: the age of reason; c. 11: the age of seven; c. 97: adulthood.
[19] CIC, c. 865.2.
[20] CIC, c. 867: within 'the first few weeks' of birth, or, if in danger of death, 'without delay'; c. 868: consent.
[21] CIC, cc. 867, 868.1 and 2; the Congregation for the Doctrine of the Faith in 1970 decreed that delay should occur in relation to parents 'who are polygamous, unmarried, married lawfully but lapsed altogether from the regular practice of the faith, or those who request their child's baptism as a purely social convention'.
[22] CIC, c. 867; c. 862: death; c. 868.2: lack of consent; J.W. Robertson, 'Canons 867 and 868 and baptising against the will of parents', 45 *The Jurist* (1985) 631; cc. 870–871: a foundling is to be baptised unless upon investigation proof of baptism is established; if aborted foetuses are alive, they are to be baptised if possible.

all non-baptised persons may receive the sacrament, '[to] be baptised, it is required that an adult have manifested the will to receive baptism', and those in danger of death may be baptised if 'the person has in any way manifested an intention of receiving baptism and promises to observe the commandments of the Christian religion' in the event of survival.[23] A lay person may validly baptise in cases of necessity, but baptism is not to be administered in a private house outside the case of necessity – the normal place for baptism is on a Sunday in church.[24] Baptism should be administered in accordance with the order prescribed in the liturgical books, except in a case of urgent necessity when only what is required for the validity of the sacrament must be observed: 'washing with true water together with the required form of words'.[25] If there is doubt as to whether one was baptised, or whether baptism was conferred validly, and after serious enquiry this doubt persists, the person is baptised conditionally; and for those of the age of reason, confirmation may immediately follow baptism.[26] A baptism must be registered, and the parents and/or sponsors must nurture the baptised person in the faith.[27] Similar rules apply to the Oriental Catholic Churches.[28]

According to Orthodox canon law: 'In the Sacrament of baptism, a person is incorporated into the crucified, resurrected and glorified Christ and is reborn to participate in the divine life'; moreover: 'Baptism is necessary for salvation and in accordance with Tradition must be performed by triple immersion in the Name of the Father, the Son and the Holy Spirit, according to the form in the Service Book. It is conferred only once.'[29] The Orthodox Church in America is typical of rules applicable to the administration of the rite. Baptism and Chrismation (see below) are 'common liturgical actions of the whole people of God, witnessed, celebrated and accomplished by all, together in one place, at one time',[30] normally in a church building at the baptismal font[31] and in accordance with the appropriate order of service.[32] The candidate for baptism should bear the name of a recognized Orthodox saint,[33] and a baptismal sponsor must be appointed to nurture the candidate in the faith – to be eligible for appointment as a sponsor a person must be a practising

---

[23] CIC, cc. 864–5; adults; c. 865.2: survival.
[24] CIC, cc. 861, 863: reservation to the bishop; c. 860: private houses and hospitals; c. 856–857: Sundays.
[25] CIC, c. 850: prescribed order; c. 849: the formula. [26] CIC, cc. 866, 869.
[27] CIC, cc. 875–878; c. 872: parents and sponsors; c. 873: one sponsor, male or female, is sufficient, but there may be two, one of each sex; c. 874: the sponsor must be no younger than 16 (unless exempted), a catholic who has been confirmed and received the Eucharist, and not be the mother or father of the candidate.
[28] CCEO, cc. 675–691.
[29] SCOBA: GOCER, Pt. I, Sacraments and Other Liturgical Services, II.1.
[30] OCIA: GC, The Mystery of Baptism, Preamble.
[31] Ibid., 1: 'Baptism is normally performed in the temple'; 'an adult baptism ... may take place outdoors at a suitable aquatic site'; 'each deanery should have [a] baptismal font ... for the immersion of adult catechumens'.
[32] Ibid., 3: 'Baptism is administered in full accordance with the Office of the Service. No exorcism or prayer is to be shortened or omitted'; it is performed by 'triple immersion'; 'mere pouring is not normally permitted'.
[33] Ibid., 2: 'This matter should be discussed with the prospective parents long before the birth of the child. An adult convert to the Church should also bear the name of an Orthodox saint.'

Orthodox Christian.[34] In the case of infant baptism, the priest must instruct the parents and sponsors in their responsibilities.[35] It is also a principle of Orthodox canon law that the ordinary minister for baptism is a cleric, though in an emergency a layman may baptise.[36] For adults, participation in the Eucharist should follow baptism and chrismation.[37] Baptismal certificates may be issued and the baptism must be registered in the parish register.[38] If there is a doubt about a previous baptism, after due investigation of the matter, a person may be baptised conditionally.[39]

According to the principles of Anglican canon law, the sacrament of baptism, instituted by Christ, is a sign of regeneration or new birth by which those who receive it are incorporated into the Church of Christ.[40] A valid baptism is administered with water, by pouring, sprinkling, immersion, submersion or other similar means, simultaneously with the form of words 'I baptize you in the name of the Father and of the Son and of the Holy Spirit'.[41] Baptism by ordained ministers is the norm, but it may be administered by a lay person in an emergency, such as danger of death. Baptism should be administered publicly in the presence of the congregation but may be administered privately if permitted by law. Baptisms must be recorded in a register maintained especially for this purpose. Valid baptism is indelible and cannot be repeated.[42] The number of godparents (or other sponsors) is customarily two – at least one should be of the same sex as the candidate, and both of an age prescribed by law. Parents or guardians may be sponsors. Subject to any permitted dispensations, sponsors must be baptised persons and should be

---

[34] Ibid., 5. See also SCOBA: GOCER, Pt. I, Sacraments and Other Liturgical Services, III.4: a sponsor is 'to provide for the Christian formation of the baptised as a representative of the Orthodox community of faith'.

[35] OCIA: GC, The Mystery of Baptism, 6: sponsor and parents 'should be prepared to receive the Eucharist ... with the newly baptized person'; 7: an excommunicate is 'ineligible to be a sponsor'; 8: a non-Orthodox may be a witness. See also SOCA: Const., Art. 143: a godparent should make confession and receive Holy Communion before the baptism; UOCIA: Instructions, Baptism.

[36] SCOBA: GOCER, Pt. I, Sacraments and Other Liturgical Services, II.3: 'In the absence of an Orthodox clergyman, an Orthodox layman or any other Christian may baptise the infant.'

[37] OCIA: GC, The Mystery of Baptism, 4.

[38] ROC: Statute, XI.20; ROMOC: Statutes, Art. 50; GOAA: Regs., Art. 17.3; MOSC: Const., Art. 43.

[39] SCOBA: GOCER, Pt I, Sacraments and Other Liturgical Services II.5: 'Proof of ... baptism must be established by an authentic document or ... a qualified witness'; OCIA: GC, Reception of Converts, 5: if there is 'reasonable doubt ... after approval ... by the hierarch, the Office of Holy Baptism is performed conditionally'.

[40] PCLCCAC, Principles 61.1 and 61.3; AR, Arts. 25, 27: a dominical sacrament, baptism is 'a sign of Regeneration or new Birth, whereby ... they that receive [it] are grafted into the Church'; by it the promises of forgiveness of sin, and adoption as sons of God by the Holy Spirit, are signed and sealed, 'Faith is confirmed, and Grace increased by ... prayer unto God'. See e.g. South East Asia: Const., Fundamental Declaration, 1; Melanesia: Can. A.1.A: it is 'the rite by which we become members of the Church ... the Body of Christ'.

[41] PCLCCAC, Principle 61.2. See e.g. Papua New Guinea: Anglican Prayer Book 1991, 198: in 'baptism water shall be poured on the head of the candidate three times, or he may be dipped in the water three times'.

[42] PCLCCAC, Principle 61.5–10; 5: if present, the bishop may administer baptism; if a bishop or priest is unavailable it may be administered by a deacon. See e.g. TEC: BCP 1979: it is 'indissoluble'; Melanesia: Cans. A.1.B-K: lay people; Scotland: Can. 27.3: public and private baptism; Korea: Cans. 12, 13: registration.

communicants.[43] Their function is to help the baptised person grow in the knowledge and love of God and in the fellowship of the church. Parents and sponsors of infants are to receive instruction prior to the baptism as to the sacrament itself and the Christian life entered by it, as are adults or others able to answer for themselves.[44] No minister may without lawful cause refuse or unduly delay baptism of a child if the parents desire baptism. However, a minister may postpone it until the parents and sponsors are instructed and able to undertake their obligations. A minister should not baptise a child without parental consent. If a minister refuses or unduly delays to baptise any child, the parents may apply to the bishop for directions. A minister who refuses to baptise without lawful cause may be subject to disciplinary process. When adults are baptised, they should be presented to the bishop for confirmation either at the same time or as soon as possible thereafter.[45] Due to the indelibility of baptism, if there is uncertainty or other reasonable doubt as to whether a candidate has been baptised previously, such person may be baptised conditionally.[46]

There is remarkable juridical symmetry between the norms of Catholics, Orthodox and Anglicans and those that appear in the regulatory instruments of Protestant churches. In Lutheranism, baptism constitutes incorporation into the church universal,[47] and is administered with water and the words 'N., I baptize you in the Name of the Father, and of the Son, and of the Holy Spirit'.[48] Both infant and adult baptism is permitted.[49] Parents should bring their children for

---

[43] PCLCCAC, Principle 62.1–4. See e.g. Scotland: Can. 27.2: in 'cases of necessity', one sponsor 'shall be deemed sufficient'; Australia: Can. P5 1992, 8: 'usually' three godparents; Wales: BCP 1984, 654: they 'shall be baptized Christians' and 'should be regular communicants'; England: Can. B23.4: dispensation.

[44] PCLCCAC, Principle 62. See e.g. Southern Africa: Can. 35.4: sponsors' duties; West Indies: Can. 28.2: it is the minister's duty 'before baptizing infants or children to prepare the sponsors by instructing both the parents and godparents concerned'; Australia: Can. P5 1992, 4: '[t]he minister shall instruct and prepare or cause to be instructed or prepared ... any person able to answer for himself or herself before baptizing that person'.

[45] PCLCCAC, Principle 63. See e.g. England: Can. B22.4: 'No minister shall refuse or ... delay to baptize any infant within his cure that is brought to the church to be baptized' (*Bland v Archdeacon of Cheltenham* [1972] 1 All ER 1012); Southern Africa: Cans. 35.1–3: adults 'shall be presented to the Bishop for Confirmation at the same time or as soon as possible thereafter'; Ireland: Const., IX.26.2: 'If the Minister shall refuse or unduly delay to baptize any such child, the parents or guardians may apply to the bishop who shall, after consultation with the minister, give such directions as he shall think fit.'

[46] PCLCCAC, Principle 64; see e.g. Melanesia: Cans. A.1.B-K: conditional baptism is administered if it is not 'certain' that a person has already been baptised validly; Philippines: Can. II.5.4: baptismal certificate.

[47] LCGB: RAR, Statement of Faith, 5: 'in Baptism we are incorporated into Christ'; 6; ELCA: Model Const. for Congregations, Ch. 8.01: baptised members are those 'received by the Sacrament of Holy Baptism'; ELCSA: G., 1.1: 'Christ Himself has instituted Baptism with the words of His command to baptize' (Matt 28, 18–20).

[48] ELCF: Catechism (2000) 68–73: 'Baptismal water ... washes us clean from all sin' and 'is administered in the name of the Triune God. The minister pours water on the candidate three times, saying: I baptise you in the name of the Father and of the Son and of the Holy Spirit'; LCGB: RAR, Baptised Member, 1: 'A baptised member is a person who has been duly baptised in the name of the Father and of the Son and of the Holy Spirit.'

[49] ELCSA: G., 1.4 and 1.7; 1.6: 'Children are baptized during the first weeks after their birth. The Baptism should be personally announced to the minister by the parents in due time. The

baptism,[50] and: 'the rite of baptism is most fittingly celebrated in the context of the Sunday liturgy' so that 'the whole congregation witnesses the admission of the newly-baptised persons ... and welcomes them into the body of Christ'; indeed: 'The normal practice should be that the pastor of the local congregation ... conducts the baptismal rite'.[51] Sponsors, who teach the child the basics of the Christian faith, must be 'baptised, practising Christians who are mature in faith and piety'.[52] Moreover: 'A pastor should not refuse a request to baptise a child simply because he suspects the motives of the parents' (such as those who consider that baptism has a merely 'socio-religious' significance) and a pastor 'should never baptise a child against the will and wishes of the parents'.[53] However, if the parents lack understanding of the significance of baptism, the pastor must weigh the situation carefully, and should consult with others, before making a decision to refuse baptism.[54] Candidates for adult baptism must also be instructed in the Christian faith.[55] In cases of danger of death, any Christian may administer emergency baptism, but it must be reported to the responsible minister together with the names of witnesses and sponsors.[56] Baptism is indelible; and, as such: 'This excludes the repetition of Baptism.'[57]

For Methodism, 'Baptism is the sacrament of initiation and incorporation into the body of Christ', 'a sign of regeneration or the new birth' open to both infants and adults;[58] 'water is administered in the name of the triune God (specified in the ritual as Father, Son, and Holy Spirit) by an authorized person, and the Holy Spirit is invoked with the laying on of hands, ordinarily in the presence of the congregation'.[59] The pastor must exhort parents/guardians 'to present their children to the Lord in baptism at an early age' and must 'diligently instruct [them] regarding the

---

minister discusses the purpose and meaning of Baptism with the parents and, if possible, also with the sponsors.'

[50] ELCIC: Const., Art. V: 'members of this church are to be constant in ... presenting their children for Holy Baptism and providing for their Christian instruction'; ELCF: Catechism (2000) 68–73.

[51] LCA: Pastoral Practice in Reference to Holy Baptism (PPHB), adopted by General Synod, 1984 (Pts. I and II) and by CTIR 1986 (Pt. III), ed. 2001: II. Guidance in Pastoral Practice, 1–2; see Pt. I for the nature of baptism.

[52] ELCSA: G., 1.9: 'The sponsor (or godparent) is a witness of the Baptism and, representing the congregation', promises 'to help the child to remain with Christ and His congregation'; at least one sponsor 'should be a member of a congregation'; a person may not become a sponsor who: (a) does not belong to a Christian church; (b) has joined a sect; (c) has publicly caused annoyance; or (d) rejects infant baptism; LCA: PPHB, 3.

[53] LCA: PPHB, 5: 'Such refusal may give the impression that the sacrament and its blessings are dependent upon persons and things outside of baptism itself'; 4: 'The pastor needs to be aware that ... baptism is in danger of being abused if parents or sponsors think [it] is just a socio-religious act or a magical rite'; 6: parental wishes.

[54] LCA: PPHB, 7; 8: 'In the case of parents ... not known to him, the pastor should find out whether another pastor has refused baptism, and if so, on what grounds the refusal was based'; 9: pastors must educate the faithful in the importance of baptism; ELCSA: G., 1.10: baptism is 'to be deferred if the parents (and sponsors) publicly despise the Gospel and refuse to accept the commitment towards a Christian upbringing'.

[55] ELCSA: G., 1.5. [56] ELCSA: G., 1.8. [57] ELCSA: G., 1.3.

[58] UMCNEAE: BOD, pars. 103, 216; AR, Art. XVII; MCNZ: LAR, s. 1, Introduction.

[59] UMCNEAE: BOD, par. 128: 'In this sacrament the church claims God's promise and the seal of the Spirit' (this cites Eph. 1:13); par. 122: the faithful should lead others to baptism; MCI: RDG, 1.01.

meaning of this sacrament and the vow that they assume'.[60] Sponsors (or godparents) must nurture the child in the faith assisted by the local church.[61] It is administered at a public service in church.[62] The pastor must issue a certificate of baptism and maintain a baptismal record.[63] Baptism 'cannot be repeated'.[64] A particularly full treatment of the rite of baptism is found in the law of the Methodist Church of Great Britain. Both infant and adult baptism is permitted.[65] 'Except in an emergency, baptism shall be administered only after instruction has been given to the candidate or to the parents/guardians of a candidate who is a young child.'[66] Normally, baptism is celebrated by a minister; however, in 'an emergency baptism may be administered by any person'.[67] It must be administered at a service of public worship, but in exceptional circumstances (e.g. prolonged or serious illness) it may take place at another time. Where candidates are able to answer for themselves, the minister must be satisfied as to the candidates' repentance, faith and desire for baptism.[68] It is administered by pouring water on the candidate or by dipping in water with the words: 'N, I baptize you in the Name of the Father, and of the Son, and of the Holy Spirit.'[69] However: 'It is contrary to the principles and usage of the Methodist Church to confer what purports to be baptism on any person known to have been already baptized at any time.'[70] If it is uncertain whether a candidate has already been baptised, a conditional baptism may be administered.[71] Baptisms must be recorded in a baptismal register.[72]

By way of contrast, normally, Presbyterian law confines baptism to professing adults and the children of professing members; there is no provision for sponsors or godparents.[73] Typically: 'Baptism is an act of the Church, and at the same time an act of God' in which 'individuals are received into the fellowship of the Church' and which

---

[60] UMCNEAE: BOD, par. 226.1: parents must also bring up their children 'in conformity to the Word of God'.

[61] UMCNEAE: BOD, par. 226.1.

[62] UMCNEAE: BOD, par. 226.3; 226.4: the duty of all the faithful to nurture the child.

[63] UMCNEAE: BOD, par. 226.2: certificates and nurture; par. 230: register of baptised persons.

[64] UMCNEAE: BOD, par. 216; see also par. 341.7: 'No pastor shall re-baptize'; 'rebaptism does not conform with God's action in baptism and is not consistent with Wesleyan tradition and the historic teachings of the church'; the pastor should counsel anyone seeking re-baptism to participate in re-affirmation of baptismal vows.

[65] MCGB: CPD, DU 6: 'According to Methodist usage the sacrament of baptism is administered to infants and regular oversight should be given by the Local Church and its minister to all who have been dedicated to God by this sign'; see also SO 010A and 054(2).

[66] MCGB: CPD, SO 010A(1); for almost identical rules, see MCI: RDG, 3.04; MCNZ: LAR, Introductory Documents, II Pastoral Resolutions: the church 'will give adequate preparation for Baptism'.

[67] MCGB: CPD, SO 010A(2): it may also be administered by e.g. a ministerial probationer or a deacon.

[68] MCGB: CPD, SO 010A(3); see also SO 634: the role of stewards.

[69] MCGB: CPD, SO 010A(4).   [70] MCGB: CPD, SO 010A(5).

[71] MCGB: CPD, SO 010A(6): 'N, if you are not already baptized, I baptize you in the Name of the Father' etc.

[72] MCGB: CPD, SO 054: a roll of baptised children must be reviewed periodically by the local Church Council.

[73] PCANZ: BO, 4.4: members have a right 'to receive baptism for [their] children'; PCA: BCO, 56.1: 'Baptism is not to be unnecessarily delayed'.

signifies God's 'gracious purpose to save us into eternal life through Jesus Christ'.[74] Infant baptism is justified.[75] It is the duty of elders to encourage parents to bring their children for baptism; also: 'In the event of parents, neither of whom is a communicant member but who express willingness to become members, seeking baptism of a child, the baptism may take place immediately, but the Kirk Session is required to appoint an elder to shepherd them into membership.'[76] Ordinarily, baptism is administered at a public service and extraordinarily it may be administered in private or in an emergency by sprinkling of water or by immersion in the name of the Father, Son and Holy Spirit.[77] The parents or guardians of a child must profess their own faith and promise to bring up the child in the faith and life of the church – if they do so, baptism must not be delayed – if they do not, baptism may be refused with the consent of the Session; the congregation also undertakes to support the child – but there are no godparents.[78] Adult baptism is normally combined with admission and confirmation, and vows are taken by the person baptised.[79] Normally baptism is administered by a minister, but an elder may do so if authorised to administer the sacraments.[80] An elder is to make arrangements for baptism and is to provide

---

[74] PCANZ: BO, 6.1.4: 'Baptism invites us to share in God's mission'; UFCS: MPP, App. 6: it 'is a sign and seal that ... declares ... union with Christ ... forgiveness of sins by washing ... new life [and] adoption as His children ... By this sacrament we are brought into Christ's Church'; PCA: BCO, 56.4: 'regeneration, adoption'.

[75] PCW: HOR, 9.1: with infants, 'baptism precedes personal faith, and its purpose is to engender faith' which 'will develop through the instruction and nurture received in the home and in the church'; with adults, 'it presupposes that through the hearing of the Word they already believe in Christ, and [baptism] is a public declaration of their professing Christ, their Saviour'; CLCS: 31; Act XVII, 1963; PCA: BCO, 56.

[76] CLCS: 108; PCI: Code, I.I.II.7(1): 'The children of believers are ... called to be part of the visible Church. Hence they are entitled to baptism and to nurture by the Church'; 39: baptism 'shall be administered in all cases by a minister and, as far as possible ... publicly'; PCW: HOR, 2.2.

[77] CLCS: 32 and 109; Acts XVII, 1963 and IV, 1975. See also UFCS: MPP, I.III.4: 'baptism should be administered during public worship; and parents ought to bring their children to the house of God for this purpose; but the Session may, where it sees cause, authorise the administration of baptism elsewhere than in the church'; PCW: HOR, 9.2: it is 'publicly administered ... by sprinkling with water ... or ... immersion, in the name of the Father, the Son and the Holy Spirit'; PCA: BCO, 56.2: it 'is not to be privately administered, but in the presence of the congregation under the supervision of the Session'; 56.4: sprinkling and washing with water.

[78] PCI: Code, I.I.II.7(2): 'the Session should be informed that a baptism is to take place' and the elder 'should visit the home. Refusal is the prerogative of the Session'; par. 83: 'A minister shall encourage baptism of the children of all such as may make a credible profession of faith'; UFCS: MPP, I.III.4: 'It is the duty of the Session to see that all the children of church members are baptised without unnecessary delay'; PCW: HOR, 9.2: those 'admitted to baptism are' the children/wards of professing believers and non-members who promise solemnly to give the church opportunity to teach the children and to whom the church is 'to explain the true meaning of Baptism, and ... importance of owning Christ themselves so that they may fully meet their obligation to their children' – 'such children should not be deprived of the privilege of baptism' as 'children can lead their parents to Christ even as parents lead their children to Him'; PCA: BCO, 56.4: parental duties; CLCS: 33.

[79] CLCS: 34; PCA: BCO, 57; UFCS: MPP, I.III.5: it is 'administered to adults upon their profession of faith'.

[80] PCANZ: BO, 6.11; PCA: BCO, 56.1: baptism is 'not to be administered, in any case, by any private person; but by a minister of Christ, called to be steward of the mysteries of God'.

spiritual guidance of applicants for baptism.[81] The minister provides a certificate of baptism and records details in the baptismal register.[82]

United Reformed Churches agree that baptism is instituted by Christ, constitutes incorporation into the church universal and represents the forgiveness of sins; also, it must ordinarily be administered publicly, and it cannot be repeated;[83] baptism in infancy is permitted, however (typically): 'The rights of conscience allow that no particular minister shall be compelled to administer baptism in a form to which s/he "has a conscientious objection".'[84] In some Congregational churches suspension of parents from the Lord's Supper may raise problems for the baptism of their children.[85] By way of contrast, Believers' Baptism lies at the heart of the Baptist tradition. The constitutions of Baptist Unions and Conventions commonly provide: 'That Christian Baptism is the immersion in water into the Name of the Father, the Son and the Holy Ghost, of those who have professed repentance towards God and faith in our Lord Jesus Christ who "died for our sins according to the Scriptures"; was buried and rose again the third day.'[86] Believers' baptism is 'an act of obedience to our Lord Jesus Christ and a sign of personal repentance, faith and regeneration; it consists of the immersion in water into the name of the Father, Son and Holy Spirit'.[87] Moreover: 'Only those who genuinely profess faith in Christ should be

---

[81] PCANZ: BO, 6.13–14. See also UFCS: MPP, I.III.2.

[82] CLCS: 34, 108; PCANZ: BO, 4.4; PCI: Code, I.II.II.39(3) and par. 255. See also UCC: Man., BL, 153(b)xi.

[83] URC: Man., A.14: 'the gospel sacrament of baptism into Christ [is] a gift of God to his Church, and ... an appointed means of grace', is 'administered with water in the name of the Father and of the Son and of the Holy Spirit' (by 'pouring or immersion'), effects 'entry into the Church and is therefore administered once only' and makes explicit 'the forgiveness of sins, the sanctifying power of the Holy Spirit and newness of life in the family of God'; in it 'the church affirms its faith, takes corporate responsibility for those received in baptism, and promises to support and nourish them into its fellowship'; Man., E: 'Baptism is an unrepeatable act', and '"rebaptism" must be avoided'; RCA: BCO, Pt. I, Ch. I, Art. 2.11: 'baptism shall be administered, if possible, at a time and place of public worship' at which 'the Office for the Administration of Baptism shall be read'.

[84] URC: BU 14; also, Man., A.14: 'Baptism may be administered in infancy or at an age of responsibility' on profession of faith; when 'administered to infants, upon profession of faith by their parent(s), they are placed under the nurture of the Church'; profession by one baptised in infancy should be at the Lord's Supper.

[85] UCCSA: Const., 15.1: as to 'administration of baptism to the children of disciplined but believing parents', discipline 'does not cancel faith'; UCA: Regs., 1.1.3: 'The sacrament shall be administered by water and in the name of the Father and of the Son and of the Holy Spirit according to an order which meets the requirements of the Assembly'; 'Normally' it is 'administered in the presence of the Congregation'; 1.1.4: records; 1.1.5: certificate; 1.1.6: the local church 'shall seek to ensure that all baptised persons are nurtured within the fellowship of the Church, equipped for witness and service in the community and prepared for confirmation'.

[86] BUGB: Const., 3.2; MTC 2003, 2.8.2. For an identical formula, see BUS: Const., III.2, JBU: Const., Art. III, and BUSA: Const., 4.2; CNBC: Const., 3.VII: 'It is an act of obedience symbolizing the believer's faith in a crucified, buried and risen Saviour, the believer's death to sin, the burial of the old life, and the resurrection to ... life in Christ'; Bethel Baptist Church (Choctaw): Const., Art. V.1: 'where the pastor is physically incapable ... and no other ordained minister is available', an elder/deacon may be chosen to baptise.

[87] BUSA: Model Const., 4.2.3. Riverside Baptist Church (Baltimore): BL, Art. I.2: to be members, 'Individuals must have made a public profession of faith in Jesus Christ ... and have undergone

baptized'; candidates are presented to the church for approval; and only ordained ministers should baptise.[88] In short, all the traditions agree that baptism constitutes incorporation of a person into the Body of Christ and they require strict observance of the conditions for its valid administration: the application of water with the invocation of the triune God. They also agree that ordinarily baptism is administered at a public service in the presence of the congregation by an ordained minister, though all have exceptions and they recognise as valid baptisms those administered by lay persons in cases of necessity. Most traditions allow both infant and adult baptism – but the Baptist tradition reserves it to believers; for infants, sponsors may be appointed to nurture the candidate in the faith, and in some traditions baptism is normally reserved to the children of professing believers. A baptism should be registered. A valid baptism cannot be repeated and if there is doubt about a previous baptism, provision is made for conditional baptism.

The rite of confirmation

By the rite of confirmation, which takes place broadly at puberty, the grace of the Holy Spirit is conveyed in a fuller manner to those who have already received it at baptism. There has been much theological discussion as to its precise significance and method of administration. Some consider it an integral stage in the process of Christian initiation (such as Catholics), whilst others do not practise confirmation (such as Presbyterians). In some traditions the rites of baptism and confirmation are separate (such as Anglican) and in others they represent a single rite (such as Orthodox Christian). The following deals with the churches *seriatim*.

Confirmation in Catholicism is treated as the second of the initiatory rites. In the Roman Catholic Church: 'the sacrament of confirmation impresses a character and by it the baptised, continuing on the path of Christian initiation, are enriched by the gift of the Holy Spirit'; confirmation binds the person 'more perfectly to the church' and it strengthens and obliges them more firmly 'to be witnesses of Christ by word and deed and to spread and defend the faith'.[89] The principal responsibility to ensure that confirmation is conferred on those who 'properly and reasonable request it' rests with the diocesan bishop; and parents and pastors are to see that the faithful are properly instructed to receive confirmation and that it is approached at the appropriate time, namely at 'about the age of discretion'. All baptised persons are capable of receiving confirmation; and, outside the danger of death, to be lawfully confirmed it is required that, for any person with the use of reason, candidates be suitably instructed, properly disposed and able to renew their baptismal promises.[90] The sacrament of confirmation is conferred by anointing with chrism on the forehead by the laying on of the hand and by the words prescribed in the liturgical books; it is desirable that it is celebrated in a church during the

---

believers' baptism by immersion'; Bethel Baptist Church (Choctaw): Const., Art. III: members are admitted through baptism by immersion administered by 'a duly authorized administrator on the profession of their faith'.

[88] NBC: PAP, Baptism; BUSA: Model Const., 10.1: 'the Pastor shall be free to baptise by immersion any believer who desires thus to confess the Lord Jesus'.

[89] CIC, c. 879; see generally W.H. Woestman, *Sacraments: Initiation, Penance, Anointing of the Sick: Commentary on Canons 840-1007* (St Paul University, Ottawa, 1996) 75-96.

[90] CIC, cc. 885, 890, and 899; cc. 889-891: the Episcopal Conference may specify an age.

Mass.[91] The ordinary minister of confirmation is a bishop, but a priest may validly confer the sacrament if he has a faculty to do so.[92] Confirmation candidates must have a sponsor who performs those functions carried out by baptismal sponsors, and the confirmation must be registered in the confirmation register.[93] Similar rules apply to chrismation with the Holy Myron (a mixture of olive oil and balsam) in the Oriental Catholic Churches,[94] and the Orthodox churches; it is administered after baptism.[95] The Patriarch consecrates and bishops distribute the Myron.[96] A register of the rite is kept.[97]

In Anglicanism, only a baptised person who has attained the age of discretion may be confirmed. Confirmation is a rite in which a person makes a profession of the faith and a mature expression or reaffirmation of the commitment to Christ made at baptism (either by the candidate in the case of adults, or on behalf of the candidate in the case of infant baptism). The minister of confirmation is the bishop. Confirmation is effected by episcopal laying on of hands and invocation of the Holy Spirit to strengthen the candidate in the Christian life. Confirmation should be administered at a celebration of the Eucharist. The duty to encourage a person to be confirmed rests upon the baptismal sponsors and sometimes with or in collaboration with the parents or guardians. A special duty to seek out candidates for confirmation may be placed on clergy.[98] An ordained minister presents candidates to the bishop for confirmation and the rite should be witnessed and recorded in a certificate or other document. All confirmation candidates must receive instruction, from an ordained minister or other authorised person, in the Christian faith. This may include the Lord's Prayer, the Creed, the Ten Commandments and church catechism, so that candidates may render an account of their faith and the bishop may be assured by the presenting minister of their

---

[91] CIC, c. 880: the chrism must have been consecrated by a bishop; c. 881: the norm is for celebration in church but for a just cause it may be celebrated apart from mass and in any fitting place.

[92] CIC, c. 882: a priest equivalent in law to a bishop, who has the mandate of the bishop or, in danger of death, any priest, has the faculty to confirm automatically by universal law.

[93] CIC, c. 892: the sponsor must fulfil the conditions set out in c. 874; cc. 875–878: proof and registration.

[94] CCEO, cc. 692–697; c. 692: 'It is necessary for those who have been baptised to be chrismated with holy Myron, so that signed with the seal of the gift of the Holy Spirit they may become more suitable witnesses and co-builders of the Kingdom of Christ'; c. 693: holy Myron is made from the oil of olives or other plants and aromatics and is confected only by a bishop; c. 694: 'According to the traditions of the Eastern Churches, chrismation with holy Myron is administered by a presbyter either in conjunction with baptism or separately.'

[95] OCIA: GC, The Mystery of Chrismation, 1: it is 'to take place immediately after the Mystery of Baptism according to the prescribed ritual'; SCOBA: GOCER, Pt. I, Sacraments and other Liturgical Services, III.1–2.

[96] GOAA: Charter, Art. 7.7; Regs., Art. 10.2: the Myron is received from the Ecumenical Patriarchate through the Archbishop; ROMOC: Statutes, Art. 26: the Patriarch consecrates the 'Holy Great Myrrh' and (Art. 88) the diocesan bishop distributes this.

[97] GOAA: Regs., Art. 17.3; Art. 18.1: chrismation confers the status of parishioner.

[98] PCLCCAC, Principle 65.1–8. See also AR, Art. 25: confirmation is 'not to be counted for [a sacrament] of the Gospel' for it has 'not any visible sign or ceremony ordained of God'; West Indies: Can. 30.1: it is a sacrament and ministers should seek out candidates; Scotland: Can. 30.1: it is administered by the bishop; Papua New Guinea: Anglican Prayer Book 1991, 198: baptismal sponsors and parents must present candidates.

faith, repentance and resolve to live the Christian life. In cases of the baptism of adults and of children able to answer for themselves, baptism and confirmation should be administered as a single rite, failing which confirmation should follow baptism as soon as is convenient.[99]

Lutherans also practise the rite of confirmation.[100] By way of illustration, in the Evangelical Lutheran Church in Southern Africa, confirmation involves the affirmation of the confession of faith at baptism through the laying on of hands.[101] Candidates for confirmation must be instructed in the faith by means of the catechism. The age for confirmation is determined by the congregation and the candidates present themselves to the congregation to indicate their own development in understanding the faith. The minister may, in exceptional cases and after consultation with the Church Committee, exclude a person from confirmation if the minister has well-founded reasons to do so. The congregation is also to provide continuing care of the confirmed person.[102] The Methodist model runs along the same lines. For example, in the episcopal United Methodist Church, at confirmation 'the pledges of baptism are accepted through profession of faith, and renewed for life and mission'.[103] Therefore: 'Confirmation is both a human act of commitment and the gracious action of the Holy Spirit strengthening and empowering discipleship.' In preparation for confirmation, baptised children are 'to be instructed and nurtured in the meaning of the faith, the rights and responsibilities of their baptism, and spiritual and moral formation' using materials approved by the church. The relationship of confirmation to baptism is underscored by the fact that both are treated as services of the 'Baptismal Covenant'. However: 'Unlike baptism, which is a once-made covenant and can only be reaffirmed and not repeated, confirmation is a dynamic action of the Holy Spirit that can be repeated.'[104] Parents must encourage their children 'to participate in preparation for their profession of faith and confirmation at the appropriate time'.[105] A register of confirmations must be kept by the pastor.[106] Confirmation is also practised in traditional Methodist Churches (without bishops).

---

[99] PCLCCAC, Principle 65. See e.g. Ireland: Const., IX.28: the minister should endeavour to instruct candidates 'in the Christian faith and life as set forth in the Holy Scriptures, the Book of Common Prayer and the Church Catechism'; Korea: Can. 10: 'Baptism and Confirmation shall normally be administered as a single rite' in the case of adults and children able to answer for themselves.

[100] ELCA: Model Const. for Congregations, Ch. 8.02: 'Confirmed members are baptized persons who have been confirmed in this congregation, those who have been received by adult baptism or by transfer as confirmed members from other Lutheran congregations, or baptized persons received by affirmation of faith.'

[101] ELCSA: G., 6.10: 'Confirmation implies that the confession of faith spoken at Baptism is confirmed, the blessing is imparted ... by laying on of hands and the confirmand is admitted to Holy Communion.'

[102] ELCSA: G., 6.7–6.9 and 6.11.

[103] UMCNEAE: BOD, par. 128; see also par. 215: professed members come into membership by 'profession of faith through appropriate services of the baptismal covenant in the ritual'.

[104] UMCNEAE: BOD, par. 216; 217: in the order of profession of the faith the candidates 'covenant together with God and ... local church to keep the vows which are a part of the order of confirmation and reception'.

[105] UMCNEAE: BOD, par. 226.

[106] UMCNEAE: BOD, par. 230: this must include the name of the officiating minister and sponsors.

For instance, the law of the Methodist Church of New Zealand provides that: 'By personal decision and profession of faith, associated with either adult baptism or confirmation, a person is initiated into responsible membership in the Church Universal, such membership being made specific within the Methodist Church of New Zealand.'[107] The rite is administered 'through the laying on of hands with prayer of a person baptised in infancy or as an older person'. Normally, confirmation is administered to those not less than 14 years of age and 'should be preceded by appropriate preparation'. Each local church must maintain a Register of Baptisms and Confirmations, and 'a Certificate shall be issued to the person confirmed'.[108]

By way of marked contrast, Presbyterians do not practise the rite of confirmation as such, but there is a rite for admission to full membership, particularly for the purposes of receiving Holy Communion. For example, in the Church of Scotland there is 'no "sacrament of confirmation"'; 'The sacrament of baptism, being complete in itself, requires no subsequent confirmation.'[109] However, the church has 'an order of service for Confirmation and Admission to the Lord's Supper', namely 'a service of public profession of faith and admission to the Lord's Table'.[110] Similarly, for Reformed churches, the affirmation (or profession) of faith by which a person is publicly admitted to full membership is by the laying on of hands and giving and receiving the right hand of fellowship.[111] Similar rules are found in Congregational churches.[112] Nor is the rite of confirmation a feature of the Baptist tradition – needless to say, at Believers' Baptism candidates confirm their own faith.[113] In short, for several churches which practise infant baptism, the rite of confirmation is designed after due preparation to enable the baptised person and the church to confirm the faith of the individual by means of a ceremony which involves laying on of hands (by the bishop in e.g. Anglicanism and/or by a deputed ordained minister in e.g. Catholicism, Lutheranism and Methodism) and, in the Catholic and Orthodox traditions, the application of chrism. However, in Presbyterianism the rite does not confirm a baptism administered in infancy, but confirmation may be employed as a mature profession of faith to receive a person into full church membership. In those Protestant churches which do not practise infant baptism, the equivalent to confirmation is the profession of the faith at Believers' Baptism.

---

[107] MCNZ: LAR, s. 1, Introduction; Introductory Documents, II Pastoral Resolutions: the church 'will give adequate preparation for ... Confirmation'. See also MCGB: CPD, DU 8(a)–(c).

[108] MCNZ: s. 1.3.1–3. See also MCGB: CPD, SO 054: 'confirmation register' of the local church.

[109] CLCS: 32–33: also, at infant baptism, the parents take vows confessing their own faith, and promising to bring up the child in the faith, but they 'do not vicariously promise anything "in the name of the child", so there can be no question of these vows being confirmed by the baptised person' (Calvin, Institutes, Bk. IV. Ch. XIX).

[110] CLCS: 33 and 128. See also PCI: Code, par. 40(2): persons proposing to take communion for the first time shall be carefully instructed by the minister.

[111] URC: Man., A., Sch. A.

[112] UCCSA: MCLC, 3. UCA: 1.1.7–1.1.10: candidates for confirmation who have not been previously baptised 'shall be baptised either prior to or in conjunction with the confirmation'.

[113] See Chapter 2 for Believers' Baptism and for profession of the faith on admission as church member.

The Eucharist, Holy Communion or Lord's Supper

The nature of the Eucharist, Holy Communion or Lord's Supper, and the mode of its administration, has been the subject of intense doctrinal disagreement historically in Christianity. The Reformation of the sixteenth century and beyond in particular witnessed theological division about the position of the Catholic Church on transubstantiation – that the elements of bread and wine are transformed into the body and blood of Jesus Christ at the time of consecration – and that of Protestantism on consubstantiation – that after their consecration the substances of bread and wine are in union with the body and blood of Christ, who is present at the celebration, but not transformed into the body of Christ. Theological divisions persist and, as we shall see in Chapter 8, still form the basis of division. However, a study of the juridical instruments of these separated traditions indicates that they all require, forbid or permit – in terms of action – much the same as to the basics of this sacrament. Given that the sacrament is one instituted by Christ himself, it is not surprising to find that all the churches studied here across the traditions have complex bodies of rules on the subject.

For the Roman Catholic Church: '[t]he most august sacrament is the blessed Eucharist, in which Christ the Lord himself is contained, offered and received, and by which the Church continually lives and grows'. Instituted by Christ, it is 'the memorial of the death and resurrection of the Lord, in which the sacrifice of the cross is forever perpetuated' and 'the summit and the source of all worship and Christian life'; by means of it 'the unity of God's people is signified and brought about, and the building up of the body of Christ perfected'.[114] The faithful must hold the Eucharist in the highest honour, take an active part in its celebration, receive the sacrament frequently, and reverence it with the greatest adoration.[115] In the Eucharist, Christ, 'through the ministry of the priest, offers himself, substantially present under the appearances of bread and wine, to God the Father, and gives himself as spiritual nourishment to the faithful'.[116] Therefore: 'The only minister, who, in the person of Christ, can bring into being the sacrament of the Eucharist, is a validly ordained priest.'[117] A priest may not celebrate the Eucharist without the participation of at least one of the faithful, unless there is a good and reasonable cause for doing so; deacons and lay persons are not permitted to perform actions in it, especially the Eucharistic prayer, proper to the priest; and the ordinary minister is a bishop, priest or deacon, though the laity may be permitted to distribute.[118] Any

---

[114] CIC, c. 897; SC 47–48.

[115] CIC, c. 898: pastors must instruct the faithful about this duty. See generally Woestman, *Sacraments*, 97–215.

[116] CIC, c. 899: in it, 'the people of God are called together under the presidency of the bishop or of a priest under his authority, who acts in the person of Christ'; the faithful present unite to participate in their own way according to their orders and liturgical roles; all derive from it the fruits Christ instituted; SC 7 and LG 26.

[117] CIC, c. 900; c. 904: daily celebration by priests is suggested; c. 905: a priest cannot celebrate more than once a day unless the bishop permits; c. 1378.2: laity attempting to confect it are automatically excommunicated.

[118] CIC, c. 906; SC 14; c. 907: prayers; c. 908: concelebration; c. 909: the priest must prepare himself by prayer; c. 910: ordinary minister; the extraordinary minister is an acolyte or other member of the faithful deputed under c. 203.3; c. 911: bringing the sacrament to the sick (as viaticum).

baptised person not forbidden by law is admitted to Holy Communion, and children may be admitted if they have sufficient knowledge and are carefully prepared so that they understand the sacrament and are able to receive the body of the Lord with faith and devotion.[119] Excommunicates and those who obstinately persist in manifest grave sin are not to be admitted, nor is anyone who is conscious of grave sin without previously having been to sacramental confession.[120] There are provisions about the number of times daily upon which a person may receive, preparation for it, and reception by the elderly, the infirm and those in danger of death; each member of the faithful is obliged to receive Holy Communion once a year.[121] The Eucharist must be offered in bread and in wine; but Holy Communion is to be given 'under the species of bread alone or, in accordance with the liturgical laws, under both species or, in the case of necessity, even under the species of wine alone'.[122] The Eucharist may be celebrated on any day and hour in a sacred place (unless necessity requires otherwise), and there is provision for reservation and veneration of the Eucharist.[123] Similar rules are to be found in the Code of Canons of the Oriental Catholic Churches.[124]

In is a fundamental principle of Orthodox canon law that: 'The celebration of the Holy Eucharist and the reception of the Holy Communion in the Divine Liturgy is the final end and goal of the Christian life.'[125] At the Divine Liturgy the faithful partake of the body and blood of Christ.[126] To be admitted to Holy Communion a person must be baptised, chrismated and profess the Orthodox Faith – and parishioners must take Holy Communion regularly.[127] The faithful should make confession before receiving Holy Communion.[128] Priests may perform two masses on one

[119] CIC, c. 912: admission; c. 913: it may be administered to children in danger of death 'if they can distinguish the Body of Christ from ordinary food and receive communion with reverence'; c. 914: parents and priests are to ensure that children of the age of reason are prepared and after confession nourished by it.
[120] CIC, cc. 915–916.
[121] CIC, cc. 917–919; c. 920: reception once a year, which must be fulfilled during the paschal time; c. 921: reception in danger of death; c. 922: the viaticum for the sick must not be unduly delayed.
[122] CIC, c. 924: a small quantity of water may be added to the wine; the bread must be wheaten, recently made, and (c. 926) unleavened; the wine must be natural, made from grapes and not corrupt (i.e. turned to vinegar); c. 927: it is absolutely wrong to consecrate one element alone; cc. 928–930: language, vesture and posture.
[123] CIC, c. 931: time; c. 932: place (the sacrifice must be carried out at the altar); c. 933: for a good reason, with the bishop's consent, and if all scandal is eliminated, a priest may celebrate in the church of another tradition; cc. 934–944: reservation; cc. 945–958: offerings for the celebration of the Mass for a specific intention.
[124] CCEO, cc. 689–717: Divine Eucharist.
[125] SCOBA: GOCER, Pt. I, Worship with Non-Orthodox, 3.
[126] OCIA: GC, Divine Services, A.1: 'the Divine Body and Blood of Christ'.
[127] ROC: Statute, XI.32; SOCA: Const., Art. 143: 'Adult believers ... should ... receive the Holy Communion at least twice a year'; GOAA: Regs., Art. 18.1: parishioners must 'faithfully attend the Divine Liturgy' and 'participate regularly'; SCOBA: GOCER, Pt. I, Sacraments and other Liturgical Services, 1: the church admits to Communion only 'baptised and chrismated children who confess the full Orthodox Faith'.
[128] SOCA: Const., Art. 145: the metropolitan may permit a person 'to partake of the Holy Sacraments after a public confession and the receiving of absolution, provided they fast at least three hours' before; UOCIA: Statutes, Art. XI.5: to qualify to vote a person must partake of Holy Communion at least once a year.

day and at the same church,[129] should not abstain themselves from the Eucharist[130] and must fast beforehand.[131] The Divine Liturgy should be celebrated on Sundays and on the prescribed feast days,[132] normally in a consecrated building, but in cases of necessity (with the consent of the diocesan hierarch) outdoors or in a suitable place other than a consecrated building.[133] There are detailed rules on the preparation and nature of the elements.[134] Major excommunication or anathema (permanent expulsion from the church) and temporary expulsion from the Eucharist are the most severe ecclesiastical penalties.[135]

For Anglicans, the Holy Communion, Eucharist or Lord's Supper is a sacrament instituted by Christ, the central act of worship and an act of the whole church, and it must be maintained and duly administered by each church. Every confirmed person should receive it frequently and regularly. Holy Communion should be administered in a church building, except for the communion of the sick or housebound, or in other cases with the consent of the bishop. The authorised forms of service must be used. The elements consecrated for Holy Communion are bread and wine and are to be received in both kinds as 'the normal practice, according to the example and precept of our Lord'. Presidency at the Holy Communion is reserved to a priest or bishop who, when present, is to be the principal celebrant; a deacon or authorised lay minister may assist in the distribution of the elements.[136] The sacrament may be reserved for the sick and housebound, those dying or in special need, and for devotional services, with the lawful permission of the bishop; the reserved sacrament must be kept in a safe and fitting place in church.[137] To receive Holy Communion, a person must be baptised and, where required by law, confirmed or ready and desirous of being confirmed. Where confirmation remains a requirement for admission to Holy Communion, a bishop may authorise such admission of baptised but unconfirmed persons to the

---

[129] SOCA: Const., Art. 144; see also OCIA: GC, The Divine Services, 17.
[130] OCIA: GC, A Selection of Clergy Disciplines, 6; this cites Trullo, c. 80; Holy Apostles, c. 8.
[131] OCIA: GC, The Divine Services, 3.   [132] Ibid., 5.   [133] Ibid., 9.
[134] Ibid., 11: for the bread, pure wheat flour, water, salt and yeast: 'It is carefully prepared, usually with appropriate scriptural readings and personal prayer by a person designated for [this purpose]. The bread must be well baked'; 12: 'The wine should be sweet, made from red grapes, without additives or fortifications.'
[135] MOCL: 112: 'The most severe of all ecclesiastical penalties is the anathema or major excommunication ... the total and continual expulsion of the guilty person from the Church'; based on divine law, it is a last resort.
[136] PCLCCAC, Principle 66. AR, Arts. 25, 28: the sacrament is instituted by Christ. See e.g. Chile: Can. D.7: central act of worship; Southern Africa: Prayer Book 1989, 363: 'Christian initiation is fulfilled in the Holy Communion'; England: Can. B15.1: 'It is the duty of all who have been confirmed to receive the Holy Communion regularly, and especially at ... Christmas, Easter and Whitsun or Pentecost'; Can. B17.2: the bread may be leavened or unleavened but 'of the best and purest wheat flour', and the wine 'fermented juice of the grape and of good quality'; TEC: BCP 1979, 311: 'It is the bishop's prerogative, when present, to be the principal celebrant at the Lord's Table'; Melanesia: Can. A.2.A.I: lay assistance.
[137] PCLCCAC, Principle 67. See e.g. West Indies: Can. 32.4: 'It is the right and duty of a Priest with a cure of souls ... to reserve the ... Sacrament permanently in his Church, subject to such regulations as the Bishop from time to time shall make'; Ireland: Const., IX.14: administration to the sick in private homes.

extent lawfully permitted.[138] No minister shall without lawful cause deny the Holy Communion to any baptised Christian who devoutly and humbly desires it. However, a person, in the absence of repentance and amendment of life, may be denied Holy Communion, for living openly in grievous sin or contention, causing scandal to the congregation or bringing the church into disrepute.[139] Churches provide for appeals to the bishop. Restoration to Holy Communion is reserved to the bishop or priest, as the case may be under church law, or in cases of appeal to the competent authority. The effects of excommunication are such as may be prescribed by law.[140]

Whilst there remain profound doctrinal differences between the Catholic and Protestant understandings of the nature of the sacrament (in terms of transubstantiation and consubstantiation), there are remarkable juridical similarities in terms of sacramental discipline. As with Catholics, Orthodox and Anglicans, the Lutheran faithful should participate in Holy Communion regularly.[141] For instance, the Evangelical Lutheran Church of Australia teaches that Holy Communion is 'the true body and blood of our Lord Jesus Christ given with bread and wine, instituted by Christ himself'; its benefits are 'the forgiveness of sins, life, and salvation'.[142] In consequence: 'the Lord's Supper is "a means of grace". It nourishes and strengthens God's people.'[143] Only repentant baptised and confessing persons may be admitted; therefore, 'responsible celebration of the Lord's Supper requires that we do not admit to the Lord's table people who (a) are not baptised or do not believe in the Triune God; (b) do not confess Christ as their only Saviour; (c) do not repent of sin and do not ask to live in accordance with the confession of faith in Christ; and (d) do not confess the real presence in the sacrament of Christ's body and blood, given and shed for the forgiveness of sins. Such people would be in danger of receiving the supper in an unworthy manner,

---

[138] PCLCCAC, Principle 68. See e.g. TEC: Cans. I.17.7: 'No unbaptised person shall be eligible to receive Holy Communion'; England: Can. B15A: 'There shall be admitted to the Holy Communion ... members of the Church ... who have been confirmed ... or are ready and desirous to be confirmed'; Scotland: Can. 25: the bishop may allow unconfirmed persons to be admitted to Holy Communion in relaxation of 'the normal rule'.

[139] PCLCCAC, Principle 69. See e.g. England: Can. B16: summary exclusion to prevent e.g. scandal; Scotland: Can. 26: 'it is the inherent right of a Bishop of a Diocese to repel offenders from Communion'; Southern Africa: Can. 35.8: if a person fails to heed admonition, the priest 'may' suspend.

[140] PCLCCAC, Principle 69.6–9. See e.g. Southern Africa: Can. 35.8: investigation by the bishop and restoration; Scotland: Can. 26: a right of appeal against the decision of the bishop to the College of Bishops.

[141] ELCIC: Const., Art. V: 'members ... are to be constant in ... regularly nourishing their life in Christ in the Sacrament of the Altar'; ELCA: Model Const. for Congregations, Ch. 8.04: 'regular use'; ELCIRE: Const., Art. 6: 'Members ... have the right to ... the use of the sacraments.'

[142] LCA: Some Pastoral Guidelines for Responsible Communion Practice (SPGRCP), adopted by the General Pastors' Conference 1990, edited 2001, 1: 'Every communicant, even an impenitent and unbelieving one, receives Christ's body and blood in this sacrament. But the benefits ... are received only by penitent believers who accept Christ's words and trust his promises expressed in the words of institution'; Large Catechism V.68. For a similar formula, see ELCSA: G., 3.1.3.3; LCGB: RAR, Statement of Faith, 5; ELCF: Catechism, 74–79.

[143] LCA: SPGRCP, 2.

and so bringing God's judgment on themselves.'[144] The ordained pastor determines who is to be admitted, presides at the sacrament and so 'represents Christ and acts on his behalf'; the pastor may be aided by 'lay assistants in the distribution of the sacrament'.[145] Provision is also made for the distribution of the sacrament to the sick outside church.[146] With regard to the ritual sequence, the 'normal practice' is for first communion to be celebrated at the rite of confirmation; however, those persons, particularly children, who have not been confirmed may be admitted if the congregation agrees, they are instructed, for example, in the doctrines of sin and grace and have reached 'a stage of spiritual development at which they can understand what is necessary ... to receive the sacrament to their blessing'; in the case of children, the parents are to be counselled and each case is to be considered individually.[147]

These same principles are to be found in Methodist law: 'The Supper of the Lord is not only a sign of the love that Christians ought to have among themselves one to another, but rather is a sacrament of our redemption by Christ's death'; when a person 'rightly, worthily, and with faith receive the same, the bread which we break is a partaking of the body of Christ; and likewise the cup of blessing is a partaking of the blood of Christ'.[148] Both bread and wine are to be received.[149] For example, the Methodist Church of Ireland recognises an obligation upon itself to make 'due provision for the regular and ordered Service of Holy Communion'; moreover: 'It is the duty and privilege of all its members to avail themselves of every opportunity to partake reverently and in faith of the Lord's Supper', for 'in His Sacraments the presence of Christ, through His Spirit, is realised in response to the obedient faith of His People'.[150] The Lord's Supper is administered by a minister in

---

[144] LCA: SPGRCP, 5 (1 Cor. 11.29). See also ELCSA: G., 3.8: 'Holy Communion has to be denied to the person who rejects the confession of ... Christ or who causes the congregation gross annoyance through word or deed.'

[145] LCA: Distribution of the Sacrament at the Altar, Department of Liturgics and adopted by the Commission on Worship, 1995 and 1998, edited 2001, 1–3; AC, 14; the pastor is responsible to Christ (Heb. 8:1–2, 6).

[146] LCA: The Distribution of the Lord's Supper to the Sick by Deacons, Elders, or Lay Servers, CTIR, 1995, edited 2001; see also LCA: The Service with Holy Communion for Ministry to those who are Sick, Department of Liturgics 1988, adopted by the Commission on Worship, 1998, edited 2001.

[147] LCA: Guidelines for Introducing the Practice of Separating First Communion from Confirmation, Board for Congregational Life, adopted by General Synod (Guidelines 1–9, 1981; Guidelines 10–11, 1984), edited 2000; but: 'Congregations should remain strongly committed to ... confirmation ... and ... make [it] as effective as possible.' ELCA: G., 3.7: 'Unconfirmed children, who come to the altar, may be blessed by laying on of hands'; pastor and council must take 'a joint general decision if children are to participate in Holy Communion'.

[148] UMCNEAE: BOD, par. 103, AR, Art. XVIII: 'Transubstantiation, or the change of the substance of bread and wine ... cannot be proved by Holy Writ, but is repugnant to the plain words of Scripture'; 'The body of Christ is given, taken, and eaten ... only after a ... spiritual manner. And the mean whereby the body of Christ is received and eaten in the Supper is faith' and must not be 'reserved, carried about, lifted up, or worshipped'.

[149] UMCNEAE: BOD, par. 103, AR, Art. XIX: 'The cup of the Lord is not to be denied to the lay people; for both the parts of the Lord's Supper, by Christ's ordinance and commandment, ought to be administered to all Christians alike.' See also MCGB: CPD, SO 922(2): 'wine used shall be non-alcoholic'.

[150] MCI: RDG, 1.01 and 2.06. See also UMCNEAE: BOD, par. 103: General Rules, par. 340.

full connexion; furthermore: 'Admission to the Lord's Supper shall be the privilege of members of the Church, and such members of the congregation, including children who wish to communicate, as the minister may judge to be eligible. The wine used in the ordinance shall be unfermented.'[151] However, a circuit which considers that any of its churches or a significant number of church members are deprived of reasonably frequent and regular celebrations of the Lord's Supper through lack of ministers, may apply in writing for the authorisation of fully accredited local preachers to preside at the sacrament when appointed to do so on the plan of that circuit, or on other occasions within the circuit when authorised by the superintendent in consultation with the district superintendent; authorisation is given by the Representative Session of the Conference as to a named person, place and period.[152] Similar arrangements are to be found in the Methodist Church of New Zealand.[153] Sometimes provision is made for the minister or class leader to visit those who are 'persistently absent from the Lord's Supper'; and a person who 'by prolonged absence severs himself or herself from Christian fellowship' is to be removed from the class book of the local church and so ceases membership of the church.[154]

For Presbyterians: 'In the Sacrament of the Lord's Supper, the Church commemorates the Lord Jesus Christ and His sacrifice for us' – Christ's offering of himself to the faithful and their acceptance of this gift are 'represented' by the breaking of bread, the pouring of wine and the distributing of both by the minister: 'In the celebration the Church acts for Christ, and Christ acts through her.' Moreover: 'The validity of the Sacrament depends on its proper administration with a sincere aim, namely, to show the Lord's death till He come'; its 'efficacy depends on our acceptance of the gift of our Lord by faith'.[155] As to the proper administration of the sacrament, the Church of Scotland is typical. The Kirk Session decides when the Lord's Supper will be celebrated but only an ordained minister is authorised to administer it;[156] an elder may assist if

---

[151] MCI: RDG, 3.05: there are exceptions to the admissions rule in pars. 4B.31 and 4G.16-21.

[152] MCI: RDG, 4G.16-4G.21; the appointee must be instructed in presidency at the Lord's Supper; in emergencies arising after the Conference (e.g. death of a minister), the president, consulting the Authorisations Committee may grant an authorisation until 30 June next. For similar rules, see MCGB: CPD, SO 011.

[153] MCNZ: LAR, s. 1.4.1-3: 1: 'The bread and the wine of the Lord's Table are perpetual reminders of Christ's atoning death, and emblems of the life he imparts. Through these tokens Christ's presence, through his Spirit, is discerned by his faithful people'; 2: 'The Lord's Supper shall be administered according to the form or forms authorised by the Conference, or by other appropriate liturgical expression, by a Presbyter or other duly authorised person, at Divine Worship' or such other time as arranged; 3: for 'imperative pastoral considerations', Conference may annually authorise a person (other than a Presbyter) of 'good character and standing' to act; authorization may at any time be withdrawn (7.11.2.21).

[154] MCGB: CPD, SO 054.

[155] PCW: HOR, 9.3: the sacrament was instituted by Christ (Matt. 26.26-28). See also PCA: BCO, 58.1: it is 'to be observed frequently' at times determined by the Session of each congregation; 58.4: it is observed 'in remembrance of Christ' and is of 'inestimable benefit' e.g. 'to strengthen His people against sin'.

[156] CLCS: 31. See also UFCS: MPP, I.III.2: the Session 'provides for ... the observance of the Lord's Supper'; 6: communion may be distributed in homes to sick and aged members; PCI: Code, I.II.II.37: public administration.

THE EUCHARIST, HOLY COMMUNION OR LORD'S SUPPER   253

authorised to administer the sacraments.[157] Members are entitled to (and should) receive communion and may do so by the 'common cup' in 'the ordinary elements of bread and wine', but an 'individual cup and unfermented wine are permitted'.[158] Baptised children may be admitted if their parents request this.[159] Presbyterian laws also provide for the exclusion of prescribed classes.[160] Similar rules are to be found in the regulatory instruments of the United,[161] Reformed[162] and Congregational churches.[163]

Finally, for Baptists the Lord's Supper is defined, typically, as: 'a symbolic act of obedience whereby members of the church, through partaking of the bread and the fruit of the vine, memorialize the death of the redeemer and anticipate His second coming'.[164] Some Baptist churches operate a liberal policy towards admission: 'Attendance shall be open to all who love the Lord Jesus as Lord and Saviour.'[165] Others confine admission to baptised persons.[166] The Lord's Supper should be observed as often as possible and at least once each quarter – the elements should include bread with or without yeast (but biscuits and wafers may be used) and a non-alcoholic beverage; only ordained ministers should administer it; and: 'Only

---

[157] PCANZ: BO, 6.11. See also UFCS: MPP, I.III.7: if there are insufficient ordained ministers, a presbytery may authorise an elder to preside at the Lord's Supper.
[158] CLCS: 109. See also PCANZ: BO 4.4: members have a right 'to participate in communion'; UFCS: MPP, I.III.6: 'Only members in full communion are entitled to participate' in the Lord's Supper; See also PCI: Code, I.II.II.40: 'The Kirk Session shall admit to the Lord's Supper only those who have been baptised, who make profession of faith in the Lord Jesus Christ, and whose character is consistent with such a profession' (see also par. 84(2)). PCW: HOR, 2.2: a member must partake 'regularly of the Lord's Supper'.
[159] CLCS: 109; Act XV, 1992: children; Act III, 1985: the mentally disabled; PCANZ: BO, 4.5: members have a right 'to have any child participate in communion'; PCW: HOR, 9.3: 'General Assembly is ... in favour of giving Ministers/Licensed Elders the power to administer communion to baptised children [and] freedom to respond to requests from parents, and neither ministers nor congregations are compelled to act on this'; the age is decided by the minister, elders and parents who 'should provide the children with instruction on receiving' Communion.
[160] PCA: BCO, 58.2: 'The ignorant and scandalous are not to be admitted to the Lord's Supper.'
[161] URC: Man., A.15: 'When in obedience to the Lord's command his people show forth his sacrifice on the cross by the bread broken and the wine outpoured for them to eat and drink, he himself, risen and ascended, is present and gives himself to them for their spiritual nourishment and growth in grace.'
[162] RCA: BCO, Pt. I, Ch. 1, Art. 2.11: 'the Lord's Supper shall be administered, if possible, at least once every three months in every church' and the approved Office used; 'All baptised Christians ... admitted to the Lord's Supper are ... invited to participate'; 13: private administration in sickness or emergency.
[163] UCCSA: Const., 15.1; UFCS: MPP VI.I: 'excommunication'; UCC: Man., BU 2.16.2.
[164] CNBC: Const 3, VII.
[165] BUSA: Model Const., Art. 10.2: 'The Lord's Supper shall be observed – as far as possible – on the first and third Sundays of the month – or at such times as the Church shall decide'; Riverside Baptist Church (Baltimore): BL Art. IV.1(c): 'at least one Sunday a month'; Bethel Baptist Church (Choctaw): Const., Art. V.2: 'a memorial Ceremony of the Lord's death, [it] is to be observed ... until the Lord comes. Unleavened bread and the fruit of the vine are ... used as symbols of His body and blood. Only members of [the church]' may receive.
[166] CNBC: Const., 3.VII: 'Being a church ordinance, [baptism] is a prerequisite to the privileges of church membership and to the Lord's Supper.'

Christians who are baptised by immersion may participate.'[167] In other words, regardless of the doctrinal differences between the traditions, all the churches studied here recognise the centrality of the sacrament in the life of the faithful – all the faithful should participate in its celebration regularly; the ordained ministers are responsible for its proper administration; prescribed classes may be denied admission to the sacrament – but provision exists for their restoration; and children may be admitted to the extent permitted by the law of a church.

Marriage and divorce

In many churches, rules on marriage have undergone considerable change in recent years. The stimulus for these has in part been the shift in secular society and law towards the greater incidence and availability of civil divorce. This has resulted in reconsideration by churches of fundamental questions about the nature of marriage and the treatment of 'remarriages' of divorced persons in church. This has led in turn to the emergence of sometimes profoundly different ecclesiastical norms on matrimonial discipline. These regulate the exercise of discretion by ordained ministers and others who have conscientious objections to the solemnisation of second marriages on the basis of the theological doctrine of indissolubility.

Marriage

The juridical instruments of all the churches in the Christian traditions studied here address the nature of marriage (particularly its covenantal character), the formation of marriage (such as the rights and capacity of the parties to marry) and the ritual solemnisation of marriage (including the role of the minister). The laws of some churches also address the conduct of the parties during the life of the marriage and the nurture of children born within marriage.

According to Roman Catholic canon law, Christian marriage is a divine institution: 'The marriage covenant, by which a man and a woman establish between themselves a partnership of their whole life, and which of its own very nature is ordered to the well-being of the spouses and to the procreation and upbringing of children, has, between the baptised, been raised by Christ the Lord to the dignity of a sacrament' – if two baptised persons marry validly, their marriage is a sacrament and 'essential properties of marriage are unity and indissolubility'.[168] A marriage is brought into being by 'the lawfully manifested consent of persons who are legally capable' – matrimonial consent is 'an act of will by which a man and a woman by an irrevocable covenant mutually give and accept one another for the purpose of establishing a marriage'.[169] Indeed: '[a]ll persons who are not prohibited by law

---

[167] NBC: PAP, Lord's Supper; BUSA: Model Const., Art. 4.1: 'the partaking of bread and wine [is] symbolical of the Saviour's mutilated body and shed blood, in remembrance of His sacrificial death till He come'.

[168] CIC, c. 1055: 'a valid marriage contract cannot exist between baptised persons without its being by that very fact a sacrament'; c. 1056: essential properties; see also GS 48. See generally R. Ombres, 'The nature of marriage and the right to marry in the Latin Code: canons 1055-1062', in N. Doe (ed.), *Marriage in Anglican and Roman Catholic Canon Law* (Centre for Law and Religion, Cardiff, 2009) 17.

[169] CIC, c. 1057: this consent cannot be supplied by any other human power.

have a right to marriage'; and baptism is a general prerequisite to sacramental marriage in church.[170] The 'diriment impediments' prevent a person from validly contracting marriage: lack of age, physical impotence, prior marriage bond, consanguinity and affinity.[171] Persons incapable of contracting marriage include those who lack the sufficient use of reason, suffer from a grave lack of judgment concerning the essential matrimonial rights and duties and, through causes of a psychological nature, are unable to assume the essential obligations of marriage.[172] Other grounds vitiating consent include ignorance, error about the identity of the partner, fraud, simulation of consent, fear and force.[173] As a general rule, only those marriages are valid which are contracted in the presence of a priest or deacon and two witnesses; the rite must be conducted in accordance with the liturgical books and the essential element of the rite is the exchange of consents.[174] When there is doubt about the validity of a marriage there is a presumption it is valid until the contrary is proven; the annulment of marriages is the function of the tribunals of the church.[175] Pastors must provide assistance in the preparation of couples for marriage and the faithful must support marriage and assist in the provision of pastoral care to spouses.[176] Similarly complex rules apply to Oriental Catholic Churches.[177]

The sacrament of marriage is defined in Orthodox canon law as a permanent union of one man and one woman.[178] Moreover: 'The Church's vision of marriage

---

[170] CIC, c. 1058; c. 53: '[o]ne who has not received baptism cannot be validly admitted to the other sacraments'; c. 1059: the marriage of Catholics (even if only one party is Catholic) is governed by divine law and canon law, 'without prejudice to the competence of civil authority in respect of the merely civil effects of the marriage'.

[171] CIC, cc. 1083–5: age, impotence and prior marriage; cc. 1091–2: consanguinity and affinity.

[172] CIC, c. 1095. See A. McGrath, 'On the gravity of causes of a psychological nature in the proof of inability to assume the essential obligations of marriage', 22 Studia Canonica (1988) 67.

[173] CIC, cc. 1096–1099, 1101–1103.

[174] CIC, c. 1108; cc. 1115–1116: place; cc. 1119–1120: local rites may be approved by the Episcopal Conference.

[175] CIC, c. 1087: 'Those ... in ... orders invalidly attempt marriage'; c. 1088: chastity; c. 1086: disparity of cult.

[176] CIC, cc. 1063–1064; c. 1065: unconfirmed Catholics must receive confirmation before marriage (if possible), and should approach confession and Eucharist; c. 1066: 'Before a marriage ... it must be established that nothing stands in the way of its valid and lawful celebration'; c. 1067: the Episcopal Conference is to issue norms as to preliminaries (e.g. banns); c. 1069: the faithful must reveal to the parish priest or local ordinary impediments they know about. See F. Gavin, 'An outline of marriage preparation in Roman Catholic discipline', in Doe, Marriage in Anglican and Roman Catholic Canon Law, 47.

[177] CCEO, cc. 776–866; cc. 783–789: preparation for marriage and pastoral care; cc. 790–799: diriment impediments; cc. 800–812: specific impediments; cc. 813–816: mixed marriages; cc. 817–827: consent; cc. 828–842: the form for its celebration; cc. 843–852: convalidation; cc. 853–866: separation of the spouses.

[178] MOCL: 123: 'Marriage is the union of man and woman' ('natural element'), sharing 'the same lot in life forever' ('moral element'), and 'the communion of divine and human law' ('religious/legal element'); see also OOCL: 187; SOCA: Const., Art. 147(a): 'matrimony is a Holy Sacrament and a lawful bond between a Syrian Orthodox man and woman. It is concluded by the designated priest who blesses the wedding in the presence of righteous Christian witnesses'; 148: it is permitted 'to perform a wedding if one of the two parties is a non-Syrian Orthodox Christian'; UOCIA: Instructions, Policy on Marriages.

is as an icon of the Trinitarian life of God Himself. In such a union, human love and desire for companionship become a love pervaded and sanctified by Divine Grace. God unites in body and spirit, heart and mind. Love unites in such a way that two lives become one life ... that is total in character'; also: 'the Christian family must be firmly established in the faith' and the parish priest must teach the faithful about the place of marriage in church life.[179] The requirements for a valid marriage are mutual consent voluntarily given by a capable party of requisite age. Absolute impediments include mental incapacity, impotence, lack of consent, prior marriage, pregnancy before marriage, ordination (and a widowed priest may not remarry), vows of chastity, widowhood after a third marriage (a fourth marriage is forbidden), and deceit, force or fear. Relative impediments include lack of requisite age, celebration on a forbidden day, and blood, spiritual (e.g. marriage between a sponsor and the baptised person), adoption and marital relationships. Absolute impediments invalidate marriage; relative impediments render it dissoluble until the impediment is lifted; and children born of an invalid marriage are illegitimate.[180] Prior to the marriage, the consent of the diocesan bishop or other hierarch must be obtained,[181] the parties should make confession and take Holy Communion,[182] and the priest must instruct them in the teaching and discipline of the church on marriage;[183] this should include instruction about the place of children in marriage and that procreation of children is not the sole purpose of marriage.[184] The couple must consult the parish priest as to the date and details of the wedding, and respect the seasons, times and holy days upon which a marriage should not be celebrated (such as in Lent).[185] Marriages should be celebrated on Sunday after the Divine Liturgy but this rule may be relaxed by the hierarch.[186] Marriage must be celebrated in an

---

[179] OCIA: GC, The Mystery of Marriage; Orthodox marrying outside the Orthodox Church exclude themselves from the Eucharist, but, after penance, may be restored if the priest so recommends and the hierarch approves; 'Normally ... restoration includes ... confirmation of the marriage through a rite approved by the hierarch.'

[180] MOCL: 123–127; see also OOCL: 194–198; UOCIA: Instructions, Policy on Marriages, 1; to be 'sacramentally valid ... No impediments to the marriage may exist, or the necessary dispensations must be obtained beforehand from the hierarch of the diocese'; parties must be in 'good standing' for at least a year before marriage; the prohibited relationships are e.g. parents marrying their children.

[181] SOCA: Const., Art. 109: 'A priest is not to conclude ... a marriage without ... a permit from the Metropolitan of the Archdiocese after submission of the necessary documents'; GOAA: Charter, Art. 7.6: the metropolitan may 'issue permits for the celebration of the sacrament of marriage'; OCIA: GC, Mystery of Marriage, 7.

[182] See e.g. SOCA: Const., Art. 143.   [183] OCIA: GC, Mystery of Marriage, 2.

[184] OCIA: GC, Mystery of Marriage, 3: 'Counselling and teaching should include ... Procreation of children is not in itself the sole purpose of marriage; nevertheless, marriage presupposes a desire to have children. The couple should pray for God to grant them the blessings of childbirth and wise nurturing of the family.'

[185] SOCA: Const., Art. 149: 'It is forbidden to perform a wedding ... during the fasts of Christmas ... Lent and all other fasts'; but, the metropolitan may permit marriages 'in urgent cases'; OCIA: GC, Mystery of Marriage, 5–6: e.g. Saturday evenings; UOCIA: Instructions, Policy on Marriages: e.g. Advent, Lent and Holy Week – but marriage may be celebrated then 'if absolutely necessary and for reasons of urgent import only with special dispensation from the diocesan hierarch'; ACROD: Guidelines, Marriages.

[186] OCIA: GC, Mystery of Marriage, 7: 'marriages are normally celebrated on Sunday after the Divine Liturgy'; Saturday weddings need the consent of the hierarch; 'The couple must be

Orthodox Church building by a cleric in accordance with the service books,[187] and witnessed.[188] Marriage certificates are issued following the ceremony which must be recorded in the marriage register of the parish.[189] Some Orthodox regulatory instruments also address the need for compliance with State law on marriage.[190]

The Anglican model of matrimonial discipline is not dissimilar. Marriage, an honourable estate instituted by God, is an exclusive life-long union, signifying the mystical union that is between Christ and his Church. It is constituted on the free exchange of consents between one man and one woman joined together by God as husband and wife and lasting until the death of one spouse. Marriage is a creative relationship to share life together in the spirit of Christ for the: (1) development of their personalities; (2) procreation and nurture of children; (3) right use of the natural instincts and affections; (4) mutual society, help and comfort which the one ought to have for the other, both in prosperity and adversity; and (5) establishment of a home and family life. All members of a church share according to their circumstances in the obligation to uphold Christian standards of marriage in society, especially by care for their own families and by neighbourly care for the families of others.[191] Ministers must comply with civil law as to the formation of marriage and with church law as to its solemnisation.[192] An ecclesiastical marriage is presumed valid if both parties: (1) have a right under civil law to contract a marriage; (2) freely and knowingly consent to marry, without fraud, coercion or mistake as to the identity or mental condition of the other party; (3) do not fall within the prohibited degrees of relationship; (4) have attained the required age for marriage; and (5) in the case of minors, have obtained the consent of their parents or guardians.[193] A church is free to impose for spiritual purposes such conditions for admission to ecclesiastical marriage as are prescribed by its law. While a Christian marriage is one between baptised persons, the law may provide for marriage where the normal requirement of baptism is not met. Generally, a minister may refuse to solemnise a marriage for such cause,

---

exhorted to attend the Divine Liturgy on the following Sunday so that the marriage can be sealed by the reception of the Holy Eucharist.'

[187] UOCIA: Instructions, Policy on Marriages, 3: marriage 'must be celebrated by an Orthodox priest in the church of the bride in accordance with the liturgical tradition of the Orthodox Church'; ACROD: Guidelines, Marriages; OCIA: GC, Mystery of Marriage, 8; SCOBA: GOCER, Pt I, Sacraments and other Liturgical Services IV.4: marriage in church; 13: the Service for Holy Matrimony.

[188] UOCIA: Instructions, Policy on Marriages, 12: one witness (a practising Orthodox) is required for the sacrament (two for civil recognition).

[189] ROC: Statute, XI.20: the rector must issue marriage certificates; GOAA: Regs., Art. 17.3: the priest must 'personally maintain the register books for all marriages ... that take place in the Parish', and submit marriage licences to the hierarch and civil marriage licences to the appropriate public authority; OCIA: GC, Mystery of Marriage, 10; MOSC: Const., Art. 43; ROMOC: Statutes, Art. 50.

[190] UOCIA: Instructions, Policy on Marriages, 2: a civil marriage licence must be obtained prior to the marriage.

[191] PCLCCAC, Principle 70; see also AR, Art. 25. See e.g. West Indies: Can. 29.1: 'the ideal of a Christian Marriage as a lifelong union'; England: Can. B30.1; New Zealand: Can. G.III.1.1.1.

[192] PCLCCAC, Principle 71.1; 71.2: 'The parties to a marriage must satisfy the civil and ecclesiastical requirements for a valid marriage. Otherwise the minister should refuse solemnisation.'

[193] PCLCCAC, Principle 71.3. See e.g. West Africa: Can. 7.4; England: Can. B31–32; West Indies: Can. 29.3.

which may include conscientious objection, as is provided by the law.[194] As to preliminaries, a minister should instruct prospective spouses in the nature, significance, purpose and responsibilities of marriage in a manner consistent with church doctrine and any requirements prescribed by ecclesiastical authority. Lawful notice of the date of the marriage must be given to the minister, who must establish that no impediment obstructs its valid celebration under canon law and civil law; if any impediment is alleged, marriage should be deferred until the truth is established.[195] The ordinary minister of matrimony is a priest or bishop, but the man and woman may also be understood as both recipients and ministers of marriage; deacons, too, may be authorised to solemnise marriage. The liturgical books must be used. A marriage is created by the free, competent and open consent of the parties in the presence of at least two witnesses. The marriage is recorded in registers maintained in the church for this purpose. A civil marriage may be followed by a blessing of that marriage in church.[196]

The Protestant churches also treat marriage as a divine institution and they provide for its formation and solemnisation. Within Lutheranism,[197] the Evangelical Lutheran Church in Southern Africa is typical: 'God has installed marriage as an order of creation. He unites man and woman towards an inseparable communion, in which they love and assist one another. The married couple is responsible to God

---

[194] PCLCCAC, Principle 71: a church may relax baptismal requirements for marriage by way of e.g. dispensation of a bishop; a person, being a member of, associated with, or resident in a parish of, a church, may be entitled to a church marriage. See e.g. Church of England Marriage Measure 2008: the common law right of parish residents extends to persons with a 'qualifying connection' to the parish; TEC: Can. I.18.4: 'It shall be within the discretion of any Member of the Clergy ... to decline to solemnize any marriage'; New Zealand: Can. G.III.2.8: 'No minister shall solemnize matrimony between two persons neither of whom has been baptized'; West Africa: Can. 7.3: if one or both parties are non-baptised, 'a dispensation [may] be granted by the Bishop' if e.g. they 'recognize [it] will be a Christian marriage identical ... to a marriage' between two baptised persons.

[195] PCLCCAC, Principle 72.1-6; 72.4: it may be solemnised following publication of banns, episcopal licence or other permission. See e.g. Southern Africa: Can. 35.6: there is no marriage 'until [the parties] have received such instruction on Christian Marriage as ... approved by the Bishop'; West Africa: Can. 7.4: the minister may not proceed unless he ascertains 'both parties understand that Holy Matrimony is a physical and spiritual union'; New Zealand: Can. G. III.2.1: notice of 30 days; Philippines: Cans. III.16.4: enquiry as to impediments.

[196] PCLCCAC, Principle 73. See e.g. Papua New Guinea: Can. No. 2 of 1995, Arts. 1–5: the man and woman are the ministers and the priest or deacon confects the marriage; Scotland: Can. 31.6: marriage must be solemnized in a church building unless the bishop permits otherwise; Central Africa: Can. 22.5: no marriages in Lent (without episcopal consent); New Zealand: Can. G.III.1.1.2: 'A marriage is created by the free, competent and open consent of the parties who contract it, in the presence of witnesses and of an authorized minister.'

[197] LCA: Marriage, Divorce and Re-Marriage, I, prepared by the CTIR, adopted by General Synod 1978, edited 2001: God 'instituted marriage. It is part of the created social order. So society, through custom or legislation, decides when a man and a woman are in fact married'; 'Marriage is the union of a man and a woman. This union excludes all other people. It is publicly and voluntarily entered into for the whole of life'; its purpose is 'to unite one man and one woman (that is, husband and wife) so that they become "one flesh"', 'to produce children and to care for their upbringing within the framework of a family' and 'to provide an appropriate place and context for a man and a woman to have sexual relations'; AC 16 and 28; Matt. 19:6; 1 Cor. 7:39.

in their way of life'; parents should educate their children about this doctrine. A couple must approach the minister in good time, and the minister must counsel them on the meaning of marriage and the Christian way of married life. The marriage must take place in the context of a public service which includes solemn promises and a blessing; no wedding celebrations should be held in Lent and Holy Week. Marriage is to be denied: (1) if both spouses are not members of a Christian church; (2) if one of the spouses publicly rejects the Christian faith; (3) if a wedding ceremony has been performed or is intended to be performed by an office bearer of another Christian religion or philosophic association; or (4) when bigamy is being committed.[198] These essentials are echoed in Methodist law: 'the sanctity of the marriage covenant ... is expressed in love, mutual support, personal commitment, and shared fidelity between a man and a woman'; moreover: 'God's blessing rests upon such marriage, whether or not there are children of the union', and the church rejects 'social norms that assume different standards for women than for men in marriage'.[199] Marriage may be open to those beyond the church membership.[200] The marriage ceremony occurs after due counsel with the parties involved.[201] It is solemnised by a minister in accordance with the laws of the state (as to validity) and the rules and service books of the church,[202] but the 'decision to perform the ceremony shall be the right and responsibility of the pastor'.[203] For the Methodist Church of Great Britain, if a request is received 'to conduct prayers for a same-sex couple the person approached should respond sensitively, pastorally and with due regard to established good practice'; 'no minister or layperson is required to act in any way contrary to his or her own conscience', and 'Methodist premises may not be used for the blessing of same-sex relationships'.[204]

Much the same approach is found in Presbyterianism. The Presbyterian churches in Wales, Scotland and Ireland respectively typify the approach as to the nature, formation and administration of marriage. For the Welsh church, marriage is 'a holy estate instituted by God. It is based on natural tendencies and needs, and it

---

[198] ELCSA: G., 7.2–7.8.
[199] UMCNEAE: BOD, Part IV: Social Principles, par. 161: marriage is 'the union of one man and one woman'; the family is 'the basic human community through which persons are nurtured and sustained in mutual love, responsibility, respect, and fidelity'; MCGB: CPD, SO 011A: marriage is 'a gift of God and that it is God's intention that a marriage should be a life-long union in body, mind and spirit of one man and one woman'.
[200] MCGB: CPD, SO 011A: 'The Methodist Church welcomes everyone, whether or not a member, who enquires about an intended marriage in any of its places of worship.'
[201] MCGB: CPD, Bk. VI, Pt. 2, s. 9: Christian Preparation for Marriage: Methodist Church Policy and Guidelines, s. 10, Guidelines for Inter-Faith Marriages, s. 14: the 'traditional teaching of the Church on human sexuality' is 'chastity for all outside marriage and fidelity within it'; MCNZ: LAR, Introductory Documents, II, Pastoral Resolutions: the church 'will give adequate preparation for ... Marriage'.
[202] See e.g. MCI: RDG, 2.09: 'Marriages solemnised according to the usages of the [church] shall be conducted by a minister in full connexion with ... Conference. The form of service ... authorised by ... Conference'; App. 5.02: Civil Registration Act 2004 (Republic of Ireland) and Marriage (Northern Ireland) Order 2003 (UK).
[203] UMCNEAE: BOD, par. 340; 341.6: 'Ceremonies that celebrate homosexual unions shall not be conducted by our ministers and shall not be conducted in our churches.'
[204] MCGB: CPD, Bk. VI, Pt. 2, s. 15: 'If there is any doubt over how to respond, the Superintendent and possibly also the Chair of District should be consulted.'

is an expression of the Divine intention in our creation, to realise moral and spiritual ends'. It is 'the duty' of the church to 'explain the true nature of marriage to its members, to impress upon them the sacred responsibilities and obligations of married life, and to show how divine grace can help to maintain and enrich the marriage bond' – marriage 'essentially permanent in character should be upheld to the utmost'.[205] For the Scottish church, a minister may not conduct a marriage service unless in receipt of a marriage schedule issued by the civil registrar and banns are then published, and the parties must disclose any impediments.[206] Only an ordained minister may solemnise a marriage and ministers are 'obliged to solemnise the marriages of parishioners'.[207] For the Irish church, every ordained minister is qualified to celebrate marriage but (unlike the Orthodox) should not celebrate marriage on a Sunday. The minister must endeavour to ascertain that there is no lawful impediment to a marriage. If difficulties arise as to whether marriage by the church is advisable, the minister may consult the Kirk Session or refer the matter to the Assembly's Committee on Marriage and the Family. However, a minister should not conduct the marriage of a church member with a person whose church membership is incompatible with the Christian witness of the Protestant Reformation until careful instruction has been given in the doctrines and obligations of the evangelical faith and the conditions approved by the Committee on Marriage and the Family have been observed. A congregation must maintain marriage registers.[208] Very few rules about marriage are to be found in the instruments of Baptist churches studied here, save to the extent that church members should marry under the marriage ordinance, that marriage ceremonies should not be expensive and that they should not be celebrated with alcohol.[209]

Divorce and remarriage

There are considerable juridical differences between the churches as to the practice of marriage annulment, divorce amongst the faithful and the solemnisation of a church marriage following a civil dissolution. The Catholic Church employs a system of marriage annulment and a restrictive approach to dissolution and second

---

[205] PCW: HOR, 9.4. See also PCA: BCO, 59.1: 'Marriage is a divine institution though not a sacrament, nor peculiar to the Church of Christ. It is proper that every commonwealth, for the good of society, make laws to regulate marriage, which all citizens are bound to obey'; 59.2: 'Christians should marry in the Lord; therefore it is fit that their marriage be solemnized by a lawful minister'; 59.3: 'Marriage is between one man and one woman, in accordance with the Word of God'; 59.4: 'The parties should be of such years of discretion as to be capable of making their own choice; and if they be under age, or live with their parents, the consent of the parents and others, under whose care they are, should be previously obtained, and well certified to the minister before he proceeds to solemnize the marriage'; 59.6: 'Marriage is of a public nature' and should be sufficiently published before solemnization and the minister must be careful not to transgress 'neither the laws of God, nor the laws of the community' and be assured that 'no just objections lie against their marriage'.

[206] Marriage Scotland Act 1977. For similar provisions see UFCS: MPP, IV.III.65.

[207] CLCS: 35; Act I, 1977. See also RCA: BCO, Pt. II, Art. 14: a pastor must perform 'a service of Christian marriage when approved by consistory and subject to state and provincial law'.

[208] PCI: Code, par. 85(1)–(5); for marriage registers, par. 255. See also UCC: Man., BL 153(b) xi.

[209] NBC: PAP, Marriage.

marriages. In the Latin Church: 'From a valid marriage there arises between the spouses a bond which of its own nature is permanent and exclusive';[210] and the 'essential properties of marriage are unity and indissolubility'.[211] When a marriage has been annulled by the church (because the criteria of validity have not been met), the parties are free to (re)marry.[212] However, if the union is terminated by a civil divorce, the canonical bond continues to exist; thus, a ratified and consummated marriage (between two baptised persons) cannot be dissolved by any human power or for any reason other than death – but the Pontiff may dissolve a non-consummated, ratified marriage for just cause at the request of both parties or one if the other is unwilling.[213] Also, a marriage of two non-baptised persons is dissolved under the Pauline Privilege if one party becomes baptised as a convert and the other no longer wishes to cohabit; the convert is then free to marry another person.[214] The Oriental Churches have parallel provisions.[215]

An Orthodox parish priest should assist if a married couple experiences marital difficulties.[216] According to Orthodox canon law, a marriage is dissolved only through the death of one of the spouses or an event which revokes 'the ecclesiastical significance of the marriage' and constitutes 'the religious or moral death of the marriage' – in such cases, divorce is tolerated on the basis of the doctrine of economy.[217] The consent of the bishop must be obtained.[218] Canonical grounds for divorce include adultery, apostasy and (if the other spouse consents) entering a monastery.[219] Following divorce, a party is free to enter a second or third

---

[210] CIC, c. 1134.
[211] CIC, c. 1056: the essential properties; c. 1134: permanence and exclusivity.
[212] CIC, cc. 1157, 1159: convalidation validates a marriage which was canonically valid *ab initio*.
[213] CIC, c. 1141; c. 1142. See e.g. M. Hilbert, 'Dispensation for non-consummated marriages: *de processu super ratio*', in Doe, *Marriage in Anglican and Roman Catholic Canon Law*, 797.
[214] CIC, c. 1143; c. 1144: the non-baptised party must be questioned as to whether he/she wishes also to receive baptism and to cohabit; c. 1146: second marriage; cc. 1151–1155: separation while the bond remains.
[215] CCEO, cc. 776–866.
[216] OCIA: GC, Mystery of Marriage, 9: 'The priest ... must ... be available to counsel those already married, who are experiencing difficulties'; UOCIA: Instructions, Policy on Marriages: 'the spiritual father or parish pastor must exert every effort to reconcile the couple and avert a divorce if this is spiritually and humanly possible'.
[217] MOCL: 135–136: indissolubility is the norm; but: 'Divorce by religious or moral death occurs by itself when the ... marriage ceases to function and the purpose of the marital bond is therefore frustrated'; thus: 'it is not the competent authority which dissolves the marriage' but 'only formally certifies that the legitimate marriage has lost its basis and has dissolved itself'; OCIA: GC, Mystery of Marriage, B. Second Marriages and Marriage between Divorced Persons, 1: 'The Orthodox norm for those who marry is one marriage. A second marriage is tolerated under certain conditions. A third marriage is extended under certain precise circumstances.'
[218] OCIA: GC, ibid., 2: 'The Church does not grant divorces. However, it recognizes that because of human weaknesses and sin marriages sometimes disintegrate and are ended by civil decree (divorce)'; 3: 'In her mercy and wisdom, the Church may grant permission to remarry' by petition to the hierarch through the parish priest; repentance from the divorced party, whether or not culpable, and reasons why a second marriage is necessary for salvation, must be addressed to the hierarch; ROMOC: Statutes, Art. 88: dispensations for remarriage.
[219] MOCL: 137–138: through divorce the bond is dissolved and the parties are free to enter a new marriage – a first marriage is considered canonical and holy, and a second marriage is

marriage – but cannot enter a fourth marriage.[220] The bishop may be involved in the quasi-judicial resolution of issues as to marriage and divorce or else these are determined by the church courts.[221] There are special orders of service to be used in the case of second marriages.[222]

The Anglican model is not unlike that of Orthodoxy. A church may provide that any person whose marriage has been terminated by divorce or annulment under civil law may apply, in the manner prescribed by church law, to the bishop or other competent ecclesiastical authority for a judgment which may declare the nullity of the marriage for ecclesiastical purposes.[223] The matrimonial bond is intended to be dissolved only by the death of one spouse. When a marriage is dissolved by the death of one of the parties, the surviving spouse is free to marry in church. However, when marital unity is imperilled, before recourse to civil law, the spouses are to approach the church, which should labour that they may be reconciled. If a harmonious or even tolerable relationship has in fact ceased to exist, a church may hold that while divorce is undesirable, it may be preferable to the continuance of a destructive relationship.[224] Following the civil dissolution of a marriage, a church may permit a person whose former spouse is still alive to be married in church, and may stipulate conditions required for the solemnisation of such a marriage which it judges necessary to safeguard the holiness of marriage and the respect due to it. An ordained minister may refuse for reasons of conscience or other lawful cause to solemnise the marriage of a divorced person whose former spouse is still alive. A church may provide that the decision to solemnise the marriage of a divorced person whose former spouse still lives is to be made by a member of the clergy, as the case may be, either alone, or in consultation with the bishop, or with the consent of the bishop or such other

exceptional (permitted by *oikonomia*); thus, those entering a second marriage ought not to be crowned as are those entering a first marriage.

[220] OCIA: GC, Mystery of Marriage, B. Second Marriages etc, 4: 'Under no circumstances can there be a fourth marriage'; MOCL: 137–8: A fourth marriage is forbidden': local synod of Constantinople 920; OOCL: 199–201; ACROD: Guidelines, Marriages, 7: 'No more than a total of three valid marriages are permitted by the Church.'

[221] ROC: Statute, X.19(d): the bishop must 'solve problems pertaining to church marriages and divorces'; SOCA: Const., Art. 147(b): 'The Personal Status Code ... is to be implemented in cases of betrothal, marriage, conflicts between couples, and ... alimonies, separations, marriage annulments, and divorces'; the Spiritual Courts deal with annulment and divorce; GOAA: Charter, Art. 9: the Spiritual Court hears cases of 'family problems' and 'divorce'; Art. 7.6: the Metropolitan may issue 'decrees of ecclesiastical divorce in the event of the dissolution'; UOCIA: Instructions, Policy on Marriages, 8: 'When one or both parties is divorced, they must obtain a decree of annulment or of spiritual death of former marriage from the Diocesan Tribunal'; Statutes, Art. XII.5: the Diocesan tribunal may issue annulment and divorces for e.g. apostasy, adultery and desertion.

[222] OCIA: GC, Mystery of Marriage, B. Second Marriages, 5: 'Order of Service: If one ... is being married for the first time' the order for first marriage is used; 'If both ... are divorced and/or widowed', the second order.

[223] PCLCCAC, Principle 74.1; 74.2: grounds for an ecclesiastical declaration of nullity may include: absence of consent freely given and received, or of an intention to be married until death; lack of the required age to marry; or being within the prohibited degrees of relationship; 3: 'Marriage in church may follow an ecclesiastical or a civil declaration of nullity'. For ecclesiastical annulment proceedings, available in only a small number of Anglican churches, see e.g. Southern Africa: Can. 34.4; TEC: Cans. I.19.1–2; Canada: Can. 21.16–33.

[224] PCLCCAC, Principle 75.1–4.

competent authority prescribed by law. A person who has a civil divorce should not by virtue of that fact alone be excluded from Holy Communion. Persons who remarry during the lifetime of a former spouse and those married to them may receive Holy Communion subject to conditions operative under the law.[225]

There is little to distinguish between these Orthodox and Anglican models and those of Protestantism. This is certainly the case in Lutheranism and Methodism. For instance, for the Evangelical Lutheran Church of Australia, divorce is 'against the will of God'; however, 'a marriage break may become a necessity'.[226] As such: 'A pastor may marry a divorced person or persons provided that the situation has been thoroughly worked through in the light of the church's teaching on marriage and divorce, and the pastor can officiate with a good conscience.' The parties are under an obligation to seek reconciliation and the church, principally through the pastor, is to facilitate this by counselling and other pastoral means.[227] This approach is typical.[228] Some Lutheran churches make provision as to the divorce of ordained pastors.[229] Likewise, for Methodism: 'God's plan is for lifelong, faithful marriage' and the church must support reconciliation between spouses in danger of marital breakdown. However: 'when a married couple is estranged beyond reconciliation ... divorce

---

[225] PCLCCAC, Principle 75.5–9; 10: lack of parity of religion is not of itself a reason for seeking divorce. See e.g. Australia: Can. 7, 1985, 4: 'A minister ... may refuse to solemnize the marriage of any divorced person during the life of the person's former spouse'; Scotland: College of Bishops Guidelines (1981): no priest is 'required to officiate ... contrary to his conscience'; Southern Africa: Can. 34.3: no cleric 'shall solemnize the marriage of any person whose marriage has been annulled or dissolved by secular authority during the lifetime of the partner' unless the marriage has been declared invalid by the bishop or the cleric has obtained a licence from the bishop; Ireland: Const., IX.31.3–6: consult the bishop; West Africa: Can. 7.6: consent of the bishop.

[226] LCA: Marriage, Divorce and Re-Marriage, II, CTIR, adopted by General Synod 1978, edited 2001: 'Divorce is against the will of God. God wants husband and wife to live together in marriage until ... separated by death' (e.g. Mk. 10:11); 'Our Lord, in Matthew 5:32 and 19:9, does not teach that failure in marriage *must* be followed by divorce ... even in the case of infidelity'; the passages 'simply indicate that in these circumstances divorce becomes a possibility'. Also, NALC: SFPM (2011) pp. 4–6: divorce is 'a violation of God's plan for marriage'.

[227] LCA: Marriage, Divorce and Re-Marriage, III.1–3; IV.B: matters of concern include the attitude of the divorced person to their former spouse; the possibility of reconciliation; God's will; repentance for any failure of the previous marriage; the extent to which the person has fulfilled responsibilities to children of the former marriage, made efforts to remove/correct factors contributing to the divorce, is willing to build a new Christian marriage; and the extent to which these concerns are understood/accepted by the prospective partner.

[228] ELCSA: G., 7.10–7.11: 'Marriage, according to God's will, is inseparable'; but: 'If a marriage is endangered, every effort should be made to heal the damage and to lead ... to reconciliation'; if a couple divorces, 'the congregation should not judge but assist'; 'The church wedding of a divorcee stands in conflict with the given solemn promise. It may only take place when the divorced partner realizes and affirms the meaning of repentance and absolution as a possibility for a new beginning and when ... the minister ... can justify the wedding before God. An appropriate space of time should elapse between divorce and re-marriage.'

[229] NALC: SFPM, pp. 4–6: the pastor must make every effort at reconciliation and with the bishop devise a plan for e.g. public disclosure to the congregation; possible leave of absence; repentance, healing and reconciliation (e.g. personal absolution, counselling); adequate attention to the spouse and children; the bishop must consult a small panel of pastors and lay people to implement this plan; 'Failure to fulfil these may result in discipline.'

is a regrettable alternative'; the church recommends mediation in such cases and should not resort to the courts of the State.[230] Nevertheless: 'Divorce does not preclude a new marriage' and the church must minister compassionately to divorced and remarried couples.[231] For instance, in the Methodist Church of Great Britain: 'Divorce does not of itself prevent a person being married in any Methodist place of worship.' However: 'Under no circumstances does the Conference require any person authorised to conduct marriages who is subject to the discipline of the Church as a minister, deacon, probationer or member to officiate at the marriage of a particular couple should it be contrary to the dictates of his or her conscience to do so.' Therefore: those authorised to conduct marriages 'but who for reasons of conscience will never officiate at the marriages of couples in particular circumstances shall refer such couples to an authorised colleague who is not so prevented'. Accordingly, if a couple seeks to be married in a Methodist place of worship, no objection to the performance by a particular minister, deacon, probationer or member of any duty in respect of their proposed marriage shall be entertained on such a ground. No minister, deacon, probationer or member shall perform the relevant duty or duties in place of the other person concerned or otherwise assist the couple to make the objection effective.[232]

This approach is also used in some Presbyterian churches: 'When a disagreement between husband and wife becomes apparent, an earnest endeavour should be made [by ministers and elders] to effect reconciliation ... in wisdom and gentleness' and to avoid resort to 'a court of law'. However: 'If and when all genuine efforts at reconciliation have failed and the husband and wife in all conscience have to accept the fact that the marriage bond has been irrevocably broken in spirit and in truth, then the Church, in accordance with the spirit of the New Testament teaching, cannot condemn persons for seeking a divorce.'[233] Nevertheless: 'The Church ... does not lay down rigid rules regarding the re-marriage in Church of divorced persons'; if the minister and elders are satisfied that 'both the reasons for the previous divorce and for the re-marriage are genuine and sincere', then remarriage may take place, but a minister may on grounds of conscience refuse to solemnise this and the Presbytery may be approached to find another.[234] Divorced persons may be admitted to Holy Communion.[235]

---

[230] UMCNEAE: BOD, Part IV: Social Principles, par. 161: 'The welfare of each child is the most important consideration.'

[231] UMCNEAE: BOD, Part IV: Social Principles, par. 161: 'The church must be on the forefront of premarital, marital, and post-marital counselling in order to create and preserve strong marriages.' See also MCGB: CPD, Book VI, Guidelines for Good Practice in Confidentiality and Pastoral Care.

[232] MCGB: CPD, SO 011A.   [233] PCW: HOR, 9.4.

[234] PCW: HOR, 9.4: 'It is important to state that the Connexion does not lay on any minister the duty of officiating at the marriage of a divorced person if, in so doing, he would be acting against his own conscience and judgment, and that of the elders.' See also CLCS: 35; Act XXVI, 1959. PCI: Code, 85(6)-(8): 'While this Church does not prohibit the marriage of a divorced person or persons, it is strongly recommended that a minister does not join in marriage a person who has been divorced, except in circumstances recognised by the Committee on Marriage and the Family as justifying such action'; also: if a divorced minister wishes to remain in office after remarriage 'the approval of the Presbytery shall be obtained'; URC: Man., M.

[235] PCW: HOR, 9.4: the church 'does not refuse Communion to a divorced person who is morally innocent in the case, or who is sincerely repentant'.

In short, the Catholic Church, and some Orthodox and Anglican churches provide for the ecclesiastical annulment of marriage, but most other traditions do not. However, on the basis of the doctrine of the indissolubility of marriage, whilst the Catholic Church operates a very restrictive approach to the dissolution of marriage, Orthodox, Anglican and Protestant churches allow remarriage after a civil dissolution subject to the satisfaction of prescribed conditions. In the Orthodox tradition, remarriage is tolerated by way of economy, and in Anglicanism and Protestantism, a minister may solemnise the marriage of a divorced person whose former spouse still lives if that minister has no conscientious objection to the marriage.

Confession and funerals

Whilst the Catholic Church and the Orthodox Church require that the faithful participate in the sacrament of penance, reconciliation or confession, the Reformation led to the juridical abandonment of obligatory private auricular confession for many churches that emerged in and beyond the sixteenth century. Nevertheless, many churches retain confession and absolution as a fundamental but voluntary facility available to the faithful. This section deals with the administration of confession and the final rite of passage for Christians – funerals.

The rite of confession

The Catholic Church practises the rite of confession. For the Roman Catholic Church: 'In the sacrament of penance the faithful who confess their sins to a lawful minister, are sorry for their sins and have a purpose of amendment, receive from God, through the absolution given by that minister, forgiveness of sins they have committed after baptism, and at the same time they are reconciled with the Church, which by sinning they wounded.'[236] All the faithful have a duty to celebrate the sacrament, confessing serious sins, at least once each year; to be validly celebrated, the penitent must be properly disposed and have the intention to amend; the penitent has a right to choose a confessor.[237] Individual confession and absolution is the ordinary method of reconciliation and only moral or physical impossibility relieves (for a limited time) a person of the duty to confess individually. General absolution may be given to a group if each one in it has confessed individually beforehand – but a priest may absolve generally without prior individual confession if the penitent is in danger of death or in cases of serious necessity when there are insufficient confessors.[238] Absolution may be given only by a validly ordained priest – if 'the confessor has no doubt about the disposition of a penitent who asks for absolution, absolution is not to be refused or delayed'; and in danger of death

---

[236] CIC, c. 959; LG 11. See generally Woestman, *Sacraments*, 217–297.

[237] CIC, cc. 988–9; c. 916: those wishing to celebrate the Eucharist must confess beforehand; see also. J.H. Provost, 'First penance and first Eucharist', 43 *The Jurist* (1983) 450; CIC, c. 987: validity; c. 991: choice of confessor and the use of an interpreter; cc. 992–997: indulgences.

[238] CIC, cc. 960–963; c. 964: the proper place for confession is in churches, or elsewhere for just cause.

cases, every priest has a duty to absolve.[239] In its administration, the priest acts as a judge and must enjoin a salutary and suitable penance in keeping with the quality and number of sins confessed, and the penitent must perform the penance personally.[240] There is a prohibition against the disclosure of any information given in the sacrament: '[t]he sacramental seal is inviolable; therefore it is a crime for a confessor in any way to betray a penitent by word or in any other manner or for any reason'; a confessor who directly violates the seal of the confessional incurs an automatic excommunication and indirect disclosure may be punished with a penalty in accord with the seriousness of the offence.[241] Similar rules apply in the Oriental Catholic Churches.[242] There is also provision for exorcism.[243]

In the Orthodox tradition, the faithful must make confession regularly.[244] Clergy must also make confession, and each should have a father confessor in order to do so,[245] and they should encourage the faithful to participate frequently in confession,[246] particularly before reception of the Holy Communion.[247] Acts of penance may include fasting, works of charity and pilgrimage.[248] Some churches address confessional secrecy explicitly; for instance: 'The secrecy of the Mystery of Penance

---

[239] CIC, c. 965; c. 979: the priest in posing questions must proceed with prudence and discretion and with attention to the age and condition of the penitent; he must refrain from asking names of accomplices; c. 986: the priest has discretion as to times for confession; c. 980: the right to absolution; c. 986: danger of death.

[240] CIC, cc. 978, 981; c. 959: the penance consummates the sacrament; c. 981: personal performance.

[241] CIC, c. 983; the duty also applies to interpreters and any third-party recipient; c. 984: the confessor must not use knowledge acquired from confession when this might harm the penitent; c. 1388: excommunication.

[242] CCEO, cc. 718–736; c. 732: the priest 'is placed by God as a minister of divine justice and mercy; as a spiritual father he should also offer appropriate counsel so the penitent might progress ... to sanctity'.

[243] CIC, c. 1172: no one may lawfully exorcise the possessed without the special and express permission of the local ordinary; this is granted only to a priest endowed with piety, knowledge, prudence and integrity of life.

[244] ROC: Statute, XI.32; SOCA: Art. 143: at least twice p.a.; OCIA: GC, The Mystery of Penance, Preamble: 'Confession, the mystery of reconciliation with the Church, must be regular and frequent ... an abiding element in the lives of the faithful'; SCOBA: GOCER, Pt. I, Sacraments and Other Liturgical Services, VI; UOCIA: Statutes, Art. XI.5: to qualify as a voting parishioner a person must partake of 'the Sacraments of Confession and Holy Communion at least once a year'.

[245] SOCA: Const., Art. 142: 'All clergy shall submit to the lawful Sacrament of Confession'; OCIA: GC, The Mystery of Penance, 5: clergy must confess 'regularly and faithfully' and may choose their own 'spiritual father' or a senior priest appointed by the hierarch as 'diocesan confessor'.

[246] OCIA: GC, A Selection of Clergy Disciplines, 7: 'Clergy should ... be diligent and sensitive in encouraging pious repentance and ... a sincere confession (Holy Apostles, c. 52; Trullo, c. 102)'; OCIA: GC, The Mystery of Penance, 1. 'The priest ... must determine the frequency with which the spiritual child confesses his/her sins.'

[247] Ibid., 2: also, 'the Spiritual Father should be prepared to hear [a] person's confession at all times'.

[248] MOCL: 111–112: 'Such acts are recommended by the holy canons'; e.g. 'more rigid fasting than what is usual, acts of charity, the reading of spiritual books, pilgrimages and the frequently imposed minor excommunication; judicial authority is exercised in the sacrament by the bishop personally or by a priest [under] a letter of authorisation (*entalterion gramma*) from the bishop'.

is considered an unquestionable rule in the entire Orthodox Church. Theologically, the need to maintain the secrecy of confession comes from the fact that the priest is only a witness before God.' Also: 'One could not expect a sincere and complete confession if the penitent has doubts regarding the practice of confidentiality. Betrayal of the secrecy of confession will lead to canonical punishment of the priest.'[249]

The Anglican model provides that only a priest or bishop may pronounce absolution. General confession and absolution may be administered at a public service, and private confession and absolution to an individual person. Priests should instruct the faithful in the use of private confession. A person who, unable to quiet his conscience by general confession or otherwise to find the assurance of the forgiveness of God, repents of his sinful past and intends amendment of life, may offer private confession to God in the presence of a priest. At a private confession the priest may give advice and must pronounce absolution except for good reason. Absolution may not be exercised without the permission of the minister having cure of souls of the parish in which it is performed, except in cases of danger of death.[250] The seal of the confessional is inviolable. The secrecy of confession is morally absolute for the confessor, an historic obligation, a solemn bond and a sacred trust so that the penitent is able to confess in the assurance that the priest will not disclose or refer again to the matter confessed. It is not abrogated on the death of the penitent. However, a priest may disclose information received in confession with the consent or at the request of the penitent who at any time may withdraw such permission, to the extent provided by the law of a church. The extent to which the seal is protected and priest-penitent communications are privileged in civil courts is a matter of civil law. Any obligation to give evidence under compulsion of a civil court or other authorised body is enforceable in secular law, but priests compelled to testify must always have in mind the historic obligation of the seal of the confessional. If a priest is required by a civil court to breach the seal of the confessional, the priest should seek permission to consult the bishop for advice and direction. A priest who violates the seal may be subject to judicial or other disciplinary proceedings carried out in accordance with church law, but no communication privileged under civil law shall be required to be disclosed.[251]

The legal evidence examined for this book suggests that confession is only practised in a small number of Protestant churches. For Lutheranism, confession

---

[249] OCIA: GC, The Mystery of Penance, 6.
[250] PCLCCAC, Principle 76. See e.g. Melanesia: Cans. A.6.A.1–5: public and private confession; Scotland: Can. 29.1: 'All priests ... shall make themselves available for the ministration of the Sacrament of Penance'; England: Can. B29: 'If there be any who ... cannot quiet his own conscience, but requires further comfort or counsel, let him come to some discreet and learned minister ... that ... he may receive the benefit of absolution.'
[251] PCLCCAC, Principle 77. See e.g. TEC: Cans. IV.14.23: 'the secrecy of a confession is morally absolute for the confessor, and must under no circumstances be broken'; Southern Africa: Prayer Book 1989, 448: 'Every priest in exercising the ministry of reconciliation ... is solemnly bound to observe secrecy concerning all those matters which are confessed before him'; Scotland: Can. 29.2: 'The seal is absolute and is not abrogated on the death of the penitent'; Australia: Can. 10 1992, 2: disclosure may occur with the consent of the penitent; Canada: Const., 156, App. M: if a secular court requires a priest to disclose, 'the priest should seek permission to consult the diocesan [bishop] and the chancellor'; England: Canons Ecclesiastical 1603, Can. 113.

and absolution have a place in the liturgy for Holy Communion and provision may exist for private confession to a pastor.[252] The church has the authority to absolve,[253] as sin which is not forgiven destroys communion with God.[254] Confession includes 'the acknowledgement of sin, the repentance towards the Father and the confession of guilt, and the forgiveness of sins, a new life in communion with God'; indeed: 'Jesus commanded His disciples to offer and to impart this forgiveness to the people. This takes place in the act of confession'; and in confession 'Christ Himself acts through His disciples whom He has authorized'.[255] Likewise: 'Christ has commanded his disciples to deny forgiveness of sins to those who are not prepared to repent ... their sin, by turning to God and by confessing their guilt.'[256] The act of (public) confession takes place during the mutual confessional service, which may also serve as preparation for Holy Communion; the rite consists of: (1) the confessional prayer in which the penitent confesses his guilt as sinner among sinners; (2) the open acknowledgement of the confessional prayer by the distinct reply to the confessional question; and (3) the absolution by the authorized servant of God.[257] Besides public confession there is private confession: 'Although the Lutheran Church does not compel anyone to participate in private confession, it acknowledges its special blessing.' Moreover: 'The penitent, who confides in his minister in private confession, shall know that the minister is bound by his ordination vow to keep secret what has been confessed.'[258] The minister is called in a special way through his ordination to take confession. Every Christian may, however, render this service if this is done in a responsible way and in absolute discretion.[259] Some Lutheran churches also explicitly impose a duty of confidentially on pastors in the ordinary course of their ministry.[260] In the Methodist

---

[252] LCA: The Service with Holy Communion for Ministry to those who are Sick, prepared in 1988 by the Department of Liturgics, adopted by the Commission on Worship 1998, edited 2001: 'Confession and absolution are therefore an important part of the church's public ministry to people who are sick'; the Order for Confession and Absolution must be used; ELCF: Catechism, 82: 'In the confession God forgives us all our sins'; 'We can confess our sins to God in the common worship service, in private confession, or in silent prayer. We can confess our sins to a pastor or to another Christian when our conscience bothers us ... The one who hears our confession is bound to confidentiality ... In the confession the words of forgiveness ... are ours to hold on to. The words of absolution are certain, for they are, according to God's promise, his own words. God wipes away all our sins on account of Christ. His unconditional pardon makes us free and gives us a good conscience.'

[253] ELCSA: G., 4.1: 'God has not only instituted the Office of Preaching and given the Sacrament, but has also established the Office of the Keys. He has granted full authority to His congregation to forgive and to retain sins through the power of the Holy Spirit'; this cites Matt. 18.15-18; John 20.21-23.

[254] ELCSA: G., 4.2.   [255] ELCSA: G., 4.3-4.4.

[256] ELCSA: G., 4.5-4.6: this cites John 20.22-23; 4.7: 'In confession the main thing is not that we are able to confess each single sin before God, but that we confess ourselves as sinners and express the desire to return from the remoteness to the nearness of God.'

[257] ELCSA: G., 4.8.

[258] ELCSA: G., 4.9; this also applies in a court of justice; what is confessed is confessed to God not to man.

[259] ELCSA: G., 4.10.

[260] ELCIC: ABL, Pt. III.4: 'No ordained minister of this church shall divulge any confidential disclosure given in the course of the care of souls or otherwise in a professional capacity, except with the express permission of the person involved, or where required by law, or in order to prevent the commission of a crime'; ELCA: Const., Ch. 7.45: 'In keeping with the historic

tradition, too, an elder may hear confessions and must 'maintain all confidences inviolate, including confessional confidences except in the cases of suspected child abuse or neglect, or in cases where mandatory reporting is required by civil law'.[261]

Funeral rites

Needless to say, all the traditions studied here practise funeral rites. Roman Catholic canon law classifies a funeral as a sacramental,[262] and it provides for the anointing of the sick and dying.[263] Christ's faithful who have died are to be given a church funeral which must be celebrated according to the norms of the liturgical books; in its funeral rites 'the Church prays for the spiritual support of the dead, it honours their bodies, and at the same time it brings to the living the comfort of hope' – whilst the church recommends burial it does not forbid cremation.[264] A funeral should normally be carried out in the parish church of the deceased and the deceased should be buried in the parish cemetery if there is one, unless another cemetery has been chosen.[265] A burial is entered in the register of the dead.[266] For funerals, catechumens are considered among the faithful, and children who die before baptism but whose parents had intended their baptism may be allowed a church funeral by the local ordinary. However, unless they gave some sign of repentance before death, funeral rites are to be denied to: notorious apostates, heretics and schismatics; those who for anti-Christian motives chose their bodies to be cremated; other manifest sinners to whom a funeral could not

---

discipline and practice of the Lutheran church and to be true to a sacred trust inherent in the nature of the pastoral office, no ordained minister ... shall divulge any confidential disclosure received in the course of the care of souls or otherwise in a professional capacity, nor testify concerning conduct observed by the ordained minister while working in a pastoral capacity, except with the express permission of the person who has given confidential information to the ordained minister or who was observed by the ordained minister, or if the person intends great harm to self or others.'

[261] UMCNEAE: BOD, par. 340. See also MCNZ: LAR, Introductory Documents, III Ethical Standards: a minister undertakes to 'respect the rights of people to privacy and confidentiality of information obtained during pastoral ministry, except when there is a clear danger to the personal safety of themselves or others'.

[262] CIC, c. 1166: 'Sacramentals are signs by which, somewhat after the fashion of the sacraments, effects, especially spiritual ones, are signified and are obtained through the intercession of the Church'; c. 1167: only the Apostolic See may establish them; c. 1168: the minister is a cleric but some sacramentals may be administered by qualified lay people; c. 1169: consecrations, dedications and blessings; cc. 1173–1175: liturgy of the hours; cc. 1186–1190: the cult of saints, sacred images and relics; cc. 1191–1204: vows and oaths.

[263] CIC, cc. 998–1007: the sacrament of anointing of the sick.

[264] CIC, c. 1176: 'the pious custom of burial'; cremation is forbidden if 'chosen for reasons contrary to Christian teaching'; SC 81: 'funeral rites should express more clearly the paschal character of Christian death'.

[265] CIC, c. 1177: however, the faithful may choose another church with the consent of its minister and notice to the priest of the deceased; c. 1178: the funeral of a bishop is in his own cathedral unless he has chosen another church; c. 1179: funerals of religious; c. 1180: 'All may, however, choose their cemetery ... unless prohibited by law'; c. 1242: permission must be obtained to bury in a church unless it is a pontiff, cardinal or diocesan bishop.

[266] CIC, c. 1182; c. 1181: funeral offerings may be made but 'the poor are not deprived of a proper burial'.

be granted without public scandal – in cases of doubt, the local ordinary must be consulted and his judgment followed.[267] Similar rules apply to Oriental Catholic Churches.[268]

Orthodox laws provide for the administration of holy unction when a person is sick or dying,[269] as well as preparation by way of confession and Holy Communion.[270] Some churches address the time which should pass between death and burial.[271] At a funeral, the priest should use the form of service prescribed, including the Divine Liturgy.[272] Funerals are not generally to be conducted on a Sunday.[273] Memorials to the dead may be the subject of detailed regulation.[274] A register of funerals must be kept in the parish.[275] Special funeral rites should be administered in the case of non-communicants,[276] and, after consulting the hierarch, non-Orthodox persons,[277] suicides[278] and those upon whom an

---

[267] CIC, c. 1183: baptised non-Catholics may also be allowed a funeral if their own minister is not available in accordance with the judgment of the local ordinary unless the person did not wish this; c. 1184: heretics etc.

[268] CCEO, c. 867–895: sacramentals; cc. 874–879: funerals; cc. 737–742: anointing of the sick.

[269] OCIA: GC, The Mystery of Unction: 1: it is 'administered to Orthodox Christians for the healing of soul and body' (2) 'especially ... for the sick and dying'; the 'dead must not be anointed'; 3: it is performed in public or private; 4: 'confession precedes' anointing; 6: there may be a 'custom' to anoint on fasting and festal seasons; 7: sanctified oil should be used; 8: 'The custom of allowing the faithful to take oil home ... to anoint others should not be encouraged.' SCOBA: GOCER Pt. I, Sacraments and Other Liturgical Services, VI: Holy Unction.

[270] OCIA: GC, Funeral Guidelines, 4: 'Prayers at the Departing of a Soul'; 5: if not present at the time of death, the priest 'must ... contact ... the family, offering to assist them [in] grieving and mourning' (1 Thess. 4.13–18).

[271] Ibid., 1: 'The Church has no specific rules determining the length of time between death and the burial. Interment varies according to the climate, civil ordinances, customs, and circumstances, and may be held immediately following death, or after a number of days'; 2: nor is the hour fixed.

[272] Ibid., 6: 'The Service for the Departed (*panikhida*) is sung on the eve of the burial'; 7: the body may be brought into the temple before the service; 8: according to 'traditional practice', the casket is left open; 9: the foot of the casket faces the iconostasis; 10: the Funeral Service is conducted on the day of burial.

[273] Ibid., 12. See also UOCIA: Instructions, Funerals: with the consent of the hierarch; ACROD: Guidelines.

[274] Ibid., 16: prayers for the dead are usually offered immediately after burial at the memorial meal, on the 3rd, 9th and 40th day after death, and every year thereafter; 17: Saturday is the usual day for memorial services; 20: these are not permitted on feast days or over Christmas and Easter. See also UOCIA: Instructions, Memorials.

[275] ROMOC: Statutes, Art. 50; GOAA: Regs., Art. 17.3; MOSC: Const., Art. 43: burial register.

[276] OCIA: GC, Funeral Guidelines, A.1: 'unless there is reason to assume that [a non-communicant] has returned to Christ at the end of his/her earthly existence, that person will not be buried from the temple'; 2. 'The burial service of such a person should only be a Service for the Departed (*panikhida*).'

[277] Ibid., B.1: 'If a priest is asked to bury a non-Orthodox person, he must consult with his diocesan hierarch.'

[278] Ibid., C.1-2: 'The Orthodox Church normally denies a Church burial to a person who has committed suicide. However, factors ... may become known to the priest who must share this information with the diocesan hierarch; the hierarch will consider the factors and make the decision concerning Funeral Services.'

ecclesiastical penalty has been imposed.[279] Cremation is discouraged by the Orthodox Church.[280]

Anglican churches have the most rudimentary of principles applicable to funerals. To prepare a person for death, a church may offer anointing or imposition of hands. Disposal of a body may be either by burial or by cremation. No minister may without lawful cause refuse or delay disposal, in accordance with the funeral rites of a church, of the remains of any person brought to the designated place. The administration of funeral rites for the non-baptised, suicides and excommunicates may be subject to direction from the diocesan bishop. The minister of funeral rites is normally a bishop or priest or, if neither is available, a deacon. Lay ministers also may conduct funerals if authorised. The choice of funeral rites, when alternatives are authorised, belongs to the officiating minister in consultation with the family or friends of the deceased. The remains of a Christian should be disposed of in a consecrated place or, if the place is not consecrated, in a place which has been blessed.[281] The ministry of deliverance (or exorcism) is reserved to the bishop or those appointed by him. All who exercise this ministry should do so with great care to ensure they act only with the knowledge and authority of the bishop. The ministry should be followed by appropriate pastoral care.[282]

There is not a great deal of material on funerals in the Protestant juridical instruments studied here. However, in the Evangelical Lutheran Church in Southern Africa, Holy Communion should be offered to a dying person.[283] The minister may officiate at a burial or cremation and the rite is, as a rule, held for members of the Christian congregation only. However, for the purposes of pastoral care, exceptions may be made, but the decision rests with the minister. Individuals, including children, who die before their baptism, are to be buried in accordance with the prescribed form of service.[284] The funeral service is denied where the deceased has openly rejected or despised the confession of Jesus Christ, or where the

---

[279] MOCL 113–114: forfeiture of an ecclesiastical burial arises automatically for those subject to the penalty of anathema (if it has not been reversed) and those who have committed suicide (unless it can be proven that this was the result of a mental disorder). See also OCIA: GC, Funeral Guidelines, D: the rite should not be used for the funerals of members of Masonic or other 'secret fraternal societies'; F: autopsy and organ donation.

[280] Ibid., E.1: 'The practice of cremation is not a Christian one and is to be discouraged. Cremated remains are not to be brought into the temple for a burial service or for any other reason.'

[281] PCLCCAC, Principle 79. See e.g. Melanesia: Cans. A.4.D–G: holy anointing may be administered by a priest to a seriously ill or dying person with oil consecrated by the bishop; England: Can. B38.2: 'It shall be the duty of every minister to bury, according to the rites of the Church of England, the corpse or ashes of any person deceased within his cure of souls or of any parishioners or persons whose names are entered on the electoral roll' of the parish; B38.2: special rites may be permitted for suicides of unsound mind.

[282] PCLCCAC, Principle 78. See e.g. Australia: Can. P6 1992, 10: 'No minister may exorcise except when authorised ... by the bishop of the diocese'; Wales: BCP 1984, 770: 'co-operation with the medical profession'.

[283] ELCSA: G., 8.4: 'By accepting Holy Communion, the dying person may be reassured in a special way of the forgiveness of his sins and may prepare himself for death'; 8.1: 'Through the hope of resurrection, death becomes the entrance into eternal life for the Christian'; 8.2: 'The good news of hope stands in the centre of a Christian funeral and not the praise for the deceased.'

[284] ELCSA: G., 8.5.

relatives demand a form of burial ceremony which contradicts the order of the Christian congregation. The decision in such cases rests with the minister.[285] In the Methodist tradition: 'Care for dying persons is part of our stewardship of the divine gift of life when cure is no longer possible.'[286] An elder may 'conduct funeral and memorial services and provide care and grief counselling' for the bereaved.[287] In Presbyterianism, burial or cremation is lawful, but a funeral service is not required – though this is the practice.[288] There is insufficient evidence from the instruments studied here to construct principles about funeral rites in the Baptist tradition; though one Baptist Convention forbids the practice of wakes.[289]

Conclusion

The rites of passage represent an important aspect of the Christian journey through life. All of the Christian traditions studied in this chapter provide in their regulatory instruments for the administration of baptism, the mature profession of the faith, the Eucharist, Holy Communion or Lord's Supper, marriage (and divorce), and funerals. However, only the Catholic, Orthodox, Anglican and Lutheran Churches make provision for private confession of sins to God in the presence of an ordained or other authorised person. All agree that baptism and the Eucharist, Holy Communion or Lord's Supper are sacraments instituted by Christ. Their administration is a matter of divine law. Yet, Catholics and some Orthodox consider that marriage, ordination, confession and anointing of the sick are also sacraments. For all churches, equally, marriage is a divine institution. The juridical instruments of churches describe the nature of each of these rites of passage, regulate their administration and control who may and who may not enjoy the spiritual benefits associated with them. To this extent, clear principles of Christian law emerge about these rites of passage. Baptism constitutes incorporation of a person into the church of Christ; it is administered with water in the name of the triune God. The ordinary minister of baptism is an ordained person, but in cases of necessity lay people, too, may baptise. Most churches practise infant and adult baptism; in those which hold to infant baptism, parents should bring their children to church for baptism and, along with the sponsors, they should be instructed in their duties to nurture the candidate in the faith which the parents, too, should share; only those adults who profess the faith should be baptised. Baptism cannot be repeated and baptisms must

---

[285] ELCSA: G., 8.6; 8.7: 'The Christian congregation bears witness of its belief in a new life in Christ also through symbols and inscriptions on the tombstones and by caring for its own cemetery.'

[286] UMCNEAE: BOD, par. 161; the church is also to provide pastoral care to the families of suicides.

[287] UMCNEAE: BOD, par. 340.

[288] CLCS: 36: the Directory for the Public Worship of God provides that a dead body should be interred 'without any ceremony'; PCA: BCO 61: the services proper for the burial of the dead are singing psalms or hymns, reading Scripture, and prayer, but: 'The funeral services are to be left largely to the discretion of the minister performing them, but he should always remember that the proper object of the service is the worship of God and the consolation of the living.' See also UCC: Man., BL, 153(b)xi: burial registers.

[289] NBC: PAP, Burial: 'There may be no wake keeping for any Baptist since there is no spiritual benefit derived from it. Where it is observed it should be done only as [a] service of songs.'

be registered. Baptism may be followed by confirmation or other rite in which there is a mature profession of the faith. The Eucharist, Holy Communion or Lord's Supper is central in the life of the church and the faithful should regularly participate in its celebration. It is administered by ordained persons or those otherwise deputed normally in a public church service and exceptionally in private, for example to the sick by means of the distribution of bread and wine or equivalent elements. The church may exclude from admission to this sacrament those whom it judges to be unworthy to receive the sacrament – though due process must be followed in this regard. Marriage must be upheld by the faithful. It is a lifelong union between one man and one woman, instituted for the mutual affection and support of the parties and may be ordered to procreation. To be married validly in the eyes of the church, the parties must satisfy the conditions prescribed by church law, and the parties should be instructed in the nature and obligations of marriage. It is celebrated at a public service ordinarily in the presence of an ordained minister and witnesses. A marriage must be registered. A marriage is dissolved ordinarily by the death of one of the spouses and extraordinarily when recognised as such by competent ecclesiastical authority. A minister may solemnise the marriage of a divorced person whose former spouse is alive to the extent that this is authorised by the law of a church and the conscience of the minister. Forgiveness of sins after repentance is a fundamental of Christianity. A church may practise private confession in the presence of a minister and a duty of confidentiality attaches to all information disclosed in this rite. Funeral rites are open to all who sincerely seek them.

8

Ecumenical relations

As we have seen, the Great Schism between east and west (in the eleventh century), the Reformation (in the sixteenth century and beyond) and doctrinal controversies within church families since these landmark events, have all resulted in the fragmentation of the undivided Christian church into a profusion today of separate institutional churches. The aim of ecumenism, a movement which matured in the twentieth century particularly, is the recovery of Christian unity through the establishment of greater visible communion between the separated denominations worldwide.[1] To date, the main focus of the practice of ecumenism (through inter-church dialogues and the work of institutions like the World Council of Churches), and of academic study which accompanies it (ecumenical theology), has been the search for agreement at the level of doctrine achieved through theological debate. The juridical instruments of churches, their laws or other regulatory instruments have not so far played a role in ecumenical practice or theology. Indeed, church law and its equivalents are seen by some commentators, across the church families,[2] as the 'missing link' in ecumenism – though 'ecumenical law' (created unilaterally by churches and addressing an ecumenical topic) is recognised by scholars as a juridical category.[3] This chapter examines the treatment of ecumenism in the juridical instruments of the separated Christian traditions: the church universal and Christian disunity; the nature of ecumenism and the ecumenical obligation; institutional structures for ecumenism; ecclesial, ministerial and sacramental communion; and conciliar ecumenism and covenantal communion. It proposes that these ecclesial regulatory instruments should have a more prominent place in ecumenical practice and theology in so far as they tell us much about the scope of both the commitment of churches to and their participation in the ecumenical enterprise. Juridical ecumenism defines what ecclesial communion is possible or not, either enabling or restricting the development of greater visible communion between separated churches in the quest for Christian unity. Whilst there are many differences between the traditions, the

---

[1] See generally e.g. N. Lossky, J.M. Bonino, J. Pobee, T.F. Stransky, G. Wainwright and P. Webb (eds.), *Dictionary of the Ecumenical Movement* (WCC Publications, Geneva, 2002).

[2] Catholic scholars include Robert Ombres OP: see Colloquium of Anglican and Roman Catholic Canon Lawyers, 'A decade of ecumenical dialogue in canon law' (2009) 11 *Ecclesiastical Law Journal* 284. See also the Protestant scholar Leo J. Koffeman, *Het goed recht van de kerk: Een theologische inleiding op het kerkrecht* (Kok, Kampen, 2009).

[3] See e.g. N. Doe, *Canon Law in the Anglican Communion* (Clarendon Press, Oxford, 1998) Ch. 12. See also the seminal work of H. Dombois, 'Ökumenisches Kirchenrecht heute' (1979) 24 *Zeitschrift für Evangelisches Kirchenrecht* 225: this recognises the ecumenical dimension of church law.

following principles of Christian law on ecumenical relations can also be inferred from the similarities between the instruments of churches.

The church universal and Christian disunity

Christian teaching about the nature of the church (ecclesiology) proposes that there is one undivided church – the church universal, the Body of Christ – the one, holy, catholic and apostolic church of the Nicene Creed.[4] This teaching is not only expressed in the doctrinal documents of the separated churches themselves, but also appears in a great many ecumenical statements resulting from dialogue between these churches.[5] The juridical instruments of churches bind them to this understanding of the existence and unity of the church universal. Catholic canon law presents the church as 'the people of God', and 'Christ bestowed unity on his Church from the beginning';[6] Orthodox instruments speak of 'the unity of the Christian Church' and 'the visible church of Christ' – 'Jesus Christ founded the one true Church' which is 'united in one Apostolic Faith';[7] and according to the principles of canon law common to the churches of the Anglican Communion, 'the "church universal" means the One, Holy, Catholic and Apostolic Church'; it is the indivisible body of Christ.[8] These marks of the oneness and indivisibility of the church universal are also commonplace in the regulatory instruments of Protestant churches. For Lutherans 'the One Holy Christian Church, the *Una Sancta*, the Church Universal, is the people of God ... the communion or congregation of saints ... gathered through the Holy Spirit' – it is 'One, Holy, Catholic, and Apostolic', and its unity is a gift of God; or else, the Church of Christ is the communion of pardoned sinners, 'the household of God'.[9] The Reformed and Presbyterian churches similarly see the church universal as the people of God united in the one, holy, catholic and apostolic church – there is 'but one Church of the one God', a gift of God.[10] Much the same outlook surfaces in the juridical instruments of Methodist churches: the church universal is the people of God, the

---

[4] See typically A.V. Dulles, *Models of the Church* (2nd edn., Gill and Macmillan, Dublin, 1988).
[5] N. Doe, 'The concept of Christian law – a case study: the concept of "a church" in a comparative and ecumenical context', in N. Doe and R. Sandberg (eds.), *Law and Religion: New Horizons* (Peeters, Leuven, 2010) 243.
[6] CIC, c. 204; CCEO, c. 7; CCC par. 820; UR 4.3; Ecumenical Directory (ED) 1993, 13.
[7] OCIA: GC, Ecumenical Witness; SCOBA: GOCER, Introduction; see also OOCL, 5–8.
[8] PCLCCAC, Definitions, p. 95; Principles 9.2 and 93.1: 'The church universal is indivisible'; TACC, 1.1; 3.2.3 (Body of Christ). See e.g. New Zealand: Const., Preamble: one, 'because it is one body, under one head, Jesus Christ'; holy, 'because the Holy Spirit dwells in its members and guides it in mission'; catholic, 'because it seeks to proclaim the whole faith to all people to the end of time'; apostolic 'because it presents the faith of the apostles and is sent to carry Christ's mission to all the world'.
[9] LCA: Theses on the Church, pars. 1, 17, 20; ELCSA: G., 11.1 and 12.6: the church as the body of Christ; ELCA: Const., Introduction and Ch. 4; see also Lutheran World Federation as a Communion (Geneva, 2003) 8: Lutherans affirm 'the unity of the one universal church, which is the body of Christ in this world'.
[10] URC: Man., A.18.5: 'the one, holy, catholic and apostolic Church, united in heaven and on earth' is 'the Body of Christ'; A.1: 'The Church is catholic or universal because Christ calls into it all people and because it proclaims the ... Gospel to the whole world'; RCA: BCO, Preamble: the 'church of Christ in the world is one church, the "Holy Catholic Church" ... the living

'one body of Christ'; 'Christ constitutes the church as his body by the power of the Holy Spirit'; it is the company of his disciples, the 'One Holy Catholic and Apostolic Church united in the faith and knowledge of the Son of God';[11] Baptist churches also speak of 'Christ's people',[12] as do the United and Uniting Churches: 'the unity of the one holy catholic and apostolic church'.[13] It is a principle of Christian law and order that there is unity in the church universal – the one, holy, catholic and apostolic church – an indivisible church. This juridical principle is merely a reflection of the doctrinal positions of churches.

A key feature of the juridical instruments of churches is their assertion that the institutional church in question is a part of the church universal, the body of Christ. Several different images of this relationship to the church universal are used – from the existence of the church universal in the institutional church, to the existence of an institutional church in the church universal. The former approach is used in the Catholic Church. Whilst for Pope Pius XII, 'the Mystical Body of Christ and the Roman Catholic Church are one and the same',[14] today the Catholic canonical position is that 'the church' (universal), 'established and ordered in this world as a society, subsists (*subsistit*) in the catholic Church, governed by the successor of Peter and the bishops in communion with him';[15] moreover, in the particular church 'the one, holy, catholic and apostolic Church of Christ truly exists and functions' in both the diocese (with its bishop) and in local congregations.[16] Orthodox churches share this view: the church universal is one and 'remains visible in the Orthodox communion [of churches]' – 'the fullness of grace and truth abides in the Orthodox Church';[17] moreover: the local ecclesial community (around its bishop) is 'a true and eucharistic manifestation of the Church of God'.[18] By way of contrast, 'the Anglican Communion is a [worldwide] fellowship of churches within the One, Holy, Catholic and Apostolic Church', and each church affirms 'its communion in

---

communion of the one people of God'; PCANZ: BO, 1.1; PCI, Code 1–4: 'the one catholic or universal Church' is both visible and invisible; UCCSA: Const., Art. 3.5.5.

[11] UMCUSA: Const., Preamble: 'The church is a community of all true believers' which consists of the 'people' of the Lord; UMCNEAE: BOD, par. 5; see also par. 103, AR, Art. XIII: 'The visible church of Christ is a congregation of faithful men'; par. 104: 'the one body of Christ'; par. 129: 'the people of God'; par. 215: Christ constitutes the church; MCI: Const., s. 1: 'The Church of Christ is the Company of His Disciples'; it is 'One Holy Catholic and Apostolic united in the faith and knowledge of the Son of God'; s. 2: 'the Holy Catholic Church, which is the Body of Christ'; MCNZ: LAR, Nature of New Zealand Methodism; s. 1.2: 'God's people'; MCGB: CPD, DU, 4 and SO 701: 'the Church of God'; FMCNA: PACLM, I.A.1: 'The church is the body of Christ in the world'; BOD, 6010: 'The church is created by God. It is the people of God.'

[12] CNBC: Const., 3 (Statement of Faith, XIV); ABCUSA: TCOR, I.A.6.

[13] UCA: Const., 2; UCC: Man., BU, 2.15: 'one Holy Catholic Church, the innumerable company of saints of every age and nation, who being united by the Holy Spirit to Christ their Head are one body in Him and have communion with their Lord and with one another'.

[14] *Humani generis* (1950).

[15] CIC, c. 204.2; LG, 8; CLLS par. 428: not wishing to identify the Church of Christ with the Roman Catholic Church to exclude other churches and communities; see also CCEO, c. 7.2.

[16] CIC, c. 369; see also c. 368 and LG, 26: the church universal is present in congregations.

[17] SCOBA: GOCER, Pt. 1, Orthodox Ecumenical Guidelines, 1; and 6: 'Orthodoxy is the wholeness of the people of God sharing the true Apostolic Faith'; see also OCIA: GC, Ecumenical Witness.

[18] G. Limouris, *Orthodox Visions of Ecumenism* (WCC, Geneva, 1994) 66f.

the one, holy, catholic, and apostolic Church' as well as its commitment to 'the catholic and apostolic faith';[19] more particularly, some Anglican churches see themselves as a 'member', 'branch' or 'portion' of, or 'belonging' to, the church universal.[20] Lutheran regulatory instruments employ both images: these instruments present a Lutheran church as an expression of the church universal,[21] and a local church or congregation gathered for the Word and Sacrament is a 'realisation' of, enjoys the presence of, or participates in, the church universal.[22] This twofold approach is common in Reformed, Presbyterian and Baptist churches.[23] Methodist laws, too, commonly speak of a Methodist church as a 'part of the church universal', or a 'branch' of it, or as having a 'place' in it;[24] and it is in the circuit that 'Local Churches express and experience their interconnexion in the Body of Christ'.[25]

Christian disunity and denominational divisions in the visible church universal on earth are often recognised in the juridical instruments of churches. Moreover, such recognition, alongside the use of concepts of the otherness of denominations which exist outside the tradition, may be understood to represent a juridical wall of separation which institutionalises ecclesial divisions within the church universal. Catholic regulatory instruments recognise the 'divisions' between Christians, and they refer to '"other Churches and ecclesial communities" ... who are not in full communion with the Catholic Church', as well as 'non-Catholics' in terms of

---

[19] PCLCCAC, Principle 10.1; see also TACC, 1.1.1.

[20] Church of India, Pakistan, Burma and Ceylon: Constitution, Prefatory Statement, 1: member; Scotland: Can. 1.1: branch; Canada: Const., Declaration of Principles, 1: portion; England: Can. A1: 'belongs'.

[21] ELCIC: Const., Art. IV.1. See also ELCA: Const., Introduction: 'part of the whole Church of Christ'.

[22] LWF 2003, 14: '[e]very local church gathered around the preaching of the gospel and the celebration of the sacraments is a realization of the universal church of all God's people'; LCA: Theses on the Church, 10: 'The local assembly of believers is essentially "church"'; ELCA: Const., Ch. 3: 'the universal Church exists in and through congregations'; ELCIC: Const., Art. III.1–3; ELCSA: G., 11.1: 'The Congregation is the body of Christ'; 12.6: 'The Church is present where people gather around the Word and Sacrament'; see also 2.1: 'The risen Lord acts within His congregation through Word and Sacrament'; LCGB: RAR, 2.

[23] UCCSA: Const., Preamble; UCCSA 'takes its stand alongside the other branches of the Christian Church'; UFCS: MPP, IV.III.1.8: branch; UCA: Const., 2: the church affirms that 'it belongs to the people of God' and works 'within' the church universal; ibid., 3: the congregation is 'the embodiment in one place of the one holy catholic and apostolic church'; URC: Man., A.11: the URC is 'within' the church universal; PCANZ: BO 1.1(1): the church is 'part' of the church universal; PC (USA): BO G-4.0102: 'The particular church is, therefore, to be understood as a local expression of the universal Church'; ABCUSA: Bylaws, prologue: the American Baptist Churches in the U.S.A. is 'a manifestation of the church universal'.

[24] UMCUSA: Const., I. Art. VI: it is a 'part of the church universal'. UMCNEAE: BOD, par. 214: 'part'; MCI: Const., s. 1: 'Among the living branches of the Church of Christ, the Methodist Church ... holds a responsible and influential place'; s. 2: 'The Methodist Church claims and cherishes its place in the Holy Catholic Church, which is the Body of Christ'; MCGB: CPD, DU, 4; and MCNZ: LAR, The Nature of New Zealand Methodism, s. 1: 'The Methodist Church is part of the Community of faith'; FMCNA: BOD, 100, Const., Ch. 1: branch; COTN: Man., 33.2: the church is 'an international expression of the Body of Christ'.

[25] MCGB: CPD, SO 500: 'The Circuit is the primary unit in which the Local Churches express and experience their interconnexion in the Body of Christ'; see also UMCNEAE: BOD, par. 201.

persons.²⁶ Within 'the disunity of Christendom', Orthodox churches recognise the existence of 'non-Orthodox communions', 'non-Orthodox churches' and 'other Christian denominations',²⁷ in some of which 'certain basic elements are lacking which constitute the reality of the fullness of the Church', namely 'the Faith of the ancient, united, and indivisible Church of the Seven Ecumenical Councils'.²⁸ Similarly, Anglican churches recognise 'the divided Christians of the world' in 'separated churches' – 'parts of the Church of Christ' but nevertheless 'other churches'.²⁹ Much the same is found in Protestant regulatory instruments. Lutheran churches recognise 'divisions in the body of Christ' in the form of 'other churches' – 'the deplorable disunity among Christians' is not 'a division of the body of Christ' – thus, a distinction must be made between the church universal and 'the visible organized Churches'.³⁰ Reformed churches understand the church universal to include 'many particular churches' (or 'other churches'), a 'division which has made it impossible for Christians fully to know, experience and communicate the life of the one, holy, catholic, and apostolic Church' – but 'the visible unity of the body of Christ, though obscured, is not destroyed by its division into different denominations of professing Christians'; and, indeed: 'It is according to scriptural example that the Church should be divided into many individual churches.'³¹ Similarly, for Methodist churches, the 'very dividedness' of the church of Christ is

²⁶ ED 9, 17, 19; 18: 'sects and new religious movements must be distinguished from churches and ecclesial communities'; 106: 'other Communions'; CIC, c. 383.3; c. 1170: 'non-catholics'; CCEO, c. 906: 'other churches or ecclesial communities'. In ecumenical dialogues too Catholics speak of baptised Christians who do not profess the full Catholic faith and are not in full communion with the See of Rome: 'a Church outside of communion with the ... Pontiff lacks more than just the visible manifestations of unity with the Church of Christ which subsists in the ... Catholic Church': Official Response of the Roman Catholic Church to the Final Report of the First Anglican-Roman Catholic International Commission, printed in *The Tablet* (December 1991).

²⁷ SCOBA: GOCER, Pt. I, Orthodox Ecumenical Guidelines, 1, 7, 13; Worship with Non-Orthodox: 'separated brethren'; Preaching on Ecumenical Occasions, 4: 'other communions'; OCIA: GC, Ecumenical Witness, B.5; ATGB: Instructions, Baptism; UOCIA: Statutes, Art. II.6: 'non-Orthodox religious bodies'; ROMOC: Statutes: 'other Christian Churches'; GOAA: Charter: 'any Christian denomination'.

²⁸ Statement of Orthodox Delegates, 2nd Assembly of WCC (Evanston, 1954): G. Limouris, *Orthodox Visions of Ecumenism* 29: a return 'to the pure and unchanged and common heritage of the forefathers of all divided Christians, shall alone produce the desired reunion of all separated Christians'.

²⁹ PCLCCAC, Principle 94.1; 95: the category 'non-member church'; 98.1: 'faith communities of other Christian traditions'; West Indies: Can. 33: 'other Churches'.

³⁰ LCA: Theses on the Church, 24–25: disunity is not a division of the one body of Christ; ELCSA: G., 3.9: other churches; 11.8: divisions; ELCA: Const., Ch. 8.72.12: 'faith communion' with another 'church body'; Ch. 11.32: 'other churches'; Ch. 12.04: 'non-Lutherans'; ELCIC: Const., Art. IV.2: 'other Christian churches'.

³¹ PCA: BCO, 1.2.2–3. See also PC (USA): BO, G-4.0201: denominationalism does not destroy the unity of the church universal; URC: Man., A.7: divisions; UFCS: MPP, IV.III.III.4: another church; UCOC: BL, 229: 'other expressions of the Church'; UCCSA: Const., Art. 6.4.9: 'other communions of the Christian Church'; Art. 6.4.11: 'other Churches'; UCA: Reg., 1.1.11: 'another Christian denomination'; PCW: HOR, IV.4.18; UCC: Man., BU, 8.6.9–10: 'other Churches'; BL, 031: other 'Christian traditions'; RCA: BCO, Preamble: 'other churches of Christ'; Ch. 1, Pt. 1, Art. 5, s. 2.b and 3: 'another Christian church'; PCANZ: BO, 9.40: 'another Christian denomination'; PCI: Code, 108(a): 'other churches'; 106(d): 'other denominations'.

found in the existence of 'other Christian communions', 'Christians of other communions', 'other Christian churches', 'other Christian traditions' and 'other denominations'.[32] Much the same applies in Baptist Unions.[33] Moreover, each church's own understanding of its individual identity (its ecclesiality), particularly robust assertions of denominational autonomy, may also contribute to the image of a juridical wall of separation between the divided churches of Christendom.[34] In short, there is juridical unity amongst churches in their recognition of the indivisible church universal, their relationship to it (and its presence in the local church) and its denominational divisions. These three juridical facts are fundamental to understand the need for ecumenism.

The nature of ecumenism and the ecumenical obligation

The juridical instruments of the separated churches share much in common in terms of their recognition of the reasons for Christian unity (as a divine imperative), their definition of ecumenism (including the nature of ecumenical communion), their obligation to participate in it (the ecumenical obligation) and their protection of the marks of the church universal; several churches also make express provision for constitutional union with other churches, and the united churches are themselves fruits of juridical union. First, regulatory instruments in most separated churches recognise that Christian unity is a divine imperative (the will of Christ: John 17.21) and that the existence of denominational divisions is a breach of divine law. Catholic canon law, Latin and Oriental, presents Christian unity as the will of Christ, a gift of God and a call of the Holy Spirit.[35] This is echoed in Anglican instruments: Christian unity is 'the will of God' – a gift and vocation.[36] The same idea is found in the juridical instruments of the Protestant traditions: for Lutherans, Christian unity is a 'divine imperative' and 'the call of the

---

[32] UMCUSA: Const., Preamble. See also UMCNEAE: BOD, Const., Preamble; MCGB: CPD, DU 8 (e); SO 051–053; FMCNA: BOD, 3401: this is 'one denomination among many other legitimate visible churches in the world'; UMCNEAE: BOD, 101 and 333: communions; and 207f: churches and traditions; MCI: RDG, 2.03 and 4B.36: other churches; 4E.04: 'another denomination'; MCNZ: LAR, s. 3.1: 'another Church or Churches'.

[33] BUGB: Const., 1.4.6: communities; JBU: Const., IV.10; BUNZ: EPGP, 2.2: 'other denominations'; NABC: Ordination Guidelines, II: 'other churches'; ABC: Standing Rules (SR) 1111: 'other Christian bodies'.

[34] See Chapter 4 for autonomy. UOCIA: Statutes, Art. I; LCA: Const., Art. VI.3: power and authority; LCGB: RAR, Congregations within LCGB, 3: self-governance; ELCIC: Const., Art. XI: the Convention is the 'highest legislative authority'; LCMS: BL, I.3.5: the autonomy of the congregation; Methodist: MCGB: CPD, DU 11: the authority of the Conference; FMCNA: BOD, 4010: the 'powers' of General Conference; URC: Man., 2(6): General Assembly is the 'final authority'; PCANZ: BO, 1.1(6): the right of self-governance; UCOC: Const., Art. V.18: 'The autonomy of the Local Church is inherent'; Baptist: NABC: Ordination Guidelines (2004) II.

[35] CCC, par. 820: 'the will of Christ'; CCEO, c. 902: it is brought about by 'the grace of the Holy Spirit'; ED 9: ecumenism is 'the plan of God' and it seeks 'to overcome what divides Christians'; 22: a grace of God.

[36] PCLCCAC, Principle 93.1; TACC, 2.1.5: the prayer of Christ that 'all may be one'; LC 2008, Reflections, 71: 'the ecumenical vocation is one which comes directly from the Lord'; Southern Africa: Resolution of Permanent Force of the Provincial Synod, 1 (1973): 'it is God's will that His Church should be visibly one'.

Gospel';[37] for Methodists, it is 'the will of our Lord' and 'a call towards unity';[38] for Reformed churches, it is 'the will of Christ that His Church on earth should exist as a visible and sacred brotherhood' and unity is a gift of God;[39] and Baptist instruments speak of 'the biblical imperative for Christian unity'.[40] Consequently, juridical instruments condemn Christian disunity. For example, some Orthodox churches see Christian disunity as a 'sin before God, a scandal to the people and an obstacle to the acceptance of the Gospel'; also, 'Christian division hinders the mission of the Church';[41] for Anglicans, too, because 'the Church is divided its mission is impaired';[42] and for Methodists, the 'very dividedness' of the church of Christ is 'a hindrance to its mission in [the] world'.[43]

Secondly, there is juridical agreement in the definition of ecumenism. In Catholic canon law, ecumenism is 'the restoration of unity between all Christians which, by the will of Christ, the Church is bound to promote'; moreover, 'the full visible communion of all Christians is the ultimate goal of the ecumenical movement'.[44] The recovery of unity is also a feature of the juridical instruments of several Orthodox churches – Guidelines of the Standing Conference of the Canonical Orthodox Bishops in the Americas provide: 'the ecumenical movement involves renewal, unity, common witness and joint action amongst Christians' and 'the recovery of the biblical-patristic synthesis of faith which is constitutive of the one church'.[45] Similarly, in Anglicanism, the ecumenical movement seeks 'the full visible unity of the Church', 'a meeting in truth in Christ' – it is important because Christian reconciliation offers a paradigm for a broken world; as such, the constitution of the Anglican Church in Korea (for example) speaks of 'the restoration of the catholic faith and principles of unity of the early Church before the Great Schism'.[46] Some Lutheran instruments understand 'unity, reconciliation and healing' as at the heart of ecumenism, as well as 'official church-to-church

---

[37] LCA: Theses on the Church, 23; see also 20: 'The unity of the Church is a gift and a task'; 23: 'the divine imperative'; ELCSA: G., 11.8; LCGB: RAR, Statement of Faith, 8: call of the Gospel.

[38] UMCUSA: Const., Preamble: the church is obedient 'to the will of our Lord that his people be one, in humility for the present brokenness of the Church'; see also UMCNEAE: BOD, Const., Preamble and par. 104: 'Christian unity is not an option; it is a gift to be received and expressed.'

[39] UCC: Man., BU 2.15; also UCCSA: Const., Preamble: 'Christ's will'; UCA: Regs., 3.1.1(b)(i): 'God's will'; PCNZ: BO 1.6: 'Jesus' prayer'; PC (USA): BO G-4.0201: unity finds expression in mission.

[40] ABCUSA: TCOR, I.A.7.

[41] SCOBA: GOCER, Pt. I, Orthodox Ecumenical Guidelines, 1, 7, 13; OCIA: GC, Ecumenical Witness, B.5; see also A Selection of Clergy Disciplines, 1; ATGB: Instructions, Baptism; UOCIA: Statutes, Art. II.6: 'non-Orthodox religious bodies'; ROMOC: Statutes: 'other Christian Churches'.

[42] TACC, Introduction, par. 6; see also LC 2008, Reflections, 71: the need to acknowledge 'our divisions in the Church of Christ'; PCLCCAC, Principle 93.1: separated churches; England: Can. A8: 'separations and schisms' and 'divisions'; New Zealand: GS Standing Resolution [on] Intercommunion (1992): the 'parts of the Church of Christ'; see also LC 2008, Reflections, 75: 'Because the Church is divided its mission is impaired.'

[43] UMCUSA: Const., Preamble; see also UMCNEAE: BOD, Const., Preamble.

[44] CIC, c. 755.1; ED 20.

[45] SCOBA: GOCER, Introduction and Pt. 1, 7–8; OCIA: GC, Ecumenical Witness.

[46] LC 2008, Reflections, 73, 76, 77, 80, 84; Korea: Const., Fundamental Declaration of Faith and Rites.

relationships'.⁴⁷ The understanding of ecumenism in several Methodist instruments is that ecumenism is a 'calling of Christians everywhere to strive towards unity' – and Methodists participate in it on the basis that they 'share a common heritage with Christians of every age and nation'; as such, 'ecumenical convergence' involves 'the healing of churches' with 'the Holy Spirit at work in making the unity among us more visible' as well as the development of 'formal relations'.⁴⁸ Parallel ideas are found in Reformed and Baptist juridical instruments.⁴⁹

Thirdly, there is juridical unity in terms of the assumption by each church of its own corporate obligation to promote and participate in ecumenism. Under Catholic canon law, Latin and Oriental, 'the Church is bound to promote' the ecumenical movement,⁵⁰ and Orthodox juridical instruments speak of 'our ecumenical duty'.⁵¹ Similarly, according to the principles of canon law common to the churches of the Anglican Communion, '[a] church should promote mutual understanding, foster reciprocal fellowship, seek ecumenical cooperation, and strive for visible unity amongst the separated churches';⁵² moreover, Anglicans are committed to seek to give themselves as servants of 'a greater unity among the divided Christians of the world'; and each church affirms 'the ecumenical vocation of Anglicanism to the full visible unity of the Church in accordance with Christ's prayer that "all may be one"'.⁵³ The ecumenical duty is shared by the Protestant churches. The juridical instruments of Lutherans commonly recognise a duty to 'promote and maintain true Christian unity in the bond of peace', and to 'dialogue with other Christian church bodies'.⁵⁴ Methodist instruments speak of 'commitment' to 'the cause of Christian unity' or 'to contribute to unity in the church'.⁵⁵ Some Reformed churches likewise present the ecumenical duty prescriptively: 'The Presbyterian Church (U.S.A.) will seek to initiate, maintain, and strengthen its relations to, and to engage in mission with, other Presbyterian and Reformed bodies and with other Christian churches, alliances, councils, and

---

[47] LCGB: RAR, Statement of Faith, 8: reconciliation; ELCA: Const., Ch. 8.70: church-to-church relationships.
[48] UMCUSA: Const., Div. 1, Art. VI; UMCNEAE: BOD, pars. 5, 101, 104; 2402: 'formal relations'.
[49] PCW: HOR, III.3.4.4: 'church unity'; BUGB: Baptists and Ecumenism, Faith and Unity Department (2006).
[50] CIC, c. 755.2; see also CCEO, cc. 902 and 903: 'The Eastern Catholic Churches have a special duty of fostering unity among all Eastern Churches' (i.e. to foster ecumenism with Orthodox churches).
[51] OCIA: GC, Ecumenical Witness.
[52] PCLCCAC, Principle 93.3; Korea: Const., Fundamental Declaration of Faith and Rites: the duty to 'strive' for unity; Lusitania: Can. X.
[53] TACC, Introduction, par. 6; LC 2008, Reflections, 72: 'the commitment of the Anglican Communion to the full visible unity of the Church'.
[54] LCA: Const., Art. III. See also ELCA: Const., Ch. 4.03: fostering unity; LCGB: RAR, Statement of Faith, 8: a commitment; ELCSA: G., 10.11 and 11.8: 'Efforts towards unity with the Church of . . . Christ remain a constant task'; LCMS: Const., Art. III: 'Conserve and promote the unity of the true faith' and 'work through its official structure towards fellowship with other Christian church bodies'; ELCIRE: Const., 3: ecumenical dialogue.
[55] UMCNEAE: BOD, par. 104; MCNZ: LAR, Introductory Documents, II Pastoral Resolutions: the pledge to break down 'religious barriers'; it also seeks to 'foster networks and relationships with communities of faith having similar goals'; it has a 'commitment' to 'ecumenical relations'; FMCNA: BOD, 160.

consortia.'[56] However, other Reformed churches present the duty descriptively: 'In obedience to its understanding of Christ's will, [the United Congregational Church of Southern Africa] participates in the ecumenical movement and shares in the task of world evangelism and social transformation.'[57] The (United) Church of South India provides that the church 'should continually seek ... to work towards the goal of full union in one body of all parts of the Church of Christ'.[58] The ecumenical obligation is less evident in Baptist instruments.[59]

Fourthly, there is considerable agreement between juridical instruments as to the types of activity or processes involved in ecumenical work. That ecumenism involves open and frank dialogue, consultation and co-operation, common witness (including joint action for social justice), reciprocity (in ministry, worship and sacrament), perhaps through intercommunion, and ultimately full communion (see below in the section on 'Ecclesial, ministerial and sacramental communion'), appears in the juridical instruments of the Catholic (Latin and Oriental),[60] Orthodox,[61] Anglican,[62] Lutheran[63] and Methodist churches (and some of the latter provide that ecumenism involves development of 'a self-critical view of our own tradition and accurate appreciation of other traditions').[64] Typically, for example, Reformed churches are to contribute to 'the ecumenical movement through dialogue and cooperation in ministry' and through the transformation of the world by promoting social justice, peace and reconciliation.[65] However, ecclesial norms impose restraints on the discharge of the ecumenical obligation. For example, the instruments of Catholics provide that there must be mutual respect of each other church's discipline; moreover, ecumenical action should involve 'lawful reciprocity' and prudence, and should not be indiscriminate nor involve 'indifferentism' or

---

[56] PC (USA): BO, G-15.0102; see also G-4.0201: the church is 'committed to the reduction of that obscurity' of the visible oneness of the church universal.

[57] UCCSA: Const., Preamble; see also WCRC, Const., Art. III.F; UFCS: MPP, App. 3, V.

[58] South India: Const., II.2.

[59] See e.g. BUGB: Const., 1.4.6: the union is 'to confer and cooperate with other Christian communities as occasion may require'; for a similar formula, see JBU: Const., XII.

[60] ED 106: consultation and lawful reciprocity; 107: 'Catholics ought to show a sincere respect for the liturgical and sacramental discipline of other Churches and ecclesial Communities and these in turn are asked to show the same respect for Catholic discipline'; each church should have a 'greater understanding of each other's discipline and even agreement on how to manage a situation in which discipline of one Church calls into question or conflicts with the discipline of another'; for 'indifferentism' see CIC, c. 844.2; CCEO, c. 905.

[61] OCIA: GC, Ecumenical Witness: 'unity in faith, sacramental life and the wholeness of truth'; SCOBA: GOCER, Pt. 1, Orthodox Ecumenical Guidelines, 13, Orthodoxy and Other Churches, 3, Preaching on Ecumenical Occasions, 4: 'the principle of reciprocity'.

[62] PCLCCAC, Principle 93.3: '[a] church should promote mutual understanding, foster reciprocal fellowship, seek ecumenical cooperation, and strive for visible unity amongst the separated churches'.

[63] ELCA: Const., Ch. 4.03: the church is to '[f]oster Christian unity by participating in ecumenical activities, contributing to its witness and work and cooperating with other churches which confess God the Father, Son and Holy Spirit'; dialogue and conversations on matters of 'faith, doctrine and practice', pulpit and altar fellowship; Ch. 8.60: 'dialogue and common action'; Ch. 8.70–71: agreements; LCA: Some Pastoral Guidelines for Responsible Communion Practice (2001); and Guidelines for Dialogue with Other Churches (2001).

[64] MCGB: CPD, SO 729: communion; SO 330: inter-communion; UMCNEAE: BOD, par. 104.

[65] WCRC, Const., Art. III.F; UCOC: BL, 239; URC: Man., B.2(5).

proselytism.⁶⁶ Likewise, Orthodox churches provide that ecumenism cannot involve 'doctrinal reductionism' nor does it require denial of the belief 'that the fullness of grace and truth abides in the Orthodox Church';⁶⁷ and Anglican churches may allow reciprocal acts of inter-communion or full communion if there is agreement on apostolic faith and order and then only 'to the extent permitted by the discipline of each church involved'.⁶⁸ For some Lutheran churches, ecumenism should be conducted 'in accordance with adopted policies' – but it must not involve 'syncretism or unionism' or full fellowship with 'Churches with which we are not one in doctrine and practice'.⁶⁹ Similar restraints appear in the norms of Reformed,⁷⁰ and Baptist, churches.⁷¹

Fifthly, the juridical instruments of churches provide a range of mechanisms designed to symbolise or protect a church's loyalty to the church universal. Typical are norms by which a church affirms its loyalty to scripture (as the ultimate standard in matters of faith and order), to proclamation of the Word, to administration of the sacraments, to worship as fundamental to Christian life, to the maintenance of ministry and to the priesthood of all believers.⁷² The field of mission is a good example of norms in which the separated churches underscore their apostolicity: for instance, each Anglican church affirms 'its participation in the apostolic mission of the whole people of God, and that this mission is shared with other Churches and traditions' – thus, each church is called 'to explore ways of being involved in the mission co-operatively with other

---

[66] ED 23, 106, 107. See also CCEO, c. 905: 'In fulfilling ecumenical work especially through open and frank dialogue and common undertakings with other Christians, due prudence has to be kept avoiding the dangers of false irenicism, indifferentism and immoderate zeal'; ED 6, 20, 23: indifferentism and proselytism.

[67] SCOBA: GOCER, Introduction, Pt. 1, Ecumenical Guidelines, 7–8; OCIA: GC, Ecumenical Witness.

[68] PCLCCAC, Principle 98.1; LC 1968, Res. 47; LC 1998, Res. IV.1: the process to visible unity may entail temporary anomalies which may be bearable when there is an agreed goal of visible unity; New Zealand: 'inter-communion does not require the acceptance of all doctrinal opinion, sacramental devotion or liturgical practice characteristic of the other, but implies that each believes the other to hold all the essentials of the faith': General Synod Standing Resolution [on] Intercommunion; LC 1998, IV.2 (Chicago-Lambeth Quadrilateral (1888)).

[69] ELCA: Const., Ch. 8.60: adopted policies; LCA: Theses on the Church, 27: syncretism; for an almost identical formula, see LCMS: Const., Art. VI; see also BL, 2.1–2.4; see also ELCA: Const., Ch. 9.91.02; ELCIC: Const., Art. IX: churches which have 'a full communion agreement' with ELCIC.

[70] UCOC, BL, 295: ecumenism should be conducted in accordance with 'policies'; UCC: Community Ministry Standards and Best Practice (2007) 35: 'ecumenical partnership'; PC (USA): BO, G-15.0101: the church 'seeks to manifest more visibly the unity of the church of Jesus Christ and will be open to opportunities for conversation, cooperation, and action with other ecclesiastical bodies'; G-15.0201: 'full communion'.

[71] CNBC: Const., 3, Statement of Faith, XIV: 'Christian unity in the New Testament sense is spiritual harmony and voluntary cooperation for common ends by various groups of Christian denominations when the end to be attained is itself justified, and when such cooperation involves no violation of conscience or compromise of loyalty to Christ and His Word as revealed in the New Testament'; see also ED 87 for respect for conscience.

[72] E.g. UFCS: MPP, IV.III.1.8: scripture; FMCNA: BOD, 3107: holiness; URC: Man., A.12: Word and Sacrament; UMCNEAE: BOD, par. 104: Bible as 'sacred canon'; MCGB: CPD, DU 4: priesthood of believers.

Christians'.[73] The catholicity and apostolicity of an institutional church is spelt out no better than in juridical lists of the objects of that church; typically: 'The Purpose of the Reformed Church in America, together with all other churches of Christ, is to minister to the total life of all people by preaching, teaching, and proclamation of the gospel of Jesus Christ.'[74] Above all, the apostolicity of each church is expressed in juridical statements about the headship of Christ of the church universal.[75] Finally, the juridical instruments of churches make explicit provision for constitutional union with other churches (and they prescribe the use of special majorities for this);[76] even United churches provide for the possibility of wider union with other churches outside that union.[77] In sum, the juridical instruments studied in this section reveal principles of Christian law and order that the restoration of Christian unity is a divine imperative, that each church has a duty to promote the ecumenical movement through dialogue and co-operation moving ultimately towards full ecclesial communion, that ecumenical activity must be lawful and prudent, and that each church should protect in its juridical system the marks of the church universal.

Institutional structures for ecumenism

Various ecumenical functions (in the nature of powers and duties) are distributed to different levels in the institutional church depending on the tradition in question and its adopted system of government and polity. In Roman Catholic canon law:

[73] TACC, 1.1.8; see also 2.1, 2.2; 3.2.4: on co-operation in mission: Anglicans need 'the stimulation, the critique and the encouragement of sisters and brothers in Christ of other traditions'; LC 2008, Reflections, 75: ecumenism is linked intimately to mission; PCLACC, Principle 93.2: 'The mission of a church is part of the wider mission of all Christians.' For Lutheranism, see e.g. ELCIC: Const., IV.2: 'The mission of this church, as an expression of the universal Church' is to share the gospel etc.

[74] RCA: BCO, Preamble. See also: Australia: Constitution, I.I.1–3: 'The Anglican Church of Australia, being a part of the ... Church of Christ, holds the Christian Faith', receives the scriptures, and 'will ever obey the commands of Christ, teach His doctrine, administer His sacraments, follow and uphold His discipline and preserve the three orders of bishops, priests and deacons in the sacred ministry'.

[75] LCA: Const., Art. VI.1: 'The Church acknowledges that Jesus Christ is its one Lord and Head'; ELCSA: G., 11.8; LCGB: RAR, Statement of Faith, 1; ELCA: Const., Chs. 3 and 4; RCA: BCO, Preamble; PCANZ: BO 1.1; UMCUSA: Const., Preamble: 'The church is a community of all true believers under the Lordship of Christ'; TACC, Preamble: Anglican churches are 'under the Lordship of Jesus Christ'.

[76] MCGB: CPD, DU 46: Conference has power over schemes for 'unification, amalgamation or association of the Methodist Church or any body thereof with any other Christian church or organisation'; UCCSA: MCLC, 11: 'The Church has the right to negotiate a union with another local church, either of UCCSA or another denomination, and to take steps necessary to give effect thereto'; see also Const., Art. 6.4.11; URC: Man., A.3(2): 'union with other churches' – this requires a two-thirds vote in the General Assembly.

[77] North India: Const., II.IV.35: the Synod 'shall have power to enter into negotiations with other Churches with a view to wider union and to do all that is necessary to bring such wider union to consummation'; see also South India: Const., XV; UCC: Man., BU 1.2: 'It shall be the policy of [this church] to foster the spirit of unity in the hope that this sentiment of unity may in due time, so far as Canada is concerned, take shape in a Church which may fittingly be described as national'; PCA: BCO. 26.5: 'full organic union' with 'any other ecclesiastical body' (with the approval of three-quarters of the General Assembly); PCANZ: BO. 1.6: a description of union.

'It is a matter for the Bishops and, in accordance with the law, for Bishops' Conferences, to promote this unity and, in line with the various needs and opportunities of the circumstances, to issue practical norms which accord with the provisions laid down by the supreme authority of the church' (namely, the Apostolic See); moreover, the bishop is to be solicitous for all Christ's faithful (regardless of age, condition or nationality) and the bishop is, in particular, 'to act with humanity and charity to those who are not in full communion with the catholic Church; he should also foster ecumenism as it is understood by the Church'; importantly, the bishop may also invite (if he considers it opportune) to the diocesan synod 'as observers some ministers or members of Churches or ecclesial communities which are not in full communion with the catholic Church'.[78] Similarly, in the Oriental Catholic Churches, 'concern for the restoration of the unity of all Christians belongs to the entire Church, all [the] Christian faithful, especially pastors of the church'; these must pray and work 'zealously participating in the ecumenical work brought about by the grace of the Holy Spirit'; bishops have a special ecumenical responsibility and particular laws are to be made on ecumenism by each individual church *sui iuris*.[79] In Orthodox churches, too, the patriarch, a holy synod or a bishop has primary responsibility 'in external relations with non-Orthodox communions'.[80]

By way of contrast, in Anglican synodical government (representative of bishops, clergy and laity), ecumenical relations may be authorised centrally (but administered locally); the authority to recognise a non-Anglican church (for ecumenical relations) vests in the central assembly or other lawfully designated body of a church.[81] However, a church is free to establish relations of ecclesial communion with other churches if permitted by the discipline of each ecumenical partner. It is for a church in agreement with its ecumenical partner to determine when dialogue reaches a stage which allows establishment of ecclesial communion. If an Anglican church enters a relation of ecclesial communion with a non-Anglican church, this effects a relationship between such non-Anglican church and other Anglican churches only to the extent provided in their own laws and the regulatory instruments of the non-Anglican church.[82] Protestant churches have similar arrangements. The central assemblies of Lutheran churches have competence over ecumenical relations,[83] and in the Evangelical Lutheran Church in America the

---

[78] CIC, c. 755.2; for the bishop, c. 383.3; for invitations, c. 463.3; see also ED 37: this suggests that it is important to know the 'highest religious authority of other Churches and ecclesial Communities'.

[79] CCEO, c. 902; c. 903: the Oriental Catholic Churches have 'a special duty to foster ecumenism among all Eastern Churches [i.e. Orthodox churches]'; c. 192.2: the episcopal responsibility; c. 904: particular laws; the Pope directs the movement for the universal church.

[80] SCOBA: GOCER, Pt. 1, Orthodox Ecumenical Witness, 1: Ecumenical Patriarch; UOCIA: Statutes, Art. II.6: the Holy Synod and 'the establishment of general policies in relation to ... non-Orthodox religious bodies'.

[81] PCLCCAC, Principle 96.1–3. See e.g. New Zealand: Cans. G.XIII.6: General Synod determines if and when it is in full communion with another church; Central Africa: Res. of Provincial Synod 1972: the bishops decide if the other holds the apostolic faith; Scotland: Cans. Sch.: this lists churches with which it is in full communion.

[82] PCLCCAC, Principle 95.1–3.

[83] LCA: Handbook, B38–39: General Synod decides 'about entering into formal relations with another church'; ELCA: Const., Ch. 8.70–71: church-to-church relationships of full communion may be recommended, reviewed by the Conference of Bishops, and adopted by the Church

bishop is the 'chief ecumenical officer' and must 'cultivate communion in faith and mission with appropriate Christian judicatory leaders functioning within the territory of [the] synod'.[84] The Reformed Church in America is typical of the Reformed tradition: 'the General Synod shall maintain a friendly correspondence and cooperative relationship with the highest judicatories or assemblies of other Christian denominations';[85] and in the Presbyterian Church (USA): 'All governing bodies of the church, in consultation with the next higher governing body, shall be authorized to work with other Christian denominations in the creation and strengthening of effective ecumenical agencies for common mission.'[86] Methodist juridical instruments also sometimes list ecumenism as a function of their central assemblies and in some Methodist churches with bishops, those bishops must have a 'passion for the unity of the church [universal]'.[87]

As well as ecumenical bodies of global ecclesial communities,[88] the central assemblies of churches are assisted in the promotion of ecumenism by various commissions, boards and other bodies charged with ecumenical tasks and the provision of advice on ecumenism. Catholic norms provide that the bishop (or eparchial bishop in the Oriental churches) should set up a diocesan ecumenical commission (composed of clergy, religious, lay people and ecumenical experts) to implement episcopal directives on ecumenism, to assist the diocesan ecumenical officer (also appointed by the bishop) and to foster ecumenism by various prescribed means (such as workshops, seminars and advice);[89] institutes of consecrated

Council; 8.14: the Churchwide organisation may authorise 'entering into relationship with . . . ecumenical . . . agencies'; LCMS: BL, 1.1.1: Synod shall 'work through its official structure toward fellowship with other Christian church bodies'; ELCIC: ABL, Pt. IX: the National Church Council is 'responsible for the implementation of all ecumenical and inter-church relations of this church and its agencies, which have been approved by the convention'.

[84] ELCA: Const., Ch. 10.31 and 13.21–22: bishop as chief ecumenical officer; LCA: BL, VIII.F.3(b): the president 'officially represents the church in relations with other church bodies'.

[85] RCA: BCO, Ch. 1, Pt. IV, Art. 2.5. See also PCI: Code, 113; UCOC: Const., Art. IX.54: General Synod is 'to encourage conversations with other communions and where appropriate to authorize and guide negotiations with them, looking to formal union'; UCCSA: Const., Art. 6.4.9: the Assembly is 'to encourage co-operation and conversations with other communions of the Christian church and to enter negotiations with them with a view to full organic union'; UCA: Regs., 3.5.54: the Assembly determines ecumenical matters; URC: Man., 2(6): General Assembly is 'to conduct and foster the ecumenical relationships' of the URC; UCC: Man., BU, 8.6.

[86] PC (USA): BO, G-15.0103. See also WCRC: Const., BL, I.C.6: the General Council consists of 'ecumenical delegates' to represent 'a recognized ecumenical fraternal organization'.

[87] MCGB: CPD, DU, 46: Conference has authority over 'association' with other churches; SO 300: the Conference Secretary leads on 'the Church's vision of unity'; UMCNEAE: BOD, 403; see also 414: the bishop must provide leadership 'in the search for strengthened relationships with other living faith communities'.

[88] In the Catholic Church the Pontifical Council for Promoting Christian Unity must cultivate relations with other churches and ecclesial communities implementing the principles of ecumenism; it organises official dialogues on the 'international level', delegates Catholic participants and issues guidelines and directives to the whole Catholic Church: ED 53. The Inter-Anglican Standing Commission on Ecumenical Relations promotes Anglican participation in multilateral and bilateral dialogues: see LC 1998, Res. IV.3.

[89] ED 41–47: they must comply with papal directions; CCEO, c. 904: eparchies may have a joint council.

life and societies of apostolic life (many of which pre-date ecclesial division) should also promote ecumenical activity.[90] Similarly, like some Orthodox bodies,[91] in Anglicanism each 'church should establish commissions with such membership and functions as may be prescribed under its law to enable ecumenism by stages or other process' and central assemblies often have a standing commission on ecumenical relations.[92] Equivalent commissions may be found in the Protestant churches – Lutheran,[93] Reformed,[94] Methodist[95] and Baptist.[96] In turn, ecumenical functions may be assigned to institutions at the most local levels of churches (typically parishes or congregations). Catholic parishes should be encouraged to participate in ecumenical initiatives at their level;[97] Orthodox parishes should have 'a Parish Council on Ecumenical Affairs' which may work with similar bodies in 'other communions';[98] the Anglican parish council must promote the 'ecumenical' mission of the church;[99] the Lutheran Church Session must consider 'ecumenical relationships', and congregations (and their councils) must engage in 'ecumenical cooperation' and 'participate in ecumenical relationships consistent with churchwide policy';[100] the Methodist local church must participate in

[90] ED 50: within their rules of life, they contribute to ecumenical understanding, organise ecumenical meetings for spiritual exercises, maintain relations with similar bodies in other 'Christian Communions', engage in ecumenical work for social justice and for the protection of creation and peace, and establish ecumenical commissions.

[91] SCOBA: Const., IV.2.4: the American Orthodox Committee on Relations with Non-Orthodox Bodies.

[92] PCLCCAC, Principle 96.3; see e.g. TEC: Cans. I.1(2): the General Convention's Standing Commission on Ecumenical Relations is to: 'develop a comprehensive and coordinated policy and strategy on relations between this Church and other Churches'; advise on 'interchurch cooperation and unity'; carry out 'such instructions on ecumenical matters as may be given ... by the General Convention'; nominate to the presiding bishop persons 'to serve on the governing bodies of ecumenical organizations to which this Church belongs by action of the General Convention' and participate in their conferences; West Indies: Can. 33: the Provincial Standing Commission on Ecumenism advises Provincial Synod on 'interchurch cooperation and unity'.

[93] LCA: Handbook, B38f : Constitution of CTIR; ELCA: Const., Ch. 15.12.B10: 'the executive for ecumenical' relations assists the bishop; 15.31.A07: the Conference of Bishops must promote 'ecumenical worship, fellowship and interaction'.

[94] UFCS: MPP, App. 3, V: the General Assembly Ecumenical Relations Committee; UCOC: BL, 229, 295: Council for Ecumenism; 239–240: the Office of General Ministries 'nurtures' ecumenism; PCW: HOR, III.3.4.4: the Ecumenical Panel of General Assembly is 'to promote further discussions on "church unity" according to [Assembly] decisions'; UCC: Man., BL, 570–572: the Conference Committee on Inter-Church and Inter-Faith Relations; RCA: BCO Ch. 3, Pt. 1, Art. 5, s.2: 'ecumenical observers' on the Commission on Christian Action.

[95] MCI: RDG, 41: Conference's Committee for Ecumenical Relations reports annually to it, addresses and keeps itself informed on national, international and world level ecumenical issues; MCNZ: LAR, s.5.4.2: the Mission and Ecumenical Committee is to 'promote the ecumenical relationships' of the church; MCGB: CPD, SO 330: the Faith and Order Committee of the Conference deals 'with proposals and projects for inter-communion'; SO 334: the 'ecumenical officer' of the Methodist Council.

[96] ABCUSA: SR, 11.11: the General Board of the American Baptist Churches has a Committee on Christian Unity; the BUGB has a Baptists and Ecumenism, Faith and Order Department.

[97] ED 67.   [98] SCOBA: GOCER, Pt. 1, Council of Churches, 10.

[99] PCLCCAC, Principle 21.6; Wales: Const., IV.C.8.

[100] LCGB: RAR, The Church Session, 1 and 2; ELCA: Const., Ch. 8.16, 8.75, 9.10–11, 9.41, and Model Const. for Congregations, Ch 4: congregations.

ecumenism;[101] and in the Presbyterian Church of Aotearoa, New Zealand, the Presbytery must 'maintain ties with ecumenical partners'; in other churches, each synod may determine 'ecumenical cooperation'; and in the United Church of Canada each Presbytery has a committee on inter-church relations.[102] In Baptist polity the local congregation determines 'the nature of its relationship with other congregations and/or ecclesiastical bodies'.[103]

Not only do juridical instruments assign ecumenical functions to ecclesial institutions; legislation and quasi-legislation may also impose ecumenical duties on the ordained ministers of the churches. This applies across the different ecclesial traditions. Catholic pastors have a duty to pray for and participate in ecumenism;[104] Orthodox clergy may engage in ecumenism to promote true Christian unity (as may the laity), and chaplains in educational institutions are 'in a special position to make real contributions to ecumenism';[105] Anglican 'ministers should seek to foster and participate in ecumenical partnership with faith communities of other Christian traditions, especially those with which their church already has formal relations'.[106] Much the same is found in Protestant juridical instruments. Lutheran bishops must ensure that the church is represented at ecumenical events 'to further the cause of Christian unity', and pastors must 'maintain good relationships with other Christian churches';[107] Reformed ministers must participate in ecumenical activities 'as possible and appropriate' and show respect to their ecumenical colleagues; ministers may also serve in ecumenical projects.[108] The New Zealand Baptist Union requires pastors to maintain 'contact' with pastors 'from other denominations, through personal meetings and regular support of pastors' meetings and conferences'.[109] Moreover, Methodist ordained ministers 'exercise their ministry in covenant with all Christians' and must participate in ecumenical concerns 'and encourage the people to become so involved and to pray and labour for the unity of the Christian community'; and ministers in the Methodist Church in Great Britain

---

[101] UMCNEAE: BOD, 202: the local church is 'to cooperate in ministry with other local churches'; MCNZ: LAR, s. 3.1 and 3.3: the congregational Leaders' Meeting is to 'foster participation and partnership with other Churches within the area'; MCGB: CPD, SO 412: the District Synod designates local ecumenical partnerships; SO 604: Local Church committees are to engage in their activities 'ecumenically'; and SO 614.

[102] PCANZ: BO, 8.4; see also PCI: Code 70(c); URC: Man., B.1(2)(a) and B.2; UCC: BL, 385.

[103] ABCUSA: TCOR, I.A.4. [104] CCEO, c. 902.

[105] OCIA: GC, Ecumenical Witness: common witness, supporting religious freedom, collaborating for social justice; ibid., B.1: the laity; SCOBA: GOCER, Pt. 1, Orthodox Ecumenical Witness, 6: chaplains.

[106] PCLCCAC, Principle 98.1: 'to the extent permitted by the discipline of each church involved'; 2: 'Ministers should in ecumenical affairs collaborate, co-operate and where appropriate consult with ministers of other faith communities and in all dealings with them act courteously and with respect for their corporate traditions'; 3: 'Ministers (a) should minister to members of other faith communities if authorised by the discipline of their own church and of the other community; and (b) should not solicit membership of their own church.'

[107] LCGB: RAR, Role of the Bishops, 3; Responsibilities and Duties of Pastors, 1–24; compare ELCA: Const., Ch. 7.31.12: no ecumenical duty is listed.

[108] UCC: ESMP, Standards of Practice, 4(d), and Ethical Standards, 4(a); URC: Man., K.

[109] BUNZ: EPGP (2008) 2.2.

undertake 'to seek to work together with the churches of all denominations within the neighbourhood'.[110]

Importantly, sometimes juridical instruments provide for the ecumenical formation of both clergy and laity. Catholic norms are particularly well developed on this matter. Teachers and pastors should undergo ecumenical formation in the history of ecclesial divisions and the doctrinal positions of other churches and ecclesial communities, especially the eastern (Orthodox) and Reformation churches.[111] In turn, Roman Catholic seminarians must be instructed in dealing with non-Catholics (and unbelievers) and in 'ecumenical questions';[112] and those in the Oriental Catholic churches who control the means of communication (e.g. preachers and teachers) must ensure that the faith is presented accurately to ecumenical partners.[113] Indeed, in the Catholic Church, 'all the faithful are called upon to make a personal commitment towards promoting increasing communion with other Christians',[114] and ordained ministers should cultivate 'an authentically ecumenical disposition'.[115] Similarly, some Orthodox churches prescribe that, for example: 'the true spirit of ecumenism should be developed through education in the home, the Church and the schools'; moreover, priests are to prepare programmes of education on ecumenism for adults and youth in the parish, and 'if the laity become involved in ecumenism, they must be well-grounded in the Orthodox faith and ecclesiology and possess at least a rudimentary knowledge of comparative theology, discipline and practice'. Therefore, not only is it the case that 'the parish priest must inform the faithful in these matters', but also clergy 'are encouraged to establish and maintain better relations with clergy and faithful of other churches', as well as to accept invitations to explain the Orthodox faith 'whenever possible'.[116]

---

[110] UMCNEAE: BOD, par. 303 (covenant) and 340; MCNZ: LAR, Introductory Documents, III Ethical Standards for Ministry: ministers must 'promote co-operation and mutuality' with colleagues 'outside the Methodist Connexion'; MCGB: CPD, Bk. VI, Pt. 1, Resolutions on Pastoral Work (1971).

[111] ED 57; 72–78: there should be an ecumenical dimension in doctrinal formation and theological disciplines, with formation in 'the elements of the Christian patrimony of truth and holiness which are common to all Churches and ecclesial Communities' (including liturgy, spirituality and doctrine proper to each communion and points of disagreement on matters of faith and morals); formation in 'canon law, which must distinguish clearly between divine law and those ecclesiastical laws which change with time, culture, or local tradition'.

[112] CIC, c. 256; see also Congregation for Catholic Education, Basic Norms for Priestly Formation 1985, no. 96; and its *The Ecumenical Dimension in the Formation of Those Engaged in Pastoral Work* (Vatican, 1995).

[113] CCEO, c. 906: 'That it may become clearer to the Christian faithful what is truly taught and handed down by the Catholic Church and other Churches or ecclesial communities, a special effort is to be made by preachers of the word, those who control the means of social communication, and all who dedicate themselves as teachers or as directors to Catholic schools and especially in institutes of higher studies'.

[114] ED 55–56; 'Catechesis must have an ecumenical dimension, presenting a true image of other Churches and Ecclesial Communities; however, care is to be taken in every way that the correct dimension of Catholic catechesis is maintained': CCEO, c. 625; thus, ecumenism should be part of clerical formation: 'ecumenism should be one of the necessary dimensions of any theological discipline': CCEO, c. 350.4; see also UR 10.

[115] ED 70.

[116] SCOBA: GOCER, Pt. 1, Orthodox Ecumenical Witness, 3, 7; Orthodoxy and other Churches, 3; OCIA: GC, Ecumenical Witness, B.1.

Ecumenical formation appears to be less obvious in the juridical instruments of Anglicans and Protestants; however, in the North American Lutheran Church: 'A pastor shall possess a sense of the wholeness of the Christian church.'[117] Indeed, the Assembly of the Uniting Church in Australia has a Ministerial Education Committee which is 'to encourage the several theological colleges to participate in ecumenical theological education'; and in the United Church of Canada each Presbytery is to have an ecumenical committee 'to promote within the presbytery a knowledge of and concern for ecumenical affairs, and to assist ... in ecumenical outreach'.[118] There is, then, ample juridical evidence of institutional structures for ecumenism in the separated churches of Christianity: ecumenism is normally in the keeping of the central authorities of churches; these may be assisted by commissions and similar advisory bodies, and duties to participate in ecumenism are also distributed to the institutions of the local churches as well as to ordained ministers; but ecumenical formation is more evident in the juridical instruments of the Catholic and Orthodox churches than in those of Protestantism.

Ecclesial, ministerial and sacramental communion

The juridical instruments of separate churches deal with matters of crucial importance to the ecumenical relationship of communion between churches – the recognition of churches as such, baptism as creating a fundamental communion between Christians, the recognition of ministers of other churches, Eucharistic fellowship, mixed marriages, common worship, funerals, sharing property and joint collaboration in the field of mission and social justice. In each of these areas we see the juridical ebb and flow of reciprocity, facility and restriction.

The recognition of churches and ecclesial communion

Whether a church of one tradition is in communion (full communion or some lesser or imperfect species of communion) with a church of another tradition depends on the extent to which that church recognises the essential marks of the church universal in the other church. Around this principle, the juridical instruments of each church studied here contain a range of conditions which must be satisfied before another denomination is recognised as a church for the purposes of the development of greater visible communion. For Catholicism, on the one hand, there are 'churches' in full communion with the Catholic Church and churches with which there is a weaker form of communion; the latter may 'possess true sacraments, above all – by apostolic succession – the priesthood and the Eucharist, whereby they are still linked with us in closest intimacy'; such a church 'retains a certain communion with the Catholic Church'.[119] For example, the Orthodox (the 'eastern churches') while not 'in perfect communion with the Catholic Church, remain united to her by means of the closest bonds, i.e. by apostolic succession and a valid Eucharist, [and] *are true particular Churches*'; the Church of Christ 'is present and operative' in them but 'they lack full communion ... since they do not accept the Catholic doctrine of Primacy, which, according to the will of God, the

---

[117] NALC: SFPM (2011) p. 2.
[118] UCA: Regs., 2.2.18(h): UCC: Man., BL 385: ecumenical outreach.   [119] ED 17, 18; UR 15.

Bishop of Rome objectively has and exercises over the entire Church'. On the other hand, 'a Church outside of communion with the Roman Pontiff lacks more than just the visible manifestations of unity with the Church of Christ which subsists in the Roman Catholic Church'.[120] Many 'communities of Christians' proclaim the gospel, announce the kingdom and celebrate baptism and other sacraments, through which 'we know that God saves and sanctifies them'; but it is difficult to determine their relationship with the Catholic Church. Consequently: '"Churches" and "other Churches and ecclesial communities" ... refer to those who are not in full communion with the Catholic Church'; that is, 'ecclesial communities which have not preserved the valid Episcopate and the genuine and integral substance of the Eucharistic mystery, *are not Churches in the proper sense*'.[121] Eucharistic and ecclesial communion are 'considered inseparable',[122] since the Eucharist is a 'church-making' sacrament: Anglican communities fall into this category.[123] Yet such communities commemorate the Holy Supper and 'profess it signifies life in communion with Christ'; their worship 'displays notable features of a liturgy once shared in common'; their way of life 'is nourished by faith', and for them the Word is a 'source of Christian virtue'.[124] While 'these separated churches and communities ... suffer from defects', they have not been 'deprived of significance and importance in the mystery of salvation'; 'the spirit of Christ has not refrained from using them as means of salvation';[125] indeed, they 'derive their efficacy from the fullness of grace and truth entrusted to the Catholic Church'.[126]

Similarly, the Orthodox refer to 'holy Churches of God', the 'Church of the Protestants', the 'Anglican Church' and 'Christian Churches'; their ecclesiality is found 'in their common history, in their common ancient and apostolic tradition, from which all of them derive their existence'. However, if reluctant to 'pass

---

[120] Official Response of the Roman Catholic Church to *The Final Report* of the First Anglican-Roman Catholic International Commission, printed in *The Tablet* (December, 1991).

[121] *Dominus Iesus* (DI) (2000) 17; OE 1–4; ED 122.   [122] ED 129.

[123] Catholic Bishops' Conference of England and Wales, Ireland and Scotland, *One Bread, One Body* (London, 1998) 53. See also House of Bishops, Church of England response to *One Bread, One Body*: '[T]he Church of England is not correctly referred to as one of those "Christian communities rooted in the Reformation". The Church of England traces its origins back to the beginnings of Christianity in England and is continuous with the Church of the Apostles and Fathers. The particular churches of the Anglican Communion belong to the one holy catholic and apostolic Church of Christ, reformed and renewed at the Reformation (though not, of course, only then).' 'Anglicans look for clarification of the unresolved ambiguities in the official stance of the Roman Catholic Church towards various "ecclesial communities", as Vatican II calls them.' House of Bishops, *The Eucharist: Sacrament of Unity* (Church House Publishing, London, 2001).

[124] UR, 23.

[125] DI, 17: the Christian faithful are therefore 'not permitted to imagine that the Church of Christ is nothing more than a collection – divided yet in some way one – of Churches and ecclesial communities'; nor 'hold that today the Church of Christ nowhere really exists, and must be considered only as a goal to which all Churches and ecclesial communities strive to reach'; see also UR, 3.

[126] DI, 16. For Pope John Paul II, their members were 'brothers and sisters', and 'the elements of sanctification and truth' in them, varying from one to the other, constituted 'the objective basis for communion, albeit imperfect, which exists between them and the Catholic Church'; '[t]o the extent that these elements are present in the other Christian Communities, the one Church of Christ is effectively present in them'. *Ut unum sint* (1995) 11; see 52 for 'canonical communion'.

judgment upon those of the separated communions', the Orthodox do not accept 'parity of denomination' (or 'equality of confessions'). Rather, 'in these communions certain basic elements are lacking which constitute the reality of the fullness of the Church', namely: 'the Faith of the ancient, united, and indivisible Church of the Seven Ecumenical Councils'. The church (universal) 'is not necessarily present in every Eucharistic assembly but in the episcopal diocese through which each Eucharistic gathering acquires its catholic nature'; a local community is 'a true manifestation' of the church 'only if it is catholic in its composition and structure'; 'there can be no churches ... except as manifestations of the one true Church'.[127] For Anglicans, ecclesial communion between two or more churches exists when 'a relationship is established in which each church believes the other to hold the essentials of the Christian faith and recognises the apostolicity of the other'. Full communion involves 'the recognition of unity in faith, sacramental sharing, the mutual recognition and inter-changeability of ministries, and the reciprocal enjoyment of shared spiritual, pastoral, liturgical and collegial resources'. In turn, inter-communion is 'an ecclesial relationship in which at least one but not all of the elements of full communion is present. Churches in communion become interdependent but remain autonomous'. But communion does not require 'the acceptance of all theological opinion, sacramental devotion or liturgical practice characteristic of another church'.[128]

Protestant juridical criteria to recognise churches for the purposes of ecclesial communion are not dissimilar. In the development of full ecclesial communion with 'sister churches', which exist in 'reconciled diversity', Lutherans (with their ecumenical partners), have employed a methodological paradigm for seeking unity by stages: in this, ecclesiality is recognised by agreement as to the goal of full visible unity on the basis of shared faith and common order, a declaration of mutual acknowledgment (of the authenticity of ministries, sacraments and oversight) and mutual commitments.[129] Thus: 'true Christians are found in every denomination in which to a greater or lesser degree the marks of the [church universal] are present'; and 'mutual recognition as brethren, altar and pulpit fellowship and resultant cooperation in the preaching of the Gospel and the administration of the Sacraments, presupposes unanimity in the pure doctrine of the Gospel and in the right administration of the Sacraments'.[130] The norms of Reformed churches also speak of 'recognised churches' in full communion,[131] as do those of Methodist churches: 'full communion' may be established with other churches which 'recognize in each other the one, holy, catholic and apostolic faith as expressed in the Holy Scriptures and confessed in the church's historic creeds' and when 'the authenticity of each other's baptism and Eucharist' is acknowledged;[132] 'covenantal relationships with

---

[127] For the various official statements, see Limouris, *Orthodox Visions of Ecumenism*, 2–9, 29, 31, 66, 103.

[128] PCLCCAC, Principle 94.1–5; see CLAC: 256–258.

[129] P. Avis (ed.), *The Christian Church: An Introduction to the Major Traditions* (SPCK, London, 2002) 150.

[130] LCA: Theses on the Church, 26; ELCA: Const., 8.60, and 70–71: 'official church-to-church relationships'.

[131] UCCSA: MCLC, 3.3; RCA: BCO Ch. 1, Pt. I, Art. 2, s. 4: recognised by the General Synod; PC (USA): BO, G-15.0201: full communion is achieved by ecumenical agreements approved by the General Assembly.

[132] UMCNEAE: BOD, par. 2402.

churches ... of other denominational traditions' may also be established.[133] At the other end of the legal spectrum, the United Church of Canada recognises 'as part, more or less pure, of this universal brotherhood, every particular church throughout the world which professes faith in Jesus Christ and obedience to Him as divine Lord and Saviour'.[134] However, for Baptists, a local congregation determines 'the nature of its relationships with other congregations and/or ecclesiastical bodies'.[135]

Baptismal communion

The juridical instruments of churches commonly recognise that baptism generates a spiritual communion between all Christians regardless of tradition (and regardless of formal ecclesial communion between them);[136] therefore, many provide for: the recognition of a baptism administered in another church outside the tradition; the baptism within the tradition of those from other traditions; the role of ministers in such baptisms; and the appointment of baptismal sponsors from other churches. The Roman Catholic Church recognises that baptism provides 'a real, if imperfect, communion among Christians': 'All the baptized ... though not professing the full Roman Catholic faith and not in full communion with the See of Rome, are seen as "joined to the Church in many ways"' (that is, in shared faith, sacramental and spiritual life, liturgy, devotion and virtue).[137] However, normally only Catholic ministers may baptise those from the Catholic community – but baptism may be administered by a member of a non-Catholic church or ecclesial community if the ordinary Catholic minister is absent or impeded, and the non-Catholic who administers the baptism has the requisite intention and satisfies the manner and form for valid baptism; there is also a presumption of the validity of a baptism administered by a non-Catholic unless there is serious doubt that the non-Catholic minister intended to do what the Church does.[138]

Moreover, whilst the general rule is that to be a sponsor for a baptismal candidate the person must be a Catholic, a 'baptised person who belongs to a non-catholic ecclesial community may be admitted only in company with a catholic sponsor, and then simply as a witness to the baptism'.[139] Catholics may also, 'in common celebration with other Christians', commemorate the baptism which unites them by renewal of baptismal promises.[140] Catholic canon law also provides for the reception of members of other churches and ecclesial communities,[141] as do

---

[133] UMCUSA: Const., Div. I, Art. VI; UMCNEAE: BOD, par. 5.
[134] UCC: Man., BU, 2.15.   [135] ABCUSA: TCOR, I.A.6.
[136] On the basis that baptism, theologically and juridically, is incorporation into the church universal.
[137] ED 104; LG, 15; but: 'Christ ... founded one church ... yet many Christian communities present themselves as the true inheritors of Jesus Christ ... such division openly contradicts the will of Christ.'
[138] CIC, c. 861; for the prohibition on administration of the sacraments to and by non-Catholics, see c. 844.1; for the presumption of validity and the general prohibition against conditional baptism (to which there are exceptions) see c. 869.2; ED 95: baptism by immersion or pouring, with the Trinitarian formula.
[139] CIC, c. 864.1.3 and 2; this does not apply to the eastern churches; see also ED 98.
[140] ED 96: they may also pledge 'to cooperate with the grace of the Holy Spirit in striving to heal the divisions which exist among Christians'.
[141] ED 99ff.

the legal and other regulatory instruments of Orthodox, Anglican and Protestant churches – but reception is not of itself an ecumenical action.[142]

Each of these rules on baptism finds to a greater or lesser extent an echo in the juridical instruments of other Christian traditions. According to Orthodox norms, Orthodox churches recognise baptisms administered elsewhere in the name of the Holy Trinity in a manner acknowledged as authentic by the church.[143] Orthodox clergy are the normal ministers of baptism, and non-Orthodox clergy present at a baptism administered by the Orthodox Church may not participate in any part of the service.[144] Only Orthodox Christians may act as baptismal sponsors, being 'a representative of the Orthodox faith' – 'members of communions other than the Orthodox Church may not act as sponsors in an Orthodox baptismal or chrismation service'; conversely, 'Orthodox Christians may not act as sponsors in baptism or chrismation in non-Orthodox communions' – but they may act as witnesses.[145] It is rarely the case that the juridical instruments of the other churches studied here address expressly the mutual recognition of baptisms, possible mutual administration and ecumenical sponsorship.[146] However, some Lutheran churches provide for the mutual recognition of baptisms,[147] as well as for administration (in emergencies) by 'any Christian';[148] moreover: 'Normally, sponsors are Lutherans whose confession of Christian faith and life is that of the evangelical Lutheran church'.[149] Similarly, in some Reformed churches baptism may be administered to adults and to 'the children of parents, one or both of whom are members of the Church';[150] in Methodist churches baptism shall be administered 'in general' only to the children of members on the congregational register;[151] and, in Britain: 'No minister of the United Reformed Church shall be compelled to administer a baptism in a form to which he has a conscientious objection.'[152] The prohibition against infant baptism in some Baptist churches is understood as a significant issue in ecumenical relations by Baptists themselves, as well as the rule that: 'Only ordained Baptist Ministers should baptise.'[153]

---

[142] ATGB: Instructions, Baptism: Reception of Non-Orthodox; OCIA: GC, Reception of Converts, 2: those baptised 'in a manner recognised as authenticate by the Church' may be received; PCLCCAC, Principle 99.

[143] OCIA: GC, The Reception of Converts, 2.

[144] SCOBA: GOCER, Pt. 1, Sacraments and Other Liturgical Services, II.1–2; for baptisms administered by non-Orthodox, see OCIA: GC, Ecumenical Witness, B.12.

[145] SCOBA: GOCER, Pt. 1, Sacraments and Other Liturgical Services, III.4; ATGB: Instructions, Baptism, 3; UOCIA: Instructions, Baptisms; ACROD: Spiritual and Sacramental Guidelines, Baptisms.

[146] See e.g. PCLCCAC, Principle 98.4: if called upon to provide ministry at a baptism of a person belonging to another faith community, the minister should as appropriate suggest they approach a minister of that other community; consult with a minister of that community for advice; and consult within their own church.

[147] LCA and the Australian (Catholic) Episcopal Conference, Decision 1977. [148] ELCSA: G., 1.7.

[149] LCA: Pastoral Practice in Reference to Holy Baptism (1984); see also ELCSA: G., 1.9: at least one sponsor should be a Lutheran.

[150] UFCS: MPP, I.III.5; compare PCW: HOR, IX.9.2: baptism is open also to children of 'non-members'.

[151] MCI: RDG, 3.04; see also MCGB: CPD, SO 010A; MCNZ: LAR, s. 1. [152] URC: Man., E.

[153] NBC: PAP, Baptism, C.

The mutual recognition of ministries

The Catholic Church determines whether to recognise orders and ministries conferred within other churches and ecclesial communities by reference to the apostolic succession.[154] The Orthodox approach is much the same. Moreover, Orthodox clergy must not take an active part in a non-Orthodox ordination and should consult the bishop before accepting an invitation to attend such an event; however, non-Orthodox clergy may be invited to Orthodox ordinations, yet they, too, must not take 'an active part' but may be given a place of honour.[155] The laws of Anglican churches provide for 'the mutual recognition and inter-changeability of ministries'; orders conferred in another church are recognised if the ordination was administered episcopally (in the historic succession) and the other church is in communion with the Anglican church in question.[156] Likewise, Lutheran churches may establish with other churches 'a mutual recognition of ministers'; moreover, ordained ministers from other churches with which a relationship of full communion has been established may be invited to serve in the Lutheran church, and Lutheran ordained ministers may serve in other churches with which a relationship of full communion has been established.[157]

Whilst many churches also have extensive provisions for the reception of ministers (and laity) from other churches (not itself an ecumenical action),[158] some Protestant churches provide for associate membership for people of other churches or they offer 'guest membership to Christians' not involving 'a change of confession'.[159] Methodist laws provide for the 'recognition of valid ordination' performed in other churches,[160] the creation of 'ecumenical shared ministries' with a 'congregation of other Christian traditions'[161] and for bishops and ministers from other churches with which there is a relationship of communion to join in the laying on of

---

[154] See the studies in N. Doe (ed.), *The Formation and Ordination of Clergy in Anglican and Roman Catholic Canon Law* (Centre for Law and Religion, Cardiff, 2009): the Catholic Church considers Anglican orders null and void.

[155] SCOBA: GOCER, Pt. 1, Sacraments and Other Liturgical Services, V.1-2.

[156] PCLCCAC, Principle 94.2; see e.g. TEC: Cans. I.16.2; III.10-11: this deals with ministers ordained 'by other than a Bishop in the Historical Succession to minister in a Christian body not in communion with this Church'.

[157] ELCA: Const., Art. VII.4-5; Ch. 7.31.20-21, and Ch. 8.72; see also Art. IX: ordained ministers of other churches with which there is a 'communion agreement' have the same rights as ministers of the host church; see also UCA: Regs., 2.7.22: secondment of ministers from other churches 'recognised by the Church'.

[158] UOCIA: Statutes, Art. II.6; ELCSA: G., 9.3; UMCNEAE: BOD, par. 225; MCI: RDG, 2.03; MCGB: CPD, DU 8(e) and SO 051-053; UFCS: MPP, IV.III.III.4; UCA: Const., 17; URC: Man., K; PCW: HOR, II.2.2; IV.4.18: the church does not encourage the transfer of ministers from other churches; RCA: BCO Ch. 1 Pt. 1 Art. 5, s. 2.b; United Church of North India: Const., III. VIII.1-3.

[159] ELCIRE: Const., 5; see also UMCNEAE: BOD, par. 227: affiliate membership for a member of another denomination; UCA: Regs., 1.1.11: associate members from 'another Christian denomination'.

[160] UMCNEAE: BOD, par. 346; see also MCGB: CPD, SO 729: 'a person ordained to the ministry of the word and sacraments in a church whose ministry is recognised by the Methodist Church'.

[161] UMCNEAE: BOD, pars. 207-211; see also MCNZ: LAR, 2.6; and UCC: Man., BL. 001 and 348: ecumenical shared ministries.

hands at ordinations.¹⁶² Similarly, according to the law of the Reformed Church in America: 'A consistory shall recognize as valid only such ordination to the office of elder or deacon in another denomination as is able to meet the following conditions: intended to be within and to the ministry of the catholic or universal church performed by a duly organized body of Christian churches, and by the authority within such body charged with the exercise of this specific power; accompanied by prayer and the laying on of hands.'¹⁶³ The basic principle emerging is summed up by the United Free Church of Scotland: 'The Church recognises the ordination of ministers of all denominations provided that the ordination has been carried out by an authority representing a recognised branch of the Universal Church.'¹⁶⁴ However, one Baptist Convention provides that: 'Any Baptist trained in a non-Baptist theological Institution, as a minister of the Gospel, should not serve as pastor in any Baptist Church.'¹⁶⁵

Eucharistic fellowship

Eucharistic communion or fellowship is, needless to say, still a subject of intense ecumenical debate. The juridical instruments of the different churches offer a range of approaches to mutual Eucharistic hospitality – from the restrictive to the more liberal. The rules of no church studied here exclude absolutely the admission to the Eucharist, Holy Communion or Lord's Supper of the faithful of other churches outside the tradition or the participation of the faithful in such celebrations in other churches outside the tradition. As a general rule, under Catholic canon law: 'Catholic ministers may lawfully administer the sacraments only to catholic members of Christ's faithful, who equally may lawfully receive them only from catholic ministers.' However, Catholics may receive the Eucharist (and penance and anointing of the sick) from non-Catholic ministers if there is a necessity or a genuine spiritual advantage commends, there is no danger of error or indifferentism and when it is physically or morally impossible to approach a Catholic minister; and the church or ecclesial community of the minister approached must have valid sacraments and order recognised as such by the Catholic Church.¹⁶⁶ In turn, Catholic ministers may lawfully administer the Eucharist (penance and anointing) to members of the eastern churches (Orthodox) and to members of other churches not in full communion with Rome which the Apostolic See judges to be in the same position as the eastern churches as to the sacraments, if those members spontaneously ask for them and are properly disposed; there is also provision for special cases of danger of death or other grave and pressing need.¹⁶⁷ Catholic priests are

---

¹⁶² UMCNEAE: BOD, par. 333; MCGB: CPD, SO 729.   ¹⁶³ RCA: BCO, Ch. 1, Pt. I, Art. 2, s. 17.
¹⁶⁴ UFCS: Statement of the General Assembly, Special Constitutional Features; 'not exclusively to a denomination': UFCS: MPP, IV.III.1.8; UCOC: Const., Art. VII.31ff: mutual recognition of ordinations.
¹⁶⁵ NBC: PAP, Pastors Attending Non-Baptist Theological Institutions.
¹⁶⁶ CIC, c. 844.1 and 2; for recognition of sacraments and orders see ED 132: i.e. those churches which have 'preserved the substance of the Eucharist, the Sacrament of Orders and apostolic succession'; see 104–6.
¹⁶⁷ CIC, c. 844.3; ED 125; *Ecclesia de Eucharistia* (Vatican, 2003) 30: the Reformation ecclesial communities 'have not preserved the genuine and total reality of the Eucharistic mystery'; the

forbidden to concelebrate the Eucharist with ministers of churches not in full communion with Rome.[168]

In similar vein, the Orthodox Divine Liturgy is 'a closed Eucharistic assembly being restricted to the active participation of Orthodox Christians alone'.[169] If non-Orthodox are present for the Divine Liturgy of the Eucharist, it is prudent to announce who is permitted to partake of the Eucharist prior to its distribution. Even after offering this specific information, it should not be presumed that the guests will necessarily understand or heed it. Therefore, it is prudent for the priest to ask one or more questions of a person he does not know to ascertain his/her Orthodox standing. In any case, the priest is reminded that he is the guardian of the Eucharist. Deacons who have been given the blessing to distribute the Eucharist to the faithful must defer to the priest in uncertain situations.[170] However, in Anglicanism, communicant members of an Anglican church may receive Holy Communion in a church outside the Anglican Communion which subscribes to the doctrine of the Holy Trinity and upholds the apostolic faith, in such circumstances permitted by the discipline both of their own church and of the host church; conversely, there may be admitted to the Holy Communion in an Anglican church, to the extent permitted by its discipline, baptised persons who are communicants of good standing in a church outside the Anglican Communion which upholds the apostolic faith and subscribes to the doctrine of the Holy Trinity.[171]

The topic is dealt with in some detail in Lutheran churches: responsible communion practice includes refraining from taking part in any celebration of the sacrament involving 'a denial of the gospel or of the nature and benefits of the Lord's supper, or which gives the impression of fellowship which does not, in fact, exist'; 'a Lutheran congregation may not be involved in a joint celebration of the Lord's supper with a congregation of another denomination'. As to admission of non-Lutherans to Lutheran altars, the fundamental principle is: 'Lutheran altars for Lutheran communicants only'; but non-Lutherans may be admitted not only if there is 'inter-communion' with another church – 'individual participation' is permitted in 'special situations and contexts' when the person has the requisite

---

bishop should make norms (taking into account those of the Bishops' Conference) to judge situations of grave and pressing need: ED 130.

[168] CIC, c. 908; breach is 'against religion and the unity of the church': c. 933; see also CCEO, cc. 670-671.

[169] SCOBA: GOCER, Pt. 1, Preaching on Ecumenical Occasions, 1; Sacraments and other Liturgical Services, 1.1 and 2; ATGB: Instructions, Holy Communion: admission is restricted to those baptised members in good standing in churches 'in Eucharistic communion with the Ecumenical Patriarchate or a patriarchate in communion with our Mother Church'.

[170] OCIA: GC, Ecumenical Witness, B.11; SCOBA: GOCER, Pt. 1, Preaching on Ecumenical Occasions, 2.

[171] PCLCCAC: Principle 99: the normal requirements for church membership should be presented before any person who regularly receives Holy Communion over a long period likely to continue indefinitely when such person is from a church not in the Anglican Communion but which upholds the apostolic faith and subscribes to the doctrine of the Holy Trinity. See e.g. New Zealand: Cans. G.IX–XIII: all 'baptised Anglicans' are free to attend the Eucharist in other churches 'as conscience dictates', and all Christians duly baptised in the name of the Trinity are 'welcome to receive the sacrament' of holy communion.

disposition.[172] Some Reformed churches are more liberal: 'Members of other Churches are welcomed to communion and ministers of other Churches may, on invitation, administer the sacraments'; thus: 'Only members in full communion are entitled to participate' in the Lord's Supper; but the Session may grant 'occasional communion to members of other churches who desire to join in it, when nothing is known concerning them inconsistent with their profession as members of the Church of Christ'.[173] However, for the Presbyterian Church in Ireland: 'the minister presiding at any celebration of the Lord's Supper may invite all communicant members of other congregations and of other Christian Churches who are present to partake of the sacrament'.[174] Methodists also 'extend sacramental hospitality' to other churches with which there is full communion.[175]

Mixed marriages

All the churches studied here make provision for mixed marriages (between a baptised person within the tradition and one in a church outside the tradition) as an exception to the general rule; the conditions vary. The general rule in Catholic canon law provides: 'Without the express permission of the competent authority, marriage is prohibited between two baptised persons, one of whom was baptised in the catholic Church or received into it after baptism, the other of whom belongs to a church or ecclesial community not in full communion with the catholic Church.'[176] However, the local ordinary may permit a mixed marriage if there is a just and reasonable cause, and permission cannot be granted unless three conditions are met: the Catholic party must declare that he or she is prepared to remove dangers of defecting from the faith and makes a sincere promise to do all in their power that the children be baptised and brought up in the catholic Church; the other party is to be informed in good time of these promises (so that the non-Catholic party is certain that he/she is truly aware of the promise and of the obligation of the Catholic party); and both parties are to be instructed about the purposes and essential properties of marriage, which are not to be excluded by either party;

---

[172] LCA: Some Pastoral Guidelines for Responsible Communion Practice (1990, 2001) 9–14; see 4–5 for detail on special situations; see also ELCSA: G., 3.9: 'members of other churches may only be admitted as guests to the Lord's Supper'; decisions on this matter are taken by the minister; and Lutherans 'are allowed to participate in Holy Communion in other churches as guests' provided there is a prior agreement with the host minister.

[173] UFCS: Statement of the General Assembly, Special Constitutional Features of the UFCS; MPP, I.III.6.

[174] PCI: Code, 84(2): but this does not extend to a person excommunicated by a Kirk Session. See also PCA: BCO, 56.4: 'the minister, at the discretion of the Session, before the observance begins, may invite all those who profess the true religion, and are communicants in good standing of any evangelical church, to participate in the ordinance'; URC: Man., F: the duty 'to be sensitive to the ecumenical dimensions of presidency at the sacraments' and so a minister must preside where possible; PC (USA) BO, W-2.4006: celebration of the Lord's Supper at 'ecumenical assemblies'.

[175] UMCNEAE: BOD, par. 2402; MCI: RDG, 4A.02: generally, only members receive communion; MCGB: CPD, SO 011: a circuit which considers that 'other Christians' in the locality are deprived of the reasonably frequent and regular celebration of the Lord's Supper may apply for persons other than ministers to preside.

[176] CIC, c. 1124; see also Pope Paul VI, *Matrimonia Mixta* (1970).

provision also exists for mixed marriages to be celebrated in a Eucharistic context (if there is a just cause).[177] A Catholic minister may take part in the celebration of a marriage between two Orthodox or a Catholic and an Orthodox if invited by the relevant Orthodox authority.[178] A non-Catholic may act as a witness at a Catholic celebration of marriage, as can Catholics at marriages in other churches.[179]

The juridical position in Orthodox churches is very similar. The norm in Orthodox churches is to celebrate only the marriage of two Orthodox; an Orthodox marriage must be solemnised by an Orthodox priest but '[a] marriage performed by a priest in communion with the Orthodox Church is recognized as valid by the entire Orthodox Church'.[180] However, a mixed marriage (between an Orthodox and a non-Orthodox Christian who is baptised and confesses the Lordship of Christ) is tolerated by means of the principle of economy for pastoral concern and love for the faithful – 'it is permitted in the hope that the non-Orthodox spouse will seek entrance into the [Orthodox] Church'; the Orthodox partner 'should not consent to have children of the union baptized outside the orthodox Church as a pre-marriage agreement'; and the active participation of non-Orthodox clergy in the marriage service, as in all the mysteries of the Orthodox Church, is not allowed (but they may attend). Conversely, 'Orthodox clergy may not participate in non-Orthodox services and rites'.[181] 'Orthodox Christians who marry outside the Orthodox Church thereby exclude their marital life from the life of the Church, exclude themselves from the Holy Eucharist, and therefore from full membership of the Church'; but they may be restored to Eucharistic fellowship by recommendation from the priest and the approval of the hierarch; normally, such restoration includes the confirmation of the marriage through the rite approved by the hierarch.[182] Anglicans also relax the general norm in the case of mixed marriages.[183]

---

[177] CIC, c. 1125; ED 150; the Episcopal Conference is to prescribe the manner in which these declarations and promises (which are always required) are to be made, and to determine how they are to be established, and how the non-Catholic party is to be informed of them: CIC, c. 1126; see c. 1127.2 for dispensations and c. 1127.3 for double marriage celebrations; local ordinaries and other pastors of souls must ensure that the Catholic spouse and the children born of a mixed marriage are not without the spiritual help needed to fulfil their obligations; they are to assist the spouses to foster the unity of conjugal and family life: c. 1128; ordinarily, a mixed marriage is celebrated outside the Eucharist, except for just cause; see ED 159.

[178] ED 127.   [179] ED 136.

[180] UOCIA: Joint Statement of Hierarchs, Living the Sacramental Life of the Church: Practical Instructions for the Diocesan Faithful, Policy on Marriages, 3.

[181] OCIA: GC, Mystery of Marriage, A.1–4: a petition for a mixed marriage must be submitted to the bishop. OCIA: GC, Ecumenical Witness, B.12: non-Orthodox clergy present at an Orthodox wedding, funeral, baptism or similar event may not participate in any part of the service, but, after a wedding, they may offer a prayer or blessing at the reception or at another appropriate time outside the church; SOBA: GOCER, Sacraments and Other Liturgical Services, IV.9: Orthodox priests may attend as a guest; ATGB: Instructions, Weddings: the non-Orthodox should sign a declaration that 'the children will be baptised and brought up within the Orthodox faith and in accordance with her traditions'; UOCIA: Instructions, Policy on Marriages, 9–12 and (for identical provisions) ACROD: Spiritual and Sacramental Guidelines, Marriages; GOA(AUS): Instructions, Weddings.

[182] OCIA: GC, Mystery of marriage, C.1–4; see also SCOBA: GOCER: Pt. 1, Sacraments and Other Liturgical Services, IV.

[183] N. Doe, 'Inter-church and inter-faith marriages in Anglican canon law', in N. Doe (ed.), *Marriage in Anglican and Roman Catholic Canon Law* (Centre for Law and Religion, Cardiff, 2009) 95; the Principles do not deal with the matter.

In the Protestant churches studied here, three in particular have detailed norms on the matter. The Lutheran Church of Australia prescribes that a Lutheran pastor may take part in a marriage service conducted by a minister of another denomination not in altar and pulpit fellowship with the Lutheran church as 'an exception' only after consultation with the president of the district of the Lutheran minister – the Lutheran pastor may read the Word of God, give an address and pronounce a blessing provided the service does not contain 'doctrinal aberrations'; however, 'a Lutheran pastor will not invite a minister of a church which is not in altar and pulpit fellowship with the [Lutheran church], to preach at a marriage service conducted by a Lutheran pastor', but such a guest minister may be invited to read from the Word of God and give a blessing or greeting.[184] The Presbyterian Church in Ireland stipulates: 'A minister should not join in marriage a member of the Church with one holding beliefs or having a Church membership incompatible with the witness of the Protestant Reformation, until careful instruction has been given in the doctrines and obligations of our evangelical faith or until other conditions approved by the General Assembly's Committee on marriage and the family have been observed.'[185] The Methodist Church in Great Britain provides that it may welcome 'everyone who enquires about an intended marriage service in a Methodist church' to be solemnised by a minister 'who is not prevented by conscience from considering their request',[186] but 'the participation of a priest or religious leader from another faith community' is the exception.[187] In short, from the churches studied here the juridical principle which emerges is that mixed marriages are permitted as exceptions to the rule.

Common prayer, worship, preaching and funerals

Common prayer and worship (outside the Eucharist) are much less sensitive issues and the juridical instruments of the different traditions are generally liberal with regard to them. According to Catholic norms,[188] Christians may be encouraged to share in spiritual activities such as common prayer (particularly prayer for Christian unity, and ecumenical partners should collaborate on the preparation of common prayer), spiritual exercises, blessings and funerals. Catholics may read lessons in Orthodox sacramental liturgical services and *vice versa*; in the case of other churches, a non-Catholic may read from scripture at a Catholic Eucharist on an

---

[184] LCA: Guidelines for Inter-Church Marriages (1988, edited 2000); see also ELCSA: G., 7.6: if one party belongs to 'a different denomination', there must be instruction about 'the problems that might follow'.

[185] PCI: Code, 85(5).

[186] MCGB: CPD, Book VI, Part 2 Guidance, Section 9: Christian Preparation for Marriage, Methodist Church Policy and Guidelines, A.

[187] MCGB: CPD, Bk. VI, Sect. 10: Guidance for Inter-Faith Marriages.

[188] CIC, c. 825.2: 'With the permission of the Bishops' Conference, catholic members of Christ's faithful, in cooperation with separated brethren, may prepare and publish versions of the Scriptures, with appropriate explanatory notes'; see also DV 22: the council approved scriptural translations 'in a joint effort with the separated brethren' with the agreement of the authorities of the church; in so doing the guidelines issues by the Secretariat for Christian Unity and the United Bible Society (2 June 1968) should be observed: Secretariat for Christian Unity, *Information Service* 5 (1968) 22–25 (see 35 *Irish Theological Quarterly* (1968) 388–394).

exceptional occasion if the bishop permits this for just cause. Indeed, liturgy should be used as an agent of unity (with prayer for Christian unity).[189] Moreover, while blessings are 'to be imparted primarily to Catholics, they may be given also to catechumens and, unless there is a prohibition by the Church, even to non-Catholics'.[190]

The general rule in Orthodox churches is that Orthodox services are 'restricted to the members of the Orthodox Church and must not be understood or implemented as means towards [Christian] unity' as they represent 'the official prayer and devotional action of the Orthodox Church'; however, non-liturgical prayer for Christian unity is encouraged and an Orthodox priest should not hesitate to provide a blessing for a non-Orthodox if requested.[191] Orthodox services may be celebrated at which non-Orthodox are present but the readings, hymns and responses must be led by Orthodox Christians; and non-Orthodox clergy may attend non-Orthodox services as guests of honour.[192] Orthodox Christians may participate in an ecumenical service but must first ask the diocesan hierarch for 'his blessing'; the Orthodox participants should also review the text of the service so they can determine whether or not an Orthodox presence might be misconstrued; if the contents of the service compromise or offend the Orthodox faith or ecclesiology 'there can be no Orthodox participation' – reasons should be given. Orthodox clergy, in the context of ecumenical services, may preach, offer a prayer in the Orthodox Tradition and read from Holy Scripture.[193] Some Anglican churches have detailed ecumenical rules for mutual ministerial participation in divine worship.[194]

The matter is not treated in the juridical instruments of the Protestant churches studied here, but preaching by ministers from other churches is addressed in some detail. For example, ministers from other prescribed churches may be invited to preach at Lutheran churches,[195] Methodist churches[196] and Reformed churches.[197] Moreover, in Orthodox churches, as a general rule, preaching at Orthodox services is reserved to Orthodox clergy (but non-Orthodox may be invited to preach as an exception to this rule),[198] and with the knowledge and blessing of his diocesan

---

[189] ED 62–65: Catholics should value e.g. 'the worship and piety of Anglicans'; the settings for ecumenical formation are the parish, family, schools, associations and other ecclesial movements.

[190] ED 111–121, 126, 133; for blessings see CIC, c. 1170.

[191] SCOBA: GOCER, Pt. 1, Worship with Non-Orthodox, 3 and Blessings etc.

[192] OCIA: GC, Ecumenical Witness, A.4; i.e., Vespers, Service of Intercession, etc; non-Orthodox choral groups may not be invited to give the responses or sing the hymns of the services; SCOBA: GOCER, Pt. 1, Worship with Non-Orthodox.

[193] OCIA: GC, Ecumenical Witness, C: Ecumenical Religious Services; there are also provisions on vesture; see also SCOBA: GOCER, Pt. 1, Special Common Prayer Occasions, 1; 'Although a service of prayer may be tailored for a particular occasion, it must be clearly demonstrated that it is the prayer of the Orthodox to God for the spiritual enlightenment and wellbeing of all the participants': OCIA: GC, Ecumenical Witness, A.5.

[194] See e.g. England: Cans. B43 and B44.   [195] LCGB: RAR, Appendix A.

[196] MCI: RDG, 10.69.

[197] RCA: BCO Ch. 1, Pt. 1, Art. 2, s. 11.e: provided their character and standard are known; see also PC (USA) BO W-3.5301: common prayer.

[198] SCOBA: GOCER, Pt. 1, Preaching on Ecumenical Occasions, 1: the bishop is consulted for exceptions; reciprocity requires extending invitations only if these can be reciprocated; OCIA: GC, Ecumenical Witness, B.4: non-Orthodox clergy may not preach in an Orthodox church,

hierarch, an Orthodox clergyman may deliver a sermon in a non-Orthodox church which will in no way compromise the tenets of the faith and Orthodox Tradition.[199]

The juridical instruments of churches also allow reciprocity in ministry at funerals, normally as an exception to the general rule. According to Catholic norms, provided their own minister is not available, baptised persons belonging to a non-Catholic church or ecclesial community may, in accordance with the prudent judgment of the local ordinary, be allowed church funerals unless it is established that they did not wish this.[200] An Orthodox clergyman may not take part in a funeral for a non-Orthodox even if that person is related to a parishioner; if invited, however, he may offer some words of consolation at the graveside or funeral meal. Moreover, if an Orthodox priest is asked to bury a non-Orthodox person, he must consult with his diocesan hierarch, and 'with the hierarch's blessing bury the person according to the services prescribed in the Book of Needs'.[201] In turn, a non-Orthodox cleric may not be invited to participate in an Orthodox funeral service or offer any form of homily or public statement in the temple, or participate in the graveside service; the officiating priest, however, cannot control what takes place after the Orthodox service of burial has been concluded in a public cemetery.[202] In Anglicanism, if called upon to provide ministry at a funeral, for persons belonging to another faith community, ministers should as appropriate suggest they approach a minister of that other community; consult with a minister of that community for advice; and consult within their own church. Ministers may approach colleagues in another faith community to minister to a member of their own church only in exceptional cases at the request of that member.[203] Some Lutheran churches also provide for ministers to perform funerals for members of other churches.[204]

The sharing of church buildings

The juridical instruments provide as a general rule that places of worship must be used only for the purposes of the church in question. However, exceptions are made to allow in prescribed circumstances the sharing of places of worship with other churches outside the tradition. Catholic churches which are consecrated or blessed have an important theological and liturgical significance for Catholics and are therefore generally reserved for Catholic worship. Nevertheless, if priests, ministers or communities not in full communion with the Catholic Church do not have a place or the liturgical objects necessary for celebrating worthily their religious ceremonies, the bishop may allow them the use of a church or a Catholic building and also lend them what may be necessary for their services. Under similar circumstances, permission may be given to them for interment or for the celebration of services at Catholic cemeteries; moreover, where there is a good ecumenical relationship, the shared ownership or use of church premises

---

but they may be invited to give lectures or presentations in the educational facilities of the church; the diocesan hierarch is to be consulted for his blessing.
[199] OCIA: GC, Ecumenical Witness, B.5. [200] CIC, c. 1183.3.
[201] OCIA: GC, Funeral Guidelines, 14 and B.1. [202] OCIA: GC, Funeral Guidelines, 15 and B.13.
[203] PCLCCAC: Principle 98.4. [204] ELCSA: G., 8.5.

may be permitted over an extended period by agreement.[205] Similarly, Orthodox properties must be used for the purposes of the Orthodox faith.[206] However, whilst an ecumenical service, as such, is not to be conducted in an Orthodox church, prior to an Orthodox service being held for the benefit of true ecumenical witness, and at which there is to be a major attendance by non-Orthodox clergy and laity, the permission and blessing of the diocesan hierarch must be secured.[207] Express provision also exists in relation to some Anglican churches for the sharing of church buildings.[208]

The juridical instruments of Protestant churches also facilitate the sharing of church buildings subject to the satisfaction of prescribed procedural requirements. For example, a congregation of the Lutheran Church of Australia may make its church 'available to another denomination' with which 'close relationships' have been developed and provided the other denomination worships the Triune God 'as confessed in the ecumenical creeds'; but 'it is not appropriate that the sanctuary is made available for use by a non-sacramental church'; the other denomination must also undertake not to alter the buildings' appointments or to proselytise amongst the members of the local Lutheran congregation.[209] Likewise, in the Reformed tradition a church building must be used for the purposes of the denomination but also for purposes which are of 'a religious, ecclesiastical, or charitable nature, though not connected with the congregation', including the conduct of worship 'by any minister of any other religious denomination' (subject to the necessary consents).[210] Similarly, whilst as a general rule Methodist places of worship shall be used 'according to the established forms and usages of Methodism', they may be shared with other churches subject to satisfaction of the prescribed consents.[211] Once again, ecumenical sharing is the exception to the rule.

Mission, social justice and ecumenism

The juridical instruments of churches often provide for ecumenical collaboration in mission to the wider world, particularly in the promotion of social justice. Under the canon law of the Oriental Catholic churches: 'With due regard for the norms on *communicatio in sacris*, it is desirable that the Catholic faithful, undertake any project in which they could cooperate with other Christians, not alone but together, such as works for charity and social justice, defence of the dignity and the

---

[205] ED 137–140: the agreement should deal with reservation of the sacrament, finance and civil law matters; see also CCEO, c. 670.2.
[206] GOAA: Regs., Art. 16.1.
[207] Local Orthodox clergy fellowships, guided by their hierarchs, should come to one mind as to ecumenical activity and uniformity of practice: OCIA: GC, Ecumenical Witness, C. Ecumenical Religious Services.
[208] In the UK the matter is governed by the Sharing of Church Buildings Act 1969 which applies not only to the Anglican churches but also, *inter alia*, to the Roman Catholic Church and the Methodist Church.
[209] LCA: Statement on the Use of Lutheran Churches by other Church Groups (1975, edited 2001).
[210] UFCS: MPP, I.III.23; UCC: Man., App. II, Sch. B, Model Trust Deed, 4(a); see also URC: Man., D, Parts I and II; UCC: Community Ministry Standards and Best Practices (2007) 21; PCI: Code, 230(5).
[211] MCNZ: LAR, s. 1.5.1–3; see also MCGB: CPD, MT 1492 and SO 920(2); UMCNEAE: BOD, par. 2550.

fundamental rights of the human person, promotion of peace, days of commemoration for the country, and national holidays.'[212] Moreover, for the promotion of religious liberty: 'Directors of schools, hospitals and other similar Catholic institutions are to see to it that other Christians who are visiting or working in the institution are able to receive spiritual aid and the sacraments from their own ministers.'[213] In Catholic schools and institutions, every effort should be made to respect the faith and conscience of students or teachers who belong to other Churches or ecclesial communities. In accordance with their own approved statutes, the authorities of these schools and institutions should take care that clergy of other communities have every facility for giving spiritual and sacramental ministration to their own faithful who attend such schools or institutions. As far as circumstances allow, with the permission of the diocesan bishop, these facilities can be offered on Catholic premises, including the church or chapel.[214] In hospitals, homes for the aged and similar institutions conducted by Catholics, the authorities should promptly advise priests and ministers of other communities of the presence of their faithful and afford them every facility to visit these persons and give them spiritual and sacramental ministrations under dignified and reverent conditions, including the use of the chapel.[215] For some Orthodox churches, 'participation and cooperation in work for the good of society in such areas as educational opportunities, morality, responsible citizenship, Christian charity, social services, and other areas of concern to the community are acceptable'.[216] Co-operation in humanitarian work,[217] and mission, also features in Orthodox,[218] and Protestant norms.[219]

Conciliar ecumenism and covenantal communion

The juridical instruments of separated churches commonly provide for the participation of those churches in the external institutional structures of the ecumenical movement. This is usually achieved through permissive norms allowing membership of local, national and international ecumenical bodies, such as the World Council of Churches.[220] Such norms exist in churches across the traditions studied here.[221] Norms may also explain the nature of permissible conversation

---

[212] CCEO, c. 908; cf. c. 930; collaborating ecumenically in charitable activities (e.g. schools, hospitals, prisons) and for human rights and liberty: ED 64.

[213] CCEO, c. 907.

[214] ED 141; for ecumenism in Methodist schools, see MCI: RDG, 20.02.   [215] ED 142.

[216] OCIA: GC, Ecumenical Witness, A.2; see also SCOBA: GOCER, Pt. 1, Secular Ecumenism, 1: inter-denominational activities as to 'social, moral and political issues'.

[217] UCC: Community Standards and Best Practices: Administrative Standards for Community and Social Service Ministries (2007) 27.

[218] Co-operation may include education, social justice, racial tensions, human development and moral issues: SCOBA: GOCER, Pt. 1, Council of Churches, 6.

[219] PCI: Code, 113.

[220] For membership of the WCC, see e.g. UMCNEAE: BOD, par. 1905ff; ELCA: Const., Ch. 15.12. B10. The WCC itself, beyond the scope of this chapter, has a constitution which deals, *inter alia*, with the objects of the WCC, membership (and the rules require submission of the principal juridical instrument of the applicant church or communion) and the functions of its assemblies and bodies.

[221] For Catholic norms, see ED 166f; for Orthodox norms, see SCOBA: GOCER, Pt. 1, Council of Churches, 7–8: 'conciliar ecumenism': 'Where membership is considered desirable by a local

and co-operation, as well as official representation on the wider ecumenical councils and bodies.[222] However, these norms on conciliar ecumenism, as with all those studied in the previous sections, are made unilaterally by each church. This may be contrasted with norms which result from joint action on the part of ecumenical partners from different traditions in the form of an ecumenical covenant which enables and regulates ecclesial communion – either full communion or a lesser communion, depending on the extent of the relationship that has been reached by the parties involved. Thus, such covenants represent ecumenical norms properly so called – joint norm-making – though the juridical instruments of churches across the separate traditions commonly provide for the making of such agreements, which are operative usually upon approval by their central assemblies.[223]

First, ecumenical covenants may be bilateral or multilateral. Bilateral covenants are entered between a single institutional church and another church from a different tradition, and often they present themselves as articulating current practice: one Anglican-Methodist covenant endorses formally (and seeks to go some way beyond) what is already a reality in many local situations.[224] Not unlike the Anglican–Lutheran Concordat of Agreement in the USA,[225] the Lutheran–Anglican Covenant in Australia is a *national* covenant which enables further *regional* agreements to develop by stages.[226] A covenant may be tripartite,[227] or it may be multipartite – the Australian Churches Covenanting Together (ACCT) involves fifteen different churches.[228] Other covenants are continental, such as the *Charta Oecumenica* (2001) between the Conference of European Churches and the (Roman Catholic) Council of European Bishops' Conferences. Or else covenants may be local in nature.[229]

---

congregation or parish, the Orthodox priest should encourage his parish council to enter into a working relationship or full membership in the Councils of Churches'; 'When invited, Orthodox priests may accept leadership positions in a council. It is desirable to enlist the support and interest of capable laity. Such elections or appointments must be brought to the attention of the bishop'; GOAA: Charter, Art. 6.9: national representation in ecumenical relations; for Lutheran norms: ELCA: Const., Ch. 15.12.B10: membership of the National Council of the Churches of Christ in the USA; see also UCC: Man., BL 385: Canadian Council of Churches; URC: Man., K: working with the Council for World Mission; MCI: RDG, 20.02: 'world level' ecumenical issues.

[222] See e.g. ED 172 ff; OCIA: GC, Ecumenical Witness, B.2-3.
[223] See e.g. UMCNEAE: BOD, par. 2402.
[224] *An Anglican-Methodist Covenant, Common Statement of the Formal Conversations between the Methodist Church of Great Britain and the Church of England* (London, 2001) v.
[225] TEC: Office of Ecumenical and Interfaith Relations, *A Beginner's Guide to the Concordat of Agreement* (2003).
[226] Anglican Church of Australia: General Synod Resolution, 78/04(a)–(b).
[227] Such as the Lutheran–Anglican–Roman Catholic (Virginia) Covenant 1990.
[228] Australian Churches Covenanting Together (ACCT) (2004), p.4: The Covenanting Document, Part A, Declaration of Intent. The parties are: the Anglican Church of Australia, Antiochian Orthodox Church, Armenian Apostolic Church, Assyrian Church of the East, Church of Christ in Australia, Congregational Federation of Australia, Coptic Orthodox Church, Greek Orthodox Archdiocese of Australia, Lutheran Church of Australia, Religious Society of Friends, Roman Catholic Church in Australia, Romanian Orthodox Church, Salvation Army, Syrian Orthodox Church, Uniting Church in Australia.
[229] Such as the Kilcoy Covenant (Queensland, Australia) 2001.

Secondly, ecumenical covenants are solemn voluntary and relational agreements which spell out the commitments which each ecclesial party has made towards greater visible communion: typically, the agreement 'gathers together in pilgrimage ... churches and Christian communities' in which they 'agree' to collaborate for greater Christian unity.[230] In the Lutheran–Anglican Covenant in Australia, for example, the parties pledge to work together to develop joint participation in mission and witness – they 'solemnly covenant together' and 'undertake' to continue to work towards a Concordat for full communion and reconciliation of ministries.[231] Such covenants may also seek to engage in secular ecumenism – working together in the field of politics and social justice.[232] Unity and co-operation are typical goals of ecumenical covenants such as the concordat between the Evangelical Lutheran Church of America and the Episcopal Church USA.[233] Inter-church agreements may also have a penitential goal, like the Leuenberg Agreement of the Community of Protestant Churches in Europe: in it the parties seek to confess the guilt and suffering that have accompanied and accompany the struggle for truth and unity in the church.[234] Ecumenical covenants also commonly describe the qualities which the parties recognise in each other – that they each share the essential marks of the church universal.[235]

Thirdly, ecumenical covenants are often prescriptive. Whilst some are 'permissive',[236] most contain 'commitments' in the form of duties and correlative rights: to welcome members of the partner churches to receive sacramental and pastoral ministrations; to regard baptised members of the churches as members of the partner churches; and to welcome persons ordained as bishop, priest or deacon to serve in the ministry of the partner churches.[237] Also, some churches formally incorporate ecumenical covenants in their juridical systems,[238] or otherwise adopt them formally;[239] but the signatories to the Lutheran–Anglican–Roman Catholic

---

[230] ACCT, pp. 3, 7: Covenanting Document, Part B.
[231] Anglican Church of Australia: General Synod Res. 78/04. See also ACCT, p. 11, Part C: the churches 'pledge e.g. to continue to discuss and articulate ... the meaning and significance of our involvement in the quest for a more visible expression of unity and the possibilities for further engagement in ecumenical partnership'.
[232] See e.g. *Charta Oecumenica, between the Conference of European Churches and the Roman Catholic Council of European Bishops' Conferences* (2001).
[233] TEC: Office of Ecumenism and Interfaith Relations, *A Beginner's Guide to the Concordat of Agreement* (2003).
[234] Preamble, 1.
[235] In the Porvoo Common Statement (1992) Anglican and Lutheran churches recognise: one another as churches belonging to the one Church of Christ, and as truly participating in the apostolic mission of the whole people of God; that, in each of them, the Word of God is authentically preached, and the sacraments of baptism and Eucharist are duly administered; and that each shares in the common confession of the apostolic faith.
[236] ACCT, p.1: it is 'permission-giving' but also contains 'commitments'; the *Charta Oecumenica* (2001) spells out mischiefs and curative commitments.
[237] Church in Wales: Can. 28-9-1995, Sch. 1; The Lutheran–Anglican Covenant Australia (pledges, commitments).
[238] Church in Wales: Can. 28-9-1995 (Porvoo); Can. 1-5-1974: Covenant of Churches in Wales.
[239] Anglican–Lutheran Covenant in Australia: the 'Anglican Church formally commits itself to enter into this Covenant with the Lutheran Church'; it was 'adopted' by General Synod and

Covenant (Virginia) merely 'recommend' it to their 'respective judicatories', and *Charta Oecumenica* has 'no magisterial or dogmatic character, nor is it legally binding under church law'.[240] Significantly, however, ecumenical covenants protect the juridical autonomy of the participating churches.[241] Indeed, the notion of 'reconciled diversity' is used by the Community of Protestant Churches in Europe: it is perfectly acceptable to have a state of 'reconciled diversity' in which there is fellowship between churches that maintain their own distinct identity and traditions.[242] In any event, covenants are the result of a process of both vocation and negotiation. For instance, the Lutheran–Anglican–Roman Catholic (Virginia) Covenant 1990 is based not only on the parties having felt 'impelled' by 'powerful experiences' to covenant together, but also on recognition that the Spirit 'calls us to ... consensus so that we can advance toward the goal of unity willed by Christ'; it has a section styled 'A Call into Covenant', and the bishops in turn call on their respective faithful to commit to the terms of the covenant.[243]

Finally, ecumenical covenants sometimes provide for tiers of membership of different covenantal commitments as between the alliance members. For example, in the Australian Churches' Covenant, fifteen churches are party to the declaration of intent and are committed to common prayer, to intercede and care for one another and to explore Christian convictions and their application.[244] Eleven agree to support an initiative for sharing physical resources, such as buildings, and to encourage consultation between the appropriate governing bodies of the churches before new major developments are undertaken.[245] Eight agree to explore strategies for mission;[246] nine agree to mutual recognition of baptisms;[247] two churches agree to Eucharistic sharing;[248] and four pairs of churches agree to work towards mutual recognition of ordained ministry.[249] All

provides that '[e]ach church enacts the Covenant by whatever measures are appropriate for each church': GS Resolution, 78/04(d) and (f).

[240] See the Preamble of both instruments.

[241] Cold Ash Statement (1983), *Growth in Communion*, par. 113: in 'this new relation, churches become interdependent while remaining autonomous'; par. 117: 'Full communion is ... a relationship between two distinct churches or communions in which each maintains its own autonomy while recognising the catholicity and apostolicity of the other, and believing the other to hold the essentials of the Christian faith': S. Oppegaard and G. Cameron (eds.), *Anglican-Lutheran Agreements: Regional and International Agreements 1972-2002* (Lutheran World Federation and Anglican Consultative Council, Geneva, 2004).

[242] The Leuenberg Fellowship (European Lutheran and Reformed churches): *The Church of Jesus Christ* (Frankfurt am Main, 1996).

[243] See also Covenant of Churches in Wales 1975 for the notion of the churches as called to covenant.

[244] ACCT: The Covenanting Document, Part B, The Proposed Commitment, (a) General (e.g. Romanian Orthodox Church is not party to this; Anglicans, Lutherans and Roman Catholics (e.g.) are).

[245] Ibid: Anglicans, Lutherans, Greek Orthodox and Roman Catholics (e.g.) are party to this.

[246] Ibid: e.g. Romanian Orthodox Church is not party to this, but the Anglicans, Lutherans and Roman Catholics (e.g.) are.

[247] Ibid: Anglicans, Lutherans, Greek Orthodox and Roman Catholics are party (e.g.).

[248] Ibid: Churches of Christ in Australia with Uniting Church in Australia (e.g.).

[249] Ibid: Anglican with Lutheran; Anglican with Uniting Church; Churches of Christ with Uniting Church; Lutheran with Uniting Church.

fifteen churches pledge to discuss and articulate the meaning of their involvement in the quest for more visible unity and to explore further steps to make more clearly visible the unity of all Christian people.[250] The churches name each other 'as a sign of what we can covenant to do together'.[251] All of these ecumenical covenants are by-products of the unilaterally created juridical norms described in the previous sections. Above all, in so far as they are the result of joint ecclesial action – bilateral or multilateral norm-making – they represent ecumenical laws properly so-called.

Conclusion

The juridical instruments of churches tell us much about the commitment of churches to and their participation in the ecumenical movement. First, they tell us about the indivisibility of the church of Christ, about how each church sees its relationship with the church universal, and about how Christian disunity itself is in part a result of and sustained by juridical walls between the separated churches. Secondly, from a comparative study of these juridical instruments, and the profound similarities between them, it is possible to induce common principles of Christian law and church order on ecumenism: the restoration of Christian unity is a requirement of divine law; each church has a duty to engage in the ecumenical enterprise; ecumenism involves dialogue and co-operation towards greater visible communion; each church should protect the marks within it of the church universal; and each church should have institutional structures for the promotion of ecumenism – its central assemblies, commissions, congregations, ministers and laity should all promote ecumenism. Thirdly, the juridical instruments define what ecclesial communion and reciprocity is possible between the divided churches: they tell us about the conditions that must be satisfied before one church recognises the ecclesiality and ministry of another; they tell us about the spiritual communion between all baptised Christians; and they tell us about the limits of mutual hospitality in the administration of the sacraments, worship and the sharing of property. However, interestingly, ecumenical norms on the administration of baptism, the Eucharist, mixed marriages and sharing property are most usually in the nature of exceptions to general rules which confine such facilities to the enjoyment of the faithful within the tradition; such norms do not reflect ecumenism as a priority. All of these unilaterally made norms may be contrasted with ecumenical covenants which represent a clear quasi-judicial form of joint ecumenical norm-making. Furthermore, needless to say, a more extensive survey of legal texts beyond the fifty or so churches examined here may reveal not only very different juridical patterns in the fields studied, but also that there may be other areas for exploration. Further work is also needed to determine how the norms discussed here relate to the method and practice of ecumenism today – whether they reflect accurately the current methodological principles developed in ecumenical theology and practice. Equally, empirical work needs to be done on how the juridical norms studied here are actually used in practice, whether they are effective or problematic. In any event, what seems to emerge is

---

[250] Ibid: Part C: The Future Pledge.   [251] Ibid: Affirmation of Commitment.

that the juridical implementation of ecumenism by churches is essential for the translation of ecumenical commitment into practical norms of action. In this respect, juridical ecumenism, the study and practical deployment of laws and other regulatory instruments of churches on ecumenism, offers both a theoretical and a practical framework to complement but not to replace the current (and dominant) doctrinal and theological focus in contemporary ecumenical method and practice.

9

Church property and finance

The juridical instruments of the Christian traditions studied here all contain elaborate rules which apply to church property and finance. The interplay between these and civil law is also evident with regard to the administration of church property and finance. Generally, as individual churches need the capacity under the civil laws of the States within which they exist to acquire, administer and dispose of property, they utilise trusts and trustees and other entities acting as representatives of the church with juridical personality under civil law. The doctrine of Christian stewardship is shared by all the churches and provides a central theological principle around which legal rules are devised. Ownership of property is vested in institutions at various ecclesiastical levels – but the focus of this chapter is property held and administered at the level of the local church. The chapter compares the rules of churches on the acquisition and disposal of church property, places of worship (and their contents, particularly those objects needed for the administration of worship), the control of finance, income in the form of offerings, taxes and investment, and expenditure in the form of the insurance of ecclesiastical property, and the stipends and pensions of ordained ministers. The chapter elucidates the key differences between the laws of churches, as well as the similarities between them, from which it is possible to induce common principles of Christian law. It is also evident that a study of the laws of churches indicates that Christians across our traditions are engaged in fundamentally the same actions with regard to church property and finance.

The ownership of property

Whilst the objects of Christian churches are essentially spiritual, even though these are played out in the public sphere of the visible church, their engagement in the management of property reveals the temporal aspects of ecclesial life. Key to these activities is the juridical concept of ownership. The laws of most churches deal with the right to acquire, own, administer and dispose of property, the need for juridical personality under civil law to enable these, the right of a church to frame norms on the acquisition, administration and disposal of property, adherence to these norms by church units particularly at the local level, and the distribution of property on the dissolution of an institutional church or its units.

The Catholic Church claims for itself 'the inherent right, independently of any secular power, to acquire, retain, administer and alienate temporal goods, in pursuit of its proper objectives', namely: 'the regulation of divine worship, the provision of fitting support for the clergy and other ministers, and the carrying out of works of the sacred apostolate and of charity, especially for the needy'. The universal church, Apostolic See, particular churches and all other juridical persons are capable of acquiring, retaining, administering and alienating temporal goods in accordance with canon law. Under the supreme authority of the Roman Pontiff, ownership of goods belongs to that juridical person which has lawfully acquired them.[1] The church may acquire temporal goods in any way in which by either natural or positive law it is lawful for others to do this – and the civil law of contract must be observed in this regard unless contrary to divine law or canon law; the permission of the competent authority is required for the valid alienation of goods which constitute the church's 'stable patrimony'.[2] The Episcopal Conference sets the minimum and maximum values of property. Property over the maximum value is alienated only with the permission of the competent authority and, if it is of special artistic or historical interest, that of the Holy See. Property between the minimum and maximum values may be alienated with the permission of the bishop who must obtain the consent of the finance council and interested parties; if parish property is below the minimum, the competent authority is the pastor. To alienate goods over the minimum value there must be 'a just cause such as urgent necessity, evident usefulness, charity or some other serious reason'. Written evaluations must be obtained from experts to determine a suitable price, and property must not be sold for less than its estimated value; the proceeds are to be applied as the competent authority directs.[3] If permission has not been obtained the disposal is canonically invalid.[4] Stable patrimony whose value falls below the minimum may be alienated by the owner without the permission of a higher authority.[5] Canon law forbids absolutely the disposal of certain sacred objects.[6] Ordinaries supervise the administration of temporal goods subject to the Pontiff who is 'the supreme administrator and steward of all ecclesiastical goods'.[7] Similar rules apply to the Oriental Catholic Churches.[8]

It is a fundamental principle of Orthodox law that a church has the right to acquire, own, administer and dispose of property,[9] as well as persons and units

---

[1] CIC, c. 1254: the right to and objects of property; c. 1255: juridical persons; c. 1256: ownership; see also c. 1257: all temporal goods are 'ecclesiastical goods and are regulated by the canons' and by the statutes of the juridical person in question; c. 1258: the 'church' for these purposes means the relevant juridical person.

[2] CIC, c. 1259; c. 1290: civil contract law must be observed; c. 1291: permission of the competent authority.

[3] CIC, cc. 1292–1294.

[4] CIC, c. 1296: if the alienation is valid in civil law, the competent authority must decide whether to vindicate the rights of the church; c. 1377: a person who alienates without the required consents incurs a just penalty.

[5] CIC, c. 1285.   [6] CIC, c. 1190: 'It is absolutely forbidden to sell sacred relics.'

[7] CIC, cc. 1273–1289: administration of goods; c. 1276: the ordinary; c. 1284: duties of administrators.

[8] CCEO, c. 1010: the right to acquire goods; cc. 909–930: juridical persons; c. 1020: temporal goods must be registered in the name of the juridical person to whom they belong; cc. 1022–1033: administration; c. 1022: the eparchial bishop has oversight of the administration of temporal goods; c. 1026: inventory of ecclesiastical goods; cc. 1034–1042: contracts and alienations and respect for civil law.

[9] ROC: Statute, XV.4–7; see e.g. Dioc. of Sourozh: Statutes I.4: 'The Diocese ... may own, use free of charge or otherwise exercise its proprietary rights over its property'; SOCA: Const., Art. 155: the right to own churches, monasteries, cemeteries and schools; ROMOC: Statutes, Art. 169: all goods of e.g. parishes, monasteries, dioceses, archdioceses and the patriarchy constitute the patrimony of the church; UOCIA: Statutes, Art. VI.1: the Major Archbishop may 'purchase property and/or buildings for ecclesiastical use'; Art. VII.4: bishops.

within it, such as a parish.[10] However, a central assembly (e.g. a Holy Synod) may issue norms about the acquisition, administration and disposal of church property,[11] and the diocesan bishop and assembly may be charged with resolution of disputes about diocesan property,[12] or else a bishop may have oversight of these matters.[13] At the local level, the parish should acquire legal personality under civil law to hold property for the benefit of the parishioners,[14] and it acts 'as trustee of God's, not man's, property'.[15] In turn, the parish decides on the acquisition, administration and disposal of church property (real and personal) and must ensure that all objects necessary for worship are available.[16] Typically: 'The parish priest is the administrator of the entire real estate and movable goods together with the Parochial Council, under the control of the Eparchial Centre'; the priest must *inter alia* maintain 'the precious goods and documents of the parish'.[17] The parish priest administers the patrimony of the parish in accordance with the decisions of the parish assembly and must maintain an inventory of parish goods.[18] Certain sacred items may be inalienable.[19] In some Orthodox churches, the parish inventory of property (movable and immovable) is reviewed annually by the parish stewards and/or other officers.[20] In the event of indiscipline or defection by a

---

[10] OOCL 179; this cites cc. 24 and 25, Synod of Antioch; cc. 26 and 33, Synod of Cartagena: the bishop cannot use the property of one parish for the purposes of another; see also MOCL 106–107.

[11] ROC: Statute, Art. XV.7: Holy Synod; UOCIA: Statutes, Art. V.4: the Prime Bishop's Council 'decides on the purchase, sale, or mortgaging of property of the Church'; Art. VIII.3: the Diocesan Assembly may authorise the Diocesan Council 'to acquire, encumber, or otherwise dispose of diocesan properties'; ROMOC: Statutes, Art. 30: the Church National Council decides on property disposal; Art. 37: Patriarchal Patrimony Department.

[12] ROC: Statute, X.18(z); bishop; X.44(l): assembly; ROMOC: Statutes, 98: the Eparchial Council decides on sales in accord with decrees of the Eparchial Assembly to which it must report annually on eparchial property.

[13] GOAA: Regs., Art. 10: the metropolitan approves the purchase, sale and lease of parish property; ROC: Dioc. of Sourozh: Statutes V.21: the bishop is 'to manage and control the property and funds of the Diocese'; IX.43: 'No real property of the Diocese and of the Diocesan Canonical Units shall be acquired or disposed of without the preliminary written permission of the Patriarch of Moscow.'

[14] GOAA: Regs., Art. 21.1; Art. 9.2: each metropolis likewise; ROC: Statute, XI.2.

[15] UOCIA: Statutes, Art. XI.9: 'all decisions concerning parish property must be inspired by that care'.

[16] ROMOC: Statutes, Art. 55: the Parochial Council submits proposals to the Eparchial Council for the purchase, sale and lease of parish real estate; GOAA: Regs., Art. 16: a parish may acquire, sell, mortgage or otherwise encumber its real property on approval by two-thirds vote at its Parish Assembly; MOSC: Const., 2.23: parish property; 4.91: trustees; ROC: Statute XI.43(l): disposals; (m): objects for worship; XI.46: parish council.

[17] ROMOC: Statutes, Art. 64.1: the priest is responsible 'to the civil courts for … maladministration'.

[18] ROMOC: Statutes, Art. 50(j).

[19] ROMOC: Statutes, Art. 170: 'The sacred goods, namely those which after consecration are designed directly and exclusively to rites, are inalienable' (e.g. places of worship, objects and vestments, ritual books, and cemeteries); the Metropolitan Synod determines if something is a sacred good; 'common goods' are designed to maintain the church and its servants, cultural, social and philanthropic activities (e.g. school buildings).

[20] MOSC: Const., 2.37: 'For every Parish there shall be a register of the movable and immovable properties of the parish Church'; it is updated every year, signed by the vicar and Kaikaran (steward), kept in the custody of the latter, and signed by the diocesan metropolitan on his parish visit; 4.76: the Association property register.

parish, provision is made normally for all parish property to vest in the superior authorities and entities of the church.[21]

This approach resonates with Anglicanism. Churches should satisfy those requirements of civil law which apply to the acquisition, ownership, administration and alienation of church property, both real and personal; property is held by those authorities within a church which enjoy legal personality as trustees or other entities of a fiduciary nature under civil law and competence under church law.[22] Ecclesiastical authorities are the stewards of church property which they hold and administer to advance the mission of a church, and for the benefit and use of its members, from generation to generation, in accordance with church law.[23] As property is held in trust for a church, it should not be alienated or encumbered without such consents as may be prescribed by church law; ecclesiastical trustees may sell, purchase and exchange property in the manner and to the extent authorised by that law.[24] A central assembly of a church, or other designated body, may frame laws for the management and the use of property held in trust for that church.[25] The management and day-to-day administration of church property at local level are vested in parish assemblies or other legal entities subject to such rights of the clergy as may be provided by law.[26] National, regional, provincial, diocesan, parish or other trustees perform their functions under the order and control of the appropriate assembly to which church law renders them accountable.[27]

The principles which emerge from Catholic, Orthodox and Anglican laws blend well with those operative in Protestantism. A fundamental principle of Lutheran property law is that: 'The Church shall have power to acquire, accept, hold, dispose of, lease, let, mortgage or otherwise deal with real and personal property and any estate or interest in real or personal property ... for the effective promotion of any

---

[21] GOAA: Regs., Art. 16.6: if a parish engages in e.g. schism, its property vests in the Archdiocese; UOCIA: Statutes, Art. XI.9: if a parish is abolished, its property is disposed of in accord with the parish bylaws; ROC: Dioc. of Sourozh: Statutes, IX.45: if dissolved, the disposal of diocesan property is decided by the Holy Synod.

[22] PCLCCAC, Principle 80.1–2. See e.g. Wales: Const., II.20, III.2–5, 13–31, 26: the Representative Body is incorporated by Royal Charter and holds property as trustees at provincial level.

[23] PCLCCAC, Principle 80.3–4. See e.g. Indian Ocean: Const., Art. 18: the Provincial Synod may acquire property the administration of which is delegated to the diocese where the property is situated.

[24] PCLCCAC, Principle 80.5–6. See e.g. Ireland: Const., XI.11: the Representative Body holds property subject to the control of General Synod; it may lease or sell property in a diocese with the consent of the Diocesan Council; X.11: all movable property for use in services vests in it 'subject to any trusts affecting the same'.

[25] PCLCCAC, Principle 80.7. See e.g. Southern Africa: Const., Arts. XVI–XX: if practicable, property is transferred to the Provincial Trustees acting on behalf of the Provincial Synod and as the latter directs.

[26] PCLCCAC, Principle 80.9. See e.g. England: M. Hill, *Ecclesiastical Law* (3rd edn., Oxford University Press, 2007) 3.76: archbishops, bishops, archdeacons and incumbents are corporations sole, and a parochial church council is a corporation aggregate; nationally, the Church Commissioners acquire and hold a wide range of properties.

[27] PCLCCAC, Principle 80.10. See e.g. New Zealand: Cans. F.I–VIII: the Diocesan Trusts Board (appointed by the Diocesan Synod) holds diocesan property; 'the specific application [of property] shall be determined by the Diocesan Synod, subject to the control of the General Synod'; the Board is to 'carry out the objects of each trust in such manner ... as the Diocesan Synod shall ... direct'; see also the Anglican Church Trusts Act 1981.

or all of its activities.'[28] Therefore: a church or bodies within it may be incorporated as a juridical person under civil law;[29] a church may appoint trustees to hold property,[30] as well as standing committees to provide advice on property matters;[31] and in disputes about the ownership or control of property, action in the civil courts must be avoided.[32] Property rights may vest in a national church institution,[33] its legal representatives (which are subject to the control of that institution),[34] as well as in a regional body,[35] or a local body such as a parish.[36] As to the latter, for instance, in the Evangelical Lutheran Church in America, 'title to property shall reside in the congregation' which 'may dispose of its property as it determines, subject to any ... self-accepted restrictions'; if a congregation is no longer recognized by the church as a result of discipline, title to its property nevertheless continues to reside in the congregation.[37] The Congregation Council is responsible for the 'property matters of [the] congregation' and acts as the board of trustees in 'maintaining and protecting its property'; but it has 'no authority to buy, sell, or encumber real property unless specifically authorized to do so by a [congregation] meeting'.[38] The church also provides for the distribution of property on its dissolution.[39]

[28] LCA: Const., Art. IV.5. See also ELCA: Articles of Incorporation, Art. II: the church has 'powers to acquire and receive funds and property of every kind and nature ... whether by purchase, conveyance, lease, gift, grant, bequest, legacy' etc; LCMS: Const., Art. IV: 'The Synod shall have legal powers ... [t]o purchase, hold, administer, and sell property of every description in the interest of the Synod.'

[29] LCA: Const., Statement to Preamble and Art. I: the church is '[a]n association incorporated under the Associations Incorporation Acts 1956-65'; ELCIC: Const., Art. I: Evangelical Lutheran Church in Canada Act.

[30] LCGB: RAR, The Annual General Meeting, 1.

[31] LCA: BL, VIII.G-H: standing committees on church properties.

[32] LCA: BL, IV.2: 'where it cannot reach an amicable settlement [as to] ownership or control of any of its property, it shall in keeping with 1 Cor. 6 make every effort to avoid action in the civil courts by first seriously seeking to settle any differences through mediation and adjudication of the judicial system of the Church'.

[33] ELCA: Const., Ch. 15.14.A10: the treasurer, within policies established by the Churchwide Assembly and Church Council, may 'purchase or otherwise acquire title to real property ... mortgage, lease, sell, or otherwise dispose of the same; and ... act on behalf of the churchwide organization regarding real property'.

[34] LCMS: Const., Art. XI.E: its Board of Directors is 'custodian of all the property of the Synod'; BL, 1.4: trust entities; 1.5: any issue as to the laws of the State of Missouri is resolved under the Synod Constitution and Bylaws; financial records must be disclosed to a congregation in accord with 'church's laws and state law'.

[35] LCA: Const., App., Const. of Districts, Art. VI. LCMS: Const., Art. XII.11: Board of Directors.

[36] LCA: Const., Art. VI.7. See also NALC: CDC, Ch. 7; LCMS: Guidelines for Constitutions and Bylaws of Lutheran Congregations, IV: Board of Directors; ELCIRE: Const., Art. 20: 3-5 Parish Trustees.

[37] ELCA: Const., Ch. 9.70-71; Ch. 9.24: 'A recognized and received congregation that is part of this church shall, when legally possible, be incorporated and may ... own property and be responsible for its care.'

[38] ELCA: Model Const. for Congregations, Ch. 12.05.

[39] ELCA: Articles of Incorporation, Art. XIII: under the Internal Revenue Code of 1954, s. 501(c)(3); see also ELCIRE: Const., Art. 22: a decision to dissolve the church is taken by the central assembly (under Art. 18.4) and assets may be used for the Evangelical Church in Germany (EKD); ELCIC: Const., Art. VI.5-11.

The position in Methodist law is broadly the same. First, a church itself may have no legal capacity and 'does not and cannot hold property', but 'Conferences, councils, boards, agencies, local churches, and other units bearing the name "United Methodist" are, for the most part, legal entities capable of suing and being sued and possessed of legal capacities' (e.g. as boards of trustees).[40] Secondly, such bodies are entrusted with property and their activities are governed by the principle of stewardship.[41] For example, for the Methodist Church in New Zealand: 'Property is a means of expressing and assisting the Church to be the Body of Christ in the world through worship, nurture, teaching, witness and service. The acquisition and administration of property by the Church is therefore not an end in itself, but is to be used for the manifestation of Christian love and liberality and to support the Church's mission.' As a consequence: 'The Church administers property on trust from God and is called to the stewardship of its property resources. This involves privilege, responsibility and accountability and should demonstrate the Christian way of using material resources to serve God's purpose for people'; moreover: 'All property of the Church is held for the ultimate benefit of the Church and is under the final authority of the Conference.'[42] Indeed, the Conference or its Property Board may authorise the purchases, sales and leases of church property – the Board receives applications from districts and circuits, for example, and these and the Board must agree on the allocation of proceeds of any sale.[43] Thirdly, the authority of a Conference may apply to property held at national, district, circuit and local levels,[44] and title 'shall be held and administered in accordance with the Book of Discipline'.[45] Fourthly, a local church may have authority over property. For example, in the United Methodist Church a local charge conference may instruct its board of trustees to purchase, sell, mortgage, construct, maintain and repair property. Also, subject to

---

[40] UMCNEAE: BOD, par. 140; par. 2512: an annual conference may be incorporated under 'local law' with a board of trustees reporting to annual conference; par. 2517: incorporation of the district board of trustees.

[41] UMCNEAE: BOD, par. 103, Confession of Faith, Art. XV: 'God is the owner of all things and that the individual holding of property is lawful and is a sacred trust under God ... All forms of property ... are to be held in solemn trust and used responsibly for human good under the sovereignty of God.'

[42] MCNZ: LAR, Introduction, 1 and 9: title vests in the Board of Administration and other incorporated boards or under the model deed; Conference consent through the Board is required for purchases, sales, leases and mortgages; prior to Conference consenting to any parish property proposal, the synod or regional court must be satisfied it is e.g. financially viable; proceeds of sales are lodged with the Church Building and Loan Fund in the name of the parish; 3.12.1–5 and 9.4.1–5: parish property; MCGB: CPD, DU 21: Conference manages all connexional property; SO 901–903; SO 940: 'The Church Council shall transact all business required of it as managing trustees of the local property.'

[43] MCI: RDG, 29.

[44] MCGB: CPD, MT 2-11: property is either local, circuit, district, connexional, conference or general; 13: trustees are authorised to apply property for e.g. charitable purposes, religious worship or services in accordance with Methodist practice, as a day school, manse etc.; UMCNEAE: BOD, par. 2523: district property.

[45] UMCUSA: Const., Div. 1, Art. VII; see also UMCNEAE: BOD, pars. 7 and 2501: 'All properties of United Methodist local churches ... are held, in trust, for the benefit of the entire denomination, and ownership and usage of church property is subject to the Discipline'; MCI: Const., s. 7: trusts of church property.

the direction of the charge conference, the board has 'the supervision, oversight, and care of all real property owned by the local church and of all property and equipment acquired directly by the local church' or an organization connected with it; the board must not prevent or interfere with the pastor in the use of any of this property for religious services or other meetings recognised by 'the laws, usages, and customs of the United Methodist Church'.[46] Provision may be made for 'an annual visual inspection' of local property.[47] Consents may be prescribed for disposal of property.[48] Fifthly, there is also provision for dissolution of a church and its units.[49]

Various approaches to these matters are used in Presbyterianism. By way of illustration, the property belonging to congregations of the Presbyterian Church of Scotland is held for them at national level by the General Trustees or by local trustees (the office-holders of the local church such as the minister); the General Trustees must approve the sale of most forms of church property and determine the use of the proceeds of sale.[50] Many churches replicate this pattern of both general trustees and congregational trustees appointed 'to receive and hold the property of the congregation on trust for the congregation and subject to its directions' and those of the Congregational Committee.[51] For instance, in New Zealand 'the church courts are responsible for the day-to-day management of property held in trust by the trustees' who must act 'in accordance with the relevant trusts and rules of the Church' and exercise 'due care and prudence in making and carrying out decisions'.[52] More particularly, at local level, the Church Council is responsible for

---

[46] UMCNEAE: BOD, par. 244; see also par. 258 and for its duties pars. 2524–2550; par. 401: the bishop is to ensure that 'temporal' matters are administered in such a way as to serve the mission of the church.

[47] MCI: RDG, 2.15.

[48] UMCNEAE: BOD, par. 2514–2515: e.g. sale of an episcopal residence must be approved by conference.

[49] MCNZ: LAR, s. 9.1 (and 1.6–1.7): if a parish, synod, or other entity should dissolve, and property remains after this and settlement of all debts and liabilities, that property is transferred to Conference for the charitable purposes of the church; *mutatis mutandis*, if the Church or Conference should dissolve or be wound up, its property is given or transferred to another organisation that is charitable under New Zealand law.

[50] CLCS: 141; Church of Scotland (Property and Endowments) Act 1925; Acts XXVI, 1933 and VII, 1995 (as amended by Act XIII, 1996): these regulate the sale of buildings. See also PCW: HOR, 5: custodian and managing trustees, sales and leases, and application of proceeds; PCA: BCO, 25.6: 'A particular church which is not incorporated ... may select from among its membership trustees ... to buy, sell, or mortgage property for the church'; they must comply with instructions of the congregation electing them; 25.7: if it is incorporated, its officers or trustees are elected by the congregational meeting to buy, sell, and mortgage property.

[51] PCI: Code, 53–57: compliance with trust terms and the Code; 47(2): the Congregational Committee administers congregational property; 76: Presbytery must 'examine and sanction transactions affecting the congregational ownership of or financial interest in any lands or buildings', and may intervene in the 'appointment or renewal of trustees'; 241–245: congregational property; 122: the Trustees of the PCI are 'a body incorporated under Royal Charter in 1871' with functions under the Irish Presbyterian Church Acts 1871 and 1901 'for management of certain trust properties'; General Assembly appoints these general trustees.

[52] PCANZ: BO, 16.2: properties are vested in either the Presbyterian Church Property Trustees or the Otago Foundation Trust Board under the Presbyterian Church Property Act 1885 and Otago Foundation Trust Board Act 1992; 16.1: 'To enable the Church to fulfil its ... mission, it requires both financial and spiritual resources.'

'the management and administration of all property of the congregation ... associated with the life, worship, and mission of the congregation' including purchases, sales and leases for which the required approvals from the relevant trustees must be obtained – the council must also review annually the state of repair of property and adequacy of insurance cover.[53] In turn, the functions of the Presbytery include approval of the purchase, sale, exchange or lease of Presbytery property;[54] the General Assembly Commission must approve all dealings in property of which the Assembly or a Presbytery is the beneficial owner, including any variations of trusts and the disposal of property.[55] All funds received from the sale of property from either a congregation or Presbytery must vest with the trustees who must place the net proceeds of sale in a property account in the name of the congregation or Presbytery concerned.[56] There is also provision for the distribution of property in the event a church or its units are dissolved or wound up.[57]

The United, Uniting and Congregational Churches similarly provide for incorporation of ecclesial bodies under civil law,[58] recognise the right of the church to legislate on property matters,[59] advise model trust deeds,[60] and require

---

[53] PCANZ: BO, 16.2: e.g. it must obtain the consent of the congregation for 'any proposal concerning property that would have a significant effect on [its] use'; also: 'The church council must ensure, and regularly monitor that it complies with, all requirements of legislation ... which affect the use and maintenance of real property.' See also PCA: BCO, 12.5: the Session approves 'actions of special importance affecting church property'.

[54] PCANZ: BO, 16.4: Presbytery must not approve works in excess of the Assembly Council sum unless those who drew up the plans for this are competent and recognised by the appropriate industry; it must also obtain and be satisfied with the report of the Church Architecture Reference Group on any proposal as to the erection, alteration, addition, or purchase of buildings; 16.5: it may delegate functions to its Property Committee. See also PCW: HOR, 3.2.2: Presbytery supervises 'buildings and all financial requirements concerning them'; UFCS: MPP, II.I.III: 'The Deacons' Court has the management and charge of the whole property [of] the congregation or held for [its] use by trustees appointed in terms of deeds which ... General Assembly has sanctioned.'

[55] PCANZ: BO, 16.6.   [56] PCANZ: BO, 16.7.

[57] PCANZ: BO, 16.14: this is in much the same terms as that applicable to MCNZ (see above). See also PCA: BCO, 25.12: 'If a church is dissolved by the Presbytery at the request of the congregation and no disposition has been made of its property ... within six months ... those who held the title ... at ... dissolution shall ... transfer to the Presbytery ... all the property of the church' and Presbytery applies the proceeds at its discretion.

[58] UCCSA: Const., 2.2: the church is incorporated in civil law and has 'to own and hold property (immovable, movable and incorporeal) in its own name and independently of its members'; 3.5.9: the local church may acquire, hold, mortgage and dispose of property; UCA: Regs., 3.5.34: incorporation of church bodies; 3.5.52: the Synod appoints members of the corporate trust under the Uniting Church in Australia Act 1977.

[59] UCC: Man., BL, 505: the General Council is 'to legislate on all matters respecting property, subject to the limitations' in the BU and approval of the Conference in which it is situated; UCA: Const., par. 50: 'The beneficial ownership of all property ... shall be vested in the Church'; 51: the Synod is a corporation and its property vests in a Synod Property Trust; 52–53: property is managed under rules made by the Assembly.

[60] UCC: Man., BU 5: 'all property ... held in trust for or to the use of a church, charge, circuit, or congregation ... shall be held by trustees appointed by or on behalf of such church, charge, circuit, or congregation, upon trusts ... declared in a Model Trust Deed' and shall not be sold, exchanged or encumbered unless Presbytery at the instance of the church, charge, circuit or congregation, consents, subject to appeal to the Conference; 205: the Church Board (Court of

property to be held for the objects of the church.[61] They also assign property functions amongst bodies at the various levels of the church – national,[62] regional[63] and local.[64] For example, in the United Church of Christ in the Philippines, the local church is free 'to acquire, own, manage and dispose of property and funds' in accordance with the principle of stewardship and 'the statutes of the UCCP and the applicable [civil] laws'; the Board of Trustees oversees 'the acquisition, management, repair, maintenance and disposition of church properties'.[65] Similarly, Baptist Unions and Conventions assert the right to own and administer property through trustees – their function is to receive, purchase, administer and dispose of property.[66] Local Baptist churches also have trustees. As is the case in the Baptist Union of Great Britain, this may be in the form, for example, of a Baptist Trust Corporation which must permit the church 'to use and manage the Church property in accordance with the Church Constitution and these Trusts'; such property may be used for a place of public worship, the promotion of the Christian faith, the practice of the rite of baptism, the instruction of children and adults in the Christian faith, and the mission of the church.[67] The holding trustees may permit the local church to erect buildings on church property or 'alter, improve, carry out

the Pastoral Charge) directs the congregation's Board of Trustees; 250: this Board must carry out the lawful directions of the Church Board, Church Council, Presbytery or Conference; 270: if a congregation ceases to exist, the Conference determines the application of its property.

[61] UCCP: Const., Art. II.9: the church 'shall observe responsible Christian stewardship by utilizing the properties under its care towards self-reliance and support of its various ministries'.

[62] UCA: Regs., 4.10: Assembly property; 4.12.5: the Synod must keep a register of properties.

[63] UCA: Regs., 4.2: each Synod Property Board advises Synod as to 'policies relating to property', supervises their implementation, and advises Presbyteries and Church Councils; 4.3: the Presbytery Property Committee advises Church Councils on property matters for which the latter are responsible, submits Council proposals to the Synod Property Board, and inspects properties for which a Presbytery or Church Council is responsible.

[64] UCA: Regs., 4.4: the Church Council is responsible for the management, administration, care and maintenance of property acquired or held for the use of the Congregation (i.e. 'congregational property'); 4.6: purchase, sale, lease etc; 4.8.1: proceeds of sale may go towards e.g. the mission of the church; UCOC: Const., Art. V.18: the local church is free 'to acquire, own, manage and dispose of property and funds'.

[65] UCCP: Const., Art. V.4, 8, 14. See also URC: Man., D Pt. I.2: the trustees of a local place of worship may sell or mortgage it and apply the money as the Church Meeting directs.

[66] BUSA: Const., 11: 'All immovable property of the Union shall be registered in the name of the Trustees of the Union'; 6.9: the Union may receive, purchase, hold, sell, donate, lease and exchange movable and immovable property; Model Const., 19.1: 'The Church shall have power to buy, sell, let' etc; 20.4: disposals must be approved by a Special General Meeting; CNBC: Const., 2(b): the Convention is 'to receive bequests, trusts, funds and property and to hold, invest, administer and distribute funds and property for the purposes of the Society'; 62: Society property 'shall be managed by the board' of directors; 119: 'The trustees of institutions and agencies shall report to and be accountable to the Convention through the National Leadership Board'; JBU: Const., Art. VII.6: the Union acts through e.g. 'A Statutory Corporation established by Act 16 of 1969'.

[67] BUGB: MTC 2003: 'The Baptist Union Corporation Limited is the Holding Trustee for many churches' under the Baptist and Congregational Trusts Act 1951 (UK); 2.7: '"Church property" means the land and buildings to which these Trusts relate . . . under the day to day management of the [local] church'; 4: management; 5: use of premises; BUSA: Model Const., 3.3.1: 'The Church shall exist as a legal entity in its own right'; 20.2: BUSA trustees act as trustees of local churches; see e.g. Central Baptist Church (Pretoria): Const., Art. 21.

repairs to, enlarge, add to or pull down and rebuild the buildings ... forming part of the Church property in such manner as the Church shall decide and the Holding Trustees shall approve'.[68] With the consent of the Church Meeting, the trustees may sell, lease, exchange or mortgage church property; the proceeds from a disposal may be applied as the church requests and as the trustees approve, for example towards the costs of work, the purchase of land and the cost of repairs.[69] On the dissolution of a local church sometimes provision is made for its property to be vested in the Union.[70]

Sacred buildings and objects

The principal forms of real and personal property used at the most local level of the church include places of worship and their contents, associated buildings (such as church halls), churchyards and burial grounds, residences for ordained ministers, and registers and records. The churches of almost all the Christian traditions studied here have detailed rules on these items of church property in terms of their definition, administration, care and maintenance.

Under Roman Catholic canon law, sacred places are those assigned to divine worship or burial by a dedication or blessing administered by the diocesan bishop (or deputy) which is then recorded.[71] Only those things are permitted in sacred places which serve worship, piety and religion: 'Anything out of harmony with the holiness of the place is forbidden'. Sacred places 'are desecrated by acts done which are gravely injurious and give scandal to the faithful when, in the judgment of the local Ordinary, these acts are so serious and so contrary to the sacred character of the place that worship may not be held there until the harm is repaired by means of the penitential rite prescribed in the liturgical books'.[72] No new church may be built without the consent of the diocesan bishop who must be satisfied that this is for the good of souls and that the means to build it are available; before consenting, he must consult the Presbyteral Council and neighbouring rectors. The principles and norms of liturgy and sacred art must be observed in the erection (and restoration) of a church, and as soon as possible afterwards it is dedicated or blessed.[73] Each church

---

[68] BUGB: MTC 2003, 7. See also JBU: Const., Art. IV.6: the Union may build or assist in building 'Churches, manses, schools or any other project that the Union may approve'.

[69] BUGB: MTC 2003, 8-9. Also, Riverside Baptist Church (Baltimore): BL Art. II.B: 'Three trustees elected by the church will hold in trust the church property'; they have 'no power to buy, sell, mortgage, lease, or transfer any property, without a specific vote of the church'; Central Baptist Church (Pretoria): Const., 22: immovable property must be registered in trustees; 23: an alienation must be approved by a Special General Meeting; 24: the application of proceeds of sale is determined by the church; 25: on dissolution the property vests in BUSA.

[70] BUSA: Model Const., 23.4.

[71] CIC, cc. 1205-1209: the dedication/blessing used is that prescribed in liturgical books; blessing a church is reserved to the bishop or delegate; the dedication or blessing is witnessed and recorded.

[72] CIC, c. 1210: the ordinary may permit for individual cases other uses not 'contrary to the sacred character of the place'; c. 1211: desecration; c. 1212: a sacred place loses its dedication/blessing if destroyed or permanently made over to secular uses (by decree/fact); c. 1213: the church freely exercises its powers in sacred places.

[73] CIC, c. 1215: consent; c. 1216: architecture – experts are to be used; c. 1217: dedication or blessing; cathedrals and parish churches must be dedicated by a solemn rite; c. 1218: a church has its own title.

must be maintained in a way which 'befits the house of God' (and the vicar forane oversees this), and entry for sacred functions must be free of charge.[74] When a church cannot be used for worship and there is no possibility of restoration, the diocesan bishop may allow it to be used for some secular but not unbecoming purpose.[75] There are also provisions on oratories and private chapels, shrines, altars and cemeteries,[76] as well as the maintenance of parish records of baptisms, confirmations and marriages, for example.[77] The Oriental Catholic Churches are subject to similar rules.[78]

In the Orthodox tradition, sacred goods include objects consecrated (e.g. a church building, altar and utensils) and those blessed by a simple blessing (e.g. liturgical books and vestments).[79] For instance, in the Russian Orthodox Church the Holy Synod is responsible for 'the proper state' of church architecture, iconography, monuments and antiquities, and for the production of utilities, candles, vestments and 'other items necessary to maintain the liturgical traditions, beauty and good order in churches'.[80] The diocesan bishop consecrates churches and oversees iconography, and with the diocesan assembly oversees the construction, maintenance and restoration of churches.[81] At annual inspection, the dean ensures that each church in the deanery is in decent order, and that it has all the objects necessary for worship.[82] On a day-to-day basis, the parish meeting and council must ensure the safety, decency and beauty of church property,[83] but the priest

---

[74] CIC, cc. 1219–1221: worship, preservation, entry; c. 553: vicars forane must ensure that 'the good appearance and condition of the churches and of sacred furnishings are carefully maintained'.

[75] CIC, c. 1222: if for other grave reason it should not be used for divine worship, the bishop may act similarly but must consult the council of priests and obtain the consent of those with rights over the church.

[76] CIC, cc. 1223–1234; cc. 1235–1239: the altar or table for the Eucharistic sacrifice should be fixed and dedicated in accord with 'ancient tradition'; cc. 1240–1243: where possible the church (and parish) is to have its own cemeteries or at least an area in a public cemetery which is blessed and reserved for the deceased faithful.

[77] CIC, c. 535: the parish must also keep such others registers as prescribed by the Episcopal Conference.

[78] CCEO, cc. 1022–1033.

[79] MOCL: 108–109: 'All sacred objects (those consecrated or blessed) are excluded from the sphere of exchange, whereas objects labelled holy can be sold or bought.'

[80] ROC: Statute, V.28.(k)-(m). See also UOCIA: Statutes, Art. II.5: Holy Synod supervises the 'ecclesiastical arts: architecture, iconography, choral music, and other applied arts'; ROMOC: Statutes, Art. 14(x).

[81] ROC: Statute, X.18(z). See also GOAA: Charter, Art. 7.3: Metropolitans 'consecrate and sanctify churches'; OCIA: GC, Divine Services, 8; UOCIA: Statutes, Art. IV.2: Archbishops 'provide the diocesan bishops with Holy Relics necessary for the consecration [VII.4] of Church altars and Holy Antimensia [portable altars]'.

[82] ROC: Statute, X.52–53.

[83] ROC: Statute, XI.43 and 46. See also GOAA: Regs., Art. 16.4: the parish must maintain 'the architectural, iconographic and artistic integrity of all Church edifices in accordance with Orthodox tradition'; all plans to erect or alter a church, and for icons, must be approved by the local hierarch whose approval is 'limited solely to aesthetic and dogmatic issues' not 'architectural or mechanical plans ... or ... other structural matter'; ROMOC: Statutes Art. 55: the Parochial Assembly decides on 'building, repairing, restoring and maintaining the church'; Art. 61: the Parochial Council approves proposals as to 'vestments, icons, religious objects and books'.

is responsible for the maintenance of vestments, sacred vessels, and registers.[84] Some Orthodox churches have very detailed rules about the maintenance of specific objects, particularly the Holy Table for the Divine Liturgy and the Holy Chrism; about who may enter what parts of a church;[85] and about the residences of clergy and other property associated with the parish church.[86]

Many of these Catholic and Orthodox themes are shared by Anglicans. Buildings may be designated as places of public worship which, with places for Christian burial, may be set aside for the purposes of God by consecration or dedication customarily performed by a bishop.[87] Consecrated or dedicated property may not be used for purposes inconsistent with the uses of God for which it is set aside; wardens or other stewards must not allow churches to be profaned by any temporal use inconsistent with the sanctity of the place and sound doctrine.[88] The day-to-day control, direction and administration of places of worship vests in the parish council or other local assembly which, subject to national, provincial or diocesan bodies, must ensure that proper care is taken of them, and their contents, and endeavour to keep them decent, clean and in good repair.[89] Episcopal or other lawful consent, whether executive or judicial, must be obtained for any alteration or addition to or removal of property from places of worship to such extent and in such manner, and subject to such appeals, as may be prescribed by law.[90] An inventory should be kept of the contents of places of worship, and a competent ecclesiastical authority should inspect places of worship and their contents at such regular intervals as may be prescribed by law.[91] There are also norms on the

---

[84] ROC: Statute, XI.20(l). See also ROMOC: Statutes, Art. 65; SOCA: Const., 54 and GOAA: Regs., Art. 17.3: records; OCIA: GC, Divine Services, 8; MOSC: Const., 2.44.

[85] OCIA: GC, Divine Services, 13–16: e.g. 'The Holy Table and Table of Oblation are to be covered with clean cloths'; the priest must ensure that 'the sanctuary ... and ... its appointments are clean and well maintained at all times'; 'No one is permitted to enter the sanctuary unnecessarily' except with 'the blessing of the priest'.

[86] ROMOC: Statutes, Art. 178: e.g. the parish office and house; 179, 186–188: a parish cemetery is managed by the Parochial Council (under the Eparchial Centre) and supervised by the parish priest.

[87] PCLCCAC, Principle 81.1–3. See e.g. Ireland: Const., IX.36: 'As often as churches are newly built or rebuilt, or churchyards are appointed for burial, they shall be dedicated and consecrated' by the bishop.

[88] PCLCCAC, Principle 81.5–6. See e.g. Ireland: Const. IX.27: if used for e.g. a performance, 'the minister shall take care that the words, music, pictures and performance are such as befit the house of God, are consonant with sound doctrine, and contribute to the edifying of the people'; the minister must obey the ordinary in this regard.

[89] PCLCCAC, Principle 81.7. See e.g. Southern Africa: Can. 28.4: the parish council has 'direction and control of the properties ... of the Parish' subject to that of e.g. Provincial Trustees; Scotland; Can. 35.3: the vestry and rector 'shall cause all proper and reasonable care' to be taken of places of worship within its charge and of the furniture and ornaments and they must endeavour to keep them 'decent, clean and in good repair'.

[90] PCLCCAC, Principle 81.8. See e.g. Wales: Rules of the Diocesan Courts: the Diocesan Chancellor deals with such matters under the faculty jurisdiction; West Indies: Can. 27: 'No Church ... shall be erected, demolished, removed or substantially altered, externally or internally, without the written approval ... of the Bishop.'

[91] PCLCCAC, Principle 81; 80.11: 'No-one shall deny or obstruct access to any ecclesiastical person or body lawfully entitled to enter or use church property.' See e.g. England: Can. F17: inventory; F18: the archdeacon must survey at least once in 3 years the churches and

maintenance of and access to records.[92] Moreover, provision is to be made for clergy in full-time ministry to have appropriate accommodation which should be inspected periodically and whose occupation may be terminated or otherwise restricted only in accordance with law.[93]

Consecration or dedication of property is also practised in many Protestant churches – and the status of such property has prescribed consequences for its administration. For Lutheranism, typically: 'The consecration of particular places for divine worship symbolises and looks forward to the final sanctification of all creation for divine worship.'[94] Thus, a congregation should set aside 'a building exclusively for worship to express reverence for God and to acknowledge the priority of worship' or, if resources are limited, a 'separate worship space' with 'the visible pointers to the means of grace, such as the altar, font, and lectern and pulpit'.[95] The sanctuary of a church is 'dedicated for word and sacrament ministry'.[96] Some norms spell out the theological significance of required items; for instance, in the Evangelical Lutheran Church in Southern Africa: 'In the place of worship the baptismal font, pulpit and altar indicate the threefold gift of the Lord – the Baptism, Word and the Lord's Supper. The cross – as a sign of justice and mercy – unites the believers with God and their fellowmen'; altar flowers point to God as Creator; the opened Bible indicates that the Word of God became flesh; candles 'symbolize Christ who is the Light of the world and who sends His disciples as light into the world through the power of the Holy Spirit'; church bells 'announce the invitation to all people'; and pictures, symbols and altar cloths visibly underline the proclamation of the Gospel.[97] Moreover, it is often the responsibility of the pastor to ensure that 'the facilities and buildings owned or used by the congregation are properly maintained and are suitable for Christian worship'.[98] Typically, when a congregation is considering the development of an additional site to be used regularly for worship, it must confer with the bishop and perhaps with national

---

churchyards and 'give direction for the amendment of all defects in the fabric, ornaments and furniture'; see also the Inspection of Churches Measure 1955.

[92] PCLCCAC, Principle 83. See e.g. Philippines: Cans. III.16.3: the minister must record all baptisms, confirmations, marriages, burials and names of communicants; Scotland: Can. 42, Res. 1: the dean must inspect registers of each parish once every 4 years and report to the bishop; Southern Africa: Can. 32: the incumbent and churchwardens must keep an inventory of all movable property; New Zealand: Can. B.V.6 and B.X.1–7: the Archives Committee of the General Synod administers 'all non-current records of permanent value'.

[93] PCLCCAC, Principle 82; e.g. Ireland: Const., IV.51.5: a vicar is 'entitled to ... enjoyment of a free residence'.

[94] LCA: A Lutheran Approach to the Theology of Worship, prepared in 1990 and reviewed by the CTIR and College of Presidents, adopted by the Commission on Worship 1998, and edited 2001, Pt. 4: Rev. 21.2–22.5.

[95] LCA: The Use of Multi-Purpose Worship Centres, prepared by the Department of Visual Arts, adopted by the Commission on Worship 1988, revised 1998, edited October 2001: 'for a congregation with limited resources, a multi-purpose worship centre can be the means of providing the best range of facilities'.

[96] LCA: Statement on the Use of Lutheran Churches by other Church Groups, prepared by the CTIR, approved by the General Pastors Conference 1975, adopted by General Synod 1975, and edited 2001.

[97] ELCSA: G., 2.5.   [98] LCGB: RAR, Responsibilities and Duties of Pastors, 1–24.

institutions before taking action to build a new church.⁹⁹ Rules may also regulate the administration of parish cemeteries and church archives.¹⁰⁰

Each Methodist church has a large body of law on the use and administration of places of worship and associated properties. The following rules illustrate Methodist approaches to the subject. First, the construction of a new church: in the United Methodist Church, if any local church wishes to purchase or build a new church, or remodel an existing one, it must establish a study committee to address the need for the proposed facility, preliminary architectural plans and estimated costs (and how to meet these). The report is submitted to the Charge Conference for examination by its building committee and the District Board of Church Location and Building. These comment on the plan and the Charge Conference finally approves the project. On acquisition or completion of 'any church-owned building, a service of consecration may be held' – but 'Before any church-owned building is formally dedicated, all indebtedness shall be discharged'.¹⁰¹ Secondly, the maintenance of local church property rests with its assembly. In the Methodist Church of Ireland, for instance, the Church Council is responsible for the 'maintenance, letting and insurance of all the property entrusted to the Society, subject to such rights and obligations, if any, as may be vested in Local Trustees'.¹⁰² The Council must appoint a Property Steward 'who shall be responsible to the Council for the proper maintenance of all property'.¹⁰³ Also, a schedule of trust property in the circuit showing its condition, for example, as to debt, state of repair and insurance must be submitted by the circuit trustees to the Circuit Executive annually and forwarded to the District Property Secretary; any structural alteration (and expenditure incurred in this) must be approved by the District Synod and Property Board; the circuit superintendents must ensure that all renovations and repairs of trust property are considered by the trustees.¹⁰⁴

Thirdly, it is a principle of Methodist law that: 'No Minister shall permit anything to be done in any Church under the responsibility of such Minister which is not in accordance with the laws and usages of the Church'.¹⁰⁵ The same duty applies to trustees. Once again, the Methodist Church in Ireland provides that: 'Trustees shall take care that Church property is restricted to Church uses only, in accordance with the provisions of the Trust Deed of the premises'; thus: 'the greatest possible care must be taken not to allow premises set apart for religious purposes

---

⁹⁹ ELCA: Const., Ch. 9.53.08.
¹⁰⁰ ELCSA: G., 8.7: cemeteries; ELCA: Const., Ch. 10.21: archives; Ch. 11.20–21: the churchwide organisation must: 'Provide archives for the retention of its valuable records, and coordinate archival activity in the synods, regions, institutions, and agencies of this church'; Ch. 13.40–42: the Secretary maintains them; ELCIC: ABL, Pt. X.III.7: the ELCIC secretary has charge of records, registers and archives.
¹⁰¹ UMCNEAE: BOD, par. 2518–2544; par. 2532: access for disabled people. See also MCI: RDG, 29.
¹⁰² MCI: RDG, 10.06. See also MCGB: CPD, SO 941–942: quinquennial inspection; SO 332: the Methodist Council must appoint annually a Listed Buildings Advisory Committee to advise on the development and use of Methodist chapels, liturgy and worship, archaeology, architecture and care of historic buildings.
¹⁰³ MCI: RDG, 10.22.   ¹⁰⁴ MCI: RDG, 10.61–10.63.
¹⁰⁵ MCNZ: LAR, s. 2.26.1. Also, MCGB: CPD, SO 920–928 and 970–978: managing trustees may not sponsor meetings in support of e.g. political parties, the sale of intoxicants, smoking, gambling, dances or entertainment.

to be used for entertainments which would bring offence to our people generally'; these include card playing, gambling, the sale, consumption or supply of alcohol, and preaching contrary to Methodist beliefs.[106] Fourthly, there are extensive provisions about the maintenance of records; for example, in the Methodist Church in Great Britain all minute books, account books, and baptismal, burial and marriage registers and any other records relating to district, circuit and local church affairs must be preserved by designated officers in each of these units, and when no longer needed for current reference must be deposited on permanent loan with a public authority.[107] Fifthly, Methodist laws deal in some detail with residences for ministers (manses). In Irish Methodism, for instance, the Circuit Executive must 'ensure that suitable comfortable and properly furnished residences with adequate sanitary facilities are provided for the ministers appointed to that Circuit', that residences and furniture in them are kept in proper repair, and that all rates and taxes relating to ministers' residences are paid; the circuit superintendent must make an annual report to the District Synod in relation to their condition and repair.[108] The Circuit Executive must also allocate a reasonable sum each year to maintain the fabric and quality of decor of the manse. This amount shall be identified in a separate manse account and must be included in the circuit accounts.[109] The minister is responsible for: the care of all items provided by the circuit as listed in the Furniture Book; the provision of general furnishings not provided by the circuit; and damage, breakage or loss arising from neglect or fault by the resident minister – such damage must be repaired and made good by the minister at the time of the occurrence.[110]

Presbyterian laws require much the same action as in the traditions outlined thus far. As to construction of new churches, typically, the functions of the Presbytery include approval of plans for and the erection of new buildings, and for renovation of and alterations and additions to buildings when this involves costs in excess of a sum determined by the Assembly Council.[111] However, the maintenance of

---

[106] MCI: RDG, 10.65-69: this also forbids political meetings.

[107] MCGB: CPD, SO 015; the responsible supervisor of such archives for e.g. the circuit is the superintendent. See also MCI: RGD, 4A.04 and 2.17: the circuit superintendent must ensure that Membership, Congregational and Junior Registers are accurately maintained; UMCNEAE: BOD, par. 230-234; 340: 'care for church records'.

[108] MCI: RDG, 12.01-03: the Circuit Executive must appoint a manse inspection committee to assist the manse steward; the circuit must provide a Furniture Book for each manse on the circuit in which is entered a full and proper inventory and description of the furniture and effects in the house, with the signature of the circuit steward or manse steward to the inventory. See also MCGB: CPD, SO 803: entitlement to a manse.

[109] MCI: RDG, 12.04; 12.05: when leaving a circuit a minister must obtain the signature of the circuit steward or manse steward to the inventory and is accountable for any want of good order and condition.

[110] MCI: RDG, 12.06-08: as prescribed by the document Manses – Basic Accommodation Required (approved by Conference); 12.10-12.14: the circuit is responsible for maintenance of vacant manses; 12.18-12.22: inspection before handover. See also UMCNEAE: BOD, 2518-2523.

[111] PCANZ: BO, 16.4-6; it must also consult the General Assembly's Church Architecture Reference Group on any proposal which concerns the erection, alteration, addition or purchase of buildings; it may delegate functions to its Property Committee. See also PCW: HOR, 3.2.2: the Presbytery supervises 'buildings and all financial requirements concerning them'; PCI: Code, 57, 76: the site and plans of all new buildings proposed to be erected on congregational

property is the responsibility of the local church. For example, the congregation in the Presbyterian Church of Scotland is responsible for the maintenance of its buildings. It must hold an annual inspection of its property and keep a Property Register to record the inspection and work carried out; the register is submitted annually to the Presbytery, which instructs full inspections of congregational property every 5 years. Again, if a congregation proposes to carry out work on a building it must obtain the approval of the Presbytery – but the Presbytery may waive this requirement, provided the work costs no more than the financial limit, namely, a figure fixed by the Assembly on the recommendation of the General Trustees; if the work costs more than this figure, and this is approved, the Presbytery must refer the matter to the Consultative Committee on Church Properties whose recommendation must be given due consideration by the Presbytery.[112] In other Presbyterian Churches, the Deacons have a special responsibility for the care of church property. For example, in America, the deacons 'shall have the care of the property of the congregation, both real and personal, and shall keep in proper repair the church edifice and other buildings belonging to the congregation. In matters of special importance affecting the property of the church, they cannot take final action without the approval of the Session and consent of the congregation'.[113] There are detailed rules about particular objects within a church building; for instance, the table for the administration of the Lord's Supper, 'on which the elements are placed' should be 'decently covered, and furnished with bread and wine'.[114] The use of a church building is also subject to regulation. Under Irish Presbyterian law: 'The minister shall be entitled to use the place of worship and other church buildings for the purposes of his office, subject to any direction of the Presbytery' but has 'no right to use the buildings or grant the use of them for any other purposes without the authority of the Kirk Session'.[115] Presbyterian laws also provide in some detail for the maintenance of Session, Presbytery and Assembly records and archives and manses.[116] Similar rules

---

property, demolition and structural alterations or additions to existing buildings must be submitted for the approval of the Committee on Church Architecture and of the Presbytery.

[112] CLCS: 142; Act IX, 1979. See also UFCS: MPP, II.I.III.4: the Deacons' Court must 'see that the place of worship and other ecclesiastical buildings are kept in good condition and repair' and secure funding for this.

[113] PCA: BCO, 9.2; 12.5: the Session controls 'uses to which the church building and associated properties may be put'.

[114] PCA: BCO, 58.5.

[115] PCI: Code, 82(1)-(2). See also UFCS: MPP, I.III.23: 'the minister is allowed, subject to the Presbytery, a large discretion'; 'Worship and other ecclesiastical buildings belonging to the congregation are at his disposal for the purposes of his office' to 'use them, and grant permission to use them, for all purposes connected with the congregation or ... its organisations' and for, with the consent of Session and Deacons' Court, uses of 'a religious, ecclesiastical or charitable nature, though not connected with the congregation'.

[116] PCANZ: BO, 7.2.3: the church council must maintain congregational rolls; PCA: BCO, 10.4: the Session, Presbytery and General Assembly Clerks are 'to preserve the records carefully, and to grant extracts from them whenever properly required'; 12.7: 'Every Session shall keep an accurate record of its proceedings' (submitted at least once a year for inspection by Presbytery); 13.7: Presbytery 'book of records'; 13.10: the Presbytery must keep an accurate record of its proceedings to be submitted to General Assembly annually for review; PCI: Code, 41; PCW: HOR, 4.10: 'A Manse, free of rent, Council Tax and water rates is to be provided by the pastorate.'

are to be found in Reformed, United, Congregational and Baptist churches worldwide on maintenance of churches,[117] church records[118] and manses.[119]

The control of finance – budgets, accounts and audit

Christian laws that regulate the control of finance are in many key respects a mirror image of those that deal with the administration of real and personal property. Rules address: those authorities charged to manage finances; the preparation and the approval of budgets; and accounts and their audit. As with the regulation of movable and immovable property, the foundation which underlies rules about finance is the principle of Christian stewardship – designed not least to honour those who give to the church by systems of accountability; and many of these rules are shaped by standards set by the civil law applicable to the churches. The following section focuses in the main on the control of finance in the local church.

In the Catholic Church the Apostolic See regulates its own finances.[120] Each diocese has an institute to collect and manage funds, including a 'common fund' through which the bishop is to satisfy those who serve the church and to meet the needs of the diocese. The ordinary is assisted in this by a finance council composed of at least three members of the faithful, 'truly skilled in financial affairs as well as in civil law and of outstanding integrity', appointed by the bishop to hold office for a 5-year term. Administrators of temporal goods must present to the ordinary an annual report which in turn he is to present to the finance council for consideration. The council must prepare each year, according to directions given by the bishop, a budget of the income and expenditure foreseen for the governance of the diocese in the coming year. At the end of the year, it must examine a report of receipts and expenditure. The bishop must also appoint a finance officer, for a renewable 5-year term, to administer funds under the authority of the bishop in accordance with the budget determined by the finance council; the officer must report receipts and expenditure at the end of the year to the council. Moreover, each parish (like every other juridical person) is to have its own finance council obliged to act in

---

[117] URC: Man., B.2: the Elders' Meeting recommends to the Church Meeting as to 'the proper maintenance of buildings ... of the local church'; D, Pt. I: the trustees must permit churches to be used for e.g. public worship, instruction, and charitable purposes not inconsistent with the 'principles and usages' of the church. With the consent of the Church Meeting and (if the work substantially alters the character, appearance or value of the building) the Provincial Synod, the trustees may permit the building to be altered, enlarged, improved, rebuilt, supplemented or demolished (under the United Reformed Church Acts 1972, 1981 and 2000).

[118] UCA: Regs., 3.4.32: the Presbytery Secretary must maintain a record of its proceedings; UFCS: MPP, II.I.III.6: the Deacons' Court is 'to preserve carefully all Minute Books, Acts of Assembly ... and other volumes'; Riverside Baptist Church (Baltimore): BL Art. III.7: the Administrative Committee is 'to give attention to ... the condition, state of repair, and appearance of the buildings and grounds' of the church and make 'repairs and improvements authorized by the church and/or included in the church budget'.

[119] UCC: Man., BL, 386: the Presbytery Manse Committee must record the state of repair of the manse, report annually to the Presbytery on its condition, and oversee the Manse Committees of Pastoral Charges.

[120] *Pastor Bonus* (1988), Arts. 172–175: the Administration of the Patrimony of the Apostolic See is 'to administer the properties owned by the Holy See in order to underwrite the expenses [of] the Roman Curia'.

accordance with universal law and episcopal directions.[121] The Oriental Catholic Churches operate much the same system under their Code of Canons.[122]

The Russian Orthodox Church may be used as an example of the Orthodox approach to these matters. At the level of the patriarchate, the Patriarch has general oversight of the church's assets,[123] and the Bishops' Council considers financial reports presented by the Holy Synod and approves the budget for income and expenditure.[124] The bishop submits an annual report about the financial state of the diocese to the Patriarch and approves parish financial reports and audits.[125] Moreover, the bishop is to dispose of the financial assets of the diocese, and exercises oversight of the financial activities of the diocese, monasteries, educational institutions and other diocesan units.[126] The Diocesan Assembly assists in raising funds to meet the needs of the diocese.[127] At the local level, the Parish Meeting prepares a financial plan, elects the parish Audit Commission, approves the annual budget and considers the financial reports of the Parish Council.[128] In turn, the Parish Council is responsible for proposing the annual budget and disposal of assets with the consent of the rector.[129] The Council chair and treasurer must sign all financial documents and keep accounts and records of all financial transactions and donations.[130] The Audit Commission, accountable to the Parish Meeting, carries out an annual audit and reports on this to the Parish Meeting.[131] Much the same arrangements are found at parish level in the Romanian Orthodox Church,[132] Greek Orthodox Archdiocese of America[133] and Ukrainian Orthodox Church in America.[134] Stewardship in the Orthodox Church in America is designed not least to honour donors: 'responsibility, accountability, ethics and fair-dealing [are] of the

---

[121] CIC, cc. 1271–77: diocesan funds; cc. 228, 492–494, 1276–1277, 1287: diocesan finance council; c. 537: parish finance council; c. 1280: every juridic person must have a finance council.

[122] CCEO, cc. 262–263: eparchies; c. 516: parishes.

[123] ROC: Statute, XV.3. See also SOCA: Const., Art. 12: the Patriarch supervises finances of the archdioceses; Art. 55: budget and audit; Art. 68: maintenance of financial records;

[124] ROC: Statute, III.4(s): Bishops' Council; V.30; approval of budgets. See also ROMOC: Statutes, Art. 14(y): the Holy Synod oversees e.g. the Missionary Fund; Art. 22: the Church National Assembly approves the general budget of the Patriarchal Administration; Art. 29: this is drafted by the Church National Council.

[125] ROC: Statute, X.16 and X.18(q). See also ROMOC: Statutes, Art. 92: the Eparchial Assembly approves the annual budget and accounts which are (Art. 98) prepared by the Eparchial Council.

[126] ROC: Statute, X.18(z); see also XV.16; see e.g. Dioc. of Sourozh: Statutes IX.37: the 'assets of the Diocese shall be managed and controlled by the Diocesan Hierarch'; 42: 'The Diocese shall keep its accounts and conduct its ... financial ... activity with reference to its accountability to the Patriarch of Moscow.'

[127] ROC: Statute, X.44(f). [128] ROC: Statute, XI.43. [129] ROC: Statute, XI.46.

[130] ROC: Statute, XI.51–54. [131] ROC: Statute, XI.58.

[132] ROMOC: Statutes, Art. 55: the Parochial Assembly approves the annual budget and accounts; Art. 61: the Parochial Council prepares the annual budget; Art. 66: the Parochial Committee prepares the accounts.

[133] GOAA: Regs., Art. 33 the parish Board of Auditors reports to the Parish Assembly (with copies to the hierarch); Art. 34: the Parish Council, 'custodian of all parish funds', presents a financial report to the Parish Assembly for the preceding year and a budget (for approval) for the next year.

[134] ROMOC: Statutes, Art. 65.

highest importance' and are therefore subject to elaborate 'policies and procedures'; the church's 'annual financial statements shall be audited by an independent external certified public accountant'.[135]

The principle of 'financial stewardship' is equally pivotal in Anglicanism. A church should be financially independent and self-supporting and each unit within it should be entrusted with a share in the responsibilities for, and control and direction of, the finances in that church. An ecclesiastical organisation must comply with such financial procedures and controls as are prescribed by church law, keep financial accounts and submit an annual report with the audited accounts to the appropriate church assembly in order for that assembly to review the financial management and affairs of that organisation.[136] Also, ministers must exercise propriety in financial matters.[137] Oversight of finance in an ecclesiastical unit in a church resides in its assembly, and day-to-day administration of funds by a lawfully constituted financial executive is under the general direction and control of the relevant assembly (such as a parish council). The bishop has no unilateral general control over diocesan finance. Funds must be used according to the terms of any gift by which they are acquired, and investigation of complaints of financial mismanagement should be carried out by an independent body with an appeal lying to an appropriate ecclesiastical authority.[138]

Lutheran churches employ a similar pattern of budgets, accounting and audit at each level of the institutional church – all founded in the principle of stewardship.[139] At national level, the Evangelical Lutheran Church in Canada is typical. The National Council consists of the directors of the corporation and trustees who exercise 'stewardship' of resources. The Council is to: (1) recommend annual budgets to the Convention; (2) supervise expenditure subject to adoption of budgets by the Convention; (3) exercise 'general oversight and control of the finance and business management' (*via* its Department of Finance and Administration); (4) provide for budgetary procedures, accounting and auditing; (5) administer church funds; (6) ensure that the officers, committees and institutions of the church exercise 'sound and responsible fiscal management'; (7) review periodically the receipts, expenditures and financial conditions of the church; and (8) recommend to the church when adjustments are needed to ensure that expenditures do not exceed the funds available in the current fiscal year. The Treasurer, the fiscal officer

---

[135] OCIA: Best Practice Principles and Policies for Financial Accountability (2008): this deals with e.g. responsible stewardship, fundraising, confidentiality, and the functions of the Internal Audit Committee.

[136] PCLCCAC, Principle 84. See e.g. LC 1958, Res. 64: this encourages churches to be self-supporting.

[137] PCLCCAC, Principle 85.1–5: a minister must: ensure the highest standards, of honesty and care, in financial activities (e.g. keep separate church and personal finances). See e.g. TEC: Cans. I.1.2: General Convention's Standing Commission on Stewardship and Development must 'hold up before the Church the responsibility of faithful stewardship'; Cans. I.7: standards on business methods in church affairs.

[138] PCLCCAC, Principle 86. See e.g. Papua New Guinea: Const., Arts. 6–8: Provincial trustees must keep 'true accounts' audited annually with a report to Provincial Council; Jerusalem and the Middle East: Const., Art. 15(iii): variation of gifts; Wales: Const., IV.C.8: the parochial church council controls parish finance.

[139] ELCA: Const., Ch. 5.01: '[a]s a steward of the resources that God has provided, this church shall organize itself to make the most effective use of its resources to accomplish its mission'.

THE CONTROL OF FINANCE – BUDGETS, ACCOUNTS AND AUDIT   329

of the church, must make full report of the financial affairs of this church to Conventions and the National Church Council.[140] At regional level, the Lutheran Church in Australia is typical: the District Church Council recommends to the District Synod adoption of the annual budget; and the District Finance Council reviews the district financial policy, examines annually the financial position of the district, receives financial statements, ensures procedures are followed and manages funds.[141] At local level, the Evangelical Lutheran Church in Ireland is typical: the Parish Council establishes the annual budget, oversees its implementation and produces financial statements at the end of the fiscal year; the Church Assembly receives the annual accounts of the Parish Council and approves the budget for the next fiscal year; and the accounts are audited annually and disclosed on request to the civil Revenue Commission.[142] Moreover: 'Pastors are expected to conduct their fiscal affairs in accordance with ethical and legal requirements.' Among those fiscal activities which may be considered 'incompatible with the character of the ministerial office' are: indifference to or avoidance of legitimate and neglected personal debts; embezzlement of money or improper appropriation of the property of others; and using the ministerial office improperly for personal financial advantage.[143]

The Methodist approach to fiscal management mirrors this at central,[144] regional[145] and local level.[146] For instance, the Conference of the Methodist Church

---

[140] ELCIC: Const., Art. XII–XV; Corporate Bylaws, 20-24. See also LCGB: RAR, Annual General Meeting: this elects trustees, receives their annual report and audited accounts, and appoints (and remunerates) an auditor; ELCA: Const., Ch. 12-14: the Assembly adopts a budget presented by the Presiding Bishop, prepared by the Church Council, and recommended by its Budget and Finance Committee (which has an Audit Committee).

[141] LCA: District By-Laws, VIII.7. See also ELCA: Const., Ch. 10.72-74: 'Each synod shall arrange to have an annual audit of its financial records conducted by a certified public accountant firm selected by the Synod Council'; it is submitted by synod to e.g. the LCA Treasurer; Const. for Synods, Ch. 11.05: Audit Committee.

[142] ELCIRE: Const., Arts. 12,15,24. See also ELCA: Model Const. for Congregations, Ch. 12.05: the Congregation Council must 'prepare an annual budget for adoption by [the] congregation', 'supervise the expenditure of funds in accordance therewith', and ascertain whether its financial affairs are conducted efficiently; it also has an Audit Committee; LCGB: RAR, Congregations, 1: stewardship of resources.

[143] NALC: SFPM, B.5.

[144] See e.g. UMCNEAE: BOD, par. 803-805: the General Council holds trust general funds contributed by local churches; it submits budgets to each quadrennial General Conference, disburses them in accord with the directives of that Conference, and conducts an annual audit of all treasuries in receipt of general church funds.

[145] UMCNEAE: BOD, pars. 611-617: the Annual Conference Council on Finance and Administration is 'to develop, maintain, and administer a comprehensive and coordinated plan of fiscal and administrative policies' for the conference; it recommends budgets for adoption by conference and accounts to it for disbursement of funds; the council must have the conference accounts audited annually by a certified public accountant; par. 604: the conference may 'make inquiry into the financial status of the local churches, and where there is a deficit in finances, it may require the pastor and lay member to appear before the appropriate committee and make explanation'; it must help the church overcome the deficit; MCI: RDG, 13.08-13.11: all departments, institutions and circuits under the Conference must prepare annual accounts for the Conference to review.

[146] UMCNEAE: BOD, pars. 243, 244, 252, 340, 2548: the local Church Council must establish the budget on recommendation of its finance committee; elders 'certify the accuracy of all financial'

in Great Britain has authority to issue norms about finance. According to these, accounts must be kept of all moneys held at connexional, district, circuit or local church level. These accounts must be audited annually in accordance with civil law. The treasurer of any fund must oversee that fund, ensure that it is administered in accordance with the lawful instructions of the body to which the treasurer is responsible, assist in the preparation of budgets and monitor income and expenditure.[147] These rules apply to district, circuit and local funds. The circuit superintendent must ensure that auditors are appointed as to funds under the jurisdiction of the Circuit Meeting or Church Councils in the circuit. As to the latter, the local Church Council is 'to exercise responsible stewardship of its property and finance'.[148] The treasurer must: receive 'all collections, gifts, donations, subscriptions and other moneys raised for the general church fund, the benevolence fund or the model trust fund and any money arising for such other accounts as the Church Council may direct'; meet all financial obligations on behalf of the Church Council; and present a statement of all such funds and accounts to the Church Council and to such other committee or committees as the Council may direct.[149] Moreover, the Council must appoint annually an auditor or independent examiner for all funds in its jurisdiction.[150] The local church must pay its contribution to the Methodist Church Fund: 'The first charge on the general church fund shall be the sums required of the Local Church by the assessment of the Circuit Meeting, which shall be paid into the circuit fund quarterly eight working days before the beginning of the quarter to which they relate'.[151]

It is a fundamental principle of Presbyterian law that budgets must be prepared, accounts kept and an annual audit of these made at each ecclesiastical level, Congregation, Presbytery and Assembly.[152] For example, in the Presbyterian Church in New Zealand, the Church Council must oversee the funds of the congregation, appoint a treasurer responsible for its accounts[153] and ensure that these are

---

    reports submitted by the local church to the annual conference; MCI: RDG, 4A.04: the circuit superintendent must ensure the accounts of the circuit, society treasurers, trustees and 'all other accounts pertaining to any department of Circuit work are properly kept and duly audited'; 10.22: the local Church Council Treasurer is 'responsible to the Council for all financial income of the Society' and must 'keep accurate accounts and submit them for annual audit, according to the requirements of ... Conference'; 10.30–10.31: the Circuit Executive is responsible for the management and annual financial audit of circuit and society accounts; 13.05–13.11: duties of auditors and circuit account book; MCNZ: LAR, s. 3.5–.3.13: parish accounts and audit.

[147] MCGB: CPD, SO 012 and 012A; the applicable civil law is the Charities Act 1993, s. 43 (amended).
[148] MCGB: CPD, SO 640; see also SO 621: the General Church Meeting (held annually) meets to discuss 'the condition of the Local Church, including its financial affairs'.
[149] MCGB: CPD, SO 635; for the funds, see SO 650–652, for the administration of accounts, SO 012.
[150] MCGB: CPD, SO 636; see also SO 012. [151] MCGB: CPD, SO 532, 635, 650.
[152] PCI: Code, 76: Presbytery must 'examine the ... accounts of each congregation ... in accordance with directions issued by the General Assembly'; 240: the Congregational Committee prepares annual accounts 'duly audited by auditors appointed by the congregation'; 286: the Board of Finance of General Assembly; UFCS: MPP, III.II.12: the Annual Congregational Meeting examines the independently audited accounts.
[153] PCANZ: BO, 7.12; PCI: Code, 47(2)(a): the Congregational Meeting must 'administer all funds [of] the congregation or held by trustees for its use and apply these [to] the purposes for which they have been created'.

prepared and audited at least once each year by 'a suitably qualified person'.[154] Moreover, the Church Council must annually prepare a budget of the congregation's projected income and expenditure for the forthcoming financial year and submit this to the annual meeting of the congregation for approval.[155] Similarly, a Presbytery must exercise oversight of all funds received or held on its own behalf, and appoint a treasurer to prepare an annual account and audit for approval by the Presbytery.[156] In turn, the General Assembly must 'exercise responsibility for the financial management and resourcing of the life, worship, and mission of the Church'; and the Assembly Council prepares the budget and accounts for annual approval by the General Assembly.[157]

Similar arrangements operate at the various territorial levels of the United Church of Christ in the Philippines,[158] the United Church of Canada,[159] the United Congregational Church of Southern Africa[160] and the United Reformed Church in Great Britain.[161] For example, in the Uniting Church in Australia, at national level the Assembly must raise and establish funds to meet Assembly expenditure and 'prescribe for budgeting and reporting procedures required in relation to such funds'. Similarly, as at regional level, at local level the Church Council is responsible for 'managing the financial affairs ... of the Congregation, including the reception, preparation and presentation of all necessary budgets, statements and reports'; the treasurer is to keep accounts and record in them all monies received and all payments made. Also, the Church Council 'shall make arrangements for audit, presentation and examination of the accounts of all the funds of the Congregation' and 'approved methods of accounting [are] required in relation to all funds of the Church'; thus: 'The books of account shall be audited and certified by the auditors at least once in every year'; and: 'Comprehensive and detailed budgets should be prepared during the current year for the next succeeding year for' the bodies of the Congregation, Presbytery, Synod and Assembly.[162] In Baptist polity,

---

[154] PCANZ: BO, 16.8: this must be done in accordance with the civil Financial Reporting Act.
[155] PCANZ: BO, 16.8: before contracting any debt exceeding a sum determined by the Assembly Council, the church council must obtain the approval of the congregation, Presbytery and general trustees.
[156] PCANZ: BO, 16.10. See also PCW: HOR, 3.2: the Presbytery examines the income and expenditure of its churches and prepares an annual report for the Association; 3.2.3; PCA: BCO, 9.4.
[157] PCANZ: BO, 16.11; see also 16.12: appeals for funds. See also PCW: HOR, 3.3,4: Association funds; 3.4.2: financial matters, insurance and property; PCI: Code, 122: 'The Auditors of Accounts of the General Assembly shall annually audit the accounts of all the funds held by the [General] Trustees' and report to the Assembly.
[158] UCCP: Const., Art. VI.4: the Conference annual budget; Art. V.8: the congregation annual budget.
[159] UCC: Man., BL, 384: the Presbytery annual budget, accounts and audit; 184: 'a full statement of receipts and expenditures' for the ensuing year must be submitted to the Congregation.
[160] UCCSA: Const., 3.5.7: the local church is free '[t]o raise and expend funds'; 4.5–7: the Regional Council has the same power and a Finance Committee; 5.7–9: Synod; 9.1: Assembly.
[161] URC: Man., B.2(1): the (local) Church Meeting is 'to adopt financial reports'; B.2(2): the Elders' Meeting recommends to the Church Meeting as to the 'oversight of all the financial responsibilities of the local church'.
[162] UCA: Regs., 3.6.5 and 5.1: Assembly Funds; 5.3: Synod Funds; 5.4: Presbytery Funds; 3.1.13, 3.1.27: Church Council; 5.5.10: accounting and audit.

likewise, the local church should be self-supporting,[163] and there are elaborate rules on the approval of budgets and accounts by Unions, or Conventions,[164] and by the local church.[165] A Baptist Union may have a central fund to enable it and its Associations and Churches 'to discharge more adequately the task of the care of all churches and of fostering the evangelical witness'.[166] In short, it is a principle of Christian law that a church is free to make rules for the administration and control of finance, that the relevant civil law should be complied with, and that each ecclesiastical unit, including the local church, through designated bodies should prepare an annual budget for approval by its own assembly, provide for the keeping of accounts by a treasurer for similar approval and ensure that these accounts are audited annually by qualified persons in order to promote proper stewardship in the church.

The lawful sources of income

The regulatory instruments of churches provide for a variety of lawful sources of income. The most common are: offerings made as a responsibility of church membership; donations of funds and other gifts; the imposition of assessments or other form of ecclesiastical tax on ecclesial units; fees payable for the provision of prescribed services; and investments. As with norms on budgets, accounts and audit, the tenor of which may be set by the standards of civil law, there is very little theology in rules on sources of income, with the exception of the pervasive principle of stewardship and the scriptural foundations for offerings of the faithful.

The Roman Catholic Church has a particularly well-developed body of rules on these matters. First, the Church asserts for itself 'the inherent right to require from the faithful whatever is necessary for its proper objectives'. The faithful have the right to give freely to the church and the diocesan bishop must admonish them to assist so that the church has what is necessary for divine worship, apostolic works, works of charity and the sustenance of ministers. Thus, the faithful have a duty 'to contribute to the support of the church by collections ... according to the norms laid down by the conference of bishops'. Secondly, however, a minister may ask nothing for administration of the sacraments beyond the offerings defined by competent authority, always taking care that the poor are not deprived of the

---

[163] NBC: PAP, Fundraising: 'Churches should be encouraged to raise whatever funds ... from amongst the [member] Churches and other Christian bodies'; BUSA: Model Const., 18.1: 'The Church shall be supported by voluntary giving'; see e.g. Central Baptist Church (Pretoria): Const., 20.

[164] BUSA: BL 4: the Union's 'Audited accounts shall be submitted [annually] to the executive with an annual report ... to the union Assembly'; BUSA: Model Const., 11.1.3: the local church annual general meeting examines audited accounts; NABC: Const., 5.4: 'The Treasurer shall account for all funds received and disbursed by the Conference' and must 'submit a financial report at each meeting of the General Council and a report to each triennial Conference'; 6.2.2: the General Council approves the Conference annual budget.

[165] Riverside Baptist Church (Baltimore): BL, Art. II.C: the treasurer keeps 'a record of all budgeted funds of the church and pay out same, under the direction of the church, and shall regularly ... report to the church of all transactions', and annually lays before the church a statement of money received and paid for the previous year; BL, Art. III.8: the Finance Committee prepares an annual budget for approval by a church business meeting.

[166] BUGB: Const., 2: the Central Fund is administered by the Trustee Board.

sacraments. Offerings are determined by the provincial bishops, but the local ordinary may prescribe a special collection for specific parochial, diocesan, national or universal projects. Thirdly, the diocesan bishop may 'impose a moderate tax on public juridical persons subject to his authority'; *taxa* should be proportionate to income and imposed only after hearing the diocesan finance council and presbyteral council. The bishop may also impose an extraordinary (but moderate) tax on other physical and juridical persons 'only in cases of grave necessity' and with 'due regard for particular laws and customs'.[167] Fourthly, those who by natural law and canon law may freely dispose of their goods may leave them to pious causes – but the formalities of civil law must be met. The wishes of the faithful who give or leave their resources to pious causes in life or by will are 'to be fulfilled with the greatest diligence'. The ordinary is the executor of all pious gifts and must 'exercise vigilance, even through visitation, so that pious dispositions are fulfilled'. All trustees of such property must inform the ordinary of the trust and its terms, and the ordinary must exercise vigilance on behalf of the execution of the disposition. If fulfilling the trust becomes impossible, the ordinary may diminish the property equitably after consultation with the interested parties and his finance council.[168] Fifthly, with the consent of the ordinary, administrators of goods may invest money remaining after expenses are met; a report on investments is made to the ordinary at the end of the year. Moneys assigned to a particular endowment must be invested cautiously and profitably, for the benefit of the foundation in question, with the approval of the ordinary who must consult interested parties and the diocesan finance council.[169] Similar rules apply to the Oriental Catholic Churches.[170]

In Orthodox canon law, assets may be acquired by voluntary offerings, gifts and legacies.[171] For instance, assets of the Russian Orthodox Church include donations received at the Divine Liturgy and other services, those of natural and legal persons (including public bodies) and income from commercial enterprises and the sale of religious objects.[172] Orthodox law also imposes a duty on the faithful to contribute to church funds. For example, the Greek Orthodox Archdiocese in America recommends on the basis of the principle of stewardship that parishioners provide 10 per cent of their income, 'as stated in Holy Scripture, to help meet the financial obligations of the Parish, the Metropolis and the

---

[167] CIC, cc. 1260–1266; c. 1274: common fund; cc. 945–947: there must be no commerce in the sacraments.

[168] CIC, cc. 1299–1310; see D.J. Ward, 'Trust management under the new code', 44 *The Jurist* (1984) 134.

[169] CIC, cc. 1294, 1305; the parish finance council has no power to invest (c. 537); cc. 282 and 286: clerics.

[170] CCEO, c. 1011: competent authorities may acquire from the faithful those things necessary for the purposes of the church; c. 1012: the eparchial bishop may impose taxes on the faithful with the consent of the finance council but not on the offerings received at the Divine Liturgy; cc. 1013–1014: the bishop may determine offerings received at the Divine Liturgy; c. 1015: juridical persons may not collect alms without the permission of the relevant authority; c. 1016: offerings for a particular purpose may be applied only to that purpose; c. 1021.1: an eparchy must have an institute to collect offerings; cc. 1043–1054: gifts to pious causes.

[171] MOCL: 107–108: as well as by purchases and exchange.

[172] ROC: Statute, XV.1. See also ROMOC: Statutes, Art. 174: assets are derived from e.g. 'contributions, donations, successions, testamentary stipulations'.

Archdiocese'; this may be waived by the parish priest.[173] Indeed, all 'special contributions, bequests, gifts, and devises beyond Stewardship shall be used by the Parish only for the purposes for which they were made'.[174] Moreover, each parish must make a corporate contribution to the diocese. The Ukrainian Orthodox Church in America is typical. The Diocesan Assembly fixes the sum to be collected from the parishes and supervises its collection.[175] In other Orthodox Churches the amount assessed is determined by the Holy Synod and the dean ensures its collection.[176] Sometimes Orthodox laws also provide for investments by church bodies.[177]

The approach of Anglican churches is not dissimilar. Ministers must instruct the faithful in their responsibilities towards the missionary work of the church and give suitable opportunity for offerings to maintain that work. The faithful should make financial offerings according to their means. The duty to collect offerings at the time of public worship vests in wardens and the disposal of these is determined by a church assembly or other lawful authority. Fees payable on the performance of such ecclesiastical ministrations as marriage and burials may be levied to the extent and in the manner prescribed by church law.[178] Moreover, a diocese should make a financial contribution to the national, regional or provincial church to fund activities undertaken at these levels, and a parish should contribute, through its assembly, a parish share or other such payment toward the finances of the diocese. A church may make legal provision as to the diocesan and parish share for: the duty to pay; the assessment of the sum due which should be fair and equitable; the timing of payment; appeals against the assessment; and sanctions for non-payment.[179] Moreover, church trustees may make such investments as are authorised by law and these should be not only financially prudent but morally sound. Powers of investment enjoyed at all levels of a church are to be exercised subject to the direction and control of an ecclesiastical assembly. However, trustees are not liable

---

[173] GOAA: Regs., Art. 18.1-4: 'The Priest shall judge any cases of special circumstances justifying the waiver of a parishioner's stewardship financial obligations.' See also MOSC: Const., 10.120; ROMOC: Statutes, Art. 45.

[174] GOAA: Regs., Art. 16.5.

[175] UOCIA: Statutes, Art. VIII.3; see also Art. XI.6: 'Each year the parish shall remit to the Diocesan Treasurer its minimum financial support to the Diocese'; the sum is fixed by the number of parishioners who are 18 or over; also Art. III.5(d): the Pre-Sobor Commission is 'to fix and collect the registration fees from each parish'.

[176] ROC: Statute, XI.5: the tax; X. 52(d): the dean.

[177] Dioc. of Sourozh (ROC): Statutes, IX.37: 'The Diocese may acquire shares and other securities'.

[178] PCLCCAC, Principle 87. See e.g. Central Africa: Diocese of Mashonaland, Pastoral Regulations 1978, 19: 'Almsgiving ... should be in proportion to the giver's wealth. For very poor people, 1% of income may be the most possible. For the wealthy, 10% is not an undue sacrifice'; England: Parochial Church Councils (Powers) Measure 1956, s. 7: the council may with the minister 'determine the objects to which all moneys to be given or collected in church shall be allocated'.

[179] PCLCCAC, Principle 88. See e.g. TEC: Cans. I.4.6: 'an assessment shall be levied upon the Dioceses of the Church in accordance with a formula which the Convention shall adopt'; Scotland: Digest of Resolutions, 39: it is the secondary 'duty' of every congregation (after providing for the stipend of the cleric) 'to contribute, either directly or through such general levy or Quota as the Diocesan Synod may require, to the diocese and to the general funds of the General Synod'.

personally for any financial loss which results from an investment, unless such loss is due to their own wilful default or culpable negligence.[180]

Most Protestant laws also deal with the right of a church to receive funds, the duty of the faithful to contribute financially, charges for prescribed services, the administration of assessments on ecclesial units and the power of investment. The following provisions are typical of Lutheranism. First, the church must support its mission 'by arranging for and encouraging financial contributions for its work'.[181] Secondly, the members of a congregation must 'observe their financial obligations',[182] and therefore 'each member may be required to pay a financial contribution to the work of the church'.[183] Thirdly, a congregation must encourage its members 'in the practice of Christian ... stewardship',[184] and ordained ministers must 'endeavour to increase the support given by the congregation to the work' of the church and its units.[185] Fourthly, a congregation must '[s]hare responsibly in providing the funds needed for the life and work of this church and of [its own] synod';[186] thus: 'Each synod shall receive contributions from congregations for the work of the church and shall forward to this church a proportion thereof determined by mutual consultation between the synod and this church.'[187] Fifthly, prescribed institutions have the authority to invest: 'Within the policies established by the Churchwide Assembly and the Church Council, the management and investment of the funds of the churchwide organization and its units receiving budgetary support shall be the responsibility of the Office of the Treasurer';[188] also: 'The Congregation Council shall be responsible for this congregation's investments.'[189]

Similar arrangements are found in Methodist laws. The following are commonplace. Income may be received for disbursement towards the objects of the church.[190] Church members must engage in 'systematic giving' or 'regular giving'

---

[180] PCLCCAC, Principle 89. See e.g. Ireland: Const., X.10: the Representative Body's powers of investment are subject to the control of the General Synod; Southern Africa: Const., Art. XIX, Sch. A: the Provincial Trustees may invest 'under the special leave and sanction' of the Provincial Synod; no liability attaches to trustees unless loss occurs through their 'own wilful neglect or default'.
[181] ELCA: Const., Ch. 4.03.
[182] ELCSA: G., 9.4: congregation members must 'observe their financial obligations according to the regulations of the Congregational Constitution'.
[183] ELCIRE: Const., 8.1: 'Each member shall pay contributions' on the basis of (8.2) 'self-assessment' and 'the principle of voluntary self-sacrifice'; 8.3: 'The parish council may set a benchmark.'
[184] ELCIC: ABL, Pt. II.2.   [185] ELCA: Const., Ch. 7.31.12.
[186] ELCIC: ABL, Pt. II.2. See also ELCA: Const., Ch. 10.70–71: 'Each synod shall remit to the [national] organization a percentage of ... receipts contributed to it by the congregations ... [as] determined by the [national] Assembly. Individual exceptions may be made by the Church Council upon request of a synod.'
[187] ELCIC: ABL, Pt. V.8.   [188] ELCA: Const., Ch. 11.40.
[189] ELCA: Model Const. for Congregations, Ch. 12.05.
[190] MCNZ: LAR, 1.2: any income gained by the church must be used to advance its charitable purposes; UMCUSA: Const., Div. 2.2, Art. IV.14: Conference may 'determine and provide for raising funds and distributing funds necessary to carry on the work of the Church'; UMCNEAE: BOD, par. 2532: bequests.

which is 'a Christian duty'.[191] Officers are to 'promote faithful financial stewardship and to encourage giving as a spiritual discipline by teaching the biblical principles of giving'.[192] The circuit superintendent must 'ensure that all collections for Connexional Funds are made at the proper times, and the amounts forwarded promptly to the respective Treasurers'.[193] Furthermore, the local church must make a contribution to the Conference towards the expenses of the church by means of an apportionment determined by the Conference; typically: 'Payment in full of these apportionments by local churches is the first benevolent responsibility of the church.'[194] Also, church trustees and prescribed bodies may invest funds in schemes which are consistent with the Social Principles of the church.[195] However, it is not permissible for the church to raise funds by means of any activity which is forbidden on Methodist property.[196]

Presbyterian laws operate parallel principles. Typically, congregational funds comprise 'all offerings received for the purposes of the congregation, all donations made to the congregation for general Church purposes, all moneys raised on behalf of the church council, all legacies received by the congregation, and any other monies given to or raised by the congregation for a specific purpose'.[197] Presbytery funds comprise income received by the Presbytery from the congregations (less expenditure), its capital funds and funds held in trust by the Presbytery, including assets of congregations which are in the process of closing.[198] The General Assembly may also raise funds.[199] Moreover, 'Christian liberality' is not simply 'a matter of providing for the work of the Church, but primarily a grateful response to what

---

[191] UMCNEAE: BOD, par. 218; see also par. 220: 'the stewardship of property and accumulated resources'; par. 801: 'Participation through service and gifts is a Christian duty, a means of grace and an expression of our love of God'; MCI: RDG, 1.01 and 2.06: members are 'expected, as far as they are able, to contribute to the funds of the Church' and 'financially support the ongoing work and mission of the church through regular giving, as far as can reasonably be expected'; MCNZ: LAR, Introductory Documents, IV: General Standards for the Guidance of Members: members are accountable to God for 'the stewardship of our ... money'.

[192] UMCNEAE: BOD, par. 340; see also par. 417–425: elders must 'lead the congregation in ... its mission through full and faithful payment of all apportioned ministerial support, administrative and benevolent funds'.

[193] MCI: RDG, 4A.04; see also 13.26: gifts; UMCNEAE: BOD, par. 2512: pastors must protect gifts.

[194] UMCNEAE: BOD, par. 247.14: following the annual conference, each district superintendent must notify a local church what amounts have been apportioned to it for general church and annual conference funds, and, with pastors, and lay members, must impress on each charge conference 'the importance of these apportioned funds'. See also MCI: RDG, 13.13ff: assessments on circuits made under the authority of the Conference.

[195] UMCNEAE: BOD, par. 716: the 'policy' is that all bodies (e.g. local churches) 'shall ... make a conscious effort to invest in institutions, companies, corporations, or funds whose practices are consistent with ... the Social Principles'; they must 'avoid investments that appear likely ... to support' e.g. sweatshop labour, gambling, or the production of nuclear armaments, alcoholic beverages or tobacco; par. 806: the General Council on Finance and Management must develop 'general investment policies and guidelines' for all agencies receiving general church funds; par. 2532: the local church may invest similarly; see also MCI: RDG, 10.70 and MCGB: MT 16.

[196] MCGB: CPD, SO 014: i.e. activity which not be permitted under SO 924, 925 and 927.

[197] PCANZ: BO, 16.8; PCI: Code, 235: congregational income includes contributions to the weekly freewill offering, stipends, the Central Ministry Fund, and Sunday and other collections.

[198] PCANZ: BO, 16.10.   [199] PCANZ: BO, 16.11; see also 16.12: appeals for funds.

God has done for his people in Jesus Christ'.[200] The principle is set out in some detail in the Presbyterian Church in America: 'The Holy Scriptures teach that God is owner of all persons and all things and that we are but stewards of both life and possessions; that God's ownership and our stewardship should be acknowledged ... [in] the form ... of giving at least a tithe of our income and other offerings to the work of the Lord through the Church of Jesus Christ, thus worshipping the Lord with our possessions; and that the remainder should be used as becomes Christians.' Moreover: 'It is both a privilege and a duty, plainly enjoined in the bible, to make regular, weekly, systematic and proportionate offerings for the support of religion and for the propagation of the Gospel in our own and foreign lands, and for the relief of the poor. This should be done as an exercise of grace and an act of worship, and at such time during the service as may be deemed expedient by the Session.' It is the duty of the deacon 'to develop the grace of liberality in the members of the church, to devise effective methods of collecting the gifts of the people, and to distribute these gifts among the objects to which they are contributed'.[201] There are extensive rules on offerings and collections.[202]

Presbyterians also employ a system of assessments on the local church. For example, a congregation must make an annual contribution to the central funds of the Church of Scotland; if the congregation fails to meet the minimum required and a vacancy occurs in a congregation with current or accumulated shortfalls to central funds, the Presbytery determines whether the shortfalls are justified – if they are not, the Presbytery must not allow the congregation to call a minister until either the shortfalls have been met to the extent determined by the Presbytery, or the congregation has been united to another congregation.[203] Much the same applies in New Zealand. The local Church Council must 'make payment of levies

---

[200] CLCS: 136: under the system of Weekly Freewill Offering, members undertake to give a regular weekly amount and this enables the financial board to place a realistic figure for income in its annual budget. See also UFCS: MPP, III.1.4: 'It is the duty of members ... to contribute heartily, as the Lord shall enable them, for the maintenance of the Christian ministry, and the furtherance of the Gospel at home and abroad.'

[201] PCA: BCO, 54.1–54.2; 54.3: 'It is appropriate that the offerings be dedicated by prayer'; 9.2: elders; 4.4: the ordinances of Christ include 'making offerings for the relief of the poor and other pious uses'. See also PCI: Code, 6: members must 'give of their substance as the Lord may prosper them'; 42: the Kirk Session 'shall promote by example and exhortation the ideal of Christian Stewardship in every department of life'.

[202] PCANZ: BO, 7.12: the board of managers or deacons' court collects 'all contributions and offerings from and to the congregation'; PCI: Code, 235: weekly freewill offering; 239: 'The encouragement of contributions by the people, in a spirit of generous and responsible stewardship for the work of the Church, both within the congregation and through the Assembly, shall be the duty of the Congregational Committee'; UFCS: MPP, I.III.2: 'The Session also regulates the time and mode of taking collections in connection with public worship'; II.I.III.8: 'Ruling elders and deacons receive the Sunday Collections of the people'; 12: 'As the Deacons' Court is charged with the care of the poor of the church, it appoints special collections as often as may be necessary.'

[203] CLCS: 139: this contribution goes into the Mission and Aid Fund (for e.g. Assembly expenses and stipends); the procedure involves the Presbyteries, Board of Stewardship and Finance, and Maintenance of Ministry Committee; for shortfalls, see Act IX, 1996; PCI: Code, 76: Presbytery has 'the right to make an assessment on each of its congregations proportional to the amount of stipend paid, to meet the incidental expenses of the Presbytery; and be required to publish annually an audited statement of accounts of its Incidental Fund'.

fixed by the presbytery' and it must 'make payment of assessments fixed by the General Assembly'.[204] The General Assembly must 'assess the contributions that congregations must pay to the General Assembly for the purposes of the life, worship, and mission of the Church which the General Assembly considers important' – it must also calculate the assessment and the time for its payment; 'every congregation must pay the assessment levied upon it'; the General Assembly may in 'special circumstances' vary the amount or exempt a congregation from payment.[205] Laws also provide for investments.[206]

United and Congregational churches, too, advocate 'cheerful giving' by the faithful, charge their officers to oversee this,[207] enable investments[208] and require the local church to make contributions to the institutions of the wider church,[209] such as the United Church of Canada: 'The Conference shall have the right to assess the presbyteries within its jurisdiction an amount sufficient to meet Conference expenses'; and: 'The Presbytery shall have the right to assess Pastoral Charges within its jurisdiction an amount sufficient to meet Presbytery expenses including the Conference assessment.'[210] Members of Baptist churches must also contribute financially,[211] and in some Baptist Unions: 'An Annual Subscription shall be paid by each Church, Association, College or other Baptist organisation in membership

---

[204] PCANZ: BO, 16.8.
[205] PCANZ: BO, 16.11. See also PCW: HOR, 3.3.5: Connexional Contribution; PCI: Code, 42: the Kirk Session co-operates with the Congregational Committee to ensure 'congregation accept their full obligation under the various assessments ... of the General Assembly as well as in support of the local Church'; UFCS: MPP, II.I.III: the Deacons' Court receives 'the contributions of the congregation for the objects ... approved by ... General Assembly', disposing of them 'in accordance with the instructions of the Assembly'.
[206] PCW: HOR, 3.2.3: the Resources and Properties Board is empowered to invest the money.
[207] UCCP: Const., Art. II.9: the church 'advocates vigorous Christian stewardship expressed in the cheerful giving of tithes'; Art. V.12: the Board of Deacons implements stewardship; Art. VII.24: the Commission on Stewardship and Resource Development of the General Assembly plans Christian stewardship; UCC: Man., BL, 469: the Stewardship Committee of the Conference is 'to ensure that the principles and practice of Christian stewardship are promoted in the Presbyteries and their Pastoral Charges'; RCA: BCO, Ch. I, Pt. I, Art. 6.
[208] UCA: Regs., 5.5.9, 6.3.1; UCCSA: Const., 6.9.2.3: the Investments Committee of the Assembly.
[209] UCA: Regs., 3.4.4: Presbytery arranges 'the contribution by Congregations of funds for the purposes of the Presbytery, the Synod and the Assembly and other approved purposes'; 3.5.5: the Congregational Fund established and administered by the Church Council consists of e.g. 'all offerings received at services of worship [and] all donations ... to the Congregation'; UCOC: BL, Art. II.178: a Conference receives contributions from local churches; UCCSA: Const., 3.5.7: the local church is 'to share in the work of the whole Church by the payment of assessments as determined from time to time by the Assembly'; RCA: BCO, Ch. I, Pt. II, Art. 7.
[210] UCC: Man., BL, 420.1: Conference; 328: Presbytery.
[211] CNBC: Const., 3, Statement of Belief, XIII: 'According to the Scriptures, Christians should contribute of their means cheerfully, regularly, systematically, proportionately, and liberally'; BUSA: Model Const., 8.3: 'Members shall be expected to support the ministry and maintain the fellowship ... by conscientious giving as God's provision enables'; Riverside Baptist Church (Baltimore): Const., Art. IV: a member covenants '[t]o contribute cheerfully and regularly to the support of the ministry, the expenses of the church, the relief of the poor, and the spread of the gospel through all nations'; Bethel Baptist Church (Choctaw): Const., Art. VII.4: a member may be disciplined for not 'supporting the church financially without having any providential cause'.

with the Union not less than such amount or amounts as the Council shall from time to time determine.'[212] However, ministers must not charge fees (e.g. for weddings or funerals) other than those agreed by the leadership of the local church.[213] Provision also exists for Baptist Unions and Conventions to invest funds prudently to further their objects.[214] In other words, according to Christian laws: a church may receive funds; the faithful must contribute financially to church work; church officers should encourage the faithful in this and collect offerings; the local church and other units may be the subject of assessments made by the regional, national and sometimes international authorities; and a church is free to invest money prudently in ethical ventures which are consistent with the standards of the church.

Ecclesiastical expenditure

As has been seen, funds may be disposed of to further the purposes of each institutional church. However, in three key areas, the regulatory instruments of churches impose duties on church authorities at various ecclesiastical levels to apply funds for insurance, stipends (or other form of remuneration) for ordained ministers and pensions upon their retirement. From rules in these fields emerge principles of Christian law that churches should insure their property against loss, that they should remunerate those engaged in full-time and other forms of ministry, and that they should make financial provision for ordained ministers who retire. These obligations are an integral part of the principle of stewardship under which expenditure may be made only for the objects of a church and from its lawful sources of church income.

Insurance

Provisions on insurance cover for property, and sometimes personal cover for ministers, are found in regulatory instruments across the Christian traditions studied here. As in the Catholic Church[215] and Orthodox Churches,[216] so, too, in Anglicanism, church assemblies, officers and other bodies should be aware of the

---

[212] BUGB: Const., 7. See also BUSA: BL, 8: 'A membership fee, as determined from time to time by the Executive, shall be payable annually to the Union by each member Church and member Association'; BUS: BL, XIII.1: 'An annual contribution to the Scottish Baptist Fund of not less than 33% of the per capita amount requested by the Assembly shall be required from each church in order to ensure representation at the Assembly and on Council'. Compare: CNBC: BL 34: 'There shall be no annual membership dues.'

[213] BUNZ: EPGP 1.8; NABC: Code of Ministerial Ethics: a minister undertakes to 'confer with church leaders before accepting remuneration for work other than that normally associated with the pastorate'.

[214] CNBC: Const., par. 75: 'In investing the funds of the Society, the board [of directors] shall not be limited to ... investments in which trustees are authorized by law to invest, but may make any investments which are prudent'; they are not liable for any loss not resulting from any fault on their behalf; BUGB: MTC 2003, 11; BUSA: Const., 6.11: the Union may invest funds; Central Baptist Church (Pretoria): Const., 21.

[215] CIC, c. 1284.1: administrators of temporal goods must insure those goods. See also CCEO c. 1021.

[216] OCIA: GC, Priests and Deacons, 16: 'A clergyman should have personal liability insurance coverage and coverage for the personal contents of his rectory'; ROMOC: Statutes, Art. 92: insuring eparchial assets.

risks associated with their activities. Church property, real and personal, and its occupation and usage, and individual church officers and activities, should be insured as appropriate against loss, damage and injury. A church should identify its bodies or persons with a duty to insure, use insurers of proven competence and specify the extent of the insurance required. Insurance policies should be regularly reviewed.[217] Protestant laws provide for much the same requirements. For example, the Secretary of the Evangelical Lutheran Church in America must provide and manage insurance for the churchwide organization and make available insurance programmes to congregations, synods and other organizations; and: 'Each synod shall maintain adequate, continuous insurance coverage in accordance with standards recommended by the churchwide organization.'[218] At local level, in the Irish Methodist Church, the Church Council is responsible for the 'insurance of all the property entrusted to the Society, subject to such rights and obligations, if any, as may be vested in Local Trustees'.[219] Moreover, ministers are advised to take out insurance for their own property and liabilities, and the circuit superintendent must pay 'special attention to the insurance of churches, manses and other buildings against loss or damage by fire or any other cause'; and particulars are entered in the Circuit Schedule Book. Indeed, the Secretary of the Property Board must furnish annually the district superintendent with a list of properties considered to be inadequately insured so that inquiry may be made at the District Synod.[220] The local church must also provide for insurance in Presbyterian churches,[221] as must prescribed Baptist institutions.[222]

The remuneration of ordained ministers

That ordained ministers have a right to financial maintenance by churches, in order to liberate them to realise their vocation and ministry, is now understood to be a fundamental of ecclesiastical life. According to Roman Catholic canon law, when ordained ministers dedicate themselves to ministry, 'they deserve a remuneration consistent with their condition in accord with the nature of their responsibilities and with the conditions of time and place'; remuneration 'should enable them to provide for the needs of their own life and for the equitable payment of those whose services they need'. Similar provision is to be made for 'such social welfare as they may need

---

[217] PCLCCAC, Principle 90. See e.g. Brazil: Cans. I.7: properties must be insured with insurance companies of 'proven competence'; Ireland: Const., III.24.4: the vestry must 'keep the churches and other parochial buildings insured against fire'; Wales: Church Fabric Regulations, 5: the parochial church council must ensure that 'all churches ... and their contents are insured in accordance with the advice of the insurer'.

[218] ELCA: Const., Ch. 15.13.A10: national level; Ch. 10.72–74: synod level.

[219] MCI: RDG, 10.06.

[220] MCI: RDG, 29.16–19: personal, Sunday school insurance, and property owners' third party insurance.

[221] PCANZ: BO, 16.3.1(b): the church council must provide 'adequate insurance cover on all property' and annually review the adequacy of the cover, and make arrangements for 'public risk insurance and personal accident insurance for voluntary workers'; PCI: Code, 47(2)(b): the Congregational meeting is to insure congregation property; UFCS: MPP, II.I.III.11: the Deacons' Court is to provide for insurance.

[222] CNBC: Const., par. 124: 'All persons who handle funds or securities of the Convention or Society shall be adequately bonded or insured.'

in infirmity, sickness or old age'.²²³ However, clerics must 'cultivate a simple style of life and are to avoid whatever has a semblance of vanity'; income surplus to needs should be used for the good of the church and for works of charity.²²⁴ Each diocese has a special institute to collect and manage a fund to support the clergy,²²⁵ and the Episcopal Conference must establish norms for the provision of proper living for clerics.²²⁶ Lay people engaged in the ecclesial service also have a right to worthy remuneration befitting their condition whereby, with due regard to civil law, they may provide for their own and families' needs.²²⁷ The church also provides to compensate injury suffered in the course of ministry.²²⁸ Similar rules apply to Oriental Catholic Churches.²²⁹

Orthodoxy and Anglicanism also provide for the remuneration of clergy. For example, in the Greek Orthodox Archdiocese in America, the parish must provide clergy with remuneration (according to standards set by the Archdiocesan Council), a housing allowance or a parish house (and pay for the utilities), health care and social security; moreover: 'No Parish shall reduce, withhold or adversely alter a Priest's remuneration without the consent of the respective Hierarch.'²³⁰ Such provisions are not untypical;²³¹ in several churches the parish remunerates its clergy and determines the stipend.²³² Likewise, in Anglicanism, a church should provide for the financial maintenance of ministry, both lay and ordained. Ministers in full-time ministry have

---

[223] CIC, c. 281.1–2; c. 281.3: married deacons also deserve remuneration sufficient to provide for themselves and their families, but if they are in a secular profession they must see to these needs from their own income.

[224] CIC, c. 282; see also cc. 531 and 551 for stole fees for remuneration of clerics.

[225] CIC, c. 1274; the bishop must assist in procuring 'those means whereby the Apostolic See can properly provide for its service to the universal church according to the conditions of the times'.

[226] CIC, cc. 1272, 1274.

[227] CIC, c. 231.2; c. 1286: administrators of temporal goods in making contracts of employment must observe the civil laws relating to labour and social life; they are to pay those who work for them under contract 'a just and honest wage which would fittingly provide for their needs and those of their dependants'.

[228] CIC, c. 192: a person may be removed only 'with due regard for rights which may have been acquired by contract or by the law itself'; c. 195: 'If a person is removed from an office which is a source of financial support, not by the law itself [i.e. if removal is not automatic], but by a decree of the competent authority, this same authority is to take care such support is seen to for a suitable time, unless it is provided otherwise.'

[229] CCEO, c. 1021: each eparchy must have a common fund from which e.g. remuneration of persons is paid.

[230] GOAA: Regs., Art. 17.8; 17.9: the parish should also compensate a parish priest during illness or disability.

[231] ROC: Statute, XI.46: the parish council is responsible for clergy accommodation; UOCIA: Statutes, Art. VII.6: the bishop 'shall be entitled to adequate financial support from the diocese and an official residence . . . if this lies within the financial means of the diocese'; ROMOC: Statutes, Art. 48: accommodation for the priest.

[232] UOCIA: Statutes, Art. XI.4: 'To be free from material preoccupations and wholly committed to his sacred ministry, the priest must be compensated by the parish, the amount . . . clearly agreed upon at the time of his appointment'; Art. X.3: the dean negotiates this 'in agreement with the ability of the parish to meet these requests'; OCIA: Clergy Compensation Guide 1995: 'A full-time pastor should be paid [to] permit [him and his] family to live at the same general level-of-living as most . . . of the parish'; 'A pastor should be satisfied with such treatment and shall not want, expect, nor ask for more' (1 Cor. 9.15–19); 'The salary . . . should appear reasonable' to the lay leaders, members, pastor and pastor's spouse; there should be an annual review.

a legitimate expectation to a stipend or other remuneration payable by virtue of the office or other position held by them. Stipend funds may be held and administered at a national, regional, provincial, diocesan or other level, and, in turn, stipend rates may be determined by a national, regional, provincial, diocesan or parish assembly. Provision for non-stipendiary ordained ministry may be made within a church. A church should also make provision for the recurrent expenses of ministers.[233]

Protestant churches make elaborate provision for the maintenance of ministry. As in Lutheranism,[234] in which a church must provide 'adequate compensation',[235] so in Methodism there is a right to a stipend.[236] For instance, in the Methodist Church of Ireland: 'It is a principle of Methodism that every circuit is expected to take upon itself the responsibility of providing the funds necessary for the maintenance of its ministers, and the expenses incidental to the work within its bounds.'[237] Moreover: 'ministers receive support according to the requirements of themselves and their families, and not salaries according to the value which may be placed upon their services'.[238] Thus: 'Those in stipendiary ministry receive a stipend, in accordance with scales as laid down by the Conference'; the amount by which the income received from paid employment outside the circuit exceeds the gross amount determined from time to time by the Stipends and Allowances Board is deducted from the stipend and remitted in equal sums to the Treasurers of the Home Mission and Retirement Funds.[239] The ordinary expenditure of a circuit includes maintenance of ministers, and rent and taxes payable on their residences.[240] Non-stipendiary ministers are entitled to reimbursement of expenses in accordance with scales determined by the Stipends and Allowances Board, and retired ministers who conduct services are remunerated as directed by the Conference.[241] Similar provisions appear in the United Methodist Church.[242]

---

[233] PCLCCAC, Principle 91. See e.g. Ireland: Const., IV.51: 'all stipends ... paid to [the minister] by right of his office for the performance of his duties' are such as 'he might reasonably be expected to have'; Korea: Can. 40: Synod shall decide the basic 'salary' of the clergy; Wales: Const., VI.22: the parish should pay clergy expenses.

[234] ELCA: Const., Ch. 15.12: the presiding bishop must develop and manage policies to compensate ministers.

[235] ELCIRE: Const., Art. 21: the stipends, expenses and e.g. housing allowances for pastors; ELCA: Const., Ch. 14.20–21: 'salary structures'; ELCIC: ABL, Pt. II.2: a congregation provides for its pastor.

[236] MCGB: CPD, SO 801: ministers and deacons in active work and probationers appointed to stations 'shall ... receive stipends' prescribed by the Conference; this also deals with allowances and expenses.

[237] MCI: RDG, 13.01: Circuits may be assisted by the Home Mission Department, if there is 'necessity for it'.

[238] MCI: RDG, 13.07.

[239] MCI: RDG, 4C.10; 8.13-.8.15; 30: the Board recommends scales to Conference. See also MCNZ: LAR 2.22: 'Conference shall from time to time determine the Standard Stipend as a living allowance for its Ministers.'

[240] MCI: RDG, 13.04.

[241] MCI: RDG, 4C.12; see also 4H.04–06: employees in e.g. City Missions are remunerated in accordance with scales and expenses determined by Conference; 6.32: travelling expenses of ministers attending the Conference are paid at a rate determined by it; 6.66–67: removal expenses (from the General Purposes Fund).

[242] UMCNEAE: BOD, par. 342: 'The Church shall provide, and the ordained minister is entitled to receive, not less than the equitable compensation established by the annual conference for

By way of contrast, two approaches are used in Presbyterianism. In the Presbyterian Church of Scotland, the congregation is responsible for the stipend of its minister; if it cannot discharge this responsibility, provision for stipend is made from central funds to ensure that the minister does not receive less than the declared minimum stipend.[243] However, in the Presbyterian Church of Wales: 'A stipend structure is assured for every full-time minister, and is reviewed annually by the General Assembly'; the Life and Witness Board General Fund will be responsible for paying every full-time and part-time minister a stipend.'[244] Reformed and United churches have a similar range of provisions,[245] as do Baptists.[246]

Pensions and other benefits

Christian churches also provide for pensions for ordained ministers on retirement as well as other forms of benefit. Roman Catholic canon law requires provision to be made for ordained ministers to have social assistance by which their needs are suitably met if they suffer from illness, incapacity or old age: specific arrangements are supplied by particular norms.[247] Orthodox churches also provide for 'pensions for the clergy and church workers' and it is often mandatory for a cleric to join a pension programme.[248] Parallel arrangements are to be found in

---

clergy members.' See also MCNZ: LAR s. 2.24: accommodation is provided by the Parish on a basis determined by the Conference.

[243] CLCS: 136. See also PCANZ: BO 16.9: 'The congregation must determine the stipend and allowances for support of ministry in accordance with the current conditions of service prior to ministry settlement' and these and any variation in them must be approved by Presbytery; PCA: BCO, 10.6: 'The expenses of ministers and ruling elders in their attendance on courts shall be defrayed by the bodies which they respectively represent.'

[244] PCW: HOR, 4.11: deductions before payment include income tax, national insurance contributions and contributions to the pension scheme; 3.2.2: Presbytery is to supervise the maintenance of the ministry. See also PCI: Code, 82(3): 'A minister shall not enter any private or other arrangements with the congregation or its representatives, as to stipend ... either before or after his settlement among them, without the consent of the Presbytery and of the Union Commission'; 123: the Central Ministry Fund is 'to receive and distribute monies intended for the ministers and agents of the Church'.

[245] UCA: Regs., 2.4.20: 'A Minister called to serve an approved placement ... shall be paid a stipend'; if full-time, it must not be less than the minimum determined by Synod; if part-time, it is calculated on a proportionate basis of the minimum rate determined by the Synod; 2.4.21: housing; 3.18: a congregation must provide 'facilities and resources in support of ... stipends and allowances' and 'stipends shall be the first charge' on its funds; URC: Man., B., 2(6): General Assembly is 'to determine arrangements for payment of stipends and expenses to ministers'.

[246] CNBC: Const., par. 72: 'No director shall be remunerated for being or acting as a director ... but may be reimbursed for all expenses necessarily and reasonably incurred ... while engaged in the affairs of the Society'.

[247] CIC, c. 281.2; c. 1274: the Episcopal Conference must ensure an institute exists to provide for the social security of clergy if social insurance has not been arranged; c. 538:3: the diocesan bishop, taking into account norms of the Conference, must provide for the 'suitable support and housing' of pastors on attaining 75.

[248] GOAA: Regs., Art. 17.11; UOCIA: Statutes, Art. XV; ROMOC: Statutes, Art. 194; ROC: Statute V.28(n): Holy Synod commission on pensions; X.25: pensions for bishops; X.44(n): the Diocesan Assembly assists.

Methodist,[249] Presbyterian,[250] United and Uniting churches,[251] and in Baptist Unions.[252] By way of illustration, the following are principles about the subject in Anglicanism and Lutheranism. An Anglican church should provide financial support for clergy during their retirement. Ministers in receipt of a stipend are entitled to a pension upon their retirement on the basis of contributions made to and their membership of a clergy pension fund. A clergy pension fund should be set up at national, regional or provincial level in order to provide for pensions on retirement, maintenance for spouses and dependants, and awards during periods of disability or illness. A clergy pension fund is administered by trustees; they must keep audited accounts and make an annual report on the administration of the fund to the appropriate ecclesiastical assembly, but are not personally liable for losses to the fund unless such losses are the result of their own wilful default or culpable negligence. A proper actuarial relationship should be maintained between contributions made, levied and collected for, and the several benefits paid from, a clergy pension fund.[253] Lutheran churches also operate a system of benefits and pensions.[254] For example, the Evangelical Lutheran Church in America must provide 'adequate' benefits and pensions for those employed by the church.[255] The Board of Pensions manages and operates the Pension and Other Benefits Program and must provide pension, health and other benefits exclusively for the benefit of eligible members working within the church; it is to report periodically to the Church Council and through this to the Churchwide Assembly. The Board may make administrative changes and routine modifications to the Pension and Other Benefits Program, and changes required to comply with civil law; it also sets contribution rates for the church's Survivor Benefits Plan, Disability Benefits Plan,

---

[249] MCGB: CPD, SO 805–907: Pension Scheme; UMCUSA: Const., Div. 2.3, Art. VI: General Conference 'shall not appropriate the net income of the publishing houses, the book concerns, or the Chartered Fund to any purpose other than for the benefit of retired or disabled preachers, their spouses, widows, or widowers, and children or other beneficiaries of the ministerial pension systems'; see also UMCNEAE: BOD, par. 22.

[250] PCA: BCO, 14.1.12: one agency of General Assembly is Retirements and Benefits, Inc.; PCI: Code, 125A: the Pension Scheme (2009) Fund is fed by e.g. quarterly contributions assessed on congregations.

[251] UCA: Regs., 2.4.22: 'Assembly shall establish and maintain a retirement fund and such other beneficiary funds for Ministers as the Assembly may consider appropriate, and shall determine the conditions upon which a Minister may be required to participate or may be exempt from participation in such funds'; UCC: Man., V.

[252] BUSA: BL, 10: The BUSA Pension Fund; JBU: Const., Art. XV.5.

[253] PCLCCAC, Principle 92. See e.g. Korea: Can. 40: clergy pensions and severance pay are determined by the National Synod; TEC: Cans. I.1.8: the Church Pensions Fund, a corporation under civil law, may establish a clergy pension system including life, accident and health benefits for those clergy who are retired or disabled by age or infirmity and for their surviving spouses and children; Canada: Can. VIII: actuarial relationship.

[254] ELCIC: Const., Art. XVI and ABL, Pt. XVI: each synod, congregation, and agency must co-operate with the National Church Council to ensure that pension and benefit plans are available and that each eligible minister and lay employee is enrolled in the plan(s); Pt. II.2: a congregation must also ensure the participation of its minister, when eligible, in the benefit plan and pension plan; Pt. XIV: pension plan.

[255] ELCA: Const., Ch. 4.03 and Ch. 11.20–21. See also LCMS: Const., Art. III and BL, 1.1.1: the Synod must 'Aid in providing for the welfare of pastors, teachers, and other church workers, and their families in the event of illness, disability, retirement, special need, or death.'

Medical and Dental Benefits Plan and Retirement Plan. The Corporate Social Responsibility Committee of the Pensions Board is guided on these matters by the Advisory Committee on Corporate Social Responsibility.[256]

Conclusion

A comparative examination of the regulatory instruments of churches on property and finance tells us a great deal about the common actions in which Christians are engaged across the traditions studied here. Whatever church they may belong to, irrespective of their denominational affiliation, as a result of their laws, Christians own, administer and dispose of real and personal property, dedicate their sacred places and objects to God, forbidding activities with regard to them which are inconsistent with those sacred purposes, give, receive and account for funds, and remunerate and provide pensions and other benefits for their ordained ministers. Moreover, from the study of these regulatory instruments emerge principles of Christian law common to all churches. A church has the right to acquire, administer and dispose of property and should seek for its institutions legal personality under civil law to enable this. Property vests in prescribed institutions, which act as its stewards, holding it on trust for the benefit of the church and its work. Places of worship and prescribed objects should be dedicated to the purposes of God and activities carried out in relation to them, and work carried out on them, should not be inconsistent with their spiritual purposes. Ecclesiastical property, including records, should be maintained carefully and insured. A church has a right to receive, hold and invest income to further its objects. Budgets should be prepared, and accounts kept and audited systematically. The faithful should contribute cheerfully according to their means to sustain the work of the church, and the institutions of church government may require contributions to church expenses by means of compulsory payments, made particularly at the level of the local church. Income should be spent only to further the objects of a church, but financial provision should be made to maintain ministry, especially in the form of remuneration, benefits and pensions. In all of this, a church should comply with the civil law applicable to its property and finances.

---

[256] ELCA: Const., Ch. 17.60–61: the President of the corporation serves as chief executive.

10

Church, State and society

We have already seen that one function of the regulatory instruments of churches is to address the external relations of a church with ecclesial bodies outside its own tradition as part of the ecumenical movement, the availability to wider society of rituals such as marriage, the public dimensions of profession of the faith and worship, and civil law applicable to church property and finance. This chapter explores further the rules of churches in their external relations with the State and wider civil society, a matter upon which denominations have historically differed in terms of the neutrality that they require from the State in its own legal posture towards religion and the position of Christian churches under civil constitutions. The chapter examines the theological stance of each church towards the State, its nature and its functions, and the working out of this stance in ecclesiastical regulatory instruments. The study moves on to examine the positions of Christian churches under civil law in the European context from the perspective of the State. The juridical approaches of churches to human rights and religious freedom in society are dealt with in the third section of the chapter. The next section examines the formal structures which churches have, under their own ecclesiastical regulatory instruments, particularly their institutions, to engage with the wider society in terms of social responsibility and charitable activity. The chapter also explores how churches regulate promotion of their activities in the life of public institutions, particularly schools, hospitals, prisons and the armed forces. It draws conclusions about the degree to which the rules of the churches facilitate or hinder their engagement with the State and society. It also proposes that whilst there are profound differences between denominations, the similarities between their regulatory instruments indicate principles of Christian law common to all churches with regard to church and State relations, human rights and religious freedom, social responsibility and Christian ministry in the public institutions of the State.

Church and State

As a general pattern, the juridical instruments of the churches address: the nature and purpose of the State; the distinct identity and functions of the church as against those of the State; the need for co-operation between church and State; the recognition and applicability of civil law to the church; Christian involvement in politics; disobedience by the faithful to unjust laws; and the avoidance in disputes amongst the faithful of recourse to the courts of the State. The regulatory instruments of each of the ecclesiastical traditions are dealt with here *seriatim*.

The Catholic Church teaches that: there is no authority except from God; every human community needs an authority to endure and develop; the 'political community and public authority are based on human nature and therefore ... belong to an order established by God'; the diversity of political regimes is legitimate; political authority must be exercised within the limits of the moral order; and it is 'the role of the State to defend and promote the common good of civil society', namely: 'the sum total of social conditions which allow people, either as groups or individuals, to reach their fulfilment more fully and more easily'. However, 'in their own domain, the political community and the church are independent from one another and autonomous' but they should develop a 'mutual cooperation' in favour of the welfare of all human beings.[1] Indeed, the Latin Code recognises the qualified applicability of the law of the State to the church: 'When the law of the Church remits some issue to the civil law, the latter is to be observed with the same effects in canon law, in so far as it is not contrary to divine law, and provided it is not otherwise stipulated in canon law'.[2] In other words, for the faithful, 'unjust laws ... would not be binding in conscience'.[3] Moreover, Catholic canon law provides for the appointment of papal legates to States,[4] forbids clerics 'to assume public office whenever it means sharing in the exercise of civil power',[5] asserts that 'no rights or privileges of election, appointment, presentation or designation of bishops are conceded to civil authorities',[6] and enables an ecclesiastical tribunal to refrain from imposing a penalty if the offender has been or will be 'sufficiently punished by the civil authority'.[7] Similar ideas and norms are to be found in the Code of Canons of the Oriental Catholic Churches.[8]

The Orthodox canonical tradition proposes that church and State derive their authority from one and the same divine source: 'The Church was founded by God, the birth of the State is a product of the will of Divine Providence for the world' but each is 'self-sufficient and independent in the sphere of its jurisdiction' – the church is not limited in space and time, but States are; the church is one, but States are many; the church seeks the salvation of souls, the State, peace and order; and the church has at its disposal spiritual means, the State, material.[9] Thus, the church

---

[1] CCC, pars. 1918–1924, 1927; GS 26, 74, 76; Rom. 13.1: all authority is from God.
[2] CIC, c. 22; see e.g. c. 98.2: for 'the appointment of guardians ... the provisions of civil law are to be observed, unless it is otherwise prescribed in canon law'; c. 110: 'Children ... adopted in accordance with the civil law are considered the children of ... those persons who have adopted them'; c. 197: 'Prescription [is] accepted [as] it is ... in the civil legislation'; c. 1059: the marriage of a Catholic is 'governed not only by divine law but also by canon law, without prejudice to the competence of civil authority in respect of [its] civil effects'; c. 1062.1: 'A promise of marriage ... is governed by the ... law [of] the Bishops' Conference ... after consideration of such custom and civil laws as may exist'; c. 1284.2: administrators must 'ensure that the ownership of ecclesiastical goods is safeguarded in the ways ... valid in civil law'; c. 1290: secular contract law is to be observed if 'the civil law is not contrary to divine law, and that canon law does not provide otherwise'.
[3] CCC, pars. 1897–1942; GS 29–31.   [4] CIC, c. 362–367.
[5] CIC, c. 285.3; CLLS, par. 593: if 'it would serve a spiritual purpose' a bishop could (under c. 87) 'dispense' from c. 285.3 'in a particular case' for a 'just and reasonable cause' as demanded by c. 90.
[6] CIC, c. 377.   [7] CIC, c. 1344.2.
[8] See e.g. CCEO, c. 1504: applicability of civil law; c. 616: church teaching on civil society; cc. 98 and 100: the power of the patriarch in civil affairs; c. 910: civil law is to be observed as to guardianship.
[9] OOCL: 205–210 (citing Matt. 22.21): 'Render unto God that which is God's and unto Caesar that which is Caesar's'; the church was founded directly (Matt. 16.18) and equipped

should not be subject to the State, nor should the State be subject to the church, but they should co-exist in harmonious co-operation – 'the *symphonia* of the sacred and secular power'.[10] In turn, the juridical instruments of Orthodox churches deal with, typically, co-operation with the State and its authorities,[11] the applicability of civil law to the church,[12] the registration of a church as a legal entity in civil law,[13] determination of church–State relations by a church assembly,[14] and representation of a church in relations with the State and its institutions by bishops at national and diocesan level,[15] and by clergy at local level.[16] Orthodox laws also deal with recourse to civil courts and engagement in politics. For instance, the ordained and lay members of the Russian Orthodox Church 'cannot apply to the authorities of the State or to the civil courts on matters which pertain to the internal life of the church, including canonical governance, church order, liturgical or pastoral activities'; also: 'The canonical units of the [Church] shall not engage in political activities and shall not rent their premises for political events.'[17] One of the dioceses of the Russian Orthodox Church provides that: 'The Diocese shall not participate in political parties and movements, and shall not provide them with financial or any other assistance and support.'[18] Similarly, the Standing Conference of Orthodox

---

(Matt. 18.20; Acts 15.28) by God; States were founded by God indirectly, 'for cohabitation and union ... through human laws'.

[10] L. Patsavos, 'The canonical tradition of the Orthodox Church', in F.K. Litsas (ed.), *A Companion to the Greek Orthodox Church* (Greek Orthodox Archdiocese of North and South America, New York, 1984) 137 at 137; R. Potz, 'State and church in European countries with an Orthodox tradition', III *Derecho y Religion* (2008) 33; OOCL 206.

[11] See e.g. ROMOC: Statutes, Art. 4.2: the church 'establishes relations of dialogue and cooperation with the State' to accomplish its 'pastoral, spiritual-cultural, educational and social-charitable mission'.

[12] SOCA: Const., Art. 18: the patriarch is to notify 'civilian authorities' about prescribed ministerial appointments; UOCIA: Instructions, Policy on Marriages, 2: 'A civil marriage licence must be obtained from the appropriate civil authorities' prior to church marriage; Code of Pastoral Conduct, 2.1: information obtained by counselling is confidential, 'except ... as required by law'; Sexual Abuse Policy, I: reporting to civil authorities; ROC: Statute, XI.13: brotherhoods are subject to e.g. 'the civil statutes' of the church, diocese and parish; XI.45: dismissal from a Parish Council for breach of the parish 'civil statute'; GOAA: Regs., Art. 16: a parish holds property in its corporate name 'except as otherwise required by any applicable civil law'.

[13] ROC: Statute, I.5; see also e.g. Dioc. of Sourozh: Statutes, I.4: 'The diocese may ... sue and be sued in court'; II.11: 'The Diocese may, with the ... consent of [its] Hierarch, incorporate legal entities.'

[14] ROC: Statute, II.5(g): the Local Council is to 'determine and adjust the principles of relations between the Church and the State'; Dioc. of Sourozh: Statutes, I.7: 'The Diocese shall have the right to liaise with local authorities [as] to the matters which may affect its activities.'

[15] GOAA: Charter, Art. 6.9: the Archbishop '[r]epresents the Archdiocese and Ecumenical Patriarchate in their dealings with all ... civil authorities' in the USA; UOCIA: Statutes, Art. IV.1; ROMOC: Statutes, Art. 26(c); ROC: Statute, X.17: the bishop, for the 'bodies of State authority'.

[16] ROC: Statute, XI.20(i); see also XI.46(k): the Parish Council must maintain contact with public authorities; XI.48: the churchwarden represents the parish in court proceedings; XI.59: the parish meeting 'is entitled to bring an action in court with the prior consent of the Diocesan Bishop'.

[17] ROC: Statute, I.9–10. See also GOAA: Regs., Addendum B, Dispute Resolution Procedures: the faithful should not resort to secular courts to resolve disputes; this cites 1 Cor. 6.1, 7.

[18] ROC: Diocese of Sourozh: Statutes, I.6.

Bishops in the Americas 'shall not participate in, or intervene in (including the publication or distribution of statements), any political campaign on behalf of any candidate for public office'.[19] Clergy must not seek political office.[20] This stance is shared broadly by Anglican churches globally in terms of how they view the State,[21] co-operation with it, the applicability of civil law, political activity,[22] recourse to the courts of the State in disputes between the faithful[23] and deference to the State in its domain.[24]

The Protestant Reformation in northern Europe saw the development of the principle that subjects should follow the religion of their ruler: *cuius regio eius religio*.[25] Today, the juridical instruments of Lutheran churches refer to the doctrine of the 'two kingdoms' – earthly and heavenly – designed *inter alia* 'to guide the church in its relations with the world, especially government'. First, the doctrine 'does not call for a separation of church and state but for a proper distinction between them': God rules 'all people, Christians and non-Christians, in his earthly kingdom through the agency of secular government [and] law' and 'he rules all Christians in his spiritual kingdom ... through the gospel [and] grace'.[26] Secondly, Christians are 'citizens of two kingdoms': 'The two reigns of God are also mutually dependent'; the church needs the State to ensure freedom of religion and the State needs 'the prayers and intercessions of the church (whether it realises it or

---

[19] SCOBA: Const., Art. VII.
[20] OCIA: GC, A Selection of Clergy Disciplines, 8: 'Clergy must not run for political office' (Carthage, c. 16).
[21] For classical Anglicanism, see AR, Art. 37: Of the Civil Magistrates: the monarch has 'the chief Government of all estates ... whether ... Ecclesiastical or Civil'; 'we give not to our Princes the ministering ... of God's Word, or ... Sacraments ... but that only prerogative ... given always to all godly Princes in holy Scriptures by God himself; that is, that they should rule all estates and degrees committed to their charge by God, whether they be Ecclesiastical or Temporal, and restrain with the civil sword the stubborn and evildoers'.
[22] PCLCCAC, Principle 46.2-3: processing data is subject to civil law; 71.1-3: ministers and parties must comply with civil law as to marriage formation; 72.5-6: civil marriage; 74.1 and 3: civil nullity of marriage; 75: no recourse immediately to civil courts on breakdown of marriage; 77.5-7: civil law on disclosure of information in breach of the seal of the confessional; 80.1-2: trustees must comply with civil law.
[23] TEC: Cans. IV.14.2: 'No Member of the Clergy ... may resort to the secular courts for the purpose of delaying, hindering or reviewing any proceeding' of the church's tribunals; '[n]o secular court shall have authority to review, annul, reverse, restrain or otherwise delay any proceeding' of these tribunals; North India: Const., II.V.VII: 'No bishop, presbyter or any other member ... should go to a civil court, for enforcing any of his spiritual and religious rights under the [church] Constitution' or the rules made under it.
[24] Ireland: Const. VIII.26.4: the Court of General Synod must not determine 'any matter ... which, in the opinion of the lay judges, is within the jurisdiction and more proper to be submitted to the ... decision of a civil tribunal'.
[25] J. Witte, *Law and Protestantism: The Legal Teachings of the Lutheran Reformation* (Cambridge University Press, 1990).
[26] LCA: Statement on the Two Kingdoms, 1-2: Rom. 13:1-5 and 1 Peter 2:13,14 are cited. See also ELCSA: G., 12.4: 'The Two Regiments of God: God is the Lord of this world. In His Church He works through Word and Sacrament, in the worldly sphere through worldly orders. Both ... are clearly ... distinguished, yet may not be separated ... The state does not rule over the Church nor the Church over the state: God rules over both.'

not)' to fulfil its tasks properly.[27] Thirdly, whilst the church 'is not called to develop and implement policies for a more just and equitable society', the church has 'every right' to be 'the conscience of society' and 'hold governments ... accountable to the public, and ultimately to God'. Fourthly: 'church and state must be clearly distinguished but not separated' though 'each has its own area of competence and responsibility': secular government must not interfere with the proclamation of the gospel, and ... the church must not use the agency of the state ... to promote the gospel or Christianise society'. Thus: 'The Church ... ought not to interfere ... in the affairs of the State: but it must bear witness to the truth ... and may therefore, for the instruction of its members and as a public testimony, have to condemn or approve acts of the State' even if the consequence is 'oppression and persecution on the part of the State'.[28] As such, Lutherans may assume political office and participate in the exercise of civil power.[29] Fifthly, whilst Lutherans are subject to 'the laws of the land', 'Obedience to all forms of human government is never absolute but always limited and conditional. If it means disobedience to God, our allegiance to God must come first.'[30] In turn, whilst there should be 'institutional separation' of church and State: both need to co-operate in matters of common concern;[31] church bodies may have personality under civil law;[32] central assemblies are to '[d]etermine and implement policy for [a] church's relationship to governments';[33] civil laws apply to the church;[34] ministers must obey State law unless there are grounds in conscience for civil disobedience to

[27] LCA: Statement on the Two Kingdoms, 1-2: 'when the state becomes tyrannical ... it exceeds its God-given bounds. Then we are freed from our obligation to obey it' (1 Peter 2:13; 1 Tim. 2:1-2).

[28] LCA: Theses on the Church, par. 16: 'The Church must act according to the instruction ... "Render unto Caesar the things which are Caesar's, and unto God the things that are God's" (Matt. 22:21) ... "obey God rather than men" (Acts 5:29)'; John 18:36: 'the Lord has removed the Church from the sphere of earthly dominion, political activity, and the like, and assigned to it the spiritual sphere, with the Word as its only weapon'.

[29] AC, Art. 16: 'all government and all established rule and laws were instituted by God for the sake of good order, and ... Christians may without sin occupy civil offices and engage in ... civil affairs'; also: 'the gospel does not overthrow civil authority, the state, and marriage but requires that all these be kept as true divine orders' (or 'orders of creation'), unless to do so would mean disobeying God (Acts 5:29).

[30] LCA: Statement on the Two Kingdoms, 3: this cites Acts 5:29.

[31] ELCA: Const., Ch. 4.03: the church must e.g. 'work with civil authorities in areas of mutual endeavour, maintaining institutional separation of church and state in a relation of functional interaction', and institute processes to 'foster mutuality and interdependence' to involve people 'in making decisions that affect them'.

[32] ELCIC: Const., Art. I: Evangelical Lutheran Church in Canada Act; ELCA: Articles of Incorporation, Art. II (under 'the laws of the State of Minnesota'); LCA: Const., Art. I: the church is '[a]n association incorporated under the Associations Incorporation Acts 1956-1965 of the State of South Australia'; ELCIRE: Const., 1(1): the church is a registered charity under the Taxes Consolidation Act 1997, s. 207.

[33] ELCA: Const., 11.20-21.

[34] ELCA: Const., 17.60-61: the Board of Pensions must 'comply with federal and state law'; Model Const. for Congregations, 12.0: 'Consistent with the laws of the state', a congregation may adopt procedures to remove a Council member; LCMS: BL, 1.4.4: 'Any issues relative to ... the laws of ... Missouri shall be resolved in accord with ... the Constitution and Bylaws of the Synod'; LCGB: RAR, Congregations, 3: a congregation is 'to comply with legal requirements, for example those concerned with charity, employment and taxation law'.

'unjust law';[35] and recourse should not generally be made to secular courts: 'It is the policy of this church not to resort to the civil courts ... until all internal procedures and appeals have been exhausted, except for emergency situations involving a significant imminent risk of physical injury or severe loss or damage to property.'[36]

The Methodist position on church and State is similar to the Lutheran. A particularly full treatment of the subject is found in the United Methodist Church. First: 'civil government derives its just powers from the sovereign God', is a 'servant of God and human beings' and should be 'based on, and be responsible for, the recognition of human rights under God'.[37] Secondly: 'Separation of church and state means no organic union of the two, but it does permit interaction. The state should not use its authority to promote particular religious beliefs' nor 'attempt to control the church, nor should the church seek to dominate the state'; rather: 'The rightful and vital separation of church and state, which has served the cause of religious liberty, should not be misconstrued as the abolition of all religious expression from public life.'[38] Thirdly, the strength of a political system depends upon the participation of its citizens; as such: 'The church should continually exert a strong ethical influence upon the state, supporting policies and programs deemed to be just and opposing policies and programs that are unjust.'[39] Fourthly, Christians must obey the law of the State: 'It is the duty of all Christians, and especially of all Christian ministers, to observe and obey the laws and commands of the governing or supreme authority of the country of which they are citizens or subjects or in which they reside, and ... to encourage and enjoin

---

[35] NALC: SFPM, B.7: 'The society in which the Church ministers, has placed a high premium on the rule of law in regulating the rights and duties of individuals to promote the common good'; thus: 'being convicted ... is grounds for discipline as conduct incompatible with ... ministerial office but may not be grounds for discipline ... where the violation of law was to protest or to test a perceived unjust law or as an expression of civil disobedience'; ELCA: Const., 7.43: call to ordained ministry 'does not imply any employment relationship or contractual obligation in regard to employment on the part of the Synod Council or Church Council'.

[36] ELCA: Const., Ch. 20.16; 5.01: the composition and actions of a church assembly, council, and committee must not 'be challenged in a court of law'; LCA: Const., Art. IV.1: in property disputes a congregation must (under 1 Cor. 6) 'make every effort to avoid action in the civil courts'; 21: indemnification of church officers party to proceedings in secular courts; LCMS: BL, 1.10.1–1.10.3: 'Christians are encouraged to seek to resolve all their disputes without resorting to secular courts', e.g. in 'theological, doctrinal, or ecclesiastical issues'.

[37] UMCNEAE: BOD, par. 103, Confession of Faith, Art. XVI; par. 164: the State as servant of God; par. 103, AR, Art. XXIII: Rulers of the USA: 'The President, the Congress [etc] ... are the rulers of the [USA], according to the division of power made to them' by the Constitution and the states. See also FMCNA: BOD, par. 159: the State is a 'God-ordained institution'; par. 3331: 'God has established the state to reward right and punish evil (1 Peter 2.14)'; par. 3330: members must be 'responsible citizens'; par. 3331: the church recognizes 'the sovereign authority of government and [the] duty to obey the law' (Matt. 22.21; Rom. 13.1–7).

[38] UMCNEAE: BOD, par. 164. Compare: MCI: RDG, 10.75–10.76: 'in harmony with the non-political character of the Methodist Church ... all party political questions shall be strictly excluded from ... the Council'.

[39] UMCNEAE: BOD, par. 164. See also FMCNA: BOD, par. 3331: church members may 'actively participate in civic life ... for the improvement of social, cultural and educational conditions' and exercise the vote.

obedience' to them.[40] However, fifthly: 'governments, no less than individuals, are subject to the judgment of God'; the church recognises, therefore, 'the right of individuals to dissent when acting under the constraint of conscience and, after having exhausted all legal recourse, to resist or disobey laws that they deem to be unjust or that are discriminately enforced' – but this requires 'refraining from violence' and 'being willing to accept the costs of disobedience'.[41] Some ministers make the declaration: 'While respecting the law, I will act to change unjust laws.'[42]

Methodist churches also enjoy the protection of their trusts by State law devoted specially to them.[43] In turn, Methodist laws recognise the general applicability of civil law to the church,[44] though not the status of ministers as employees under secular employment law,[45] and they assign functions to prescribed church bodies to engage in dialogue with civil government.[46] Some Methodist

---

[40] UMCNEAE: BOD, par. 103, AR, Art. XXVI; Confession of Faith, Art. XVI: 'Christian citizens [are] to give moral strength and purpose to their respective governments through sober, righteous and godly living.'

[41] UMCNEAE: BOD, par. 164: but, the norm is that: 'Citizens have a duty to abide by laws duly adopted by orderly and just process of government'; prayers should be offered 'for those in rightful authority ... and we support their efforts to afford justice and equal opportunity for all people'; 'We assert the duty of churches to support those who suffer because of their stands of conscience represented by nonviolent beliefs or acts.'

[42] MCNZ: LAR, Introductory Documents, III Ethical Standards for Ministry, Responsibilities to the Wider Community, 2.

[43] MCGB: CPD, Bk. I, Methodist Church Act 1976 (esp. Sch. 2, Model Trusts), Methodist Church Act 1939, Methodist Church Funds Act 1960; MCI: Const., s. 7: the Methodist Church in Ireland Act (Northern Ireland) 1928 and Methodist Church in Ireland Act (Saorstat Eireann) 1928: under these e.g. it is lawful for Conference to amend the Constitution by special resolution, make, vary and revoke rules and regulations as expedient for the general conduct of its proceedings and business, and authorise vesting of property in trustees; MCNZ: LAR, 3.13: trustees administer property under the Methodist Church Property Act 1887 (as amended).

[44] UMCNEAE: BOD, par. 258.3: the local church must keep itself informed of 'personnel matters in relationship to ... civil law'; par. 2532: trust funds must be invested 'in conformity with laws of the country, state or like political unit in which the local church is located'; MCI: RDG, 4H.01-03: contracts on employment for lay employees; MCGB: CPD, SO 018: in employing lay persons, every church body must comply with the civil legislation and implement an equal opportunities policy; COTN: Man., par. 113.4: 'where the civil law requires a specific course of procedure in ... church meetings, that course should be strictly followed'; par. 142: 'where the civil law requires a specific mode of election of church trustees, that mode shall be strictly followed'.

[45] UMCNEAE: BOD, par. 142: 'clergy ... are not employees of the local church, the district, or the annual conference'; but, for certain purposes (e.g. taxation and insurance) 'governments ... may classify clergy as employees': 'Such classifications are not to be construed as affecting or defining United Methodist polity' and 'should be accepted, if at all, only for limited purposes ... with the full recognition ... that it is the responsibility of the clergy to be God's servants'; MCNZ: LAR, 2.1: 'A Minister is not an employee of the Church. Ministers are persons in a special relationship with and appointed by the Conference ... with powers, duties, rights and functions as set out in this Law Book, and entitled to such ... allowances as ... determined' by Conference.

[46] MCI: RDG, 8.10: 'In public ceremonies in which the Church should be represented, or ... appointments of a public character ... the presentation of addresses, or ... matters in which the legal rights of the Methodist people are involved ... the General Committee shall act on behalf of the Church' (or may delegate this function).

churches permit ministers to participate in the work of political parties,[47] and to stand for local civil office, subject, for example, to consideration of the effects of this on ministry and discipline, consultation with the district superintendent (who must consult, for example, the circuit officials) and the approval of the District Advisory Committee.[48] Similar rules apply with regard to parliamentary elections.[49] As a general principle, however: 'In no circumstances shall church or manse property be used for any kind or form of political electioneering.'[50] The Methodist Church in Great Britain has several rules on the subject: 'Managing trustees may not sponsor meetings in support of political parties, nor may such meetings be held in the name of any other Methodist body'; however, they may permit occasional use of Methodist property for political meetings by non-Methodist bodies and sponsor meetings to promote discussion of public issues in the context of Christian theology and ethics, provided this does not have a 'detrimental effect on the peace and unity of the Church and its witness'. Moreover: 'It is not permitted to submit resolutions, or take votes, on political matters during any Methodist meeting for public religious worship, or while the congregation is assembling or dispersing'; nor 'to invite signatures for petitions on political matters during any Methodist meeting for public religious worship, or while the congregation is assembling or dispersing, except with the consent of the Church Council or of some person or persons to whom the council has delegated authority for that purpose'.[51] However, Methodist laws are generally more permissive when it comes to proceedings in the courts of the State; for example: 'No lawsuit relating to churches, schools or other Trust property shall be commenced without the consent of the General Committee through the Property Board, except by direction of the Conference'; without such consent or direction, 'the parties proceeding shall be held responsible for all expenses incurred by such lawsuit'.[52] Sometimes, Methodist rules specify which bodies are to represent the church in legal proceedings.[53]

---

[47] MCI: RDG, 4D.19: 'In view of the deep divisions in Irish politics it believes that ministers can most effectively bear their witness by the wise and enlightened application of Biblical insights to political issues and by the encouragement and enabling of Christian laypersons to enter party politics.'

[48] MCI: RDG, 4D.20-24.

[49] MCI: RDG, 4D.25; MCNZ: LAR, s. 2.10: 'No minister, or student for ministry, shall consent to nomination for any Parliamentary, Civic, or Public Office' so as to 'interfere with ministerial duties except with the consent' of the Parish Meeting, Board and President and President's Committee of Advice; if these withhold consent and the candidate proceeds, the President may e.g. require resignation and/or Disciplinary Procedures.

[50] MCI: RDG, 4D.20-24.

[51] MCGB: CPD, SO 921: before agreeing, the church must consider, in light of advice from the Connexional Team, whether permission would have a detrimental effect on the peace and unity of the Church and its witness.

[52] MCI: RDG, 29.20.

[53] MCNZ: LAR, 9.12: 'when the Church is a party to a dispute or litigation under civil or criminal law' the General Secretary (consulting the Chair of the Board of Administration) is responsible for: engaging suitably qualified counsel; taking steps to obtain legal opinion; and carrying out the tasks set out in the Code of Disciplinary Procedures; 12. 4: in property transactions a Parish, Board, Committee or other entity requiring legal advice or action, must 'employ such professionally qualified person(s) as they may themselves choose'.

The Lutheran and Methodist approaches are broadly replicated in the Presbyterian tradition. The classical Presbyterian position is stated in the Book of Church Order of the Presbyterian Church in America: 'The power of the Church is exclusively spiritual; that of the State includes the exercise of force. The constitution of the Church derives from divine revelation; [that] of the State must be determined by human reason and the course of providential events. The Church has no right to construct or modify a government for the State, and the State has no right to frame a creed or polity for the Church.'[54] Therefore: 'No religious constitution should be supported by the civil power further than may be necessary for the protection and security equal and common to all others.'[55] However, the church must comply with the law of the State (particularly in matters of property and finance);[56] but: 'although civil rulers are bound to render obedience to Christ in their own province, yet they ought not to attempt in any way to constrain anyone's religious beliefs, or invade the rights of conscience'.[57] Some Presbyterian churches have State law devoted exclusively to them.[58] Presbyterian laws also sometimes assign to the moderator the function of representing the church in public affairs.[59]

Similar provisions are found in Reformed, United, Congregational and Baptist regulatory instruments. For the Reformed Churches, 'Christ, the only ruler and head of the Church, has therein appointed a government distinct from civil government and in things spiritual not subordinate thereto, and that civil authorities, being always subject to the rule of God, ought to respect the rights of conscience and of religious belief and to serve God's will of justice and peace for all humankind'.[60] The church should therefore exercise no authority over the State nor does the State over the church.[61] Nevertheless, some churches have State law devoted exclusively to them,[62] and, while they assert that ministers are not

---

[54] PCA: BCO, 3.4: 'They are as planets moving in concentric orbits' (Matt. 22.21); 11.1: church assemblies are 'altogether distinct from the civil magistracy, and have no jurisdiction in political or civil affairs'; PCI: Code, I.IV.15: Christ 'has appointed [in the church] a government distinct from civil authority'; His Kingdom is not of this world, 'its laws ... founded on His authority' and 'directed to the conscience'; 'their sanctions are spiritual'.

[55] PCA: BCO, Preface I.1–3; Preamble, II.1; II.8: ecclesiastical discipline is 'not attended with any civil effects'.

[56] PCA: BCO, 59.1: 'It is proper that every commonwealth, for the good of society, make laws to regulate marriage, which all citizens are bound to obey'; PCW: Const. for a Local Church, 9.17: the trustees may let or dispose of property 'in accordance with the restrictions imposed by the Charities Act 1993' (as amended).

[57] PCI: Code, I.III.13; this cites the Act of the Church of Scotland 1647.

[58] PCI: Irish Presbyterian Church Act 1871; PCANZ: Presbyterian Church Property Act 1885.

[59] PCANZ: BO, 14.17(4): the moderator also makes 'statements' on behalf of the church; PCA: BCO 59.1: 'It is proper that every commonwealth ... make laws to regulate marriage, which all citizens are bound to obey'.

[60] URC: Man., BU A, Sch. D, Version I, 8.

[61] RCA: BCO, Preamble: 'The church shall not exercise authority over the state, nor should the state usurp authority over the church' – Christ is 'the only Head of the Church'.

[62] URC: United Reformed Church Acts 1972, 1981 and 2000: these set out e.g. the trusts for places of worship and manses; RCA: the General Synod of the Reformed Protestant Dutch Church was incorporated 'by an Act of the Legislature of the State of New York ... 1819'; an Act of 1920 changed its name to its current name.

employees under civil law,[63] generally churches must comply with State law.[64] United and Congregational Churches also distinguish themselves from the State,[65] but seek 'to uphold the just authority of the State'.[66] United Churches may be legal entities under civil law,[67] but their members should not approach the courts of the 'civil power' in order to resolve their disputes.[68]

Baptist instruments also propose the separation of church and State. For example, the Baptist Union of Southern Africa affirms 'the principle of separation of church and state, in that, in the providence of God, the two differ in their respective natures and functions'. Thus: 'The Church is not to be identified with the State nor is it, in its faith or practice, to be directed or controlled by the State. The State is responsible for administering justice, ensuring an orderly community, and promoting the welfare of its citizens. The Church is responsible for preaching the Gospel and for demonstrating and making known God's will and care for all mankind.'[69] Similarly, for the Canadian National Baptist Convention: 'Church and state should be separate'; moreover: 'The state owes every church protection and full freedom in the pursuit of its spiritual ends. In providing for such freedom no ecclesiastical group or denomination should be favoured by the state more than others.' Also: 'Civil government being ordained of God, it is the duty of Christians to render loyal obedience thereto in all things not contrary to the revealed will of God. The church should not resort to the civil power to carry out its work.'[70] A Baptist Union is sometimes the subject of State law exclusively devoted to it,[71] but

---

[63] URC: Man., M.

[64] RCA: BCO, Ch. I, Pt. II, Art. 14.5: pastors must perform marriages 'subject to state and provincial law'.

[65] UCCSA: Const., Preamble: the church 'calls all people, society and states . . . to accept and obey Jesus Christ'.

[66] UCC: Man., BU 2.20; UCNI: Const., App. XIV: 'While the Church is autonomous [with] its own marriage laws . . . these must be carried out with due regard to the laws of the State', so Christian marriages are recognised.

[67] UCCSA: Const., 2.2: 'The legal status of the Church is that of a corporate body'; ABCUSA: BL, Art. XIII.6: 'The General Board shall determine appropriate Denominations Functions for each corporation managed by a national board, in the light of such corporation's charter or act of incorporation.'

[68] UFCS: Const., V.II.8: 'Application by office-bearers or members to the civil power or Courts for reduction, restraint, review, alteration, or control of the procedure in the . . . Courts of the Church, or of their decisions, is excluded. Parties . . . before the Church Courts, or affected by their decisions, are . . . precluded from recourse to the civil Courts'; UCCP: Const., Art. VIII.5: 'All questions of state policies and . . . the public justice of the State are beyond the jurisdiction of the Commission [on Discipline and Conflict Resolution]'; BL, Art. VI.4: 'No member . . . who is party to any controversy with another member or with the Church may institute any suit or proceeding or apply for remedy before any civil court . . . without . . . exhausting all intrachurch remedies.'

[69] BUSA: BL, 4.2.7. See also e.g. NABC: Statement of Beliefs, 7: 'Church and state exist by the will of God. Each has distinctive concerns and responsibilities, free from control by the other (Matthew 22.21).'

[70] CNBC: Const., 3, Statement of Faith, Art. XVII: 'The state has no right to impose taxes for the support of any form of religion. A free church in a free state is the Christian ideal, and this implies the right of free and unhindered access to God on the part of all men . . . without interference by the civil power.'

[71] BUGB: Baptist and Congregational Trusts Act 1961. Compare e.g. JBU: Const., Art. VII.6: the Union acts through e.g. a Statutory Corporation established by Act 16 of 1969.

some churches refuse submission to State laws as to matters properly pertaining to the autonomy of the church.[72] Sometimes instruments also forbid recourse to the civil courts.[73] They also provide for civil disobedience: a minister should undertake to be a 'good citizen' and 'to obey the laws of [the] government unless they require disobedience to the law of God' (New Zealand);[74] 'God alone is Lord of the conscience, and He has left it free from the doctrines and commandments of men, which are contrary to His Word or not contained in it' (Canada);[75] again: 'Christians should pray for civil leaders, and obey and support [the] government in matters not contrary to Scripture' (North America).[76]

In sum, according to the principles of Christian law which emerge from the similarities between the regulatory instruments of churches: the State is instituted by God; its function is to promote and protect the temporal and common good of society; the functions of the State are fundamentally different from those of the church; there should be a basic separation between church and State; church and State should co-operate in matters of common concern; the faithful may participate in politics to the extent permitted by church law; the church should comply with State law, but disobedience by the faithful to unjust laws is permitted; and the faithful should not resort to State courts unless all ecclesiastical process is exhausted.

The position of churches under State law

As we have seen above, churches across the Christian traditions studied here accept that church and State are distinct in their own spheres and that they should be institutionally separate. Equally, however, they all agree that there should be co-operation between church and State in matters of common concern.

[72] Bethel Baptist Church (Choctaw): Const., Art. XI: 'While Bethel Baptist Church recognizes the authority of the state over members of the church in those areas in which God has specifically granted the state authority in His Word (the Bible), the church maintains it is not subject to the state or any of its officers in its doctrines, offices, government, discipline, property, and practices. The state has no business in the affairs of the church other than what pertains to property, buildings, and codes affecting the same.' Asserting its rights under the US constitution, 'Bethel Baptist Church refuses to incorporate as a corporation under the laws of the State of Oklahoma, since such an incorporation subjects the Church of Jesus Christ to the laws of the state'.

[73] NBCUSA: Const., Art. IV.8: 'Under no circumstances shall a member [church] or group of members have the right to litigate, adjudicate, or arbitrate disputes and questions regarding membership rights, privileges, and procedures of this Body in the secular courts or any other forum other than that prescribed by this constitution'; NBC: PAP, Court Cases: 'Crises within the Baptist family should be resolved in accordance with the Convention Constitution ... All cases in Court instituted by individuals, churches, associations or conference or group of persons against the Convention or any of its components should be withdrawn from Court', otherwise exclusion follows until 'the conduct is purged'; BUSA: BL 2(b): 'It shall be a condition for ministry that every Minister ... shall accept without resort to a Court of Law the decision of the Executive and the Assembly.'

[74] BUNZ: EPGP, 6: 'I will be a good citizen'; 'I will endeavour to obey the laws of my government unless they require disobedience to the law of God'; NABC: Code of Ministerial Ethics: 'I will obey the laws of my government as long as they do not conflict with the laws of God and will practice Christian citizenship without engaging in partisan or political activities that would discredit the integrity of the ministry.'

[75] CNBC: Const., 3, Statement of Faith, XVII.

[76] NABC: Statement of Belief, 7: this cites 1 Timothy 2.1–4; Romans 13.1–7; 1 Peter 2.13–16.

Co-operation is no better illustrated than by State laws which deal with the position under civil law of the churches themselves. There is ample evidence from State laws to indicate the preparedness of churches for co-operation on this matter. However, the degree of co-operation may vary as between the Christian traditions. What follows examines the position of churches under the national laws of States in Europe. In broad terms, at least at the level of constitutional law, there are three European approaches to this subject: the State–church model (such as Denmark and Malta); the separation model (such as France and Slovenia); and the co-operation model (such as Italy and Spain).[77] All the traditions studied here participate directly or indirectly in one or other of these models.

As the mission of the Catholic Church determines the nature of its relationship with the political community, so it may enter agreements (*conventiones*) with States to fulfil that mission. These may include concordats with sovereign States entered on the basis that the Holy See has personality in international law (with treaty-making capacity), as does the Vatican City.[78] Consequently, the canons of the Latin Code do not abrogate nor derogate from 'agreements entered into by the Apostolic See with nations or other civil entities'; for this reason, 'these agreements continue in force as hitherto, notwithstanding any contrary provisions of this Code'.[79] Concordats between the Holy See and a State cover a range of subjects and other agreements may deal with discrete matters.[80] The concordat between the Holy See and Poland is typical: 'The Republic of Poland and the Holy See reaffirm that the State and the Catholic Church are, each in its own domain, independent and autonomous, and that they are fully committed to respecting this principle in all their mutual relations and in co-operating for the promotion of the benefit of humanity and the good of the community'.[81] In Italy, amendments to concordats with the Church must be agreed by both parties and their parliamentary ratification is subject to scrutiny by the Italian Constitutional Court.[82] Equally,

---

[77] See generally N. Doe, *Law and Religion in Europe: A Comparative Introduction* (Oxford University Press, 2011).
[78] See e.g. I. Brownlie, *Principles of Public International Law* (6th edn., Oxford University Press, 2003) 63–64: in a Treaty and Concordat of 1929, Italy recognised 'the Sovereignty of the Holy See in the international domain' and its exclusive jurisdiction over the City of the Vatican which, for Brownlie, is 'proximate to a state'.
[79] CIC c. 3; c. 113.1: the 'Church and the Apostolic See have the status of a moral person by divine disposition'.
[80] See e.g. Spain: Const., Art. 16.1: 'No religion shall have a state character. Public authorities shall take the religious beliefs of Spanish society into account and shall in consequence maintain appropriate cooperation with the Catholic Church and the other religious communities'; Agreement with the Holy See, 28 July 1976; Agreement on Legal Affairs, 4 Dec. 1979; Agreement on Educational and Cultural Affairs, 2 Jan. 3 1979.
[81] Concordat 1993, Art. 1; Const., Art. 25.4: 'The relations between [Poland] and the Roman Catholic Church shall be determined by international treaty concluded with the Holy See, and by statute.'
[82] Const., Art. 7: they are 'according to its own order, independent and sovereign' and their 'relations are ruled by the Lateran Treaties'; the Lateran Concordat 1929 was replaced with another in 1984; subsequent agreements have been entered (e.g. on church holidays (1985) and cultural and religious heritage (1996)); Constitutional Court, Decision no 30 of 1971. See also e.g. Lithuania: Agreement with the Holy See on Legal Affairs 2000, Art. 4: the church is free to carry out its activities 'in accordance with Canon Law' and the laws of the Republic.

the Catholic Church may in some States be recognised as the official State religion (e.g. Malta and Lichtenstein),[83] but in others have the status of a private voluntary association, or else its civil legal personality may be recognised by way of legislation or registration.[84]

By way of contrast, Orthodox churches do not have formal concordats with States. However, in some European countries, an Orthodox church is the State church. The Greek constitution provides that the 'prevailing religion' is that of the Orthodox Church of Greece; united with the Ecumenical Patriarchate of Constantinople, the church is autocephalous and administered by its Holy Synods.[85] There is a low level of State control. The church has personality in public law and a statutory charter approved by parliament; and its holy canons are invulnerable from challenge in State courts as to doctrine and liturgy.[86] Moreover, the President of Greece must take a Christian oath.[87] The Council of State has a supervisory jurisdiction over the church in matters of administration and may determine the competence of a church body to decide the matter and ensure that the decision complies with State law.[88] However, it has no jurisdiction over matters which relate to doctrine and worship or those which have 'spiritual and purely religious content' (such as a decision about the suitability of a candidate for ordination).[89] The Council of State has held that the decisions of the ecclesiastical courts are reviewable in so far as they are disciplinary bodies,[90] and it has reviewed cases involving the transfer and dismissal of clergy.[91] By way of contrast, in separation systems Orthodox churches have the status of a private voluntary association, and in co-operation systems they may enjoy the protection of laws specifically devoted to them: this is the case in Belgium[92] and Lithuania, for example.[93] However, Bulgarian law provides that: 'Religious institutions shall be

---

[83] Malta: Const., Art. 2: 'The Religion of Malta is the Roman Catholic Apostolic Religion'; Lichtenstein: Const., Art. 37: 'The Roman Catholic Church is the State Church and as such enjoys the full protection of the State.'

[84] See e.g. Ireland: Catholic canon law is classified as a species of 'foreign law' and it must be proved by expert witnesses: *Colquhoun v Fitzgibbon* [1937] IR 555; for registration, see Doe, *Law and Religion in Europe*, 33–35, 98–108.

[85] Const., Art. 3; also 'The text of the Holy Scriptures shall be maintained unaltered'; translation of the text 'without prior sanction by the ... Church of Greece and the Great Church of Christ in Constantinople, is prohibited'.

[86] For the statutory charter, see Law 590/1977, Art. 1(4) (under Const., Art. 3 in conjunction with Art. 72); see the Charter, Arts. 4, 6, 9: the competences of the Permanent Holy Synod and Holy Synod of the Hierarchy.

[87] Const., Art. 33: the oath is taken 'in the name of the Holy and Consubstantial and Indivisible Trinity'.

[88] See Ch. K. Papastathis, 'Religious self-administration in the Hellenic Republic', in G. Robbers (ed.), *Church Autonomy* (Peter Lang, Frankfurt am Main, 2001) 425 at 427.

[89] COS, Decision No. 491/1940, 583/1940: the Council declined jurisdiction to question refusal of a metropolitan to ordain a person on the basis of spiritual unsuitability; No. 545–6/1978: if a matter has both an administrative and a spiritual dimension, its administrative aspects are reviewable.

[90] COS, Decision No. 195/1987, 825/1988; No. 1534/1992: annulling a bishop's court decision.

[91] COS, Decision No. 5761/1974: transfer; No. 824/1949: discharge; No. 4625/1985: dismissal.

[92] Law of 17 April 1985.

[93] Const., Art. 43: 'There shall not be a state religion in Lithuania'; Law on Religious Communities and Associations 1995, Art. 5: this recognises nine 'traditional religions' which are not required

separate from the State' but 'Eastern Orthodox Christianity shall be considered the traditional religion'.[94] The Cypriot constitution also recognizes the autocephaly of the Orthodox Church of Cyprus and its right to administer its internal affairs 'in accordance with the Holy Canons and its Charter'.[95] For the Finnish Orthodox Church, the second largest church in Finland,[96] its synod drafts bills and the government may alter these prior to approval by parliament without the consent of synod.[97]

Most churches of the worldwide Anglican Communion engage with the State, its institutions and laws, for the purposes of their own visible organisation. With the exception of the established Church of England (see below), Anglican churches under civil law are non-established (they never were established),[98] quasi-established (with some reliance on State law)[99] or disestablished (achieved by the enactment of State law).[100] Moreover, these churches may use the facilities afforded by State law for their institutional structures and property. For example, in New South Wales (Australia), it has been held judicially that '[t]he Constitution of the Anglican Church ... came into existence formally on the enactment of the Church of England in Australia Constitution Act 1961' – 'to an extent the Act of 1961 has given statutory force' to the constitution.[101] In New Zealand, several parliamentary statutes 'declare and define the powers of the General Synod of the Church of the Province of New Zealand'; they regulate the alteration of the formularies of the church and its trust property.[102] When churches generally function in civil law as voluntary associations, their internal regulatory instruments

---

to register their statutes with the Ministry of Justice, including e.g. Orthodox, Roman Catholic, Lutheran and Reformed.

[94] Const., Art. 13.2–3. See also Romania: Law No. 178/2002, Art. 15: 'The Romanian Orthodox Church is autocephalous.' See also ROMOC: Statutes, Art. 5: the church is 'national and majority according to her apostolic age, tradition, number of faithful and special contribution to the life of the Romanian people'.

[95] Const., Art. 110–111: Orthodox marriages are 'governed by the law of the Greek Orthodox Church'.

[96] It is subject to the Ecumenical Patriarch, and decisions of its General Assembly are approved by the State.

[97] Law 521/1969 and Law 179/1970.

[98] See e.g. TEC (which must be viewed in the secular light of the US anti-establishment clause); Southern Africa: Const., Preamble: this church is 'not by law established' but it is an 'unestablished church'.

[99] See e.g. New Zealand: for elements of quasi-establishment see e.g. N. Cox, *Church and State in the Post-Colonial Era: The Anglican Church and the Constitution in New Zealand* (Polygraphia, Auckland, 2008).

[100] See e.g. Church of England in Bermuda Act 1975; Barbados, Anglican Church Act 1969; Jamaica, Church of England Disestablishment Law 1938; Grenada, Church of England Disestablishment Act 1959; Welsh Church Act 1914 which disestablished the Church of England in Wales (as from 1920) and Irish Church Act 1869.

[101] *Scandrett v Dowling* [1992] 27 NSWLR 483 at 489. See also UK: *Forbes v Eden* [1867] LR 1 HL Sc & Div 568 at 588: 'A Court of Law will not interfere with the rules of a voluntary [religious] association unless to protect some civil right or interest'; moreover: '[s]ave for the due disposal and administration of property, there is no authority in the Courts ... to take cognizance of the rules of a voluntary association.'

[102] See e.g. Church of England Empowering Act 1928 (as amended); Anglican Church Trusts Act 1981.

have the status in civil law of terms of a contract entered into by the members and as such may be enforceable in the courts of the State, particularly in property matters.[103] Indeed, the preparedness of Anglicans to engage with the State in matters of common concern is typified in continental Europe by the recognition of Anglican ecclesial communities by parliamentary statute, registration or agreements with the State to address matters of common concern.[104] However, in England, the Church of England is 'established according to the laws of this realm under the Queen's Majesty'.[105] The incidents of establishment are well-known: the monarch has 'supreme authority over all persons in all causes, as well ecclesiastical as civil'; the monarch is empowered by Act of Parliament to appoint bishops; some bishops sit in the House of Lords; the Measures of the General Synod (on parliamentary approval and royal assent) have the same force and effect as Acts of Parliament; canons created by General Synod must receive royal assent; and people who are resident in its parishes have rights to baptism, holy communion, marriage and burial.[106]

Moving along the ecclesiastical spectrum, in some countries Protestant churches are national churches and elsewhere they enjoy the benefit of State legislation especially designed for them or (as is the case in some German *länder*) they may have agreements with the authorities of the State.[107] For example, the Danish constitution provides that: 'The Evangelical Lutheran Church shall be the Folk Church of Denmark, and as such shall be supported by the State'; and the monarch must be a member of that church.[108] However, the Danish folk church has no synod, no legal personality as a corporate body and its constitution is to be laid down by statute (but this has not yet occurred). The church is subject to direct State control. The Ministry of Ecclesiastical Affairs is its governing body; its Canons are promulgated by parliament – but by convention church legislation will only be enacted with cross-party agreement.[109] The Ministry determines

---

[103] See e.g. N. Doe, *The Law of the Church in Wales* (University of Wales Press, Cardiff, 2002) Ch. 1.

[104] See e.g. Belgium: Law of 4 March 1870; Luxembourg: Law of 11 June 2004; Czech Republic: Act no 3/2002 Sb; Spain: Law 24/1992: the Federation of Protestant Churches. See also the Lambeth Commission on Communion, *The Windsor Report* (Anglican Communion Office, London, 2004) par. 119: 'At such moments when a church faces pressure from its host State(s) to adopt secular state standards ... an international Anglican Covenant might provide powerful support to the church, in a dispute with the State, to reinforce and underpin its religious liberty.'

[105] England: Canon A1.

[106] England: Canons A1 and A7; Appointment of Bishops Act 1533; Church of England Assembly (Powers) Act 1919: measures; Synodical Government Measure 1969: canons; see generally N. Doe, *The Legal Framework of the Church of England: A Critical Study in a Comparative Context* (Clarendon Press, Oxford, 1996); M. Hill, *Ecclesiastical Law* (3rd edn., Oxford University Press, 2007).

[107] In recent years in Germany, agreements have been entered between the Protestant church and the state *länder*: Saxony-Anhalt (1993), Mecklenburg-West Pomerania (1994), Saxony (1994), Thuringia (1994) and Brandenburg (1996); as well as with the Evangelical Methodist Church in North West Germany (1978): see generally R. Puza and N. Doe (eds.), *Religion and Law in Dialogue: Covenantal and Non-Covenantal Cooperation between State and Religion in Europe* (Peeters, Leuven, 2006).

[108] Const., Art. 4; Art. 6: 'The King shall be a member of the Evangelical Lutheran Church.'

[109] Const., Art. 66: 'The constitution of the established Church shall be laid down by statute.'

rules on church membership, the creation of new parishes and the appointment and dismissal of its clergy (who have the status of civil servants).[110] Local parishes operate as State agencies performing various administrative functions for the State, and all taxpayers who are members of the national church pay a church tax.[111] Nevertheless, Danish law also provides for religious freedom, prohibitions against religious discrimination and the operation of other religious organisations which may function freely in society.[112] By way of contrast, the Evangelical Lutheran Church in Finland, which enjoys constitutional status, is governed by church law enacted on the exclusive initiative of its General Synod – the government cannot interfere in the content of ecclesiastical bills introduced by the synod; parliament enacts the law but may only approve or reject the bill; the church and its parishes are autonomous; bishops are no longer appointed by the State; and its ministers are no longer State-funded.[113] There is also a national Lutheran church in Iceland,[114] and one in Norway,[115] but in Sweden it has been disestablished.[116]

On the basis that Presbyterianism calls for the separation of church and state, Presbyterian churches are not established under civil law. However, in Scotland, the relationship of the (Presbyterian) Church of Scotland to the State is regulated by the parliamentary Church of Scotland Act 1921: under this statute, the church is 'a national Church representative of the Christian Faith of the Scottish people ... [and] acknowledges its distinctive call and duty to bring the ordinances of religion to the people in every parish of Scotland through a territorial ministry'. The aim of the Act is 'to declare the right of the Church to self-government in all that concerned its own life and activity'; the church has this 'right and power subject

---

[110] 'The Ministry of Ecclesiastical Affairs is the governing body of the Danish National Evangelical Lutheran Church and [administers] grants and appropriations to that part of the Danish National Church funded out of the National Budget. The most important task of the Ministry of Ecclesiastical Affairs is to [administer] the [church] in conformity with current legislation': Statement, Ministry of Ecclesiastical Affairs, 2009.

[111] Since 1903, all members of the Danish National Church over the age of 18 are eligible to vote and stand for election to Parochial Church Councils, the functions of which include the upkeep of registers and buildings.

[112] Const., Art. 69: 'Rules for religious bodies dissenting from the established church shall be laid down by statute'; they function as private associations.

[113] Const., Art. 76 (The Church Act): 'Provisions on the organisation and administration of the Evangelical Lutheran Church are laid down in the Church Act. The legislative procedure for enactment of the Church Act and the right to submit legislative proposals relating to the Church Act are governed by the specific provisions in that Code.' The church has created for itself a Church Ordinance 1993.

[114] Const., Art. 62: 'The Evangelical Lutheran Church shall be the State Church in Iceland and ... supported and protected by the State'; the State pays clergy; whilst the church elects its bishops, the President of Iceland signs the candidate into office; the church has an Assembly, and its highest authority is its Council; a church tax is payable but non-members may pay an equivalent sum to the University of Iceland.

[115] Const., Art. 2: the Evangelical Lutheran Church is the 'official religion of the State'; the king is its titular head and it is administered by the Ministry of Culture and Church Affairs; it is regulated by law enacted by parliament, above all by the Act Concerning the Administration of the Church of Norway 1953.

[116] Church of Sweden Act 1998; Religious Communities Act 1998; see L. Friedner, 'State and Church in Sweden 2000', 8 EJCSR (2001) 255.

to no civil authority to legislate and to adjudicate finally, in all matters of doctrine, worship, government, and discipline in the Church'; however, the monarch is represented at its General Assembly, and its courts (General Assembly, Presbyteries and Kirk Sessions) are public *fora*.[117] Whilst not national churches, the foundational instruments of Methodist, Baptist and Reformed churches may also be protected by State laws specifically designed for them individually, and are enforceable as such (at least with regard to property) in the civil courts.[118] Agreements have also been established between alliances of churches and the State,[119] as well as within the European Union – such as the *Charta Oecumenica* (2001) between the Conference of European Churches and the (Roman Catholic) Council of European Bishops' Conferences ('a common commitment to dialogue and co-operation').[120]

In short, there is little difference in principle between Christian churches in Europe in the matter of their respective positions under State laws. Catholic, Orthodox, Anglican and Protestant churches all enjoy in some countries the constitutional status of a national, prevailing or official State church. In these States provision is also made to protect the religious freedom and institutional autonomy of other churches and religious organisations. Normally, however, Christian churches in Europe have no special constitutional status – they exist under State law variously as private voluntary associations, as statutory churches with law specifically designed for them individually or as covenantal churches which have agreements with the institutions of the State. All are free to legislate provided, one way or another, their rules are approved by the State explicitly or implicitly. Ultimately, the rules of all churches must not be inconsistent with State law – provided this meets the standards of relevant international law. Moreover, certain classes of instrument of national or established churches (in State–church systems) must be approved by parliament, just as the instruments of public or private religious associations (in separation and co-operation systems) must be approved by State institutions through parliamentary statutes, or covenants (perhaps ratified by statute), or in the process of registration. Importantly, however, some sources of religious law, especially those of fundamental and doctrinal significance, need no State approval.

Human rights and religious freedom

The principle that freedom is an essential characteristic of faith is a key tenet of Christianity. The principle is one claimed by Christians as a fundamental of social existence. It has also been recognised by the World Council of Churches: 'God's redemptive dealing with men is not coercive. Accordingly, human attempts by a legal enactment or by pressure of social custom to coerce or eliminate faith are

---

[117] Church of Scotland Act 1921, Sch., Articles Declaratory. For the public status of its courts, see e.g. *Ballatyne v Presbytery of Wigtown* (1936) SC 625.
[118] UK: Methodist Church Act 1976, Baptist and Congregational Trusts Act 1951, United Reformed Church Act 2000.
[119] Such as that in Poland with an alliance of the Lutheran, Orthodox, Polish Catholic, Evangelical Reformed, United Methodist, Old Catholic Mariavite Churches and Baptist Union of Poland.
[120] *Charta Oecumenica* (2001) Preamble: but it has no binding force in church law.

violations of the fundamental ways of God with men. The freedom which God has given ... implies free response to God's love.'[121] This section addresses the treatment of human rights in general and religious freedom in particular in the teaching and juridical instruments of churches across the Christian traditions studied here. To varying degrees, these instruments deal with the nature of human rights, the corporate duty of a church to promote them in civil society, the establishment of institutions to work in the human rights field and the obligation of the faithful as individuals to respect human rights.

The Catholic Church teaches that the role of the State is 'to defend and protect the common good of civil society', which consists of 'respect for and promotion of the fundamental rights of the person, prosperity, or the development of the spiritual and temporal goods of society, and the peace and security of the community and its members'.[122] Moreover, the church claims for itself a right 'to true freedom to preach the faith, to proclaim its teaching about society, to carry out its task among people without hindrance, and to pass moral judgments even in matters relating to politics, whenever the fundamental rights of man or the salvation of souls requires it'; and its canon law also recognises the inherent right of the church to own and administer property 'independently of any secular power'.[123] Indeed, the rights and duties of the faithful, as enumerated in the Code of Canon Law, derive from the fundamental dignity of the individual as a human person and include inalienable and inviolable human rights.[124] The religious freedom of the Catholic Church itself is sometimes explicitly recognised and protected in States by, variously, a concordat, constitution, sub-constitutional law and decisions of State courts. For example, in agreements with the Holy See, Spain recognises that 'the freedom of the Church is an essential principle of the relationship between the church and public authority'; moreover: 'The Spanish state recognizes the right of the Catholic Church to carry out its apostolic mission and guarantees the church free and public exercise of those activities inherent to it, especially worship, jurisdiction and teaching'.[125] However, the Catholic Church has been criticised in recent years in several cases, for instance on the applicability of human rights to the processes of its own tribunals (and fair trial standards),[126] and the dismissal of an organist (separated from his wife) on grounds of adultery and bigamy (in relation to the right to family and private life).[127]

---

[121] 'Statement on Religious Liberty', in the New Delhi Report: The Third Assembly of the World Council of Churches 1961 (New York, 1962) 159; see N. Doe and A.W. Jeremy, 'Justifications for religious autonomy', in R. O'Dair and A. Lewis (eds.), *Law and Religion*, Current Legal Issues Vol. 4 (Oxford University Press, 2001) 421.
[122] CCC, pars. 1925–1927; GS 26, 84.
[123] GS 76; DH 14; CIC, c. 1254.1: property; see also cc. 1311, 1401 on the right to discipline and conduct trials.
[124] CIC, c. 204: equality and dignity; c. 747: 'fundamental human rights'.
[125] Agreement, 19 Aug. 1979, Preamble; Agreement on Legal Affairs, 3 Jan. 1979, Art. I.
[126] *Pellegrini v Italy*, Appl. No. 30882/96, 20 July 2001: a breach of ECHR Art. 6 occurred when an Italian court did not ensure fair process in the Roman Rota before allowing enforcement of its judgment in a marriage case.
[127] *Schüth v Germany*, Appl. No. 1620/03, 23 Sept. 2010: his contract with the church was not 'an unequivocal undertaking to live a life of abstinence in the event of separation or divorce' and breached ECHR Art. 8.

Whereas the juridical instruments of some Orthodox churches expressly assert their right to freedom of religion or institutional autonomy,[128] those of global Anglicanism generally do not. However, there is a large body of Anglican teaching and quasi-legislation on the promotion of human rights in the Anglican encounter with the wider world; much of it is found in resolutions of the Lambeth Conference.[129] Five basic themes emerge. First, the Conference recognizes the existence of human rights and regards them as of 'capital and fundamental importance' not least in the context of the effects of their abuse and attacks upon human dignity.[130] Moreover, it calls upon 'all the Churches to press upon governments and communities their duty to promote fundamental human rights and freedoms among all their peoples'.[131] Secondly, for the Conference, human rights involve freedom to enable humankind to develop its relationship with God, to ensure that 'the divine dignity of every human being is respected and ... justice is pursued'.[132] The Conference commonly attacks breaches of human rights on the basis that such breaches are contrary to 'the teaching of Christ'.[133] Thirdly, it classifies human rights in terms of political rights, which include 'a fair and just share' for people in government, and economic rights, in so far as 'human rights must include economic fairness and equity, and enable local economies to gain greater control over their own affairs'.[134] Fourthly, fundamental to the Anglican approach is the idea that all humans are created in the image of God.[135] Consequently, '[t]he Christian must ... judge every social system by its effect on human personality'.[136] Fifthly, member churches are 'to speak out' against breaches of human rights, 'support all who are working for [the] implementation of human rights instruments',[137] and 'urge compliance with the United Nations Declaration of Human Rights by the nations in which our various member Churches are located, and [by] all others over whom we may exercise any influence'.[138] Individual Anglicans also have a responsibility to promote and protect human rights.[139]

The juridical instruments of churches of the Anglican Communion also promote human rights in civil society through the establishment and work of institutions of the church, such as in the Philippines where the church has a National Commission

---

[128] ROMOC: Statutes, Art. 4.1: the church is 'autonomous in regard to the State and other institutions'; ROC: Dioc. of Sourozh: Statutes, II.10: 'In order to promote the right to freedom of religion and to advance the Orthodox Christian faith, the Diocese carries out' listed activities.

[129] See generally N. Doe, 'Canonical approaches to human rights in Anglican churches', in M. Hill (ed.), *Religious Liberty and Human Rights* (University of Wales Press, Cardiff, 2002) 185.

[130] See e.g. LC 1998, Res. 1.1: the Conference affirmed and adopted the UN Declaration of Human Rights.

[131] LC 1968, Res. 16.

[132] *The Official Report of the Lambeth Conference 1998* (Morehouse Publishing, Harrisburg, PA, 1999) 77.

[133] LC 1978, Res. 3.

[134] LC 1920, Res. 75; 1920, Res. 78; 1958, Res. 110; *Called to Full Humanity*, LC 1998, *Official Report*, 79.

[135] LC 1958, Res. 110; and LC 1968, Res. 16.   [136] LC 1948, Res. 5.

[137] LC 1988, Res. 33.   [138] LC 1998, Res. 1.1(a).

[139] LC 1920, Res. 77; however, 'the Church is not to be identified with any particular political or social system': LC 1958, Res. 104.

on Social Justice and Human Rights, or in the West Indies where the Provincial Synod has a Standing Commission on Social Justice and Human Rights.[140] The Lambeth Conference call to the individual members of Anglican churches to promote human rights finds no direct echo in the actual laws of churches – for this reason the constitution of the Church of South India is exceptional; it requires 'members ... [to] contribute to the total ministry of the Church ... by responsible participation in secular organizations, legislative bodies ... and in other areas of public life', so that 'the decisions which are made in these areas may be controlled by the mind of Christ and the structures of society transformed according to His will'.[141] More commonly, catechetical instruments encourage individuals to contribute to the promotion of human rights in their work for 'justice and reconciliation' in civil society.[142] The principles of canon law common to Anglican churches also state that: 'All persons are equal in dignity before God'; and that: 'All persons have inherent rights and duties inseparable from their dignity as human beings created in the image and likeness of God and called to salvation through Jesus Christ.'[143]

Promotion of human rights and religious liberty is also pivotal in the doctrinal and juridical instruments of Protestants. At international level, one function of the Lutheran World Federation is to further 'worldwide among the churches diaconic action, alleviation of human need, promotion of peace and human rights, social and economic justice, care for God's creation and sharing of resources'.[144] At national level, typically: 'This Church affirms the God-given human dignity of all people, rejoicing in the diversity of God's creation' and commits itself to 'struggle for justice, peace and the integrity of creation'.[145] The Lutheran Church in Australia has a particularly full treatment of the subject: 'The concept of human rights is based on two convictions: that certain actions against other human beings are wrong no matter what; and that in all circumstances all people are entitled to respect and proper treatment as human beings.' The preservation of ordered human society belongs to the earthly kingdom in which God rules the world through the law: governments, as 'ministers of God', have the duty to preserve the life, liberties, property, prosperity and honour of each citizen. Christian citizens have the duty to urge their governments to honour human rights and to protest where they are either ignored or violated; and the foundation for Christian involvement in human rights is both the fundamental dignity of all human beings as creatures of God and the divine command to love our neighbour. Consequently, in accordance with the following 'guidelines', Christians should *inter alia*: (1) become informed about situations, at home and abroad, where people's human rights are being threatened or human rights abuses are taking place; (2) develop an attitude of concern and compassion toward victims; (3) increase community awareness of the need to safeguard human dignity; (4) intercede for those who suffer, especially those who cannot pray for themselves; and (5) investigate particular situations, study human-rights questions, contact politicians and

---

[140] E.g. Philippines: *Social Concerns Resolutions and Statements of the Philippine Episcopal Church* (1988); West Indies, Can. 33.1.C.
[141] E.g. South India: Const., VI.2.   [142] E.g. Southern Africa: Prayer Book 1989, 434.
[143] PCLCCAC, Principle 26.1 and 2.   [144] LWF: Const., Art. III.
[145] LCGB: RAR, Statement of Faith, 9.

embassies, organise petitions, distribute information, and support or join human-rights organisations.[146]

The United Methodist Church has a similarly robust approach to human rights. First, as 'all persons as equally valuable in the sight of God', governments should respect 'human rights under God'.[147] Civil government is 'a principal vehicle for the ordering of society', and it is responsible for 'the protection of the rights of the people' to, for example, free and fair elections, free speech and assembly, redress of grievances without fear of reprisal, privacy, adequate food, clothing, shelter, education and health care.[148] Secondly, recognising the 'inherent dignity of all persons', the church should: 'transform social structures';[149] support 'the basic rights of all persons to equal access to housing, education, communication, employment, medical care, legal redress for grievances, and physical protection'; combat acts of hate or violence against groups or persons based on race, ethnicity, gender, sexual orientation, religious affiliation, or economic status; and work for 'the recognition, protection, and implementation of the principles of the Universal Declaration of Human Rights so that communities and individuals may claim and enjoy their universal, indivisible, and inalienable rights'.[150] Thirdly, the church should support 'policies and practices that ensure the right of every religious group to exercise its faith free from legal, political, or economic restrictions' and condemn 'all overt and covert forms of religious intolerance'. The church asserts 'the right of all religions and their adherents to freedom from legal, economic, and social discrimination', and should 'defend religious freedom' and other freedoms; indeed: 'the rightful and vital separation of church and state, which has served the cause of religious liberty, should not be misconstrued as the abolition of all religious expression from public life'.[151] These principles are echoed in other Methodist laws which rest human rights on the equality of all,[152] promote

---

[146] LCA: Human Rights, adopted by the CTIR, 1994, edited 2001, Introduction: this sets out the history of international human rights instruments and cites Rom. 13:1–7 and 1 Peter 2:13–14; Christian Perspectives: 'Although the human rights movement has secular origins, "justice" and "right" are concepts which have a biblical basis'; Practical Considerations: these contain the 'guidelines'.

[147] UMCNEAE: BOD, par. 103, Confession of Faith, Art. XVI; par. 161: the equality of humans and genders.

[148] UMCNEAE: BOD, par. 164: e.g. detention and imprisonment 'for the harassment and elimination of political opponents or other dissidents violates fundamental human rights'; 'torture, and other cruel, inhumane, and degrading treatment or punishment of persons by governments for any purpose violates Christian teaching and must be condemned and/or opposed by Christians and churches wherever and whenever it occurs'.

[149] UMCNEAE: BOD, par. 121.

[150] UMCNEAE: BOD, par. 162: it also rejects 'inequalities and discriminatory practices [in] Church and society'.

[151] UMCNEAE: BOD, pars. 121, 162 and 164.

[152] FMCNA: BOD, par. 111: 'God created human beings in His own image, innocent, morally free and responsible to choose between good and evil, right and wrong' but 'humans are corrupted in their very nature so that from birth they are inclined to sin' though by 'God's grace and help people are enabled to do good works with a free will'; par. 112: under the law of God humans 'should strive to secure to everyone respect for their person, their rights and their greatest happiness in the possession and exercise of the right within the moral law'.

human rights in society,[153] forbid discrimination[154] and advocate freedom of belief and conscience.[155]

Like the Lutheran World Federation, the World Communion of Reformed Churches is to work for justice and promote 'the full and just partnership of men and women in church and society', 'diaconal service in church and society' and it is to engage in 'promoting and defending religious, civil, and all other human rights wherever threatened throughout the world'.[156] Similar functions are assumed by individual churches at national level. For instance, as to religious freedom, the United Reformed Church in Great Britain declares that 'civil authorities, being always subject to the rule of God, ought to respect the rights of conscience and of religious belief and to serve God's will of justice and peace for all humankind'.[157] The Presbyterian churches also hold to the view that (typically): 'although civil rulers are bound to render obedience to Christ in their own province, yet they ought not to attempt in any way to constrain anyone's religious beliefs, or invade the rights of conscience.'[158] Thus: 'the rights of private judgment in all matters that respect religion are universal and inalienable'.[159] In like fashion, the United Church of Christ in the Philippines 'affirms and upholds the inviolability of the rights of persons as reflected in the Universal Declaration of Human Rights and other agreements on human rights, [and] the international covenants on economic, social and cultural rights and on civil and political rights'.[160]

There is very little to distinguish these Reformed approaches to human rights and religious freedom from those which appear in the instruments of Baptists. As

---

[153] MCNZ: LAR, Introductory Documents, V: Some Social Principles of the Methodist Church: the 'right to freedom of conscience, constitutional liberty, secrecy of the ballot and access to the Courts'; Christians should influence 'the politics of human rights'; COTN: Man., par. 903.7: 'political and religious freedom rest upon biblical concepts of the dignity of humankind as God's creation and the sanctity of one's own individual conscience'; members should actively support these and be vigilant against threats to them.

[154] MCNZ: LAR, Introductory Documents, II, Pastoral Resolutions: the pledge to 'breaking down all racial, political and religious barriers, and of confronting all people' with fullness of life in Christ; III, Ethical Standards for Ministry, 3: human dignity and a prohibition against discrimination of grounds of 'race, colour, gender, sexual orientation, socio-economic group, disability, age, religious, theological or political belief'; COTN: Man., App., par. 903.2: the church promotes equality and prohibits discrimination.

[155] COTN: Man., par. 903.8: the church does not 'bind the conscience of its members relative to participation in military service . . . although . . . the individual Christian as a citizen is bound to give service . . . in all ways that are compatible with the Christian faith and . . . way of life'; the church claims for 'conscientious objectors within its membership the same exemptions and considerations regarding military service as are accorded members of recognized non-combatant religious organizations'; FMCNA: BOD par. 3331: 'It is our firm conviction that the consciences of our members be respected (Acts 4.19-20; 5.29). Therefore, we claim exemption from all military service for those who register officially with the church as conscientious objectors to war.'

[156] WCRC: Const., Art. V; see also Art. IV: its values include 'the dignity of every person'.

[157] URC: Man., BU A, Sch. D, Version I, 8; see also Man., G: the Equal Opportunities Committee of the General Assembly: Man., I: the Equal Opportunities Policy affirms the commitment of the URC to 'the same openness to all people in today's world' and forbids discrimination in the church.

[158] PCI: Code, I.III.13; this cites the Act of the Church of Scotland 1647.

[159] PCA: BCO, Preamble II.1.   [160] UCCP: Const., Art. II.11.

the Baptist World Alliance is to defend human rights at global level,[161] so, too, at national level Baptist Conventions and Unions recognise fundamental human rights and are 'to maintain religious liberty'.[162] For instance, the Baptist Union of Southern Africa accepts 'The principle of religious liberty, namely, that no individual should be coerced either by the State or by any secular, ecclesiastical or religious group in matters of faith'; as such: 'The right of private conscience is to be respected. For each believer this means the right to interpret the Scriptures responsibly and to act in the light of his conscience.'[163] Again, for the North American Baptist Conference religious freedom is an 'inalienable right'; and: 'The state should guarantee religious liberty to all persons and groups regardless of their religious preferences, consistent with the common good';[164] in consequence, the State has 'no right to impose penalties for religious opinions of any kind'.[165]

From the similarities between the normative instruments of churches across the Christian churches studied here, the principles of Christian law provide that all humans are created in the image of God and as such share a basic equality of dignity and fundamental rights; the State should recognise, respect and protect these basic human rights; the church should promote and defend human rights in society, and, like the church, the State and society should not discriminate against individuals on grounds of, for example, race, gender and religion; the State should also recognise, promote and protect the religious freedom of churches corporately and of the faithful individually, as well as freedom of conscience.

The church and social responsibility

In view of the provisions outlined above on the obligation of churches and the faithful to be active in the political arena for the promotion and defence of the teaching of Christ and of human rights, it is not surprising that the juridical instruments of churches place great emphasis on the pursuit of philanthropic activities in society. Christians use laws primarily to require or permit the establishment of institutions to advance social work and sometimes they oblige or exhort social work on the part of the faithful individually. The convergence of rules on this subject indicates that Christians, regardless of denomination, are engaged in

---

[161] BWA: Const., Art. II. See also R.V. Pierard (ed.), *Baptists Together in Christ 1905-2005: A Hundred-Year History of the Baptist World Alliance* (BWA, Falls Church, Virginia, 2005) 281: 18th Congress, Melbourne: 'human rights are God-given and that violations of human rights are violations of the laws of God'.

[162] BUSA: Const., Art. 5.3; NBC: PAP, Ethical Behaviour of Baptists in Public Life: 'it is the inalienable right of every citizen to take part in the government of the country through ... his civic rights'; church members may enter 'fulltime politics' but are 'under divine obligation to influence [their] party to embrace principles of morality and righteousness'; if a political party acts 'in a way displeasing to God and contrary to Christian teaching' the member should dissociate himself 'until the policies and practices are made right'.

[163] BUSA: BL, 4.2.7.

[164] NABC: Statement of Beliefs, 7: 'religious liberty, rooted in Scripture, is the inalienable right of all individuals to freedom of conscience with ultimate accountability to God (Genesis 1.27; John 8.32; II Corinthians 3.17; Romans 8.21; Acts 5.29)'; Riverside Baptist Church (Baltimore): Const., Preamble: the constitution is designed e.g. for 'preserving the liberties inherent in each individual member of the church'.

[165] CNBC: Const., 3, Statement of Faith, Art. XVII.

common action for the advancement of charitable and associated forms of social activity. Needless to say, this section does not attempt to describe the actual activities of Christians in the social field. The purpose of the section is merely to elucidate the laws which stimulate these activities.

The Catholic Church teaches that 'the human person needs to live in society'. This is not 'an extraneous addition but a requirement of his nature' in which persons develop their potential and thus respond to their vocation and end: God himself. A society is 'a group of persons bound together organically by a principle of unity that goes beyond each one of them' and '[e]ach community is defined by its purpose and consequently obeys specific rules'; but 'the human person ... is and ought to be the principle, the subject and the end of every social organization'.[166] Moreover: '[t]o promote the participation of the greatest number in the life of a society, the creation of voluntary associations and institutions must be encouraged "on both national and international levels, which relate to economic and social goals, to cultural and recreational activities, to sport, to various professions, and to political affairs"'.[167] In society, persons must engage in charity, 'the greatest social commandment', and promote the common good; and social justice requires them to respect the human person, equality and no discrimination, human solidarity and the exercise of 'social charity'.[168] In turn, according to Catholic canon law, the church carries out its sanctifying office in part through works of charity, and temporal goods are held for such works, 'especially for the needy'.[169] All the faithful must promote social justice and help the poor and they may establish associations for charitable purposes,[170] in order to 'permeate and perfect the temporal order of things with the spirit of the gospel' and in this way, 'particularly in conducting secular business and exercising secular functions, they are to give witness to Christ'.[171] Furthermore, the parish priest is 'to help the sick and especially the dying in great charity' and he is 'to endeavour to ensure that the faithful are concerned for the community of the parish', and 'to foster works which promote the spirit of the gospel, including its relevance to social justice'.[172]

Social responsibility is a key value in Orthodox law. By way of illustration, several institutions in the Russian Orthodox Church are to 'express, if need be, concern for contemporary problems' and 'pastoral concern for social problems';[173]

---

[166] CCC, pars. 1878–1881; GS 25.1.

[167] CCC, par. 1881; 1883: subsidiarity means 'a community of a higher order should not interfere in the internal life of a community of a lower order' but 'support it' and 'co-ordinate its activity with [those] of the rest of society' for the common good: *Centesimus annus*, Pope John Paul II 1991; par. 1894: neither the state nor society should substitute itself for 'the initiative and responsibility of individuals and intermediary bodies'.

[168] CCC, pars. 1897–1942; see above for the common good; par. 1928: 'Society ensures social justice when it provides the conditions that allow associations or individuals to obtain what is their due, according to their nature and their vocation. Social justice is linked to the common good and the exercise of authority.'

[169] CIC, c. 839.1 and c. 1254.2.   [170] CIC, c. 215: the faithful; c. 222.2: social justice.

[171] CIC, cc. 224–231: laity are entitled to 'insurance, social security and medical benefits duly safeguarded'.

[172] CIC, cc. 528–529; also c. 394.1: the diocesan bishop must foster and oversee works of the apostolate.

[173] ROC: Statute, II.5(h): Local Council; III.4(g): Bishops' Council; IV.4(g). See also GOAA: Charter, Art. 10: the Archdiocesan Clergy–Laity Congress may address 'the philanthropic

and the Holy Synod may establish commissions on 'works of charity and social ministry'.[174] The bishops should promote (and establish) charitable institutions and dioceses must have departments for the promotion of social and charitable activity.[175] At parish level, the rector has a responsibility for 'organizing activities in the public domain' including the 'charitable and educational activities of the parish';[176] and property may be put to social, charitable and cultural uses.[177] Similar norms are found in the Greek Orthodox Archdiocese of America: 'the Parish shall establish such educational and philanthropic activities to foster the aims and mission of the Parish and to edify its parishioners in the Faith and ethos of the Church'.[178] The Standing Conference of the Canonical Orthodox Bishops in the Americas applies the same obligation to individuals: 'Individual Orthodox Christians ... are obliged to assist in every effort or activity which embodies justice, the principles of brotherhood, and ... provides more favourable conditions for the spiritual development of both personality and community'. Whilst the Church 'cannot always endorse social systems, movements and programs, it is up to Christians enlightened by their conscience and the Christian ideal to commit themselves to social change in morally acceptable ways' as to, for example, 'social justice, racial tensions, human development and moral issues'.[179] Orthodox Christians may also co-operate with ecumenical partners in such areas as 'morality, responsible citizenship, Christian charity, [and] social services'.[180] Indeed, State funding may be employed to advance these objectives. For example, in Greece,

---

concerns of the Archdiocese'; ROMOC: Statutes, Art. 14(i),(t): the Holy Synod addresses 'matters of general interest in society' and establishes norms on 'social-charitable assistance'.

[174] ROC: Statute, V.28(i)–(j); see also VI.7: the patriarchate has a Department for Charity and Social Ministry. See also ROMOC: Statutes, Art. 37.1(b), (d): Social Charitable Department; Cultural Patrimony Dept.

[175] ROC: X. 48; see e.g. Dioc. of Sourozh: Statutes, II.10: the Diocese may engage in 'charitable activity, including the area of social care of orphans and abandoned children, old and disabled people'; VIII.38: it may 'use its funds to make charitable donations [to] individuals in need'. See also e.g. UOCIA: Statutes, Art. IV.2(i) and V.4: Major Archbishops and the Prime Bishops' Council provide 'for the establishment and maintenance of institutions of charity and education'; VII.4: the bishop must provide for '[t]he establishment of charitable organizations'; VIII.3: the Diocesan Assembly must strengthen the 'charities of the Diocese'; IX.5(l): the Diocesan Council must maintain diocesan 'institutions of charity'; ROMOC: Statutes, Art. 92: the Eparchial Assembly must sustain eparchial cultural and social-philanthropic institutions.

[176] ROC: Statute, XI.20(e). See also MOSC: Const., Art. 22: the Parish Assembly must provide for the expenses for e.g. 'Charitable Hospitals' and Orphanages.

[177] ROC: Statute, XV:4, 5, 10, 17, 18, 23. See also GOAA: Regs., Art. 16.1: parish property must be used to serve e.g. the 'cultural and philanthropic ministries of the Parish'.

[178] GOAA: Regs., Art. 15.4. See also ROMOC: Statutes, Art. 50(d): the parish priest implements the parish 'social-charitable' programme; Art. 55(f): the Parish Assembly is 'to initiate fund raising for ... social-charitable purposes'; Art. 67.2: it has a Social Department to e.g. collaborate with medical units, the poor, orphans, widows and elderly; Art. 71: the archpriest oversees the 'social-philanthropic activity of priests'; Arts. 137: the church provides 'social services' through its units and through 'NGOs functioning with the approval of the competent church authorities'; 138: the strategy for such assistance is designed by Holy Synod.

[179] SCOBA: GOCER, Pt. I, Secular Ecumenism, 4. See also ROMOC: Statutes, Art. 45: the faithful of the parish have a right to 'charitable assistance' and they must 'fulfil acts of Christian mercy'.

[180] OCIA: GC, Ecumenical Witness, A.2.

the State provides funding for the charitable work of the Orthodox Church's *Apostoliki Diakonia*, and the sum is determined jointly by the Minister of Education and Cults and Minister of Finance.[181]

The regulatory instruments of Anglicanism also generate interaction between church and society. This is the case at all ecclesial levels and in relation to all sorts of activities. A common understanding in Anglicanism is that each autonomous church exists to 'promote within each of their territories a national expression of Christian faith, life and worship'; and both clergy and the laity are under a duty 'to take part in the mission of the Church'.[182] In turn, the laws of churches sometimes spell out the mission of the church in wider society – these may include the duty to contribute to the 'moral and spiritual' welfare of society,[183] to promote justice in the world,[184] 'to transform unjust structures of society, caring for God's creation, and establishing the values of the Kingdom',[185] and to engage in 'educational, medical, social, agricultural and other service'.[186] Consequently, social service is a key function which provincial laws and other regulatory instruments assign to the assemblies of the church.[187] Typically, the governing body of each parish must 'promote the whole mission of the church, pastoral, evangelistic, social and ecumenical'.[188] Similarly, diocesan assemblies (synod, councils and conferences) stimulate service.[189] Indeed, in its treatment of mission, the Anglican Communion Covenant commits the churches 'to respond to human need by loving service', 'to seek to transform unjust structures of society' and 'to strive to safeguard the integrity of creation and to sustain and renew the life of the earth'.[190]

Social action is contemplated in various forms by Protestant laws. The Evangelical Lutheran Church in America typifies the Lutheran approach to social responsibility. One objective of the church is 'to meet human needs, caring for the sick and the aged, advocating dignity and justice for all people, working for peace and reconciliation among the nations, and standing with the poor and powerless and committing itself to their needs'.[191] Moreover, the church 'shall seek to meet human needs through encouragement of its people to individual and corporate action, and through establishing, developing, recognizing, and supporting institutions and agencies that minister to people in their spiritual and

---

[181] Law 1155/1981.   [182] LC 1930, Res. 48 and 49; LC 1958, Res. 58.
[183] Venezuela: Const., II.
[184] See e.g. Philippines: Const., Art. 1.1; Canons 1.2.2(d): one of the functions of the Provincial Synod's Commission on Social Concerns is 'to study the nature and root causes of poverty and underdevelopment in the country and review the participation of the Church in the development process'.
[185] New Zealand: Const., Preamble.
[186] North India: Const., II.I.II; see also Chile: Statutes, Art. 2.
[187] For a comparative study of national mission, see N. Doe, 'The notion of a national church: a juridical framework', 149 *Law and Justice* (2002) 77.
[188] PCLCCAC, Principle 21.6.
[189] See e.g. New Zealand: Cans. B.XXII: the duties of the inter-diocesan synod.
[190] TACC, 2.2.2; the Anglican Communion has various networks and other bodies to assist in these tasks.
[191] ELCA: Const., 4.02. See also ELCIC: Const., 2(1)(d): the church is to provide testimony in public.

temporal needs'. Through affiliated social ministry organizations, it must also 'establish affiliations and alliances within this church and within society, and carry out a comprehensive social ministry witness'.[192] As such, its central organisation must therefore respond to 'human need, caring for the sick and suffering, working for justice and peace, and providing guidance to members on social matters',[193] and its Church Council 'shall have responsibility for the corporate social responsibility of this church'.[194] Toward this end, the church must study 'social issues and trends, work to discover the causes of oppression and injustice, and develop programs of ministry and advocacy to further human dignity, freedom, justice, and peace in the world'.[195] At regional and local level, too, the synod and congregation must engage in 'service to the world' and '[r]espond to human need, work for justice and peace, care for the sick and the suffering, and participate responsibly in society'.[196] The Lutheran Churches in Australia, Canada and Southern Africa exhort similar institutional engagement in social action at national, regional and local level,[197] not least by means of the study of and statements on social problems.[198] The faithful individually must also engage directly in 'diaconic service', especially towards 'the sick, the aged, the needy, the disabled and the troubled' – this is because: 'The Christian acts according to a conscience bound to the Word of God' and 'works for justice for all, especially for the disadvantaged and bears witness of the will of God, even if one has to suffer.'[199] Bishops and pastors must 'speak publicly to the world in solidarity with the poor and oppressed, calling for justice and proclaiming God's love for the world'.[200] In short: Christian faith must be manifested in 'public life': 'The Christian is available ... for cultural, social and political tasks. In the congregation the Word of God is expressed for the specific situations and thus bears witness of the will of God in concrete circumstances. Church and congregation assist the bearers of public responsibility in [the] economy, administration, politics, law, education and other spheres with advice and deed.'[201]

---

[192] ELCA: Const., Ch. 8.33.   [193] ELCA: Const., 11.20-21   [194] ELCA: Const., 14.21.10-16.
[195] ELCA: Const., 4.03(l); see also 10.20-21: the 'interpretation of social statements' by the regional Synod.
[196] ELCA: Const., 9.10-11, 9.41: congregation; 10.20-21: synod.
[197] LCA: BL, VIII.G and H: there are boards on e.g. care for the aged, education, and commissions on social and bioethical issues; ELCIC: Const., Art. IV.2: the church may establish, maintain or support 'institutions and agencies to minister to human need ... study issues in contemporary society in the light of the Word of God and respond publicly to social and moral issues as an advocate for justice and ... agent for reconciliation'; ABL, V.5: the regional synod may provide programmes and resources for 'social ministry'; ELCSA: G., 10.10; 11.1: 'Christ uses His Church with ... its service' and is 'to live a life of charity'.
[198] LCA: BL, VIII.F: the College of Presidents has a duty to study developments in 'church and society' and give guidance to pastors and members accordingly.
[199] ELCSA: G., 11.4. See also ELCIC: ABL, Pt. II.2: a congregation must encourage members 'in works of mercy'; ELCIRE: Const., 6(1): church members 'should testify ... through words and deeds in public as in private life' to the faith and (3) undertake 'diaconal tasks'.
[200] ELCIC: Const., Art. XIII.5: the bishop is to '[s]peak publicly and witness for the gospel on behalf of this church'; ELCA: Const., 7.31.12: pastors; 7.51.05: deacons must be 'responsive to needs in a changing world'.
[201] ELCSA: G., 11.7.

It is a fundamental principle of Methodist social responsibility that the church has a duty 'to apply the Christian vision of righteousness to social, economic and political issues'.[202] The promotion of 'benevolent interests', 'social concern' or similar object is listed, typically, in the functions of a central assembly.[203] Regional assemblies may have a similar role,[204] circuits may have advisory councils on 'social welfare',[205] the local church is 'to defend God's creation and live as an ecologically responsible community',[206] and its church council is to 'give attention to local and larger community ministries of compassion, justice and advocacy' including 'church and society', 'campus ministry', 'health and welfare', 'religion and race, and the status and role of women'.[207] Moreover, the faithful individually should engage in 'healing the sick, feeding the hungry, caring for the stranger, freeing the oppressed, being and becoming a compassionate caring presence, and working to develop social structures that are consistent with the gospel'.[208] They are to carry out this service in, *inter alia*, 'daily work, recreation and social activities, and responsible citizenship'.[209] Social responsibility is also a function of ministers. Deacons have a special ministry to the poor and needy.[210] Bishops must seek to equip the faithful to serve 'in the world' and offer a 'prophetic voice for justice in a suffering and

---

[202] UMCNEAE: BOD, par. 101. See also MCNZ: LAR, Nature of New Zealand Methodism: 'Methodism particularly emphasises both personal spirituality and a concern for social action as responses to the gospel'; MCGB: CPD, SO 351: advocacy for and financial assistance to the poor.

[203] UMCUSA: Const., Div. 2.4, Art. V: jurisdictional conference; Div. 2.5, Art. IV: central conference; see also UMCNEAE: BOD, pars. 27 and 31; par. 127: 'human needs'; COTN: Man. II, Const., Articles of Faith, XI.15: 'working for justice'; App., par. 903.4: as 'God identifies with and assists the poor', so too the church's ministry includes 'acts of charity as well as the struggle to provide opportunity, equality, and justice for the poor'; FMCNA: BOD, par. 5250: annual conference may elect 'a social issues and ministries committee to assist churches in seeking justice for all, showing mercy to the poor, empowering the disenfranchised and maintaining openness and sensitivity to the social problems of all ages, race and gender'; the committee recommends resolutions for General Conference and organises resources 'to assist the local church in seeking justice for all'.

[204] MCNZ: LAR, 4.2: a regional synod must encourage engagement in 'community concerns and social justice'.

[205] MCI: RDG, 10.75.

[206] UMCNEAE: BOD, par. 202; FMCNA: BOD, par. 6010: 'the local church corporately cares for the needs of its own and others'.

[207] UMCNEAE: BOD, par. 252; see also par. 254: the charge conference may appoint annually a co-ordinator for e.g. advocacy for persons with special needs; MCNZ: LAR, 3.4: the local leaders are to 'initiate, research and promote dialogue and action on matters of community concern and social justice'.

[208] UMCNEAE: BOD, par. 122.

[209] UMCNEAE: BOD, par. 220; see also par. 253: specialist ministries to the disabled; par. 256: the local Mission and Ministry Groups allow the faithful to 'participate in small groups to serve the needs of the poor and marginalized' and e.g. 'advocate for social justice'; MCNZ: LAR, Introductory Documents, IV, General Standards for the Guidance of Members: 'we are called both to active participation in civic and national affairs and to service directed towards the attainment of world peace and justice'; MCGB: CPD, SO 604: a local church must help 'those in need'; SO 651: its Church Council maintains a Benevolence Fund for the relief of poverty.

[210] UMCNEAE: BOD, par. 328: a ministry of 'love, justice, and service' and of 'connecting the church with the most needy, neglected, and marginalized among the children of God'; par. 337: elders and 'social services'.

conflicted world through the tradition of social holiness'.[211] Ministers must participate 'in the shaping of social policies advocating the promotion of social justice, improved social conditions and a fair sharing of the community's resources'.[212] Methodist instruments sometimes present an agenda for social action,[213] and their 'social principles' aim 'to speak to the human issues in the contemporary world from a biblical and theological foundation' and are intended to stimulate a 'dialogue of faith and practice'.[214] Engagement in social ministry is carried out by a host of institutions at the various levels of a Methodist church.[215] The Methodist Church in Ireland is typical.[216] Its Council on Social Responsibility must undertake, on behalf of the Connexion, 'informed study and analysis of social, economic, political and international issues ... with theological insight ... in a manner which effectively both represents and resources the Church'; the Council must report annually to Conference: 'In connection with any of the issues being addressed, the Council or its Executive Committees are authorised to take action in harmony with existing declarations or resolutions of the Conference, and to communicate regarding these matters with the Governments of each jurisdiction in Ireland.' Areas of interest included in its work are: environmental issues; health and well-being; medical ethics and bio-ethics; EU and international affairs; political developments and parliamentary business; age, gender and inter-cultural issues; and social justice and equality.[217]

The normative instruments of the Reformed traditions have equally explicit treatment of the social responsibilities of Christians. The World Communion of

---

[211] UMCNEAE: BOD, pars. 401 and 403; MCNZ: LAR, 7.5: the Conference President, as chief pastor, is to exercise 'a prophetic voice in its pursuit of justice'.

[212] MCNZ: LAR, Introductory Documents, III Ethical Standards for Ministry, Responsibilities to the Wider Community, 2; MCGB: CPD, Bk. VI, Pt. I, Resolutions on Pastoral Work (1971): ministers are 'to encourage and train members ... to be representatives of Christ in the world, that by their faith and deeds of service they may show Christ's compassion' and must 'seek every opportunity to minister ... to those who work in industry, local government, and other sectors of the life of community'.

[213] MCNZ: LAR, Introductory Documents, V, Some Social Principles of the Methodist Church: the sacredness of human personality and the equal value of all in the sight of God; adequate opportunities for employment, and reasonable standards of living for those unable to work; the right to a just return for services, good housing, and a healthy environment; and promoting social and industrial reforms by lawful means.

[214] UMCNEAE: BOD, Pt. IV, Social Principles; pars. 1001–1011: the General Board of Church and Society is to 'provide forthright ... action on issues of human well-being, justice, peace, and the integrity of creation' to the goal of 'personal, social, and civic righteousness', and work on a 'strategy and methodology for social change'.

[215] MCNZ: LAR, s. 5.7.10: the Churches Agency on Social Issues seeks, on 'social, economic, ecological and political matters' e.g. to: resource and encourage the church at national, regional, local and individual levels to discuss such matters; advocate on them from the Christian perspective 'as promptly, clearly, publicly, and effectively as possible'; be 'agents for ... justice'; the agency is a joint venture of MCNZ, PCANZ, Churches of Christ NZ, and Society of Friends.

[216] MCI: RDG, 7, 35: the objects of the Methodist Church Child Care Society (MCI) are 'to provide financial assistance in the maintenance, welfare and safety of children in need who are connected with the Methodist Church'; the management of the Society is under the Department of Youth and Children's Work Executive.

[217] MCI: RDG, 34.01.

Reformed Churches is to promote 'economic and ecological justice, global peace, and reconciliation in the world', relief and sustainable development and the eradication of poverty.[218] Within this, the United Reformed Church in Great Britain is typical. At national level, the General Assembly takes action in the interests of 'the well-being of the community in which the Church is placed',[219] the regional synod is 'to encourage in the local churches concern for youth work and social service'[220] and the local elders' meeting is 'to foster in the congregation concern for witness and service to the community'.[221] Ministers should have 'an informed and passionate involvement in the issues of the contemporary world',[222] church-related community workers work for peace and justice in society,[223] and deacons have a special responsibility to the poor and needy.[224] Similarly, in Presbyterianism, the General Assembly may take action for 'the well-being of the community',[225] and it has commissions to assist in this task, such as the Church and Society Department of the Presbyterian Church of Wales, which is 'to consider the Connexion's response to social, national and international issues'.[226] The Presbytery must provide for pastoral care 'within the wider community'.[227] The Kirk Session must seek to further Christian witness and service in the local community and raise funds for prescribed 'philanthropic objects'.[228] Ruling elders are responsible for 'practical witness', including in 'the wider world',[229] ministers must visit the sick and provide leadership in the humanitarian activity of the local church[230] and church members must themselves witness to society.[231]

---

[218] WCRC: Const., Art. V.
[219] URC: Man., B., 2(6). See also RCA: BCO, Ch. I, Pt. IV.2: the General Synod oversees 'benevolent work'.
[220] URC: Man., B., 2(5). [221] URC: Man., B., 2(2). [222] URC: Man., K, 3.
[223] URC: Man., BU, A, Confessional Statement, 22: these are 'to care for, to challenge and to pray for the community, to discern with others God's will for the well-being of the community, and to endeavour to enable the church to live out its calling ... through working with others in both church and community for peace and justice in the world'; Man., G: Church-Related Community Work Management Sub-Committee.
[224] RCA: BCO Ch. I, Pt. I., Arts. 1.10, 6: the Board of Deacons ministers to 'the sick, the hurt, and the helpless'.
[225] PCI: Code, VII.II.104; PCW: HOR, 3.4.2: social issues; PCA: BCO: General Assembly is 'to recommend measures for the promotion of charity ... through all the churches under its care'.
[226] PCI: Code, XVII.I, par. 281: the Board of Social Witness of General Assembly must 'concern itself with all questions affecting the social welfare of the members ... and the community'; PCW: HOR, 2.12.1.2.
[227] PCANZ: BO, 8.4(4).
[228] PCI: Code, II.II.35 and 38: provided the philanthropic objects do not include 'balloting, raffling, or lottery causes'; see also III.I.46: the Congregational Meeting may raise funds for 'charitable objects'; PCW: HOR, I.1: one object of the church is 'serving our communities and our country through practical activity', 'taking a stand for justice and peace in our world' and 'safeguarding our environment in every possible way'; PCA: BCO, 4.4: the local church must make offerings 'for the relief of the poor'; PCANZ: BO, 5.2(2): 'mission to the world'.
[229] PCI: Code, II.I.30.
[230] PCI: Code, IV.73: Presbytery must ensure that visits to the sick are carried out; PCW: HOR, 4.2: humanitarian activity in 'the local community, nation and world'; PCA: BCO, 8.4: pastors; 9.2: deacons; PCANZ: BO, 6.6: a minister must provide for and support 'the wider community'.
[231] PCW: HOR, 2.2: members must 'give freely of their service to society'; PCANZ: BO, 6.1(3): the commitment of baptism takes shape in a range 'of activities in society'.

Much the same arrangements are required or permitted by United, Congregational and Baptist regulatory instruments. In the United and Congregational churches, one function of a central assembly is to 'issue or approve statements on important public issues and concerns'.[232] Similarly, the functions of a regional council include bringing 'the influence of the churches to bear upon such public and general questions as may demand their collective action',[233] initiating and exercising 'oversight of Church-related educational, medical, welfare and other work within its bounds' and, through its Mission Council, engaging in 'Justice and Social Responsibility'.[234] Designated ministries may also engage directly with social justice,[235] and the local church and its members are to care for the poor.[236] Like the Baptist World Alliance globally,[237] a national Baptist Union or Convention may be called to be 'a prophetic community, confronting injustice and challenging human concepts of power, wealth, status and security' and engage in 'simpler, greener, fairer living'.[238] For instance, according to the North American Baptist Conference: 'Christians, individually and collectively ... [must] promote truth, justice and peace ... [and] aid the needy and preserve the dignity of all races and conditions';[239]

---

[232] UCCP: Const., Art. VII.3(a): General Assembly. See also UCA: Const., 4: the church is 'to assist in human development and toward the improvement of human relationships, [and] to meet human need through charitable and other services'; UCNI: Const., II.II: the church is to provide 'educational, medical, social, agricultural and other services' for e.g. 'social justice'.

[233] UCCSA: Const., 4.5.3 and 4.7.3. See also UCCP: Const., Art. II.5: 'The fundamental values of love, justice, truth and compassion are at the heart of our witness to the world'; 8: the church has a 'prophetic witness in the life and culture of the Filipino people'; 12: it is to 'protect, promote and enhance ... the integrity of creation'; UCA: Const., 26: Presbytery assists congregations in 'wider aspects of the work of the Church'.

[234] UCCSA: Const., 5.7.4 and 5.9.3.1.

[235] UCOC: Const., par. 66: Justice and Witness Ministries are to encourage local churches, associations, conferences and national expressions of the church 'to engage in God's mission by direct action for the integrity of creation, justice and peace'; UCA: Regs., 2.4.2: the minister must 'equip [members] for their ministry in the community'; 2.12: community workers; UCC: ESMP, 2: in 'a church committed to social justice', ministers must 'encourage and support the development and pursuit of social justice' and 'lay leadership on social justice issues'; BL, App. II, Sch. B: Model Trust Deed: property may be used for charitable and social purposes; Community Ministry Standards and Best Practices: Administrative Standards for Community and Social Justice Ministries; UCNI: Const., I.VIII.14: deacons must serve 'the poor and needy'.

[236] UFCS: Const., I.III.22: the Kirk Session and 'care for the poor'; II.III.1: the Deacons' Court has a special responsibility for 'the temporal wants of poor persons connected with the congregation'; UCCP: Const., Art. V.4: the congregation must 'respond to the life and concerns of society'; UCA: Regs., 3.1.1: the congregation must equip members for 'service in the world'; UCC: BL 153: the Session is responsible for 'the care of the poor, and the visiting of the sick'; UCNI: Const., I.VII.2: the faithful are to offer to engage in 'social welfare'.

[237] BWA: Const., Art. II and BL 6: the Alliance must respond to human need. See also ABF: Const., III.5.

[238] BUGB: Mission Executive: A Vision for the Environment; BUS: Const., IV.4: the member churches must act together in matters of common concern which relate to e.g. 'the state of the nation'.

[239] NABC: Statement of Beliefs, 8: this cites e.g. Matt. 5.13–16, Hebrews 13.5, Luke 9.23, and Titus 2.12.

and the American Baptist Churches in the USA are to seek the mind of Christ on 'political, economic, [and] social' matters and express this 'to the rest of society'.[240] In similar vein, a Baptist pastor must 'support biblical morality in the community through prophetic witness and social action',[241] and (for the Canadian National Baptist Convention): 'Every Christian is under obligation to seek to make the will of Christ supreme in his own life and in human society'; thus: 'Every Christian should seek to bring industry, government, and society as a whole under the sway of the principles of righteousness, truth and brotherly love' without 'compromising their loyalty to Christ and His truth'.[242] Increasingly, Christian churches are also developing rules on interfaith relations as to their engagement with other major world religions represented in wider society.[243] So, the principles of Christian law which emerge from the similarities of the regulatory instruments of the churches studied here provide: a church must promote social justice; it should have institutions to guide, initiate and implement programmes for action in wider society; its ministers are to lead by example in this field; and the faithful are to engage directly in the promotion of social justice and charitable work: this is a requirement of the Christian faith. Further research is needed to determine how and in what ways these legal provisions are actually implemented in practice and to study the constitutions etc. of each Christian charity.

The church and public institutions

The presence of Christianity in the public institutions of the State, a topical and controversial subject, is stimulated in some measure by the regulatory instruments of the churches and it is regulated by the laws of State, themselves often the result of co-operation between church and State in this field. What follows examines the instruments of churches, across the Christian traditions, which either require or permit a Christian contribution to religious education in State schools and those which require or permit ministry in hospitals, prisons and the armed forces, and, briefly, the accommodation of these activities by State laws in Europe.

---

[240] ABCUSA: BL, Statement of Purpose. [241] BUNZ: EPGP, 6.4.
[242] CNBC: Const., 3, Statement of Faith, XV; BMPP, 216, App. III, SCBC, Type A: Art. II: the church must minister 'to human need in the name of Christ'; Art. VI.5: the Benevolence Treasurer administers funds for 'the benevolent purposes'; Art. VII: Committee on Christian Social Concern.
[243] See e.g. CIC, c. 1086: interfaith marriages; CCC pars. 839–856; GOAA: Charter, Art. 2: in 'inter-religious activities' the church must follow the guidance of Constantinople; ROMOC: Statutes, Art. 14(s): the Holy Synod governs 'inter-religious cooperation'; Art. 37(f): the Department for Interreligious Relations; LC 2008, Reflections, Section F: Relations with Other World Religions: mutual respect, dialogue and co-operation; the Anglican Communion's Network for Inter-Faith Concerns (NIFCON) is to e.g. develop relations with other faiths; ELCA: Const., 4.03(f), 8.60, 11.20–21, 15.12.B10: the church should have a 'policy' towards other faiths and 'interfaith activities'; ELCIRE: Const., 3(4): the church is to engage in 'interreligious dialogue'; UMCNEAE: BOD, pars. 121, 252, 340, 2001–2008: 'respect for persons of all religious faiths' and the work of the Committee on Christian Unity and Interreligious Concerns; MCGB: CPD, Bk. VI, s. 10: Guidelines for Inter-Faith Marriages; UCC: BL 385, 570: Inter-Faith Committee.

Christian education and the schools of the State

The regulatory instruments of some of the church families studied here address, but with differences of emphasis, the provision of Christian or other forms of religious education in State schools and the rights of the faithful in this regard. Under Roman Catholic canon law, parents have the right to educate their children, to choose the means and institutes which, in their local circumstances, may best promote the Catholic education of their children, and 'to avail themselves of that assistance from civil society which they need to provide a catholic education for their children'.[244] Education must pay regard to 'the formation of the whole person, so that they may attain their eternal destiny and at the same time promote the common good of society', and children are to be formed, inter alia, 'to take an active part in social life'.[245] Parents are free to choose for the education of their children and 'must be watchful that the civil society acknowledges this freedom of parents and, in accordance with the requirements of distributive justice, even provides them with assistance'.[246] Therefore, parents must send their children to schools which will provide for their Catholic education and if they cannot do this they must ensure 'the proper catholic education of their children outside the school'; moreover: 'Christ's faithful are to strive to secure that in the civil society the laws which regulate the formation of the young also provide a religious and moral education in the schools that is in accord with the conscience of the parents.'[247] Similar norms appear in the Code of Canons of the Oriental Catholic Churches.[248]

Some Orthodox churches have departments devoted to the provision of religious education in State schools and some of their juridical instruments assert the right of the church to provide for the religious education of Orthodox children in State schools.[249] Orthodox churches may also have education departments at the national level[250] and in the diocese.[251] Similarly, many Anglican churches have bodies involved in an advisory capacity concerning religious education in State schools.[252] Ireland is a good example. The principal duty of the Board of Education

---

[244] CIC, cc. 793–794: 'The Church has in a special way the duty and the right of educating, for it has a divine mission of helping all to arrive at the fullness of Christian life'; GE 6: civil society should allocate funds so that 'parents are truly free to select schools for their children in accordance with their conscience'.

[245] CIC, c. 795; GE 1.   [246] CIC, c. 797.

[247] CIC, cc.798–799; see also cc. 800–806: the administration of Catholic schools; GE 8.

[248] CCEO, cc. 627–630: the rights of parents; cc. 631–639: schools (including Catholic schools).

[249] SCOBA: Const., Art. IV.2: it has an Orthodox Christian Education Commission. See also GOAA: Charter, Art. 19–20: the Archdiocese may establish educational institutions with the consent of the Eparchial Synod and Archdiocesan Council or Local Council; ROC: Dioc. of Sourozh: Statutes, II.13: 'The Diocese shall have the right to teach the fundamentals of the Orthodox faith to junior pupils in government educational institutions subject to the relevant request from the parents and in the manner prescribed by [civil] law.'

[250] ROC: Statute, V.28(i): Holy Synod and (VI.7) Patriarchal Commissions on Education.

[251] ROC: Statute, X.48.

[252] Melanesia: Cans. E.16: the Education Board of the church acts under the secular Education Act 1978 of the Solomon Islands, proposes education policy for adoption by General Synod, advises on education and funding and liaises with secular government; Australia: Can. 1 1989: the General Board of Religious Education.

of the General Synod of the Church of Ireland is 'to define the policy of the Church in education both religious and secular', and, in promotion of this policy, 'to take steps to co-ordinate activities in all fields of education affecting the interests of the Church of Ireland'. The Board must maintain close contact with secular government, diocesan boards of education and schools. The Board has a special duty 'to study any [secular] legislation or proposed legislation likely to affect the educational interests of the Church of Ireland and to act as necessary'. There is an obligation to report annually to the General Synod.[253] Echoing this, the Board of Education of the Conference of the Methodist Church in Ireland has 'the direction and statement of the education policy of the Church and oversight of matters affecting the education of young people in schools, colleges and universities', especially their 'religious education'. The Board is responsible for all matters which concern 'the educational welfare of the young people connected with' the church. It must consult other churches as to the provision of religious education, provide for the visitation of such schools and arrange meetings of teachers engaged in religious education in them.[254] The Education Board of the Presbyterian Church of Ireland has parallel functions. It acts under instruction from the Assembly in all matters affecting education in Ireland, administers funds for this, and seeks 'to promote the religious education of school children generally'; it may call ministers to serve as teachers and act as advisers on religious education.[255] Carrying out work in schools may also be a function of a Baptist Union.[256] Lutheran churches sometimes claim for the right to establish and maintain their own schools,[257] and the Lutheran Church in Australia, for example, has several instruments on the administration of these.[258]

In turn, the States of Europe have extensive laws on the provision of Christian teaching in State schools. Five models are evident: (1) compulsory Christian knowledge which the State designs, teaches and funds, but from which parents or pupils may opt out (e.g. Finland); (2) compulsory denominational education which religious organisations design (perhaps in collaboration with the State) and teach,

---

[253] Ireland: Const., approved by General Synod 1965–1994.
[254] MCI: RDG, 20.01; 20.02: it also administers the General Education Fund; 20.03: it includes the Conference President; 20.06–07: the Education Secretary of the District Synod must visit schools; 20.08: the Board may withdraw aid from schools; for schools under Methodist management, see 20.12–14. See also MCGB: CPD, SO 500: the circuit must deploy resources for 'local schools and colleges'; FMCNA: BOD, par. 6340: the church shall 'encourage and promote the establishing of Christian day schools' (see also pars. 4320 and 5270).
[255] PCI: Code, XVII.1.284. [256] JBU: Const., Art. IV.3.
[257] ELCIC: Const., Art. IV.2: the church may establish, maintain, recognize and support schools for the education of 'members and others for leadership in church and society'; LCMS: BL, 1.1.1: the church may '[a]id congregations . . . to establish agencies of Christian education such as elementary and secondary schools'.
[258] The Lutheran Church of Australia and Its Schools, adopted by General Church Council 1999, edited 2001; The Public Ministry in the Lutheran School, adopted by the Board for Lutheran Schools 1995, edited 2001; The Teacher in the Lutheran School, prepared by the Board for Lutheran Schools, endorsed by General Church Council 1992, edited 2001: these deal with e.g. partnership with the State, the duties of governing bodies, principals, and teachers, and the rights of parents and children; the Lutheran school is an 'agency' of the church 'to make available . . . a formal education in which the gospel of Jesus Christ informs all learning and teaching, all human relationships, and all activities in the school'.

but which the State funds and from which pupils may opt out (e.g. Malta – Catholic education; Greece – Orthodox education); (3) opt-in denominational education which religious organisations design (perhaps in collaboration with the State) and deliver, but the State funds (e.g. Spain and Italy); (4) opt-in non-denominational education which the State designs, delivers and may fund (e.g. Sweden and Estonia); and (5) the prohibition of religious education on the premises of State schools, but the State makes provision for pupils to receive religious education externally (e.g. France and Slovenia). States also have laws which enable and regulate the establishment of church schools.[259]

Prisons, hospitals and the armed forces

The regulatory instruments of churches commonly require or permit the work of chaplaincies to provide spiritual or other care in hospitals, prisons, residential homes and the armed forces. Rules deal with the appointment of chaplains, their tenure and functions and their relationship with the public institution in question. For Catholic canon law, a chaplain is 'a priest to whom is entrusted in a stable manner the pastoral care, at least in part, of some community or special group of Christ's faithful, to be exercised in accordance with universal and particular law'; a chaplain is normally appointed by the local ordinary 'to whom also it belongs to appoint one who has been presented or to confirm one elected'.[260] A chaplain must be given all the faculties which due pastoral care demands and has by virtue of his office the faculty to hear the confessions of the faithful entrusted to his care, to preach to them the word of God, to administer the viaticum and the anointing of the sick, and to confer the sacrament of confirmation when they are in danger of death. Moreover: 'In hospitals and prisons and on sea voyages, a chaplain has the further faculty to be exercised only in those places, to absolve from *latae sententiae* censures.'[261] As far as possible, a chaplain is appointed 'for those who, because of their condition of life, are not able to avail themselves of the ordinary care of parish priests, as for example migrants, exiles, refugees, nomads and seafarers'; armed forces chaplains are ruled by special laws, as are military ordinariates.[262]

Some Orthodox laws list as one of the objects of a church the provision of spiritual care in hospitals, orphanages and residential homes, prisons and the armed

---

[259] Doe, *Law and Religion in Europe*, 191–196: religious education; 199–203: church schools.
[260] CIC, c. 564; CLLS, par. 1106: a community includes e.g. 'a school, a hospital, etc'; c. 565: appointment is by the local ordinary unless the law provides otherwise or unless special rights lawfully belong to someone else; c. 567: the local ordinary must not appoint a chaplain to a house of a lay religious institute without consulting the superior; the chaplain may conduct liturgy but not involve himself in the internal governance of the institute. See also c. 572: c. 563 applies to the removal of chaplains for 'just reasons'.
[261] CIC, c. 566; c. 567: absolution of those in danger of death may occur without faculty.
[262] CIC, c. 568: migrants etc; c. 569: the armed forces; the special laws are those contained e.g. in the apostolic constitution *Spirituali militum curae* (1986); see R. Ombres, 'The pastoral care of the armed forces in canon law', 2 *Priests and People* (1988) 234–239; cc. 368–369: military ordinariates are equivalent to dioceses; c. 570: this deals with a non-parochial church attached to an establishment of a community or group; c. 571: in the exercise of his pastoral office, a chaplain is to maintain the due relationship with the parish priest.

forces when requested by the faithful and in accordance with the relevant provisions of civil law.[263] On a visit to a hospital, prison, home for the aged or similar institutions, 'an Orthodox priest should not hesitate to bless or pray with members of other faiths and communions who make such a request' – but the priest should not seek these out and must inform the authorities of the institution which should also be informed of 'the presence and availability of the nearest Orthodox clergyman for spiritual and sacramental ministrations'.[264] For the Standing Conference of the Canonical Orthodox Bishops in the Americas: 'Orthodox chaplains in the armed forces or on the staff of schools, colleges and medical and social services institutions' should address problems to the bishop.[265] Orthodox clergy may participate in observances of a civic nature, but must not wear any liturgical vestment.[266] The assemblies of some Orthodox churches have jurisdiction over the provision of chaplains (for whom one in episcopal orders may have responsibility) as well as departments devoted to the provision of spiritual care in public institutions.[267] For instance, the Holy Synod of the Russian Orthodox Church has a Department of Relations with the Armed Forces and Law Enforcement Agencies.[268] Again, the Romanian Orthodox Church is responsible, through its eparchies, to provide religious assistance 'in the army, prisons, medical units, social centres and educational units, according to law, [and] the protocols or agreements concluded with the public authorities'; general norms on such religious assistance are set by the Holy Synod; those who provide such assistance are to be appointed, transferred or dismissed with the agreement of the eparchy and the public institution in question in accordance with the laws of both the church and the State, and they are to provide assistance upon request by the faithful in these public institutions.[269]

Similar provisions are found in some Protestant laws.[270] For example, Methodism requires the faithful to visit and help 'them that are sick or in prison'.[271] The

---

[263] ROC: Dioc. of Sourozh: Statutes, II.10: provision of church services, sacraments and devotions in hospitals 'shall be carried out upon request of their residents and subject to the consent of the [body's] administration' and in military units 'subject to the requirements of military regulations'.

[264] SCOBA: GOCER, Pt. I, Blessings, Hospital Ministrations and Chaplaincies, 1-2.

[265] SCOBA: GOCER, Pt. I, Blessings, Hospital Ministrations and Chaplaincies, 3.

[266] SCOBA: GOCER, Pt. I, Special Common Prayer Practices, 1.

[267] UOCIA: Statutes, Art. II.6(p): Holy Synod has '[g]eneral supervision over Armed Forces Chaplaincies, with the Archbishops of each country being particularly and immediately responsible in this field'; SCOBA: Const., Art. IV. 2.6: the Committee on Chaplaincies in the Armed Forces and Welfare Institutions.

[268] ROC: Statute, VI.7. [269] ROMOC: Statutes, Arts. 14, 135-136.

[270] ELCA: Const., 13.21-22: responsibility for 'the chaplaincies of this church in federal agencies, institutions and armed forces' and for 'the pastoral care of those called to these ministries'; Ch. 15.12.C10: these functions are carried out by an assistant to and appointed by the presiding bishop to: supervise the Bureau for Federal Chaplaincy Ministries of ELCA; fulfil the requirements for endorsement of candidates for chaplaincy service; seek periodically the advice of the inter-Lutheran committee for federal chaplaincies, whose members from ELCA are appointed by the presiding bishop; ELCIC: ABL, V.5: the regional synod is responsible for providing chaplaincies to institutions on its territory.

[271] MCI: General Rules of the Society; UMCNEAE: BOD, par. 103, General Rules, 5; FMCNA: BOD, par. 4700: the church 'provides ministry to persons in special situations beyond the local church, such as in the military, prisons, institutions and law enforcement agencies, through

Methodist Churches in Ireland and Great Britain have extensive rules on chaplaincy work. For the Methodist Church in Ireland: 'When a Methodist Chaplain is appointed in any public institution, the District Synod within whose bounds the appointment is made shall have the right, subject to the authority of the Conference, of determining which minister shall be appointed'. Each Spring, District Synod must make careful inquiry concerning the work of the chaplains within its area, consider additional appointments as circumstance may require and report to the General Committee.[272] The Conference must appoint a Prison and Healthcare Chaplaincy Committee 'to support and promote Christian chaplaincy ministries of healing, care and restoration among vulnerable people'. The membership of the Committee must reflect the number and diversity of chaplaincies throughout Ireland with no less than two representatives from either Northern Ireland or the Republic of Ireland, two representatives from either hospital or prison ministries, and two lay persons or ministers.[273] The Methodist Council of the Methodist Church in Great Britain must annually appoint a Royal Navy, Army and Royal Air Force Board through which it exercises general oversight of: the work of all ministers set apart to serve under the direction of the council as chaplains to the forces; the work of all deacons serving in support of chaplains; all lay workers employed by the council to serve in support of chaplains; and declared Methodists in the forces.[274] The Board through its secretary makes such arrangements with the relevant government authorities as may be necessary for the well-being of Methodist members of the forces and their families; the government provides funding for armed forces chaplains and other personnel.[275] Some Methodist churches also make provision for the appointment of 'workplace chaplains'.[276] Similar provisions are to be found in Presbyterian

---

ordained ministers who are chaplains'; rules on their appointment are approved by the Board of Bishops and the Board of Administration (see Guidelines for Ecclesiastical Chaplain Credentials); chaplains must be approved by the Board of Bishops and accredited by the FMCNA Chaplain Endorsing Agent; chaplains have their own association.

[272] MCI: RDG, 9.13–9.14.

[273] MCI: RDG, 40. See also MCGB: CPD, SO 354: the Connexional Team has the oversight of 'chaplains in pastoral care of Methodist inmates of prisons and prison staff'. These chaplains must report on their work to the Synod and the Superintendent Chaplain of Prisons appointed by the Methodist Council. The Team is responsible for the nomination of prison chaplains. The Superintendent Chaplain of Prisons consults the chair of the district in which a prison is situated as to a suitable nomination to be forwarded to the prison governor for appointment as Methodist chaplain. In the case of a minister to be appointed to full-time chaplaincy, the Superintendent Chaplain must first secure the agreement of the Stationing Committee, and, after selection has been made by the appropriate authority, must forward the name of the person to be appointed to the Stationing Committee.

[274] MCGB: CPD, SO 355: 'Declared Methodists' is a category used by the Ministry of Defence to determine the number of chaplaincy appointments; the Forces Board also oversees the work of ministers appointed to serve as Reserve Chaplains, Officiating Chaplains and Cadet Force Chaplains.

[275] MCGB: CPD, SO 355: the board secretary is responsible for recommending both to the government department concerned and to the Stationing Committee the name of a person to be appointed as a full-time chaplain, for maintaining the Forces Membership Roll and for making the annual return of members on it.

[276] MCGB: CPD, SO 355A: these function in 'industry, business and commerce'.

churches,[277] and Baptist bodies.[278] The States in Europe make extensive accommodation for chaplaincy care in public institutions.[279]

Conclusion

The regulatory instruments of churches across the Christian traditions studied here indicate that all Christians should be engaged in co-operation with the State, compliance with its laws, political activity for the common good, the promotion of human rights, the advancement of social justice and the provision of spiritual care in the public institutions of the State. From the similarities between the laws of churches emerge clear principles of Christian law. The State is instituted by God. Church and State are distinct and discharge separate functions. Church and State must co-operate with each other in matters of common concern. The faithful, both lay and ordained, may engage in political activity in wider society to the extent permitted by the law of a church. Each church and its faithful must comply with State law in so far as obedience is just and conscionable. Christian churches may enjoy under State law the position of State churches, statutory churches and covenantal churches. All humans are created in the image of God. They are therefore equal and bearers of fundamental or human rights. The State should uphold human rights, including religious freedom, and the church corporately and the faithful individually should promote human rights. A key function of the church is to engage directly in social justice. A church should have institutions devoted to the study and advancement of social justice, and, at each of its levels, must engage directly in works of charity; the faithful must do likewise, and the ordained ministers must provide leadership in this matter. Churches may promote the teaching of Christianity in State schools, and they may enable the provision of spiritual care through chaplains in the public institutions of the State, including hospitals, prisons and the armed forces. Christian churches are only recently developing norms on their relation with other major world faiths.

---

[277] PCI: Code, XVII.1.281(3): the Board of Social Witness of the Presbyterian Church in Ireland may 'call ministers recommended by their Presbyteries who have been offered full-time chaplaincies in HM Forces, in hospitals, prisons, universities, colleges or schools' and to nominate to 'the appropriate authorities' ministers as part-time chaplains in such institutions.

[278] NABC: Serving the Lord as a Chaplain in the Armed Forces of the USA, adopted by the Home Commission (2000): candidates must hold a recognised degree and have undertaken 'professional pastoral duties'; they must: receive 'ecclesiastical endorsement' from the Armed Forces Chaplain Board; be 'sensitive to the religious pluralism of the military environment and be willing to support the free exercise of religion for all military members'; and 'maintain the highest moral, spiritual, ethical, and financial standards at all times' and if they do not this may result in 'revocation of ecclesiastical endorsement'; the Conference must sustain the chaplain in 'regular prayer' and 'administrative support as required', and visit the chaplain at least once every 5 years.

[279] Doe, *Law and Religion in Europe*, 203–212.

General conclusion

Christians are prolific legislators. The laws they make are a meeting-place of faith and action. Of the twenty-two world church families, the churches of the ten studied here all have laws and other regulatory instruments. Alongside the Bible and service books for worship, these law books are central to the institutional lives of these churches. A comparison of the juridical instruments of churches, in a global compass, reveals profound similarities between the Christian traditions in their treatment, as to both internal and external relations, of church ministry, governance, doctrine, worship, ritual, ecumenism, property and public activity in the State and wider society. From these similarities emerge principles of Christian law common to the churches studied. This is a category which has not hitherto been suggested by scholarship in this area. The existence of these shared principles may be factually established as a result of careful observation. Every Christian tradition, and each institutional church within it, contributes through its own legal system, and whenever it legislates on a matter, to this store of principles. The principles have the appearance of laws (they may be preceptive, prohibitive or permissive), but they are not themselves laws: they are principles of law – as such they have a strong dimension of weight and are fundamental to the self-understanding of Christianity. The principles also have a living force and contain in themselves the possibility for further development through the continuing legislative activity of each church in an exercise of its own autonomy. Moreover, the existence of the principles both demonstrates and promotes juridical unity in Christianity in terms of its identity and global witness. The principles seem to rest on three fundamental maxims: law is the servant of the church; laws should reflect faith in the revealed will of God; and dogmas divide but laws link Christians in common action. Flowing from these maxims of juridical Christianity worldwide – about service, faith, and action – the principles themselves are capable of articulation as general normative propositions which operate in relation to a very wide range of subjects directly related to the visible lives of Christians. A statement of these is proposed in the Appendix.

The study of church law is not part of the staple diet of theologians, and the study of theology is not an established feature of the study of church laws. This state of affairs needs to be addressed. Theology and law, in the life of the Christian church, are intimately related. All the traditions accept the category divine law, and they all accept the value of Holy Scripture as a vital norm in standards of faith and practice. Reflection by the institutional churches on the revelation of God, as expressed in Holy Scripture, results in the formulation of theological propositions and values that go to the heart of the mission of the church. All the churches studied here implement theological propositions in the form of norms of conduct. As a result, the laws of the church are, essentially, applied theology. They are designed both to facilitate and to order the life of the church as it seeks to fulfil its divine mission. In turn, both theologians and lawyers need to understand this interaction. Comparative church law allows both classes working within a single Christian tradition, in their service to the church, to contextualise their work. Theology shapes law, and law implements theology. In light of the persistent doctrinal disagreements between the separated churches of Christianity, it is also a particular challenge for both lawyers and theologians to explore the place of law in these disagreements, and perhaps to justify the continued significance of divisions in doctrine when the laws of churches, of all traditions, converge so deeply in these shared principles of law. The materials presented in this book show time and time again how theological ideas surface in juridical form in the regulatory instruments of the churches – though, needless to say, not every rule studied here has an obvious theological dimension. However, we await a full-bodied exploration of not only the incidence of theology in church law across the various denominational divides, but also a Christian conception of the theology of church law.

The discussions presented in this book, and the very wide range of topics treated, indicate clearly the pervasiveness of law in the institutional life of the church. This is the case, once again, irrespective of the ecclesiastical tradition in question. All churches have rules on the ministry of the faithful (ordained and lay), governance (and its institutions and processes), doctrine, worship and those rites of passage which mark the Christian journey of the faithful through life. Whatever the title churches ascribe to particular regulatory instruments – from canon laws to books of church order – all the traditions, though to varying extents, explicitly use the term 'law' to describe generically these binding norms of conduct. This goes to the heart of Christianity as a religion of belief and action, faith and law. It is undoubtedly the case that the divided churches have developed different doctrinal reasons for their own juridical arrangements. However, the similarities between the laws of churches, as norms of conduct, reveal that Christians all over the world today should engage in much the same actions whatever their actual denominational affiliation. It must be assumed that, generally, Christians act in compliance with the laws which they have created for themselves. In all of the traditions, therefore, the members of the faithful engage in Christian service, ordain and appoint persons set apart for ministry, assemble in institutions to govern the visible church, resolve disputes amongst them in accordance with procedures consistent with universal standards of fairness, and discipline those amongst them who are in serious violation of Christian standards. They also formulate doctrine, proclaim the Gospel, engage in worship, use forms of service consistent with doctrine, administer the sacraments and other authorised rites, acquire, maintain and account for their property and finances, and work with the State and society in matters of common concern to further their mission. As norms of conduct do not displace but rather seek to translate faith into action, Christianity is a religion of law.

The study has also disclosed major juridical differences between the churches. These are in part the product of the historical, political and cultural forces which have shaped the churches. The various traditions operate sometimes very different models of church polity. The Episcopal model vests governmental authority in the bishops, exclusively in the case of the Catholic Church, and in the Orthodox Church with regard to doctrine, but in Anglicanism and in many Lutheran and some Methodist churches this is an authority shared with the clergy and laity. However, the Protestant models are different. In Presbyterianism, the Presbytery is pivotal, but authority is exercised nevertheless by national institutions and the local church. In the Congregational and Baptist models, authority does not descend from a Union or Convention, but it ascends to these from the local church – though the local church is the primary manifestation of the church universal and its autonomy is protected legally. The juridical unity of churches is time and time again the result of their common reliance on Scripture, or the adaptation of their own institutional inheritance, and, embodied in a shared principle, it is often the case that legal differences are found in exceptions to that principle, or in the conditions that must be satisfied in its application; it is in these details that we find juridical disunity. In other words, juridical differences often exist in terms of the detailed conditions under which churches particularise shared overarching principles to concrete cases. Beneath the constitutional level of polity, distinctions cannot so easily be found. At this level, the dominant model is that of co-operation between ordained ministers and the laity in fields such as worship, the provision of funds and the enjoyment of the rites of passage. All churches regulate the admission of members, but the admission conditions vary. All churches require the faithful to contribute financially to the work of the church, but amounts vary. All churches regulate public worship, but the bodies empowered to regulate it vary. Conversely, there may be fundamental juridical differences, not least in the juristic vocabulary used by churches, and yet juridical unity is found in common action: Catholic bishops share much the same functions as Methodist superintendents; Orthodox Synods discharge much the same functions as Presbyterian Assemblies; and Anglican churchwardens are engaged in much the same functions as the stewards of local Lutheran congregations.

The principles of Christian law provide an obvious resource for dialogue between Christians themselves, between Christians and the State, and between Christianity and other major world faiths. Development of the category is important to support a church when it is required in the context of religious freedom to explain the pervasiveness of the principles to which it adheres in its relations with the State when the institutions of government pressurise that church to adopt the standards of secular society. The category of Christian law may also be of value in interfaith relations for the partners to comprehend the freedoms enjoyed by and the constraints imposed on Christians in their dealings with those other faiths. Moreover, it offers a point of comparison for scholars working in the field of religious law, such as Jewish law and Islamic law, not least to stimulate greater understanding of the concept and role of law, and the attendant debates about legal pluralism, in the field of religion generally. Above all, the principles of Christian law provide the missing link in ecumenical practice and discourse. Juridical ecumenism – the deployment of church laws as an instrument of ecumenism – tells us a great deal about the opportunities available to and the limits upon the movement towards greater visible communion between the divided churches of Christianity. Whilst the doctrinal postures of churches are often divisive, appreciation of the juridical dimension of ecumenism is of enormous assistance to translate the ecumenical commitment into one which focuses on what Christians share in terms of action based on their common norms of conduct. In short, the principles of Christian law represent an obvious framework to complement but not to displace the current and dominant doctrinal and theological focus in contemporary ecumenical method and practice. Further work is needed to enable this.

Finally, this book does not purport to be an exhaustive study of the laws of Christians. A number of important matters have emerged which suggest the need for further comparative study and reflection. One such matter is the denominational coverage of the book. Its focus has been the churches of ten traditions or church families worldwide. A more ambitious study of all the global church families represented in and beyond the World Council of Churches would be an important contribution to the secondary literature in this field and a worthy project for the Council itself to take forward the recommendations of its Faith and Order Commission in 1974. Another matter is the legal history of the Christian churches. A study of the legal antecedents to the juridical instruments examined in this book would help to explain how the instruments have acquired their current shape and to expose the influence of political, social and cultural forces on their development. It would also establish the incidence (or not) of adoption and adaptation by churches of legal material from within their own tradition (particularly from their mother church) as well as between the different traditions. This transportation of legal material, its export and import, would also tell us something about globalisation in the development of church law. Similarly, further study is needed on the application of laws – the extent to which they are actually complied with by those to whom they are addressed – such as the enforcement of spiritual sanctions, the practice of hospitality in spite of restrictive ecumenical norms, and the incidence of the relaxation of rules. The same applies to difficulties associated with the administration of laws – whether they obstruct the mission of the church – for example, whether rules which govern the legislative process stifle development, whether disciplinary processes actually ensure fair treatment, and whether those on the administration of sacred places enable or frustrate liturgical innovation. It would also be instructive to explore how these laws of Christians relate to the laws of States. A State perspective on the laws of Christians could tell us whether the principles enunciated here are relative or universal, whether Christian standards reflect those of the secular world, and whether civil law has actually shaped the laws of churches and *vice versa*. In any event, it seems that in 2007 the speculation of John Witte was correct, and my scepticism quite unfounded, about the existence and development of the theological and juridical category of the contemporary principles of Christian law.

Appendix

The principles of law common to Christian churches

A principle of law common to the churches of the Christian traditions studied here is a foundational proposition or maxim of general applicability which has a strong dimension of weight, is induced from the similarities of the regulatory systems of churches, derives from their juridical tradition or the practices of the church universal, expresses a basic theological truth or ethical value, and is implicit in, or underlies, the juridical systems of the churches.

Principle 1: Ecclesiality: An institutional church: (1) defines itself by reference to its territoriality, polity and objects; (2) is a community with a defined geographical compass (international, national, regional or local); (3) has a distinct membership organised in ecclesiastical units (such as provinces, districts, or congregations); (4) is autonomous in polity and its system of governance; (5) has objects to advance mission which include proclaiming the Gospel, administering the sacraments and serving the wider community.

Principle 2: The forms of ecclesiastical regulation: (1) An institutional church may employ the term 'law' to describe its regulatory instruments; (2) The presence of law in an institutional church does not mark out its doctrinal posture; (3) Laws are found in a variety of formal sources, including codes of canon law, charters and statutes, constitutions and bylaws, and books of church order; (4) Ecclesiastical customs may have juridical force to the extent permitted by the law of a church; (5) Ecclesiastical quasi-legislation, which includes guidelines and codes of practice, is designed to complement law and consists of informal rules that are nevertheless prescriptive in form and generate the expectation of compliance.

Principle 3: The servant law: (1) Law exists to serve a church in its mission and witness to Christ; (2) Laws are necessary to constitute the institutional organisation of a church and facilitate and order its public activities but cannot encompass all facets and experiences of the Christian faith and life; (3) Laws are the servant of the church and must promote the mission of the church universal; (4) Theology shapes law, and law implements theological propositions in the form of norms of conduct; (5) Church laws should conform and are subject ultimately to the law of God, as revealed in Holy Scripture and by the Holy Spirit.

Principle 4: The structure, effect and relaxation of norms: (1) In their treatment of ministry, government, doctrine, worship, rites and property, regulatory instruments consist of a variety of juridical formulae, including precepts, prohibitions and permissions cast as principles and rules, rights and duties, functions and powers; (2) Regulatory instruments are binding and/or exhortatory; (3) No person in a church is above its law; (4) A church should have in place mechanisms for the enforcement and vindication of the rights and duties of the faithful; (5) A law may be relaxed by means of dispensation, economy or other form of equity for the spiritual good of the individual and the common good of the community.

Principle 5: The interpretation of law: (1) Laws should be interpreted by reference to their text and context; (2) Laws are to be understood according to the proper meaning of their words; (3) The church has authority to interpret its own law; (4) If there is doubt about the meaning of a law, that law does not bind; (5) For interpretation, recourse may be had to the purposes of the law, the mind of the legislator, and the faith and practice of the church.

Principle 6: The people of God: (1) The Christian faithful constitute the people of God; (2) All the faithful are equal in dignity; (3) The basis of their equality is their creation in the image of God; (4) The members of the faithful consist of lay and ordained persons; (5) All members of the faithful share in the threefold ministry of Christ: king, prophet and priest.

Principle 7: Church membership: (1) A church should serve, in appropriate ways, all who seek its ministry regardless of membership; (2) A church may admit into its membership any person who qualifies under its law; (3) Membership in a church, for the purposes of participation in its governance, may be based on any or all of the following: baptism; baptism and confirmation or other mature demonstration of faith; and such other conditions as may be prescribed by the law of that church; (4) The names of persons may be entered on a roll or other register of membership subject to such conditions as may be prescribed by law; (5) Names may be removed from such rolls and registers in accordance with the law.

Principle 8: The functions of the laity: (1) Members of the laity have such rights and duties as are recognised by the law of their church; (2) The laity must promote the mission of the church; (3) A lay person must engage in the collective ecclesial life, in proclaiming the Word, participation in worship and celebration of the sacraments; (4) Lay persons must witness to the Christian faith in their public activities; (5) Lay persons must maintain such Christian standards and spiritual practices in their private lives as are prescribed by law.

Principle 9: Lay public ministry: (1) Ministry is a gift of God exercised by persons, called by God and recognised as such by lawful authority, to serve the church in its mission and witness to the Gospel; (2) The law of a church should enable the laity to exercise ministry in those offices and other positions lawfully open to them; (3) Lay persons may be admitted to such offices and positions provided they are suitable, qualified, selected and admitted by competent ecclesiastical authority for such term as is prescribed by law; (4) Lay ministers and officers exercise such public and representative ministry within and on behalf of a church with such functions as may be prescribed by its law; (5) The authority to discipline, dismiss or reappoint a lay minister or officer depends on, and its exercise must comply with, the law.

Principle 10: Associations of the faithful: (1) The faithful may freely associate in a religious community or other association; (2) The establishment of a religious community or other association may be governed by the law of church to which it is affiliated; (3) A religious community or other association enjoys such autonomy in its governance as is permitted by its own statutes or other regulatory instrument; (4) The regulatory instruments applicable to a religious community or other association are to provide for the admission, rights and duties, and termination of association of its members; (5) The relationship of a religious order or association to the church to which it may be affiliated, and any provision for visitation, are governed by the mutual acceptance of their respective regulatory systems.

Principle 11: Ordination: (1) Ordained ministry is divine in origin and persons are set apart for this; (2) Ordained ministers exist in a variety of grades, which may include bishops, priests, deacons, superintendents, pastors, ministers and elders; (3) Candidates for ordination must be called by God to this and their vocation and suitability are tested by the church through a process of selection, examination and training; (4) Persons are admitted to ordained ministry through the rite of ordination administered by competent authority by means of the laying-on-of-hands and invocation of the Holy Spirit; (5) Ordination cannot be repeated.

Principle 12: The tenure of ministerial office: An ecclesiastical office: (1) is a stable substantive position constituted by law and held in succession; (2) exists independently of the person who occupies it; (3) enables the discharge of functions of the particular ordained ministry attaching to it; (4) is filled either by appointment or by election by competent ecclesiastical authority; (5) is terminated by death, resignation, retirement or removal.

Principle 13: The functions of ordained ministers: Ordained ministers, when duly authorised by their church, are: (1) to preach the Word, administer the Sacraments and provide pastoral care to and where required beyond the faithful; (2) to lead their private lives in a manner which befits their sacred calling; (3) to reside in the territorial boundaries of their pastoral charge unless lawfully permitted to be absent; (4) to engage only in such other occupations, including offices held beyond the local church, as are permitted by law; (5) to account for the exercise of their ministry to competent authority prescribed by law.

Principle 14: The exercise of oversight: (1) Oversight of a regional ecclesial unit is carried out by those in senior ordained ministries, such as diocesan bishops, district superintendents, presbytery moderators or other ecclesiastical persons, as designated by law; (2) The person with regional oversight is either elected or otherwise appointed to the relevant office with the participation of the faithful by means of consent or consultation; (3) Admission to office is by means of such ritual as may be prescribed by law and the tenure of office terminates on death, resignation, retirement or removal; (4) The person assigned to a regional ministry is to exercise leadership and oversee the governance, teaching and ritual life of the region to the extent permitted by law; (5) Ecclesial units beyond the region, such as at provincial or national level, are overseen by metropolitans, archbishops, presidents, moderators or other such officers whose authority and its exercise are determined by the relevant law.

Principle 15: Personal international oversight and leadership: (1) A senior ordained minister may enjoy such international functions of oversight or leadership as are permitted under the law of a church; (2) The international ecclesiastical offices include those of pope, patriarch, primate or president; (3) Those who exercise international oversight or leadership are elected to that office by competent ecclesial authority; (4) A church may assign to such an office a coercive jurisdiction or a moral or persuasive authority; (5) Tenure of an office which involves international ministry terminates on the death, resignation, retirement or removal of the minister or the satisfaction of such other condition as may be prescribed by church law.

Principle 16: Systems of church polity: (1) A church may employ an Episcopal, Presbyterian, Congregational or other form of government permitted by its conception of divine law with Christ as the ultimate head of the church universal in all its manifestations; (2) A church should have institutions to legislate, administer and adjudicate for its own governance; (3) An institution has such power or authority as may be assigned to it by law; (4) An institution must comply with the rule of law and may be subject in the exercise of its functions to such substantive and procedural limitations as may be prescribed by law; (5) Ecclesial institutions may be organised at international, national, regional and/or local level composed of such members or representatives of the faithful as are prescribed by law.

Principle 17: International ecclesial communities: (1) An ecclesial tradition may have an international organisation in the form of a communion, federation or other global association; (2) An institutional church may be coincidental with or associate in such an international organisation; (3) A global ecclesial community has such institutional organisation as may be constituted by it or assigned to it under its doctrine and law; (4) An international ecclesial institution has such functions and authority over its autonomous constituent parts as are assumed by the institutional church represented in it or conferred upon it by those churches associated within it; (5) An international ecclesial institution is composed of such persons on such terms of tenure as are assigned to them in accordance with its own juridical instruments.

Principle 18: National church structures: (1) An ecclesial tradition may have a national organisation; (2) National ecclesiastical organisation may be in the form of an institutional church or of churches associated together at that level; (3) A church or other ecclesial community organised at national level may have such institutional organisation as is prescribed by the regulatory instrument applicable to it; (4) The autonomy and functions of a national ecclesial entity, and its conference, synod, council or other form of central assembly, may include the authority to legislate, administer and adjudicate on matters within its competence; (5) A national ecclesial assembly or other such institution is composed of such members of the faithful as are elected or otherwise appointed to it in accordance with law.

Principle 19: Regional church structures: (1) Within national ecclesiastical entities, an ecclesial tradition may have regional structures; (2) Regional ecclesiastical organisation may be in the form of a diocese, eparchy, synod, district, association or other regional unit; (3) A regional ecclesiastical unit may have such institutions, in the form of a synod, council, presbytery, or other assembly, as are prescribed by the law applicable to it; (4) A regional institution enjoys such authority and functions as are conferred on it by the wider ecclesial community to which it belongs or the constituent churches associated in it; (5) A regional ecclesial assembly or other such institution is composed of such members of the faithful as are elected or otherwise appointed to it by those competent to do so under the law.

Principle 20: The local church: (1) Regional ecclesial units may be divided into or constituted by local churches or congregations existing at the most localised level of church life; (2) The local church is a manifestation of the church universal; (3) A local church may be in the form of a parish, circuit, congregation or other ecclesial unit; (4) A local church, its assembly and other institutions, such as a council, meeting, session or other body, has such authority and functions as are lawfully inherent to it or conferred upon it by the institutions of the wider ecclesial entity to which it belongs; (5) The assembly of a local church is composed of those members of the faithful who are lawfully elected or otherwise appointed to it.

Principle 21: Ecclesiastical discipline: (1) An institutional church has the right to enforce discipline and to resolve conflicts amongst the faithful; (2) The right to exercise discipline over the faithful is based on divine and spiritual authority; (3) A church may exercise discipline in relation to both lay and ordained persons to the extent provided by law; (4) The purpose of discipline is to glorify God, to protect the integrity of the church, to safeguard the vulnerable from harm and to promote the spiritual benefit of its members through just structures; (5) Discipline may be exercised by competent authority in accordance with law.

Principle 22: Informal dispute resolution: (1) Ecclesiastical disputes may be settled by means of administrative process and/or quasi-judicial power; (2) A complainant with a sufficient interest in the matter may challenge a decision by means of appeal to the relevant and competent authority; (3) The competent authority may settle the matter in a process short of formal judicial process in the manner and to the extent provided by law; (4) Visitation may be exercised pastorally by a regional or other competent authority in relation to the local church or other such entity in the manner and to the extent provided by law; (5) The aim of visitation is to monitor, affirm and improve the life and discipline of the entity visited.

Principle 23: Church courts and tribunals: (1) A church or other ecclesial community may have a system of courts or tribunals to provide for the enforcement of discipline and the formal and judicial resolution of ecclesiastical disputes; (2) Church courts and tribunals may exist at international, national, regional and/or local level to the extent permitted by the relevant law; (3) The establishment, composition and jurisdiction of judicial bodies are determined by the law applicable to them; (4) Church courts and tribunals are established by competent authority, administered by qualified personnel and may be tiered in terms of their original and their appellate jurisdiction; (5) Church courts and tribunals exercise such authority over the laity and ordained ministers as is conferred upon them by law.

Principle 24: Due process: (1) Every effort must be made by the faithful to settle their disputes amicably, lawfully, justly and equitably; (2) Recourse to church courts and tribunals is a last resort; (3) Judicial process may be composed of informal resolution, investigation, a hearing and/or other stages as may be prescribed by law, including an appeal; (4) Disciplinary procedures at trial must secure fair, impartial and due process on the basis of natural justice; (5) The parties, particularly the accused, have the right to notice, to be heard, to question evidence, to silence, to an unbiased hearing and, where appropriate, to appeal.

Principle 25: Ecclesiastical offences and sanctions: (1) A church may institute a system of ecclesiastical offences; (2) Ecclesiastical offences and defences to them are to be clearly defined in writing and a court, tribunal or other body acting in a judicial capacity must give reasons for its finding of breach of church discipline; (3) The church has an inherent right to impose spiritual and other lawful censures, penalties and sanctions upon the faithful provided a breach of ecclesiastical discipline has been established objectively; (4) Sanctions must be lawful and just and may include admonition, rebuke, suspension, excommunication and ultimately removal from office or membership or other withdrawal from spiritual privileges for the remedial or medicinal purpose of the reform of the offender and the welfare of the church; (5) A church should enable the removal of sanctions on the basis of the principle of forgiveness or other value and restoration to the full benefits of ecclesial association.

Principle 26: Doctrinal definition: (1) Doctrine is the teaching of the church on matters of faith and practice; (2) The doctrine of a church is rooted in the revelation of God as recorded in Holy Scripture, summed up in the historical Creeds, and expounded in instruments, texts and pronouncements issued by ecclesiastical persons and institutions with lawful authority to teach; (3) Doctrinal instruments include Catechisms, Articles of Religion, Confessions of Faith and other statements of belief; (4) The doctrinal instruments of churches may have normative elements which themselves may generate norms of conduct; (5) The doctrines of a church may be interpreted and developed afresh to the extent and in the manner prescribed by law provided this accords with the catholic and apostolic faith of the church universal.

Principle 27: Proclamation of the faith: (1) The proclamation of the Word of God is a fundamental action of the church and a divine imperative incumbent on all the faithful; (2) A church is responsible for the instruction of the faithful and the evangelisation of the world; (3) Preaching is inherent to ordained ministry and ordained ministers and authorised lay persons may deliver sermons or other forms of preaching for the glory of God, the edification of the people and the consistent exposition of church doctrine; (4) Instruction by the church, by its ministers and amongst the faithful in general may be by means of catechesis, Sunday school or other such classes and the faithful should study Holy Scripture; (5) Biblical texts must be treated respectfully and coherently, building on tradition and scholarship so that scriptural revelation may continue to illuminate, challenge and transform thinking and doing.

Principle 28: Doctrinal discipline: (1) The church has a right to enforce its own doctrinal standards and discipline; (2) The faithful should believe church doctrine and ordination candidates and others may be required to subscribe, assent or otherwise affirm their belief in or loyalty to that doctrine; (3) The faithful should not publicly manifest, in word or deed, a position contrary to church doctrine; (4) Any person who offends church doctrine may be subject to disciplinary process; (5) Determining permissible theological opinion and the interpretation of its own doctrine and doctrinal standards vests in each church.

Principle 29: The nature and forms of worship: (1) The worship of God is a fundamental action of the church and divinely instituted; (2) Worship involves an intimate encounter between the church corporately and the faithful individually with the presence of God; (3) Each church and those bodies within it which are competent to do so are to develop liturgical texts or other forms of service for the public worship of God provided these are consistent with the Word of God and church doctrine; (4) Forms of service may be found in a book of rites or liturgy, a book of common prayer, a directory of worship and such other service books as are lawfully authorised for use in a church; (5) The rubrics or other directions in a service book are to be interpreted flexibly in order to enable meaningful worship.

Principle 30: The administration of public worship: (1) A church must provide for public worship; (2) Ordained ministers are particularly responsible for the conduct of public worship in accordance with the authorised forms of service; (3) The faithful must engage in regular attendance at divine worship, particularly on the Lord's Day, Sunday; (4) The administration of worship is subject to supervision by those local and regional authorities designated by law to provide this; (5) The performance of music is an essential feature of Christian worship.

Principle 31: Baptism: (1) Baptism is a divinely instituted sacrament and constitutes incorporation of a person into the church of Christ; (2) Baptism is validly administered with water in the name of the triune God; (3) Baptism is administered ordinarily in public in the presence of the faithful by an ordained minister, but extraordinarily in cases of necessity by a lay person; (4) A church may practise infant and/or believers' baptism and a baptised person should be nurtured in the faith by duly qualified sponsors or other designated entity; (5) A baptism should be registered in books kept for this purpose and it cannot be repeated, but, in the absence of proof of a prior valid baptism, a conditional baptism may be administered.

Principle 32: Confirmation and profession: (1) Baptism may be constituted by, accompanied by or followed by a rite in which candidates make a public and mature demonstration of their faith; (2) Such a rite may be conceived as a sacrament or as sacramental in nature provided this is consistent with church doctrine; (3) The rite may be styled confirmation, profession of the faith or admission to full membership; (4) Candidates must undergo preparation and instruction prior to the administration of the rite; (5) The rite is administered by means of laying on of hands or other ritual action administered by an authorised ordained minister in the presence of the faithful at a public service.

Principle 33: The Eucharist, Holy Communion or Lord's Supper: (1) The Eucharist, Holy Communion or Lord's Supper is a sacrament instituted by Christ; (2) It is central to ecclesial life and the faithful should participate in it regularly; (3) It is administered by ordained persons, or those otherwise lawfully deputed, normally in a public church service and exceptionally in private, such as to the sick; (4) It is administered by means of the distribution of bread and wine or equivalent elements; (5) A church by due process may exclude from admission to the sacrament those whom it judges unworthy to receive it.

Principle 34: Marriage: (1) Marriage must be upheld by the faithful; (2) It is a lifelong union between one man and one woman, instituted by God for the mutual affection and support of the parties and may be ordered to procreation; (3) To be married validly in the eyes of the church, the parties must satisfy the conditions prescribed by church law and should be instructed in the nature and obligations of marriage; (4) It is celebrated at a public service in the presence of an ordained minister and witnesses, and it must be registered; (5) A marriage is dissolved ordinarily by the death of one of the spouses and extraordinarily when recognised as such by competent ecclesiastical authority, though a minister may solemnise the marriage of a divorced person whose former spouse is still alive to the extent that this is authorised by the law of a church and the conscience of the minister.

Principle 35: Confession and funerals: (1) Forgiveness of sins after repentance is a fundamental of Christianity; (2) A church may practise private confession and absolution in the presence of an ordained minister to the extent that this is permitted by the law of a church; (3) A duty of confidentiality attaches to all information disclosed and received in the rite of confession or in the course of ministry; (4) Funeral rites are open to all who sincerely seek them; (5) Disposal of human remains may be either by burial or by cremation accompanied by the administration of any funeral service authorised for lawful use in a church.

Principle 36: The church universal: (1) There is one, holy, catholic and apostolic church universal; (2) Christ bestows unity on the church, the Body of Christ; (3) Admission to the church of Christ is by baptism; (4) An institutional church has for the purposes of law such relationship to the church universal, by being a portion, member or branch of it, or by other form of manifestation of it, as is prescribed in its doctrine and law; (5) The unity of the church universal is not destroyed by the denominational division of institutional churches.

Principle 37: The nature of ecumenism and the ecumenical obligation: (1) The restoration of Christian unity is a divine imperative of Christ; (2) Each church must promote the ecumenical movement through active dialogue and co-operation; (3) The institutional goal of ecumenism is full ecclesial communion; (4) Ecumenical activity must be prudent and in accordance with the law of all ecumenical partners involved so that the discipline of each is respected; (5) The law of a church should protect the marks of the church universal and define what ecclesial communion and reciprocity is possible between that and other churches.

Principle 38: Institutional structures for ecumenism: (1) The regulation and authorisation of ecumenical activity are in the keeping of the central authority of a church; (2) The central authority of a church may be assisted by commissions and other advisory bodies in the ecumenical enterprise; (3) Duties to participate in ecumenism may be distributed to the institutions of the local church and to ordained ministers; (4) A church should provide for the ecumenical formation of the faithful; (5) It is for a church in agreement with its ecumenical partner to determine when dialogue reaches a stage which allows ecclesial communion.

Principle 39: Ecclesial, ministerial and sacramental communion: (1) Ecclesial communion between two or more churches of different traditions exists when a relationship is established in which each church believes the other to hold the essential marks of the church universal; (2) Full communion involves the mutual recognition of unity in faith, sacramental sharing, the mutual recognition and inter-changeability of ministries, and the reciprocal enjoyment of shared spiritual, pastoral and other resources, and partial communion is an ecclesial relationship in which at least one but not all the elements of full communion is present; (3) An agreement to establish ecclesial communion between two or more churches does not affect the legal relationship between those churches and other churches not party to it; (4) The validity of an act performed in a church is determined by that church and recognition of such validity by another church is a matter for that other church; (5) Ecumenical norms on the administration of the sacraments, mixed marriages and sharing property are in the nature of exceptions to general rules which confine such facilities to the enjoyment of the faithful within the ecclesiastical tradition which created those norms.

Principle 40: Conciliar ecumenism and covenantal communion: (1) Each church is free to determine whether or not it participates in existing international, national, regional or local ecumenical initiatives; (2) The extent and terms of ecclesial communion or other relationship between a church of two or more different traditions may be set out in a constitutional union, concordat, covenant or other instrument agreed between the participant churches; (3) The establishment of ecumenical agreements is an exercise of autonomy by a church in the form of collaborative ecumenical norm-making which may be prescriptive or aspirational; (4) A church may incorporate in its own law the terms of an ecumenical agreement; (5) Ecumenical agreements may be varied or terminated only with the agreement of the participant churches.

Principle 41: The ownership of property: (1) A church has the right to acquire, administer and dispose of property; (2) A church and/or institutions or bodies within it should seek legal personality under civil law to enable ownership; (3) A church should have rules about the acquisition, ownership, administration, sale or other form of disposal of church property; (4) A church should have in place provision for its own dissolution or that of units within it and the distribution of property on dissolution; (5) Property vests in institutions prescribed by law which act as its stewards holding it on trust for the benefit of the church and its work.

Principle 42: Sacred places and objects: (1) Places of worship and prescribed objects should be dedicated to the purposes of God; (2) The activities carried out in relation to sacred property should not be inconsistent with the spiritual purposes which attach to it; (3) Items of church property include places of worship and their contents, associated buildings used for ecclesiastical purposes, and church registers and records; (4) The use, care and maintenance of sacred places and objects should reside in a designated and local person or body; (5) Oversight of the administration of church property vests in competent ecclesiastical authority and a periodic appraisal of its condition may be the object of a lawful visitation.

Principle 43: The control of finance: (1) A church has the right to make rules for the administration and control of its finances; (2) The civil law applicable to financial accountability should be complied with; (3) Each ecclesiastical unit, including the local church, through designated bodies, should prepare an annual budget for approval by its own assembly; (4) A church should provide, with regard to each unit, for the keeping of accounts by a treasurer for similar approval; (5) A church must ensure that financial accounts are audited annually by qualified persons in order to promote proper stewardship in the church.

Principle 44: Lawful income: (1) A church has a right to receive funds; (2) The faithful must contribute financially to church work; (3) Church officers should encourage the faithful in the matter of offerings and collect and distribute these in the manner and to the objects prescribed by law; (4) The local church and other units may be the subject of assessments made beyond them by regional, national, or international authorities; (5) A church may invest money prudently in ethical ventures which are consistent with the standards of the church.

Principle 45: Ecclesiastical expenditure: A church should: (1) require the designated authorities within it to insure church property against loss; (2) remunerate those engaged in full-time and other forms of ministry; (3) pay the expenses of persons engaged in ministry who are entitled to them; (4) make financial provision for ordained ministers who are in ill-health and who retire; (5) monitor that these duties are discharged in accordance with law.

Principle 46: Church–State relations: (1) The State is instituted by God to promote and protect the temporal and common good of civil society, functions fundamentally different from those of the church; (2) There should be a basic institutional separation between a church and the State but a church should co-operate with the State in matters of common concern; (3) The faithful may participate in politics to the extent permitted by church law; (4) The faithful should comply with State law but disobedience by the faithful to unjust laws is permitted; (5) The faithful should not resort to State courts unless all ecclesiastical process is exhausted.

Principle 47: The position of churches under State law: Co-operation between a church and the State may be exercised on the basis of: (1) the establishment of, or other formal relationship between, a church and the State; (2) an agreement or civil legislation negotiated freely with the State; (3) the juridical personality which a church or institutions within it may enjoy under civil law; (4) the registration of a church in accordance with the provisions of any applicable State law; (5) the fundamental institutional autonomy of the church in carrying out its lawful objects and its freedom in these areas from intervention by the State.

Principle 48: Human rights and religious freedom: (1) All humans are created in the image of God; (2) All humans share an equality of dignity and fundamental human rights; (3) The State should recognise, respect and promote basic human rights; (4) The church should protect and defend human rights in society for all people, and, like the church, the State and society should not discriminate against individuals on grounds of race, gender and colour; (5) The State should recognise, promote and protect the religious freedom of churches corporately and of the faithful individually, as well as their freedom of conscience.

Principle 49: Social responsibility: (1) The church must promote social justice; (2) A church should have institutions to guide, initiate and implement programmes for Christian action in society; (3) Ordained ministers are to lead by example in the field of social justice and responsibility; (4) The faithful are to engage directly in the promotion of social justice and charitable work; (5) Engagement in service to society is a requirement of faith and law.

Principle 50: Public institutions: (1) Churches may promote the teaching of Christianity in State schools; (2) Christian teaching provided in State schools by church entities and persons is a matter of co-operation between the relevant and competent church and civil authorities; (3) Churches should avail themselves of the opportunities under civil law for the provision of spiritual care in public institutions which include hospitals, homes, prisons and the armed forces; (4) Churches should seek lawful financial assistance from the State in the provision of spiritual care in public institutions; (5) Communion with God is the supreme law.

BIBLIOGRAPHY

The following is a thematic list of the materials used in this study. In sections 1 to 10, each tradition studied is listed alphabetically – its primary sources (their laws and other regulatory instruments) followed by the secondary sources. Section 11 lists primary and secondary sources on ecumenism, and sections 12–15 list secondary sources on the history of church law, civil law on religion, religious law, and theology and the history of Christian themes.

1. Anglican materials

Primary sources

Australia: *The Anglican Church of Australia: Constitution, Canons and Rules of the Anglican Church of Australia* (2010); *A Prayer Book for Australia* (1995)
Brazil: Episcopal Anglican Church of Brazil, *Igreja Episcopal Anglicana do Brasil: Constituciao* (1994) *and Canones Gerais* (1994)
Burundi: Church of the Province of Burundi, *Constitution* (1991)
Canada: Anglican Church of Canada, *Handbook of the General Synod of the Anglican Church of Canada* (2010); *Book of Common Prayer* (1962)
Central Africa: Church of the Province of Central Africa, *Constitution and Canons* (1996)
Chile: Diocese of Chile, Anglican Church of the Southern Cone of America, *Estatutos de la Corporacion Anglicana de Chile* (1995)
England: Church of England, *Canons of the Church of England* (1964–2011); *Book of Common Prayer* (1662); *A Directory of Religious Life* (Advisory Council on the Relations of Bishops and Religious Communities, 1990)
Indian Ocean: Church of the Province of the Indian Ocean, *Constitution and Canons* (1994)
Ireland: *The Constitution of the Church of Ireland* (2003)
Japan: Holy Catholic Church in Japan (*Nippon Sei Ko Kai*), *Constitution and Canons* (1971)
Jerusalem: *Constitution of the Central Synod of the Episcopal Church in Jerusalem and the Middle East* (1980)
Kenya: Church of the Province of Kenya, *Constitution* (1979)
Korea: *The Constitution and Canons of the Anglican Church of Korea* (1992)
Melanesia: Church of the Province of Melanesia, *Constitution and Canons* (1992)
Mexico: Anglican Church of Mexico, *Constitucion del Sinodo General de la Iglesia Anglicana de Mexico* (1996)

New Zealand: Anglican Church in Aotearoa, New Zealand and Polynesia, *Constitution and Code of Canons* (2008); *A New Zealand Prayer Book* (1989)
Nigeria: Church of Nigeria (Anglican Communion), *Constitution* (2002)
Papua New Guinea: Anglican Church of (the Province of) Papua New Guinea, *Provincial Constitution and Provincial Canons* (1996)
Philippines: Episcopal Church in the (Province of the) Philippines, *Constitution and Canons* (1996); *Social Concerns Resolutions and Statements* (1988)
Portugal: Lusitanian Church (Portuguese Episcopal Church), *Igreja Lusitana, Catolica, Apostolica, Evangelica, Canones* (1980)
Rwanda: Church of the Province of Rwanda, *Constitution* (1998)
Scotland: Scottish Episcopal Church, *Code of Canons* (2006)
South East Asia: Church of the Province of South East Asia, *Constitution and Regulations* (1997)
South India: *The Constitution of the Church of South India* (1992)
Southern Africa: Anglican Church of Southern Africa, *Constitution and Canons* (2004); *An Anglican Prayer Book* (1989)
Sudan: *The Constitution of the Province of the Episcopal Church of the Sudan* (1976: as amended, 1983)
The Anglican Communion Covenant (Anglican Communion Office, London, 2009)
The Canon Law of the Church of England, Report of the Archbishops' Commission on Canon Law [Church of England] (SPCK, London, 1947)
The Principles of Canon Law Common to the Churches of the Anglican Communion (Anglican Communion Office, London, 2008)
The Windsor Report, Lambeth Commission on Communion (Anglican Communion Office, London, 2004)
Uganda: Church of the Province of Uganda, *Provincial Constitution* (1994)
USA: The Episcopal Church in the USA, *Constitution and Canons for the Government of the Episcopal Church in the United States of America* (2000); *Book of Common Prayer* (1979); Office of Ecumenism and Interfaith Relations, *A Beginner's Guide to the Concordat of Agreement* (with the Evangelical Lutheran Church of America) (2003)
Venezuela: Extra-Provincial Diocese of Venezuela, *Constitucion y Canones de la Iglesia Anglicana en Venezuela* (1995)
Virginia Report (of the Inter-Anglican Theological and Doctrinal Commission), The Official Report of the Lambeth Conference 1998 (Morehouse Publishing, Harrisburg, Pennsylvania, 1999)
Wales: *The Constitution of the Church in Wales* (2006); *The Book of Common Prayer* (1984).
West Africa: Church of the Province of West Africa, *Constitution and Canons* (1989)
West Indies: *Constitution and Canons of the Church of the Province of the West Indies* (1991)

Secondary sources

Allchin, A.M., *The Silent Rebellion: Anglican Religious Communities 1845–1900* (SCM Press, London, 1958)

Baima, T.M., *The Concordat of Agreement between the Episcopal Church and the Evangelical Lutheran Church in America: Lessons on the Way Toward Full Communion* (Edwin Mellen Press, New York, 2003)

Coleman, E. (ed.), *Resolutions of the Twelve Lambeth Conferences 1867–1988* (Anglican Book Centre, Toronto, 1992)

Doe, N., *An Anglican Covenant: Theological and Legal Considerations for a Global Debate* (Canterbury Press, Norwich, 2008)

'Canonical approaches to human rights in Anglican churches', in M. Hill (ed.), *Religious Liberty and Human Rights* (University of Wales Press, Cardiff, 2002) 185

'Canon law and communion', 6 *Ecclesiastical Law Journal* (2002) 241

Canon Law in the Anglican Communion: A Worldwide Perspective (Clarendon Press, Oxford, 1998)

'Inter-church and inter-faith marriages in Anglican canon law', in N. Doe (ed.) *Marriage in Anglican and Roman Catholic Canon Law* (Centre for Law and Religion, Cardiff, 2009) 95

(ed.), *Marriage in Anglican and Roman Catholic Canon Law* (Centre for Law and Religion, Cardiff, 2009)

'The Anglican Covenant proposed by the Lambeth Commission', 8 *Ecclesiastical Law Journal* (2005) 147–161

'The common law of the Anglican Communion', 7 *Ecclesiastical Law Journal* (2003) 4

'The contribution of common principles of canon law to ecclesial communion in Anglicanism', in *The Principles of Canon Law Common to the Churches of the Anglican Communion* (Anglican Communion Office, London, 2008) 97

(ed.), *The Formation and Ordination of Clergy in Anglican and Roman Catholic Canon Law* (Centre for Law and Religion, Cardiff, 2009)

The Law of the Church in Wales (University of Wales Press, Cardiff, 2002)

The Legal Framework of the Church of England: A Critical Study in a Comparative Context (Clarendon Press, Oxford, 1996)

'The principles of canon law: a focus of legal unity in Anglican-Roman Catholic relations', 5 *Ecclesiastical Law Journal* (1999) 221

Hill, M., *Ecclesiastical Law* (3rd edn., Oxford University Press, 2007)

'Gospel and order', 4 *Ecclesiastical Law Journal* (1996) 659

House of Bishops, *The Eucharist: Sacrament of Unity* (Church House Publishing, London, 2001)

2. Baptist materials

Primary sources

American Baptist Churches in the USA: *Standing Rules* (2007); *Bylaws* (2007); *Common Budget Covenant, Operating Guidelines Manual* (2004); *The Covenant of Relationships and its Agreements among the General, National, and Regional Boards of the American Baptist Churches* (1984)

Asian Baptist Federation (BWA, Regional Organisation): *Constitution and Bylaws* (1994)

Baptist Churches of New Zealand: *Ethical Principles and Guidelines for Pastors of New Zealand Baptist Churches* (2000, amended 2008); *Transitional Ministry Guidelines* (2005)

Baptist Union of Great Britain: *Constitution* (undated); Baptist Union Corporation Guidelines, *Baptist Model Trusts for Churches* (2003); *Baptists in Ecumenical Partnerships* (2008)

Baptist Union of Scotland: *Constitution and Standing Orders of the Council and Assembly* (undated)

Baptist Union of Southern Africa: *Constitution and Bylaws* (1933, as amended); *Model Constitution* (2000)

Baptist World Alliance: *Constitution, and Bylaws of the General Council* (2004)

Bethel Baptist Church, Choctaw, Oklahoma, USA: *Constitution and Bylaws* (undated)

Canadian National Baptist Convention: *Constitution and Bylaws* (2008)

Central Baptist Church, Pretoria, South Africa: *Constitution* (2010)

Jamaica Baptist Union: *Constitution* (1981)

National Baptist Convention, USA, Incorporated: *Constitution* (Revised, 2002); *Bylaws* (2003)

Nigerian Baptist Convention: *Policies and Practice* (undated)

North American Baptist Conference: *Constitution* (2009); *Statement of Beliefs* (2004); *Ordination Guidelines* (2004); *Home Missions Commission, Serving the Lord as a Chaplain in the Armed Forces of the United States of America* (2000)

Orders and Prayers for Church Worship: A Manual for Ministers, compiled by E.A. Payne and S.F. Winward (BUGB and Ireland, London, 1960, Reprinted 1972)

Riverside Baptist Church, Baltimore, USA: *Constitution and Bylaws* (2003)

Southern Baptist Convention: Sunday School Board, *The Baptist Faith and Message* (Nashville, Tennessee, 1963); *The Church Constitution Guide*: www.namb.net

Secondary sources

Brackney, W.H., *Historical Dictionary of the Baptists* (Scarecrow Press, Lanham, Maryland and London, 1999)

Deweese, C.W., *Baptist Church Covenants* (Boardman Press, Nashville, Tennessee, 1990)

Gilmore, A. (ed.), *The Pattern of the Church: A Baptist View* (Lutterworth Press, London, 1963)

Goodliff, P., 'Baptist church polity and practice', 168 *Law and Justice* (2012) 5

Grenz, S.J., *The Baptist Congregation: A Guide to Baptist Belief and Practice* (Regent College Publishing, Vancouver, British Columbia, 1985)

Lumpkin, W.L., *Baptist Confessions of Faith* (Judson Press, Philadelphia, 1959)

Maring, N.H., and W.S. Hudson, *A Baptist Manual of Polity and Practice* (Judson Press, Valley Forge, Pennsylvania, 1963)

Pierard, R.V. (ed.), *Baptists Together in Christ 1905–2005: A Hundred-Year History of the Baptist World Alliance* (BWA, Falls Church, Virginia, 2005)

Sparkes, D.C., *The Constitutions of the Baptist Union of Great Britain* (BUGB, London, 1996)

Stanton Norman, R., *The Baptist Way: Distinctiveness of a Baptist Church* (Broadman and Holman, Nashville, Tennessee, 2005)
West, W.M.S., *Baptist Principles* (BUGB, London, 1960)
Wright, N.G., *Free Church, Free State: The Positive Baptist Vision* (Paternoster, London, 2005)

3. Catholic materials

Primary sources

Acta Apostolicae Sedis (Vatican, 1909–present)
Basic Norms for Priestly Formation (Vatican, 1985)
Catechism of the Catholic Church (Geoffrey Chapman, London, 1994)
Christus Dominus (Vatican II, Decree, 1965)
Codex Canonum Ecclesiarum Orientalium, Code of Canons of the Eastern Churches (1990), Latin-English Edition, Canon Law Society of America (Washington, 2001)
Codex Iuris Canonici, The Code of Canon Law (1983) (Latin Church)
Dignitatis Humanae (Vatican II, Decree, 1965)
Directory for the Application of Norms and Principles of Ecumenism (Vatican, 1993)
Directory for the Ministry and Life of Priests (Vatican, 1994)
Ecclesia de Eucharistia (Vatican, 2003)
Gaudium et Spes (Vatican II, Pastoral Constitution, 1966)
Gravissimum Educationis (Vatican II, Declaration, 1965)
Lumen Gentium (Vatican II, Dogmatic Constitution, 1965)
Matrimonia Mixta (1970)
One Bread, One Body, Bishops' Conference of England and Wales, Ireland and Scotland (London, 1998)
Pastor Bonus (Vatican, 1988)
Sacrae Disciplinae Leges (Vatican, 1983)
Sacrosanctum Consilium (Vatican II, Constitution, 1964)
The Ecumenical Dimension of Those Engaged in Pastoral Work (Vatican, 1995)
The Priest, Pastor and Leader of the Parish Community (Vatican, 2002)
Unitatis Redintegratio (Vatican II, Decree on Ecumenism, 1964)

Secondary sources

Arrieta, J.I., *Governance Structures within the Catholic Church* (Wilson and Lafleur, Montreal, 2000)
Beal, J.P., J.A. Coriden and T.J. Green (eds.), *New Commentary on the Code of Canon Law* (Paulist Press, New York, 2000)
Corecco, E., *The Theology of Canon Law: A Methodological Question* (Duquesne University Press, Pittsburgh, Pennsylvania, 1992)
Coriden, J., 'A challenge: make rights real', 45 *The Jurist* (1986) 1
Dalton, W., 'Parish councils or parish pastoral councils', 22 *Studia Canonica* (1988) 169
Euart, S.A., 'Council, code and laity: implications for lay ministry', 47 *The Jurist* (1987) 492

Flannery, A. (ed.), *Vatican Council II: The Conciliar and Post-Conciliar Documents*, Vatican Collection, 2 Volumes (Costello, New York, 1982, 1988)

Gallagher, C., *Church Law and Church Order in Rome and Byzantium: A Comparative Study* (Ashgate, Variorum, Aldershot, 2002)

Gauthier, A., 'Juridical persons in the code of canon law', 25 *Studia Canonica* (1991) 77

Gavin, F., 'An outline of marriage preparation in Roman Catholic discipline', in N. Doe (ed.), *Marriage in Anglican and Roman Catholic Canon Law* (Centre for Law and Religion, Cardiff, 2009) 27

Gerosa, L., *Canon Law* (Continuum, London, 2002)

Hilbert, M., 'Dispensation for non-consummated marriages: de *processu super ratio*', in N. Doe (ed.), *Marriage in Anglican and Roman Catholic Canon Law* (Cardiff, 2009)

Huels, J.M., *Liturgy and Law: Liturgical Law in the System of Roman Catholic Canon Law* (Wilson and Lafleur, Montreal, 2006)

'The interpretation of liturgical law', 55 *Worship* (1981) 218

Huizing, P., and K. Walf, 'What does the "right to dissent" mean in the Church?', 158 *Concilium* (1982) 3

Johnson, J.G., 'The synod of bishops: an exploration of its nature and function', 20 *Studia Canonica* (1986) 275

Lara, C., 'Some general reflections on the rights and duties of the Christian faithful', 20 *Studia Canonica* (1986) 7

Mallett, J.M. (ed.), *The Ministry of Governance* (Canon Law Society of America, Washington, D.C., 1986)

Matthews, K., 'Extra-judicial appeal and hierarchical recourse', 18 *Studia Canonica* (1984) 95

McGrath, A., 'On the gravity of causes of a psychological nature in the proof of inability to assume the essential obligations of marriage', 22 *Studia Canonica* (1988) 67

Morrisey, F., 'Papal and curial pronouncements: their canonical significance in the light of the 1983 code of canon law', 50 *The Jurist* (1990) 102

Motiuk, D., 'The code of canons of the Eastern Catholic Churches: some ten years later', 36 *Studia Canonica* (2002) 189

Nedungatt, G. (ed.), *A Guide to the Eastern Code: A Commentary on the Code of Canons of the Eastern Churches* (Pontificio Istituto Orientale, Rome, 2002)

Ombres, R., 'The nature of marriage and the right to marry in the Latin Code: canons 1055–1062', in N. Doe (ed.), *Marriage in Anglican and Roman Catholic Canon Law* (Centre for Law and Religion, Cardiff, 2009) 17

'The new profession of faith and oath', 3 *Priests and People* (1989) 339

'The pastoral care of the armed forces in canon law', 2 *Priests and People* (1988) 234

'The removal of parish priests', 1 *Priests and People* (1987) 9

Örsy, L., *Theology and Canon Law: New Horizons for Legislation and Interpretation* (Collegeville, Minnesota, 1992)

Otero, J.C., 'Church–state relations in the light of Vatican II', 8 *Concilium* (1970) 113

Pospishil, V.J., *Eastern Catholic Church Law* (St Marion, New York, 1996)

Provost, J.H., 'First penance and first Eucharist', 43 *The Jurist* (1983) 450

'The participation of the laity in the governance of the church', 17 *Studia Canonica* (1983) 417

Robertson, J.W., 'Canons 867 and 868 and baptising against the will of parents', 45 *The Jurist* (1985) 631

Sheehy, G., R. Brown, D. Kelly and A. McGrath (eds.), *The Canon Law: Letter and Spirit – A Practical Guide to the Code of Canon Law*, The Canon Law Society of Great Britain and Ireland (Veritas, Dublin, 1995)

Sullivan, F.A., 'The response to the non-definitive exercise of *magisterium*', 23 *Studia Canonica* (1989) 267

Ward, D.J., 'Trust management under the new code', 44 *The Jurist* (1984) 134

Wijlens, M., *Theology and Canon Law: The Theories of Klaus Mörsdorf and Eugene Corecco* (University Press of America, Lanham, 1992)

Witte, H., 'The local bishop and lay pastoral workers: a newly created function in the church and its impact on Episcopal collegiality', 69 *The Jurist* (2009) 84

Woestman, W.H. (ed.), *Papal Allocutions to the Roman Rota: 1939–1994* (St Paul University, Ottawa, 1994)
Sacraments: Initiation, Penance, Anointing the Sick: Commentary on Canons 840–1007 (St Paul University, Ottawa, 1996)
The Sacrament of Orders and the Clerical State (St Paul University, Ottawa, 1999)

Wood, S., 'The theological foundation of Episcopal conferences and collegiality', 22 *Studia Canonica* (1988) 327

For the Old Catholic Church

Primary sources

International Conference of Old Catholic Bishops United in the Union of Utrecht: *Statute* (2000); *Guidelines with Respect to the Recognition of a Church as an Independent Old-Catholic Church of the Utrecht Union* (2002)

Polish National Catholic Church: *Constitution and Laws* (2006)

Secondary sources

Moss, C.B., *The Old Catholic Movement: Its Origins and History* (SPCK, London, 1964)

4. Congregational materials

Primary sources

Congregational Federation: *Constitution*, in *The Congregational Year Book* (Congregational Federation, Nottingham, 2009)

United Congregational Church of Southern Africa: *Constitution (including Model Constitution for Local Churches)* (2007)

Secondary sources

Dale, R.W., *History of English Congregationalism* (Hodder & Soughton, London, 1907)

Price, E.J., *A Handbook of Congregationalism* (2nd edn., Independent Press, London, 1957)

5. Lutheran material

Primary sources

Church of Sweden: *Church Ordinance* (2000)
Evangelical Church of Finland: *Catechism* (2000)
Evangelical Lutheran Church in America: *Constitution, Bylaws, and General Resolutions* (2009); *Model Constitution for Congregations* (2005)
Evangelical Lutheran Church in Canada: *Constitution* (2009); *Administrative Bylaws* (2009); *Corporate Bylaws* (2011); *Sexual Abuse or Harassment Policy* (2006)
Evangelical Lutheran Church in Ireland: *Constitution* (2011)
Evangelical Lutheran Church of Southern Africa (Natal-Transvaal): *Guidelines for the Church Life of the Evangelical Lutheran Church in Southern Africa (Natal-Transvaal)* (2007)
International Lutheran Council: *Constitution and Guiding Principles* (2007)
Lutheran Church in Great Britain: *Rules and Regulations* (2011)
Lutheran Church of Australia: *Constitution and Bylaws* (2004); *Doctrinal Statement and Theological Opinions, Some Pastoral Guidelines for Responsible Communion Practice* (2001); *Worship Guidelines* (2005); *Women as Lay Readers: Some Guidelines* (2004); *Guidelines for Inter-Church Marriages* (2000); *Guidelines for Drawing Up a Statement of 'Recognition of Relationship' between the Lutheran Church of Australia and Another Lutheran Church Body* (2001); *Recognition of Relationship: A Confessional Agreement between the Lutheran Church of Australia and the Lutheran Church Canada* (1993); *A Lutheran Approach to the Theology of Worship* (2001); *What is a call?* (2000)
Lutheran Missouri Synod: *Handbook: Constitution, Bylaws and Articles of Association* (2010); *Guidelines for Constitutions and Bylaws of Lutheran Congregations* (2006); *Standard Operating Procedures Manual: Expulsion of Individuals from Membership in the Synod as a Result of Sexual Misconduct or Criminal Behavior* (2011), *Expulsion from Membership: Congregations or Individuals* (2011), *Dispute Resolution* (2011)
Lutheran World Federation: *Constitution and Bylaws* (2010); *The Lutheran World Federation as a Communion of Churches* (LWF, Geneva, 2003)
North American Lutheran Church: *Constitution Document for Congregations* (2011); *Standards for Pastoral Ministry* (2011)
The Book of Concord: The Confession of the Evangelical Lutheran Church, translated and edited by T.G. Toppart (Fortress Press, Philadelphia, 1959)

Secondary sources

Bergendoff, C., *The Church of the Lutheran Reformation* (Concordia Publishing, St Louis, 1967)
Bodensieck, J. (ed.), *The Encyclopedia of the Lutheran Church* (Augsburg Publishing, Minneapolis, 1965)

Church Law and Polity in Lutheran Churches, Reports of the International Consultations in Järvenpää and Baastad (LWF, Geneva, 1979)
Gassmann, G., and H. Meyer, *The Unity of the Church: Requirements and Structures* (LWF, Geneva, 1983)
Schjörring, J.H., P. Kunari and N.A. Hjelm, *From Federation to Communion: The History of the Lutheran World Federation* (Fortress Press, Minneapolis, 1997)
Witte, J., *Law and Protestantism: the Legal Teachings of the Protestant Reformation* (Cambridge University Press, 2002)

6. Methodist materials

Primary sources

Church of the Nazarene: *Manual: History, Constitution, Government, Ritual* (2009-2013)
Free Methodist Church of North America: *Book of Discipline* (2007); *Deacon Handbook* (2004); *Pastors and Church Leaders Manual* (2006)
Methodist Church in Great Britain: *The Constitutional Practice and Discipline of the Methodist Church* (2009); *Guidelines for Churches dealing with Extremist Political Parties* (2003); *Rules and Regulations for Faith and Worship: The Local Preachers' Training Course* (2006); *Handbook for Probation: Formation in Ministry* (2007)
Methodist Church in Ireland: *Constitution* (2010); *Regulations, Discipline and Government* (2010)
Methodist Church of New Zealand (Te Haahi Weteriana o Aotearoa): *Laws and Regulations* (2007)
Methodist Church of South Africa: *Laws and Discipline* (2000)
United Methodist Church in Northern Europe and Eurasia: *Book of Discipline* (2009)
United Methodist Church – USA: *Constitution* (2009)
World Methodist Council, *Constitution*

Secondary sources

Beck, B., 'The Methodist Church and the idea of a national church', 149 *Law and Justice* (2002) 105

7. Orthodox materials

Primary sources

American Carpatho-Russian Orthodox Diocese of the USA: *Spiritual-Sacramental Guidelines* (undated)
Archdiocese of Thyateira and Great Britain (Greek Orthodox): *Instructions* (2007)
Diocese of Sourozh (Russian Orthodox Church): *Statutes* (2000)
Greek Orthodox Archdiocese of America: *Charter* (2003); *Regulations* (2007)
Malankara Orthodox Syrian Church: *Constitution* (2006)

Orthodox Church in America: *Guidelines for Clergy* (1998); *Clergy Compensation Scheme* (1995); *Reducing the Risk of Child Sexual Abuse: Guidelines for Parishes and Institutions* (2002); *Policies, Standards and Procedures on Sexual Misconduct* (2003); *Best Practice Principles and Policies for Financial Accountability* (2008)
Romanian Orthodox Church: *Statutes* (undated)
Russian Orthodox Church: *Statute* (1988, as amended)
Standing Conference of the Canonical Orthodox Bishops in the Americas: *Constitution* (1961, as amended); *Guidelines for Orthodox Christians in Ecumenical Relations* (1973)
Standing Conference of Canonical Orthodox Churches of Australia: *Constitution* (undated)
Syrian Orthodox Church of Antioch: *Constitution* (1998)
The Rudder (Pedalion) of the Orthodox Christians or All the Sacred and Divine Canons, edited by C. Cummings (Orthodox Christian Educational Society, Chicago, Illinois, 1957)
Ukrainian Orthodox Church in America: *Statutes* (2005); *Joint Statements of the Hierarchs, Practical Instructions for Diocesan Faithful, Code of Pastoral Conduct, Sexual Abuse Policy* (undated)

Secondary sources

Afanasiev, N., 'The canons of the church: changeable or unchangeable?', 11 *St Vladimir's Theological Quarterly* (1967) 54
Archondonis, B., 'A common code for the Orthodox churches', I *Kanon* (1973) 45
Erickson, J.H., *The Challenge of Our Past: Studies in Orthodox Canon Law and Church History* (Crestwood, New York, 1991)
Meyendorff, J., 'Contemporary problems of Orthodox canon law', 17 *Greek Orthodox Theological Review* (1972) 41
Patsavos, L.J., *Manual for the Course in Orthodox Canon Law* (Hellenic College, Holy Cross Orthodox School of Theology, New York, 1975)
Patsavos, L., 'The canonical tradition of the Orthodox Church', in F.K. Litsas (ed.), *A Companion to the Greek Orthodox Church* (Greek Orthodox Archdiocese of North and South America, New York, 1984) 137
Rodopoulos, P., *An Overview of Orthodox Canon Law* (Orthodox Research Institute, Rollinsford, New Hampshire, 2007)
Viscuso, P., 'Canon law as an instrument for the realisation of the Church in Orthodox ecclesiology', 11 *International Journal for the Study of the Christian Church* (2011) 203
Ware, T., *The Orthodox Church* (Penguin, London, 1963, reprinted 1991)
Zizioulas, J., *Being as Communion* (St Vladimir's Seminary Press, New York, 1985)

8. Presbyterian materials

Primary sources

Presbyterian Church in America: *The Book of Church Order* (2005)
Presbyterian Church in Ireland: *The Code: Book of the Constitution and Government* (2010)
Presbyterian Church of Aotearoa New Zealand: *The Book of Order* (2011)

Presbyterian Church of Wales (*Eglwys Bresbyteraidd Cymru*): *Constitution* (2009); *Handbook of Order and Rules* (2010); *Constitution for a Local Church* (2009); *Employee Handbook* (undated)
United Free Church of Scotland: *Manual of Practice and Procedure* (2011)

Secondary sources

Herron, A., *A Guide to the General Assembly of the Church of Scotland* (St Andrew Press, Edinburgh, 1986)
  The Law and Practice of the Kirk: A Guide and Commentary (Bell and Bain, Glasgow, 1995)
Weatherhead, J.L. (ed.), *The Constitution and Laws of the Church of Scotland* (Board of Practice and Procedure, Edinburgh, 1997)
Wotherspoon H.J., and J.M. Kirkpatrick, *A Manual of Church Doctrine According to the Church of Scotland* (2nd edn., Oxford University Press, 1960)

9. Reformed Church materials

Primary sources

Église Reformée de France: *Discipline* (2003)
Reformed Church in America: *The Book of Church Order* (2010)
United Reformed Church: *Manual* (2008): *Model Constitution for Local Churches* (2010)
World Alliance of Reformed Churches: *Constitution* (2003)
World Communion of Reformed Churches: *Constitution and Bylaws* (2010)

Secondary sources

Coertzen, P., *Church and Order: A Reformed Perspective* (Peeters, Leuven, 1998)
Dombois, H., 'Ökumenisches Kirchenrecht heute', 24 *Zeitschrift für Evangelisches Kirchenrecht* (1979) 225
Huffel, M.A.P. van, 'The relevance of Reformed church polity principles', unpublished paper delivered at the conference *Protestant Church Polity in Changing Contexts, Utrecht,* 7-10 November 2011
Koffeman, L.J., *Het goed recht van de kerk: Een theologische inleiding op het kerkrecht* (Kok, Kampen 2009)
Kuhn, K.C., 'Church order instead of church law', 5 *Concilium* (1996) 29
Niemandt, N., 'Emerging missional ecclesiology in the Dutch Reformed Church in South Africa and church polity – a case study', unpublished paper delivered at the conference *Protestant Church Polity in Changing Contexts, Utrecht,* 7-10 November 2011
Steinmuller, W., 'Divine law and its dynamics in Protestant theology of law', 8 *Concilium* (1969) 13

10. United and Uniting Churches materials

United Church of Canada: *The Manual* (2010); *Ethical Standards and Standards of Practice for Ministry Personnel* (2008); *Section 429 Guidelines for Incorporated Ministries* (2008); *Ministry and Employment Policies and Benefits* (2005);

Pastoral Relations Parental Leave Policy (2010); *Financial Handbook for Congregations* (2010); *Dispute Resolution Policy Handbook* (2008); *Sexual Abuse Prevention and Response Policy and Procedures* (2011); *Community Ministry Standards and Best Practices: Administrative Standards for Community and Social Justice Ministries* (2007)
United Church of Christ: *Constitution and Bylaws* (2010)
United Church of Christ in the Philippines: *Constitution and Bylaws* (2002)
(United) Church of North India: *Constitution and Bylaws* (2006)
Uniting Church in Australia: *Constitution and Regulations* (2001)

11. Ecumenical materials

Primary sources

An Anglican-Methodist Covenant, Common Statement of Formal Conversations, Methodist Church of Great Britain and Church of England (London, 2001)
Anglican-Lutheran Covenant in Australia (2004)
Anglican-Lutheran Covenant in New Zealand (2006)
Anglican Roman Catholic International Commission: *Church as Communion* (1990)
Australian Churches Covenanting Together (2004)
Bonn Agreement (1931)
Charta Oecumenica, between the Conference of European Churches and the Roman Catholic Council of European Bishops' Conferences (2001)
Churches Together in Britain and Ireland: *Constitution* (2003)
Common Ground: Covenanting for Mutual Recognition and Reconciliation, between the Anglican Church in Aotearoa, New Zealand and Polynesia and the Lutheran Church of New Zealand (2006)
Community of Protestant Churches in Europe (Lutheran and Reformed): *Leuenberg Agreement* (1973); The Leuenberg Fellowship, *The Church of Jesus Christ* (Frankfurt am Main, 1996)
Conference of European Churches: *Constitution* (1992)
Covenant of the Churches in Wales (1975)
Growth in Communion, Report of the Anglican-Lutheran International Working Group 2000-2002 (Geneva, 2003)
Kilcoy Covenant (United, Anglican, Catholic and Lutheran Churches) (Queensland, Australia, 2001)
Lausanne Covenant (1974)
Lutheran-Anglican-Roman Catholic Covenant (Virginia, 1990)
Porvoo Common Statement (1992)
World Council of Churches, Faith and Order Commission, 'The Ecumenical Movement and Church Law', Document IV.8 (1974)
World Council of Churches: *Constitution and Rules* (2006); *Handbook of Churches and Councils* (WCC, Geneva, 2006)

Secondary sources

Arthur, G., *Law, Liberty and Church* (Ashgate, Aldershot, 2006)
Avis, P., (ed.), *The Christian Church: An Introduction to the Major Traditions* (SPCK, London, 2002)

Boldon, D.A., 'Formal church polity and ecumenical activity', 49 *Sociological Analysis* (1988) 293

Colloquium of Anglican and Roman Catholic Canon Lawyers, 'A decade of ecumenical dialogue in canon law', 11 *Ecclesiastical Law Journal* (2009) 284

Conn, J., and N. Doe, and J. Fox (eds.), *Initiation, Membership and Authority in Anglican and Roman Catholic Canon Law* (Centre for Law and Religion, Cardiff, and Pontifical Gregorian University and Pontifical University of St Thomas Aquinas, Rome, 2005)

Doe, N., 'Canonical doctrines of judicial precedent: a comparative study', 54 *The Jurist* (1994) 205

'The concept of Christian law – a case study: the concept of "a church" in comparative and ecumenical context', in N. Doe and R. Sandberg (eds.), *Law and Religion: New Horizons* (Peeters, Leuven, 2010) 243

'The notion of a national church: a juridical framework', 149 *Law and Justice* (2002) 77

Evans, G.R., *The Church and the Churches: Toward an Ecumenical Ecclesiology* (Cambridge University Press, 1994)

Leahy, B., 'The role of canon law in the ecumenical venture: a Roman Catholic perspective', 13 *Ecclesiastical Law Journal* (2011) 15

Limouris, G. (ed.), *Orthodox Visions of Ecumenism* (WCC, Geneva, 1994)

Lossky, N., 'The Orthodox Churches', in P. Avis (ed.), *The Christian Church: An Introduction to the Major Traditions* (SPCK, London, 2002) 1

Lossky, N., J.M. Bonino, J. Pobee, T.F. Stransky, G. Wainwright and P. Webb (eds.), *Dictionary of the Ecumenical Movement* (WCC Publications, Geneva, 2002)

MacLean, M.A. (ed.), *Legal Systems of Scottish Churches* (Dundee University Press, 2009)

Oppegaard, S., and G. Cameron (eds.), *Anglican-Lutheran Agreements: Regional and International Agreements 1972-2002* (Lutheran World Federation and Anglican Consultative Council, Geneva, 2004)

Reuver, M., *Faith and Law: Juridical Perspectives for the Ecumenical Movement* (WCC, Geneva, 2000)

Sagovsky, N., 'The contribution of canon law to Anglican-Roman Catholic ecumenism', 13 *Ecclesiastical Law Journal* (2011) 4

Stormon, E.J. (ed.), *Towards the Healing of Schism* (Paulist Press, New York, 1987)

Vischer, L. (ed.), *A Documentary History of the Faith and Order Movement: 1927-1963* (Bethany Press, St Louis, 1964)

12. History of church law

Brundage, J.A., *Medieval Canon Law* (Longman, London, 1995)

Helmholz, R.H., *The Canon Law and Ecclesiastical Jurisdiction from 597 to the 1640s* (Oxford University Press, 2004)

The Spirit of Classical Canon Law (University of Georgia Press, Athens and London, 1996)

O'Donovan, O., and O'Donovan, J.L. (eds.), *From Irenaeus to Grotius: A Sourcebook in Christian Political Thought 100-1625* (William B. Eerdmans, Cambridge, 1999)

Urresti, T., 'Canon law and theology: two different sciences', 8 *Concilium* (1967) 10

Witte, J., and F.S. Alexander (eds.), *Christianity and Law* (Cambridge University Press, 2008)

13. Civil law on religion

Ahdar, R., and I. Leigh, *Religious Freedom in the Liberal State* (Oxford University Press, 2005)
Brownlie, I., *Principles of Public International Law* (6th edn., Oxford University Press, 2003)
Cane, P., C. Evans and Z. Robinson (eds.), *Law and Religion in Theoretical and Historical Context* (Cambridge University Press, 2008)
Cox, N., *Church and State in the Post-Colonial Era: The Anglican Church and the Constitution in New Zealand* (Polygraphia, Auckland, 2008)
Doe, N., and A.W. Jeremy, 'Justifications for religious autonomy', in R. O'Dair and A. Lewis (eds.), *Law and Religion, Current Legal Issues*, Vol. 4 (Oxford University Press, 2001) 421
Doe, N., *Law and Religion in Europe: A Comparative Introduction* (Oxford University Press, 2011)
Edge, P., *Religion and Law* (Ashgate, Aldershot, 2006)
Friedner, L., 'Church and State in Sweden 2000', 8 *European Journal for Church and State* (2001) 255
Hamilton, C., *Family, Law and Religion* (Sweet and Maxwell, London, 1995)
Papastathis, Ch.K., 'Religious self-administration in the Hellenic Republic', in G. Robbers (ed.), *Church Autonomy* (Peter Lang, Frankfurt am Main, 2001) 425
Potz, R., 'State and church in European countries with an Orthodox tradition', III *Derecho y Religion* (2008) 33
Puza, R., and N. Doe (eds.), *Religion and Law in Dialogue: Covenantal and Non-Covenantal Cooperation between State and Religion in Europe* (Peeters, Leuven, 2006)
Rivers, J., *The Law of Organized Religions* (Oxford University Press, 2011)
Sandberg, R., *Law and Religion* (Cambridge University Press, 2011)
Taylor, P.M., *Freedom of Religion* (Cambridge University Press, 2005)
Vyver, D.D. van der, and J. Witte (eds.), *Religious Human Rights in Global Perspective: Legal Perspectives* (Martinus Nijhoff, The Hague, 1995)
Witte, J., and J.D. van der Vyver (eds.), *Religious Human Rights in Global Perspective: Religious Perspectives* (Martinus Nijhoff, The Hague, 1996)

14. Religious law

Beckford, J.A., and J.T. Richardson, 'Religion and regulation' in J.A. Beckford and N.J. Demerath (eds.), *The Sage Handbook of the Sociology of Religion* (Sage, London, 2007) 396
Hecht, N.S., B.S. Jackson, S.M. Passamaneck, D. Piattelli, and A.M. Rabello (eds.), *An Introduction to the History and Sources of Jewish Law* (Oxford University Press, 1996)
Huxley, A. (ed.), *Religion, Law and Tradition* (Routledge, Abingdon, 2002)
Menski, W.F., *Hindu Law* (Oxford University Press, 2003)

Neusner, J., and T. Sonn, *Comparing Religions Through Law: Judaism and Islam* (Routledge, London, 1999)
Schacht, J., *An Introduction to Islamic Law* (Clarendon Press, Oxford, 1982)
The First Roman Consultation on Jewish and Canon Law (Gregorian University, Rome, 2006), *Periodica de re canonica*, XCVI (2007)
Williams, R., 'Civil and religious law in England: a religious perspective' (2008) *Ecclesiastical Law Journal* 262

15. Theology and history

Brand, C.O., and R.S. Norman (eds.), *Perspectives on Church Government: Five Views of Church Polity* (Boardman and Holman, Nashville, Tennessee, 2004)
Cameron, E., *The European Reformation* (Oxford University Press, 1991)
Chadwick, H., *East and West: The Making of a Rift in the Church* (Oxford University Press, 2003)
Cross, F.L., and E.A. Livingstone (eds.), *The Oxford Dictionary of the Christian Church* (Oxford University Press, Revised, 2005)
Dulles, A.V., *Models of the Church* (2nd edn., Gill and Macmillan, Dublin, 1988)
Fahlbusch, E., J.M. Lochman, J. Mbiti, L. Pelikan and L. Vischer (eds.), *Encyclopedia of Christianity* (Eerdmans, Cambridge, 1997)
Komonchak, J.A., M. Collins and D.A. Lane (eds.), *The New Dictionary of Theology* (Gill and Macmillan, Dublin, 1987)
Lindars, B. (ed.), *Law and Religion: Essays on the Place of Law in Israel and Early Christianity* (Clarke, Cambridge, 1988)
MacCulloch, D., *A History of Christianity: The First Three Thousand Years* (Viking, New York, 2009)

INDEX

A

acolytes, 62–71
administration
  of church finances (budgets, accounts and audits), 326–32, 396
  of juridical and regulatory instruments, 38–9
administrative and quasi-judicial discipline and conflict resolution, 158, 392
admonition, 182–6
Alexander, Frank S., vii
Anglican Communion, 4
  administration and enforcement of juridical instruments, 38–9
  anointing of the sick, 270
  archbishops, presiding bishops and principal bishops, 110
  baptism, 237
  binding and enforceable nature of juridical instruments, 37–8
  bishops, 104
  Book of Common Prayer, 190, 221
  Canterbury, Archbishop of, 115, 127
  catechesis, 203
  church buildings, ecumenical sharing of, 303
  on church–State relationship, 349
  confession, 267
  confirmation, 244
  on converts from other Christian churches and ecclesial communities, 293–4
  courts and tribunals, 167
  diocesan officers, 96
  dispensation, relaxation of norms by means of, 40
  disunity and denominational divisions, recognition of, 278
  divorce and remarriage, 262, 265
  doctrinal standards, maintenance of, 211
  doctrine, definition and sources of, 190
  due process, 173
  on ecclesial communion, 292
  ecumenical covenants and councils, 305–7
  ecumenical nature, definition of ecumenism, and ecumenical obligations, 279–83
  ecumenical relations, institutions for, 285, 287–8
  ecumenical services, 301
  Eucharist, 249
  on Eucharistic fellowship, 297
  European State laws on, 359
  financial administration in, 328
  funeral rites, 271, 302
  Gospel, duty to proclaim, 197
  governance, form of, 119–20, 385–6
  hierarchical recourse, 159
  on human rights and freedom of religion, 364–5
  income, lawful sources of, 334
  institutional church, as manifestation of universal church, 276
  institutional church, concept of, 15
  insurance, 339
  international 'bonds of affection', 21
  international institutions of church governance, 127
  interpretation of law in, 42
  juridical and regulatory instruments of, 6, 21, 24
  laity, duties and rights of, 57
  Lambeth Conference, 127, 133, 364–5
  lay ministry in, 64
  local institutions of church governance, 148
  marriage, 257

Anglican Communion (cont.)
  membership in church, 50
  on ministerial communion, 295
  mission and evangelisation, 206
  mixed marriages, 299
  music and worship, 231
  national institutions of church governance, 133
  national, regional and local laws, 24
  offences, ecclesiastical, 180
  ordained ministers' functions, duties and rights, 95
  ordained ministers' remuneration, 341
  ordination, 79
  ownership of property in, 313
  pensions and benefits for ordained ministers, 344
  people of God, concept of, 47
  preaching function, 200
  Principles of Canon Law Common to the Churches of the Anglican Communion (2008), 4, 6, 21, 184
  regional institutions of church governance, 142
  on religious education in State schools, 378
  religious orders, 74–5
  sacraments, 233
  sacred buildings and objects, 321
  sanctions and penalties, 184
  on social responsibility, 371
  standard juridical formulae and structures, 36
  tenure of ministerial office in, 88
  theology/faith expressed through law, 32–3
  Thirty-Nine Articles, 190
  on universal and undivided church, 275
  visitation, 162
  on worship, 217, 221, 226
Anglican Consultative Council, 127
anointing of the sick, 269–71
apostasy, 210
Apostles' Creed, 190, 192, 194
Apostolic See. *See* papacy
Apostolic Signatura, 165
apostolic succession of ordained ministries, controversy over, 77
arbitration, 160
archbishops, 109–12

archdeacons, 96
archdioceses. *See* diocese, district and circuit
armed forces, chaplains in, 380–3, 397
Arminianism, 3
assemblies
  courts and tribunals, 169
  as international institutions of church governance, 128
  as local institutions of church governance, 146–52
  as national institutions of church governance, 133–4, 136
  as regional institutions of church governance, 140
  visitation in Protestant churches, 163
assessments, ecclesiastical, 332–9, 397
associations of the faithful (lay brotherhoods and sisterhoods), 64, 389
Athanasian Creed, 192
Augsburg Confession, 16, 192

B

baptism, 49–54, 235–43, 394
baptismal communion, 293–4, 395
Baptist World Alliance (BWA), 4–5, 18, 22, 116, 120, 368, 376
Baptists, 5
  arbitration, 161
  baptism, 235, 242
  on baptismal communion, 294
  binding and enforceable nature of juridical instruments, 37–8
  catechesis, 205
  on church–State relationship, 355
  courts and tribunals, 170
  defined, 4
  discipline, nature and purpose of, 157
  doctrinal standards, maintenance of, 215
  doctrine, definition and sources of, 195
  on ecclesial communion, 293
  ecumenical nature, definition of ecumenism and ecumenical obligations, 280–3
  ecumenical relations, institutions for, 287–8
  Eucharist, 253
  European State laws on, 362

INDEX 417

facilitating and ordering life and mission of, 31
financial administration in, 331
funeral rites, 272
Gospel, duty to proclaim, 198
governance, power and form of, 119–20, 123, 386
on human rights and freedom of religion, 368
income, lawful sources of, 338
institutional church as manifestation of universal church, 277
institutional church, concept of, 18
insurance, 340
international constitutions, 22
international officers, 116
interpretation of law in, 43
laity, duties and rights of, 61
on law of God, 35
lay ministry in, 71
local institutions of church governance, 152
marriage, 260
on ministerial communion, 296
mission and evangelisation, 209
music and worship, 232
national institutions of church governance, 138
national, regional and local laws, 28
ordained ministers' functions, duties and rights, 101
ordination, 85
ownership of property in, 318
pensions and benefits for ordained ministers, 344
people of God, concept of, 49
preaching function, 202
Presidents of Associations, 109
regional institutions of church governance, 145
relaxation of juridical norms in, 41
on religious education in State schools, 379
remuneration of ordained ministers, 343
sacraments, 234
sacred buildings and objects, 326
sanctions and penalties, 186
on social responsibility, 376
standard juridical formulae and structures, 36

tenure of ministerial office in, 92
theology/faith expressed through law, 35
union and convention presidents, moderators, and directors, 113
Belgium, church–State relations in, 358
Believers' Baptism, 235, 243, 246
benefits and pensions for ordained ministers, 343–5, 397
Bible
 doctrine, as source of, 188–95
 resolution of disputes, scriptural processes for, 171
bishops
 archbishops, 109
 catechesis, responsibility for, 202
 common principles, 390
 diocesan, 102–6
 doctrinal standards, maintenance of, 212
 doctrine, definition and sources of, 189–90
 ecumenical relations, responsibility for, 286, 288
 Episcopal form of church polity, 118, 119–21, 158, 164, 385–6, 391
 financial administration, responsibility for, 326–8
 income, lawful sources of, 332
 in international institutions of church governance, 124–5, 127
 as judges, 166–8, 171
 in national institutions of church governance, 130–4
 preaching function, 199
 presiding bishops, 110–11
 principal bishops, 110
 in regional institutions of church governance, 142
 visitation by, 161–3
 worship, responsibilities regarding, 220–1, 224–6
blasphemy, 210
Book of Common Prayer, 190, 221
Book of Concord of 1580, 192
Bulgaria, church–State relations in, 358
burial rites, 268, 269–72, 300–3
BWA (Baptist World Alliance), 4–5, 18, 22, 116, 120, 368, 376

C

canon law
  Orthodox Christianity, canonical tradition of, 20, 23
  Principles of Canon Law Common to the Churches of the Anglican Communion (2008), 4, 6, 21
  Roman and Oriental Catholic codes, 20, 22
Canterbury, Archbishop of, 115, 127
Cardinals, 114
catechesis, 202–5
Catechisms
  of the Catholic Church, 189
  Luther, Small and Large Catechisms of, 192
  Presbyterian Larger and Shorter Catechisms, 193
catholic (universal and undivided) church, concept of, 275–9
Catholicism, 3. *See also* papacy
  administration and enforcement of juridical instruments, 38–9
  anointing of the sick, 269
  archbishops and metropolitans, 109
  associations of the faithful (lay brotherhoods and sisterhoods), 72
  baptism, 235
  on baptismal communion, 293–4
  binding and enforceable nature of juridical instruments, 37–8
  bishops, 102
  catechesis, 202
  on chaplains in prisons, hospitals, and armed forces, 380
  church buildings, ecumenical sharing of, 302
  on church–State relationship, 346
  codes of canon law, 20, 22
  concelebration of Eucharist, 297
  concelebration of mixed marriages, 299
  confession, 265
  confirmation, 243
  on converts from other Christian churches and ecclesial communities, 293–4
  courts and tribunals, 63, 165
  defined, 2
  diocesan officers, 94
  discipline, nature and purpose of, 154
  dispensation, relaxation of norms by means of, 39
  disunity and denominational divisions, recognition of, 277
  divorce and remarriage, 260, 265
  doctrinal standards, maintenance of, 209
  doctrine, definition and sources of, 188
  due process, 172
  on ecclesial communion, 290
  ecumenical covenants and councils, 305–7, 362
  ecumenical nature, definition of ecumenism, and ecumenical obligations, 279–82
  ecumenical relations, institutions for, 284, 286–9
  ecumenical services, 300
  Eucharist, 247, 250
  on Eucharistic fellowship, 296
  European State laws on, 357
  facilitating and ordering life and mission of, 29
  financial administration in, 326
  free theological enquiry and expression in, 210
  funeral rites, 269, 302–3
  Gospel, duty to proclaim, 196
  governance, form of, 119, 385–6
  governance, restricted to ordained ministers, 63, 119
  hierarchical recourse, 158
  on human rights and freedom of religion, 363
  income, lawful sources of, 332
  infallible doctrine of, 209
  institutional church as manifestation of universal church, 276
  institutional church, concept of, 12
  insurance, 339
  international institutions of church governance, 124
  interpretation of law in, 41
  juridical and regulatory instruments of, 6, 20, 22
  laity, duties and rights of, 55
  on law of God, 33

lay ministry in, 63
local institutions of church governance, 146
magisterium, 188, 199, 209
marriage, 254
membership in church, 49
on ministerial communion, 295
mission and evangelisation, 205
mixed marriages, 298
music and worship, 231
national institutions of church governance, 130–2
national, regional and local laws, 22
offences, ecclesiastical, 178
ordained ministers' functions, duties and rights, 93
ordination, 78
ownership of property in, 310
patriarchs of Oriental Catholic Churches, 114, 119
pensions and benefits for ordained ministers, 343
people of God, concept of, 46
preaching function, 199
Primacy, doctrine of, 290
regional institutions of church governance, 139
on religious education in State schools, 378
religious or monastic life (institutes of consecrated life), 72, 286
remuneration of ordained ministers, 340
Roman Curia, 125
sacraments, 233
sacred buildings and objects, 319
sanctions and penalties, 182
social justice, ecumenical co-operation in promoting, 303
on social responsibility, 369
societies of apostolic life, 72, 286
standard juridical formulae and structures, 36
tenure of ministerial office in, 86
theology/faith expressed through law, 31, 33
on universal and undivided church, 275
visitation, 161
on worship, 215, 220, 224
celibacy and ordained ministry, 78–9
censure, 182–6

chaplains in prisons, hospitals, and armed forces, 380–3, 397
charitable actions. *See* social justice; State and society, relationship of churches to
Charta Oecumenica, 305–6, 362
chrismation, 236–7
Christian law, vii, 1–10, 384–7
  academic and practical purposes of studying, 1–2, 7–10
  church property and finance, 3, 310–45 (*see also* church property and finance)
  common principles, 384, 388–98
  comparative examination of, 1
  defined, 1
  discipline and conflict resolution, 3, 154–87 (*see also* discipline and conflict resolution)
  doctrine, 3, 188–232 (*see also* doctrine)
  ecumenical relations, 3, 274–309 (*see also* ecumenical relations)
  future studies in, 387
  institutions applying, 3, 118–53 (*see also* institutions of church governance)
  interfaith studies and, 8
  interpretation of, 41–4, 389
  juridical and regulatory instruments, 2, 11–45 (*see also* juridical and regulatory instruments)
  on laity, 2, 46–76 (*see also* laity)
  law of God and, 33–6
  methodological issues, 6–7
  number of churches and range of denominations studied, 3–5
  on ordained ministry, 3, 77–117 (*see also* ordained ministry)
  pervasiveness of concept of, 385
  ritual, 3, 233–73 (*see also* ritual)
  shared principles of, 1
  similarities across Christian traditions, 1
  State and society, relationship to, 3, 346–83 (*see also* State and society, relationship of churches to)
  theology/faith and, 384–5 (*see also* theology/faith)
Christian stewardship, doctrine of, 310
Christianity and Law (Witte and Alexander, eds., 2008), vii
Christianity as religion of law, 1

church buildings
    ecumenical sharing of, 302–3
    insuring, 339–40
    as sacred property, 319–26, 396
church discipline. *See* discipline and conflict resolution
church property and finance, 3, 310–45
    administration (budgets, accounts and audits), 326–32, 396
    Christian stewardship, doctrine of, 310
    expenditures, 339–45, 397
    income, lawful sources of, 332–9, 397
    insurance, 339–40
    laity, role of, 62–71
    ownership of property, 310–19, 396
    pensions and benefits for ordained ministers, 343–5, 397
    remuneration of ordained ministers, 340–3, 397
    sacred buildings and objects, 319–26, 396
    trusts, trustees, and other entities utilised to represent church, 310
church–State relations. *See* State and society, relationship of churches to
church stewards, 62–71, 386
church universal, concept of, 275–9, 394
churchwardens, 62–71, 386
circuits. *See* diocese, district and circuit
classis, 99, 151, 168
clergy. *See* ordained ministry
codes of canon law, 20, 22
Cold Ash Statement (1983), 307
common prayer and worship, 300–2
common principles of Christian law, 384, 388–98
communion, ecumenical, 290–8, 395
communion, Eucharistic. *See* Eucharist
concelebration
    of Eucharist, 297
    of mixed marriages, 298–300
conciliar and covenantal ecumenism, 304–8, 396
conferences
    international institutions of church governance, 127, 133
    national institutions of church governance, 130, 137–8
confession (penance or reconciliation), 265–9
confirmation, 235, 243–6, 394

conflict resolution. *See* discipline and conflict resolution
Congregational form of church polity, 118, 123–4, 158, 165, 391
Congregationalism, 5
    baptism, 242
    catechesis, 205
    on church–State relationship, 355
    courts and tribunals, 170
    discipline, nature and purpose of, 157
    doctrinal standards, maintenance of, 215
    doctrine, definition and sources of, 194
    due process, 177
    ecumenical nature, definition of ecumenism, and ecumenical obligations, 282
    Eucharist, 253
    Gospel, duty to proclaim, 198
    governance, power and form of, 386
    hierarchical recourse, 160
    income, lawful sources of, 338
    laity, duties and rights of, 61
    membership in church, 53
    mission and evangelisation, 209
    moderators, 108
    music and worship, 232
    national institutions of church governance, 136
    offences, ecclesiastical, 181
    ordained ministers' functions, duties, and rights, 100
    ownership of property in, 317
    preaching function, 202
    regional institutions of church governance, 145
    sacraments, 234
    sacred buildings and objects, 326
    sanctions and penalties, 186
    on social responsibility, 376
    tenure of ministerial office in, 92
    on worship, 224
conscience, freedom of, 362–8, 397
Constantinople, Ecumenical Patriarchate of, 115, 125, 167
constitutions in Protestant traditions, 21
consubstantiation, 247
conventions as national institutions of church governance, 134, 138
conventions or treaties between church and State, 357

converts from other Christian churches and ecclesial communities, 293–4
councils
  as international institutions of church governance, 128–9
  as local institutions of church governance, 146–52
  as national institutions of church governance, 135
courts and tribunals, 164–71
  common principles, 392
  lay involvement in Catholic tribunals, 63, 165
covenantal and conciliar ecumenism, 304–8, 396
Creeds
  Apostles' Creed, 190, 192, 194
  Athanasian Creed, 192
  Nicene Creed, 190, 192, 194, 210, 275
Cyprus, church–State relations in, 359

D

deacons, 77–86. *See also* ordained ministry
deans, 95–7
Denmark, church–State relations in, 357, 360
denominational divisions and disunity, recognition of, 277
diocese, district, and circuit.
  See also bishops
  deans and vicars, 94–7, 99
  ecumenical responsibilities, 286
  financial administration in, 326–8, 330
  governance, forms of, 119–20
  local institutions of church governance and, 146–52
  presidents, superintendents and moderators, 106–9, 164, 212, 390
  as regional institutions of church governance, 139–46
discipline and conflict resolution, 3, 154–87. *See also* courts and tribunals
  administrative and quasi-judicial procedures, 158, 392
  arbitration, 160
  common principles, 392
  doctrinal standards, maintenance of, 209–15, 393
  due process, 171–8, 392
  hierarchical recourse, 158–61
  judges, 164–71
  nature and purposes of church discipline, 154–8
  offences, 178–82, 393
  sanctions and penalties, 182–6, 393
  scriptural processes for resolution of disputes, 171
  visitation, 161–4
dispensation, relaxation of norms by means of, 39
dispute resolution. *See* discipline and conflict resolution
districts. *See* diocese, district and circuit
disunity and denominational divisions, recognition of, 277
divine law, 33–6
divorce, 254, 260–5
doctrine, 3, 188–232
  assent, requiring, 209
  catechesis, 202–5
  of Christian stewardship, 310
  defined, 188, 393
  enforcement or oversight of doctrinal standards, 209
  Eucharist, doctrinal disagreements regarding, 247
  maintenance of doctrinal standards, 209–15, 393
  mission and evangelisation, 205–9
  sources of, 188–95
  of 'two kingdoms', 349
donations, 332–9
due process, 171–8, 392
duties and rights
  of the faithful, 55–62, 389
  Gospel, duty to proclaim, 195–9, 393–4
  of ordained ministers, 93–101, 390
dying persons, pastoral care of, 269–72

E

Eastern Orthodoxy. *See* Orthodox Christianity
ecclesial communion, 290–3, 395
ecclesiality (institutional church), 11–19, 388
ecclesiastical discipline. *See* discipline and conflict resolution

ecclesiastical regulatory systems.
　See juridical and regulatory
　instruments
ecclesiology versus ecclesiality, 12
economic issues. *See* church property and
　finance
economy, principle of, 40, 299
Ecumenical Patriarchate of Constantinople,
　115, 125, 167
ecumenical relations, 3, 274–309
　aim and purpose of, 274
　church buildings, sharing, 302–3
　communion (ecclesial, baptismal,
　　ministerial, and Eucharistic), 290–8,
　　395
　conciliar and covenantal ecumenism,
　　304–8, 396
　disunity and denominational divisions,
　　recognition of, 277
　formation in, 289–90
　funeral rites, 300–2
　institutional churches as manifestation
　　of universal church, 276
　institutional structures for, 284–90, 394
　interfaith studies, 8, 386
　at international level, 284–6
　mixed marriages (between baptised
　　persons from different traditions),
　　298–300
　at national and regional levels, 286
　nature, definition, and obligations of
　　ecumenism, 279–84, 394
　prayer and worship in common, 300–2
　preaching and liturgy of the word, 300–2
　principles of Christian law as resource
　　for, 386
　as reason for studying Christian law, 9
　State and society, relationship of
　　churches to, 303–4
　universal and undivided church, concept
　　of, 275–9, 394
education. *See* teaching
elders, 82, 85, 136. *See also* ordained ministry
enforcement
　ability to enforce instruments, 37–8
　of doctrinal discipline, 209
　of juridical and regulatory instruments,
　　38–9
England, church–State relations in, 359–60
eparchies. *See* diocese, district, and circuit

Episcopal form of church polity, 118,
　119–21, 158, 164, 385–6, 391
Episcopal versus Protestant reformed
　traditions, ordained ministry in,
　77–8, 86
Episcopalians. *See* Anglican Communion
episcopate. *See* bishops
established/official State churches, 356–62,
　397
Estonia, church–State relations in, 380
Eucharist, 247–54
　common principles, 394
　concelebration of, 297
　doctrinal disagreements regarding, 247
　for the dying, 270–1
　ecumenical communion or Eucharistic
　　fellowship, 296–8, 395
　following baptism and chrismation in
　　Orthodox tradition, 237
　lay ministers of, 62–71
European State laws
　on chaplains in prisons, hospitals, and
　　armed forces, 383
　on church–State relations, 356–62
　on religious education in State schools,
　　379
evangelisation and mission, 205–9, 303–4
excommunication, 182–6, 210
expenditures, ecclesiastical, 339–45, 397
extreme unction, 269–71

F

facilitating and ordering life and mission of
　church, 29–31
faith. *See* theology/faith
faithful. *See* laity
fees for services, 332–9
ferendae sententiae, 182
Fidei Depositum (apostolic constitution),
　189
finance. *See* church property and finance
Finland, church–State relations in, 359,
　361, 379
France, church–State relations in, 357, 380
freedom
　of religion and conscience, 362–8, 397
　of theological enquiry and expression,
　　210
funeral rites, 268, 269–72, 300–3

G

gender issues
    lay ministries in Catholic Church, 63
    ordination, 78–80
Germany, church–State relations in, 360
God, law of, 33–6
Gospel, duty to proclaim, 195–9, 393–4
governance. *See also* institutions of church governance
    different forms of, 118–24, 385–6
    forms of, 118–24, 391
    levels of, 118–24, 391
    power restricted to ordained ministers in Catholic Church, 63, 119
government and church. *See* State and society, relationship of churches to
Great Schism, 9, 274, 280
Greece, church–State relations in, 358, 380
Greek Orthodoxy. *See* Orthodox Christianity

H

Heidelberg Confession, 194
Helwys, Thomas, 4
heresy, 210–12
hierarchical recourse, 158–61
hierarchical systems of international church government, 130
Holy Communion. *See* Eucharist
holy orders. *See* ordained ministry
Holy See. *See* papacy
holy unction, 269–71
hospital chaplains, 380–3, 397
human law versus divine law, 33–6
human rights principles, 362–8, 397

I

Iceland, church–State relations in, 361
income of church, lawful sources of, 332–9, 397
infant baptism, 235, 243, 246, 394
institutes of consecrated life, Catholic, 72, 286
institutional church, concept of, 11–19, 388
institutions of church governance, 3, 118–53
    common principles, 391
    different forms of general church polity, 118–24, 385–6
    hierarchical systems of international church government, 130
    international, 124–30, 391
    local, 146–52, 392
    national, 130–9, 391
    non-coercive jurisdiction, international church governments wielding, 130
    regional, 139–46, 391
Interfaith Legal Advisers Network, 7
interfaith studies and study of Christian law, 8, 386
international law, personality of papacy and Vatican City in, 357
international level
    common principles regarding oversight of, 390
    ecclesiastical offices, 114–16
    ecumenical relations at, 284–6
    forms of church governance, 118–24, 391
    institutions of church governance, 124–30, 391
    juridical and regulatory instruments, 19–22
interpretation of law, 41–4, 389
investments, income from, 332–9, 397
Italy, church–State relations in, 357, 380

J

John Paul II (Pope), 20, 29, 154
judges, 164–71. *See also* courts and tribunals; discipline and conflict resolution
judicial office in Catholic Church, lay involvement in, 63
judicial procedures. *See* discipline and conflict resolution
juridical and regulatory instruments, 2, 11–45
    administration and enforcement, 38–9
    binding and enforceable nature of, 37–8
    common principles, 388
    defined, 5–6, 11
    facilitating and ordering life and mission of church, 29–31
    forms of, 19

juridical and regulatory instruments (cont.)
  institutional church, concept of, 11–19, 388
  at international level, 19–22
  interpretation of, 41–4, 389
  law of God and, 33–6
  at national, regional, and local levels, 22
  purposes of, 29–36
  relaxation of norms, 39–41, 388
  servant law, 388
  standard juridical formulae and structures, 36, 388
  theology/faith expressed through, 11, 31–6

K

Kirk Sessions. *See* Presbyterianism

L

laity, 2, 46–76
  associations of the faithful (lay brotherhoods and sisterhoods), 64, 389
  duties and rights of, 55–62, 389
  ecumenical formation of, 289–90
  as judges in Catholic tribunals, 63, 165
  in local institutions of church governance, 146–52
  membership in church, concept of, 49–54, 389
  ministries and ecclesiastical offices open to, 62–71, 389
  in national institutions of church governance, 133–5
  ordained ministry, relationship to, 77
  ordained people distinguished from, 46
  people of God, concept of, 46–9, 389
  preaching by, 62–71, 200
Lambeth Conference, 127, 133, 364–5
latae sententiae, 182
Latin Church. *See* Catholicism
law. *See also* Christian law
  Christianity as religion of, 1
  of God, 33–6
  human law versus divine law, 33–6
  pervasiveness of concept of, 385
lay persons. *See* laity

lectors, 62–71
Leuenberg Agreement of the Community of Protestant Churches in Europe, 306
Lichtenstein, church–State relations in, 358
Lithuania, church–State relations in, 358
liturgy. *See* worship
local level. *See also* diocese, district, and circuit; parishes
  ecumenical relations at, 287
  financial administration, responsibility for, 328–31
  forms of church governance, 118–24, 391
  institutions of church governance, 146–52, 392
  juridical and regulatory instruments, 22
  priests and ministers (*see* ordained ministry)
Lord's Supper. *See* Eucharist
Luther, Martin, 3, 192
Lutheran–Anglican–Roman Catholic (Virginia) Covenant 1990, 306
Lutheran World Federation, 4, 15, 21, 39, 116, 120–1, 128, 365
Lutheranism, 4
  administration and enforcement of juridical instruments, 38–9
  archbishops and presiding bishops, 111
  Augsburg Confession, 16, 192
  baptism, 238
  on baptismal communion, 294
  binding and enforceable nature of juridical instruments, 37–8
  bishops, 105
  Book of Concord of 1580, 192
  catechesis, 203
  church buildings, ecumenical sharing of, 303
  on church–State relationship, 349
  confession, 267
  confirmation, 245
  courts and tribunals, 168
  defined, 3
  district officers, 97
  district presidents and vice-presidents, 106
  disunity and denominational divisions, recognition of, 278
  divorce and remarriage, 263

doctrinal standards, maintenance of, 212
doctrine, definition and sources of, 191
due process, 174-5
dying persons, pastoral care of, 271
on ecclesial communion, 292
ecumenical covenants and councils, 305-7
ecumenical nature, definition of ecumenism and ecumenical obligations, 279-83
ecumenical relations, institutions for, 285, 287-8, 290
ecumenical services, 301
Eucharist, 250
on Eucharistic fellowship, 297
European State laws on, 360
facilitating and ordering life and mission of, 30
financial administration in, 328
funeral rites, 271, 302
Gospel, duty to proclaim, 197
governance, power and form of, 120-1, 385-6
hierarchical recourse, 160
on human rights and freedom of religion, 365
income, lawful sources of, 335
institutional church as manifestation of universal church, 277
institutional church, concept of, 15
insurance, 340
international constitutions, 21
international institutions of church governance, 128
international officers, 116
interpretation of law in, 43
laity, duties and rights of, 58
on law of God, 34
lay ministry in, 66
local institutions of church governance, 148
marriage, 258
membership, 51
on ministerial communion, 295
mission and evangelisation, 207
mixed marriages, 300
music and worship, 231
national institutions of church governance, 134
national, regional and local laws, 25
offences, ecclesiastical, 180
ordained ministers' functions, duties and rights, 96
ordination, 80
ownership of property in, 313
pensions and benefits for ordained ministers, 344
people of God, concept of, 48
preaching, ecumenical, 301
preaching function, 200
regional institutions of church governance, 143
on religious education in State schools, 379
remuneration of ordained ministers, 342
sacraments, 234
sacred buildings and objects, 322
sanctions and penalties, 184
Smalcald Articles, 192
on social responsibility, 371
standard juridical formulae and structures, 36
tenure of ministerial office in, 89
theology/faith expressed through law, 32, 34
'two kingdoms' doctrine, 349
on universal and undivided church, 275
visitation, 163
on worship, 217, 221, 227

M

magisterium, 188, 199, 209
Malta, church-State relations in, 357-8, 380
marriage, 254-65
  Catholic tribunals dealing mainly with matters of, 165
  common principles, 394
  divorce and remarriage, 254, 260-5
  mixed (between baptised persons from different traditions), 298-300
  ordained ministry and, 78-9
membership in church, concept of, 49-54, 389
Methodism, 4
  administration and enforcement of juridical instruments, 38-9
  baptism, 239
  on baptismal communion, 294

Methodism (cont.)
    binding and enforceable nature of
        juridical instruments, 37–8
    catechesis, 204
    on chaplains in prisons, hospitals, and
        armed forces, 381
    church buildings, ecumenical sharing of,
        303
    on church–State relationship, 351–3
    conference presidents, 112
    confession, 268, 269–72
    confirmation, 245
    courts and tribunals, 170–1
    discipline, nature and purpose of, 157
    district and circuit officers, 99
    district superintendents, 107
    disunity and denominational divisions,
        recognition of, 278
    divorce and remarriage, 263
    doctrinal standards, maintenance of, 213
    doctrine, definition and sources of, 192
    due process, 176–7
    dying persons, pastoral care of, 272
    on ecclesial communion, 292
    ecumenical nature, definition of
        ecumenism and ecumenical
        obligations, 280–2
    ecumenical relations, institutions for,
        286–8
    ecumenical services, 301
    Eucharist, 251
    on Eucharistic fellowship, 298
    European State laws on, 362
    facilitating and ordering life and mission
        of, 30
    financial administration in, 329
    funeral rites, 272
    Gospel, duty to proclaim, 198
    governance, power and form of, 120,
        122, 385–6
    on human rights and freedom of
        religion, 366
    income, lawful sources of, 335
    institutional church as manifestation of
        universal church, 277
    institutional church, concept of, 17
    insurance, 340
    international constitutions, 22
    international institutions of church
        governance, 129
    interpretation of law in, 43
    laity, duties and rights of, 58
    on law of God, 34
    lay servant leadership in, 67–9
    local institutions of church governance,
        149
    marriage, 259
    membership in church, 52
    on ministerial communion, 295
    mission and evangelisation, 208
    mixed marriages, 300
    music and worship, 231
    national institutions of church
        governance, 137
    national, regional and local laws, 26
    offences, ecclesiastical, 181
    ordained ministers' functions, duties and
        rights, 98
    ordination, 81
    ownership of property in, 315
    pensions and benefits for ordained
        ministers, 344
    people of God, concept of, 48
    preaching, ecumenical, 301
    preaching function, 200
    regional institutions of church
        governance, 143
    remuneration of ordained ministers, 342
    sacraments, 234
    sacred buildings and objects, 323–4
    sanctions and penalties, 186
    on social responsibility, 373
    standard juridical formulae and
        structures, 36
    tenure of ministerial office in, 90
    theology/faith expressed through law,
        34
    on universal and undivided church, 275
    visitation, 164
    World Methodist Council, 17, 22, 120,
        122, 129
    on worship, 218, 222, 227
metropolises. *See* diocese, district, and
    circuit
metropolitans, 109–12
military chaplains, 380–3, 397
ministry. *See also* ordained ministry
    ecumenical communion regarding,
        295–6, 395
    lay, 62–71, 389

INDEX

mission and evangelisation, 205–9, 303–4
mixed marriages (between baptised persons from different traditions), 298–300
moderators, 106–9, 112–13, 390
music and worship, 231

N

national level
  ecumenical relations at, 286
  financial administration, responsibility for, 328–31
  forms of church governance, 118–24, 391
  institutions of church governance, 130–9, 391
  juridical and regulatory instruments, 22
Nicene Creed, 190, 192, 194, 210, 275
non-coercive jurisdiction, international church governments wielding, 130
Norway, church–State relations in, 361

O

obligations and rights. *See* duties and rights
offences, ecclesiastical, 178–82, 393
offerings, 332–9, 397
official/established State churches, 356–62, 397
Old Catholic Union of Utrecht, 3, 39
One, Holy, Catholic and Apostolic Church, 275–9, 394
ordained ministry, 3, 77–117.
  See also bishops, diocesan
  apostolic succession, controversy over, 77
  archbishops and metropolitans, 109–12
  benefits, 343–5, 397
  catechesis, responsibility for, 202–5
  celibacy and, 78–9
  concelebration of Eucharist, 297
  concelebration of mixed marriages, 298–300
  ecumenical communion regarding, 295–6
  ecumenical responsibilities, 288–90
  Episcopal versus Protestant reformed traditions, 77–8, 86
  functions, duties and rights, 93–101, 390
  gender issues, 78–80
  governance, power of, in Catholic Church, 63, 119
  at international level, 114–16
  laity distinguished from, 46
  laity, relationship to, 77
  in local institutions of church governance, 146–52
  marriage and, 78–9
  in national institutions of church governance, 133–5
  pensions, 343–5, 397
  preaching function, 199–209
  presidents, superintendents and moderators, 106–9, 112–13
  process of ordination, 77–86, 390
  at regional level, 102–13
  salaries and financial maintenance, 340–3, 397
  tenure of office, 86–93, 390
ordering and facilitating life and mission of church, 29–31
Oriental Catholic Churches. *See* Catholicism
Orthodox Christianity, 3
  administration and enforcement of juridical instruments, 38–9
  anointing of the sick, 270
  associations of the faithful (lay brotherhoods and sisterhoods), 64, 71
  baptism and chrismation, 236, 244
  on baptismal communion, 294
  binding and enforceable nature of juridical instruments, 37–8
  bishops, 103
  canonical tradition of, 20, 23
  catechesis, 202
  on chaplains in prisons, hospitals and armed forces, 380
  church buildings, ecumenical sharing of, 303
  on church–State relationship, 347
  confession, 265–6
  on converts from other Christian churches and ecclesial communities, 293–4
  courts and tribunals, 166
  defined, 3
  diocesan officers, 95
  disunity and denominational divisions, recognition of, 278

Orthodox Christianity (cont.)
  divorce and remarriage, 261, 265
  doctrinal standards, maintenance of, 210
  doctrine, definition and sources of, 189
  on ecclesial communion, 291
  economy, principle of, 40
  ecumenical nature, definition of ecumenism, and ecumenical obligations, 280–3
  Ecumenical Patriarchate of Constantinople, 115, 125, 167
  ecumenical relations, institutions for, 287–9
  ecumenical services, 301
  Eucharist, 248
  on Eucharistic fellowship, 297
  European State laws on, 358
  facilitating and ordering life and mission of, 29
  financial administration in, 327
  funeral rites, 270, 302
  Gospel, duty to proclaim, 196
  governance, power and form of, 119, 385–6
  hierarchical recourse, 158
  on human rights and freedom of religion, 364
  income, lawful sources of, 333
  institutional church as manifestation of universal church, 276
  institutional church, concept of, 13
  insurance, 339
  international institutions of church governance, 125
  interpretation of law in, 41
  juridical and regulatory instruments of, 6, 20, 23
  laity, duties and rights of, 56
  on law of God, 33
  lay ministry in, 63
  local institutions of church governance, 147
  marriage, 255
  membership in church, 50
  metropolitans, primates and archbishops, 109
  on ministerial communion, 295
  mission and evangelisation, 206
  mixed marriages, 299
  monastic life, 73–4
  music and worship, 231
  national institutions of church governance, 132
  national, regional and local laws, 23
  offences, ecclesiastical, 179
  ordained ministers' functions, duties and rights, 94
  ordination, 79
  ownership of property in, 311
  patriarchs, 120
  pensions and benefits for ordained ministers, 343
  people of God, concept of, 47
  preaching, ecumenical, 301
  preaching function, 200
  regional institutions of church governance, 140
  on religious education in State schools, 378
  remuneration of ordained ministers, 341
  sacraments, 233
  sacred buildings and objects, 320
  sanctions and penalties, 183
  social justice, ecumenical co-operation in promoting, 304
  on social responsibility, 369
  standard juridical formulae and structures, 36
  tenure of ministerial office in, 87
  theology/faith expressed through law, 32–3
  on universal and undivided church, 275
  visitation, 161
  on worship, 216, 220, 225
ownership of property, 310–19, 396

P

papacy, 114
  doctrine, definition and sources of, 189
  ecclesiastical offences associated with, 179
  financial administration, responsibility for, 326
  governance, power of, 119
  as international institution of church governance, 124, 390

ordained ministers' oath of fidelity to, 78
patriarchs of Oriental Catholic Churches and, 114
Pauline Privilege, 261
personality in international law, 357
preaching function, 199
Primacy, doctrine of, 290
as supreme judge for universal church, 165
visitation reports to, 161
worship, responsibility for, 220, 224
parishes
ecumenical responsibilities, 287
financial administration in, 326-7, 329
as local institutions of church governance, 146-9
priests and ministers in charge of (*see* ordained ministry)
patriarchs
financial administration, responsibility for, 327
international institutions of church governance, 125, 390
of Oriental Catholic Churches, 114, 119
in Orthodox Christianity, 120
Pauline Privilege, 261
payment of ordained ministers
fees for services, 332-9
pensions and benefits, 343-5, 397
salaries and wages, 340-3, 397
Pedalion, 20
penalties and sanctions for ecclesiastical offences, 182-6, 393
penance
confession or reconciliation, 265-9
as disciplinary sanction, 182-3
pensions and benefits for ordained ministers, 343-5, 397
people of God, concept of, 46-9, 389
personality of papacy and Vatican City in international law, 357
Pius XII (Pope), 276
Poland's concordat with Holy See, 357
polity. *See* governance
Pontiff
Roman Catholic (*see* papacy)
of Syrian Orthodox Church of Antioch, 115
Pope. *See* papacy
Porvoo Agreement, 306

prayer, ecumenical, 300-2
preaching and liturgy of the word, 195-202
catechesis, 202-5
duty to proclaim Gospel of Christ, 195-9, 393
ecumenical services, 300-2
as lay ministry, 62-71, 200
mission and evangelisation, 205-9
obligations and rights of ordained ministries, 93-101
by ordained ministers, 199-209
Wesley, John, sermons of, 192, 228
Presbyterian form of church polity, 118, 122-3, 158, 165, 386, 391
Presbyterianism, 5
administration and enforcement of juridical instruments, 38-9
baptism, 240
binding and enforceable nature of juridical instruments, 37-8
catechesis, 205
on church-State relationship, 354
courts and tribunals, 169
discipline, nature and purpose of, 157
divorce and remarriage, 264
doctrinal standards, maintenance of, 214
doctrine, definition and sources of, 193
due process, 175
ecumenical nature, definition of ecumenism, and ecumenical obligations, 281
ecumenical relations, institutions for, 286, 288
Eucharist, 252
on Eucharistic fellowship, 298
European State laws on, 361
facilitating and ordering life and mission of, 31
financial administration in, 330
funeral rites, 272
Gospel, duty to proclaim, 198
governance, power and form of, 122, 386
hierarchical recourse, 160
on human rights and freedom of religion, 367
income, lawful sources of, 336-8
institutional church as manifestation of universal church, 277
institutional church, concept of, 17

Presbyterianism (cont.)
  insurance, 340
  laity, duties and rights of, 60
  on law of God, 35
  local institutions of church governance, 151
  marriage, 259
  membership in church, 53
  mission and evangelisation, 208
  mixed marriages, 300
  moderators, 108, 113
  music and worship, 231
  national institutions of church governance, 136
  national, regional and local laws, 27
  offences, ecclesiastical, 180
  ordained ministers' functions, duties and rights, 100
  ordination, 83
  ownership of property in, 316
  pensions and benefits for ordained ministers, 344
  people of God, concept of, 49
  preaching function, 201
  regional institutions of church governance, 144
  relaxation of juridical norms in, 40
  on religious education in State schools, 379
  remuneration of ordained ministers, 343
  rite of admission rather than confirmation in, 246
  sacraments, 234
  sacred buildings and objects, 324
  sanctions and penalties, 185
  on social responsibility, 375
  standard juridical formulae and structures, 36
  Sunday observance, 230
  tenure of ministerial office in, 91
  theology/faith expressed through law, 35
  on universal and undivided church, 275
  visitation, 163
  Westminster Confession of Faith, 193
  on worship, 219, 223, 228–30
presidents
  conference presidents, 112, 164, 212
  district presidents, 106–9, 212
  of international bodies, 116, 390

presiding bishops, 110–11
priests, 77–86. *See also* ordained ministry
Primacy, doctrine of, 290
primates, 109
principal bishops, 110
principles of law common to Christian churches, 384, 388–98
prison chaplains, 380–3, 397
proclamation of the faith, 195–9, 393–4
property. *See* church property and finance
Protestant traditions, 4. *See also specific denominations*
  associations of the faithful (lay brotherhoods and sisterhoods), 71
  on chaplains in prisons, hospitals and armed forces, 381
  church buildings, ecumenical sharing of, 303
  on church–State relationship, 349
  confession, juridical abandonment of, 265
  confession, limited use of, 267
  on converts from other Christian churches and ecclesial communities, 293–4
  courts and tribunals, 168
  discipline, nature and purpose of, 155–8
  divorce and remarriage, 263, 265
  due process, 174
  on ecclesial communion, 292
  ecumenical covenants and councils, 304–8
  ecumenical services, 301
  Eucharist, 247, 250
  European State laws on, 360
  governance, forms of, 386
  on human rights and freedom of religion, 365
  income, lawful sources of, 335
  international constitutions, 21
  interpretation of law in, 42
  juridical and regulatory instruments of, 6
  laity, duties and rights of, 58
  on law of God, 34–6
  lay ministry in, 66
  marriage, 258
  on ministerial communion, 295
  ordained ministry in Episcopal versus Protestant reformed traditions, 77–8, 86

ownership of property in, 313
preaching, ecumenical, 301
relaxation of juridical norms in, 40
remuneration of ordained ministers, 342
sacred buildings and objects, 322
sanctions and penalties, 184
social justice, ecumenical co-operation in promoting, 304
theology/faith expressed through law, 32, 34–6
visitation, 163
public institutions of the State, 377–83, 397
punishments for ecclesiastical offences, 182–6, 393

Q

quasi-judicial discipline and conflict resolution, 158, 392

R

reconciliation (confession or penance), 265–9
Reformation, 9, 118, 247, 265, 274
Reformed Churches, 5. *See also* Congregationalism; Presbyterianism; United and Uniting Churches
administration and enforcement of juridical instruments, 38–9
baptism, 242
on baptismal communion, 294
catechesis, 205
church buildings, ecumenical sharing of, 303
on church–State relationship, 354
courts and tribunals, 168
defined, 3
discipline, nature and purpose of, 157
doctrinal standards, maintenance of, 215
doctrine, definition and sources of, 194
due process, 175
on ecclesial communion, 292
ecumenical nature, definition of ecumenism and ecumenical obligations, 280–4
ecumenical relations, institutions for, 286–8

ecumenical services, 301
Eucharist, 253
on Eucharistic fellowship, 298
European State laws on, 362
facilitating and ordering life and mission of, 31
Gospel, duty to proclaim, 198
governance, power of, 120, 122
on human rights and freedom of religion, 367
institutional church as manifestation of universal church, 277
institutional church, concept of, 17
international constitutions, 22
international institutions of church governance, 129
international officers, 116
interpretation of law in, 43
laity, duties and rights of, 60
lay ministry in, 69–70
local institutions of church governance, 150
membership in church, 53
on ministerial communion, 296
mission and evangelisation, 209
music and worship, 232
national institutions of church governance, 135
national, regional and local laws, 27
offences, ecclesiastical, 180
ordained ministers' functions, duties and rights, 99
ordination, 82
people of God, concept of, 48
preaching, ecumenical, 301
preaching function, 202
presidents, 108
regional institutions of church governance, 144
remuneration of ordained ministers, 343
sacraments, 234
sacred buildings and objects, 326
sanctions and penalties, 185
on social responsibility, 374
tenure of ministerial office in, 91
theology/faith expressed through law, 32
on universal and undivided church, 275
visitation, 163

Reformed Churches (cont.)
  World Communion of Reformed
    Churches (formerly World Alliance),
    4, 17, 22, 39, 116, 120, 122, 129, 367,
    374
  on worship, 219, 224, 230
regional level. See also diocese, district and
    circuit
  common principles regarding oversight
    of, 390
  ecclesiastical officers, 102–13
  ecumenical relations at, 286
  financial administration, responsibility
    for, 328–31
  forms of church governance, 118–24,
    391
  institutions of church governance,
    139–46, 391
  juridical and regulatory instruments, 22
regulatory instruments. See juridical and
    regulatory instruments
relaxation of juridical norms, 39–41, 388
religious education in State schools,
    378–80, 397
religious freedom, 362–8, 397
religious orders, 286
remarriage, 254, 260–5
remuneration of ordained ministers.
    See payment of ordained ministers
resolution of disputes. See discipline and
    conflict resolution
rights and duties. See duties and rights
ritual, 3, 233–73. See also Eucharist;
    marriage
  baptism, 49–54, 235–43, 394
  confession (penance or reconciliation),
    265–9
  confirmation, 235, 243–6, 394
  dying persons, pastoral care of
    (Eucharist or anointing), 269–72
  funeral rites, 268, 269–72
  sacraments, classification as, 233–4
Roman Catholic Church. See Catholicism
Roman Curia, 125
Roman Missal, 220
Roman Pontifical, 220
Roman Ritual, 220
Roman Rota, 165
Russian Orthodoxy. See Orthodox
    Christianity

S

sacramentals, 269
sacraments, classification of some rites as,
    233–4. See also ritual; specific
    sacraments
sacred buildings and objects, 319–26, 396.
    See also church buildings
salaries of ordained ministers, 340–3,
    397
sanctions and penalties for ecclesiastical
    offences, 182–6, 393
schism, 210
schools. See teaching
Scotland, church–State relations in, 361
Scots Confession, 194
Scripture
  doctrine, as source of, 188–95
  resolution of disputes, scriptural
    processes for, 171
Second Helvetic Confession, 194
Second Vatican Council, 49, 63, 189
secretariats, 128–9
sermons. See preaching and liturgy of the
    word
servant law, 388
Slovenia, church–State relations in, 357,
    380
Smalcald Articles, 192
Smyth, John, 4
social justice
  church responsibility for, 368–77, 397
  ecumenism and, 303–4
  human rights principles and freedom of
    conscience, 362–8, 397
societies of apostolic life, Catholic, 72,
    286
society and church. See State and society,
    relationship of churches to
Spain, church–State relations in, 357, 363,
    380
State and society, relationship of churches
    to, 3, 346–83. See also European State
    laws
  chaplains in prisons, hospitals, and
    armed forces, 380–3, 397
  church views on relationship between
    church and State, 346–56, 397
  conventions or treaties between church
    and State, 357

ecumenical efforts at mission and social justice, 303–4
established/official State churches, 356–62, 397
freedom of religion and conscience, 362–8, 397
human rights principles, 362–8, 397
principles of Christian law as resource for, 386
public institutions of the State, 377–83, 397
as reason for studying Christian law, 8
religious education in State schools, 378–80, 397
social responsibilities of churches, 368–77, 397
'two kingdoms' doctrine, 349
stewards, 62–71, 386
stewardship, doctrine of, 310
Sunday observance, 227–30
Sunday Schools, 202–5
superintendents, 106–9, 164, 386, 390
suspension, 182–6
Sweden, church–State relations in, 361, 380
Synods
 courts and tribunals, 168
 as international institutions of church governance, 124–5
 as national institutions of church governance, 131–2, 134–5
 as regional institutions of church governance, 139–46

T

taxes, ecclesiastical, 332–9
teaching
 catechesis, 202–5
 ecumenical formation, 289–90
 magisterium or teaching office in Catholic Church, 188, 199
 preaching, as teaching function of ordained ministry, 199–209
 religious education in State schools, 378–80, 397
theology/faith, 384–5. *See also* doctrine; worship
 divine law and human law, 33–6
 ecclesiastical discipline, nature and purpose of, 154–8

expressed through Christian law, 1, 11, 31–6
free enquiry and expression regarding, 210
Gospel, duty to proclaim, 195–9, 393
people of God, concept of, 46–9, 389
resolution of disputes, scriptural processes for, 171
servant law, 388
Thirty-Nine Articles, 190
transubstantiation, 247, 251
treaties or conventions between church and State, 357
tribunals and courts, 164–71
 common principles, 392
 lay involvement in Catholic tribunals, 63, 165
trusts, trustees, and other entities utilised to represent church, 310
'two kingdoms' doctrine, 349

U

Unions, Baptist, as national institutions of church governance, 138
United and Uniting Churches, 5
 arbitration, 160
 catechesis, 205
 on church–State relationship, 355
 courts and tribunals, 170
 doctrinal standards, maintenance of, 215
 doctrine, definition and sources of, 194
 due process, 177
 on ecclesial communion, 293
 ecumenical nature, definition of ecumenism, and ecumenical obligations, 282, 284
 ecumenical relations, institutions for, 290
 Eucharist, 253
 facilitating and ordering life and mission of, 31
 financial administration in, 331
 Gospel, duty to proclaim, 198
 governance, power of, 123
 hierarchical recourse, 160
 on human rights and freedom of religion, 367
 income, lawful sources of, 338
 institutional church, concept of, 18
 laity, duties and rights of, 61

United and Uniting Churches (cont.)
  on law of God, 35
  membership in church, 53
  mission and evangelisation, 209
  music and worship, 232
  national institutions of church governance, 136
  national, regional and local laws, 28
  ordained ministers' functions, duties and rights, 100
  ownership of property in, 317
  pensions and benefits for ordained ministers, 344
  preaching function, 202
  remuneration of ordained ministers, 343
  sacred buildings and objects, 326
  on social responsibility, 376
  tenure of ministerial office in, 92
  theology/faith expressed through law, 35
  on universal and undivided church, 276
  on worship, 224, 230
universal and undivided church, concept of, 275–9, 394
Universal Declaration of Human Rights, 364, 366–7
Utrecht, Old Catholic Union of, 3, 39

V

Vatican City, personality in international law of, 357
Vatican II, 49, 63, 189
vicars, diocesan, 94, 96, 140
Virginia (Lutheran-Anglican-Roman Catholic) Covenant 1990, 306
visitation, 161–4

W

wages of ordained ministers, 340–3, 397
WCC. *See* World Council of Churches
Wesley, John and Charles, 3–4, 192, 228
Westminster Confession of Faith, 193
Witte, John, vii, 387
women
  lay ministries in Catholic Church, 63
  ordination, 78–80
word, liturgy of. *See* preaching and liturgy of the word
World Communion of Reformed Churches (formerly World Alliance), 4, 17, 22, 39, 116, 120, 122, 129, 367, 374
World Council of Churches (WCC)
  'church family' of, vii
  definition of church, 12
  ecumenical aims of, 9
  as ecumenical covenant or communion, 304
  Faith and Order Commission on need for ecumenical discussion of church law, 1–2, 387
  on freedom of religion and conscience, 362
  nature and purpose of, 12
World Methodist Council, 17, 22, 120, 122, 129
worship, 3, 215–32. *See also* preaching and liturgy of the word; ritual
  conduct and oversight, 224–32, 394
  development of liturgical texts and forms of service, 220–4
  ecumenical services, 300–2
  music and, 231
  nature and forms of, 215–19, 393

Lightning Source UK Ltd.
Milton Keynes UK
UKOW06f0953240116

266979UK00011B/384/P